REA's Test Prep Books Are The Best!

(a sample of the hundreds of letters REA receives each year)

" REA's *SAT Subject Test: Math Level 2* test prep definitely helped boost my score.... "
Student, Portland, OR

" My students report your chapters of review as the most valuable single resource they used for review and preparation. "
Teacher, American Fork, UT

" Your book was such a better value and was so much more complete than anything your competition has produced — and I have them all! "
Teacher, Virginia Beach, VA

" Compared to the other books that my fellow students had, your book was the most useful in helping me get a great score. "
Student, North Hollywood, CA

" Your book was responsible for my success on the exam, which helped me get into the college of my choice... I will look for REA the next time I need help. "
Student, Chesterfield, MO

" Just a short note to say thanks for the great support your book gave me in helping me pass the test... I'm on my way to a B.S. degree because of you! "
Student, Orlando, FL

(more on next page)

(continued from front page)

“I am writing to congratulate you on preparing an exceptional study guide. In five years of teaching this course, I have never encountered a more thorough, comprehensive, concise and realistic preparation for this examination.”

Teacher, Davie, FL

“I have found your publications, *The Best Test Preparation...*, to be exactly that.”

Teacher, Aptos, CA

“I used your book to prepare for the test and found that the advice and the sample tests were highly relevant... Without using any other material, I earned very high scores and will be going to the graduate school of my choice.”

Student, New Orleans, LA

“I used your *CLEP Introductory Sociology* book and rank it 99% — thank you!”

Student, Jerusalem, Israel

“Your *GMAT* book greatly helped me on the test. Thank you.”

Student, Oxford, OH

“I just wanted to thank you for helping me get a great score on the AP U.S. History exam... Thank you for making great test preps!”

Student, Los Angeles, CA

“Your *AP English Literature and Composition* book is most impressive.”

Student, Montgomery, AL

“The REA *LSAT* Test Preparation guide is a winner!”

Instructor, Spartanburg, SC

The Best Test Preparation for the

SAT Subject Test United States History

7th EDITION

With REA's TEST*ware*® on CD-ROM

Gary Land, Ph.D.
Professor of History
Andrews University
Berrien Springs, Michigan

Ronald Lettieri, Ph.D.
Associate Professor of History
Mount Ida College
Newton Centre, Massachusetts

Michelle DenBeste, Ph.D.
Associate Professor and Chair, History
California State University
Fresno, California

Research & Education Association
Visit our website at
www.rea.com

Research & Education Association
61 Ethel Road West
Piscataway, New Jersey 08854
E-mail: info@rea.com

The Best Test Preparation for the
SAT SUBJECT TEST IN
UNITED STATES HISTORY
With TEST*ware*® on CD-ROM

Printed in the United States of America

Library of Congress Control Number 2006935830

International Standard Book Number 0-7386-0296-5

L06-0101

About Research & Education Association

Founded in 1959, Research & Education Association (REA) is dedicated to publishing the finest and most effective educational materials—including software, study guides, and test preps—for students in middle school, high school, college, graduate school, and beyond.

REA's Test Preparation series includes books and software for all academic levels in almost all disciplines. Research & Education Association publishes test preps for students who have not yet entered high school, as well as high school students preparing to enter college. Students from countries around the world seeking to attend college in the United States will find the assistance they need in REA's publications. For college students seeking advanced degrees, REA publishes test preps for many major graduate school admission examinations in a wide variety of disciplines, including engineering, law, and medicine. Students at every level, in every field, with every ambition can find what they are looking for among REA's publications.

REA presents tests that accurately depict the official exams in both degree of difficulty and types of questions. REA's practice tests are always based upon the most recently administered exams, and include every type of question that can be expected on the actual exams.

REA's publications and educational materials are highly regarded and continually receive an unprecedented amount of praise from professionals, instructors, librarians, parents, and students. Our authors are as diverse as the fields represented in the books we publish. They are well known in their respective disciplines and serve on the faculties of prestigious high schools, colleges, and universities throughout the United States and Canada.

Today REA's wide-ranging catalog is a leading resource for teachers, students, and professionals.

We invite you to visit us at *www.rea.com* to find out how "REA is making the world smarter."

Acknowledgments

In addition to our authors, we would like to thank Larry B. Kling, Vice President, Editorial, for his overall direction; Pam Weston, Vice President, Publishing, for setting the quality standards for production integrity and managing the publication to completion; John Cording, Vice President, Technology, for coordinating the design and development of REA's TEST*ware*® software; Anne Winthrop Esposito, Senior Editor, for project management of this edition; Heena Patel and Michelle Boykins, Technology Project Managers, for their design contributions and tireless software-testing efforts; Kaylon Goodwill for proofreading; Caragraphics for typesetting this edition; and Christine Saul, Senior Graphic Designer, for cover design.

CONTENTS

INTRODUCTION

Passing the SAT United States History Subject Test

About This Book and TEST*ware*®

If you're planning to take the SAT United States History Subject Test, this book and the accompanying software are for you. REA provides an accurate and complete representation of the test in six full-length practice exams based on official exam questions released by the College Entrance Examination Board. Our practice tests present every type of question that you can expect to encounter on the actual exam. Practice Tests 1 and 2 are also included on the enclosed TEST*ware*® CD. The software provides the benefits of instantaneous, accurate scoring and enforced timed conditions. Beyond just giving you good practice, however, we also provide *context*. All of our answers are followed by detailed explanations that will enable you to zero in on your strengths and weaknesses—a surefire confidence booster!

But we don't stop there. This book also contains an extensive topical review that will help you make better use of your study time by reinforcing your command of the subject matter.

About the Test

Developed by the College Board and administered by Educational Testing Service (ETS), the SAT United States History Subject Test is a one-hour examination that features 90 to 95 multiple-choice questions. To do well on the test, you need to be familiar with United States history from pre-Columbian times to the present. The majority of the history questions fall in the post-1763 period and cover all major facets of United States history: political, economic, social, diplomatic, intellectual, and cultural.

The test is offered throughout the year, usually in January, May, June, October, November, and December. You can obtain registration forms and specific test date information at your school's guidance or counseling office, or by contacting the College Board as follows:

College Board SAT Program
PO Box 6200
Princeton, NJ 08541-6200
Phone: (609) 771-7600
Website: www.collegeboard.com

The test's proportional coverage can and does vary from one edition of the exam to another, but this breakdown gives you a good idea of what to expect:

Political History (including Political Science and Law)	32–36%
Economic History (including Geography)	18–20%
Social History (including Sociology, Anthropology, and Social Psychology)	18–22%
Foreign Policy (including International Relations)	13–17%
Intellectual and Cultural History	10–12%

The periods covered are as follows:

Pre-Columbian History to 1789	20%
1790 to 1898	40%
1899 to present	40%

Theoretically, the only necessary preparation for the test is a thorough course in American history at the college-preparatory level, although information tested on the exam may be found in courses such as American government, economics, and problems of democracy. Keeping up with national news by regularly reading a major daily newspaper (e.g., the *Chicago Tribune*, *Miami Herald*, or *New York Times*) or, at the very least, one of the newsweekly magazines, can only help you.

The test seeks to measure many types of abilities. Sometimes there's overlap; in other words, an individual question may test more than one type of ability within its scope.

The types of abilities measured include the following:

- Knowledge of facts, terms, concepts, and generalizations; recall of basic information.

- Analyzing and interpreting presented materials.

- Selecting or relating hypotheses, concepts, principles, or generalizations to given data.

- Judging the value of data for a given purpose, either by assessing internal evidence (proof and logical consistency) or external evidence (comparison with other works, established standards, and theories).

Scoring the Practice Tests

The SAT Subject Test is scored by crediting each correct answer with one point and deducting only partial credit (one-fourth of a point) for each incorrect answer. You will neither gain nor lose credit for questions you skip. The resulting value is the "raw score." The accompanying practice-test scoring conversion table on the following page enables you to convert your raw score on each of our full-length practice tests into a total scaled score, which allows you to simulate where your performance places you on the College Board's 200–800 scale.

To get your raw score, add up all your correct responses. Then add up all the incorrect answers and divide this number by four. Subtract this number from the first number and round the result to the nearest whole number (0.5 is rounded up to the next-highest whole number; 0.4 is rounded down to the next-lowest whole number). Now find this number on the scoring table to determine your scaled score.

Here's a worksheet for figuring your practice-test scores:

______ – (______x 0.25) = ______
number right* number wrong* raw score†

SSD Accommodations for Students with Disabilities

Many students qualify for extra time to take the SAT Subject Tests, and our TEST*ware*® can be adapted to accommodate your time extension. This allows you to practice under the same extended-time accommodations that you will receive on the actual test day. To customize your TEST*ware*® to suit the most common extensions, visit our website at *www.rea.com/ssd.*

*** Do not count answers that you left blank.**

† Round to the nearest whole number.

SAT United States History
Practice-Test Scaled Score Conversion Table‡

Raw Score	Scaled Score	Raw Score	Scaled Score	Raw Score	Scaled Score
95	800	55	630	15	430
94	800	54	630	14	430
93	800	53	620	13	420
92	800	52	610	12	420
91	800	51	610	11	410
90	800	50	600	10	410
89	800	49	600	9	400
88	800	48	590	8	390
87	800	47	590	7	380
86	800	46	580	6	380
85	800	45	570	5	370
84	790	44	570	4	360
83	790	43	560	3	360
82	790	42	560	2	350
81	780	41	550	1	350
80	770	40	550	0	340
79	770	39	540	–1	330
78	760	38	540	–2	320
77	750	37	530	–3	310
76	740	36	530	–4	310
75	740	35	520	–5	300
74	730	34	510	–6	290
73	720	33	510	–7	280
72	720	32	510	–8	270
71	710	31	500	–9	260
70	710	30	500	–10	250
69	700	29	490	–11	250
68	700	28	490	–12	240
67	690	27	490	–13	230
66	690	26	480	–14	220
65	680	25	480	–15	210
64	680	24	470	–16	200
63	670	23	470	–17	200
62	670	22	460	–18	200
61	660	21	460	–19	200
60	660	20	450	–20	200
59	650	19	450	–21	200
58	650	18	450	–22	200
57	640	17	440	–23	200
56	640	16	440	–24	200

‡ Some points to bear in mind: (1) This conversion table does not necessarily reflect the scale that will be used by ETS to score the actual test. (2) Your score on REA's practice tests may be higher or lower than your score on the actual test. (3) Scoring formulations for standardized tests typically vary slightly from one edition of a test to another.

INDEPENDENT STUDY SCHEDULE
SAT U.S. HISTORY SUBJECT TEST

This study schedule is set up to thoroughly prepare you for the SAT United States History Subject Test. Although it is designed to allow you to pace yourself comfortably over an eight-week preparation period, it can be condensed into a four-week course by collapsing each two-week period into one. Be sure to set aside enough time—at least two hours each day—to study. No matter which study schedule works best for you, however, the more time you spend acquainting yourself with the subject matter and the test, the more prepared and relaxed you will feel on Test Day.

Week	*Activity*
1	Read the introduction to this book, which details critical aspccts of the SAT U.S. History Subject Test for you. Take Practice Test 1 on CD-ROM as a diagnostic to gauge your strengths and weaknesses. After comparing your answers against the answer key and reading the detailed explanations, flag any test items that were difficult for you. Review your problem areas by using appropriate textbooks, classroom notes, and this book's course review.
2 and **3**	Carefully read and study the course review included in this book. Cover all the material, but highlight those areas that gave you trouble in Practice Test 1. Go through each of the items you answered incorrectly and make sure you understand how to arrive at the correct answer.
4	Take Practice Test 2 on CD-ROM. When done, thoroughly read all the detailed explanations—not just those for the test items you answered incorrectly—and flag any sections that pose difficulty for you. Use textbooks, classroom notes, and our course review to go over those areas for which you need clarification.
5 and **6**	Take Practice Tests 3 and 4 in this book. After scoring each exam, flag your incorrect answers. For any types of questions or particular subjects that continue to pose difficulty for you, check our detailed explanations and consult our course review by way of our handy index.

Week	Activity
7	Take Practice Tests 5 and 6 in this book. After scoring your exam, carefully review the explanations for all your incorrect answers. By this point, you should be nearing mastery of the subject matter. Again, consult our course review (by way of our handy index) as often as possible to ensure that you're sufficiently at ease with our model tests.
8	This is the week you'll consolidate your gains and eliminate any continuing subject-matter weaknesses. Retake one or more of the practice tests (as you deem necessary), paying particular attention to the questions with which you had difficulty the first time around. Going through the practice tests once again will put you on completely familiar terms with the subject matter and the SAT Subject Test itself.

Good luck on the SAT Subject Test in United States History!

THE SAT SUBJECT TEST IN

United States History

COURSE REVIEW

1 PRE-COLUMBIAN HISTORY OF THE AMERICAS

The "New World" that Columbus and other explorers discovered in the late 15th and early 16th centuries was neither recently formed nor recently settled. It had actually been settled between 15,000 and 35,000 years earlier. As in other areas of the world, these aboriginal peoples formed communities but did not immediately develop a written language. The lack of any kind of written record makes interpreting this prehistorical past more difficult. Archaeologists and anthropologists working in North and South America have unearthed the remains of these early communities, and it is upon this evidence that the earliest theories about the origins, movement, and lifestyle of these people are based. It is important to remember that there is not one universally accepted theory regarding the earliest history of the people who settled North and South America. It is also important to remember that by the time Europeans came into contact with the indigenous peoples of the Americas, more than 2,000 distinct cultures and hundreds of distinct languages existed. It is therefore necessary to trace not just the origins but also the developments, affected by various factors such as the environment, that took place prior to the arrival of the Europeans. This will provide us with an understanding of the various Indian cultures and societies and the impact that contact with Europeans had upon them.

THE GREAT ICE AGE

During the Great Ice Age, which lasted over two million years, so much water was frozen that sea levels dropped drastically. One consequence of this was that a land mass between Siberia and Alaska known as Beringia, now covered in water, was exposed and formed a bridge between the Asian and American continents. This land bridge was exposed during three separate periods: the earliest was from 70,000 to 45,000 years ago, the second was from about 22,000 to 12,500, and the last was approximately 11,000 to 8,000 years ago. It is thought that several groups migrated along this path during at least two different periods, and there is strong evidence that people migrated across Beringia during the second period. These early people followed and hunted large game animals, such as mammoths, which found the climate and conditions in Beringia suitable to their needs.

About 9,000 years ago, changes in environmental conditions and ultimately the ending of the Ice Age had a number of consequences. The resulting warmer temperatures led to the development of different climates in different regions of the Americas, the loss of large areas of grassland, and the melting of ice, which once caused water to cover areas such as Beringia, thus cutting off the Americas from the other continents. Many large animals—such as mammoths, mastodons, and horses—became extinct, and the nomadic big-game hunters who had survived largely by killing and using the meat, skin, and bone of these animals were forced to accommodate the loss of such prey by making changes in their lifestyle.

Changes in Hunting and the Development of Agriculture

Archeologists refer to the period from approximately 9,000 to 3,000 B.C.E., when humans shifted away from reliance strictly on hunting and towards a more diverse lifestyle, as the archaic period. It is necessary to review general trends that occurred during this period before turning to the distinct cultures that developed in various regions and that were in existence when the Europeans arrived. One of the changes was the development of additional types of tools made from various materials. Previously, hunters had relied on the effective "Clovis" points, named after the site in Mexico where they were first discovered. They were made by chipping away flakes from the bones of large animals that had been killed. These points were an advance over earlier stone arrow points and proved more reliable and more effective. The shift away from big-game hunting, however, gave early man the time as well as the need to develop a vast array of tools besides hunting spears from other materials, such as wood. The increased amount of time that was produced by not having to constantly track and kill large animals also led to the development of artwork and ornate baskets and other crafts. Population also increased as early people spent more time in each place, although they continued to be nomadic.

The impact of environmental conditions and the introduction of farming techniques and crops, such as maize, had a tremendous impact in the Americas and led to the emergence of the distinct cultures mentioned earlier. It is not possible to describe in depth the 2,000 cultures that had developed by the time the explorers arrived. Instead, some indication of specific trends and cultures that existed in various regions and climates just prior to the arrival of the Europeans will be provided.

Indian Cultures Just Prior to the Arrival of the Europeans

In the Southwest region of North America, severe restrictions were imposed by the aridity of the climate and the fact that nothing could be planted in vast areas of the desert. The cultivation of plants was possible, however, along the banks of the several rivers that flow from the mountains through the Southwest toward the Gulf of Mexico or the Gulf of California. These rivers also provided water for irrigation and farming, and Indian farmers had been growing crops in this manner for about 3,000 years prior to contact with European explorers. The Indians cultivated crops such as corn, beans, sunflowers, and cotton.

They lived in settlements spread across the desert at intervals of approximately one mile, and trading networks extended across the entire southwest. Each settlement had a headman who managed irrigation matters, but a council of adult men made decisions with unanimous consent being required. Ceremonies were an integral part of life, and the most important ceremonies focused on bringing rain. One ceremony required everyone present to drink cactus wine until intoxicated, as this ceremony was thought to both purify the individual and bring rain for the community.

Native Communities in the South and Southwest

One group of Indians living in the Southwest, the Anasazis, lived a few hundred miles north of the area, known as the "Four Corners," where modern-day Arizona, New Mexico, Utah, and Colorado connect. Around the first century C.E., the Anasazis—or "ancient outsiders"—began to settle down and cultivate crops. A change in the climate during the eighth century C.E. presented them with a new challenge. Instead of reverting to a nomadic lifestyle, they found ways to improve their farming techniques and also implemented a system of terraced fields that were irrigated by a sophisticated canal system. In addition to farming, the Anasazis hunted, and around 500 C.E. they benefited from the introduction of a more effective bow and arrow. Although the Anasazis were very skilled at basket making and pottery, it is their architectural achievements that have received the most attention. The Anasazis built and lived in complexes of apartments that had a central plaza, along with areas for storage and religious ceremonies. One of these complexes, named Pueblo Bonito by the Spanish, was completed in the twelfth century and contains more than 650 connected rooms. Only a few of the more than 25,000 communities have been excavated but it is already clear that the Anasazis had a communication system consisting of signaling stations in the mountains and distributed food and resources over an extended network. Although the Anasazis continued to develop more complex irrigation systems and other techniques to counter the dry conditions, these measures were not enough to sustain them through a prolonged drought that occurred in the thirteenth century. The impact of the subsequent crop failures and attacks by bands of Athapascan migrants (the ancestors of the Navajos and Apaches) on the Anasazis contributed to the decline of this community.

It is thought that the cliff dwellings built at Mesa Verde, Colorado, during the 14th and 15th centuries, and later used by the Pueblo people, may have been constructed to defend the Anasazis from their enemies. The Anasazis abandoned these dwellings, however, and left the Four Corners area. There is evidence to suggest that they settled along the Rio Grande and intermarried with the local population, which led to the emergence of the Pueblo people. The Pueblo culture inherited architectural knowledge and also farming and religious practices from the Anasazis. The Pueblo people spoke several different languages, but they had a common code of behavior regulating personal conduct that was enforced by matrilineal clans and societies of both a religious and a political nature. The Pueblo were able to produce harvests of corn and squash because these plants were drought resistant and could be cultivated through the use of dry farming techniques.

Conditions in the South were less harsh and more favorable to human settlement. The winters are short and the climate is mild compared with those of other areas. Furthermore, this region has a broad fertile plain of rich soil that makes cultivation easier and less dependent upon irrigation techniques. There are also a number of rivers that provide opportunities for travel, fishing, and hunting. In the Mississippi Valley, a number of cultures thrived at different time periods. In the mid-1200s at a place archeologists have named Cahokia (near modern-day St. Louis), there was an urban center of approximately 30,000 people. There are no written records to tell us about life at Cahokia, but archeologists have unearthed the remains of a flourishing civilization. Cahokia had a huge earthwork pyramid built as a temple to the gods. The pyramid was built on top of 15 acres and was as tall as a 10-story building. The Indian chiefs and the priests of Cahokia lived in residences built on the top of the pyramid, while the rest of the population of Cahokia lived in houses along the riverbank and worked either in shops along the river bank or in the fields. Fields of corn, beans, and pumpkins covered the surrounding countryside as far as one could see while standing atop of the pyramid. Pottery, clay sculptures, and metal objects were produced at Cahokia and were traded at long distances along trading routes that reached the Great Lakes and even as far as the Atlantic coast. The civilization at Cahokia declined and disappeared in the fourteenth century. When the Europeans arrived, they came into contact with various peoples who continued some of the same patterns of life as had existed at Cahokia. Most of the peoples in the Mississippi Valley were decimated by disease almost immediately after contact with Europeans and thus little is known about them as well.

The Natchez farmers of the lower Mississippi delta, however, survived into the eighteenth century, and thus considerably more is known about their culture. The ruler of the Natchez was known as the Great Sun. He lived on a ceremonial mound in his village capitol, and when he went out among his subjects he was carried upon a litter. The wives and servants of the chief preceded the litter and swept its path clean. Natchez society was divided into classes. The members of one class, the nobles, served as advisers to the Great Sun and were appointed to serve as peace and war chiefs of the villages. The majority of the Natchez people—known as the "Stinkards"—were subordinate to the ruler and the nobles. The Natchez considered the act of warfare to elevate the status of the individual and the state; thus, the state was drawn into a number of conflicts. They also practiced public torture and human sacrifice. The Natchez, along with other Mississippian cultures, were organized into confederacies consisting of several farming towns, with the most powerful confederacies living along the floodplains. However, these highly organized confederacies, such as the Natchez, proved more vulnerable to conquest by the Europeans than the more loosely organized tribes of the continental interior, such as the Cherokees.

Native Communities in the Northeast

The Iroquois inhabited Ontario and upstate New York for at least 4,500 years before the arrival of Europeans and were among the first people in that area to rely more on cultivation of crops than on fishing and hunting. The Iroquois lived in an area featuring mountain highlands, great rivers, lakes, and valleys and also coastal plains and wooded areas. In the coastal areas and the river valleys, the growing season lasted long enough to produce a crop of maize, and from around 500 C.E., maize farming became the dominant economic pursuit. The Iroquois had a matrilineal line of descent, and it was also women who planted and harvested the corn, beans, squash, and sunflowers that fed and supported the community. The community was organized into 50 longhouses, each containing an extended family, and wooden walls were usually constructed around a village to protect it from attack. Population growth and also persistent violence and war led to the creation of the Iroquois Confederation. This confederacy outlawed warfare among member nations but encouraged violence against neighboring groups that were outside the Confederation. The Confederation was also modeled on the longhouse system. Each nation occupied a separate area but was linked by descent from a common mother, and women played important roles in choosing male leaders or chiefs who would represent them in the Confederation. The Iroquois Confederation came to be extremely significant during the period of European colonization. In addition to the tribes that spoke Iroquois and formed the Confederation, there were at least 50 different cultures created by people who all spoke a common language. These people all spoke Algonquian, and they shared some other characteristics. Unlike the Iroquois, the Algonquians were hunters and foragers who lived in bands with only loose family affiliations. The Algonquians were patrilineal, lived in smaller villages and houses, and had fewer fortifications. The Algonquians also relied more on hunting and fishing than on the cultivation of crops, and the bow and arrow and fishing spear were their most important tools. Some of the Algonquian-speaking tribes, such as the Chippewas and the Crees, came to be involved in the fur trade that developed in that region.

HISTORICAL TIMELINE

Pre-Columbian Cultures (12,000 B.C.E.–1492 C.E.)

ca. 12,000 B.C.E.	Asians begin several migrations over Bering Strait
5000 B.C.E.	Maize cultivation begins in southern Mexico
700 B.C.E.	Olmec people flourish along Gulf of Mexico
100 C.E.	Hopewell culture sets up massive trading network
300	Mayan city of Tikal features 20,000 residents and many temples
500	Teotihuacán's population reaches 100,000 at peak of culture
600	Hohokam civilization develops in present Arizona and New Mexico
800	Collapse of many Mayan cities
900	Anasazi build cliff villages in American southwest
1000	Leif Ericson and Norsemen settle Vinland in current Newfoundland
1125	City of Cahokia (near present-day St. Louis) has 15,000 residents and 100 temple mounds
1325	Aztecs build Tenochtitlán on site of current Mexico City
1438	Incas begin conquest of Andean region of South America
1492	Columbus lands at San Salvador in Bahamas

2 EUROPEAN EXPLORATION AND THE COLONIAL PERIOD (1492–1763)

THE AGE OF EXPLORATION

The Treaty of Tordesillas

Excited by the gold Columbus had brought back from America (after Amerigo Vespucci, an Italian member of a Portuguese expedition to South America whose widely reprinted report suggested a new world had been found), Ferdinand and Isabella, joint monarchs of Spain, sought formal confirmation of their ownership of these new lands. They feared the interference of Portugal, which was at that time a powerful seafaring nation and had been active in overseas exploration. In 1493, at Spain's urging, the pope drew a "Line of Demarcation" 100 leagues west of the Cape Verde Islands, dividing the heathen world into two equal parts—that east of the line for Portugal and that west of it for Spain.

Because this line tended to be unduly favorable to Spain, and because Portugal had the stronger navy, the two countries worked out the Treaty of Tordesillas (1494), by which the line was moved farther west. As a result, Brazil eventually became a Portuguese colony, while Spain maintained claims to the rest of the Americas. As other European nations joined the hunt for colonies, they tended to ignore the Treaty of Tordesillas.

The Spanish Conquistadores

To conquer the Americas the Spanish monarchs used their powerful army, led by independent Spanish adventurers known as *conquistadores*. At first the conquistadores confined their attentions to the Caribbean islands, where the European diseases they unwittingly carried with them devastated the local Indian populations, who had no immunities against such diseases.

After about 1510 the conquistadores turned their attention to the American mainland. In 1513 Vasco Núñez de Balboa crossed the isthmus of Panama and became the first European to see the Pacific Ocean. The same year Juan Ponce de León explored Florida in search of gold and a fabled fountain of youth. He found neither, but claimed Florida for Spain. In 1519 Hernando (Hernán) Cortés led his dramatic expedition against the Aztecs of Mexico. Aided by the fact that the Indians at first mistook him for a god, as well as by firearms, armor, horses, and (unbeknown to him) smallpox germs, all previously unknown in America, Cortés destroyed the Aztec empire and won enormous riches. By the 1550s other such fortune seekers had conquered much of South America.

In North America the Spaniards sought in vain for riches. In 1528 Panfilio de Narvaez led a disastrous expedition through the Gulf Coast region from which only four of the original four hundred men returned. One of them, Cabeza de Vaca, brought with him a story of seven great cities full of gold (the "Seven Cities of Cibola") somewhere to the north. In response to this, two Spanish expeditions explored the interior of North America. Hernando de Soto led a six hundred-man expedition (1539–1541) through what is now the southeastern United States, penetrating as far west as Oklahoma and discovering the Mississippi River, on whose banks de Soto was buried. Francisco Vasquez de Coronado led an expedition (1540–1542) from Mexico, north across the Rio Grande and through New Mexico, Arizona, Texas, Oklahoma, and Kansas. Some of Coronado's men were the first Europeans to see the Grand Canyon. While neither expedition discovered rich Indian civilizations to plunder, both increased Europe's knowledge of the interior of North America and asserted Spain's territorial claims to the continent.

New Spain

Spain administered its new holdings as an autocratic, rigidly controlled empire in which everything was to benefit the parent country. Tight control of even mundane matters was carried out by a suffocating bureaucracy run directly from Madrid. Annual treasure fleets carried the riches of the New World to Spain for the furtherance of its military-political goals in Europe.

As population pressures were low in 16th-century Spain, only about 200,000 Spaniards came to America during that time. To deal with the consequent labor shortages—and as a reward to successful conquistadores—the Spaniards developed a system of large manors or estates (*encomiendas*), with Indian slaves ruthlessly managed for the benefit of the conquistadores. The encomienda system was later replaced by the similar but somewhat milder *hacienda* system. As the Indian population died from overwork and European diseases, Spaniards began importing African slaves to supply their labor needs. Society in New Spain was rigidly stratified, with the highest level reserved for natives of Spain (*peninsulares*) and the next for those of Spanish parentage born in the New World (*creoles*). Those of mixed or Indian blood occupied lower levels.

English and French Beginnings

In 1497 the Italian John Cabot (Giovanni Caboto), sailing under the sponsorship of the king of England in search of a Northwest Passage (a water route to the Orient through or around the North American continent), became the first European since the Viking voyages more than four centuries earlier to reach the mainland of North America, which he claimed for England.

In 1524 the king of France authorized another Italian, Giovanni da Verrazzano, to undertake a mission similar to Cabot's. Endeavoring to duplicate the achievement of Portuguese Ferdinand Magellan, who had five years earlier found a way around the southern tip of South America, Verrazzano followed the American coast from present-day North Carolina to Maine.

Beginning in 1534, Jacques Cartier, also authorized by the king of France, mounted three expeditions to the area of the St. Lawrence River, which he believed might be the hoped-for Northwest Passage. He explored up the river as far as the site of Montreal, where—as he saw it—rapids prevented him from continuing to China. He claimed the area for France before abandoning his last expedition and returning to France in 1542. France made no further attempts to explore or colonize in America for sixty-five years.

England showed little interest in America as well during most of the 16th century. But when the English finally did begin colonization, commercial capitalism in England had advanced to the point that the English efforts were supported by private rather than government funds, allowing the English colonists to enjoy a greater degree of freedom from government interference.

Partially as a result of the New World rivalries and partially through differences between Protestant and Catholic countries, the 16th century was a violent time both in Europe and in America. French Protestants, called Huguenots, who attempted to escape persecution in Catholic France by settling in the New World were massacred by the Spaniards. One such incident led the Spaniards, nervous about any possible encroachment on what they considered to be their exclusive holdings in America, to build a fort that became the beginning of a settlement at St. Augustine, Florida, the first city in North America. Spanish priests ventured north from St. Augustine, but no permanent settlements were built in the interior.

French and especially English sea captains made great sport of—and considerable profit from—plundering the Spaniards of the wealth they had first plundered from the Indians. One of the most successful English captains, Francis Drake, sailed around South America and raided the Spanish settlements on the Pacific coast of Central America before continuing on to California, which he claimed for England and named Nova Albion. Drake then returned to England by sailing around the world. England's Queen Elizabeth, sister and Protestant successor to Mary, had been quietly investing in Drake's highly profitable voyages. On Drake's return from his round-the-world voyage, Elizabeth openly showed her approval.

Angered by this, as well as by Elizabeth's support of the Protestant cause in Europe, Spain's King Philip II in 1588 dispatched a mighty fleet, the Spanish Armada, to conquer England. Instead, the Armada was defeated by the English navy and largely destroyed by storms in the North Sea. This victory established England as a great power and moved it a step closer to overseas colonization, although the war with Spain continued until 1604.

Gilbert, Raleigh, and the First English Attempts at Colonization

English nobleman Sir Humphrey Gilbert believed England should found colonies and find a Northwest Passage. In 1576 he sent English sea captain Martin

Frobisher to look for such a passage. Frobisher scouted along the inhospitable northeastern coast of Canada and brought back large amounts of a yellow metal that turned out to be fool's gold. In 1578 Gilbert obtained a charter allowing him to found a colony with his own funds and guaranteeing the prospective colonists all the rights of those born and residing in England, thus setting an important precedent for future colonial charters. His attempts to found a colony in Newfoundland failed, and while pursuing these endeavors he was lost at sea.

With the queen's permission, Gilbert's work was taken up by his half-brother, Sir Walter Raleigh. Raleigh turned his attention to a more southerly portion of the North American coastline, which he named Virginia, in honor of England's unmarried queen. He selected as a site for the first settlement Roanoke Island just off the coast of present-day North Carolina.

After one abortive attempt, a group of 114 settlers—men, women, and children—landed in July 1587. Shortly thereafter, Virginia Dare became the first English child born in America. Later that year the expedition's leader, John White, returned to England to secure additional supplies. Delayed by the war with Spain, he did not return until 1590, when he found the colony deserted. It is not known what became of the Roanoke settlers. After this failure, Raleigh was forced by financial constraints to abandon his attempts to colonize Virginia. Hampered by unrealistic expectations, inadequate financial resources, and the ongoing war with Spain, English interest in American colonization was submerged for fifteen years.

THE BEGINNINGS OF COLONIZATION

Virginia

In the first decade of the 1600s, Englishmen, exhilarated by the recent victory over Spain and influenced by the writings of Richard Hakluyt (who urged American colonization as the way to national greatness and the spread of the gospel), once again undertook to plant colonies.

Two groups of merchants gained charters from James I, Queen Elizabeth's successor. One group of merchants was based in London and received a charter to North America between what are now the Hudson and the Cape Fear rivers. The other was based in Plymouth and was granted the right to colonize in North America from the Potomac to the northern border of present-day Maine. They were called the Virginia Company of London and the Virginia Company of Plymouth, respectively. These were joint-stock companies, which raised their capital by the sale of shares of stock. Companies of this sort had already been used to finance and carry on English trade with Russia, Africa, and the Middle East.

The Plymouth Company, in 1607, attempted to plant a colony in Maine, but after one winter the colonists became discouraged and returned to Britain. Thereafter the Plymouth Company folded.

The Virginia Company of London, in 1607, sent out an expedition of three ships with 104 men to plant a colony some forty miles up the James River from

Chesapeake Bay. Like the river on which it was located, the new settlement was named Jamestown in honor of England's king. It became the first permanent English settlement in North America, but for a time it appeared to be going the way of the earlier attempts. During the early years of Jamestown, the majority of the settlers died of starvation, various diseases, or hostile action by Indians. Though the losses were continuously replaced by new settlers, the colony's survival remained in doubt for a number of years.

There were several reasons for these difficulties. The entire colony was owned by the company, and all members shared the profits regardless of how much or how little they worked; thus, there was a lack of incentive. Many of the settlers were gentlemen, who considered themselves too good to work at growing the food the colony needed to survive. Others were simply unambitious and little inclined to work in any case. Furthermore, the settlers had come with the expectation of finding gold or other quick and easy riches and wasted much time looking for these while they should have been providing for their survival.

For purposes of defense, the settlement had been sited on a peninsula formed by a bend in the river; but this low and swampy location proved to be a breeding ground for all sorts of diseases and, at high tide, even contaminated the settlers' drinking supply with sea water. To make matters worse, relations with Powhatan, the powerful local Indian chief, were at best uncertain and often openly hostile, with disastrous results for the colonists.

In 1608 and 1609 the dynamic and ruthless leadership of John Smith kept the colony from collapsing. Smith's rule was, "He who works not, eats not." After Smith returned to England in late 1609, the condition of the colony again became critical.

In 1612, a Virginia resident named John Rolfe discovered that a superior strain of tobacco, native to the West Indies, could be grown in Virginia. There was a large market for this tobacco in Europe, and Rolfe's discovery gave Virginia a major cash crop.

To secure more settlers and boost Virginia's shrinking labor force, the company moved to make immigration possible for Britain's poor, who were without economic opportunity at home or financial means to procure transportation to America. This was achieved by means of the indenture system, by which a poor worker's passage to America was paid by an American planter (or the company itself), who in exchange, was indentured to work for the planter (or the company) for a specified number of years. The system was open to abuse and often resulted in the mistreatment of the indentured servants.

To control the workers thus shipped to Virginia, as well as the often lazy and unruly colonists already present, the company gave its governors in America dictatorial powers. Governors such as Lord De La Warr, Sir Thomas Gates, and Sir Thomas Dale made use of such powers, imposing a harsh rule.

For such reasons, and its well-known reputation as a death trap, Virginia continued to attract inadequate numbers of immigrants. To solve this, a reform-minded faction within the company proposed a new approach, and under its leader, Edwin Sandys, made changes designed to attract more settlers. Colonists were promised the same rights they had in England. A representative assembly, the House of Burgesses, was founded in 1619—the first in America. Additionally, private ownership of land was instituted.

Despite these reforms, Virginia's unhealthy reputation kept many Englishmen away. Large numbers of indentured servants were brought in, especially young, single men. The first Africans were brought to Virginia in 1619 but were treated as indentured servants rather than slaves.

Virginia's Indian relations remained difficult. In 1622 an Indian massacre took the lives of 347 settlers. In 1644 the Indians struck again, massacring another 300 settlers. Shortly thereafter, the coastal Indians were subdued and no longer presented a serious threat.

Impressed by the potential profits from tobacco growing, King James I determined to have Virginia for himself. Using the high mortality and the 1622 massacre as a pretext, he revoked the London Company's charter in 1624 and made Virginia a royal colony. This pattern was followed throughout colonial history; both company colonies and proprietary colonies tended eventually to become royal colonies. Upon taking over Virginia, James revoked all political rights and the representative assembly—he did not believe in such things—but fifteen years later his son, Charles I, was forced, by constant pressure from the Virginians and the continuing need to attract more settlers, to restore these rights.

New France

Shortly after England returned to the business of colonization, France renewed its interest in the areas previously visited by such French explorers as Jacques Cartier. The French opened with the Indians a lucrative trade in furs, plentiful in America and much sought after in Europe.

The St. Lawrence River was the French gateway to the interior of North America. In 1608 Samuel de Champlain established a trading post in Quebec, from which the rest of what became New France eventually spread.

Relatively small numbers of Frenchmen came to America, and, partially because of this, they were generally able to maintain good relations with the Indians. French Canadians were energetic in exploring and claiming new lands for France.

French exploration and settlement spread through the Great Lakes region and the valleys of the Mississippi and Ohio rivers. In 1673 Jacques Marquette explored the Mississippi Valley, and in 1682 Sieur de la Salle followed the river to its mouth. French settlements in the Midwest were not generally real towns, but rather forts and trading posts serving the fur trade.

Throughout its history, New France was handicapped by an inadequate population and a lack of support from the parent country.

New Netherlands

Other countries also took an interest in North America. In 1609 Holland sent an Englishman named Henry Hudson to explore for them in search of a

Northwest Passage. In this endeavor Hudson discovered the river that bears his name.

Arrangements were made to trade with the Iroquois for furs, especially beaver pelts for the hats then popular in Europe. In 1624 Dutch trading outposts were established on Manhattan Island (New Amsterdam) and at the site of present-day Albany (Fort Orange). A profitable fur trade was carried on and became the main source of revenue for the Dutch West India Company, the joint-stock company that ran the colony.

To encourage enough farming to keep the colony supplied with food, the Dutch instituted the patroon system, by which large landed estates would be given to wealthy men who transported at least fifty families to New Netherlands. These families would then become tenant farmers on the estate of the patroon who had transported them. As Holland's home economy was healthy, few Dutch felt desperate enough to take up such unattractive terms.

New Netherlands was, in any case, internally weak and unstable. It was poorly governed by inept and lazy governors, and its population was a mixture of people from all over Europe as well as many African slaves, forming what historians have called an "unstable pluralism."

The Pilgrims at Plymouth

Many Englishmen came from England for religious reasons. For the most part, these fell into two groups, Puritans and Separatists. Though similar in many respects to the Puritans, the Separatists believed the Church of England was beyond saving and so felt they must separate from it.

One group of Separatists, suffering government harassment, fled to Holland. Dissatisfied there, they decided to go to America and, thus, became the famous Pilgrims.

Led by William Bradford, they departed in 1620, having obtained from the London Company a charter to settle just south of the Hudson River. Driven by storms, their ship, the Mayflower, made landfall at Cape Cod in Massachusetts. They decided it was God's will for them to settle in that area. This, however, put them outside the jurisdiction of any established government, and so, before going ashore, they drew up and signed the *Mayflower Compact*, establishing a foundation for orderly government based on the consent of the governed. After a difficult first winter that saw many die, the Pilgrims went on to establish a quiet and modestly prosperous colony. After a number of years of hard work they were able to buy out the investors who had originally financed their voyage and thus gain greater autonomy.

The Massachusetts Bay Colony

The Puritans were far more numerous than the Separatists. Contrary to stereotype, they did not dress in drab clothes and were not ignorant or bigoted. They did, however, take the Bible and their religion seriously and felt the Anglican Church still retained too many unscriptural practices left over from Roman Catholicism.

King James I had no use for the Puritans but, mindful of their growing political power, refrained from bringing on a confrontation. His son, Charles I, determined in 1629 to persecute the Puritans aggressively and to rule without the Puritan-dominated Parliament. This course would lead eventually (ten years later) to civil war, but in the meantime some of the Puritans decided to set up a community in America.

To accomplish their purpose, they sought in 1629 to charter a joint-stock company to be called the Massachusetts Bay Company. Whether because Charles was glad to be rid of the Puritans or because he did not realize the special nature of this joint-stock company, the charter was granted. Further, the charter neglected to specify where the company's headquarters should be located. Taking advantage of this unusual omission, the Puritans determined to make their headquarters in the colony itself, three thousand miles from meddlesome royal officials.

Under the leadership of John Winthrop, who taught that a new colony should provide the whole world with a model of what a Christian society ought to be, the Puritans carefully organized their venture and, upon arriving in Massachusetts in 1630, did not undergo the "starving time" that had often plagued other first-year colonies.

The government of Massachusetts developed to include a governor and a representative assembly (called the General Court) selected by the "freemen"—adult male church members. As Massachusetts' population increased (20,000 Puritans had come by 1642 in what came to be called the Great Migration), new towns were chartered, each town being granted a large tract of land by the Massachusetts government. As in European villages, these towns consisted of a number of houses clustered around the church house and the village green. Farmland was located around the outside of the town. In each new town the elect—those who testified of having experienced saving grace—covenanted together as a church.

Rhode Island, Connecticut, and New Hampshire

Puritans saw their colony not as a place to do whatever might strike one's fancy, but as a place to serve God and build His kingdom. Dissidents would be tolerated only insofar as they did not interfere with the colony's mission.

One such dissident was Roger Williams. A Puritan preacher, Williams was received warmly in Massachusetts in 1631; but he had a talent for carrying things to their logical (or sometimes not so logical) extreme. When his activities became disruptive he was asked to leave the colony. To avoid having to return to England—where he would have been even less welcome—he fled to the wilderness around Narragansett Bay, bought land from the Indians, and founded the settlement of Providence (1636), soon populated by his many followers.

Another dissident was Anne Hutchinson, who openly taught things contrary to Puritan doctrine. Called before the General Court to answer for her teachings, she claimed to have had special revelations from God superseding the Bible. This was unthinkable in Puritan theology and led to Hutchinson's banishment from the colony. She also migrated to the area around Narragansett Bay and with her followers founded Portsmouth (1638). She later migrated still farther west and was killed by Indians.

In 1644 Roger Williams secured from Parliament a charter combining Providence, Portsmouth, and other settlements that had sprung up in the area into the colony of Rhode Island. Through Williams' influence the colony granted complete religious toleration. Rhode Island tended to be populated by such exiles and troublemakers as could not find welcome in the other colonies or in Europe. It suffered constant political turmoil.

Connecticut was founded by Puritans who had slight religious disagreements with the leadership of Massachusetts. In 1636 Thomas Hooker led a group of settlers westward to found Hartford. (Hooker, though a good friend of Massachusetts Governor John Winthrop, felt he was exercising somewhat more authority than was prudent.) Others also moved into Connecticut from Massachusetts. In 1639 the *Fundamental Orders of Connecticut*, the first written constitution in America, were drawn up, providing for representative government.

In 1637 a group of Puritans led by John Davenport founded the neighboring colony of New Haven. Davenport and his followers felt that Winthrop, far from being too strict, was not being strict enough. In 1662 a new charter combined both New Haven and Connecticut into an officially recognized colony of Connecticut.

New Hampshire's settlement did not involve any disagreement at all among the Puritans. It was simply settled as an overflow from Massachusetts. In 1677 King Charles II chartered the separate royal colony of New Hampshire. It remained economically dependent on Massachusetts.

Maryland

By the 1630s, the English crown was taking a more direct interest in exercising control over the colonies, and therefore turned away from the practice of granting charters to joint-stock companies, and towards granting such charters to single individuals or groups of individuals known as proprietors. The proprietors would actually own the colony, and would be directly responsible for it to the king, in an arrangement similar to the feudalism of medieval Europe. Though this was seen as providing more opportunity for royal control and less for autonomy on the part of the colonists, in practice proprietary colonies turned out much like the company colonies because settlers insisted on self-government.

The first proprietary colony was Maryland, granted in 1632 to George Calvert, Lord Baltimore. It was to be located just north of the Potomac River and to be at the same time a reward for Calvert's loyal service to the king as well as a refuge for English Catholics, of whom Calvert was one. George Calvert died before the colony could be planted, but the venture was carried forward by his son Cecilius.

From the start, more Protestants than Catholics came. To protect the Catholic minority Calvert approved an Act of Religious Toleration (1649) guaranteeing political rights to Christians of all persuasions. Calvert also allowed a representative assembly. Economically and socially, Maryland developed as a virtual carbon copy of neighboring Virginia.

The Carolinas

In 1663 Charles II, having recently been restored to the throne after a twenty-year Puritan revolution that had seen his father beheaded, moved to reward eight of the noblemen who had helped him regain the crown by granting them a charter for all the lands lying south of Virginia and north of Spanish Florida.

The new colony was called Carolina, after the king. In hopes of attracting settlers, the proprietors came up with an elaborate plan for a hierarchical, almost feudal, society. Not surprisingly this proved unworkable, and despite offers of generous land grants to settlers, the Carolinas grew slowly.

The area of North Carolina developed as an overflow from Virginia with similar economic and cultural features. South Carolina was settled by English planters from the island of Barbados; they founded Charles Town (Charleston) in 1670. These planters brought with them their black slaves; thus, unlike the Chesapeake colonies of Virginia and Maryland, South Carolina had slavery as a fully developed institution from the outset.

New York and New Jersey

Charles II, though immoral and dissolute, was cunning and had an eye for increasing Britain's power. The Dutch colony of New Netherlands, lying between the Chesapeake and the New England colonies, caught his eye as a likely target for British expansion. In 1664 Charles gave his brother, James, Duke of York, title to all the Dutch lands in America, provided James conquered them first. To do this James sent an invasion fleet under the command of Colonel Richard Nicols. New Amsterdam fell almost without a shot and became New York.

James was adamantly opposed to representative assemblies and ordered that there should be none in New York. To avoid unrest Nicols shrewdly granted as many other civil and political rights as possible; but residents, particularly Puritans who had settled on Long Island, continued to agitate for self-government. Finally, in the 1680s, James relented, only to break his promise when he became king in 1685.

To add to the confusion in the newly renamed colony, James granted a part of his newly acquired domain to John Lord Berkeley and Sir George Carteret (two of the Carolina proprietors) who named their new proprietorship New

Jersey. James neglected to tell Colonel Nicols of this, with the result that both Nicols, on the one hand, and Carteret and Berkeley, on the other, were granting title to the same land—to different settlers. Conflicting claims of land ownership plagued New Jersey for decades, being used by the crown in 1702 as a pretext to take over New Jersey as a royal colony.

THE COLONIAL WORLD

Life in the Colonies

New England grew not only from immigration but also from natural increase during the 17th century. The typical New England family had more children than the typical English or Chesapeake family, and more of those children survived to have families of their own. A New Englander could expect to live 15 to 20 years longer than his counterpart in the parent country and 25 to 30 years longer than his fellow colonist in the Chesapeake. Because of the continuity provided by these longer lifespans, because the Puritans had migrated as intact family units, and because of the homogeneous nature of the Puritan New England colonies, New England enjoyed a much more stable and well-ordered society than did the Chesapeake colonies.

Puritans placed great importance on the family, which in their society was highly patriarchal. Young people were generally subject to their parents' direction in the matter of when and whom they would marry. Few defied this system, and illegitimate births were rare. Puritans also placed great importance on the ability to read, since they believed everyone should be able to read the Bible, God's word, himself. As a result, New England was ahead of the other colonies educationally and enjoyed extremely widespread literacy.

Since New England's climate and soil were unsuited to large-scale farming, the region developed a prosperous economy based on small farming, home industry, fishing, and especially trade and a large shipbuilding industry. Boston became a major international port.

Life in the Chesapeake colonies was drastically different. The typical Chesapeake colonist lived a shorter, less healthy life than his New England counterpart and was survived by fewer children. As a result the Chesapeake's population steadily declined despite a constant influx of settlers. Nor was Chesapeake society as stable as that of New England. Most Chesapeake settlers came as indentured servants; and since planters desired primarily male servants for work in the tobacco fields, men largely outnumbered women in Virginia and Maryland. This hindered the development of family life. The short lifespans also contributed to the region's unstable family life, as few children reached adulthood without experiencing the death of one or both parents. Remarriage resulted in households that contained children from several different marriages.

The system of indentured servitude was open to serious abuse, with masters sometimes treating their servants brutally or contriving through some technicality to lengthen their terms of indenture. In any case, 40 percent of Chesapeake region indentured servants failed to survive long enough to gain their freedom.

By the late 17th century life in the Chesapeake was beginning to stabilize, with death rates declining and life expectancies rising. As society stabilized, an elite group of wealthy families such as the Byrds, Carters, Fitzhughs, Lees, and Randolphs, among others, began to dominate the social and political life of the region. Aping the lifestyle of the English country gentry, they built lavish manor houses from which to rule their vast plantations. For every one of these, however, there were many small farmers who worked hard for a living, showed deference to the great planters, and hoped someday they, or their children, might reach that level.

On the bottom rung of Southern society were the black slaves. During the first half of the 17th century, blacks in the Chesapeake made up only a small percentage of the population and were treated more or less as indentured servants. In the decades between 1640 and 1670 this gradually changed, and blacks came to be seen and treated as lifelong chattel slaves whose status would be inherited by their children. Larger numbers of them began to be imported and with this and rapid natural population growth they came by 1750 to compose 30 to 40 percent of the Chesapeake population.

While North Carolina tended to follow Virginia in its economic and social development (although with fewer great planters and more small farmers), South Carolina developed a society even more dominated by large plantations and chattel slavery. By the early decades of the 18th century, blacks had come to outnumber whites in that colony. South Carolina's economy remained dependent on the cultivation of its two staple crops, rice and, to a lesser extent, indigo.

Mercantilism and the Navigation Acts

Beginning around 1650, British authorities began to take more interest in regulating American trade for the benefit of the mother country. A key idea that underlay this policy was the concept of mercantilism. Mercantilists believed the world's wealth was sharply limited, and therefore one nation's gain was automatically another nation's loss. Each nation's goal was to export more than it imported (i.e., to have a "favorable balance of trade"). The difference would be made up in gold and silver, which, so the theory ran, would make the nation strong both economically and militarily. To achieve their goals, mercantilists believed economic activity should be regulated by the government. Colonies could fit into England's mercantilist scheme by providing staple crops, such as rice, tobacco, sugar, and indigo, and raw materials, such as timber, that England would otherwise have been forced to import from other countries.

To make the colonies serve this purpose, Parliament passed a series of Navigation Acts (1651, 1660, 1663, and 1673). These were the foundation of England's worldwide commercial system and some of the most important pieces of imperial legislation during the colonial period. They were also intended as weapons in England's on-going struggle against its chief seventeenth-century maritime rival, Holland. The system created by the Navigation Acts stipulated that trade with the colonies was to be carried on only in ships made in Britain or America and with at least 75 percent British or American crews. Additionally, when certain "enumerated" goods were shipped from an American port, they were to go only to Britain or to another American port. Finally, almost nothing could be imported to the colonies without going through Britain first.

Mercantilism's results were mixed. Though ostensibly for the benefit of all subjects of the British Empire, its provisions benefited some at the expense of others. It boosted the prosperity of New Englanders, who engaged in large-scale shipbuilding (something Britain's mercantilist policy-makers chose to encourage), while it hurt the residents of the Chesapeake by driving down the price of tobacco (an enumerated item). On the whole, the Navigation Acts, as intended, transferred wealth from America to Britain by increasing the prices Americans had to pay for British goods and lowering the prices Americans received for the goods they produced. Mercantilism also helped bring on a series of three wars between England and Holland in the late 1600s.

Charles II and his advisors worked to tighten up the administration of colonies, particularly the enforcement of the Navigation Acts. In Virginia tempers grew short as tobacco prices plunged as a result. Virginians were also angry at Royal Governor Sir William Berkeley, whose high-handed, high-taxing ways they despised and whom they believed was running the colony for the benefit of himself and his circle of cronies.

When, in 1674, an impoverished nobleman of shady past by the name of Nathaniel Bacon came to Virginia and failed to gain admittance to Berkeley's inner circle with its financial advantages, he began to oppose Berkeley at every turn and came to head a faction of like-minded persons. In 1676 disagreement over Indian policy brought the matter to the point of armed conflict. Bacon and his men burned Jamestown, but then the whole matter came to an anticlimactic ending when Bacon died of dysentery.

The British authorities, hearing of the matter, sent ships, troops, and an investigating commission. Berkeley, who had had twenty-three of the rebels hanged in reprisal, was removed. Thenceforth Virginia's royal governors had strict instructions to nun the colony for the benefit of the mother country. In response, Virginia's gentry, who had been divided over Bacon's Rebellion, united to face this new threat to their local autonomy. By political means they consistently obstructed the governors' efforts to increase royal control.

The Half-Way Covenant

By the latter half of the seventeenth century many Puritans were coming to fear that New England was drifting away from its religious purpose. The children and grandchildren of the first generation were displaying more concern for making money than creating a godly society.

To deal with this, some clergymen in 1662 proposed the "Half-Way Covenant," providing a sort of half-way church membership for the children of members, even though those children, having reached adulthood, did not profess saving grace as was normally required for Puritan church membership. Those who embraced the Half-Way Covenant felt that in an increasingly materialistic society it would at least keep church membership rolls full and might preserve some of the church's influence in society.

Some communities rejected the Half-Way Covenant as an improper compromise, but in general the shift toward secular values continued, though slowly.

King Philip's War

As New England's population grew, local Indian tribes felt threatened, and conflict sometimes resulted. Puritans endeavored to convert Indians to Christianity. The Bible was translated into Algonquian; four villages were set up for converted Indians, who by 1650 numbered over a thousand. Still, most Indians remained unconverted.

In 1675 a Wampanoag chief named King Philip (Metacomet) led a war to exterminate the whites. Some 2,000 settlers lost their lives before King Philip was killed and his tribe subdued. New England continued to experience Indian troubles from time to time, though not as severe as those suffered by Virginia.

The Dominion of New England

The trend toward increasing imperial control of the colonies continued. In 1684 the Massachusetts charter was revoked in retaliation for that colony's large-scale evasion of the restrictions of the Navigation Acts.

The following year Charles II died and was succeeded by his brother, James II. James was prepared to go even farther in controlling the colonies, favoring the establishment of a unified government for all of New England, New York, and New Jersey. This was to be called the Dominion of New England, and the fact that it would abolish representative assemblies and facilitate the imposition of the Church of England on Congregationalist (Puritan) New England made it still more appealing to James.

To head the Dominion, James sent the obnoxious and dictatorial Sir Edmond Andros. Arriving in Boston in 1686, Andros quickly alienated the New Englanders. When news reached America of England's 1688 Glorious Revolution, replacing the Catholic James with his Protestant daughter Mary and her husband, William of Orange, New Englanders cheerfully shipped Andros back to England.

Similar uprisings occurred in New York and Maryland. William and Mary's new government generally accepted these actions, though Jacob Leisler, leader of Leisler's Rebellion in New York, was executed for hesitating to turn over power to the new royal governor. This unfortunate incident poisoned the political climate of New York for many years.

The charter of Massachusetts, now including Plymouth, was restored in 1691, this time as a royal colony, though not as tightly controlled as others of that type.

The Salem Witch Trials

In 1692 Massachusetts was shaken by an unusual incident in which several young girls in Salem Village (now Danvers) claimed to be tormented by the occult activities of certain of their neighbors. Before the resulting Salem witch trials could be stopped by the intervention of Puritan ministers such as Cotton Mather, some twenty persons had been executed (nineteen by hanging and one crushed under a pile of rocks).

Pennsylvania and Delaware

Pennsylvania was founded as a refuge for Quakers. One of a number of radical religious sects that had sprung up about the time of the English Civil War, the Quakers held many controversial beliefs. They believed all persons had an "inner light" which allowed them to commune directly with God. They believed human institutions were, for the most part, unnecessary and, since they believed they could receive revelation directly from God, placed little importance on the Bible. They were also pacifists and declined to show customary deference to those who were considered to be their social superiors. This and their aggressiveness in denouncing established institutions brought them trouble in both Britain and America.

William Penn, a member of a prominent British family, converted to Quakerism as a young man. Desiring to found a colony as a refuge for Quakers, in 1681 he sought and received from Charles II a grant of land in America as payment of a large debt the king had owed Penn's late father.

Penn advertised his colony widely in Europe, offered generous terms on land, and guaranteed a representative assembly and full religious freedom. He personally went to America to set up his colony, laying out the city of Philadelphia. He succeeded in maintaining peaceful relations with the Indians.

In the years that followed, settlers flocked to Pennsylvania from all over Europe. The colony grew and prospered and its fertile soil made it not only attractive to settlers, but also a large exporter of grain to Europe and the West Indies.

Delaware, though at first part of Pennsylvania, was granted by Penn a separate legislature, but until the American Revolution, Pennsylvania's proprietary governors also functioned as governor of Delaware.

THE 18TH CENTURY

Economy and Population

British authorities continued to regulate the colonial economy, though usually without going so far as to provoke unrest. An exception was the Molasses Act of 1733, which would have been disastrous for New England merchants. In this case, trouble was averted by the customs agents wisely declining to enforce the act stringently.

The constant drain of wealth from America to Britain, created by the mother country's mercantilistic policies, led to a corresponding drain in hard currency (gold and silver). The artificially low prices that this shortage of money created for American goods was even more advantageous to British buyers. When colonial legislatures responded by endeavoring to create paper money, British authorities blocked such moves. Despite these hindrances, the colonial American economy remained for the most part extremely prosperous.

America's population continued to grow rapidly, both from natural increases due to prosperity and a healthy environment, and from large-scale immigration, not only of English but also of such other groups as Scots-Irish and Germans.

The Germans were prompted to migrate because of wars, poverty, and religious persecution in their homeland. They found Pennsylvania especially attractive and settled there fairly close to the frontier, where land was more readily available. They eventually came to be called the "Pennsylvania Dutch."

The Scots-Irish, Scottish Presbyterians who had been living in northern Ireland for several generations, left their homes because of high rent and economic depression. In America they settled even farther west than the Germans, on or beyond the frontier in the Appalachians.

The Early Wars of the Empire

Between 1689 and 1763 Britain and its American colonies fought a series of four wars with Spain, France, and France's Indian allies, in part to determine who would dominate North America.

Though the first war, known in America as King William's War (1689–1697) but in Europe as the War of the League of Augsburg, was a limited conflict involving no major battles in America, it did bring a number of bloody and terrifying border raids by Indians. It was ended by the Treaty of Ryswick, which made no major territorial changes.

The second war was known in America as Queen Anne's War (1702–1713), but in Europe as the War of the Spanish Succession, and brought America twelve years of sporadic fighting against France and Spain. It was ended by the Treaty of Utrecht, the terms of which gave Britain major territorial gains and trade advantages.

In 1739 war once again broke out with France and Spain. Known in America as King George's war, it was called the War of Jenkins' Ear in Europe (since Captain Robert Jenkins had claimed to have lost an ear to the Spanish coast guards in the Caribbean) and later the War of the Austrian Succession. American troops played an active role, accompanying the British on several important expeditions and suffering thousands of casualties. In 1745 an all-New England army, led by William Pepperrell, captured the powerful French fortress of Louisbourg at the mouth of the St. Lawrence River. To the Americans' disgust, the

British in the 1748 Treaty of Aix-la-Chapelle gave Louisbourg back to France in exchange for lands in India.

Georgia

With this almost constant imperial warfare in mind, it was decided to found a colony as a buffer between South Carolina and Spanish-held Florida. A group of British philanthropists, led by General James Oglethorpe, obtained a charter for such a colony in 1732, to be located between the Savannah and Altamaha rivers and to be populated by such poor as could not manage to make a living in Great Britain.

The philanthropist trustees, who were to control the colony for twenty-one years before it reverted to royal authority, made elaborate and detailed rules to mold the new colony's society as they felt best. As a result, relatively few settlers came, and those who did complained endlessly. By 1752 Oglethorpe and his colleagues were ready to acknowledge their efforts a failure.

The Enlightenment

As the eighteenth century progressed, Americans came to be more or less influenced by European ways of thought, culture, and society. Some Americans embraced the European intellectual movement known as the "Enlightenment."

The key concept of the Enlightenment was rationalism—the belief that human reason was adequate to solve all of mankind's problems and, correspondingly, much less faith was needed in the central role of God as an active force in the universe.

A major English political philosopher of the Enlightenment was John Locke. Writing partially to justify England's 1688 Glorious Revolution, he strove to find in the social and political world the sort of natural laws Isaac Newton had recently discovered in the physical realm. He held that such natural laws included the rights of life, liberty, and property; that to secure these rights people submit to governments; and that governments which abuse these rights may justly be overthrown. His writings were enormously influential in America, though usually indirectly, by way of early eighteenth-century English political philosophers. Americans tended to equate Locke's law of nature with the universal law of God.

The most notable Enlightenment man in America was Benjamin Franklin. While Franklin never denied the existence of God, he focused his attention on human reason and what it could accomplish.

The Great Awakening

Of much greater impact on the lives of the common people in America was the movement known as the Great Awakening. It consisted of a series of religious revivals occurring throughout the colonies from the 1720s to the 1740s. Preachers such as the Dutch Reformed Theodore Frelinghuysen, the Presbyterians William and Gilbert Tennent, and the Congregationalist Jonathan Edwards—best known for his sermon "Sinners in the Hands of an Angry God"—proclaimed a message of personal repentance and faith in Jesus Christ for salvation from an otherwise certain eternity in hell. The most dynamic preacher of the Great Awakening was the Englishman George Whitefield, who traveled through the colonies several times, speaking to crowds of up to 30,000.

The Great Awakening had several important results. America's religious community came to be divided between the "Old Lights," who rejected the great Awakening, and the "New Lights," who accepted it—and sometimes suffered persecution because of their fervor. A number of colleges were founded (many of them today's "Ivy League" schools), primarily for the purpose of training New-Light ministers. The Great Awakening also fostered a greater readiness to lay the claims of established authority (in this case religious) alongside a fixed standard (in this case the Bible) and to reject any claims it found wanting.

The French and Indian War

The Treaty of Aix-la-Chapelle (1748), ending King George's War, provided little more than a breathing space before the next European and imperial war. England and France continued on a collision course as France determined to take complete control of the Ohio Valley and western Pennsylvania.

British authorities ordered colonial governors to resist this, and Virginia's Robert Dinwiddie, already involved in speculation on the Ohio Valley lands, was eager to comply. George Washington, a young major of the Virginia militia, was sent to western Pennsylvania to request the French to leave. When the French declined, Washington was sent in 1754 with 200 Virginia militiamen to expel them. After success in a small skirmish, Washington was forced by superior numbers to fall back on his hastily built Fort Necessity and then to surrender.

The war these operations initiated spread to Europe two years later, where it was known as the Seven Years' War. In America it later came to be known as the French and Indian War.

While Washington skirmished with the French in western Pennsylvania, delegates of seven colonies met in Albany, New York, to discuss common plans for defense. Delegate Benjamin Franklin proposed a plan for an intercolonial government. While the other colonies showed no support for the idea, it was an important precedent for the concept of uniting in the face of a common enemy.

To deal with the French threat, the British dispatched Major General Edward Braddock with several regiments of British regular troops. Braddock marched overland toward the French outpost of Fort Duquesne, at the place where the Monongahela and Allegheny rivers join to form the Ohio. About eight miles short of his goal he was ambushed by a small force of French and Indians. Two-thirds of the British regulars, including Braddock himself, were killed. However, Britain bounced back from this humiliating defeat and several others that followed, and under the leadership of its capable and energetic prime minister, William Pitt, had by 1760 taken Quebec and Montreal and virtually liquidated the French empire in North America.

By the Treaty of Paris of 1763, which officially ended hostilities, Britain gained all of Canada and all of what is now the United States east of the Mississippi River. France lost all of its North American holdings.

Americans at the end of the French and Indian War were proud to be part of the victorious British Empire and proud of the important role they had played in making it so. They felt affection for Great Britain, and thoughts of independence would not have crossed their minds.

HISTORICAL TIMELINE

The Colonial Period (1500–1763)

1517	Martin Luther challenges Roman Catholic authority, beginning Protestant Reformation in Europe
1521	Cortés conquers Aztecs in Mexico Magellan circumnavigates the globe
1533	Pizarro captures Inca capital in Peru
1539	De Soto explores southeastern U.S.
1540	Coronado explores southwestern U.S.
1555	Elizabeth I takes throne in England
1585	Roanoke Island colony established off Virginia coast, then disappears
1607	Jamestown colony founded
1608	Champlain founds Quebec
1611	First Virginia tobacco crop harvested
1619	First Africans arrive in Virginia
1620	Plymouth Colony founded House of Burgesses established in Virginia
1622	Powhatan Confederacy attacks Virginia settlers
1630	Massachusetts Bay Colony founded
1635	Roger Williams establishes Rhode Island colony
1636	Harvard College founded

1660	Anne Hutchinson expelled from Massachusetts Bay Colony
1642–1648	English Civil War
1647	Massachusetts law requires a public school in every town
1649	King Charles I executed
1660	Charles II becomes king
1662	Halfway Covenant established in New England
1676	Bacon's Rebellion in Virginia
1681	Pennsylvania established by William Penn
1688	Glorious Revolution in England William and Mary succeed James II
1692	Witchcraft trials begin in Salem
1714	George I takes throne, beginning Hanover dynasty
1734	Great Awakening begins
1739	Stono Rebellion in North Carolina George Whitefield begins preaching in America
1743	Benjamin Franklin sets up the American Philosophical Society
1754	French and Indian War begins Albany Plan of Union
1759	Britain captures Quebec
1763	Regulator movement in the Carolinas Pontiac's Revolt Treaty of Paris

3 THE AMERICAN REVOLUTION (1763–1787)

THE COMING OF THE AMERICAN REVOLUTION

Writs of Assistance

While Americans' feelings toward Great Britain were pride and affection, British officials felt contemptuous of Americans and were eager to increase imperial control over them beyond anything that had previously been attempted. This drive to gain new authority over the colonies, beginning in 1763, led directly to American independence.

Even before that time the Writs of Assistance cases had demonstrated that Americans would not accept a reduction of their freedom.

In 1761 a young Boston lawyer named James Otis argued before a Massachusetts court that Writs of Assistance (general search warrants issued to help royal officials stop evasion of Britain's mercantilist trade restrictions) were contrary to natural law. He made his point though he lost his case, and others in the colonies joined in protesting against the Writs.

Grenville and the Stamp Act

In 1763 the strongly anti-American George Grenville became prime minister and set out to solve some of the empire's more pressing problems. Chief among these was the large national debt incurred in the recent war.

Of related concern was the cost of defending the American frontier, recently the scene of a bloody Indian uprising led by an Ottawa chief named Pontiac. Goaded by French traders, Pontiac had aimed to drive the entire white population into the sea. While failing in that endeavor, he had succeeded in killing a large number of settlers along the frontier.

Grenville created a comprehensive program to deal with these problems and moved energetically to put it into effect. He sent the Royal Navy to suppress American smuggling and vigorously enforce the Navigation Acts. He also issued the Proclamation of 1763, forbidding white settlement west of the crest of the Appalachians, in hopes of keeping the Indians happy and the settlers close to the coast and thus easier to control.

In 1764, Grenville pushed through Parliament the Sugar Act (also known as the Revenue Act) aimed at raising revenue by taxes on goods imported by the Americans. It halved the duties imposed by the Molasses Act but was intended to raise revenue rather than control trade. Unlike the Molasses Act, it was stringently enforced, with accused violators facing trial in admiralty courts without benefit of jury or the normal protections of due process.

Grenville determined to maintain up to 10,000 British regulars in America to control both colonists and Indians and secure passage of the Quartering Act, requiring the colonies in which British troops were stationed to pay for their maintenance. Americans had never before been required to support a standing army in their midst.

Grenville also saw through the passage of his Currency Act of 1764, which forbade once and for all any colonial attempts to issue currency not redeemable in gold or silver, making it more difficult for Americans to avoid the constant drain of money that Britain's mercantilist policies were designed to create in the colonies.

Most important, however, Grenville got Parliament to pass the Stamp Act (1765), imposing a direct tax on Americans for the first time. The Stamp Act required Americans to purchase revenue stamps on everything from newspapers to legal documents and would have created an impossible drain on hard currency in the colonies. Because it overlooked the advantage already provided by Britain's mercantilist exploitation of the colonies, Grenville's policy was shortsighted and foolish; but few in Parliament were inclined to see this.

Americans reacted first with restrained and respectful petitions and pamphlets, in which they pointed out that "taxation without representation is tyranny." From there resistance progressed to stronger and stronger protests that eventually became violent and involved intimidation of those Americans who had contracted to be the agents for distributing the stamps.

Resistance was particularly intense in Massachusetts, where it was led first by James Otis and then by Samuel Adams, who formed the organization known as the Sons of Liberty.

Other colonies copied Massachusetts' successful tactics while adding some of their own. In Virginia, a young Burgess named Patrick Henry introduced seven resolutions denouncing the Stamp Act. Though only the four most moderate of them were passed by the House of Burgesses, newspapers picked up all seven and circulated them widely through the colonies, giving the impression all seven had been adopted. By their denial of Parliament's authority to tax the colonies they encouraged other colonial legislatures to issue strongly worded statements.

In October 1765, delegates from nine colonies met as the Stamp Act Congress. Called by the Massachusetts legislature at the instigation of James Otis, the Stamp Act Congress passed moderate resolutions against the act, asserting that Americans could not be taxed without their consent, given by their representatives. They pointed out that Americans were not, and because of their location could not practically be, represented in Parliament and concluded by calling for the repeal of both the Stamp and Sugar Acts. Most important, however, the Stamp Act Congress showed that representatives of the colonies could work together and gave political leaders in the various colonies a chance to become acquainted with each other.

Most effective in achieving repeal of the Stamp Act was colonial merchants' nonimportation (boycott) of British goods. Begun as an agreement among New

York merchants, the boycott spread throughout the colonies and had a powerful effect on British merchants and manufacturers, who began clamoring for the act's repeal.

Meanwhile, the fickle King George III had dismissed Grenville over an unrelated disagreement and replaced him with a Cabinet headed by Charles Lord Rockingham. In March 1766, under the leadership of the new ministry, Parliament repealed the Stamp Act. At the same time, however, it passed the Declaratory Act, claiming power to tax or make laws for the Americans "in all cases whatsoever."

Though the Declaratory Act denied exactly the principle Americans had just been at such pains to assert—that of no taxation without representation—the Americans generally ignored it in their exuberant celebration of the repeal of the Stamp Act. Americans continued to eagerly proclaim their loyalty to Great Britain.

The Townshend Acts

The Rockingham ministry proved to be even shorter lived than that of Grenville. It was replaced with a Cabinet dominated by Chancellor of the Exchequer Charles Townshend. Townshend had boasted that he could successfully tax the colonies, and in 1766 Parliament gave him his chance by passing his program of taxes on items imported into the colonies. These taxes came to be known as the Townshend Duties. Townshend mistakenly believed the Americans would accept this method while rejecting the use of direct internal taxes. The Townshend Acts also included the use of admiralty courts to try those accused of violations, the use of writs of assistance, and the paying of customs officials out of the fines they levied. Townshend also had the New York legislature suspended for non-compliance with the Quartering Act.

American reaction was at first slow. Philadelphia lawyer John Dickinson wrote an anonymous pamphlet entitled "Letters from a Farmer in Pennsylvania," in which he pointed out in moderate terms that the Townshend Acts violated the principle of no taxation without representation and that if Parliament could suspend the New York legislature it could do the same to others. At the same time he urged a restrained response on the part of his fellow Americans.

In February 1768 the Massachusetts legislature, at the urging of Samuel Adams, passed the Massachusetts Circular Letter, reiterating Dickinson's mild arguments and urging other colonial legislatures to pass petitions calling on Parliament to repeal the acts. Had the British government done nothing, the matter might have passed quietly.

Instead, British authorities acted. They ordered that if the letter was not withdrawn, the Massachusetts legislature should be dissolved and new elections held. They forbade the other colonial legislatures to take up the matter, and they also sent four regiments of troops to Boston to prevent intimidation of royal officials and intimidate the populace instead.

The last of these actions was in response to the repeated pleas of the Boston customs agents. Corrupt agents had used technicalities of the confusing and poorly written Sugar and Townshend Acts to entrap innocent merchants and line their own pockets. Mob violence had threatened when agents had seized the ship *Liberty*, belonging to Boston merchant John Hancock. Such incidents prompted the call for troops.

The sending of troops, along with the British authority's repressive response to the Massachusetts Circular Letter, aroused the Americans to resistance. Non-importation was again instituted, and soon British merchants were calling on Parliament to repeal the acts. In March 1770, Parliament, under the new prime minister, Frederick Lord North, repealed all of the taxes except that on tea, which was retained to prove Parliament had the right to tax the colonies if it so desired.

By the time of the repeal, however, friction between British soldiers and Boston citizens had led to an incident in which five Bostonians were killed. Although the British soldiers had acted more or less in self-defense, Samuel Adams labeled the incident the "Boston Massacre" and publicized it widely. At their trial the British soldiers were defended by prominent Massachusetts lawyer John Adams and were acquitted on the charge of murder.

The Return of Relative Peace

Following the repeal of the Townshend duties a period of relative peace set in. The tax on tea remained as a reminder of Parliament's claims, but it could be easily avoided by smuggling.

Much good will had been lost and colonists remained suspicious of the British government. Many Americans believed the events of the previous decade to have been the work of a deliberate conspiracy to take their liberty.

Occasional incidents marred the relative peace. One such was the burning, by a seagoing mob of Rhode Islanders disguised as Indians, of the *Gaspee*, a British customs schooner that had run aground offshore. The *Gaspee's* captain and crew had alienated Rhode Islanders by their extreme zeal for catching smugglers as well as by their theft and vandalism when ashore.

In response to this incident British authorities appointed a commission to find the guilty parties and bring them to England for trial. Though those responsible for the burning of the *Gaspee* were never found, this action on the part of the British prompted the colonial legislatures to form committees of correspondence to communicate with each other regarding possible threats from the British government.

The Tea Act

The relative peace was brought to an end by the Tea Act of 1773.

In desperate financial condition—partially because the Americans were buying smuggled Dutch tea rather than the taxed British product—the British East

India Company sought and obtained from Parliament concessions allowing it to ship tea directly to the colonies rather than only by way of Britain. The result would be that East India Company tea, even with the tax, would be cheaper than smuggled Dutch tea. The colonists would thus, it was hoped, buy the tea, tax and all. The East India Company would be saved and the Americans would be tacitly accepting Parliament's right to tax them.

The Americans, however, proved resistant to this approach, and, rather than seem to admit Parliament's right to tax, they vigorously resisted the cheaper tea. Various methods, including tar and feathers, were used to prevent the collection of the tax on tea. In most ports Americans did not allow the tea to be landed.

In Boston, however, pro-British Governor Thomas Hutchinson forced a confrontation by ordering Royal Navy vessels to prevent the tea ships from leaving the harbor. After twenty days this would, by law, result in the cargoes being sold at auction and the tax paid. The night before the time was to expire, December 16, 1773, Bostonians thinly disguised as Indians boarded the ships and threw the tea into the harbor.

Many Americans felt this—the destruction of private property—was going too far, but the reaction of Lord North and Parliament quickly united Americans in support of Boston and opposition to Britain.

The Intolerable Acts

The British responded with four acts collectively titled the Coercive Acts. First, the Boston Port Act closed the port of Boston to all trade until local citizens would agree to pay for the lost tea (they would not). Secondly, the Massachusetts Government Act greatly increased the power of Massachusetts' royal governor at the expense of the legislature. Thirdly, the Administration of Justice Act provided that royal officials accused of crimes in Massachusetts could be tried elsewhere, where chances of acquittal might be greater. Finally, a strengthened Quartering Act allowed the new governor, General Thomas Gage, to quarter his troops anywhere, including unoccupied private homes.

A further act of Parliament also angered and alarmed Americans. This was the Quebec Act, which extended the province of Quebec to the Ohio River, established Roman Catholicism as Quebec's official religion, and set up for Quebec a government without a representative assembly.

For Americans this was a denial of the hopes and expectations of westward expansion for which they had fought the French and Indian War. Also, New Englanders especially saw it as a threat that in their colonies too, Parliament could establish autocratic government and the hated Church of England.

Americans lumped the Quebec Act together with the Coercive Acts and referred to them all as the Intolerable Acts.

In response to the Coercive Acts, the First Continental Congress was called and met in Philadelphia in September 1774. It once again petitioned Parliament for relief but also passed the Suffolk Resolves (so called because they were first passed in Suffolk County, Massachusetts), denouncing the Intolerable Acts and calling for strict nonimportation and rigorous preparation of local militia companies in case the British should resort to military force.

The Congress then narrowly rejected a plan, submitted by Joseph Galloway of Pennsylvania, calling for a union of the colonies within the empire and a rearrangement of relations with Parliament. Most of the delegates felt matters had already gone too far for such a mild measure. Finally, before adjournment, it was agreed that there should be a Second Continental Congress to meet in May of the following year if the colonies' grievances had not been righted by then.

THE WAR FOR INDEPENDENCE

Lexington and Concord

The British government paid little attention to the First Continental Congress, having decided to teach the Americans a military lesson. More troops were sent to Massachusetts, which was officially declared to be in a state of rebellion. Orders were sent to General Gage to arrest the leaders of the resistance or, failing that, to provoke any sort of confrontation that would allow him to turn British military might loose on the Americans.

Gage decided on a reconnaissance-in-force to find and destroy a reported stockpile of colonial arms and ammunition at Concord. Seven hundred British troops set out on this mission on the night of April 18, 1775. Their movement was detected by American surveillance and news was spread throughout the countryside by dispatch riders Paul Revere and William Dawes.

At the little village of Lexington, Captain John Parker and some seventy Minutemen (militiamen trained to respond at a moment's notice) awaited the British on the village green. As the British approached, a British officer shouted at the Minutemen to lay down their arms and disperse. The Minutemen did not lay down their arms but did turn to file off the green. A shot was fired, and then the British opened fire and charged. Eight Americans were killed and several others wounded, most shot in the back.

The British continued to Concord only to find that nearly all of the military supplies they had expected to find had already been moved. Attacked by growing numbers of Minutemen, they began to retreat toward Boston. As the British retreated, Minutemen, swarming from every village for miles around, fired on the column from behind rocks, trees, and stone fences. Only a relief force of additional British troops saved the first column from destruction.

Open warfare had begun, and the myth of British invincibility was destroyed. Militia came in large numbers from all the New England colonies to join the force besieging Gage and his army in Boston.

Bunker Hill

In May 1775, three more British generals, William Howe, Henry Clinton, and John Burgoyne, arrived in Boston urging Gage to further aggressive action. The following month the Americans tightened the noose around Boston by fortifying Breed's Hill (a spur of Bunker Hill), from which they could, if necessary, bombard Boston.

The British determined to remove them by a frontal attack that would demonstrate the awesome power of British arms. Twice the British were thrown back and finally succeeded as the Americans ran out of ammunition. Over a thousand British soldiers were killed or wounded in what turned out to be the bloodiest battle of the war (June 17, 1775). Yet the British had gained very little and remained bottled up in Boston.

Meanwhile in May 1775, American forces under Ethan Allen and Benedict Arnold took Fort Ticonderoga on Lake Champlain.

Congress, hoping Canada would join in resistance against Britain, authorized two expeditions into Quebec. One, under General Richard Montgomery took Montreal and then turned toward the city of Quebec. It was met there by the second expedition under Benedict Arnold. The attack on Quebec (December 31, 1775) failed. Montgomery was killed, Arnold wounded, and American hopes for Canada ended.

The Second Continental Congress

While these events were taking place in New England and Canada, the Second Continental Congress met in Philadelphia in May 1775. Congress was divided into two main factions. One was composed mostly of New Englanders and leaned toward declaring independence from Britain. The other drew its strength primarily from the Middle Colonies and was not yet ready to go that far. It was led by John Dickinson of Pennsylvania.

Congress took action to deal with the difficult situation facing the colonies. It adopted the New England army around Boston, calling on the other colonies to send troops and sending George Washington to command it, adopted a "Declaration of the Causes and Necessity for Taking up Arms" and adopted the "Olive Branch Petition" pleading with King George III to intercede with Parliament to restore peace.

This last overture was ignored in Britain, where the king gave his approval to the Prohibitory Act, declaring the colonies in rebellion and no longer under his protection. Preparations were made for full-scale war against America.

Throughout 1775, Americans remained deeply loyal to Britain and King George III despite the king's proclamations declaring them to be in revolt. In Congress moderates still resisted independence.

In January 1776, Thomas Paine published a pamphlet entitled *Common Sense*, calling for immediate independence. Its arguments were extreme and sometimes illogical and its language intemperate, but it sold largely and may have had much influence in favor of independence. Continued evidence of Britain's intention to carry on the war throughout the colonies also weakened the moderates' resistance to independence. The Prohibitory Act, with its virtual declaration of war against America, convinced many that no further moral scruples need stand in the way of such a step.

On June 7, 1776, Richard Henry Lee of Virginia introduced a series of formal resolutions in Congress calling for independence and a national government. Accepting these ideas, Congress named two committees. One, headed by John Dickinson, was to work out a framework for a national government. The other was to draft a statement of the reasons for declaring independence. This statement, the Declaration of Independence, was primarily the work of Thomas Jefferson of Virginia. It was a restatement of political ideas by then commonplace in America, showing why the former colonists felt justified in separating from Great Britain. It was formally adopted by Congress on July 4, 1776.

Washington Takes Command

Britain, meanwhile, was preparing a massive effort to conquer the United States. Gage was removed for being too timid, and top command went to Howe. To supplement the British army, large numbers of troops were hired from various German principalities. Since many of these Germans came from the state of Hesse-Kassel, Americans referred to all such troops as Hessians.

Although the London authorities desired a quick and smashing campaign, General Howe and his brother, British naval commander Richard, Admiral Lord Howe, intended to move slowly, using their powerful force to cow the Americans into signing loyalty oaths.

In March 1776, Washington placed on Dorchester Heights, overlooking Boston, some of the large cannon that had been captured at Ticonderoga, forcing the British to evacuate the city.

The British shipped their troops to Nova Scotia and then, together with large reinforcements from Britain, landed that summer at New York City. They hoped to find many loyalists there and make that city the key to their campaign to subdue America.

Washington anticipated the move and was waiting at New York, which Congress had ordered should be defended. However, the under-trained, under-equipped, and badly outnumbered American army was no match for the powerful forces under the Howes. Defeated at the Battle of Long Island (August 27, 1776), Washington narrowly avoided being trapped there (an escape partially due to the Howes' slowness). Defeated again at the Battle of Washington Heights (August 29–30, 1776) on Manhattan, Washington was forced to retreat across New Jersey with the aggressive British General Lord Cornwallis, a subordinate of Howe, in pursuit. By December, what was left of Washington's army had made it into Pennsylvania.

With his victory almost complete, Howe decided to wait till spring to finish annihilating Washington's army. Scattering his troops in small detachments so as to hold all of New Jersey, he went into winter quarters.

Washington, with his small army melting away as demoralized soldiers deserted, decided on a bold stroke. On Christmas night 1776, his army crossed the Delaware River and struck the Hessians at Trenton. The Hessians, still groggy from their hard-drinking Christmas party, were easily defeated. A few days later Washington defeated a British force at Princeton (January 3, 1777).

Howe was so shocked by these two unexpected defeats that he pulled his outposts back close to New York. Much of New Jersey was regained. Those who had signed British loyalty oaths in the presence of Howe's army were now at the mercy of their patriot neighbors. And Washington's army was saved from disintegration.

Early in the war France began making covert shipments of arms to the Americans. This it did, not because the French government loved freedom (it did not), but because it hated Britain and saw the war as a way to weaken Britain by depriving it of its colonies. Arms shipments from France were vital for the Americans.

Saratoga and Valley Forge

For the summer of 1777 the British home authorities adopted an elaborate plan of campaign urged on them by General Burgoyne. According to the plan, Burgoyne himself would lead an army southward from Canada along the Lake Champlain corridor while another army under Howe moved up the Hudson River to join hands with Burgoyne at Albany. This, it was hoped, would cut off New England and allow the British to subdue that region, which they considered the hotbed of the "rebellion."

Howe had other ideas and shipped his army by sea to Chesapeake Bay, hoping to capture the American capital, Philadelphia, and destroy Washington's army at the same time. At Brandywine Creek (September 1, 1777) Washington tried but failed to stop Howe's advance. Yet the American army, though badly beaten, remained intact. Howe occupied Philadelphia as the Congress fled westward to York, Pennsylvania.

In early October, Washington attempted to drive Howe out of Philadelphia; but his attack at Germantown, though at first successful, failed at least partially due to thick fog and the still imperfect level of training in the American army, both of which contributed to confusion among the troops. Thereafter Howe settled down to comfortable winter quarters in Philadelphia, and Washington and his army to very uncomfortable ones at nearby Valley Forge, while far to the north, the British strategy that Howe had ignored was going badly awry.

Burgoyne's advance began well but slowed as the Americans placed obstructions on the rough wilderness trails by which his army, including numerous cannon and much bulky baggage, had to advance. A diversionary force of British troops and Iroquois Indians under the command of Colonel Barry St. Leger swung east of Burgoyne's column, but although it defeated and killed American General Nicholas Herkimer at the Battle of Oriskany (August 6, 1777), it was finally forced to withdraw to Canada.

In mid-August, a detachment of Burgoyne's force was defeated by New England militia under General John Stark near Bennington in what is now

Vermont. By autumn Burgoyne found his way blocked by an American army: continentals (American regular troops such as those that made up most of Washington's army, paid, in theory at least, by Congress); and New England militia, under General Horatio Gates, at Saratoga, about thirty miles north of Albany. Burgoyne's two attempts to break through (September 19 and October 7, 1777) were turned back by the Americans under the brilliant battlefield leadership of Benedict Arnold. On October 17, 1777, Burgoyne surrendered to Gates.

The American victory at Saratoga convinced the French to join openly in the war against England. Eventually the Spanish (1779) and the Dutch (1780) joined as well, and England was faced with a world war.

The British Move South

The new circumstances brought a change in British strategy. With fewer troops available for service in America, the British would have to depend more on loyalists, and since they imagined that larger numbers of these existed in the South than elsewhere, it was there they turned their attention.

Howe was relieved and replaced by General Henry Clinton, who was ordered to abandon Philadelphia and march to New York. In doing so, he narrowly avoided defeat at the hands of Washington's army—much improved after a winter's drilling at Valley Forge under the direction of Prussian nobleman Baron von Steuben—at the Battle of Monmouth, New Jersey (June 28, 1778).

Clinton was thenceforth to maintain New York as Britain's main base in America while detaching troops to carry out the new Southern strategy. In November 1778 the British easily conquered Georgia. Late the following year Clinton moved on South Carolina with a land and naval force, and in May 1780, U.S. General Benjamin Lincoln surrendered Charleston. Clinton then returned to New York, leaving Cornwallis to continue the Southern campaign.

Congress, alarmed at the British successes, sent General Horatio Gates to lead the forces opposing Cornwallis. Gates blundered to a resounding defeat at the Battle of Camden, in South Carolina (August 16, 1780).

The general outlook seemed bad for America at that point in the war. Washington's officers grumbled about their pay in arrears. The army was understrength and then suffered successive mutinies among the Pennsylvania and New Jersey troops. Benedict Arnold went over to the British. In short, the British seemed to be winning the contest of endurance. This outlook was soon to change.

In the West, George Rogers Clark, acting under the auspices of the state of Virginia, led an expedition down the Ohio River and into the area of present-day Illinois and Indiana, defeating a British force at Vincennes, Indiana, and securing the area north of the Ohio River for the United States.

In the South, Cornwallis began to move northward toward North Carolina, but on October 7, 1780, a detachment of his force under Major Patrick Ferguson was defeated by American frontiersmen at the Battle of Kings Mountain in northern South Carolina. To further increase the problems facing the British, Cornwallis had unwisely moved north without bothering to secure South Carolina first. The result was that the British would no sooner leave an area than American militia or guerilla bands, such as that under Francis Marion ("the Swamp Fox"), were once again in control and able to deal with those who had expressed loyalty to Britain in the presence of Cornwallis's army.

To command the continental forces in the South, Washington sent his most able subordinate, military genius Nathaniel Greene. Greene's brilliant strategy led to a crushing victory at Cowpens, South Carolina (January 17, 1781), by troops under Greene's subordinate, General Daniel Morgan of Virginia. It also led to a near victory by Greene's own force at Guilford Court House, North Carolina (March 15, 1781).

Yorktown

The frustrated and impetuous Cornwallis now abandoned the Southern strategy and moved north into Virginia. Clinton, disgusted at this departure from plan, sent instructions for Cornwallis to take up a defensive position and await further orders. Against his better judgment Cornwallis did so, selecting Yorktown, Virginia, on a peninsula that reaches into Chesapeake Bay between the York and James rivers.

Washington now saw and seized the opportunity this presented. With the aid of a French fleet which took control of Chesapeake Bay and a French army that joined him in sealing off the land approaches to Yorktown, Washington succeeded in trapping Cornwallis. After three weeks of siege, Cornwallis surrendered on October 17, 1781.

The War at Sea

Britain had other problems as well. Ships of the small but daring U.S. Navy as well as privateers (privately owned vessels outfitted with guns and authorized by a warring government to capture enemy merchant ships for profit) preyed on the British merchant marine. John Paul Jones, the most famous of American naval leaders, captured ships and carried out audacious raids along the coast of Britain itself. French and Spanish naval forces also struck against various outposts of the British Empire.

The Treaty of Paris of 1783

News of the debacle at Yorktown brought the collapse of Lord North's ministry, and the new Cabinet opened peace negotiations. The extremely able American negotiating team was composed of Benjamin Franklin, John Adams, and John Jay. The negotiations continued for some time, delayed by French and Spanish maneuvering. When it became apparent that France and Spain were planning to achieve an agreement unfavorable to the United States, the American envoys negotiated a separate treaty with Britain.

The final agreement became known as the Treaty of Paris of 1783. Its terms stipulated the following: 1) The United States was recognized as an independent nation by the major European powers, including Britain; 2) Its western boundary was set at the Mississippi River; 3) Its southern boundary was set at 31° north latitude (the northern boundary of Florida); 4) Britain retained Canada but had to surrender Florida to Spain; 5) Private British creditors would be free to collect any debts owed by U.S. citizens; and 6) Congress was to recommend that the states restore confiscated loyalist property.

THE CREATION OF NEW GOVERNMENTS

The State Constitutions

After the collapse of British authority in 1775, it became necessary to form new state governments. By the end of 1777 ten new state constitutions had been formed.

Connecticut and Rhode Island kept their colonial charters, which were republican in nature, simply deleting references to British sovereignty. Massachusetts waited until 1780 to complete the adoption of its new constitution. The constitutions ranged from such extremely democratic models as the virtually unworkable Pennsylvania constitution (soon abandoned), in which a unicameral legislature ruled with little check or balance, to more reasonable frameworks such as those of Maryland and Virginia, which included more safeguards against popular excesses.

Massachusetts voters set an important example by insisting that a constitution should be made by a special convention rather than the legislature. This would make the constitution superior to the legislature and, it was hoped, assure that the legislature would be subject to the constitution.

Most state constitutions included bills of rights—lists of things the government was not supposed to do to the people.

The Articles of Confederation

In the summer of 1776, Congress appointed a committee to begin devising a framework for national government. When completed, this document was known as the Articles of Confederation. John Dickinson, who had played a leading role in writing the Articles, felt a strong national government was needed; but by the time Congress finished revising them, the Articles went to the opposite extreme of preserving the sovereignty of the states and creating a very weak national government.

The Articles of Confederation provided for a unicameral Congress in which each state would have one vote, as had been the case in the Continental Congress. Executive authority under the Articles would be vested in a committee of thirteen, one member from each state. In order to amend the Articles, the unanimous consent of all the states was required.

The Articles of Confederation government was empowered to make war, make treaties, determine the amount of troops and money each state should contribute to the war effort, settle disputes between states, admit new states to the Union, and borrow money. More importantly, however, was that it was not empowered to levy taxes, raise troops, or regulate commerce.

Ratification of the Articles of Confederation was delayed by a disagreement over the future status of the lands that lay to the west of the original thirteen states. Some states, notably Virginia, held extensive claims to these lands based on their original colonial charters. Maryland, which had no such claim, withheld ratification until in 1781 Virginia agreed to surrender its western claims to the new national government.

Meanwhile, the country was on its way to deep financial trouble. Unable to tax, Congress resorted to printing large amounts of paper money to finance the war; but these inflated "Continentals" were soon worthless. Other financial schemes fell through, and only grants and loans from France and the Netherlands staved off complete financial collapse. A plan to amend the Articles to give Congress power to tax was stopped by the lone opposition of Rhode Island. The army, whose pay was far in arrears, threatened mutiny. Some of those who favored a stronger national government welcomed this development and in what became known as the Newburgh Conspiracy (1783) consulted with army second-in-command Horatio Gates as to the possibility of using the army to force the states to surrender more power to the national government. This movement was stopped by a moving appeal to the officers by Washington himself.

The Trans-Appalachian West and the Northwest Ordinance

For many Americans the enormous trans-Appalachian frontier represented an opportunity to escape the economic hard times that followed the end of the war.

In 1775, Daniel Boone opened the "Wilderness Road" through the Cumberland Gap and on to the "Bluegrass" region of Kentucky. Others scouted down the Ohio River from Pittsburgh. By 1790, over 100,000 had settled in Kentucky and Tennessee, despite the risk of violent death at the hands of Indians. This risk was made worse by the presence of the British in northwestern military posts that should have been evacuated at the end of the war. From these posts they supplied the Indians with guns and encouraged them to use them on Americans. The Spaniards on the Florida frontier behaved in much the same way.

The settlement of Kentucky and Tennessee increased the pressure for the opening of the lands north of the Ohio River. To facilitate this, Congress passed three land ordinances in the years from 1784 to 1787.

The Land Ordinance of 1784 provided for territorial government and an orderly system by which each territory could progress to full statehood (this ordinance is sometimes considered part of the Land Ordinance of 1785).

The Land Ordinance of 1785 provided for the orderly surveying and distribution of land in townships six miles square, each composed of thirty-six one-square-mile (640 acre) sections, of which one should be set aside for the support of education. (This ordinance is sometimes referred to as the "Northwest Ordinance of 1785").

The Northwest Ordinance of 1787 provided a bill of rights for settlers and forbade slavery north of the Ohio River.

These ordinances were probably the most important legislation of the Articles of Confederation government.

The Jay-Gardoqui Negotiations

Economic depression followed the end of the war as the United States remained locked into the disadvantageous commercial system of the British Empire but without the trade advantages that this system had provided.

One man who thought he saw a way out of the economic quagmire was Congress's secretary of foreign affairs, John Jay. In 1784, Jay began negotiating with Spanish minister Gardoqui a treaty that would have granted lucrative commercial privileges—benefiting large east-coast merchants such as Jay—in exchange for U.S. acceptance of Spain's closure of the Mississippi River as an outlet for the agricultural goods of the rapidly growing settlements in Kentucky and Tennessee. This the Spanish desired because they feared that extensive settlement in what was then the western part of the United States might lead to American hunger for Spanish-held lands.

When Jay reported this to Congress in the summer of 1786, the West and South were outraged. Negotiations were broken off. Some, angered that Jay could show so little concern for the other sections of the country, talked of dissolving the Union; this helped spur to action those who desired not the dissolution but the strengthening of the Union.

Shays' Rebellion

Nationalists were further stimulated to action by Shays' Rebellion (1786). Economic hard times coupled with high taxes intended to pay off the state's war debt drove western Massachusetts farmers to desperation. Led by war veteran Daniel Shays, they shut down courts to prevent judges from seizing property or condemning people to debtors' prison for failing to pay their taxes.

The unrest created a disproportionate amount of panic in the rest of the state and the nation. The citizens of Boston subscribed money to raise an army to suppress the rebels. The success of this army together with timely tax relief caused the "rebellion" to fizzle out fairly quickly.

Amid the panic caused by the news of the uprising, many came to feel that a stronger government was needed to control such violent public outbursts as those of the western Massachusetts farmers.

HISTORICAL TIMELINE

The American Revolution (1763–1787)

1763	Proclamation Line of 1763
1764	Sugar Act Currency Act
1765	Stamp Act Sons of Liberty formed
1767	Townshend Duties Dickinson's "Letters of a Pennsylvania Farmer"
1770	Boston Massacre Lord North becomes British prime minister
1772	H.M.S. *Gaspee* burned off coast of Rhode Island
1773	Tea Act Boston Tea Party
1774	Intolerable Acts First Continental Congress
1775	Lexington and Concord Battle of Bunker Hill
1776	*Common Sense* published by Thomas Paine Declaration of Independence Battle of New York City Battle of Trenton
1777	British surrender 5,800 men at Saratoga American army at Valley Forge
1778	French-American alliance established British begin Southern strategy and capture Savannah
1780	British capture Charleston French army lands in Connecticut
1781	Articles of Confederation approved Gen. Cornwallis surrenders at Yorktown
1783	Treaty of Paris ends war, grants American independence Newburgh Conspiracy of American army officers

4 THE UNITED STATES CONSTITUTION (1785–1789)

DEVELOPMENT AND RATIFICATION

Toward a New Constitution

As time went on, the inadequacy of the Articles of Confederation became increasingly apparent. Congress could not compel the states to comply with the terms of the Treaty of Paris of 1783 regarding debts and loyalists' property. The British used this as an excuse for not evacuating their Northwestern posts, hoping to be on hand to make the most of the situation when, as they not unreasonably expected, the new government fell to pieces. In any case, Congress could do nothing to force them out of the posts, nor to solve any of the nation's other increasingly pressing problems.

In these dismal straits, some called for disunion, others for monarchy. Others felt that republican government could still work if given a better constitution, and they made it their goal to achieve this.

In 1785 a meeting of representatives of Virginia, Maryland, Pennsylvania, and Delaware was held at George Washington's residence, Mt. Vernon, for the purpose of discussing current problems of interstate commerce. At their suggestion the Virginia legislature issued a call for a convention of all the states on the same subject, to meet the following summer in Annapolis, Maryland.

The Annapolis Convention met in September of 1786, but only five states were represented. Among those present, however, were such nationalists as Alexander Hamilton, John Dickinson, and James Madison. With so few states represented it was decided instead to call for a convention of all the states to meet the following summer in Philadelphia for the purpose of revising the Articles of Confederation.

The Constitutional Convention

The men who met in Philadelphia in 1787 were remarkably able, highly educated, and exceptionally accomplished. For the most part they were lawyers, merchants and planters. Though representing individual states, most thought in national terms. Prominent among them were James Madison, Alexander Hamilton, Gouverneur Morris, Robert Morris, John Dickinson, and Benjamin Franklin.

George Washington was unanimously elected to preside, and the enormous respect that he commanded helped hold the convention together through difficult times (as it had the Continental Army) and make the product of the convention's work more attractive to the rest of the nation. The delegates then voted that the convention's discussions should be secret, to avoid the distorting and confusing influence of the press and publicity.

The delegates shared a basic belief in the innate selfishness of man, which must somehow be kept from abusing the power of government. For this purpose the document that they finally produced contained many checks and balances, designed to prevent the government, or any one branch of the government, from gaining too much power.

Madison, who has been called the "father of the Constitution," devised a plan of national government and persuaded fellow Virginian Edmund Randolph, who was more skilled at public speaking, to introduce it. Known as the "Virginia Plan," it called for an executive branch and two houses of Congress, each based on population.

Smaller states, who would thus have seen their influence decreased, objected and countered with William Paterson's "New Jersey Plan," calling for the continuation of a unicameral legislature with equal representation for the states as well as sharply increased powers for the national government.

A temporary impasse developed that threatened to break up the convention. At this point Benjamin Franklin played an important role in reconciling the often wrangling delegates, suggesting that the sessions of the convention henceforth begin with prayer (they did) and making various other suggestions that eventually helped the convention arrive at the "Great Compromise." The Great Compromise provided for a Presidency, a Senate with all states represented equally (by two Senators each), and a House of Representatives with representation according to population.

Another crisis involved North-South disagreement over the issue of slavery. Here also a compromise was reached. Slavery was neither endorsed nor condemned by the Constitution. Each slave was to count as three-fifths of a person for purposes of apportioning representation and direct taxation on the states (the Three-Fifths Compromise). The federal government was prohibited from stopping the importation of slaves prior to 1808.

The third major area of compromise was the nature of the Presidency. This was made easier by the virtual certainty that George Washington would be the first president and the universal trust that he would not abuse the powers of the office or set a bad example for his successors. The result was a strong Presidency with control of foreign policy and the power to veto Congress's legislation. Should the president commit an actual crime, Congress would have the power to impeach him. Otherwise the president would serve for a term of four years and be re-electable without limit. As a check to the possible excesses of democracy, the president was to be elected by an Electoral College, in which each state would have the same number of electors as it did Senators and Representatives combined. The person with the second highest total in the Electoral College would be Vice-President. If no one gained a majority in the Electoral College, the President would be chosen by the House of Representatives.

The new Constitution was to take effect when nine states, through special state conventions, had ratified it.

The Struggle for Ratification

As the struggle over ratification got under way, those favoring the Constitution astutely took for themselves the name Federalists (i.e., advocates of centralized power) and labeled their opponents Antifederalists. The Federalists were effective in explaining the convention and the document it had produced. *The Federalist Papers*, written as a series of eighty-five newspaper articles by Alexander Hamilton, James Madison, and John Jay, brilliantly expounded the Constitution and demonstrated how it was designed to prevent the abuse of power from any direction. These essays are considered to be the best commentary on the Constitution by those who helped write it.

At first, ratification progressed smoothly, with five states approving in quick succession. In Massachusetts, however, a tough fight developed. By skillful maneuvering, Federalists were able to win over to their side such popular opponents of the Constitution as Samuel Adams and John Hancock. Others were won over by the promise that a bill of rights would be added to the Constitution, limiting the federal government just as the state governments were limited by their bills of rights. With such promises, Massachusetts ratified by a narrow margin.

By June 21, 1788, the required nine states had ratified, but the crucial states of New York and Virginia still held out. In Virginia, where George Mason and Patrick Henry opposed the Constitution, the influence of George Washington and the promise of a bill of rights finally prevailed and ratification was achieved there as well. In New York, where Alexander Hamilton led the fight for ratification, *The Federalist Papers*, the promise of a bill of rights, and the news of Virginia's ratification were enough to carry the day.

Only North Carolina and Rhode Island still held out, but they both ratified within the next fifteen months.

In March 1789, George Washington was inaugurated as the nation's first president.

OUTLINE OF THE UNITED STATES CONSTITUTION

Articles of the Constitution

Preamble

"We the People of the United States, in order to form a more perfect Union, establish justice, insure domestic tranquility, provide for the common defense, promote the general welfare, and secure the blessings of liberty to ourselves and our posterity, do ordain and establish this Constitution for the United States of America."

Article I – Legislature

The legislature is divided into two parts—the House of Representatives (435 members currently; determined by proportional representation of the population) and the Senate (100 members currently; two from each state).

The House of Representatives may bring impeachment charges. All bills which concern money must originate in the House. Because of the size of the body, debate is limited except in special cases, where all representatives may meet as the Committee of the Whole. The Speaker of the House presides over the proceedings. Terms of representatives are two years, re-electable without limit, to persons who are at least 25 years of age.

The Senate, originally elected by state legislatures but now by direct election (17th Amendment), approves or rejects presidential nominations and treaties, and serves as the court and jury in impeachment proceedings. Debate within the Senate is unlimited. The President pro tempore usually presides, but the Vice-President of the United States is the presiding officer, and may vote to break a tie. Senate elected terms are for six years, re-electable without limit, to persons who are at least 30 years of age.

Article II – Executive

The President of the United States is elected for a four-year term, originally electable without limit (the 22nd Amendment limits election to two terms), and must be at least 35 years old.

Responsibilities for the President as outlined in the Constitution include acting as the Chief of State, the Chief Executive, Commander-in-Chief of the Armed Forces, the Chief Diplomat, and Chief Legislature.

Article III – Judiciary

While the Constitution describes the Supreme Court in Article 111, the actual construction of the court system was accomplished by the Judiciary Act of 1789. The Supreme Court has jurisdiction for federal courts and appellate cases on appeal from lower courts.

Article IV – Interstate Relations

This article guarantees that court decisions and other legal actions (marriage, incorporation, etc.) valid in one state are valid in another. Extradition of criminals (and, originally, runaway slaves) and the exchange of citizenship benefits are likewise guaranteed. Article IV also provides for the admission of new states and guarantees federal protection against invasion and violence for each state. States admitted maintain the same status as the original states. All states are guaranteed a republican form of government.

Article V – Amendment Process

Amendments are proposed by a two-thirds vote of each house of Congress or by a special convention called by Congress upon the request of two-thirds of the state legislatures. Amendments are ratified by three-fourths of the state legislatures or state conventions.

Article VI – Supremacy Clause

Article VI sets up the hierarchy of laws in the United States. The Constitution is the "supreme law of the land," and supersedes treaties. Treaties supercede federal laws, federal laws (later to include federal regulatory agency directives) supercede state constitutions, state laws and local laws, respectively. All federal and state officials, including judges, must take an oath to support and defend the Constitution.

Article VII – Ratification

This article specified the ratification process necessary for the Constitution to take effect. Nine of the original thirteen states had to ratify the Constitution before it became operative.

Amendments to the Constitution

The Amendments to the Constitution guarantee certain individual rights and amend original dictates of the Constitution. The first ten amendments are known as the Bill of Rights, for which Thomas Jefferson provided the impetus.

1 – protects the freedom of religion, speech, press, assembly, as well as the right to petition the government for the redress of grievances (1791)

2 – protects the right to bear arms in a regulated militia (on a state basis; it was not intended to guarantee an individual's rights) (1791)

3 – ensures that troops will not be housed in private citizens' homes (1791)

4 – protects against unreasonable search and seizure (need for search warrant) (1791)

5 – protects the rights for the accused, including required indictments, double jeopardy, self-incrimination, due process, and just compensation (1791)

6 – guarantees a speedy and public trial, the confrontation by witnesses, and the right to call witnesses on one's own behalf (1791)

7 – guarantees a jury trial (1791)

8 – protects against excessive bail and cruel and unusual punishment (1791)

9 – says that all rights not enumerated are nonetheless retained by the people (1791)

10 – says that all powers not specifically delegated to the federal government are retained by the states (1791)

11 – states may not be sued by individuals (1798)

12 – dictates that electors will cast separate ballots for President and Vice-President; in the event of no clear winner, the House will select the President and the Senate the Vice-President (1804)

13 – abolished slavery (1865)

14 – extends citizenship to all persons; made Confederate debt void and Confederate leaders ineligible for public office; states which denied voting rights to qualified citizens (blacks) would have their representation in Congress reduced; conferred "dual" citizenship (both of the United States and of a specific state) on all citizens (1868)

15 – extends voting rights to blacks (1870)
16 – legalized the income tax (1913)
17 – provides for the direct election of senators (1913)
18 – prohibited the general manufacture, sale and use of alcoholic beverages (1919)
19 – extends voting rights to women (1920)
20 – changed inauguration date from March 4 to January 20; eliminated the "lame duck" session of Congress (after the November elections) (1933)
21 – repealed the 18th Amendment (1933)
22 – limits presidents to two terms (1951)
23 – gives presidential electoral votes to the District of Columbia (1961)
24 – prohibits poll taxes (1964)
25 – changed the order of the presidential line of succession and provides guidelines for presidential disability (1967)
26 – extends voting rights to eighteen-year-olds (1971)
27 – restricts the practice of congressional salary adjustment (1992)

SEPARATION AND LIMITATION OF POWERS

Powers Reserved for the Federal Government Only

- Regulate foreign commerce regulation
- Regulate interstate commerce regulation
- Mint money
- Create and establish post offices
- Regulate naturalization and immigration
- Grant copyrights and patents
- Declare and wage war, declare peace
- Admit new states
- Fix standards for weights and measures
- Raise and maintain an army and a navy
- Govern the federal city (Washington, D.C.)
- Conduct relations with foreign powers
- Universalize bankruptcy laws

Powers Reserved for the State Governments Only

- Conduct and monitor elections
- Establish voter qualifications
- Provide for local governments
- Ratify proposed amendments to the Constitution
- Regulate contracts and wills
- Regulate intrastate commerce

- Provide education for its citizens
- Levy direct taxes (the 16th Amendment permits the federal government to levy direct taxes)
- Maintain police power over public health and safety
- Maintain integrity of state borders

Powers Shared by Federal and State Governments

- Taxing, borrowing and spending money
- Controlling the militia
- Acting directly on individuals

Restrictions on the Federal Government

- No ex post facto laws
- No bills of attainder
- Two-year limit on appropriation for the military
- No suspension of habeas corpus (except in a crisis)
- One port may not be favored over another
- All guarantees as stated in the Bill of Rights

Restrictions on State Governments

- Treaties, alliances, or confederations may not be entered into
- Letters of marque and reprisal may not be granted
- Contracts may not be impaired
- Money may not be printed or bills of credit emitted
- No import or export taxes
- May not wage war (unless invaded)

Required Percentages of Voting

Actions which require a simple majority include raising taxes, requesting appropriations, declaring war, increasing the national debt, instituting a draft, and introducing impeachment charge (House).

Actions which require a two-thirds majority include overriding a presidential veto, proposing amendments to the Constitution, expelling a member of Congress (in the individual house only), ratifying treaties (Senate), acting as a jury for impeachment (Senate), ratifying presidential appointments (Senate).

The action which requires a three-fourths majority is approving a proposed constitutional amendment (states).

HISTORICAL TIMELINE

The United States Constitution (1785–1789)

1785	Land Ordinance provides for orderly development of territories Spain closes the Mississippi River to American shipping
1786	Annapolis Convention Virginia adopts Jefferson's "Statute of Religious Freedom" Shays' Rebellion
1787	Northwest Ordinance prohibits slavery in new territories Constitutional Convention meets in Philadelphia
1788	*Federalist Papers* published New Hampshire is ninth state to ratify Constitution, making it the law of the land
1789	Washington elected and inaugurated as president French Revolution begins as Bastille is stormed French National Assembly issues "Declaration of Rights of Man"

5 THE NEW NATION (1789–1824)

THE FEDERALIST ERA

The results of the first elections held under the new Constitution made it clear that the fledgling government was going to be managed by those who had drawn up the document and by their supporters. Few Antifederalists were elected to Congress, and many of the new legislators had served as delegates to the Philadelphia Convention two years before. This Federalist majority immediately set about to draft legislation which would fill in the gaps left by the convention and to erect the structure of a strong central government.

The New Executive

There had never been any doubt as to who would be the first president. George Washington received virtually all the votes of the presidential electors, and John Adams received the next highest number, thus becoming the vice president. After a triumphal journey from Mount Vernon, Washington was inaugurated in New York City, the temporary seat of government, on April 30, 1789.

Congress Erects the Structure of Government

The new national legislature immediately acted to honor the Federalist pledge of a bill of rights made to those voters who had hesitated to ratify the new Constitution. Twelve amendments were drafted which embodied the guarantees of personal liberties, most of which had been traditionally enjoyed by English citizens. Ten of these were ratified by the states by the end of 1791, and they became our Bill of Rights. The first nine spelled out specific guarantees of personal freedoms, such as religion, speech, press, assembly, petition, and a speedy trial by one's peers, and the 10th Amendment reserved to the states all those powers not specifically withheld, or granted to the federal government. This last was a concession to those who feared the potential of the central government to usurp the sovereignty of the individual states.

The Establishment of the Federal Court System

The Judiciary Act of 1789 provided for a Supreme Court, with six justices, and invested it with the power to rule on the constitutional validity of state laws. It was to be the interpreter of the "supreme law of the land." A system of district courts was established to serve as courts of original jurisdiction, and three courts of appeal were also provided for.

THE ESTABLISHMENT OF THE EXECUTIVE DEPARTMENTS

The Constitution had not specified the names or number of the departments of the executive branch. Congress established three—state, treasury, and war—and also the offices of attorney general and postmaster general. President Washington immediately appointed Thomas Jefferson, Alexander Hamilton, and Henry Knox, respectively, to fill the executive posts, and Edmund Randolph became attorney general. These four men were called upon regularly by the president for advice, and they later formed the nucleus of what became known as the Cabinet, although no provision for such was made in the Constitution.

WASHINGTON'S ADMINISTRATION, 1789–1797

Hamilton's Financial Program

Treasury Secretary Alexander Hamilton, in his "Report on the Public Credit," proposed the funding of the national debt at face value, federal assumption of state debts, and the establishment of a national bank. In his "Report on Manufactures," Hamilton proposed an extensive program for federal stimulation of industrial development, through subsidies and tax incentives. The money needed to fund these programs, proposed Hamilton, would come from an excise tax on distillers and from tariffs on imports.

Opposition to Hamilton's Program

Jefferson and others objected to the funding proposal because it obviously would benefit speculators who had bought up state and confederation obligations at depressed prices, and who would profit handsomely by their redemption at face value. The original purchasers, they claimed, should at least share in the windfall. They opposed the tax program because it would fall primarily on the small farmers. They saw Hamilton's entire program as enriching a small elite group at the expense of the more worthy common citizen.

The Appearance of Political Parties

Political parties had been considered a detrimental force by the founding fathers, since they were seen as contributing to the rise of "factions." Thus, no mention of such was made in the Constitution. But differences in philosophy very quickly began to drive the leaders of government into opposing camps—the Federalists and the Republicans.

Alexander Hamilton and the Federalists

Hamilton, as the theorist of the group who favored a strong central government, interpreted the Constitution as having vested extensive powers in the federal government. This "implied powers" stance claimed that the government was given all powers that were not expressly denied to it. This is the "broad" interpretation.

Thomas Jefferson and the Republicans

Jefferson and Madison held the view that any action not specifically permitted in the Constitution was thereby prohibited. This is the "strict" interpretation, and the Republicans opposed the establishment of Hamilton's national bank on this view of government. The Jeffersonian supporters, primarily under the guidance of James Madison, began to organize political groups in opposition to the Federalist program, and called themselves Republicans.

Sources of Partisan Support

The Federalists received their strongest support from the business and financial groups in the commercial centers of the Northeast and in the port cities of the South. The strength of the Republicans lay primarily in the rural and frontier areas of the South and West.

FOREIGN AND FRONTIER AFFAIRS

The French Revolution

When revolutionary France went to war with the European powers in 1792, Washington's response was a Proclamation of Neutrality. Citizen Genet violated that policy by trying to encourage popular support in this country for the French government, and embarrassed the president. American merchants traded with both sides, though the most lucrative business was carried on with the French West Indies. This brought retaliation by the British, who began to seize American merchant ships and force their crews into service with the British navy.

Jay's Treaty with Britain (1794)

John Jay negotiated a treaty with the British which attempted to settle the conflict at sea, as well as to curtail English agitation of their Indian allies on the western borders. The agreement actually settled few of the issues and merely bought time for the new nation in the worsening international conflict. Jay was severely criticized for his efforts, and was even hanged in effigy, but the Senate accepted the treaty as the best possible under the circumstances.

The Treaty with Spain (1795)

Thomas Pinckney was invited to the Spanish court to strengthen what Madrid perceived to be her deteriorating position on the American frontier. The result was the Pinckney Treaty, ratified by the Senate in 1796, in which the Spanish opened the Mississippi River to American traffic, including the right of deposit in the port city of New Orleans, and recognized the 31st parallel as the northern boundary of Florida.

Frontier Problems

Indian tribes on the Northwest and Southwest borders were increasingly resisting the encroachments on their lands by the American settlers. British authorities in Canada were encouraging the Indians in their depredations against frontier settlements.

In 1794, General Anthony Wayne decisively defeated the Indians at the Battle of Fallen Timbers, and the resulting Treaty of Greenville cleared the Ohio territory of Indian tribes.

INTERNAL PROBLEMS

The Whiskey Rebellion (1794)

Western farmers refused to pay the excise tax on whiskey which formed the backbone of Hamilton's revenue program. When a group of Pennsylvania farmers terrorized the tax collectors, President Washington sent out a federalized militia force of some 15,000 men, and the rebellion evaporated, thus strengthening the credibility of the young government.

Land Policy

As the original 13 states ceded their Western land claims to the new federal government, new states were organized and admitted to the Union, thus strengthening the ties of the Western farmers to the central government (Vermont, 1791; Kentucky, 1792; and Tennessee, 1796).

JOHN ADAMS' ADMINISTRATION, 1797–1801

The Election of 1796

John Adams was the Federalist candidate, and Thomas Jefferson ran under the opposition banner of the Republicans. John Adams was elected president. Since Jefferson received the second highest number of electoral votes, he became vice-president. Thus, a Federalist president and a Republican vice president served together, an obviously awkward arrangement. Adams was a brilliant lawyer and statesman, but too dogmatic and uncompromising to be an effective politician, and he endured a very frustrating and unproductive term in office.

The XYZ Affair

A three-man delegation was sent to France in 1798 to persuade the French to stop harassing American shipping. When they were solicited for a bribe by three subordinates of the French Minister Talleyrand, they indignantly refused, and their report of this insult produced outrage at home. The cry "millions for defense, but not one cent for tribute" was raised, and public feelings against the French ran high. Since Talleyrand's officials were unnamed in the dispatches, the incident became known as the "XYZ Affair."

Quasi-War, 1798–1799

This uproar moved Adams to suspend all trade with the French, and American ship captains were authorized to attack and capture armed French vessels. Congress created the Department of the Navy, and war seemed imminent. In 1800, the new French government, now under Napoleon, signed a new treaty, and the peace was restored.

REPRESSION AND PROTEST

The Alien and Sedition Acts

The elections in 1798 had increased the Federalists' majorities in both houses of Congress and they used their "mandate" to enact legislation to stifle foreign influences. The Alien Act raised new hurdles in the path of immigrants trying to obtain citizenship, and the Sedition Act widened the powers of the Adams administration to muzzle its newspaper critics. Both bills were aimed at actual or potential Republican opposition, and a number of editors were actually jailed for printing critical editorials.

The Kentucky and Virginia Resolutions

Republican leaders were convinced that the Alien and Sedition Acts were unconstitutional, but the process of deciding on the constitutionality of federal laws was as yet undefined. Jefferson and Madison decided that the state legislatures should have that power, and they drew up a series of resolutions which were presented to the Kentucky and Virginia legislatures, respectively. They proposed that John Locke's "compact theory" be applied, which would empower the state bodies to "nullify" federal laws within those states. These resolutions were adopted, but only in these two states, and so the issue died. A principle, however, had now been set forth which would later bear fruit in the nullification controversy of the 1830s and ultimately in the secession crisis of 1860–61.

THE REVOLUTION OF 1800

The Election

Thomas Jefferson and Aaron Burr ran on the Republican ticket, though not together, against John Adams and Charles Pinckney for the Federalists. All ran for the presidency; the candidate winning the second-highest number of votes would become vice-president. Jefferson and Burr received the same number of electoral votes, so the selection went to the House of Representatives. After a lengthy deadlock, Alexander Hamilton threw his support to Jefferson, and Burr had to accept the vice presidency, the result obviously intended by the electorate. This increased the ill will between Hamilton and Burr and helped set the stage for their famous duel in 1804.

Packing the Judiciary

The Federalist Congress passed a new Judiciary Act early in 1801 and President Adams filled the newly created vacancies with party supporters, many of them with last-minute commissions. John Marshall was then appointed Chief Justice of the U.S. Supreme Court, thus guaranteeing continuation of Federalist policies from the bench of the high court.

THE JEFFERSONIAN ERA

Thomas Jefferson and his Republican followers envisioned a society in vivid contrast to that of Hamilton and the Federalists. They dreamed of a nation of independent farmers, living under a central government that exercised a minimum of control over their lives and served merely to protect the individual liberties guaranteed by the Constitution. This agrarian paradise would be free from the industrial smoke and urban blight of Europe, and would serve as a beacon light of Enlightenment rationalism to a world searching for direction. That vision was to prove a mirage, and Jefferson was to preside over a nation that was growing more industrialized and urban, and which seemed to need an ever stronger hand at the presidential tiller.

The New Federal City

The city of Washington had been designed by Pierre L'Enfant and was briefly occupied by the Adams administration. When Jefferson moved in, it was still a straggling provincial town, with muddy streets and muggy summers. Most of its inhabitants moved out when Congress was not in session.

Jefferson the President

The new president tried to project an image of democratic simplicity, sometimes appearing so casually dressed as to appear slovenly. But he was a brilliant thinker and a shrewd politician. He appointed men to his Cabinet who agreed with his political philosophy: James Madison as Secretary of State and Albert Gallatin to the Treasury.

CONFLICT WITH THE JUDGES

Marbury vs. Madison

William Marbury, one of Adams' "midnight appointments," sued Secretary of State Madison to force delivery of his commission as a justice of the peace in the federal district. John Marshall, as Supreme Court justice, refused to rule on the request, claiming that the law which gave the Supreme Court jurisdiction over such matters had exceeded the Constitutional grant of powers and thus was unconstitutional. Marshall thus asserted the power of judicial review over federal legislation, a power which has become the foundation of the Supreme Court's check on the other two branches of government.

The Impeachment Episodes

Jefferson began a campaign to remove Federalist judges by impeachment. One district judge was removed, and proceedings were begun to impeach Supreme Court Justice Samuel Chase. That effort failed, but the threat had encouraged the judiciary to be less blatantly political.

DOMESTIC AFFAIRS

Enforcement of the Alien and Sedition Acts was immediately suspended, and the men convicted under those laws were released.

The federal bureaucracy was reduced and expenses were drastically cut. The size of the army was reduced and the expansion program of the Navy was cancelled.

The excise taxes were repealed and federal income was limited to land sale proceeds and customs duties. Federal land sale policy was liberalized, smaller parcels were authorized, and less cash was required—policies which benefitted small farmers.

The 12th Amendment was adopted and ratified in 1804, ensuring that a tie vote between candidates of the same party could not again cause the confusion of the Jefferson-Burr affair.

Following the Constitutional mandate, the importation of slaves was stopped by law in 1808.

The Louisiana Purchase

Napoleon, in an effort to regain some of France's New World empire, had obtained the old French trans-Mississippi territory from Spain by political pressure. Jefferson sent a delegation to Paris to try to buy New Orleans, lest the new French officials close it to American traffic. Napoleon's defeat in Santo Domingo persuaded him that Louisiana could not be exploited, and indeed was now subject to potential American incursions. So he offered to sell the entire territory to the United States for $15 million. The American delegation accepted the offer in April 1803, even though they had no authority to buy more than the city of New Orleans.

The Constitutional Dilemma

Jefferson's stand on the strict interpretation of the Constitution would not permit him to purchase land without Congressional approval. But he accepted his advisors' counsel that his treaty-making powers included the authority to buy the land. Congress concurred, after the fact, and the purchase price was appropriated, thus doubling the territory of the nation overnight.

Exploring the West

Even before Napoleon's offer, Jefferson had authorized an expedition to explore the Western territory to the Pacific. The Lewis and Clark group, with 48 men, left St. Louis in 1804, and returned two years later with a wealth of scientific and anthropological information, and having strengthened the United States' claim to the Oregon territory. At the same time, Zebulon Pike and others had been traversing the middle parts of Louisiana and mapping the land.

The Essex Junto (1804)

Some New England Federalists saw the Western expansion as a threat to their position in the Union, and they tried to organize a secessionist movement. They courted Aaron Burr's support by offering to back him in a bid for the governorship of New York. Hamilton led the opposition to that campaign and when Burr lost the election, he challenged Hamilton to a duel, which resulted in Hamilton's death.

The Burr Conspiracy

Aaron Burr was now a fugitive, without a political future. He became involved in a scheme to take Mexico from Spain and establish a new nation in the West.

In the fall of 1806, he led a group of armed men down the Mississippi River system toward New Orleans. He was arrested in Natchez and tried for treason in Richmond, Virginia. Judge John Marshall's decision for acquittal helped to narrow the legal definition of treason. Jefferson's attempts to influence and prejudice the trial were justified by his claims of "executive privilege," but they were fruitless.

John Randolph and the Yazoo Claims

Jefferson's Republican opponents, under the leadership of his cousin John Randolph of Roanoke, called themselves the "Quids." They accused the president of complicity in the Yazoo Land controversy which had followed Georgia's cession of her western lands to the federal government. This created serious strife within the Republican party and weakened Jefferson's effectiveness in his second term.

INTERNATIONAL INVOLVEMENT

The Barbary War

In 1801 Jefferson sent a naval force to the Mediterranean to break the practice of the North African Muslim rulers of exacting tribute from Western merchant ships. Intermittent undeclared war dragged on until 1805, with no decisive settlement.

The Napoleonic Wars

War continued in Europe between France under Napoleon and the European powers led by Britain. Both sides tried to prevent trade with their enemies by neutral powers, especially the United States. Napoleon's "Continental System" was answered by Britain's "Orders in Council." American ships were seized by both sides and American sailors were "impressed" into the British navy.

The Chesapeake-Leopard Affair (1807)

The British ship H.M.S. *Leopard* stopped the U.S.S. *Chesapeake* off the Chesapeake Bay, and four alleged British deserters were taken off. Public outcry for war followed, and Jefferson was hard pressed to remain neutral.

The Embargo of 1807

Jefferson's response to the cry for war was to draft a law prohibiting American ships from leaving port for any foreign destination, thus avoiding contact with vessels of either belligerent. The result was economic depression, particularly in the heavily commercial Northeast. This proved to be his most unpopular policy of both terms in office.

MADISON'S ADMINISTRATION, 1809–1817

The Election of 1808

Republican James Madison won the election over Federalist Charles Pinckney, but the Federalists gained seats in both houses of the Congress. The embargo-induced depression was obviously a heavy political liability, and Madison was to face growing pressures to deal with the international crisis. He was a brilliant man but with few social or political skills. His greatest asset was probably his wife, the vivacious and energetic Dolley.

The War of 1812

Congress had passed a modified embargo just before Madison's inauguration, known as the Non-Intercourse Act, which opened trade to all nations except France and Britain. When it expired in 1810, it was replaced by Macon's Bill No. 2, which gave the president power to prohibit trade with any nation that violated our neutrality.

The Indian tribes of the Northwest and the Mississippi Valley were resentful of the government's policy of pressured removal to the West, and the British authorities in Canada were exploiting their discontent by encouraging border raids against the American settlements.

The Shawnee chief Tecumseh set out to unite the Mississippi Valley tribes and reestablish Indian dominance in the Old Northwest. With the help of his brother, the Prophet, and the timely New Madrid earthquake, he persuaded a sizeable force of warriors to join him. On November 11, 1811, General William Henry Harrison destroyed Tecumseh's village on Tippecanoe Creek and dashed his hopes for an Indian confederacy.

Southern frontiersmen coveted Spanish Florida, which included the southern ranges of Alabama, Mississippi and Louisiana. They resented Spanish support of Indian depredations against the borderlands, and since Spain was Britain's ally, they saw Britain as the background cause of their problems.

The Congress in 1811 contained a strong pro-war group called the War Hawks, led by Henry Clay and John C. Calhoun. They gained control of both houses and began agitating for war with the British. On June 1, 1812, President Madison asked for a declaration of war, and Congress complied.

A three-pronged invasion of Canada met with disaster on all three fronts, and the Americans fell back to their own borders. At sea, American privateers and frigates, including "Old Ironsides," scored early victories over British warships, but were soon driven back into their home ports and blockaded by the powerful British ships-of-the-line.

Admiral Oliver Hazard Perry constructed a fleet of ships on Lake Erie and on September 10, 1813, defeated a British force at Put-In Bay and established control of the lake. His flagship flew the banner, "Don't Give Up the Ship." This victory opened the way for William Henry Harrison to invade Canada in October and defeat a combination British and Indian force at the Battle of the Thames.

The War in the Southwest

Andrew Jackson led a force of frontier militia into Alabama in pursuit of Creek Indians who had massacred the white inhabitants of Fort Mims. On

March 27, 1814, he crushed the Indians at Horseshoe Bend, and then seized the Spanish garrison at Pensacola.

British Strategy Changes, 1814

A British force came down Lake Champlain and met defeat at Plattsburgh, New York, in September. A British armada sailed up the Chesapeake Bay and sacked and burned Washington, D.C. It then proceeded toward Baltimore, which was guarded by Fort McHenry. That fort held firm through the British bombardment, inspiring Key's "Star Spangled Banner."

The Battle of New Orleans

The most serious British threat came at the port of New Orleans. A powerful invasion force was sent there to close the mouth of the Mississippi River, but Andrew Jackson decisively defeated it with a polyglot army of frontiersmen, blacks, creoles and pirates. The battle was fought on January 8, 1815, two weeks after a peace treaty had been signed at the city of Ghent, in Belgium.

The Treaty of Ghent, Christmas Eve, 1814

With the European wars ended, the major causes for the dispute with Britain had ceased to be important, so both sides were eager for peace. The treaty provided for the acceptance of the status quo at the beginning of hostilities and so both sides restored their wartime conquests to the other.

The Hartford Convention, December 1814

The Federalists had become increasingly a minority party. They vehemently opposed the war and Daniel Webster and other New England congressmen consistently blocked the Administration's efforts to prosecute the war effort. On December 15, 1814, delegates from the New England states met in Hartford, Connecticut, and drafted a set of resolutions suggesting nullification—and even secession—if their interests were not protected against the growing influence of the South and the West.

Soon after the convention adjourned the news of the victory at New Orleans was announced and their actions were discredited. The Federalist party ceased to be a political force from this point on.

POSTWAR DEVELOPMENTS

Protective Tariff (1816)

The first protective tariff in the nation's history was passed in 1816 to slow the flood of cheap British manufactures into the country.

Rush-Bagot Treaty (1817)

An agreement was reached in 1817 between Britain and the United States to stop maintaining armed fleets on the Great Lakes. This first "disarmament" agreement is still in effect.

Jackson's Florida Invasion (1817)

Indian troubles in the newly acquired areas of western Florida prompted General Andrew Jackson, acting under dubious authority, to invade Spanish East Florida and to hang two British subjects whom he suspected of selling guns and supplies to the Indians. Then he reoccupied Pensacola and raised the American flag, a clear violation of international law. Only wide public support prevented his arrest and prosecution by the government.

Indian Policy

The government began to systematically pressure all the Indian tribes remaining in the East to cede their lands and accept new homes west of the Mississippi, a policy which met with disappointing results. Most declined the offer.

The Barbary Wars (1815)

In response to continued piracy and extortion in the Mediterranean, Congress declared war on the Muslim state of Algiers in 1815, and dispatched a naval force to the area under Stephen Decatur. He quickly defeated the North African pirates and forced them to pay indemnities for past tribute they had exacted from American ship captains. This action finally gained the United States free access to the Mediterranean basin.

The Adams-Onis Treaty (1819)

Spain had decided to sell the remainder of the Florida territory to the Americans before they took it anyway. Under this agreement, the Spanish surrendered all their claims to the territory and drew the boundary of Mexico all the way to the Pacific. The United States in exchange agreed to assume $5 million in debts owed to American merchants.

The Monroe Doctrine

Around 1810, national revolutions had begun in Latin America, so the colonial populations refused to accept the rule of the new Napoleonic governments in Europe. Leaders like San Martin and Bolivar had declared independence for their countries and, after Napoleon's fall in 1814, were defying the restored Hapsburg and Bourbon rulers of Europe.

British and American leaders feared that the new European governments would try to restore the former New World colonies to their erstwhile royal owners.

In December 1823, President Monroe included in his annual message to Congress a statement that the American hemisphere was "henceforth not to be considered as subjects for future colonization by any European powers." Thus began a thirty-year period of freedom from serious foreign involvement for the United States.

INTERNAL DEVELOPMENT, 1820–1830

The years following the War of 1812 were years of rapid economic and social development. Too rapid, in fact, and they were followed by a severe depression in 1819. But this slump was temporary, and it became obvious that the country was moving rapidly from its agrarian origins toward an industrial, urban future. Westward expansion accelerated, and the mood of the people became very positive. In fact, these years were referred to as the "Era of Good Feelings."

The Monroe Presidency, 1817–1825

James Monroe, the last of the "Virginia Dynasty," had been hand-picked by the retiring Madison and he was elected with only one electoral vote opposed: a symbol of national unity.

Postwar Boom

The years following the war were characterized by a high foreign demand for American cotton, grain and tobacco; commerce flourished. The Second National Bank, through its overly liberal credit policies, proved to be an inflationary influence, and the price level rose rapidly.

The Depression of 1819

Inventories of British manufactured goods had built up during the war, and English merchants began to dump their products on the American market at cut-rate prices. American manufacturers suffered from this influx of imports. The U.S. Bank tried to slow the inflationary spiral by tightening credit, and a sharp business slump resulted.

This depression was most severe in the newly expanding West, partly because of its economic dependency, partly because of heavy speculation in Western lands.

THE MARSHALL COURT

John Marshall delivered the majority opinions in a number of critical decisions in these formative years, all of which served to strengthen the power of the federal government and restrict the powers of state governments.

Marbury v. Madison (1803)

This case established the Supreme Court's power of judicial review over federal legislation.

Fletcher v. Peck (1810)

The Georgia legislature had issued extensive land grants in a shady deal with the Yazoo Land Company. A subsequent legislative session repealed that action because of the corruption that had attended the original grant. The Court decided that the original action by the Georgia Assembly had constituted a valid contract which could not be broken regardless of the corruption which had followed. This was the first time a state law was voided on the grounds that it violated a principle of the U.S. Constitution.

Dartmouth College v. Woodward (1819)

The quarrel between the president and the trustees of the New Hampshire college became a political issue when the Republicans backed the president and the Federalists supported the trustees. The president tried to change Dartmouth from a private to a public institution by having its charter revoked. The Court ruled that the charter, though issued by the king during colonial days, still constituted a contract, and thus could not be arbitrarily changed or revoked without the consent of both parties. The result of this decision was to severely limit the power of state governments to control the corporation, which was the emerging form of business organization.

McCulloch v. Maryland (1819)

The state of Maryland had tried to levy a tax on the Baltimore branch of the Bank of the United States, and so protect the competitive position of its own state banks. Marshall's ruling declared that no state has the right to control an agency of the federal government. Since "the power to tax is the power to destroy," such state action violated Congress' "implied powers" to establish and operate a national bank.

Gibbons v. Ogden (1824)

The State of New York had granted a monopoly to Ogden to operate a steamboat between New York and New Jersey. Gibbons obtained a Congressional permit to operate a steamboat line in the same waters. When Ogden sued to maintain his monopoly, the New York courts ruled in his favor. Gibbons' appeal went to the Supreme Court. John Marshall ruled that commerce included navigation, and that only Congress has the right to regulate commerce among states. Thus the state-granted monopoly was void.

STATEHOOD: A BALANCING ACT

The Missouri Compromise (1820)

The Missouri Territory, the first to be organized from the Louisiana Purchase, applied for statehood in 1819. Since the Senate membership was evenly divided between slave-holding and free states at that time, the admission of a new state was obviously going to give the voting advantage either to the North or to the South. Slavery was already well-established in the new territory, so the Southern states were confident in their advantage, until Representative Tallmadge of New York proposed an amendment to the bill which would prohibit slavery in Missouri.

The Southern outcry was immediate, and the ensuing debate grew hot. The Senate was dead-locked.

Henry Clay's Compromise Solution

As the debate dragged on, the northern territory of Massachusetts applied for admission as the state of Maine. This offered a way out of the dilemma, and House Speaker Clay formulated a package that both sides could accept. The two admission bills were combined, with Maine coming in free and Missouri as a slave state. To make the package palatable for the House, a provision was added to prohibit slavery in the remainder of the Louisiana Territory, north of the southern boundary of Missouri (latitude 36° 30'). Clay guided this bill through the House and it became law, thus maintaining the balance of power.

The debates in Congress had reminded everyone of the deep division between the sections, and some saw it as evidence of trouble to come. Thomas Jefferson, in retirement at Monticello, remarked that the news from Washington was like a "fire-ball in the night."

THE EXPANDING ECONOMY

The Growing Population

Population continued to double every 25 years. The migration of people to the West increased in volume and by 1840 over one-third of all

Americans lived west of the Alleghenies. Immigration from abroad was not significant until 1820; then it began to increase rapidly, mostly from the British Isles.

The Farming Sector

The growth of markets for farm products in the expanding cities, coupled with liberal land sale policies by the federal government, made the growing of staple agricultural crops more profitable. More and more land was put into cultivation, and the prevailing system of clearing and planting became more wasteful of timber as well as of the fertility of the land.

The Cotton Kingdom

The new lands in the Southwest, then constituting Alabama, Mississippi, Louisiana and Texas, proved ideal for the production of short-staple cotton. Eli Whitney's invention of the cotton gin solved the problem of separating the seeds from the fibers, and the cotton boom was under way.

The growing market for food and work animals in the cotton South provided the opportunity for the new Western farmers to specialize in those items and further stimulated the westward movement.

Fishing

New England and Chesapeake fishing proved very profitable. Deep-sea whaling became a significant enterprise, particularly from the Massachusetts/Rhode Island ports.

Lumbering

The expanding population created a need for building materials, and timber remained a profitable export item. Shipbuilding thrived in a number of Eastern Seaboard and Gulf Coast ports.

Fur Trade

John Jacob Astor and others opened up business all the way to the Northwest coast. "Mountain men" probed deeper and deeper into the Rocky Mountain ranges in search of the beaver.

Trade with the Spanish

The Santa Fe Trail, which ran from New Mexico northeast to Independence, Missouri, became an active trading corridor, opening up the Spanish territories to American migration and influence, and also providing the basis for future territorial claims.

THE TRANSPORTATION REVOLUTION

The first half of the 19th century witnessed an extraordinary sequence of inventions and innovations which produced a true revolution in transport and communications.

River Traffic

The steamboats built by Robert Fulton, the *Clermont* in 1807 and the *New Orleans* in 1811, transformed river transport. As shipment times and freight rates both plummeted, regular steam service was established on all the major river systems.

Road Building

By 1818, the National Road, which was built with federal funds, had been completed from Cumberland, Maryland, to Wheeling, Virginia, linking the Potomac with the Ohio River. A network of privately owned toll roads (turnpikes) began to reach out from every sizeable city. They were usually built for only a few miles out, and they never accounted for a significant share of the total freight tonnage moved, but they formed the nucleus of a growing road system in the new nation.

The Canal Era

The Erie Canal, linking the Hudson River at Albany, New York, with Lake Erie, was completed in 1825 and became the first and most successful example of an artificial waterway. It was followed by a rash of construction until canals linked every major waterway system east of the Mississippi River.

Canals were the first development projects to receive large amounts of public funding. They ran east-west and so tied the new West to the old East, with later implications for sectional divisions.

The Rise of New York City

Its location as a transport hub, coupled with innovations in business practices, boosted New York City into a primary trade center, and made it America's largest city by 1830. One such innovation was the packet boats, which operated on a guaranteed schedule and helped to rationalize commerce, both internal and international.

New York soon dominated the domestic market for cotton, a situation which progressively reduced the South to the status of an economic colony.

INDUSTRIALIZATION

The Rise of the Factory System

Samuel Slater had migrated from Britain in 1789, having served as an apprentice under inventor Richard Arkwright and then as a mill manager. He used his knowledge to build the first successful cotton-spinning mill in this country. The first cotton manufacturing plant in the world to include all the elements of manufacturing under one roof was built in Boston in 1813.

Eli Whitney's development and application of the principle of interchangeable parts, first used in his firearms factories, helped to speed the growth of mass-production operations.

The expansion of markets in Latin America and the Far East, as well as domestic markets, both resulted from and helped to develop the factory system.

Manufacturers and industrialists found it necessary to organize banks, insurance companies, and real estate firms to meet the needs of their growing business organizations.

The Corporation

The corporate form, with its limited liability and its potential for raising and utilizing large amounts of capital, became the typical type of business organization. By the 1830s, most states had enacted general laws for incorporating.

The Labor Supply

In the early days, the "Lowell System" became a popular way to staff the New England factories. Young women were hired from the surrounding countryside, brought to town and housed in dormitories in the mill towns. They were paid low wages for hard work under poor conditions, but they were only working for a short time, to earn a dowry or help out with the family income, so they soon went back home. This "rotating labor supply" was ideal for the owners, since the girls were not motivated to agitate for better wages and conditions.

Labor was always in short supply in this country, so the system depended on technology to increase production. This situation always placed a premium on innovation in machinery and technique.

The Growth of Unions

The factory system separated the owners from the workers and thus depersonalized the workplace. It also made the skilled artisan less important, since the repetitive processes of the mill could be performed by relatively unskilled laborers.

Although the first organized strike took place in 1828, in Paterson, New Jersey, by child workers, periodic economic downturns helped keep workers relatively dependent and passive until the 1850s.

A major goal of early unions was the 10-hour day, and this effort sparked a period of growth in organized labor which was later effectively quenched by the depression of 1837.

EDUCATIONAL DEVELOPMENT

The Growth of Public Schools

Before 1815, there were no public schools to speak of in this country. Some states had endorsed the idea of free schools for the people, but they shrank from the task of financing such a system. Jefferson had outlined such a plan for Virginia, but it came to nothing.

Schools were primarily sponsored by private institutions—corporate academies in the Northeast and religious institutions in the South and mid-Atlantic states. Most were aristocratic in orientation, training the nation's leaders, and few had any interest in schooling the children of the poor.

Women were likewise considered unfit for academic training, and those female schools which existed concentrated on homemaking skills and the fine arts which would make "ornaments" of the young ladies enrolled.

The New York Free School, one of those rare examples of a school for the poor, experimented for a time with the Lancastrian system, in which older students tutored the younger ones, thus stretching scarce budget dollars.

Higher Education

Although the numbers of institutions of higher learning increased sharply in the early years of the nineteenth century, none was truly public. All relied upon high tuition rates for survival, so less than one in ten young men, and no women, ever attended a college or university.

The training these schools provided was very limited as well. The only professional training was in theology, and only a scattering of colleges offered brief courses of study in law or medicine. The University of Pennsylvania, for example, offered one year of medical schooling, after which a person could obtain a license to practice the healing arts. Needless to say, medical practice was quite primitive.

The Growth of Cultural Nationalism

Jeffersonian Americans tried to demonstrate their newly-won independence by championing a strong sense of cultural nationalism, a feeling that their young republic represented the "final stage" of civilization, the "last great hope of mankind."

Literary Nationalism

Although most Americans had access to one or more newspapers, the market for native authors was quite limited. Publishers preferred to print works from British authors or to import books from Europe. A few Americans who were willing to pay the costs of publishing their own works found a growing number of readers.

Significant American Authors

Washington Irving was by far the best-known native writer in America. He excelled in the telling of folk tales and local color stories, and is best remembered for his portraits of Hudson River characters.

Mercy Otis Warren, the revolutionary pamphleteer, published a multi-volume *History of the Revolution* in 1805.

"Parson" Mason Weems wrote the best-seller *Life of Washington* in 1806, which was short on historical accuracy but long on nationalistic hero-worship.

Educational Literature

Early schoolbooks, like Noah Webster's *Blue Backed Speller*, as well as his dictionary of the "American" language, reflected the intense desire to promote patriotism and a feeling of national identity.

DEVELOPMENTS IN RELIGIOUS LIFE

The Post-Revolution Years

The Revolutionary War weakened the position of the traditional, established churches. The doctrines of the Enlightenment became very popular, and its religious expression, deism, gained a considerable following among the educated classes. Rationalism, Unitarianism, and Universalism all saw a period of popularity. Thomas Paine's exposition of the rationalist posture, *The Age of Reason*, attacked the traditional Christian values and was read widely.

The Second Great Awakening

The reaction to the trend toward rationalism, the decline in church membership, and the lack of piety, was a renewal of personal, heart-felt evangelicalism. A second Great Awakening began in 1801 at Cane Ridge, Kentucky, in the first "camp meeting."

As the revival spread, its characteristics became more uniform—an emphasis on personal salvation, an emotional response to God's grace, an individualistic faith. Women took a major part in the movement. Blacks were also heavily involved, and the individualistic emphasis created unrest among their ranks, particularly in the slave-holding South.

The revival produced strong nationalistic overtones, and the Protestant ideas of a "called nation" were to flourish later in some of the Manifest Destiny doctrines of expansionism. The social overtones of this religious renewal were to spark the great reform movements of the 1830s and 1840s.

HISTORICAL TIMELINE
The New Nation (1789–1824)

1789	Judiciary Act sets up federal court system
1791	Bill of Rights approved First Bank of United States chartered
1793	Washington issues Proclamation of Neutrality Louis XVI executed in France Cotton gin patented by Eli Whitney
1794	Whiskey Rebellion
1795	Jay Treaty Pinckney Treaty Treaty of Greenville
1796	Adams defeats Jefferson for presidency
1798	XYZ Affair Alien and Sedition Acts Virginia and Kentucky Resolutions
1800	Jefferson defeats Adams for presidency Prosser's Rebellion
1801	John Marshall becomes Chief Justice Midnight judges appointed by Adams
1803	*Marbury v. Madison* decision Louisiana Purchase
1804	Lewis and Clark Expedition
1807	Chesapeake-Leopard incident Embargo Act Robert Fulton builds *Clermont*, first steamboat
1811	Battle of Tippecanoe
1812	Congress declares war on Britain

1814	British burn Washington, D.C. Treaty of Ghent ends War of 1812 Hartford Convention
1815	Jackson defeats British at New Orleans
1819	First section of Erie Canal is opened Panic of 1819 *McCullough v. Maryland* decision
1820	Missouri Compromise
1823	Monroe Doctrine
1824	Congress sets protective tariffs *Gibbons v. Ogden* decision promotes interstate trade

6 JACKSONIAN DEMOCRACY AND WESTWARD EXPANSION (1824–1850)

THE JACKSONIAN DEMOCRACY, 1829–1841

While the "Age of Jackson" did not bring perfect political, social or economic equality to all Americans, it did mark a transformation in the political life of the nation that attracted the notice of European travelers and observers. Alexis de Tocqueville observed an "equality of condition" here that existed nowhere else in the world, and an egalitarian spirit among the people that was unique. Certainly the electorate had become broadened so that all white males had access to the polls, even if blacks and women were still outside the system. It was, in that sense, the "age of the common man." As to whether Andrew Jackson and his party were actually working for the good of those common men is another matter.

THE ELECTION OF 1824

The Expansion of the Electorate

Most states had already eliminated the property qualifications for voting before the campaigns for this election began. The new Massachusetts state constitution of 1820 had led the way in this liberalization of the franchise, and most Northern states followed soon after, usually with some conservative opposition, but not violent reactions. In Rhode Island, Thomas Dorr led a bloodless "rebellion" in an effort to expand the franchise in that state, and though he was briefly imprisoned for his efforts, the incident led the conservative legislature to relent and grant the vote to non-property owners. The movement for reform was much slower in the Southern states.

Free blacks were excluded from the polls across the South, and in most of the Northern states. In those areas where they had held the franchise, they were gradually excluded from the social and economic mainstream—as well as from the political arena—in the early years of this period.

National elections had never attracted much enthusiasm until 1824. Legislative caucuses had made the presidential nominations and kept the ruling cliques in power by excluding the voters from the process. But this year the system failed, and the caucuses were bypassed.

The members of the electoral college were now being almost universally elected by the people, rather than by the state legislatures, as in the early days.

The Candidates

Secretary of the Treasury William H. Crawford of Georgia was the pick of the Congressional caucus. Secretary of State John Quincy Adams held the job which traditionally had been the stepping-stone to the executive office. Speaker of the House Henry Clay presented the only coherent program to the voters, the "American System," which provided a high tariff on imports to finance an extensive internal improvement package. Andrew Jackson of Tennessee presented himself as a war hero from the 1812 conflict. All four candidates claimed to be Republicans.

The Election

Jackson won 43 percent of the popular vote, but the four-way split meant that he only received 38 percent of the electoral votes. Under the provisions of the 12th Amendment, the top three candidates were voted on by the House of Representatives. This left Henry Clay out of the running, and he threw his support to Adams. The votes had no sooner been counted when the new president, Adams, appointed Henry Clay his Secretary of State.

Andrew Jackson and his supporters immediately cried "foul!" and accused Clay of making a deal for his vote. The rallying cry of "corrupt bargain" became the impetus for their immediate initiation of the campaign for the 1828 election.

The Adams Administration

The new president pushed for an active federal government in areas like internal improvements and Native American affairs. These policies proved unpopular in an age of increasing sectional jealousies and conflicts over states' rights.

Adams was frustrated at every turn by his Jacksonian opposition, and his unwillingness, or inability, to compromise further antagonized his political enemies. For example, his refusal to endorse and enforce the Creek Native Americans' land cession to the state of Georgia was negated by their re-cession of their lands under pressure from Georgia's Jacksonian government.

John C. Calhoun and Nullification

In 1828, Congress passed a new tariff bill which was originally supported by Southern congressmen in order to embarrass the administration. The finished bill, however, included higher import duties for many goods which were bought by Southern planters, so they bitterly denounced the law as the "Tariff of Abominations."

John C. Calhoun was serving as Adams' vice president, so to protest the tariff and still protect his position, he anonymously published the "South

Carolina Exposition and Protest," which outlined his theory of the "concurrent majority": that a federal law which was deemed harmful to the interests of an individual state could be declared null and void within that state by a convention of the people. Thus, a state holding a minority position could ignore a law enacted by the majority which they considered unconstitutional (shades of Thomas Jefferson).

The Election of 1828

Adams' supporters now called themselves the National Republicans, and Jackson's party ran as the Democratic Republicans. Andrew Jackson had aggressively campaigned since his defeat in the House in 1825.

It was a dirty campaign. Adams' people accused Jackson of adultery and of the murder of several militiamen who had been executed for desertion during the War of 1812. Jackson's followers in turn defamed Adams and his programs and accused him of extravagance with public funds.

When the votes were counted, Jackson had won 56 percent of the popular vote and swept 178 of the 261 electoral votes. John C. Calhoun was elected vice president.

Andrew Jackson as President

Jackson was popular with the common man. He seemed to be the prototype of the self-made Westerner: rough-hewn, violent, vindictive, with few ideas but strong convictions. He ignored his appointed Cabinet officers and relied instead on the counsel of his "Kitchen Cabinet," a group of partisan supporters who had the ear and the confidence of the president.

Jackson expressed the conviction that government operations could be performed by untrained, common folk, and he threatened the dismissal of large numbers of government employees, to replace them with his supporters. Actually, he talked more about this "spoils system" than he acted on it.

He exercised his veto power more than any other president before him. A famous example was the Maysville Road, a project in Kentucky which would require a federal subsidy. Jackson opposed it because it would exist only within the boundaries of a single state.

Jacksonian Indian Policy

Jackson supported the removal of all Indian tribes to west of the Mississippi River. The Indian Removal Act in 1830 provided for federal enforcement of that process.

The portion of the Cherokee Nation which occupied northern Georgia claimed to be a sovereign political entity within the boundaries of that state. The Supreme Court supported that claim in its decision in *Worcester v. Georgia* (1832), but President Jackson refused to enforce the court's decision.

The result of this policy was the Trail of Tears, the forced march, under U.S. Army escort, of thousands of Cherokees to the West. A quarter or more of the Indians, mostly women and children, perished on the journey.

THE WEBSTER-HAYNE DEBATE (1830)

Federal Land Policy

The method of disposing of government land raised sectional differences. Westerners wanted cheap lands available to the masses. Northeasterners opposed this policy because it would lure away their labor supply and drive up wages. Southerners supported the West, hoping to weaken the ties between East and West.

The Senate Confrontation

Senator Robert Hayne of South Carolina made a speech in support of cheap land and he used Calhoun's anti-tariff arguments to support his position. In his remarks, he referred to the possibility of nullification.

Daniel Webster's famous replies to this argument moved the debate from the issue of land policy to the nature of the Union and states' rights within it. Webster argued for the Union as indissoluble and sovereign over the individual states. His concluding statements have become a part of our rhetorical heritage: "It is, Sir, the people's Constitution, the people's government, made for the people, made by the people, and answerable to the people....Liberty and Union, now and for ever, one and inseparable!"

The Second Nullification Crisis

The final split between Andrew Jackson and his vice president, John C. Calhoun, came over the new Tariff of 1832, and over Mrs. Calhoun's snub of Peggy Eaton, the wife of Secretary of War John Eaton.

Mrs. Eaton was a commoner, and the aristocratic Mrs. Calhoun refused to include her on the guest lists for the Washington parties. Jackson, no doubt remembering the slights to his own dear Rachel, defended his friends Peggy and John, and demanded that they be included in the social life of the capital.

Jackson was a defender of states' rights, but within the context of a dominant Union. When he supported the higher rates of the new tariff, Calhoun resigned his office in a huff and went home to South Carolina. There he composed an Ordinance of Nullification, which was duly approved by a special convention, and the customs officials were ordered to stop collecting the duties at the port of Charleston.

Jackson's response was immediate and decisive. He obtained a Force Bill from Congress (1833), which empowered him to use federal troops to enforce the collection of the taxes. And he suggested the possibility of hanging Calhoun. At the same time, he offered a gradual reduction in the levels of the duties. Calhoun backed down, both sides claimed victory, and the crisis was averted.

THE WAR ON THE BANK

The Controversy

The Bank of the United States had operated under the direction of Nicholas Biddle since 1823. He was a cautious man, and his conservative economic policy enforced conservatism among the state and private banks—which many bankers resented. Many of the Bank's enemies opposed it simply because it was big and powerful. Many still disputed its constitutionality.

The Election of 1832

Andrew Jackson freely voiced his antagonism toward the Bank and his intention to destroy it. During the campaign for the presidency in 1832, Henry Clay and Daniel Webster promoted a bill to recharter the Bank, even though its charter did not expire until 1836. They feared that Jackson would gain support over time and could kill the Bank as a parting shot as he retired. The Congress passed the recharter bill, but Jackson vetoed it. This left that institution a lame duck agency.

Jackson soundly defeated Henry Clay in the presidential race and he considered his victory a mandate from the people to destroy the Bank. His first move was to remove the federal government's deposits from Biddle's vaults and distribute the funds to various state and local banks, called by his critics the "pet banks." Biddle responded by tightening up on credit and calling in loans, hoping to embarrass the government and force a withdrawal by Jackson. Jackson stood firm and the result was a financial recession.

The Panic of 1837

When Biddle was forced to relent through pressure from business interests, the economy immediately rebounded. With credit policies relaxed, inflation began to pick up. The government contributed to this expansion by offering millions of acres of western land for sale to settlers at low prices.

In 1836, Jackson ordered a distribution of surplus funds and thus helped to further fuel the inflationary rise in prices. Finally, even Jackson recognized the danger, and tried to slow the spiral by issuing the Specie Circular, which required payment for public land in hard money; no more paper or credit. Depression quickly followed this move.

The business recession lasted well into the 1840s. Our national economy was by this time so tied in with international business and finance that the downturn affected the entire Atlantic community, and was in turn worsened by the global impact. But most Americans blamed everyone in power, including Jackson, and our institutions and business practices. This disillusionment helped to initiate and intensify the reform movement which so occupied this nation in the 19th century's second quarter.

The Election of 1836

Jackson had handpicked his Democratic successor, Martin Van Buren of New York. The Whigs ran three regional candidates in hopes of upsetting the Jacksonians. The Whig Party had emerged from the ruins of the National Republicans and other groups who opposed Jackson's policies. The name was taken from the British Whig tradition, which simply refers to the "opposition."

Van Buren's Presidency

Van Buren, known as Old Kinderhook (O.K.), inherited all the problems and resentments generated by his mentor. He spent most of his term in office dealing with the financial chaos left by the death of the Second Bank. The best he could do was to eventually persuade Congress to establish an Independent Treasury to handle government funds. It began functioning in 1840.

THE ELECTION OF 1840

The Candidates

The Whigs nominated William Henry Harrison, "Old Tippecanoe," Western Indian fighter. Their choice for vice president was John Tyler, a former Democrat from Virginia. The Democrats put up Van Buren again, but they could not agree on a vice presidential candidate, so they ran no one.

The Campaign

This election saw the largest voter turnout to date. The campaign was a dramatic one. The Whigs stressed the depression and the opulent lifestyle of the incumbent in contrast to the simple "log cabin" origins of their candidate.

Harrison won a narrow popular victory, but swept 80 percent of the electoral vote. Unfortunately for the Whigs, President Harrison died only a month after the inauguration, having served the shortest term in presidential history.

THE MEANING OF JACKSONIAN POLITICS

The Party System

The Age of Jackson was the beginning of the modern party system. Popular politics, based on emotional appeal, became the accepted style. The practice of meeting in mass conventions to nominate national candidates for office was established during these Jackson years.

The Strong Executive

Jackson, more than any president before him, used his office to dominate his party and the government to such an extent that he was called "King Andrew" by his critics.

The Changing Emphasis Toward States' Rights

Andrew Jackson supported the authority of the states against the national government, but he drew the line at the concept of nullification. He advocated a strong union made up of sovereign states, and this created some dissonance in his political thinking.

The Supreme Court reflected this shift in thinking in its decision on the *Charles River Bridge* case in 1837, delivered by Jackson's new Chief Justice, Roger Taney. He ruled that a state could abrogate a grant of monopoly if that original grant had ceased to be in the best interests of the community. This was clearly a reversal of the *Dartmouth College* principle of the sanctity of contracts, in a case where the general welfare was perceived as being involved.

Party Philosophies

The Democrats opposed big government and the requirements of modernization: urbanization and industrialization. Their support came from the working classes, small merchants, and small farmers.

The Whigs promoted government participation in commercial and industrial development, the encouragement of banking and corporations, and a cautious approach to westward expansion. Their support came largely from Northern business and manufacturing interests, and from large Southern planters. Calhoun, Clay, and Webster dominated the Whig party during these early decades of the nineteenth century.

Tocqueville's Democracy in America

Alexis de Tocqueville, a French civil servant, traveled to this country in the early 1830s to study the American prison system, which was one of the more innovative systems in the world. His book *Democracy in America*, published in 1835, was the result of his observations, and it reflected a broad interest in the entire spectrum of the American democratic process and the society in which it had developed. His insightful commentary on the American way of life has proven to be almost prophetic in many respects, and provides the modern reader with an outsider's objective view of what this country was like in the Age of Jackson.

ANTE-BELLUM CULTURE: AN AGE OF REFORM

The American people in 1840 found themselves living in an era of transition and instability. The society was changing and traditional values were being challenged. The responses to this uncertainty were two-fold: a movement toward reform and a rising desire for order and control.

We have a fairly vivid picture of what Americans were like in this period of time, from accounts by hundreds of foreign visitors who came to this country to observe our society-in-the-making. These observers noted a restless population, always on the move, compulsive joiners of associations, committed to progress, hard-working and hard-playing, driven relentlessly by a desire for wealth. They believed in and talked about equality, but the reality was that the system was increasingly creating a class society. Americans seemed to lean toward violence, and mob incidents were common.

The Reform Impulse: Major Sources of Reform

Romanticism held a belief in the innate goodness of man, thus in his improvability. This movement had its roots in turn-of-the-century Europe, and it emphasized the emotions and feelings over rationality. It appeared as a reaction against the excesses of the Enlightenment which had put strong emphasis on reason, to the exclusion of feelings.

There was also a growing need perceived for a stable social order, and control over the forces which were threatening the traditional values.

Both of these major streams of reform activity were centered in the Northeast, especially in New England.

THE FLOWERING OF LITERATURE

Northern Writers and Themes

James Fenimore Cooper's *Leatherstocking Tales* emphasized the independence of the individual, and also the importance of a stable social order.

Walt Whitman's *Leaves of Grass* likewise celebrated the importance of individualism.

Henry Wadsworth Longfellow's epic poems *Evangeline* and *Hiawatha* spoke of the value of tradition, and the impact of the past on the present.

Herman Melville's classic stories—*Typee, Billy Budd, Moby Dick*—all lashed out at the popular optimism of his day. He believed in the Puritan doctrine of original sin and his characters spoke of the mystery of life.

Historian and nationalist Francis Parkman vividly portrayed the struggle for empire between France and Britain in his *Montcalm and Wolfe*. *The Oregon Trail* described the opening frontier of the Rocky Mountains and beyond.

James Russell Lowell, poet and editor, wrote the *Bigelow Papers* and the *Commemoration Ode*, honoring Civil War casualties of Harvard.

A writer of romances and tales, Nathaniel Hawthorne is best remembered for his criticism of Puritan bigotry in *The Scarlet Letter*.

Southern Writers and Themes

Author of *The Raven, Tamerlane*, and many tales of terror and darkness, Edgar Allan Poe explored the world of the spirit and the emotions.

South Carolina poet William Gilmore Simms changed from a staunch nationalist to a defender of the slave system and the uniqueness of the Southern way of life.

A Georgia storyteller, Augustus Longstreet used vulgar, earthy language and themes to paint the common folk of the South.

THE FINE ARTS

Artists and Themes

The Hudson River School was a group of landscape painters who portrayed the awesomeness of nature in America, the new world. George Catlin painted the American Indian, whom he saw as a vanishing race. John James Audubon painted the wide array of American birds and animals.

Music and the Theatre

The theatre was popular, but generally condemned by the church and conservatives as a "vagabond profession." The only original American contribution was the blackface minstrel show.

THE TRANSCENDENTALISTS

Major Themes

This movement had its origins in Concord, Massachusetts. The basic objective of these thinkers was to transcend the bounds of the intellect and to strive for emotional understanding, to attain unity with God, without the help of the institutional church, which they saw as reactionary and stifling to self-expression.

Major Writers

Ralph Waldo Emerson, essayist and lecturer, authored "Nature" and "Self-Reliance." Henry David Thoreau, best known for his *Walden*, repudiated the repression of society, and preached civil disobedience to protest unjust laws.

THE UTOPIANS

Their Purpose

The cooperative community was their attempt to improve the life of the common man in the face of increasing impersonal industrialism.

The Utopian Communities

Brook Farm, in Massachusetts, was the earliest commune in America, and it was short-lived. Nathaniel Hawthorne was a short-term resident, and his *Blithedale Romance* was drawn from that experience. This work and *The Scarlet Letter* were both condemnations of the life of social isolation.

New Harmony, Indiana, was founded by Robert Owen, of the New Lanark experiment in Wales, but it failed after two years. He attacked religion, marriage, and the institution of private property, so he encountered resistance from neighboring communities.

Nashoba was in the environs of Memphis, Tennessee, established by the free thinking Englishwoman Frances Wright as a communal haven for freed slaves. Needless to say, her community experiment encountered fierce opposition from her slaveholding neighbors and it survived only briefly.

Oneida Community in New York was based on free love and open marriages.

The Shakers were directed by Mother Ann Lee. The communities were socialistic experiments which practiced celibacy, sexual equality and social discipline. The name was given them by onlookers at their community dancing sessions.

Amana Community, in Iowa, was another socialist experiment, with a rigidly ordered society.

THE MORMONS

The Origins of the Religion

Joseph Smith received the "sacred" writings in New York state in 1830, and organized the Church of Jesus Christ of Latter Day Saints. They were not popular with their neighbors, primarily because of their practice of polygamy, and so were forced to move about, first to Missouri, then to Nauvoo, Illinois. There Smith was killed by a mob, and in 1847 the community was led to the valley of the Great Salt Lake by their new leader, Brigham Young, in one of the great epic migrations to the West.

The Church

They established a highly organized, centrally controlled system, which provided security and order for the faithful. They held a strong belief in human perfectability, and so were in the mainstream of romantic utopians.

REMAKING SOCIETY: ORGANIZED REFORM

Sources of Inspiration

Transcendentalism, as a branch of European Romanticism, spawned a great deal of interest in remaking society into more humane forms.

Protestant Revivalism was a powerful force for the improvement of society. Evangelist Charles G. Finney, through his "social gospel," offered salvation to all. A strong sectarian spirit split the Protestant movement into many groups (e.g., the Cumberland Presbyterians). Also evident was a strong anti-Catholic element, which was strengthened by the new waves of immigration from Catholic Ireland and southern Germany after 1830.

Temperance

The American Society for Promotion of Temperance was organized in 1826. It was strongly supported by Protestants, but just as strongly opposed by the new Catholic immigrants.

Public Schools

The motivations for the free school crusade were mixed. Some wanted to provide opportunity for all children to learn the skills for self-fulfillment and success in a republic. Others wanted to use schools as agencies for social control—to Americanize the new immigrant children as well as to Protestantize the Catholics, and to defuse the growing problems of urbanization. The stated purpose of the public schools was to instill social values: thrift, order, discipline, democracy.

Public apathy and even opposition met the early reformers: Horace Mann, the first secretary of the Massachusetts Board of Education, and Henry Barnard, his counterpart in Connecticut and Rhode Island.

The movement picked up momentum in the 1830s, but progress was very spotty. Few public schools were available in the West, fewer still for Southern whites, and none at all for Southern blacks.

Higher Education

In 1839, the first state-supported school for women, Troy Female Seminary, was founded in Troy, New York. Oberlin College in Ohio was the nation's first coeducational college. The Perkins School for the Blind in Boston was the first of its kind in the United States.

Asylums for the Mentally Ill

Dorothea Dix led the fight for these institutions, advocating more humane treatment for the mentally incompetent.

Prison Reform

The purpose of the new penitentiaries was not to just punish, but to rehabilitate. The first was built in Auburn, New York, in 1821.

Feminism

The Seneca Falls, New York, meeting in 1848, and its "Declaration of Sentiments and Resolutions," was the beginning of the modern feminist movement. The Grimké sisters, Elizabeth Cady Stanton, and Harriet Beecher Stowe were active in these early days. The movement was linked with that of the abolitionists, but suffered because it was considered to be of secondary importance.

The Abolitionist Movement

The early anti-slavery movement was benign, advocating only the purchase and transportation of slaves to free states in Africa. The American Colonization Society was organized in 1817 and established the colony of Liberia in 1830, but by that time the movement had reached a dead end.

In 1831, William Lloyd Garrison started his paper, *The Liberator*, and began to advocate total and immediate emancipation, thus giving new life to the movement. He founded the New England Anti-slavery Society in 1832, and the American Antislavery Society in 1833. Theodore Weld pursued the same goals, but advocated more gradual means.

Frederick Douglass, having escaped from his Maryland owner, became a fiery orator for the movement, and published his own newspaper, the *North Star*.

There were frequent outbursts of anti-abolition violence in the 1830s, against the fanaticism of the radicals. Abolitionist editor Elijah Lovejoy was killed by a mob in Illinois.

The movement split into two wings: Garrison's radical followers, and the moderates who favored "moral suasion" and petitions to Congress. In 1840, the Liberty Party, the first national anti-slavery party, fielded a presidential candidate on the platform of "free soil," non-expansion of slavery into the new western territories.

The literary crusade continued with Harriet Beecher Stowe's *Uncle Tom's Cabin* being the most influential among the many books which presented the abolitionist message.

Educating the Public

This was the golden age of oratory. Speechmaking drew huge and patient crowds, and four-hour-long orations were not uncommon, especially at public events like Fourth of July celebrations.

Newspapers and magazines multiplied and were available to everyone.

Women more and more became the market for magazines oriented to their interests. Periodicals like *Godey's Ladies Book* reached mass circulation figures.

Colleges sprang up everywhere, the products of religious sectarianism as well as local pride, which produced "booster colleges" in every new community as population moved west. Many of these were poorly funded and managed, and thus did not survive.

DIVERGING SOCIETIES—LIFE IN THE NORTH

Although the United States was a political entity, with all of the institutions of government and society shared among the peoples of the various states, there had always been a wide diversity of cultural and economic goals among the various states of the union. As the nineteenth century progressed, that diversity seemed to grow more pronounced, and the collection of states seemed to polarize more into the two sections we call the North and the South, with the expanding West becoming ever more identified with the North.

Population Growth, 1790–1860

The new West was the fastest growing area of the country, with population tending to move along parallels westward. From four million in 1790, population had reached 32 million in 1860 with one-half living in states and territories which did not even exist in Washington's administration.

Increase in Median Age

Birth rates began to drop after 1800, more rapidly in the cities than in the rural areas. Families who had averaged six children in 1800 only had five in 1860. Some of the reasons were economic: children were becoming liabilities rather than assets. The new "cult of domesticity" reflected a shift in family responsibilities. Father was out of the home working, and the burden of child-rearing fell more heavily on mother. Primitive birth control methods were used, and abortion was becoming common enough that several states passed laws restricting it. One result of all this was an aging population, with the median age rising from 16 to 20 years.

Immigration

The influx of immigrants had slowed during the conflicts with France and England, but the flow increased between 1815 and 1837, when the economic downturn again sharply reduced their numbers. Thus the overall rise in population during these years was due more to incoming foreigners than to natural increase. Most of the newcomers were from Britain, Germany and southern Ireland. The Germans usually fared best, since they brought more money and more skills. Discrimination was common in the job market, primarily directed against the Catholics. "Irish Need Not Apply" signs were common. However, the persistent labor shortage prevented the natives from totally excluding the foreign elements. These newcomers huddled in ethnic neighborhoods in the cities, or those who could moved west to try their hand at farming.

Growth of the Cities

In 1790, 5 percent of the U.S. population lived in cities of 2,500 or more. By 1860, that figure had risen to 25 percent. This rapid urbanization created an array of problems.

Problems of Urbanization

The rapid growth in urban areas was not matched by the growth of services. Clean water, trash removal, housing and public transportation all lagged behind, and the wealthy got them first. Bad water and poor sanitation produced poor health, and epidemics of typhoid fever, typhus and cholera were common. Police and fire protection were usually inadequate and the development of professional forces was resisted because of the cost and the potential for political patronage and corruption.

Social Unrest

Rapid growth helped to produce a wave of violence in the cities. In New York City in 1834, the Democrats fought the Whigs with such vigor that the state militia had to be called in. New York and Philadelphia witnessed race riots in the mid-1830s, and a New York mob sacked a Catholic convent in 1834. In the 1830s, 115 major incidents of mob violence were recorded. Street crime was common in all the major cities.

THE ROLE OF WOMEN AND MINORITIES

Women

Women were treated as minors before the law. In most states a woman's property became her husband's with marriage. Political activity was limited to the formation of associations in support of various pious causes, such as abolition, and religious and benevolent activity. Professional employment was largely limited to schoolteaching; that occupation became dominated by women. The women's rights movement focused on social and legal discrimination, and women like Lucretia Mott and Sojourner Truth became well-known figures on the speakers' circuit.

Blacks

By 1850, 200,000 free blacks lived in the North and West. Their lives were restricted everywhere by prejudice, and "Jim Crow" laws separated the races. Black citizens organized separate churches and fraternal orders. The African Methodist Episcopal Church, for example, had been organized in 1794 in Philadelphia, and flourished in the major Northern cities. Black Masonic and Odd Fellows lodges were likewise established. The economic security of the free blacks was constantly threatened by the newly-arrived immigrants, who were willing to work at the least desirable jobs for less wages. Racial violence was a daily threat.

THE NORTHEAST LEADS THE WAY

The Growth of Industry

By 1850, the value of industrial output had surpassed that of agricultural production. The Northeastern states led the way in this movement. Over one-half of the manufacturing establishments were located there, and most of the larger enterprises. Seventy percent of the workers who were employed in manufacturing lived in New England and the middle states, and the Northeast produced more than two-thirds of the manufactured goods.

Inventions and Technology

The level of technology used in American manufacturing already exceeded that of European industry. Eli Whitney's applications of interchangeable parts were being introduced into a wide variety of manufacturing processes. Coal was replacing water as the major source of industrial power. Machine tools were reaching a high level of sophistication. Much of this progress was due to the contributions of America's inventors. Between 1830 and 1850 the number of patents issued for industrial inventions almost doubled. Charles Goodyear's process of vulcanizing rubber was put to 500 different uses and formed the basis for an entire new industry. Elias Howe's sewing machine was to revolutionize the clothing industry. The mass production of iron, with its new techniques and uses, created a new array of businesses, of which the new railroad industry was the largest consumer. Samuel B. Morse's new electric telegraph was first used in 1840 to transmit business news and information.

The Rise of Unions

The growth of the factory system was accompanied by the growth of the corporate form of business ownership, which in turn further separated the owners from the workers. One result was the organization of worker groups to fight for benefits, an early example of which was the 10-hour day. In 1835,

Boston construction craftsmen struck for seven months to win a 10-hour work day, and Paterson, New Jersey, textile workers became the first factory workers to strike for shorter hours. The federal government's introduction of the 10-hour day for federal projects, in 1840, helped to speed the acceptance of this goal. The influx of immigrants who were willing to work for low wages helped to spur the drive for unions, and in turn their numbers helped to weaken the bargaining position of union members.

The Revolution in Agriculture

Farm and industry reinforced each other and developed simultaneously. As more urban workers became dependent on food grown by others, the potential profits of farming increased. Many of the technological developments and inventions were applied to farm machinery, which in turn enabled farmers to produce more food more cheaply for the urban workers. As in industry, specialization and mechanization became the rule in agriculture, particularly on the newly opening western prairies of Illinois, Iowa, and Kansas.

Inventions and Technology

Large-scale farming on the prairies spurred critical inventions. McCormick's mechanical reaper, patented in 1834, enabled a crew of six men to harvest in one day as much wheat as 15 men could using older methods. John Deere's steel plow, patented in 1837, provided a more durable tool to break the heavy prairie sod. Jerome Case's threshing machine multiplied the bushels of grain that could be separated from the stalk in a day's time.

The New Market Economy

These developments not only made large-scale production possible—they also shifted the major emphasis from corn to small grain production, and made farming for the international market feasible, which in turn made the Western farmer dependent on economic forces over which he had no control. This dependence produced the rising demand for government provision of free land and the agricultural colleges which later were provided by the Homestead and Morrill bills during the Civil War.

In the East, the trend was toward truck farming for the nearby burgeoning urban areas, and the production of milk, fruits, and berries. Here, as in the West, there was much interest in innovative practices which could increase production efficiency and profits.

The Revolution in Commerce

Before the coming of the railroad, coastal sailing ships practically monopolized domestic trade. The canal construction boom of the 1830s had taken commercial traffic from the river systems, but by 1840 the railroad had begun to emerge as the carrier of the future. Pennsylvania and New York State contained most of the 3,328 miles of track, but the rail system was rapidly expanding across the northern tier of states, tying the industrializing East to the expanding, agricultural West.

EVERYDAY LIFE IN THE NORTH

Between 1800 and 1860 output of goods and services increased twelve fold and the purchasing power of the average worker doubled. The household labor system was breaking down, and the number of wage-earners exceeded for the first time the numbers of independent, self-employed Americans. Even so, everyday living was still quite primitive. Most people bathed only infrequently, washed clothes and dishes even less. Housing was primitive for most, consisting of one- or two-room cabins heated by open fireplaces, with water carried in from springs or public faucets. For the working man, rural or urban, life was hard.

DIVERGING SOCIETIES—LIFE IN THE SOUTH

The Southern states experienced dramatic growth in the second quarter of the nineteenth century. The economy grew more productive and more prosperous, but still the section called the South was basically agrarian, with few important cities and scattered industry. The plantation system, with its cash crop production driven by the use of slave labor, remained the dominant institution. In the words of one historian, "The South grew, but it did not develop." The South grew more unlike the North, and it became more defensive of its distinctive way of life.

The Cotton Kingdom

The most important economic phenomenon of the early decades of the nineteenth century was the shift in population and production from the old "upper South" of Virginia and the Carolinas to the "lower South" of the newly opened Gulf States of Alabama, Mississippi, and Louisiana. This shift was the direct result of the increasing importance of cotton. In the older Atlantic states, tobacco retained its importance, but had shifted westward to the Piedmont, and was replaced in the east by food grains. The southern Atlantic coast continued to produce rice and southern Louisiana and east Texas retained their emphasis on sugar cane. But the rich black soil of the new Gulf states proved ideal for the production of short-staple cotton, especially after the invention of the gin, and cotton became the center of the Southern economy. Nearly three million bales were being produced annually by 1850.

By 1860, cotton was to account for two-thirds of the value of U.S. exports. In the words of a Southern legislator of that era, "Cotton is King!"

Classes in the South

Although the large plantation with its white-columned mansion and its aristocratic owners is frequently seen as typical of Southern life, the truth is quite different.

The Planter Class

Owners of large farms who also owned 50 or more slaves actually formed a small minority of the Southern population. Three-fourths of Southern whites owned no slaves at all, almost half of slave-owning families owned fewer than six, and 12 percent owned 20 or more. But this minority of large slave owners exercised political and economic power far beyond what their numbers would indicate. They became a class to which all others paid deference, and they dominated the political and social life of their region.

The Yeoman Farmers

The largest group of Southern whites was the independent small farmers who worked their land with their family, sometimes side-by-side with one or two slaves, to produce their own food, with sometimes enough surplus to sell for a little extra cash. These simple folk predominated in the upland South and constituted a sizeable element even in the lower cotton-producing states. Their major crop was corn, and indeed the South's corn crop was more valuable than its cotton. The corn was used at home for dinner tables and for animal feed, however, and so ranked behind cotton as an item of export. These people were generally poorer than their Northern counterparts.

The Poor Whites

Perhaps a half-million white Southerners lived on the edge of the agrarian economy, in varying degrees of poverty. These "crackers," or "sandhillers," occupied the barren soils of the red hills or sandy bottoms, and they lived in squalor worse than the slaves. They formed a true underclass.

The Institution of Slavery

As the necessary concomitant of this expanding plantation system, the "Peculiar Institution" of black slavery fastened itself upon the Southern people, even as it isolated them from the rest of the world.

Slavery as a Labor System

The utilization of slave labor varied according to the region and the size of the growing unit. The large plantations growing cotton, sugar or tobacco used the gang system, in which white overseers directed black drivers, who supervised large groups of workers in the fields, all performing the same operation. In the culture of rice, and on the smaller farms, slaves were assigned specific tasks, and when those tasks were finished, the worker had the remainder of the day to himself.

House servants usually were considered the most favored since they were spared the hardest physical labor and enjoyed the most intimate relationship with the owner's family. This could be considered a drawback, since they were frequently deprived of the social communion of the other slaves, enjoyed less privacy, and were more likely to suffer the direct wrath of a dissatisfied master or mistress.

It is still debated as to whether the living conditions of the Southern plantation slaves were better or worse than the Northern wage laborers. Certainly their lot was better than their counterparts in South America and the Carribean.

Urban Slavery in the Southern City

A sizeable number of black slaves worked in the towns, serving as factory hands, domestics, artisans, and construction workers. They lived fairly independent lives and indeed a good number purchased their freedom with their savings, or quietly crossed the color line and disappeared into the general population. As the 19th century progressed, these people were increasingly seen as a bad model and a threat to the institution, and so urban slavery practically disappeared.

The Slave Trade

The most significant demographic shift in these decades was the movement of blacks from the Old South to the new Southwest. Traders shipped servants by the thousands to the newly opened cotton lands of the gulf states. A prime field hand fetched an average price of $800, as high as $1,500 in peak years. Families were frequently split apart by this miserable traffic. Planters freely engaged in this trade, but assigned very low status to the traders who carried it out.

Although the importation of slaves from abroad had been outlawed by Congress since 1808, they continued to be smuggled in until the 1850s. The import ban kept the price up and encouraged the continuation of the internal trade.

Slaves' Reaction to Slavery

Blacks in bondage suffered varying degrees of repression and deprivation. The harsh slave codes were comprehensive in their restrictions on individual freedom, but they were unevenly applied, and so there was considerable variety in the severity of life. The typical slave probably received a rough but adequate diet and enjoyed crude but sufficient housing and clothing.

But the loss of freedom and the injustice of the system produced a variety of responses. Many "soldiered" on the job, and refused to work hard, or they found ways to sabotage the machinery or the crops. There was an underground system of ridicule toward the masters which was nurtured, as reflected in such oral literature as the "Br'er Rabbit" tales.

Violent reaction to repression was not uncommon. Gabriel Prosser in Richmond (1800), Denmark Vesey in Charleston (1822), and Nat Turner in coastal Virginia (1831) all plotted or led uprisings of blacks against their white masters. Rumors of such uprisings kept whites in a state of constant apprehension.

The ultimate rebellion was to simply leave, and many tried to run away, some successfully. Especially from the states bordering the North, an ever increasing number of slaves fled to freedom, many with the aid of the "underground railroad" and smugglers such as Harriet Tubman, who led over 300 of her family and friends to freedom after she herself had escaped.

Most of those in bondage, however, were forced simply to adapt, and they did. A rich culture was developed within the confines of the system, and included distinctive patterns of language, music and religion.

COMMERCE AND INDUSTRY

The lack of manufacturing and business development has frequently been blamed for the South's losing its bid for independence in 1861–1865. Actually the South was highly industrialized for its day, and compared favorably with most European nations in the development of manufacturing capacity. Obviously, it trailed far behind the North, so much so that when war erupted in 1861, the Northern states owned 81 percent of the factory capacity in the United States.

Manufacturing

The Southern states saw considerable development in the 1820s and 1830s in textiles and iron production and in flour milling. Richmond's Tredegar Iron Works compared favorably with the best in the North. Montgomery Bell's forges in Tennessee produced a good proportion of the ironware used in the upper South. Even so, most of the goods manufactured in these plants were for plantation consumption rather than for export, and they never exceeded two percent of the value of the cotton crop.

Commercial Activity

The businessmen of the South worked primarily with the needs and products of the plantation and the factors of New Orleans and Charleston had to serve as bankers and insurance brokers as well as the agents for the planters. An organized network of commerce never developed in the South, even though the planters themselves must be recognized as businessmen, since they operated large, complex staple-producing units.

Voices for Change

There were those who saw their native South sinking ever more into the position of dependency upon Northern bankers and businessmen, and they cried out for reform. James B.D. DeBow's *Review* advocated commercial development and agricultural diversification, but his cries fell largely on deaf ears.

Why were Southerners so wedded to the plantation system, in the face of much evidence that it was retarding development? Certainly one reason is that cotton was profitable. Over the long run, capital return on plantation agriculture was at least as good as on Northern industrial capital. Even though skilled slaves abounded and could have manned factories, they were more profitable in the field.

Since most of the planter's capital was tied up in land and slaves, there was little left to invest in commerce or manufacturing. Most important, perhaps, was the value system of the Southern people, who put great store in traditional rural ideals: chivalry, leisure, genteel elegance. Even the yeoman farmer held these values, and hoped someday to attain to the position the planters held.

LIFE IN THE SOUTHERN STATES

The Role of Women

The position of the Southern woman was similar in many ways to her Northern counterpart, but also very different. She had fewer opportunities for anything but home life. The middle-class wife was heavily involved in the operation of the farm, and served as supervisor and nurse for the servants, as well as manager of the household, while the upper class women served merely as ornaments. Education was rare, and centered on the "domestic arts." High birth and death rates took their toll on childbearing women, and many men outlived several wives. The half-breed slave children were constant reminders of the planters' dalliances and produced constant tension and frustration among plantation wives.

Education

Schooling beyond literacy training was available only to the sons of the well-to-do. Academics and colleges abounded, but not for the working classes, and what public schools there were were usually inferior and ill-supported. By 1860, one-half of all the illiterates in the United States lived in the South.

Daily Life in the South

The accounts of travelers in the Southern states provide us with vivid pictures of living conditions on the average homestead. Housing was primitive, one- or two-room cabins being the rule. Corn, sweet potatoes, and pork formed the staples of the Southern diet and health problems reflected the resulting vitamin deficiencies. Rickets and pellagra were common ailments.

Although the prevalence of violence has probably been overstated, it certainly existed and the duel remained an accepted avenue for settling differences well into the nineteenth century.

Southern Response to the Anti-Slavery Movement

As the crusade for abolition intensified in the North, the South assumed an ever more defensive position. Biblical texts were used to justify the enslavement of an "inferior race." Scientific arguments were advanced to prove the inherent inferiority of the black African. Southern postal authorities refused to deliver any mail that contained information antagonistic to the slave system. Any kind of dissent was brutally suppressed, and the South became more and more a closed society. Literature and scholarship shriveled, and creative writers like Edgar Allan Poe and William Gilmore Simms became the rare exception.

The last serious Southern debate over the institution of slavery took place in the Virginia legislature in 1832, in the aftermath of Nat Turner's revolt. That discussion squelched any move toward emancipation. In 1836 Southern members of the U.S. House of Representatives pushed through the infamous "gag rule," which forbade any discussion on the question of slavery on the floor of the House. That rule remained in effect until 1844.

The most elaborate product of this ferment was John C. Calhoun's theory of the "concurrent majority," in which a dual presidency would insure a South independent of Northern dominance, and would forever keep majority rule at bay.

Beginning in 1837, regular conventions were held across the South to discuss ways to escape Northern economic and political hegemony.

As the decade of the 1840s opened, the two sections were becoming more and more estranged, and the channels of compromise were becoming more and more poisoned by the emotional responses to black slavery. The development which contributed most to keeping the sore festering was westward expansion.

MANIFEST DESTINY AND WESTWARD EXPANSION

Although the term "Manifest Destiny" was not actually coined until 1844, the belief that the American nation was destined to eventually expand all the way to the Pacific Ocean, and to possibly embrace Canada to the North, and Mexico to the South, had been voiced for years by many who believed that American liberty and ideals should be shared with everyone possible, by force if necessary. The rising sense of nationalism which followed the War of 1812 was fed by the rapidly expanding population, the reform impulse of the 1830s, and the desire to acquire new markets and resources for the burgeoning economy of "Young America."

Louisiana and the Far West Fur Trade

The Lewis and Clark expedition had scarcely filed its reports before a variety of adventurous entrepreneurs began to penetrate the newly acquired territory and the lands beyond. "Mountain men" like Jim Bridges trapped the Rocky Mountain streams and the headwaters of the Missouri River system for the greatly prized beaver pelts, while explorers like Jedediah Smith mapped the vast territory which stretched from the Rockies to the Sierra Nevada range and on into California. John Jacob Astor established a fur post at the mouth of the Columbia River which he named Astoria, and challenged the British claim to the northwest. Though he was forced to sell out his establishment to the British, he lobbied Congress to pass trade restrictions against British furs, and eventually became the first American millionaire from the profits of the American Fur Company. The growing trade with the Orient in furs and other specialty goods was sharpening the desire of many businessmen for American ports on the Pacific coast.

The Oregon Country

The Adams-Onis Treaty of 1819 had set the northern boundary of Spanish possessions near the present northern border of California. The territory north of that line and west of the vague boundaries of the Louisiana Territory had been claimed over the years by Spain, England, Russia, France, and the United States. By the 1820s, all these claims had been yielded to Britain and the United States. The Hudson's Bay Company had established a fur trading station at Fort Vancouver, and claimed control south to the Columbia. The United States claimed all the way north to the 54° 40' parallel. Unable to settle the dispute, they had agreed on a joint occupation of the disputed land.

In the 1830s American missionaries followed the traders and trappers to the Oregon country, and began to publicize the richness and beauty of the land, sending back official reports on their work which were published in the new, inexpensive "penny press" papers. Everyone read these reports, and the result was the "Oregon Fever" of the 1840s, as thousands of settlers trekked across the Great Plains and the Rocky Mountains to settle the new Shangri-La.

The Texas Question: 1836–1845

Texas had been a state in the Republic of Mexico since 1822, following the Mexican revolution against Spanish control. The United States had offered to buy the territory at the time, since it had renounced its claim to the area in the Adams-Onis agreement of 1819. The new Mexican government indignantly refused to sell, but immediately began to invite immigration from the north by offering land grants to Stephen Austin and other Americans. They needed to increase the population of the area and to produce revenue for the infant government. The Americans responded in great numbers, and by 1835 approximately 35,000 "gringos" were homesteading on Texas land.

The Mexican officials saw their power base eroding as the foreigners flooded in, and so they moved to tighten control, through restrictions on new immigration, and through tax increases. The Texans responded in 1836 by proclaiming independence and establishing a new republic. The ensuing war was short-lived. The Mexican dictator Antonio López de Santa Anna advanced north and annihilated the Texan garrisons at the Alamo and at Goliad. On April 23, 1836, Sam Houston defeated him at San Jacinto, and the Mexicans were forced to let Texas go its way.

Houston immediately asked the American government for recognition and annexation, but President Andrew Jackson feared the revival of the slavery issue since the new state would come in on the slave-holding side of the political balance, and he also feared war with Mexico, so he did nothing. When Van Buren followed suit, the new republic sought foreign recognition and support, which the European nations eagerly provided, hoping thereby to create a counterbalance to rising American power and influence in the Southwest. France and England both quickly concluded trade agreements with the Texans.

New Mexico and California

The district of New Mexico had, like Texas, encouraged American immigration, and for the same reasons. Soon that state was more American than Mexican. The Santa Fe Trail—from Independence, Missouri, to the town of Santa Fe—created a prosperous trade in mules, gold and silver, and furs which moved north in exchange for manufactured goods which went south. American settlements sprung up all along the route.

Though the Mexican officials in California had not encouraged it, American immigration nevertheless had been substantial. First traders and whaling crews, then merchants, arrived to set up stores and developed a brisk trade. As the decade of the 1830s passed, the number of newcomers increased. Since the Missouri Compromise had established the northern limits for slavery at the 36° 30' parallel, most of this Mexican territory lay in the potential slave-holding domain, and many of the settlers had carried their bondsmen with them.

Manifest Destiny and Sectional Stress

The question of expansion was universally discussed. Although the strongest sentiment was found in the North and West, the South had its own ambitions, and they usually involved the extension of their "peculiar institution."

The Democrats generally favored the use of force, if necessary, to extend American borders. The Whigs favored more peaceful means, through diplomacy. Some Whigs, like Henry Clay, feared expansion under any circumstances, because of its potential for aggravating the slavery issue.

Clay was closest to the truth. As the decade of the 1840s opened, the questions of Texas, California and the New Mexican territory were increasingly prominent, and the sectional tension which they produced was destined to light the fires of civil war.

TYLER, POLK, AND CONTINUED WESTWARD EXPANSION

Tyler and the Whigs

When William Henry Harrison became president, he immediately began to rely on Whig leader Henry Clay for advice and direction, just as Clay had planned and expected he would. He appointed to his Cabinet those whom Clay suggested, and at Clay's behest he called a special session of Congress to vote the Whig legislative program into action. To the Whigs' dismay, Harrison died of pneumonia just one month into his term, to be replaced by Vice President John Tyler.

A states' rights Southerner and a strict constitutionalist who had been placed on the Whig ticket to draw Southern votes, Tyler rejected the entire Whig program of a national bank, high protective tariffs, and federally funded internal improvements (roads, canals, etc.). Clay stubbornly determined to push the program through anyway. In the resulting legislative confrontations, Tyler vetoed a number of Whig-sponsored bills.

The Whigs were furious. Every Cabinet member but one resigned in protest. Tyler was officially expelled from the party and made the target of the first serious impeachment attempt. (It failed.) In opposition to Tyler over the next few years the Whigs, under the leadership of Clay, transformed themselves from a loose grouping of diverse factions to a coherent political party with an elaborate organization.

One piece of important legislation that did get passed during Tyler's administration was the Preemption Act (1841), allowing settlers who had squatted on unsurveyed federal lands first chance to buy the land (up to 160 acres at low prices) once it was put on the market.

The Webster-Ashburton Treaty

The member of Tyler's Cabinet who did not immediately resign in protest was Secretary of State Daniel Webster. He stayed on to negotiate the Webster-Ashburton Treaty with Great Britain.

There were at this time several causes of tension between the U.S. and Great Britain:

1) The Canada-Maine boundary in the area of the Aroostook Valley was disputed. British efforts to build a military road through the disputed area led to reaction by Maine militia in a bloodless confrontation known as the "Aroostook War" (1838).

2) The Caroline Affair (1837) involved an American ship, the *Caroline*, that had been carrying supplies to Canadian rebels. It was burned by Canadian loyalists who crossed the U.S. border in order to do so.
3) In the Creole Incident, Britain declined to return escaped slaves who had taken over a U.S. merchant ship, the *Creole*, and sailed to the British-owned Bahamas.
4) British naval vessels, patrolling the African coast to suppress slave-smuggling, sometimes stopped and searched American ships.

The Webster-Ashburton Treaty (1842) dealt with these problems in a spirit of mutual concession and forbearance:

1) Conflicting claims along the Canada-Maine boundary were compromised.
2) The British expressed regret for the destruction of the *Caroline*.
3) The British promised to avoid "officious interference" in freeing slaves in cases such as that of the *Creole*.
4) Both countries agreed to cooperate in patrolling the African coast to prevent slave-smuggling.

The Webster-Ashburton Treaty was also important in that it helped create an atmosphere of compromise and forebearance in U.S.-British relations.

After negotiating the treaty, Webster too resigned from Tyler's Cabinet.

The Texas Issue

Rejected by the Whigs and without ties to the Democrats, Tyler was a politician without a party but not without ambitions. Hoping to gather a political following of his own, he sought an issue with powerful appeal and believed he had found it in the question of Texas annexation.

The Republic of Texas had gained its independence from Mexico in 1836 and, since most of its settlers had come from the U.S., immediately sought admission as a state. It was rejected because anti-slavery forces in Congress resented the presence of slavery in Texas and because Mexico threatened war should the U.S. annex Texas.

To excite American jealousy and thus hasten annexation, Texas President Sam Houston made much show of negotiating for closer relations with Great Britain. Southerners feared that Britain, which opposed slavery, might bring about its abolition in Texas and then use Texas as a base from which to undermine slavery in the American South. Other Americans were disturbed at the possibility of a British presence in Texas because of the obstacle it would present to what many Americans were coming to believe—and what New York journalist John L. O'Sullivan would soon express—as America's "manifest destiny to overspread the continent."

Tyler's new secretary of state, John C. Calhoun, negotiated an annexation treaty with Texas. Calhoun's identification with extreme pro-slavery forces and his insertion in the treaty of pro-slavery statements brought the treaty's rejection by the Senate (1844). Nevertheless, the Texas issue had been injected into national politics and could not be made to go away.

The Election of 1844

Democratic front-runner Martin Van Buren and Whig front-runner Henry Clay agreed privately that neither would endorse Texas annexation and that it would not become a campaign issue, but expansionists at the Democratic convention succeeded in dumping Van Buren in favor of James K. Polk. Polk, called "Young Hickory" by his supporters, was a staunch Jacksonian who opposed protective tariffs and a national bank but, most important, favored territorial expansion, including not only annexation of Texas but also occupation of all the Oregon country (up to latitude 54° 40′) hitherto jointly occupied by the U.S. and Britain. The latter claim was expressed in his campaign slogan, "Fifty-four forty or fight."

Tyler, despite his introduction of the issue that was to decide that year's presidential campaign, was unable to build a party of his own and withdrew from the race.

The Whigs nominated Clay, who continued to oppose Texas annexation but, sensing the mood of the country was against him, began to equivocate. His wavering cost him votes among those Northerners who were extremely sensitive to the issue of slavery and believed that the settlement, independence, and proposed annexation of Texas was a gigantic plot to add slave states to the Union. Some of these voters shifted to the Liberty party.

The anti-slavery Liberty party nominated James G. Birney. Apparently because of Clay's wavering on the Texas issue, Birney was able to take enough votes away from Clay in New York to give that state, and thus the election, to Polk.

Tyler, as a lame-duck president, made one more attempt to achieve Texas annexation before leaving office. By means of a joint resolution, which unlike a treaty required only a simple majority rather than a two-thirds vote, he was successful in getting the measure through Congress. Texas was finally admitted to the Union (1845).

Polk as President

Though a relatively unknown "dark horse" at the time of his nomination for the Presidency, Polk had considerable political experience within his home state of Tennessee and was an adept politician. He turned out to be a skillful and effective president.

As a good Jacksonian, Polk favored a low, revenue-only tariff rather than a high, protective tariff. This he obtained in the Walker Tariff (1846). He also opposed a national debt and a national bank and re-established Van

Buren's Independent Sub-Treasury system, which then remained in effect until 1920.

The Settlement of Oregon

A major issue in the election campaign of 1844, Oregon at this time comprised all the land bounded on the east by the Rockies, the west by the Pacific, the south by latitude 42°, and the north by the boundary of Russian-held Alaska at 54° 40′. Oregon had been visited by Lewis and Clark and in later years by American fur traders and especially missionaries such as Jason Lee and Marcus Whitman. Their reports sparked interest in Oregon's favorable soil and climate. During the first half of the 1840s, some 6,000 Americans had taken the 2,000-mile, six-month journey on the Oregon Trail, from Independence, Missouri, across the plains along the Platte River, through the Rockies at South Pass, and down the Snake River to their new homesteads. Most of them settled in the Willamette Valley, south of the Columbia River.

The area had been under the joint occupation of the U.S. and Great Britain since 1818, but Democrats in the election of 1844 had called for U.S. ownership of all of Oregon. Though this stand had helped him win the election, Polk had little desire to fight the British for land he considered unsuitable for agriculture and unavailable for slavery, which he favored. This was all the more so since trouble seemed to be brewing with Mexico over territory Polk considered far more desirable.

The British, for their part, hoped to obtain the area north of the Columbia River, including the natural harbor of Puget Sound (one of only three on the Pacific coast), with its adjoining Strait of Juan de Fuca.

By the terms of the Oregon Treaty (1846), a compromise solution was reached. The existing U.S.-Canada boundary east of the Rockies (49°) was extended westward to the Pacific, thus securing Puget Sound and shared use of the Strait of Juan de Fuca for the U.S. Some northern Democrats were angered and felt betrayed by Polk's failure to insist on all of Oregon, but the Senate readily accepted the treaty.

The Mormon Migration

Aside from the thousands of Americans who streamed west on the Oregon Trail during the early 1840s, and the smaller number who migrated to what was then Mexican-held California, another large group of Americans moved west but to a different destination and for different reasons. These were the Mormons.

Mormonism is a unique religion founded in 1832 by Joseph Smith at Palmyra, New York. Mormons were often in trouble with their neighbors, and had been forced to migrate to Kirtland, Ohio, then Clay County, Missouri; and finally, Nauvoo, Illinois. There, on the banks of the Mississippi River, they built the largest city in the state, had their own militia, and were a political force to be reckoned with.

In 1844 Mormon dissidents published a newspaper critical of church leader Smith and his newly announced doctrine of polygamy. Smith had their printing press destroyed. Arrested by Illinois authorities, Smith and his brother were confined to a jail in Carthage, Illinois, but later killed by a crowd of hostile non-Mormons who forced their way into the jail.

The Mormons then decided to migrate to the Far West, preferably someplace outside U.S. jurisdiction. Their decision to leave was hastened by pressure from their non-Mormon neighbors, among whom anti-Mormon feeling ran high as a response to polygamy and the Mormons' monolithic social and political structure.

Under the leadership of new church leader Brigham Young, some 85,000 Mormons trekked overland in 1846 to settle in the valley of the Great Salt Lake in what is now Utah (but was then owned by Mexico). Young founded the Mormon republic of Deseret and openly preached (and practiced) polygamy.

After Deseret's annexation by the U.S. as part of the Mexican Cession, Young was made territorial governor of Utah. Nevertheless, friction developed with the federal government. By 1857 public outrage over polygamy prompted then-President James Buchanan to replace Young with a non-Mormon governor. Threats of Mormon defiance led Buchanan to send 2500 army troops to compel Mormon obedience to federal law. Young responded by calling out the Mormon militia and blocking the passes through which the army would have to advance. This standoff, known as the "Mormon War," was resolved in 1858, with the Mormons accepting the new governor and Buchanan issuing a general pardon.

The Coming of War with Mexico

For some time American interest had been growing in the far western lands then held by Mexico:

1) Since the 1820s Americans had been trading with Santa Fe and other Mexican settlements along the Rio Grande by means of the Santa Fe Trail. Though not extensive enough to be of economic importance the trade aroused further American interest in the area.
2) Also, since the 1820s, American "mountain men," trappers who sought beaver pelts in the streams of the Rockies, had explored the mountains of the Far West, opening new trails and discovering fertile lands. They later served as guides for settlers moving west.
3) At the same time whaling ships and other American vessels had carried on a thriving trade with the Mexican settlements on the coast of California.
4) Beginning in 1841, American settlers came overland to California by means of the California Trail, a branch from the Oregon Trail that turned southwest in the Rockies and crossed Nevada along the Humboldt River. By 1846 several hundred Americans lived in California.

The steady flow of American pioneers into Mexican-held areas of the Far West led to conflicting territorial desires and was thus an underlying cause of the Mexican War. Several more immediate causes existed:

1) Mexico's ineffective government was unable to protect the lives and property of American citizens in Mexico during the country's frequent and recurring revolutions and repeatedly declined to pay American claims for damages even when such claims were supported by the findings of mutually agreed upon arbitration.
2) Mexico had not reconciled itself to the loss of Texas and considered its annexation by the U.S. a hostile act.
3) The southern boundary of Texas was disputed. Whereas first the independent Republic of Texas and now the U.S. claimed the Rio Grande as the boundary, Mexico claimed the Nueces River, 130 miles farther north, because it had been the boundary of the province of Texas when it had been part of Mexico.
4) Mexican suspicions had been aroused regarding U.S. designs on California when, in 1842, a U.S. naval force under Commodore Thomas Catsby Jones had seized the province in the mistaken belief that war had broken out between the U.S. and Mexico. When the mistake was discovered, the province was returned and apologies made.
5) Mexican politicians had so inflamed the Mexican people against the U.S. that no Mexican leader could afford to take the risk of appearing to make concessions to the U.S. for fear of being overthrown.

Though Mexico broke diplomatic relations with the U.S. immediately upon Texas' admission to the Union, there still seemed to be some hope of a peaceful settlement. In the fall of 1845 Polk sent John Slidell to Mexico City with a proposal for a peaceful settlement of the differences between the two countries. Slidell was empowered to cancel the damage claims and pay $5 million for the disputed land in southern Texas. He was also authorized to offer $25 million for California and $5 million for other Mexican territory in the Far West. Polk was especially eager to obtain California because he feared the British would snatch it from Mexico's extremely weak grasp.

Nothing came of these attempts at negotiation. Racked by coup and countercoup, the Mexican government refused even to receive Slidell.

Polk thereupon sent U.S. troops into the disputed territory in southern Texas. A force under General Zachary Taylor (who was nicknamed "Old Rough and Ready") took up a position just north of the Rio Grande. Eight days later, on April 5, 1846, Mexican troops attacked an American patrol. When news of the clash reached Washington, Polk sought and received from Congress a declaration of war against Mexico, on May 13, 1846.

The Mexican War

Americans were sharply divided about the war. Some favored it because they felt Mexico had provoked the war or because they felt it was the destiny of America to spread the blessings of freedom to oppressed peoples. Others opposed the war. Some, primarily Polk's political enemies the Whigs, accused the president of having provoked it. Others, generally Northern abolitionists, saw in the war the work of a vast conspiracy of Southern slaveholders greedy for more slave territory.

In planning military strategy, Polk showed genuine skill. American strategy consisted originally of a three-pronged attack, consisting of a land movement westward through New Mexico into California, a sea movement against California, and a land movement southward into Mexico.

The first prong of this three-pronged strategy, the advance through New Mexico and into California, was led by Colonel Stephen W. Kearny. Kearny's force easily secured New Mexico, entering Santa Fe on August 16, 1846, before continuing west to California. There American settlers, aided by an Army exploring party under John C. Fremont, had already revolted against Mexico's weak rule in what was called the Bear Flag Revolt.

As part of the second prong of U.S. strategy, naval forces under Commodore John D. Sloat had seized Monterey and declared California to be part of the United States. Forces put ashore by Commodore Robert Stockton joined with Kearny's troops to defeat the Mexicans at the Battle of San Gabriel in January 1847, and complete the conquest of California.

The third prong of the American strategy, an advance southward into Mexico, was itself divided into two parties:

1) Troops under Colonel Alexander W. Doniphan defeated Mexicans at El Brazito (December 25–28, 1846) to take El Paso, and then proceeded southward, winning the Battle of Sacramento (February 28, 1847) to take the city of Chihuahua, capital of the Mexican province of that name.
2) The main southward thrust, however, was made by a much larger American army under General Zachary Taylor. After badly defeating larger Mexican forces at the battles of Palo Alto (May 7, 1846) and Resaca de la Palma (May 8, 1846), Taylor advanced into Mexico and defeated an even larger Mexican force at the Battle of Monterey (September 20–24, 1846). Then, after substantial numbers of his troops had been transferred to other sectors of the war, he successfully withstood, though badly outnumbered, an attack by a Mexican force under Antonia Lopez de Santa Anna at the Battle of Buena Vista, February 22–23, 1847.

Despite the success of all three parts of the American strategy, the Mexicans refused to negotiate. Polk therefore ordered U.S. forces under General Winfield Scott to land on the east coast of Mexico, march inland, and take Mexico City.

Scott landed at Veracruz March 9, 1847, and by March 27 had captured the city with the loss of only twenty American lives. He advanced from there, being careful to maintain good discipline and avoid atrocities in the countryside. At Cerro Cord (April 18, 1847), in what has been called "the most important single battle of the war," Scott outflanked and soundly defeated a superior enemy force in a seemingly impregnable position. After beating another Mexican army at Churubusco (August 19–20, 1847), Scott paused outside Mexico City to offer the Mexicans another chance to negotiate. When they declined, U.S. forces stormed the fortress of Chapultepec (September 13, 1847) and the next day entered Mexico City. Still Mexico refused to negotiate a peace and instead carried on guerilla warfare.

Negotiated peace finally came about when the State Department clerk Nicholas Trist, though his authority had been revoked and he had been ordered back to Washington two months earlier, negotiated and signed the Treaty of Guadalupe-Hidalgo (February 2, 1848), ending the Mexican War. Under the terms of the treaty Mexico ceded to the U.S. the territory Polk had originally sought to buy, this time in exchange for a payment of $15 million and the assumption of $3.25 million in American citizens' claims against the Mexican government. This territory, the Mexican Cession, included the natural harbors at San Francisco and San Diego, thus giving the U.S. all three of the major west-coast natural harbors.

Despite the appropriation of vast territories, many, including Polk, felt the treaty was far too generous. There had been talk of annexing all of Mexico or of forcing Mexico to pay an indemnity for the cost of the war. Still, Polk felt compelled to accept the treaty as it was, and the Senate subsequently ratified it.

On the home front many Americans supported the war enthusiastically and flocked to volunteer. Some criticized the war, among them Henry David Thoreau, who, to display his protest, went to live at Walden Pond and refused to pay his taxes. Jailed for this, he wrote "Civil Disobedience."

Although the Mexican War increased the nation's territory by one-third, it also brought to the surface serious political issues that threatened to divide the country, particularly the question of slavery in the new territories.

HISTORICAL TIMELINE

Jacksonian Democracy and Westward Expansion (1824–1850)

1825	John Quincy Adams wins Corrupt Bargain presidential election
1828	Tariff of Abominations Jackson wins presidency
1830	Jackson vetoes Maysville Road extension Baltimore & Ohio becomes first railroad company Joseph Smith publishes *Book of Mormon*
1831	*Cherokee Nation v. Georgia* denies Indian claim of nationhood Nat Turner's Rebellion
1832	Jackson vetoes U.S. Bank re-charter Nullification crisis in South Carolina
1834	Women workers at Lowell, Massachusetts, stage first strike
1836	Texas independence fight Gag rule prevents discussion of slavery in Congress
1837	Panic of 1837
1838	Trail of Tears
1842	*Commonwealth v. Hunt* legalizes unions
1845	Annexation of Texas
1846	U.S. declares war on Mexico Oregon Treaty
1847	Winfield Scott captures Mexico City
1848	Gold discovered in northern California Treaty of Guadalupe Hidalgo Seneca Falls statement of women's rights
1849	California gold rush

7 SECTIONAL CONFLICT AND THE CAUSES OF THE CIVIL WAR (1850–1860)

THE CRISIS OF 1850 AND AMERICA AT MID-CENTURY

The Wilmot Proviso

The Mexican War had no sooner started when, on August 8, 1846, freshman Democratic Congressman David Wilmot of Pennsylvania introduced his Wilmot Proviso as a proposed amendment to a war appropriations bill. It stipulated that "neither slavery nor involuntary servitude shall ever exist" in any territory to be acquired from Mexico. It was passed by the House, and though rejected by the Senate it was reintroduced again and again amid increasingly acrimonious debate.

The Wilmot Proviso aroused intense sectional feelings. Southerners, who had supported the war enthusiastically, felt they were being treated unfairly. Northerners, some of whom had been inclined to see the war as a slaveholders' plot to extend slavery, felt they saw their worst suspicions confirmed by the Southerners' furious opposition to the Wilmot Proviso. There came to be four views regarding the status of slavery in the newly acquired territories.

The Southern position was expressed by John C. Calhoun, now serving as senator from South Carolina. He argued that the territories were the property not of the U.S. federal government, but of all the states together, and therefore Congress had no right to prohibit in any territory any type of "property" (by which he meant slaves) that was legal in any of the states.

Anti-slavery Northerners, pointing to the Northwest Ordinance of 1787 and the Missouri Compromise of 1820 as precedents, argued that Congress had the right to make what laws it saw fit for the territories, including, if it so chose, laws prohibiting slavery.

A compromise proposal favored by President Polk and many moderate Southerners called for the extension of the 36° 30′ line of the Missouri Compromise westward through the Mexican Cession to the Pacific, with territory north of the line to be closed to slavery and territory south of it open to slavery.

Another compromise solution, favored by Northern Democrats such as Lewis Case of Michigan and Stephen A. Douglas of Illinois, was known as "squatter sovereignty" and later as "popular sovereignty." It held that the residents of each territory should be permitted to decide for themselves whether or not to allow slavery, but it was vague as to when they might exercise that right.

The Election of 1848

Both parties sought to avoid as much as possible the hot issue of slavery in the territories as they prepared for the 1848 election campaign.

The Democrats nominated Lewis Cass, and their platform endorsed his middle-of-the-road popular sovereignty position with regard to slavery in the territories.

The Whigs dodged the issue even more effectively by nominating General Zachary Taylor, whose fame in the Mexican War made him a strong candidate. Taylor knew nothing of the current political issues, had never voted, and liked to think of himself as above politics. He took no position at all with respect to slavery in the territories.

Some anti-slavery Northern Whigs and Democrats, disgusted with their parties' failure to take a clear stand against the spread of slavery, deserted the party ranks to form another antislavery third party. They were known as "Conscience" Whigs (because they voted their conscience) and "Barnburner" Democrats (because they were willing to burn down the whole Democratic "barn" to get rid of the pro-slavery "rats"). Their party was called the Free Soil Party, since it stood for keeping the soil of new western territories free of slavery. Its candidate was Martin Van Buren.

The election excited relatively little public interest. Taylor won a narrow victory, apparently because Van Buren took enough votes from Cass in New York and Pennsylvania to throw those states into Taylor's column.

Gold in California

The question of slavery's status in the Western territories was made more immediate when, on January 24, 1848, gold was discovered at Sutter's Mill, not far from Sacramento, California. The next year gold-seekers from the eastern U.S. and from many foreign countries swelled California's population from 14,000 to 100,000.

Once in the gold fields these "forty-niners" proved to contain some rough characters, and that fact, along with the presence, or at least the expectation, of quick and easy riches, made California a wild and lawless place. No territorial government had been organized since the U.S. had received the land as part of the Mexican Cession, and all that existed was an inadequate military government. In September 1849, having more than the requisite population and being much in need of better government, California petitioned for admission to the Union as a state.

Since few slaveholders had chosen to risk their valuable investments in human property in the turbulent atmosphere of California, the people of the area not surprisingly sought admission as a free state, touching off a serious sectional crisis back east.

The Compromise of 1850

President Zachary Taylor, though himself a Louisiana slaveholder, opposed the further spread of slavery. Hoping to sidestep the dangerously divisive issue of slavery in the territories, he encouraged California as well as the rest of the Mexican Cession to organize and seek admission directly as states, thus completely bypassing the territorial stage.

Southerners were furious. They saw admission of a free-state California as a backdoor implementation of the hated Wilmot Proviso they had fought so hard to turn back in Congress. They were also growing increasingly alarmed at what was becoming the minority status of their section within the country. Long outnumbered in the House of Representatives, the South would now find itself, should California be admitted as a free state, also outvoted in the Senate.

Other matters created friction between North and South. A large tract of land was disputed between Texas, a slave state, and the as-yet-unorganized New Mexico Territory, where slavery's future was at best uncertain. Southerners were angered by the small-scale but much-talked-of efforts of Northern abolitionists' "underground railroad" to aid escaped slaves in reaching permanent freedom in Canada. Northerners were disgusted by the presence of slave pens and slave markets in the nation's capital. Radical southerners talked of secession and scheduled an all-Southern convention to meet in Nashville in June 1850 to propose ways of protecting Southern interests, inside or outside the Union.

At this point the aged Henry Clay attempted to compromise the various matters of contention between North and South. He proposed an eight-part package deal that he hoped would appeal to both sides.

For the North, the package contained these aspects: California would be admitted as a free state; the land in dispute between Texas and New Mexico would go to New Mexico; New Mexico and Utah Territories (all of the Mexican Cession outside of California) would not be specifically reserved for slavery, but its status there would be decided by popular sovereignty; and, the slave trade would be abolished in the District of Columbia.

For the South, the package offered the following: A tougher Fugitive Slave Law would be enacted; the federal government would pay Texas' $10,000,000 pre-annexation debt; Congress would declare that it did not have jurisdiction over the interstate slave trade; and, Congress would promise not to abolish slavery itself in the District of Columbia.

What followed the introduction of Clay's compromise proposal was eight months of heated debate, during which Clay, Calhoun, and Daniel Webster, the three great figures of Congress during the first half of the 19th century—all three aged and none of them with more than two years to live—made some of their greatest speeches. Clay called for compromise and "mutual forbearance." Calhoun gravely warned that the only way to save the Union was for the North to grant all the South's demands and keep quiet on the issue of slavery. Webster abandoned his previous opposition to the spread of slavery (as well as most of his popularity back in his home state of Massachusetts) to support the Compromise in an eloquent speech.

The opponents of the Compromise were many and powerful and ranged from President Taylor, who demanded admission of California without reference to slavery, to Northern extremists such as Senator William Seward of New York, who spoke of a "higher law" than the Constitution, forbidding the spread of slavery, to Southern extremists such as Calhoun or Senator Jefferson Davis of Mississippi. By mid-summer all seemed lost for the Compromise, and Clay left Washington exhausted and discouraged.

Then the situation changed dramatically. President Taylor died (apparently of gastroenteritis) July 9, 1850, and was succeeded by Vice President Millard Fillmore, a quiet but efficient politician and a strong supporter of compromise. In Congress the fight for the Compromise was taken up by Senator Stephen A. Douglas of Illinois. Called the "Little Giant" for his small stature and large political skills, Douglas broke Clay's proposal into its component parts so that he could use varying coalitions to push each part through Congress. This method proved successful, and the Compromise was adopted.

The Compromise of 1850 was received with joy by most of the nation. Sectional harmony returned, for the most part, and the issue of slavery in the territories seemed to have been permanently settled. That this was an illusion became apparent within a few years.

The Election of 1852

The 1852 Democratic convention deadlocked between Cass and Douglas and so instead settled on dark horse Franklin Pierce of New Hampshire. The Whigs, true to form, chose General Winfield Scott, a war hero of no political background.

The result was an easy victory for Pierce, largely because the Whig Party, badly divided along North-South lines as a result of the battle over the Compromise of 1850, was beginning to come apart. The Free Soil Party's candidate, John P. Hale of New Hampshire, fared poorly, demonstrating the electorate's weariness with the slavery issue.

Pierce and "Young America"

Americans eagerly turned their attention to railroads, cotton, clipper ships, and commerce. The world seemed to be opening up to American trade and influence.

President Pierce expressed the nation's hope that a new era of sectional peace was beginning. To assure this he sought to distract the nation's attention from the slavery issue to an aggressive program of foreign economic and territorial expansion known as "Young America."

In 1853 Commodore Matthew Perry led a U.S. naval force into Tokyo Bay on a mission to open Japan—previously closed to the outside world—to American diplomacy and commerce.

By means of the Reciprocity Treaty (1854) Pierce succeeded in opening Canada to greater U.S. trade. He also sought to annex Hawaii, increase

U.S. interest in Central America, and acquire territories from Mexico and Spain.

From Mexico he acquired in 1853 the Gadsden Purchase, a strip of land in what is now southern New Mexico and Arizona along the Gila River. The purpose of this purchase was to provide a good route for a trans-continental railroad across the southern part of the country.

Pierce sought to buy Cuba from Spain. When Spain declined, three of Pierce's diplomats, meeting in Ostend, Belgium, sent him the Ostend Manifesto urging military seizure of Cuba should Spain remain intransigent.

Pierce was the first "doughface" president—"a northern man with southern principles"—and his expansionist goals, situated as they were in the South, aroused suspicion and hostility in anti-slavery northerners. Pierce's administration appeared to be dominated by southerners, such as Secretary of War Jefferson Davis, and whether in seeking a southern route for a trans-continental railroad or seeking to annex potential slave territory such as Cuba, it seemed to be working for the good of the South.

Economic Growth

The chief factor in the economic transformation of America during the 1840s and 1850s was the dynamic rise of the railroads. In 1840 America had less than 3000 miles of railroad track. By 1860 that number had risen to over 30,000 miles. Railroads pioneered big-business techniques, and by improving transportation helped create a nationwide market. They also helped link the Midwest to the Northeast rather than the South, as would have been the case had only water transportation been available.

Water transportation during the 1850s saw the heyday of the steamboat on inland rivers and the clipper ship on the high seas. The period also saw rapid and sustained industrial growth. The factory system began in the textile industry, where Elias Howe's invention of the sewing machine (1846) and Isaac Singer's improved model (1851) aided the process of mechanization, and spread to other industries.

Agriculture varied according to region. In the South, large plantations and small farms existed side by side for the most part, and both prospered enormously during the 1850s from the production of cotton. Southern leaders referred to the fiber as "King Cotton," an economic power that no one would dare fight against.

In the North the main centers of agricultural production shifted from the Middle Atlantic states to the more fertile lands of the Midwest. The main unit of agriculture was the family farm, and the main products were grain and livestock. Unlike the South, where 3.5 million slaves provided abundant labor, the North faced incentives to introduce labor-saving machines. Cyrus McCormick's mechanical reaper came into wide use, and by 1860 over 100,000 were in operation on Midwestern farms. Mechanical threshers also came into increasing use.

Decline of the Two-Party System

Meanwhile, ominous developments were taking place in politics. America's second two-party system, which had developed during the 1830s, was in the process of breaking down. The Whig Party, whose dismal performance in the election of 1852 had signaled its weakness, was now in the process of complete disintegration. Partially this was the result of the issue of slavery, which tended to divide the party along North-South lines. Partially, though, it may have been the result of the nativist movement.

The nativist movement and its political party, the American, or, as it was called, the Know-Nothing Party, grew out of alarm on the part of native-born Americans at the rising tide of German and Irish immigration during the late 1840s and early 1850s. The Know-Nothing Party, so called because its members were told to answer "I know nothing" when asked about its secret proceedings, was anti-foreign and, since many of the foreigners were Catholic, also anti-Catholic. It surged briefly to become the country's second-largest party by 1855 but faded even more quickly due to the ineptness of its leaders and the growing urgency of the slavery question, which, though ignored by the Know-Nothing Party, was rapidly coming to overshadow all other issues. To some extent the Know-Nothing movement may simply have benefitted from the already progressing disintegration of the Whig Party, but it may also have helped to complete that disintegration.

All of this was ominous because the collapse of a viable nationwide two-party system made it much more difficult for the nation's political process to contain the explosive issue of slavery.

THE RETURN OF SECTIONAL CONFLICT

Continuing Sources of Tension

While Americans hailed the apparent sectional harmony created by the Compromise of 1850 and enjoyed the rapid economic growth of the decade that followed, two items which continued to create tension centered on the issue of slavery.

The Strengthened Fugitive Slave Law

The more important of these was a part of the Compromise itself, the strengthened federal Fugitive Slave Law. The law enraged Northerners, many of whom believed it little better than a legalization of kidnapping. Under its provisions blacks living in the North and claimed by slave catchers were denied trial by jury and many of the other protections of due process. Even more distasteful to anti-slavery Northerners was the provision that required all U.S. citizens to aid, when called upon, in the capture and return of alleged fugitives. So violent was Northern feeling against the law that several riots erupted as a result of attempts to enforce it. Some Northern states passed personal liberty laws in an attempt to prevent the working of the Fugitive Slave Law.

The effect of all this was to polarize the country even further. Many Northerners who had not previously taken an interest in the slavery issue now became opponents of slavery as a result of having its injustices forcibly brought home to them by the Fugitive Slave Law. Southerners saw in Northern resistance to the law further proof that the North was determined to tamper with the institution of slavery.

Uncle Tom's Cabin

One Northerner who was outraged by the Fugitive Slave Act was Harriet Beecher Stowe. In response, she wrote *Uncle Tom's Cabin*, a fictional book depicting what she perceived as the evils of slavery. Furiously denounced in the South, the book became an overnight best-seller in the North, where it turned many toward active opposition to slavery. This, too, was a note of harsh discord among the seemingly harmonious sectional relations of the early 1850s.

The Kansas-Nebraska Act

All illusion of sectional peace ended abruptly when in 1854 Senator Stephen A. Douglas of Illinois introduced a bill in Congress to organize the area west of Missouri and Iowa as the territories of Kansas and Nebraska. Douglas, who apparently had no moral convictions on slavery one way or the other, hoped organizing the territories would facilitate the building of a trans-continental railroad on a central route, something that would benefit him and his Illinois constituents.

Though he sought to avoid directly addressing the touchy issue of slavery, Douglas was compelled by pressure from Southern senators such as David Atchison of Missouri to include in the bill an explicit repeal of the Missouri Compromise (which banned slavery in the areas in question) and a provision that the status of slavery in the newly organized territories be decided by popular sovereignty.

The bill was opposed by most Northern Democrats and a majority of the remaining Whigs, but with the support of the Southern-dominated Pierce administration it was passed and signed into law.

The Republican Party

The Kansas-Nebraska Act aroused a storm of outrage in the North, where the repeal of the Missouri Compromise was seen as the breaking of a solemn agreement. It hastened the disintegration of the Whig Party and divided the Democratic Party along North-South lines.

In the North, many Democrats left the party and were joined by former Whigs and Know-Nothings in the newly created Republican Party. Springing to life almost overnight as a result of Northern fury at the Kansas-Nebraska Act, the

Republican party included diverse elements whose sole unifying principle was the firm belief that slavery should be banned from all the nation's territories, confined to the states where it already existed, and allowed to spread no further.

Though its popularity was confined almost entirely to the North, the Republican Party quickly became a major power in national politics.

Bleeding Kansas

With the status of Kansas (Nebraska was never in much doubt) to be decided by the voters there, North and South began competing to see which could send the greatest number. Northerners formed the New England Emigrant Aid Company to promote the settling of anti-slavery men in Kansas, and Southerners responded in kind. Despite these efforts the majority of Kansas settlers were Midwesterners who were generally opposed to the spread of slavery but were more concerned with finding good farm land than deciding the national debate over slavery in the territories.

Despite this large anti-slavery majority, large-scale election fraud, especially on the part of heavily armed Missouri "border ruffians" who crossed into Kansas on election day to vote their pro-slavery principles early and often, led to the creation of a virulently pro-slavery territorial government. When the presidentially-appointed territorial governor protested this gross fraud, Pierce removed him from office.

Free-soil Kansans responded by denouncing the pro-slavery government as illegitimate and forming their own free-soil government in an election which the pro-slavery faction boycotted. Kansas now had two rival governments, each claiming to be the only lawful one.

Both sides began arming themselves and soon the territory was being referred to in the Northern press as "Bleeding Kansas" as full-scale guerilla war erupted. In May 1856, Missouri border ruffians sacked the free-soil town of Lawrence, killing two, and destroying homes, businesses, and printing presses. Two days later a small band of antislavery zealots under the leadership of fanatical abolitionist John Brown retaliated by killing and mutilating five unarmed men and boys at a pro-slavery settlement on Pottawatomie Creek. In all, some 200 died in the months of guerilla fighting that followed.

Meanwhile, violence had spread even to Congress itself. In the same month as the Sack of Lawrence and the Pottawatomie Massacre, Senator Charles Sumner of Massachusetts made a two-day speech entitled "The Crime Against Kansas," in which he not only denounced slavery but also made degrading personal references to aged South Carolina Senator Andrew Butler. Two days later Butler's nephew, Congressman Preston Brooks, also of South Carolina, entered the Senate chamber and, coming on Sumner from behind, beat him about the head and shoulders with a cane, leaving him bloody and unconscious.

Once again the North was outraged, while in the South, Brooks was hailed as a hero. New canes were sent to him to replace the one he had broken over

Sumner's head. Denounced by Northerners, he resigned his seat and was overwhelmingly re-elected. Northerners were further incensed and bought thousands of copies of Sumner's inflammatory speech.

The Election of 1856

The election of 1856 was a three-way contest that pitted Democrats, Know-Nothings, and Republicans against each other.

The Democrats dropped Pierce and passed over Douglas to nominate James Buchanan of Pennsylvania. Though a veteran of forty years of politics, Buchanan was a weak and vacillating man whose chief qualification for the nomination was that during the slavery squabbles of the past few years he had been out of the country as American minister to Great Britain and therefore had not been forced to take public positions on the controversial issues.

The Know-Nothings, including the remnant of the Whigs, nominated Millard Fillmore. However, choice of a Southerner for the nomination of vice president so alienated Northern Know-Nothings that many shifted their support to the Republican candidate.

The Republicans nominated John C. Frémont of California. A former officer in the army's Corps of Topographical Engineers, Frémont was known as "the Pathfinder" for his explorations in the Rockies and the Far West. The Republican platform called for high tariffs, free Western homesteads (160 acres) for settlers, and, most important, no further spread of slavery. Their slogan was "Free Soil, Free Men, and Frémont." Southerners denounced the Republican Party as an abolitionist organization and threatened secession should it win the election.

Against divided opposition Buchanan won with apparent ease. However, his victory was largely based on the support of the South, since Frémont carried most of the Northern states. Had the Republicans won Pennsylvania and either Illinois or Indiana, Frémont would have been elected. In the election the Republicans demonstrated surprising strength for a political party only two years old and made clear that they, and not the Know-Nothings, would replace the moribund Whigs as the other major party along with the Democrats.

The *Dred Scott* Case

Meanwhile, there had been, rising through the court system, a case that would give the Supreme Court a chance to state its opinion on the question of slavery in the territories. The case was *Dred Scott v. Sanford*, which involved a Missouri slave, Dred Scott, who had been encouraged by abolitionists to sue for his freedom on the basis that his owner, an Army doctor, had taken him for a stay of several years in a free state, Illinois, and then in a free territory, Wisconsin. By 1856 the case had made its way to the Supreme Court, and by March of the following year the Court was ready to render its decision.

The justices were at first inclined to rule simply that Scott, as a slave, was not a citizen and could not sue in court. Buchanan, however, shortly before his inauguration, urged the justices to go farther and attempt to settle the whole slavery issue once and for all, thus removing it from the realm of politics where it might prove embarrassing to the president.

The Court obliged. Under the domination of aging pro-Southern Chief Justice Roger B. Taney of Maryland, it attempted to read the extreme Southern position on slavery into the Constitution, ruling not only that Scott had no standing to sue in federal court, but also that temporary residence in a free state, even for several years, did not make a slave free, and that the Missouri Compromise (already a dead letter by that time) had been unconstitutional all along because Congress did not have the authority to exclude slavery from any territory whatsoever. Nor did territorial governments, which were considered to receive their power from Congress, have the right to prohibit slavery.

Far from settling the sectional controversy, the *Dred Scott* case only made it worse. Southerners were encouraged to take an extreme position and refuse compromise, while anti-slavery Northerners became more convinced than ever that there was a pro-slavery conspiracy controlling all branches of government, and expressed an unwillingness to accept the Court's dictate as final.

Buchanan and Kansas

Later in 1857 the pro-slavery government in Kansas, through largely fraudulent means, arranged for a heavily pro-slavery constitutional convention to meet at the town of Lecompton. The result was a state constitution that allowed slavery. To obtain a pretense of popular approval for this constitution the convention provided for a referendum in which the voters were to be given a choice only to prohibit the entry of additional slaves into the state.

Disgusted free-soilers boycotted the referendum, and the result was a constitution that put no restrictions at all on slavery. Touting this Lecompton constitution, the pro-slavery territorial government petitioned Congress for admission to the Union as a slave state. Meanwhile the free-soilers drafted a constitution of their own and submitted it to Congress as the legitimate one for the prospective state of Kansas.

Eager to appease the South, which had started talking of secession again, and equally eager to suppress anti-slavery agitation in the North, Buchanan vigorously backed the Lecompton constitution. Douglas, appalled at this travesty of popular sovereignty, broke with the administration to oppose it. He and Buchanan became bitter political enemies, with the president determined to use all the power of the Democratic organization to crush Douglas politically.

After extremely bitter and acrimonious debate the Senate approved the Lecompton constitution, but the House insisted that Kansans be given a chance to vote on the entire document. Southern congressmen did succeed in managing to apply pressure to the Kansas voters by adding the stipulation that, should the

Lecompton constitution be approved, Kansas would receive a generous grant of federal land, but should it be voted down, Kansas would remain a territory.

Nevertheless, Kansas voters, when given a chance to express themselves in a fair election, turned down the Lecompton constitution by an overwhelming margin, choosing to remain a territory rather than become a slave state. Kansas was finally admitted as a free state in 1861.

The Panic of 1857

In 1857 the country was struck by a short but severe depression. There were three basic causes for this "Panic of 1857": several years of overspeculation in railroads and lands, faulty banking practices, and an interruption in the flow of European capital into American investments as a result of the Crimean War. The North blamed the Panic on low tariffs, while the South, which had suffered much less than the industrial North, saw the Panic as proof of the superiority of the Southern economy in general and slavery in particular.

The Lincoln-Douglas Debates

The 1858 Illinois senatorial campaign produced a series of debates that got to the heart of the issues that were threatening to divide the nation. In that race incumbent Democratic Senator and front-runner for the 1860 presidential nomination Stephen A. Douglas was opposed by a Springfield lawyer, little known outside the state, by the name of Abraham Lincoln.

Though Douglas had been hailed in some free-soil circles for his opposition to the Lecompton constitution, Lincoln, in a series of seven debates that the candidates agreed to hold during the course of the campaign, stressed that Douglas's doctrine of popular sovereignty failed to recognize slavery for the moral wrong it was. Again and again Lincoln hammered home the theme that Douglas was a secret defender of slavery because he did not take a moral stand against it.

Douglas, for his part, maintained that his guiding principle was democracy, not any moral standard of right or wrong with respect to slavery. The people could, as far as he was concerned, "vote it up or vote it down." At the same time he strove to depict Lincoln as a radical and an abolitionist who believed in racial equality and race mixing.

At the debate held in Freeport, Illinois, Lincoln pressed Douglas to reconcile the principle of popular sovereignty with the Supreme Court's decision in the *Dred Scott* case. How could the people "vote it up or vote it down," if, as the Supreme Court said, no territorial government could prohibit slavery? Douglas, in what came to be called his "Freeport Doctrine," replied that the people of any territory could exclude slavery simply by declining to pass any of the special laws that slave jurisdictions usually passed for their protection.

Douglas's answer was good enough to win him re-election to the Senate, although by the narrowest of margins, but hurt him in the coming presidential campaign. The Lecompton fight had already destroyed Douglas's hopes of uniting the Democratic Party and defusing the slave issue. It had also damaged his 1860 presidential hopes by alienating the South. Now his Freeport Doctrine hardened the opposition of Southerners already angered by his anti-Lecompton stand.

For Lincoln, despite the failure to win the Senate seat, the debates were a major success, propelling him into the national spotlight and strengthening the backbone of the Republican Party to resist compromise on the free-soil issue.

THE COMING OF THE CIVIL WAR

John Brown's Raid

On the night of October 16, 1859, John Brown, the Pottawatomie Creek murderer, led eighteen followers in seizing the federal arsenal at Harpers Ferry, Virginia (now West Virginia), taking hostages, and endeavoring to incite a slave uprising. Brown, supported and bankrolled by several prominent Northern abolitionists (later referred to as "the Secret Six"), planned to arm local slaves and then spread his uprising across the South. His scheme was ill-conceived and had little chance of success. Quickly cornered by Virginia militia, he was eventually captured by a force of U.S. Marines under the command of Army Colonel Robert E. Lee. Ten of Brown's eighteen men were killed in the fight, and Brown himself was wounded.

Charged under Virginia law with treason and various other crimes, Brown was quickly tried, convicted, sentenced, and, on December 2, 1859, hanged. Throughout his trial and at his execution he conducted himself with fanatical resolution, making eloquent and grandiose statements that convinced many Northerners that he was a martyr rather than a criminal. His death was marked in the North by signs of public mourning.

Though responsible Northerners such as Lincoln denounced Brown's raid as a criminal act that deserved to be punished by death, many Southerners became convinced that the entire Northern public approved of Brown's action and that the only safety for the South lay in a separate Southern confederacy. This was all the more so because Brown, in threatening to create a slave revolt, had touched on the foremost fear of white Southerners.

Hinton Rowan Helper's Book

The second greatest fear of Southern slaveholders was that Southern whites who did not own slaves, by far the majority of the Southern population, would come to see the continuation of slavery as not being in their best interest. This fear was touched on by a book, *The Impending Crisis in the South*, by a North Carolinian named Hinton Rowan Helper. In it Helper argued that slavery was economically harmful to the South and that it enriched the large planter at the expense of the yeoman farmer.

Southerners were enraged, and more so when the Republicans reissued a condensed version of the book as campaign literature. When the new House of Representatives met in December 1859 for the first time since the 1858 elections, angry Southerners determined that no Republican who had endorsed the book should be elected speaker.

The Republicans were the most numerous party in the House although they did not hold a majority. Their candidate for speaker, John Sherman of Ohio, had endorsed Helper's book. A rancorous two-month battle ensued in which the House was unable even to organize itself, let alone transact any business. Secession was talked of openly by Southerners, and as tensions rose congressmen came to the sessions carrying revolvers and Bowie knives. The matter was finally resolved by the withdrawal of Sherman and the election of a moderate Republican as speaker. Tensions remained fairly high.

The Election of 1860

In this mood the country approached the election of 1860, a campaign that eventually became a four-man contest.

The Democrats met in Charleston, South Carolina. Douglas had a majority of the delegates, but at that time a party rule required a two-thirds vote for the nomination. Douglas, faced with the bitter opposition of the Southerners and the Buchanan faction, could not gain this majority. Finally, the convention split up when Southern "fire-eaters" led by William L. Yancey walked out in protest of the convention's refusal to include in the platform a plank demanding federal protection of slavery in all the territories.

A second Democratic convention several weeks later in Baltimore also failed to reach a consensus, and the sundered halves of the party nominated separate candidates. The Southern wing of the party nominated Buchanan's vice president, John C. Breckinridge of Kentucky, on a platform calling for a federal slave code in all the territories. What was left of the national Democratic Party nominated Douglas on a platform of popular sovereignty.

A third presidential candidate was added by the Constitutional Union Party, a collection of aging former Whigs and Know Nothings from the southern and border states as well as a handful of moderate Southern Democrats. It nominated John Bell of Tennessee on a platform that sidestepped the issues and called simply for the Constitution, the Union, and the enforcement of the laws.

The Republicans met in Chicago, confident of victory and determined to do nothing to jeopardize their favorable position. Accordingly they rejected as too radical front-running New York Senator William H. Seward in favor of Illinois favorite son Abraham Lincoln. The platform was designed to have something for all Northerners, including the provisions of the 1856 Republican platform as well as a call for federal support of a trans-continental railroad. Once again its centerpiece was a call for the containment of slavery.

Douglas, believing only his victory could reconcile North and South, became the first U.S. presidential candidate to make a vigorous nationwide speaking tour. In his speeches he urged support for the Union and opposition to any extremist candidates that might endanger its survival, by which he meant Lincoln and Breckinridge.

On election day the voting went along strictly sectional lines. Breckinridge carried the Deep South; Bell, the border states; and Lincoln, the North. Douglas, although second in popular votes, carried only a single state and part of another. Lincoln led in popular votes, and though he was short of a majority in that category, he did have the needed majority in electoral votes and was elected.

The Secession Crisis

Lincoln had declared he had no intention of disturbing slavery where it already existed, but many Southerners thought otherwise. They also feared further raids of the sort John Brown had attempted and felt their pride injured by the election of a president for whom no Southerner had voted.

On December 20, 1860, South Carolina, by vote of a special convention made up of delegates elected by the people of the state, declared itself out of the Union. By February 1, 1861, six more states (Alabama, Georgia, Florida, Mississippi, Louisiana, and Texas) had followed suit.

Representatives of the seven seceded states met in Montgomery, Alabama, in February 1861 and declared themselves to be the Confederate States of America. They elected former Secretary of War and U.S. Senator Jefferson Davis of Mississippi as president, and Alexander Stephens of Georgia as vice president. They also adopted a constitution for the Confederate States which, while similar to the U.S. Constitution in many ways, contained several important differences:

1) Slavery was specifically recognized, and the right to move slaves from one state to another was guaranteed.
2) Protective tariffs were prohibited.
3) The president was to serve for a single non-renewable six-year term.
4) The president was given the right to veto individual items within an appropriations bill.
5) State sovereignty was specifically recognized.

In the North reaction was mixed. Some, such as prominent Republican Horace Greeley of the *New York Tribune*, counseled, "Let erring sisters go in peace." President Buchanan, now a lame duck, seemed to be of this mind, since he declared secession to be unconstitutional but at the same time stated his belief that it was unconstitutional for the federal government to do anything to stop states from seceding. Taking his own advice, he did nothing.

Others, led by Senator John J. Crittenden of Kentucky, strove for a compromise that would preserve the Union. Throughout the period of several weeks as the Southern states one by one declared their secession, Crittenden worked desperately with a congressional compromise committee in hopes of working out some form of agreement.

The compromise proposals centered on the passage of a constitutional amendment forever prohibiting federal meddling with slavery in the states where it existed as well as the extension of the Missouri Compromise line (36° 30′) to the Pacific, with slavery specifically protected in all the territories south of it.

Some Congressional Republicans were inclined to accept this compromise, but President-elect Lincoln urged them to stand firm for no further spread of slavery. Southerners would consider no compromise that did not provide for the spread of slavery, and talks broke down.

HISTORICAL TIMELINE

Sectional Conflict and the Causes of the Civil War (1850–1860)

1850	Compromise of 1850 Fugitive Slave Law passed
1852	*Uncle Tom's Cabin* published
1854	Ostend Manifesto Kansas-Nebraska Act Republican Party formed
1856	"Bleeding Kansas"
1857	*Dred Scott* decision Lecompton Constitution in Kansas
1858	Lincoln-Douglas debates
1859	John Brown's raid
1860	Lincoln elected president

8 THE CIVIL WAR AND RECONSTRUCTION (1860–1877)

HOSTILITIES BEGIN

Fort Sumter

Lincoln did his best to avoid angering the slave states that had not yet seceded. In his inaugural address he urged Southerners to reconsider their actions but warned that the Union was perpetual, that states could not secede, and that he would therefore hold the federal forts and installations in the South.

Of these only two remained in federal hands: Fort Pickens, off Pensacola, Florida; and Fort Sumter, in the harbor of Charleston, South Carolina. Lincoln soon received word from Major Robert Anderson, commanding the small garrison at Sumter, that supplies were running low. Desiring to send in the needed supplies, Lincoln informed the governor of South Carolina of his intention but promised that no attempt would be made to send arms, ammunition, or reinforcements unless Southerners initiated hostilities.

Not satisfied, Southerners determined to take the fort. Confederate General P. G. T. Beauregard, acting on orders from President Davis, demanded Anderson's surrender. Anderson said he would if not resupplied. Knowing supplies were on the way, the Confederates opened fire at 4:30 a.m. on April 12, 1861. The next day the fort surrendered.

The day following Sumter's surrender Lincoln declared the existence of an insurrection and called for the states to provide 75,000 volunteers to put it down. In response to this, Virginia, Tennessee, North Carolina, and Arkansas declared their secession.

The remaining slave states, Delaware, Kentucky, Maryland, and Missouri, wavered to varying degrees but stayed with the Union. Delaware, which had few slaves, gave little serious consideration to the idea of secession. Kentucky declared itself neutral and then sided with the North when the South failed to respect this neutrality. Maryland's incipient secession movement was crushed by Lincoln's timely imposition of martial law. Missouri was saved for the Union by the quick and decisive use of federal troops as well as the sizeable population of pro-Union, anti-slavery German immigrants living in St. Louis.

Relative Strengths at the Outset

An assessment of available assets at the beginning of the war would not have looked favorable for the South.

The North enjoyed at least five major advantages over the South. It had overwhelming preponderance in wealth and thus was better able to finance the enormous expense of the war. The North was also vastly superior in industry and thus capable of producing the needed war materials; the South, as a primarily agricultural society, often had to improvise or do without.

The North furthermore had an advantage of almost three-to-one in manpower, and over one-third of the South's population was composed of slaves, whom Southerners would not use as soldiers. Unlike the South, the North received large numbers of immigrants during the war. The North retained control of the U.S. Navy, and thus would command the sea and be able, by blockading, to cut the South off from outside sources of supply.

Finally, the North enjoyed a far superior system of railroads, while the South's relatively sparse railroad net was composed of a number of smaller railroads, often not interconnected and with varying gauges of track. They were more useful for carrying cotton from the interior to port cities than for moving large amounts of war supplies or troops around the country.

The South did, however, have several advantages of its own. It was vast in size, and this would make it difficult to conquer; it did not need to conquer the North, but only resist being conquered itself. Its troops would also be fighting on their own ground, a fact that would give them the advantage of familiarity with the terrain, as well as the added motivation of defending their homes and families. Its armies would often have the opportunity of fighting on the defensive, a major advantage in the warfare of that day.

At the outset of the war the South drew a number of highly qualified senior officers, such as Robert E. Lee, Joseph E. Johnston, and Albert Sidney Johnston, from the U.S. Army. By contrast, the Union command structure was already set when the war began, with the aged Winfield Scott, of Mexican War fame, at the top. It took young and talented officers, such as Ulysses S. Grant and William T. Sherman, time to work up to high rank. Meanwhile, Union armies were often led by inferior commanders as Lincoln experimented while in search of good generals.

At first glance, the South might also have seemed to have an advantage in its president. Jefferson Davis had extensive military and political experience and was acquainted with the nation's top military men and, presumably, with their relative abilities. On the other hand, Lincoln had been, up until his election to the presidency, less successful politically and had virtually no military experience. In fact, Lincoln was much superior to Davis as a war leader, showing firmness, flexibility, mental toughness, great political skill, and, eventually, an excellent grasp of strategy.

Opposing Strategies

Both sides were full of enthusiasm for the war. In the North the battle cry was "On to Richmond," the new Confederate capital established after the secession of Virginia. In the South it was "On to Washington." Yielding to popular demand, Lincoln ordered General Irvin McDowell to advance on Richmond with his army. At a creek called Bull Run near the town of

Manassas Junction, Virginia, just southwest of Washington, D.C., they met a Confederate force under generals P. G. T. Beauregard and Joseph E. Johnston, July 21, 1861. In the First Battle of Bull Run (called First Battle of Manassas in the South) the Union army was forced to retreat in confusion back to Washington.

Bull Run demonstrated the unpreparedness and inexperience of both sides. It also demonstrated that the war would be long and hard, and, particularly in the North, that greater efforts would be required. Lincoln would need an overall strategy. To supply this, Winfield Scott suggested his Anaconda Plan to squeeze the life out of the Confederacy. This plan included a naval blockade to shut out supplies from Europe, a campaign to take the Mississippi River, thereby splitting the South in two, and the taking of several strategic points, then waiting for pro-Union sentiment in the South to overthrow the secessionists. Lincoln liked the first two points of Scott's strategy but considered the third point unrealistic.

He ordered a naval blockade, an overwhelming task considering the South's long coastline. Yet under Secretary of the Navy Gideon Welles the Navy was expanded enormously and the blockade, derided in the early days as a "paper blockade," became increasingly effective.

Lincoln also ordered a campaign to take the Mississippi River. A major step in this direction was taken when naval forces under Captain David G. Farragut took New Orleans in April 1862.

Rather than waiting for pro-Unionists in the South to gain control, Lincoln hoped to raise huge armies and apply overwhelming pressure from all sides at once until the Confederacy collapsed. The strategy was good; the problem was finding good generals to carry it out.

THE UNION PRESERVED

Lincoln Tries McClellan

To replace the discredited McDowell, Lincoln chose General George B. McClellan. McClellan was a good trainer and organizer and was loved by the troops, but was unable to effectively use the powerful army (now called the Army of the Potomac) he had built up. Despite much prodding from Lincoln, McClellan hesitated to advance, badly overestimating his enemy's numbers.

Finally, in the spring of 1862, he took the Army of the Potomac by water down Chesapeake Bay to land between the York and James rivers in Virginia. His plan was to advance up the peninsula formed by these rivers directly to Richmond.

The operations that followed were known as the Peninsula Campaign. McClellan advanced slowly and cautiously toward Richmond, while his equally cautious Confederate opponent, General Joseph E. Johnston, drew back to the outskirts of the city before turning to fight at the Battle of Seven Pines.

May 31–June 1, 1862. In this inconclusive battle Johnston was wounded. To replace him Jefferson Davis appointed his military advisor, General Robert E. Lee.

Lee summoned General Thomas J. "Stonewall" Jackson and his army from the Shenandoah Valley (where Jackson had just finished defeating several superior federal forces, causing consternation in Washington) and with the combined forces attacked McClellan.

After two days of bloody but inconclusive fighting, McClellan lost his nerve and began to retreat. In the remainder of what came to be called the Battle of the Seven Days, Lee continued to attack McClellan, forcing him back to his base, though at great cost in lives. McClellan's army was loaded back onto its ships and taken back to Washington.

Before McClellan's army could reach Washington and be completely deployed in northern Virginia, Lee saw and took an opportunity to thrash Union General John Pope, who was operating in northern Virginia with another Northern army, at the Second Battle of Bull Run.

Union Victories in the West

In the western area of the war's operations, (essentially everything west of the Appalachian Mountains,) matters were proceeding in a much different fashion. The Northern commanders there, Henry W. Halleck and Don Carlos Buell, were no more enterprising than McClellan, but Halleck's subordinate, Ulysses S. Grant, definitely was.

Seeking and obtaining permission from Halleck, Grant mounted a combined operation—army troops and navy gunboats—against two vital Confederate strongholds, Forts Henry and Donelson, which guarded the Tennessee and Cumberland rivers in northern Tennessee, and which were the weak point of the thin-stretched Confederate line under General Albert Sidney Johnston. When Grant captured the forts in February 1862, Johnston was forced to retreat to Corinth in northern Mississippi.

Grant pursued but, ordered by Halleck to wait until all was in readiness before proceeding, Grant halted his troops at Pittsburg Landing on the Tennessee River, twenty-five miles north of Corinth. On April 6, 1862, Johnston, who had received reinforcements and been joined by General P. G. T. Beauregard, surprised Grant there, but in the two-day battle that followed (Shiloh) failed to defeat him. Johnston himself was among the many killed in what was, up to this point, the bloodiest battle in American history.

Grant was severely criticized in the North for having been taken by surprise. Yet with other Union victories and Farragut's capture of New Orleans, the North had taken all of the Mississippi River except for a 110-mile stretch between the Confederate fortresses of Vicksburg, Mississippi, and Port Hudson, Louisiana.

The Success of Northern Diplomacy

Many Southerners believed Britain and France would rejoice in seeing a divided and weakened America. The two countries would likewise be driven by the need of their factories for cotton and thus intervene on the Confederacy's behalf. So strongly was this view held that during the early days of the war, when the Union blockade was still too weak to be very effective, the Confederate government itself prohibited the export of cotton in order to hasten British and French intervention.

This view proved mistaken for several reasons. Britain already had on hand large stocks of cotton from the bumper crops of the years immediately prior to the war. During the war the British were successful in finding alternative sources of cotton, importing the fiber from India and Egypt. British leaders may also have weighed their country's need to import wheat from the northern United States against its desire for cotton from the Southern states. Finally, British public opinion opposed slavery.

Skillful Northern diplomacy had a great impact. In this, Lincoln had the extremely able assistance of Secretary of State William Seward, who took a hard line in warning Europeans not to interfere, and of Ambassador to Great Britain Charles Francis Adams. Britain therefore remained neutral and other European countries, France in particular, followed its lead.

One incident nevertheless came close to fulfilling Southern hopes for British intervention. In November 1861 Captain Charles Wilkes of the U.S.S. *San Jacinto* stopped the British mail and passenger ship *Trent* and forcibly removed Confederate emissaries James M. Mason and John Slidell. News of Wilkes' action brought great rejoicing in the North but outrage in Great Britain, where it was viewed as a violation of Britain's rights on the high seas. Lincoln and Seward, faced with British threats of war at a time when the North could ill afford it, wisely chose to release the envoys and smooth things over with Britain.

The Confederacy was able to obtain some loans and to purchase small amounts of arms, ammunition, and even commerce-raiding ships such as the highly successful C.S.S. *Alabama*. However, Union naval superiority kept such supplies to a minimum.

The War at Sea

The Confederacy's major bid to challenge the Union's naval superiority was based on the employment of a technological innovation, the ironclad ship. The first and most successful of the Confederate ironclads was the C.S.S. *Virginia*. Built on the hull of the abandoned Union frigate *Merrimac*, the *Virginia* was protected from cannon fire by iron plates bolted over her sloping wooden sides. In May 1862 she destroyed two wooden warships of the Union naval force at Hampton Roads, Virginia, and was seriously threatening to destroy the rest of the squadron before being met and fought to a standstill by the Union ironclad U.S.S. *Monitor*.

The Home Front

The war on the home front dealt with the problems of maintaining public morale, supplying the armies of the held, and resolving constitutional questions regarding authority and the ability of the respective governments to deal with crises.

For the general purpose of maintaining public morale but also as items many Republicans had advocated even before the war, Congress in 1862 passed two highly important acts dealing with domestic affairs in the North.

The Homestead Act granted 160 acres of government land free of charge to any person who would farm it for at least five years. Much of the West was eventually settled under the provisions of this act. The Morrill Land Grant Act offered large amounts of the federal government's land to states that would establish "agricultural and mechanical" colleges. Many of the nation's large state universities were founded in later years under the provisions of this act.

Keeping the people relatively satisfied was made more difficult by the necessity, apparent by 1863, of imposing conscription in order to obtain adequate manpower for the huge armies that would be needed to crush the South. Especially hated by many working class Northerners was the provision of the conscription act that allowed a drafted individual to avoid service by hiring a substitute or paying $300. Resistance to the draft led to riots in New York City in which hundreds were killed.

The Confederacy, with its much smaller manpower pool on which to draw, had instituted conscription in 1862. Here, too, it did not always meet with cooperation. Some Southern governors objected to it on doctrinaire states' rights grounds, doing all they could to obstruct its operation. A provision of the Southern conscription act allowing one man to stay home as overseer for every twenty slaves led the non-slaveholding whites who made up most of the Southern population to grumble that it was a "rich man's war and a poor man's fight." Draft-dodging and desertion became epidemic in the South by the latter part of the war.

Scarcity of food and other consumer goods in the South as well as high prices led to further desertion as soldiers left the ranks to care for their starving families. Discontent also manifested itself in the form of a "bread riot" in Richmond.

Supplying the war placed an enormous strain on both societies, but one the North was better able to bear.

To finance the Northern side of the war, high tariffs and an income tax (the nation's first) were resorted to, yet even more money was needed. The Treasury Department, under Secretary of the Treasury Salmon P. Chase, issued "greenbacks," an unbacked fiat currency that nevertheless fared better than the Southern paper money because of greater confidence in Northern victory. To facilitate the financing of the war through credit expansion, the National Banking Act was passed in 1863.

The South, with its scant financial resources, found it all but impossible to cope with the expense of war. Excise and income taxes were levied and some small loans were obtained in Europe, yet the Southern Congress still felt compelled to issue paper money in such quantities that it became virtually worthless. That, and the scarcity of almost everything created by the war and its disruption of the economy, led to skyrocketing prices.

The Confederate government responded to the inflation it created by imposing taxes-in-kind and impressment, the seizing of produce, livestock, etc., by

Confederate agents in return for payment according to an artificially set schedule of prices. Since payment was in worthless inflated currency, this amounted to confiscation and soon resulted in goods of all sorts becoming even scarcer than otherwise when a Confederate impressment agent was known to be in the neighborhood.

Questions of constitutional authority to deal with crises plagued both presidents.

To deal with the emergency of secession, Lincoln stretched the presidential powers to the limit, or perhaps beyond the limit, of the Constitution. To quell the threat of secession in Maryland, Lincoln suspended the writ of *habeas corpus* and imprisoned numerous suspected secessionists without charges or trial, ignoring the insistence of pro-Southern Chief Justice Roger B. Taney in *ex Parte Merryman* (1861) that such action was unconstitutional.

"Copperheads," Northerners such as Clement L. Vallandigham of Ohio who opposed the war, denounced Lincoln as a tyrant and would-be dictator but remained a minority. Though occasionally subject to arrest and/or deportation for their activities, they were generally allowed a considerable degree of latitude.

Davis encountered obstructionism from various state governors, the Confederate Congress, and even his own vice president, who denounced him as a tyrant for assuming too much power and failing to respect states' rights. Hampered by such attitudes, the Confederate government proved less effective than it might have been.

The Emancipation Proclamation

By mid-1862, Lincoln, under pressure from radical elements of his own party and hoping to create a favorable impression on foreign public opinion, determined to issue the Emancipation Proclamation, declaring free, as of January 1, 1863, all slaves in areas still in rebellion. In order that this not appear an act of panic and desperation in view of the string of defeats the North had recently suffered on the battlefields of Virginia, Lincoln, at Seward's recommendation, waited to announce the proclamation until the North should win some sort of victory. This was provided by the Battle of Antietam, September 17, 1862.

Though the Radical Republicans, pre-war abolitionists for the most part, had for some time been urging Lincoln to take such a step, Northern public opinion as a whole was less enthusiastic, as the Republicans suffered major losses in the November 1862 congressional elections.

The Turning Point in the East

After his victory of the Second Battle of Bull Run, August 27–30, 1862, Lee moved north and crossed into Maryland, where he hoped to win a decisive victory that would force the North to recognize Southern independence.

He was confronted by the Army of the Potomac, once again under the command of General George B. McClellan. Through a stroke of good fortune early in the campaign, detailed plans for Lee's entire audacious operation fell into McClellan's hands, but the Northern general, by extreme caution and slowness, threw away this incomparable chance to annihilate Lee and win—or at least shorten—the war.

The armies finally met along Antietam Creek, just east of the town of Sharpsburg in western Maryland. In a bloody but inconclusive day-long battle, known as Antietam in the North and as Sharpsburg in the South, McClellan's timidity led him to miss another excellent chance to destroy Lee's cornered and badly outnumbered army. After the battle Lee retreated to Virginia, and Lincoln, besides issuing the Emancipation Proclamation, removed McClellan from command.

To replace him, Lincoln chose General Ambrose E. Burnside, who promptly demonstrated his unfitness for command by blundering into a lopsided defeat at Fredericksburg, Virginia, December 13, 1862.

Lincoln then replaced Burnside with General Joseph "Fighting Joe" Hooker. Handsome and hard-drinking, Hooker had bragged of what he would do to "Bobby Lee" when he got at him; but when he took his army south, "Fighting Joe" quickly lost his nerve. He was out-generaled and soundly beaten at the Battle of Chancellorsville, May 5–6, 1863. At this battle the brilliant Southern General "Stonewall" Jackson was accidentally shot by his own men and died several days later.

Lee, anxious to shift the scene of the fighting out of his beloved Virginia, sought and received permission from President Davis to invade Pennsylvania. He was pursued by the Army of the Potomac, now under the command of General George G. Meade, whom Lincoln had selected to replace the discredited Hooker. They met at Gettysburg, and in a three-day battle (July 1–3,1863) that was the bloodiest of the entire war, Lee, who sorely missed the services of Jackson and whose cavalry leader, the normally reliable J. E. B. Stuart, failed to provide him with timely reconnaissance, was defeated. However, he was allowed by the victorious Meade to retreat to Virginia with his army intact if battered, much to Lincoln's disgust. Still, Lee would never again have the strength to mount such an invasion.

Lincoln Finds Grant

Meanwhile, Grant undertook to take Vicksburg, one of the two last Confederate bastions on the Mississippi River. In a brilliant campaign, he bottled up the Confederate forces of General John C. Pemberton inside the city and placed them under siege. After six weeks of siege, the defenders surrendered, July 4, 1863. Five days later Port Hudson surrendered as well, giving the Union complete control of the Mississippi.

After Union forces under General William Rosecrans suffered an embarrassing defeat at the Battle of Chickamauga in northwestern Georgia, September 19–20, 1863, Lincoln named Grant overall commander of Union forces in the West.

Grant went to Chattanooga, Tennessee, where Confederate forces under General Braxton Bragg were virtually besieging Rosecrans, and immediately took control of the situation. Gathering Union forces from other portions of the western theater and combining them with reinforcements from the East, Grant won a resounding victory at the Battle of Chattanooga (November 23–25, 1863), in which federal forces stormed seemingly impregnable Confederate positions on Lookout Mountain and Missionary Ridge. This victory put Union forces in position for a drive into Georgia, which began the following spring.

Early in 1864 Lincoln made Grant commander of all Union armies. Grant devised a coordinated plan for constant pressure on the Confederacy. General William T. Sherman would lead a drive toward Atlanta, Georgia, with the goal of destroying the Confederate army under General Joseph E. Johnston (who had replaced Bragg). Grant himself would accompany Meade and the Army of the Potomac in advancing toward Richmond with the goal of destroying Lee's Confederate army.

In a series of bloody battles (the Wilderness, Spotsylvania, Cold Harbor) in May and June of 1864, Grant drove Lee to the outskirts of Richmond. Still unable to take the city or get Lee at a disadvantage, Grant circled around to try to take both by way of the back door, attacking Petersburg, Virginia, an important railroad junction just south of Richmond and the key to that city's—and Lee's—supply lines. Once again turned back by entrenched Confederate troops, Grant settled down to besiege Petersburg and Richmond in a stalemate that lasted some nine months.

Sherman had been advancing simultaneously in Georgia. He maneuvered Johnston back to the outskirts of Atlanta with relatively little fighting. At that point Confederate President Davis lost patience with Johnston and replaced him with the aggressive General John B. Hood. Hood and Sherman fought three fierce but inconclusive battles around Atlanta in late July, then settled down to a siege of their own during the month of August.

The Election of 1864 and Northern Victory

In the North discontentment grew with the long casualty lists and seeming lack of results. Yet the South could stand the grinding war even less. By late 1864 Jefferson Davis had reached the point of calling for the use of blacks in the Confederate armies, though the war ended before black troops could see action for the Confederacy. The South's best hope was that Northern war-weariness would bring the defeat of Lincoln and the victory of a peace candidate in the election of 1864.

Lincoln ran on the ticket of the National Union Party, essentially the Republican party with loyal or "War" Democrats. His vice-presidential candidate was Andrew Johnson, a loyal Democrat from Tennessee.

The Democratic Party's presidential candidate was General George B. McClellan, who, with some misgivings, ran on a platform labeling the war a failure and calling for a negotiated peace settlement even if that meant Southern independence.

The outlook was bleak for a time, and even Lincoln himself believed that he would be defeated. Then in September 1864 came word that Sherman had taken Atlanta. The capture of this vital Southern rail and manufacturing center brought an enormous boost to northern morale. Along with other Northern victories that summer and fall, it insured a resounding election victory for Lincoln and the continuation of the war to complete victory for the North.

To speed that victory, Sherman marched through Georgia from Atlanta to the sea, arriving at Savannah in December 1864 and turning north into the Carolinas, leaving behind a 60-mile-wide swath of destruction. His goal was to impress on southerners that continuation of the war could mean only ruin for all of them. He and Grant planned that his army should press on through the Carolinas and into Virginia to join Grant in finishing off Lee.

Before Sherman's troops could arrive, Lee abandoned Richmond (April 3, 1865) and attempted to escape with what was left of his army. Pursued by Grant, he was cornered and forced to surrender at Appomattox, Virginia, on April 9, 1865. Other Confederate armies still holding out in various parts of the South surrendered over the next few weeks.

Lincoln did not live to receive news of the final surrenders. On April 14, 1865, he was shot in the back of the head while watching a play at Ford's Theater in Washington. His assassin, pro-Southern actor John Wilkes Booth, injured his ankle in making his escape. Hunted down by Union cavalry several days later, he died of a gunshot wound, apparently self-inflicted. Several other individuals were tried, convicted, and hanged by a military tribunal for participating with Booth in a conspiracy to assassinate not only Lincoln, but also Vice President Johnson and Secretary of State Seward.

THE ORDEAL OF RECONSTRUCTION

Lincoln's Plan of Reconstruction

Reconstruction began well before the fighting of the Civil War came to an end. It brought a time of difficult adjustments in the South.

Among those who faced such adjustments were the recently freed slaves, who flocked into Union lines, followed advancing Union armies, or whose plantations were part of the growing area of the South that came under Union military control. Some slaves had left their plantations, and thus their only means of livelihood, in order to obtain freedom within Union lines. Many felt they had to leave their plantations in order to be truly free, and some sought to find relatives separated during the days of slavery. Some former slaves also seemed to misunderstand the meaning of freedom, thinking they need never work again.

To ease the adjustment for these recently freed slaves, Congress in 1865 created the Freedman's Bureau, to provide food, clothing, and education, and generally look after the interests of former slaves.

Even before the need to deal with this problem had forced itself on the Northern government's awareness, steps had been taken to deal with another major adjustment of Reconstruction, the restoration of loyal governments to the seceded states. By 1863 substantial portions of several Southern states had come under Northern military control, and Lincoln had set forth a policy for re-establishing governments in those states.

Lincoln's policy, known as the Ten Percent Plan, stipulated that Southerners, except for high-ranking rebel officials, could take an oath promising future loyalty to the Union and acceptance of the end of slavery. When the number of those who had taken this oath within any one state reached ten percent of the number who had been registered to vote in that state in 1860, a loyal state government could be formed. Only those who had taken the oath could vote or participate in the new government.

Tennessee, Arkansas, and Louisiana met the requirements and formed loyal governments but were refused recognition by Congress, which was dominated by Radical Republicans.

The Radical Republicans, such as Thaddeus Stevens of Pennsylvania, believed Lincoln's plan did not adequately punish the South, restructure Southern society, and boost the political prospects of the Republican Party. The loyal southern states were denied representation in Congress and electoral votes in the election of 1864.

Instead, the Radicals in Congress drew up the Wade-Davis Bill. Under its stringent terms a majority of the number who had been alive and registered to vote in 1860 would have to swear an "ironclad" oath stating that they were now loyal and had never been disloyal. This was obviously impossible in any former Confederate state unless blacks were given the vote, something Radical Republicans desired but Southerners definitely did not. Unless the requisite number swore the "ironclad" oath, Congress would not allow the state to have a government.

Lincoln killed the Wade-Davis bill with a "pocket veto," and the Radicals were furious. When Lincoln was assassinated the Radicals rejoiced, believing Vice President Andrew Johnson would be less generous to the South or at least easier to control.

Johnson's Attempt at Reconstruction

To the dismay of the Radicals, Johnson followed Lincoln's policies very closely, making them only slightly more stringent by requiring ratification of the 13th Amendment (officially abolishing slavery), repudiation of Confederate debts, and renunciation of secession. He also recommended the vote be given to blacks.

Southern states proved reluctant to accept these conditions, some declining to repudiate Confederate debts or ratify the 13th Amendment (it nevertheless received the ratification of the necessary number of states and was declared part of the Constitution in December 1865). No Southern state extended the vote to blacks (at this time no Northern state did, either). Instead the Southern states promulgated Black Codes, imposing various restrictions on the freedom of the former slaves.

Foreign Policy Under Johnson

On coming into office Johnson had inherited a foreign policy problem involving Mexico and France. The French Emperor, Napoleon III, had made Mexico the target of one of his many grandiose foreign adventures. In 1862, while the U.S. was occupied with the Civil War and therefore unable to prevent this violation of the Monroe Doctrine, Napoleon III had Archduke Maximilian of Austria installed as a puppet emperor of Mexico, supported by French troops. The U.S. had protested but for the time could do nothing.

With the war over, Johnson and Secretary of State Seward were able to take more vigorous steps. General Philip Sheridan was sent to the Rio Grande with a military force. At the same time Mexican revolutionary leader Benito Juarez was given the tacit recognition of the U.S. government. Johnson and Seward continued to invoke the Monroe Doctrine and to place quiet pressure on Napoleon III to withdraw his troops. In May 1866, facing difficulties of his own in Europe, the French emperor did so, leaving the unfortunate Maximilian to face a Mexican firing squad.

Johnson's and Seward's course of action in preventing the extension of the French Empire into the Western Hemisphere strengthened America's commitment to and the rest of the world's respect for the Monroe Doctrine.

In 1866 the Russian minister approached Seward with an offer to sell Alaska to the U.S. The Russians desired to sell Alaska because its fur resources had been largely exhausted and because they feared that in a possible war with Great Britain (something that seemed likely at the time) they would lose Alaska anyway.

Seward, who was an ardent expansionist, pushed hard for the purchase of Alaska, known as "Seward's Folly" by its critics, and it was largely through his efforts that it was pushed through Congress. It was urged that purchasing Alaska would reward the Russians for their friendly stance toward the U.S. government during the Civil War, at a time when Britain and France had seemed to favor the Confederacy.

In 1867 the sale went through and Alaska was purchased for $7.2 million.

Congressional Reconstruction

Southern intransigence in the face of Johnson's relatively mild plan of Reconstruction manifested in the refusal of some states to repudiate the Confederate debt and ratify the 13th Amendment. The refusal to give the vote to blacks, the passage of black codes, and the election of many former high-ranking Confederates to Congress and other top positions in the Southern states, played into the hands of the Radicals, who were anxious to impose harsh rule on the South. They could now assert that the South was refusing to accept the verdict of the war.

Once again Congress excluded the representatives of the Southern states. Determined to reconstruct the South as it saw fit, Congress passed a Civil Rights Act and extended the authority of the Freedman's Bureau, giving it both quasi-judicial and quasi-executive powers.

Johnson vetoed both bills, claiming they were unconstitutional; but Congress overrode the vetoes. Fearing that the Supreme Court would agree with Johnson and overturn the laws, Congress approved and sent on to the states for ratification (June 1866) the 14th Amendment, making constitutional the laws Congress had just passed. The 14th Amendment defined citizenship and forbade states to deny various rights to citizens, reduced the representation in Congress of states that did not allow blacks to vote, forbade the paying of the Confederate debt, and made former Confederates ineligible to hold public office.

With only one Southern state, Tennessee, ratifying, the amendment failed to receive the necessary approval of three-fourths of the states. But the Radicals in Congress were not finished. Strengthened by victory in the 1866 elections, they passed, over Johnson's veto, the Military Reconstruction Act, dividing the South into five military districts to be ruled by military governors with almost dictatorial powers. Tennessee, having ratified the 14th Amendment, was spared the wrath of the Radicals. The rest of the Southern states were ordered to produce constitutions giving the vote to blacks and to ratify the 14th Amendment before they could be "readmitted." In this manner the 14th Amendment was ratified.

Realizing the unprecedented nature of these actions, Congress moved to prevent any check or balance from the other two branches of government. Steps were taken toward limiting the jurisdiction of the Supreme Court so that it could not review cases pertaining to congressional Reconstruction policies. This proved unnecessary as the Court, now headed by Chief Justice Salmon P. Chase in place of the deceased Taney, readily acquiesced and declined to overturn the Reconstruction acts.

To control the president, Congress passed the Army Act, reducing the president's control over the Army. In obtaining the cooperation of the Army the Radicals had the aid of General Grant, who already had his eye on the 1868 Republican presidential nomination. Congress also passed the Tenure of Office Act, forbidding Johnson to dismiss Cabinet members without the Senate's permission. In passing the latter act, Congress was especially thinking of Radical Secretary of War Edwin M. Stanton, a Lincoln holdover whom Johnson desired to dismiss.

Johnson obeyed the letter but not the spirit of the Reconstruction acts, and Congress, angry at his refusal to cooperate, sought in vain for grounds to impeach him until in August 1867, Johnson violated the Tenure of Office Act (by dismissing Stanton) in order to test its constitutionality. The matter was not tested in the courts, however, but in Congress, where Johnson was impeached by the House of Representatives and came within one vote of being removed by the Senate. For the remaining months of his term he offered little further resistance to the Radicals.

The Election of 1868 and the 15th Amendment

In 1868 the Republican convention, dominated by the Radicals, drew up a platform endorsing Radical Reconstruction. For president, the Republicans nominated Ulysses S. Grant, who had no political record and whose views—if any—on national issues were unknown. The vice-presidential nominee was Schuyler Colfax.

Though the Democratic nomination was sought by Andrew Johnson, the party knew he could not win and instead nominated former Governor Horatio Seymour of New York for president and Francis P. Blair Jr. of Missouri for vice president. Both had been Union generals during the war. The Democratic platform mildly criticized the excesses of Radical Reconstruction and called for continued payment of the war debt in greenbacks, although Seymour himself was a hard-money man.

Grant, despite his enormous popularity as a war hero, won by only a narrow margin, drawing only 300,000 more popular votes than Seymour. Some 700,000 blacks had voted in the Southern states under the auspices of Army occupation, and since all of these had almost certainly voted for Grant, it was clear that he had not received a majority of the white vote.

The narrow victory of even such a strong candidate as Grant prompted Republican leaders to decide that it would be politically expedient to give the vote to all blacks, North as well as South. For this purpose the 15th Amendment was drawn up and submitted to the states. Ironically, the idea was so unpopular in the North that it won the necessary three-fourths approval only with its ratification by Southern states required to do so by Congress.

Postwar Life in the South

Reconstruction was a difficult time in the South. During the war approximately one in ten Southern men had been killed. Many more were maimed for life. Those who returned from the war found destruction and poverty. Property of the Confederate government was confiscated by the federal government, and dishonest Treasury agents confiscated private property as well. Capital invested in slaves or in Confederate war bonds was lost. Property values fell to one-tenth of their pre-war level. The economic results of the war stayed with the South for decades.

The political results were less long-lived but more immediately disturbing to Southerners. Southerners complained of widespread corruption in governments sustained by federal troops and composed of "carpetbaggers," "scalawags" (the Southern names for Northerners who came to the South to participate in Reconstruction governments and for southerners who supported the Reconstruction regimes, respectively), and recently freed blacks.

Under the Reconstruction governments, social programs were greatly expanded, leading to higher taxes and growing state debts. Some of the financial problems were due to corruption, a problem in both North and South in this era when political machines, such as William Marcy "Boss" Tweed's Tammany Hall machine in New York, dominated many Northern city governments and grew rich.

Southern whites sometimes responded to Reconstruction governments with violence, carried out by groups such as the Ku Klux Klan, aimed at intimidating blacks and white Republicans out of voting. The activities of these organizations were sometimes a response to those of the Union League, an organization used by Southern Republicans to control the black vote. The goal of Southerners not allied with the Reconstruction governments, whether members of the Ku Klux Klan or not, was "redemption" (i.e., the end of the Reconstruction governments).

By 1876 Southern whites had been successful, by legal means or otherwise, in "redeeming" all but three Southern states.

Reconstruction ended primarily because the North lost interest. Corruption in government, economic hard times brought on by the Panic of 1873, and general weariness on the part of Northern voters with the effort to remake Southern society all sapped the will to continue. Diehard Radicals such as Thaddeus Stevens and Charles Sumner were dead.

Corruption Under Grant

Having arrived in the presidency with no firm political positions, Grant found that the only principle he had to guide his actions was his instinctive loyalty to his old friends and the politicians who had propelled him into office. This principle did not serve him well as president. Though personally of unquestioned integrity, he naively placed his faith in a number of thoroughly dishonest men. His administration was rocked by one scandalous revelation of government corruption after another. Not every scandal involved members of the executive branch, but together they tended to taint the entire period of Grant's administration as one of unparalleled corruption.

The "Black Friday" Scandal

In the "Black Friday" scandal, two unscrupulous businessmen, Jim Fiske and Jay Gould, schemed to corner the gold market. To further their designs, they got Grant's brother-in-law to persuade the president that stopping government gold sales would be good for farmers. Grant naively complied, and many businessmen were ruined as the price of gold was bid up furiously on "Black Friday." By the time Grant realized what was happening, much damage had already been done.

The Credit Mobilier Scandal

In the Credit Mobilier scandal, officials of the Union Pacific Railroad used a dummy construction company called Credit Mobilier to skim off millions of dollars of the subsidies the government was paying the Union Pacific for building a transcontinental railroad. To ensure that Congress would take a benevolent attitude toward all this, the officials bribed many of its members lavishly. Though much of this took place before Grant came into office, its revelation in an 1872 congressional investigation created a general scandal.

The "Salary Grab Act"

In the "Salary Grab Act" of 1873, Congress voted a 100 percent pay raise for the president and a 50 percent increase for itself and made both retroactive two years. Public outrage led to a Democratic victory in the next congressional election and the law was repealed.

The Sanborn Contract Fraud

In the Sanborn Contract fraud, a politician named Sanborn was given a contract to collect $427,000 in unpaid taxes for a 50 percent commission. The commission found its way into Republican campaign funds.

The Whiskey Ring Fraud

In the Whiskey Ring fraud, distillers and treasury officials conspired to defraud the government of large amounts of money from the excise tax on whiskey. Grant's personal secretary was in on the plot, and Grant himself naively accepted gifts of a questionable nature. When the matter came under investigation, Grant endeavored to shield his secretary.

The Bribing of Belknap

Grant's secretary of war, W. W. Belknap, accepted bribes from corrupt agents involved in his department's administration of Indian affairs. When the matter came out, he resigned to escape impeachment.

The Liberal Republicans

Discontentment within Republican ranks with regard to some of the earlier scandals as well as with the Radicals' vindictive Reconstruction policies led a faction of the party to separate and constitute itself as the Liberal Republicans. Besides opposing corruption and favoring sectional harmony, the Liberal Republicans favored hard money and a laissez-faire approach to economic issues. For the election of 1872 they nominated *New York Tribune* editor Horace Greeley for president. Eccentric, controversial, and ineffective as a campaigner, Greeley proved a poor choice. Though nominated by the Democrats as well as the Liberal Republicans, he was easily defeated by Grant, who was again the nominee of the Radicals.

Economic Issues Under Grant

Many of the economic difficulties the country faced during Grant's administration were caused by the necessary readjustments from a wartime back to a peacetime economy.

The central economic question was deflation versus inflation or, more specifically, whether to retire the unbacked paper money, greenbacks, printed to meet the wartime emergency, or to print more.

Economic conservatives, creditors, and business interests usually favored retirement of the greenbacks and an early return the gold standard.

Debtors, who had looked forward to paying off their obligations in depreciated paper money worth less than the gold-backed money they had borrowed, favored a continuation of currency inflation through the use of more greenbacks. The deflation that would come through the retirement of existing greenbacks would make debts contracted during or immediately after the war much harder to pay.

Generally, Grant's policy was to let the greenbacks float until they were on par with gold and could then be retired without economic dislocation.

Early in Grant's second term the country was hit by an economic depression known as the Panic of 1873. Brought on by the overexpansive tendencies of railroad builders and businessmen during the immediate post-war boom, the Panic was triggered by economic downturns in Europe and, more immediately, by the failure of Jay Cooke and Company, a major American financial firm.

The financial hardship brought on by the Panic led to renewed clamor for the printing of more greenbacks. In 1874 Congress authorized a small new issue of greenbacks, but it was vetoed by Grant. Pro-inflation forces were further enraged when Congress in 1873 demonetized silver, going to a straight gold standard. Silver was becoming more plentiful due to Western mining and was seen by some as a potential source of inflation. Pro-inflation forces referred to the demonetization of silver as the "Crime of '73."

In 1875 Congress took a further step toward retirement of the greenbacks and return to a working gold standard when, under the leadership of John Sherman, it passed the Specie Resumption Act, calling for the resumption of specie payments (i.e., the redeemability of the nation's paper money in gold) by January 1, 1879.

Disgruntled proponents of inflation formed the Greenback Party and nominated Peter Cooper for president in 1876. However, they gained only an insignificant number of votes.

The Disputed Election of 1876

In the election of 1876, the Democrats campaigned against corruption and nominated New York Governor Samuel J. Tilden, who had broken the Tweed political machine of New York City.

The Republicans passed over Grant, who was interested in another term and had the backing of the remaining hard-core Radicals, and turned instead to Governor Rutherford B. Hayes of Ohio. Like Tilden, Hayes was decent, honest, in favor of hard money and civil service reform, and opposed to government regulation of the economy. In their campaigning, the Republicans resorted to a tactic known as "waving the bloody shirt." Successfully used in the last two presidential elections, this meant basically playing on wartime animosities, urging Northerners to vote the way they had shot, and suggested that a Democratic victory and a Confederate victory would be about the same thing.

This time the tactic was less successful. Tilden won the popular vote and led in the electoral vote 184 to 165. However, 185 electoral votes were needed for election, and 20 votes, from the three Southern states still occupied by Federal troops and run by Republican governments, were disputed.

Though there had been extensive fraud on both sides, Tilden undoubtedly deserved at least the one vote he needed to win. Congress created a special commission to decide the matter. It was to be composed of five members each from the Senate, the House, and the Supreme Court. Of these, seven were to be Republicans, seven Democrats, and one an independent. The Republicans arranged, however, for the independent justice's state legislature to elect him to the Senate. When the justice resigned to take his Senate seat, it left all the remaining Supreme Court justices Republican. One of them was chosen, and in a series of eight-to-seven votes along straight party lines, the commission voted to give all 20 disputed votes—and the election—to Hayes.

When outraged congressional Democrats threatened to reject these obviously fraudulent results, a compromise was worked out. In the Compromise of 1877, Hayes promised to show consideration for Southern interests, end Reconstruction, and withdraw the remaining Federal troops from the South in exchange for Democratic acquiescence in his election.

Reconstruction would probably have ended anyway, since the North had already lost interest in it.

HISTORICAL TIMELINE

THE CIVIL WAR AND RECONSTRUCTION (1860–1877)

1860	Crittenden Compromise proposed South Carolina secedes
1861	Confederacy formed Firing on Ft. Sumter First Battle of Bull Run
1862	Shiloh Antietam Homestead Act Emancipation Proclamation announced
1863	Vicksburg Gettysburg New York City draft riots
1864	Grant takes command of all Union armies Sherman captures Atlanta
1865	Lee surrenders at Appomattox Lincoln assassinated 13th Amendment ends slavery Freedmen's Bureau established
1867	Alaska purchased from Russia Grange founded
1868	President Johnson impeached 14th Amendment passed Grant elected president
1869	Transcontinental railroad completed Knights of Labor formed
1873	Slaughterhouse case Panic of 1873

1875	Dwight L. Moody begins urban revivalism movement
1876	Custer defeated by Sioux at Little Big Horn
1877	Compromise of 1877 Reconstruction ends

9 INDUSTRIALISM, WAR, AND THE PROGRESSIVE ERA (1877–1912)

THE NEW INDUSTRIAL ERA, 1877–1882

The structure of modern American society was erected by democratic, capitalistic and technological forces in the post–Civil War era. Between the 1870s and 1890s, "Gilded Age" America emerged as the world's leading industrial and agricultural producer.

POLITICS OF THE PERIOD, 1877–1882

The presidencies of Abraham Lincoln and Theodore Roosevelt mark the boundaries of a half century of relatively weak executive leadership, and legislative domination by Congress and the Republican Party.

The Compromise of 1877

With Southern Democratic acceptance of Rutherford B. Hayes' Republican presidency, the last remaining Union troops were withdrawn from the Old Confederacy (South Carolina, Florida, Louisiana), and the country was at last reunified as a modern nation-state led by corporate and industrial interests. The Hayes election arrangement also marked the government's abandonment of its earlier vague commitment to African-American equality.

Republican Factions

"Stalwarts" led by New York Senator Roscoe Conkling favored the old spoils system of political patronage. "Half-Breeds" headed by Maine Senator James G. Blaine pushed for civil service reform and merit appointments to government posts.

Election of 1880

James A. Garfield of Ohio, a Half-Breed, and his vice presidential running mate, Chester A. Arthur of New York, a Stalwart, defeated the Democratic candidate, General Winfield S. Hancock of Pennsylvania and former Indiana congressman William English. Tragically, the Garfield administration was but an interlude, for the president was assassinated in 1881 by a mentally disturbed patronage seeker, Charles Guiteau. Although without much executive experience, the Stalwart Arthur had the courage to endorse reform of the political spoils system by supporting passage of the Pendleton Act (1883) which established open competitive examinations for civil service positions.

The Greenback-Labor Party

The Greenback-Labor Party movement polled over one million votes in 1878, and elected 14 members to Congress in an effort to promote the inflation of farm prices, and the cooperative marketing of agricultural produce. In 1880, the party's presidential candidate, James Weaver of Iowa, advocated public control and regulation of private enterprises such as railroads in the common interest of more equitable competition. Weaver theorized that because railroads were so essential, they should be treated as a public utility. He polled only 3 percent of the vote.

THE ECONOMY, 1877–1882

Industrial expansion and technology assumed mayor proportions in this period. Between 1860 and 1894 the United States moved from the fourth-largest manufacturing nation to the world's leader through capital accumulation, natural resources (especially in iron, oil and coal) an abundance of labor helped by massive immigration, railway transportation and communications (the telephone was introduced by Alexander Graham Bell in 1876), and major technical innovations such as the development of the modern steel industry by Andrew Carnegie, and electrical energy by Thomas Edison. In the petroleum industry, John D. Rockefeller controlled 95 percent of the U.S. oil refineries by 1877.

The New South

By 1880, Northern capital erected the modern textile industry in the New South by bringing factories to the cotton fields. Birmingham, Alabama, emerged as the South's leading steel producer, and the introduction of machine-made cigarettes propelled the Duke family to prominence as tobacco producers.

Standard of Living

An elite class rose during this period which accumulated vast family fortunes, while many Americans, especially immigrants and newly freed slaves, suffered crushing poverty.

Social Darwinism

Many industrial leaders used the doctrines associated with the "Gospel of Wealth" to justify the unequal distribution of national wealth. Self-justification by the wealthy was based on the notion that God had granted wealth as He had given grace for material and spiritual salvation of the select few. These few, according to William Graham Sumner, relied heavily on the survival-of-the-fittest philosophy associated with Charles Darwin.

Labor Unrest

When capital over-expansion and over-speculation led to the economic panic of 1873, massive labor disorders spread through the country leading to the paralyzing railroad strike of 1877. Unemployment and salary reductions caused major class conflict. President Hayes used federal troops to restore order after dozens of workers were killed. Immigrant workers began fighting among themselves in California where Irish and Chinese laborers fought for economic survival.

Labor Unions

The depression of the 1870s undermined national labor organizations. The National Labor Union (1866) had a membership of 600,000 but failed to withstand the impact of economic adversity. The Knights of Labor (1869) managed to open its membership to not only white native American workers, but immigrants, women and African-Americans as well. Although they claimed one million members, they too could not weather the hard times of the 1870s, and eventually went under in 1886 in the wake of the bloody Haymarket Riot in Chicago.

Agricultural Militancy

Agrarian discontent expressed through the activities of the National Grange and the Farmers' Alliances in the West and South showed greater lasting power. During the Civil War, many farmers had over-expanded their operations, purchased more land and machinery, and gone heavily into debt. When the relatively high wartime agricultural prices collapsed in the decades after the war, farmers worked collectively to promote currency inflation, higher farm prices, silver and gold bimetalism, debt relief, cooperative farm marketing ventures, and regulation of monopolies and railroads by the federal and state governments. Although not very successful in the 1870s, farmer militancy continued to be a powerful political and economic force in the decades of the 1880s and 1890s.

SOCIAL AND CULTURAL DEVELOPMENTS, 1877–1882

Urbanization was the primary social and cultural phenomenon of the period. Both internal and external migrations contributed to an industrial urban state that grew from 40 million people in 1870 to almost 80 million in 1900. New York, Chicago, and Philadelphia emerged as cities of over 1 million people.

Skyscrapers and Immigrants

Cities grew both up and out as the skyscraper made its appearance after the introduction of the mechanical elevator by Elisha Otis. The city also grew outward into a large, impersonal metropolis divided into various business, industrial and residential sectors, usually segregated by ethnic group, social class and race. Slums and tenements sprang up within walking distance of department stores and townhouses. Two million immigrants from northern Europe poured into the U.S. during the 1870s. In the 1880s another 5 million entered the country, but by this time they were coming from southern and eastern Europe.

Lack of Government Policy

There were few programs to deal with the vast influx of humanity other than the prohibition of the criminal and the insane. City governments soon developed the primary responsibility for immigrants—often trading employment, housing and social services for political support.

Social Gospel

In time, advocates of the "social gospel" such as Jane Addams and Washington Gladden urged the creation of settlement houses and better health and education services to accommodate the new immigrants. New religions also appeared, including the Salvation Army, and Mary Baker Eddy's Church of Christian Science in 1879.

Education

Public education continued to expand, especially on the secondary level. Private Catholic parochial schools and teaching colleges grew in number as well. Adult education and English instruction became important functions of both public and private schooling.

African-American Leaders

Booker T. Washington emerged in 1881 as the president of Tuskegee Institute in Alabama, a school devoted to teaching and vocational education for African-Americans with a mission to encourage self-respect and economic equality of the races. It was at Tuskegee that George Washington Carver emerged in subsequent years as an agricultural chemist who did much to find industrial applications for agricultural products.

Feminism

The new urban environment encouraged feminist activism. Millions of women worked outside the home, and continued to demand voting rights. Many women became active in social reform movements such as the prohibitionist Women's Christian Temperance Movement, planned parenthood, humane societies, anti-prostitution crusades, and equal rights for all regardless of gender, race, or class.

Literature

Important books appeared such as Henry George's *Progress and Poverty* (1879), a 3-million-copy seller that advocated one single tax on land as the means to redistribute wealth for greater social and economic justice. In fiction Lew Wallace's *Ben Hur* (1880), and the many Horatio Alger stories promoting values such as hard work, honesty, and a touch of good fortune sold many millions of copies. Other famous works of the era included Mark Twain's *The Gilded Age* (1873), and *The Adventures of Tom Sawyer* (1876), Bret Harte's stories of the Old West, William Dean Howell's social commentaries, and Henry James's *Daisy Miller* (1879) and *Portrait of a Lady* (1881).

FOREIGN RELATIONS, 1877–1882

The United States gradually became involved in the "new imperialism" of the 1870s geared to finding markets for surplus industrial production, access to needed raw materials, and opportunities for overseas investment during a time of domestic economic depression. Unlike European territorial colonialism, however, the United States preferred market expansion without the political liability of military occupation.

Latin America

President Hayes recognized the government of dictator Porfirio Diaz in Mexico, thus encouraging not only trade expansion, but U.S. investment in railroads, mines, agriculture and oil.

Pan Americanism

In 1881 Secretary of State James G. Blaine advocated the creation of an International Bureau of American Republics to promote a customs union of trade and political stability for the Western Hemisphere. The assassination of President Garfield temporarily kept Blaine from forming this organization until 1889. The Bureau subsequently evolved into the Pan American Union in 1910, and the Organization of American States in 1948.

Mediation of Border Disputes

The United States offered its good offices to promote the peaceful resolution of border conflicts between a number of states: in 1876 between Argentina and Paraguay; in 1880 between Colombia and Chile; and in 1881 between Mexico and Guatemala, Argentina and Chile, and Peru and Chile. The United States also worked to bring an end to the War of the Pacific (1879–1884) fought between Chile and the alliance of Peru and Bolivia.

Canal Project

In 1876 the Interoceanic Canal Commission recommended a Nicaraguan route for a canal to link the Atlantic and Pacific oceans. In the 1880s, the U.S. officially took a hostile position against the French Panama Canal project.

The Pacific

In 1878, the United States ratified a treaty with Samoa giving the U.S. trading rights and a naval base at Pago Pago.

Japan

In 1878, the United States was the first country to negotiate a treaty granting tariff autonomy to Japan, and set a precedent for ending the practice by Western nations of controlling customs house collections in Asian states.

Korea

Commodore Robert Wilson Shufeldt opened trade and diplomatic relations with the Hermit Kingdom in 1882. The United States promoted the principles of equal opportunity of trade, and the sovereignty of Korea (later known as open door policies) which had earlier been advocated as desirable in China.

Native Americans

Westward expansion and the discovery of gold in South Dakota in the early 1870s led to the Sioux War, 1876–1877, and George A. Custer's "last stand." In 1877 the Nez Perce War in Idaho resulted from similar causes. The Apache in Arizona and New Mexico fought as well.

Reservations

The Indian tribes were eventually vanquished and compelled to live on isolated reservations. In addition to superior U.S. military force, disease, railway construction, alcoholism, and the virtual extermination of the bison contributed to their defeat. In 1881 Helen Hunt Jackson's *A Century of Dishonor* chronicled the tragic policy pursued against Native Americans.

THE REACTION TO CORPORATE INDUSTRIALISM, 1882–1887

The rise of big business and monopoly capitalism—especially in banking, railroads, mining, and the oil and steel industries—generated a reaction on the part of working class Americans in the form of new labor organizations and collective political action. Most Americans, however, were not opposed to free enterprise economics, but simply wanted an opportunity to share in the profits.

POLITICS OF THE PERIOD, 1882–1887

The only Democrat elected president in the half century after the Civil War was Grover Cleveland.

Election of 1884

The Republicans nominated James G. Blaine (Maine) for president and John Logan (Illinois) for vice president. The Democrats chose New York governor Grover Cleveland and Thomas A. Hendricks (Indiana). The defection of Independent Republicans supporting civil service reforms, known as "Mugwumps" (such as E.L. Godkin and Carl Schurz) to the Cleveland camp cost Blaine, the former Speaker of the House, the election. The Democrats held control of the House and the Republicans controlled the Senate.

Presidential Succession Act of 1886

The death of Vice President Hendricks in 1885 led to a decision to change the line of succession (established in 1792) from the president *pro tempore* of the Senate to the Cabinet officers in order of creation of their departments to maintain party leadership. This system lasted until 1947 when the Speaker of the House was declared third in line.

Executive Appointments

President Cleveland insisted that executive appointments and removals were the prerogative of the executive and not the Senate. This was the first time since Andrew Johnson that a president had strengthened the independence of his office.

THE ECONOMY, 1882–1887

Large, efficient corporations prospered. Captains of industry, or robber barons, such as John D. Rockefeller in oil, J. P. Morgan in banking, Gustavus Swift in meat processing, Andrew Carnegie in steel, and E. H. Harriman in railroads, put together major industrial empires.

Big Business

The concentration of wealth and power in the hands of a relatively small number of giant firms in many industries led to monopoly capitalism that minimized competition. This process, in turn, led to a demand by smaller businessmen, farmers and laborers for government regulation of the economy in order to promote capital competition for the salvation of free enterprise economics.

The Interstate Commerce Act (1887)

Popular resentment of railroad abuses such as price fixing, kickbacks, and discriminatory freight rates created demands for state regulation of the railway industry. When the Supreme Court ruled individual state laws unconstitutional (*Wabash* case, 1886) because only Congress had the right to control interstate commerce, the Interstate Commerce Act was passed providing that a commission be established to oversee fair and just railway rates, prohibit rebates, end discriminatory practices, and require annual reports and financial statements. The Supreme Court, however, remained a friend of special interests, and often undermined the work of the I.C.C.

Expanding Cultivation

Agrarians and ranchers continued their westward expansion. The amount of land under cultivation between 1870 and 1890 more than doubled from 408 to 840 million acres. Transcontinental railroads, modem farm machinery, and soil conservation practices contributed to national prosperity.

Low Farm Prices

Despite success many farmers were concerned about capital indebtedness, low farm prices resulting from surplus production, railroad rate discrimination, and the lack of sufficient silver currency to promote price inflation. Agrarian groups such as the National Grange and the Farmers' Alliances called for government of the economy to redress their grievances. To a certain extent, however, many of these problems were determined by participation of American agriculture in global markets. Farmers did not completely understand all the risks in an international free market economy.

American Federation of Labor, 1886

Confronted by big business, Samuel Gompers and Adolph Strasser put together a combination of national craft unions to represent the material interests of labor in the matter of wages, hours, and safety conditions. The American Federation of Labor philosophy was pragmatic and not directly influenced by the dogmatic Marxism of some European labor movements. Although militant in its use of the strike and its demand for collective bargaining in labor contracts with large corporations such as those in railroads, mining and manufacturing, the American Federation of Labor did not intend violent revolution or political radicalism.

Scientific Management

Frederick W. Taylor, an engineer credited as the father of scientific management, introduced modern concepts of industrial engineering, plant management, and time and motion studies. This gave rise to efficiency experts and a separate class of managers in industrial manufacturing.

SOCIAL AND CULTURAL DEVELOPMENTS, 1882–1887

The continued growth of urban America contributed to the dissemination of knowledge and information in many fields.

Newspapers and Magazines

The linotype machine (1886) invented by Otto Mergenthaler cut printing costs dramatically. Press associations flourished and publishing became big business. In 1884, Joseph Pulitzer, a Hungarian-born immigrant, was the first publisher to reach a mass audience selling 100,000 copies of the *New York World*. New magazines such as *Forum* appeared in 1886 with a hard-hitting editorial style that emphasized investigatory journalism and controversial subjects.

Higher Education

Colleges and universities expanded and introduced a more modern curriculum. Graduate study emphasized meticulous research and the seminar method as pioneered in the United States at Johns Hopkins University.

Women's Colleges

Bryn Mawr (1885) was established and soon found a place among such schools as Vassar, Wellesley, and Mount Holyoke in advancing education for women.

Natural Science

Albert Michelson at the University of Chicago, working on measuring the speed of light, contributed in the 1880s to theories which helped prepare the way for Einstein's Theory of Relativity. In 1907, Michelson was the first American to win a Nobel Prize.

The New Social Science

Richard T. Ely studied the ethical implications of economic problems. Henry C. Adams and Simon Patten put forth theories to justify government regulation and planning in the economy. In sociology, Lester Frank Ward's *Dynamic Sociology* (1883) stressed intelligent planning and decision making over genetic determinism as promoted by Social Darwinists such as William Graham Sumner. Woodrow Wilson's *Congressional Government* was a critique of the committee system in Congress and called for a better working relationship between the executive and legislative branches of government. After winning the presidency in 1912, Wilson would be in a position to put his ideas into practice.

Literary Realism

Romanticism declined in favor of a more realistic approach to literature. Novelists explored social problems such as crime and political corruption, urban ghetto life, class conflict, evolution, and the environment. Mark Twain's masterpiece *Huckleberry Finn* appeared in 1884. In 1885, William Dean Howell's *The Rise of Silas Lapham* presented the theme of business ethics in a competitive society. *The Bostonians* (1886) by Henry James attempted a complex psychological study of female behavior.

Art

Realism could also be seen in the artistic works of Thomas Eakins, Mary Cassatt, Winslow Homer, and James Whistler. Museums and art schools expanded. Wealthy patrons spent fortunes on personal art collections.

FOREIGN RELATIONS, 1882–1887

Contrary to popular belief, the United States was not an isolationist nation in the 1880s. Trade expansion and the protection of markets were primary concerns.

Modern Navy

In 1883 Congress authorized the construction of new steel ships that would take the U.S. Navy in a 20-year period from twelfth to third in world naval ranking. In 1884, the U.S. Naval War College was established in Newport, Rhode Island—the first of its kind.

Europe

Problems existed with Britain over violence in Ireland and England. In 1886, the U.S. refused to extradite an Irish national accused of terrorist activity in London.

Diseased meat products in the European market led to British and German bans against uninspected American meat exports. Congress soon provided for government regulation and inspection of meat for export. This action would set a precedent for systematic food and drug inspection in later years.

Africa

The United States participated in the Berlin Conference (1884) concerning trade in the Congo. The U.S. also took part in the Third International Red Cross Conference.

Asia and the Pacific

In 1882, Congress passed a law suspending Chinese immigration to the U.S. for ten years. The act reflected racist attitudes and created friction with China.

In 1886, the U.S. obtained by treaty with Hawaii the Pearl Harbor Naval Base.

Missionaries

American Christian missionaries were active in the Pacific, Asia, Africa, Latin America and the Middle East. Missionaries not only brought religion to many third world regions, but also Western education, exposure to science and technology, and commercial ventures. Some missionaries also took with them racist concepts of white supremacy.

Latin America

In 1884, the U.S. signed a short-lived pact with Nicaragua for joint ownership of an isthmian canal in Central America.

THE EMERGENCE OF REGIONAL EMPIRE, 1887–1892

Despite a protective tariff policy, the United States became increasingly international as it sought to export surplus manufactured and agricultural goods. Foreign markets were viewed as a safety valve for labor employment problems and agrarian unrest. The return of Secretary of State James G. Blaine in 1889 marked a major attempt by the United States to promote a regional empire in the Western Hemisphere and reciprocal trade programs.

POLITICS OF THE PERIOD, 1887–1892

National politics became more controversial and turbulent in this era.

Election of 1888

Although the Democrat Grover Cleveland won the popular vote by about 100,000 over the Republican Benjamin Harrison, Harrison carried the electoral college 233 to 168, and was declared president after waging a vigorous campaign to protect American industrial interests with a high protective tariff. In Congress, Republicans won control of both the House and Senate.

House Rules of Operation

Republican Thomas B. Reed became Speaker of the House in 1890, and changed the rules of operation to make himself a veritable tsar with absolute control in running the House.

Force Bill (1890)

Senate objections kept Congress from protecting African-American voters in the South through federal supervision of state elections.

Dependent Pensions Act (1890)

Congress granted service pensions to Union veterans and their dependents for the first time.

THE ECONOMY, 1887–1892

Anti-monopoly measures, protective tariffs and reciprocal trade, and a billion dollar budget became the order of the day.

Sherman Anti-Trust Act, 1890

Corporate monopolies (trusts) which controlled whole industries were subject to federal prosecution if they were found to be combinations or conspiracies in restraint of trade. Although supported by smaller businesses, labor unions and farm associations, the Sherman Anti-Trust Act was in time interpreted by the Supreme Court to apply to labor unions and farmers' cooperatives as much as to large corporate combinations.

Sherman Silver Purchase Act, 1890

Pro-silver interests passed legislation authorizing Congress to buy 4.5 million ounces of silver each month at market prices, and issue Treasury notes redeemable in gold and silver. This act created inflation and lowered gold reserves.

McKinley Tariff, 1890

This compromise protective tariff promised by the Republicans in 1888, and introduced by William McKinley of Ohio was passed and extended to industrial and agricultural goods. The act also included reciprocal trade provisions that allowed the president to retaliate against nations that discriminated against U.S. products, and reward states that opened their markets to American goods. Subsequent price increases led to a popular backlash, and a Democratic House victory in the 1890 congressional elections.

Billion-Dollar Budget

Congress depleted the Treasury surplus with the first peacetime billion-dollar appropriation of funds for state tax refunds, infrastructure improvements, Navy modernization, and pension payments. The loss of Treasury reserves put the economy in a precarious position when an economic panic occurred in 1893.

SOCIAL AND CULTURAL DEVELOPMENTS, 1887–1892

Entertainment for the masses became increasingly differentiated.

Popular Amusements

In addition to the legitimate stage, vaudeville shows presenting variety acts became immensely popular. The circus expanded when Barnum and Bailey formed a partnership to present "the greatest show on earth." Distinctively American Wild West shows toured North America and Europe. To record these activities, George Eastman's newly invented roll-film camera became popular with spectators.

Sports

In 1888, professional baseball sent an all-star team to tour the world. Boxing adopted leather gloves in 1892. Croquet and bicycle racing were new crazes. Basketball was invented in 1891 by James Naismith, a Massachusetts Y.M.C.A. instructor. Organized inter-collegiate sports such as football, basketball, and baseball created intense rivalries between colleges that attracted mass spectator interest.

Childrearing Practices

Parents became more supportive and sympathetic to their children and less authoritarian and restrictive. The 1880s were something of a golden age in children's literature. Mary Wells Smith depicted an agrarian ideal; Sidney Lanier wrote tales of heroic boys and girls; Howard Pyle's *Robin Hood* gained wide readership and Joel Chandler Harris' characters Br'er Rabbit, Br'er Fox, and Uncle Remus became very popular.

Religion

Many churches took issue with the growing emphasis on materialism in American society. Dwight Lyman Moody introduced Urban revivalism comparable to earlier rural movements among Protestant denominations. In addition, the new immigrants generated significant growth for Roman Catholicism and Judaism. By 1890, there were about 150 religious denominations in the United States.

FOREIGN RELATIONS, 1887–1892

Following in the footsteps of William Seward as a major architect of American foreign policy, James G. Blaine promoted hemispheric solidarity with Latin America and economic expansionism.

Pan Americanism

As Secretary of State, Blaine was concerned with international trade, political stability and excessive militarism in Latin America. His international Bureau of American Republics was designed to promote a Pan American customs union and peaceful conflict resolution. To achieve his aims, Blaine opposed U.S. military intervention in the hemisphere. To a certain extent, his policies were in the tradition of President James Monroe and his Secretary of State, John Quincy Adams.

Haiti

After the Haitian revolution of 1888–1889, Blaine resisted pressure for U.S. intervention to establish a naval base near Port-au-Prince. The noted African-American Frederick Douglass played a key role in advising Blaine as U.S. minister to Haiti.

Chilean Revolution

When American sailors from the U.S.S. *Baltimore* were killed in Valparaiso (1891), President Harrison threatened war with the anti-American revolutionary government of President Balmaceda. Secretary Blaine helped to bring about a Chilean apology and preserve his Pan American policy.

Asia and the Pacific

The medical missionary/diplomat Horace Allen promoted peaceful American investment and trade with Korea.

In 1889, the United States upheld its interests against German expansion in the Samoan Islands by establishing a three-party protectorate over Samoa with Britain and Germany. The United States retained the port of Pago Pago.

In 1891, Queen Lydia Kamekeha Liliuokalani resisted American attempts to promote a protectorate over Hawaii. By 1893, pro-American sugar planters overthrew the native Hawaiian government and established a new government friendly to the United States.

Africa

The United States refused (1890) naval bases in the Portuguese colonies of Angola and Mozambique when Portugal was looking for allies against British expansion in Africa. Blaine opposed territorial expansion for the U.S. in Africa, but favored the development of commercial markets.

Theoretical Works

In 1890, naval Captain Alfred Thayer Mahan published *The Influence of Sea Power on History* which argued that control of the seas was the means to world power. Josiah Strong's *Our Country* presented the thesis that Americans had a mission to fulfill by exporting the word of God around the world, especially to non-white populations. Frederick Jackson Turner's "Frontier Thesis" (1893) justified overseas economic expansion as a way to secure political power and prosperity. In *The Law of Civilization and Decay* (1895), Brooks Adams postulated that a nation must expand or face inevitable decline.

Europe

The murders of eleven Italian citizens in New Orleans (1891) brought the United States and Italy into confrontation. The United States defused the situation by compensating the families of the victims.

ECONOMIC DEPRESSION AND SOCIAL CRISIS, 1892–1897

The economic depression that began in 1893 brought about a collective response from organized labor, militant agriculture and the business community. Each group called for economic safeguards, and a more humane free enterprise system that would expand economic opportunities in an equitable manner.

Election of 1892

Democrat Grover Cleveland (New York) and his vice presidential running mate, Adlai E. Stevenson (Illinois), regained the White House by defeating the

Republican President Benjamin Harrison (Indiana) and Vice President Whitelaw Reid (New York). Voters generally reacted against the inflationary McKinley Tariff. Cleveland's conservative economic stand in favor of the gold standard brought him the support of various business interests. The Democrats won control of both houses of Congress.

Populist Party

The People's Party (Populist) nominated James Weaver (Iowa) for president and James Field (Virginia) for vice president in 1892. The party platform put together by such Populist leaders as Ignatius Donnally (Minnesota), Thomas Watson (Georgia), Mary Lease (Kansas), and "Sockless" Jerry Simpson (Kansas) called for the enactment of a program espoused by agrarians, but also for a coalition with urban workers and the middle class. Specific goals were the coinage of silver to gold at a ratio of 16 to 1; federal loans to farmers; a graduated income tax; postal savings banks; public ownership of railroads, telephone and telegraph systems; prohibition of alien land ownership; immigration restriction; a ban on private armies used by corporations to break up strikes; an 8-hour working day; a single six-year term for president, and direct election of senators; the right of initiative and referendum; and the use of the secret ballot.

Although the Populists were considered radical by some, they actually wanted to reform the system from within, and allow for a fairer distribution of wealth. In a society with vast differences in income and wealth, the Populists were able to garner about one million votes (out of 11 million votes cast), and 22 electoral votes. By 1894, Populists had elected 4 senators, 4 congressmen, 21 state executive officials, 150 state senators, and 315 state representatives, primarily in the West and South. After the 1893 depression, the Populists planned a serious bid for national power in the 1896 election.

Repeal of Sherman Silver Purchase Act (1893)

After the economic panic of 1893, Cleveland tried to limit the outflow of gold reserves by asking Congress to repeal the Sherman Silver Act which had provided for notes redemptive in either gold or silver. Congress did repeal the act, but the Democratic Party split over the issue.

Election of 1896

The Republicans nominated William McKinley (Ohio) for president and Garrett Hobart (New Jersey) for vice president on a platform calling for maintaining the gold standard and protective tariffs. The Democratic Party repudiated Cleveland's conservative economics and nominated William Jennings Bryan (Nebraska) and Arthur Sewell (Maine) for president and vice president on a platform similar to the Populists: 1) coinage of silver at a ratio of 16 to 1; 2) condemnation of monopolies, protective tariffs and anti-union court injunctions;

3) criticism of the Supreme Court's removal of a graduated income tax from the Wilson-Gorman tariff bill (1894). Bryan delivered one of the most famous speeches in American history when he declared that the people must not be "crucified upon a cross of gold."

The Populist Party also nominated Bryan, but chose Thomas Watson (Georgia) for vice president. Having been outmaneuvered by the Silver Democrats, the Populists lost the opportunity to become a permanent political force.

McKinley won a hard-fought election by only about one-half million votes as Republicans succeeded in creating fear among business groups and middle class voters that Bryan represented a revolutionary challenge to the American system. The manipulation of higher farm prices, and the warning to labor unions that they would face unemployment if Bryan won the election helped to tilt the vote in favor of McKinley. An often forgotten issue in 1896 was the Republican promise to stabilize the ongoing Cuban revolution. This pledge would eventually lead the U.S. into war with Spain (1898) for Cuban independence. The Republicans retained control over Congress which they had gained in 1894.

THE ECONOMY, 1892–1897

The 1890s was a period of economic depression and labor agitation.

Homestead Strike, 1892

Iron and steel workers went on strike in Pennsylvania against the Carnegie Steel Company to protest salary reductions. Carnegie employed strike-breaking Pinkerton security guards. Management-labor warfare led to a number of deaths on both sides.

Depression of 1893

The primary causes for the Depression of 1893 were the dramatic growth of the federal deficit; withdrawal of British investments from the American market and the outward transfer of gold; loss of business confidence. The bankruptcy of the National Cordage Company was the first among thousands of U.S. corporations that closed banks and businesses. As a consequence, 20 percent of the work force was eventually unemployed. The depression would last four years. Recovery would be helped by war preparation.

March of Unemployed (1894)

The Populist businessman Jacob Coxey led a march on Washington of hundreds of unemployed workers asking for a government work relief program. The government met the marchers with force and arrested their leaders.

Pullman Strike (1894)

Eugene V. Debs' American Railway Union struck the Pullman Palace Car Co. in Chicago over wage cuts and job losses. President Cleveland broke the violent strike with federal troops. Popular opinion deplored violence and militant labor tactics.

Wilson-Gorman Tariff (1894)

This protective tariff did little to promote overseas trade as a way to ease the depression. A provision amended to create a graduated income tax was stricken by the Supreme Court as unconstitutional (*Pollack v. Farmers' Loan and Trust Co.*, 1895).

Dingley Tariff (1897)

The Dingley Tariff raised protection to new highs for certain commodities.

Surplus Production and Foreign Trade

Anxiety over domestic class warfare, and the desire to sell surplus manufactured goods overseas led many business interests to encourage the U.S. government to find new international markets. Carnegie Steel and Standard Oil lobbied the State Department for better trade promotion policies as a way to recover from the depression, and provide jobs for American workers. Ironically, special business interests often undercut efforts to establish reciprocal trade agreements and free trade in favor of politically motivated tariff protection.

SOCIAL AND CULTURAL DEVELOPMENTS, 1892–1897

Economic depression and war dominated thought and literature in the decade of the 1890s.

Literature

Lester Frank Ward of Brown University presented a critique of excessive competition in favor of social planning in *The Psychic Factors of Civilization,* 1893. William Dean Howells' *A Hazard of New Fortunes,* 1890, was a broad attack on urban living conditions in industrial America, and on the callous treatment of workers by wealthy tycoons. Stephen Crane wrote about society's abuse of women in *Maggie, A Girl of the Streets,* 1892, and the pain of war in *The Red Badge of Courage,* 1895. Edward Bellamy's *Looking Backward* presented a science fiction look into a prosperous, but regimented future.

Americans also began to read such European realists as Dostoevsky, Ibsen, Tolstoy and Zola.

William James' *Principles of Psychology* introduced the discipline to American readers as a modern science of the human mind.

Prohibition of Alcohol

The Anti-Saloon League was formed in 1893. Women were especially concerned about the increase of drunkenness during the depression.

Immigration

Immigration declined by almost 400,000 during the depression. Jane Addams' Hull House in Chicago continued to function as a means of settling poor immigrants from Greece, Germany, Italy, Poland, Russia and elsewhere into American society. Lillian Wald's Henry Street Settlement in New York, and Robert Wood's South End House in Boston performed similar functions. Such institutions also lobbied against sweatshop labor conditions, and for bans on child labor.

Chautauqua Movement

Home study courses growing out of the Chautauqua Movement in New York State became popular.

Chicago World's Fair (1893)

Beautifying the cities was the fair's main theme. One lasting development was the expansion of urban public parks.

Radio and Film

Nathan Stubblefield transmitted voice over the air without wires in 1892. Thomas Edison's kinetoscope permitted the viewing of motion pictures in 1893.

FOREIGN RELATIONS, 1892–1897

In addition to the economic depression, three international events in 1895 that propelled the United States foreign policy were the Cuban war for independence against Spain, Britain's boundary dispute with Venezuela, and the settlement of the Sino-Japanese War.

Cuba and Spain

The Cuban revolt against Spain in 1895 impacted on the U.S. in that Americans had about $50 million invested in the Cuban economy, and did an annual business of over $100 million in Cuba. During the election of 1896, McKinley promised to stabilize the situation and work for an end to hostilities. Sensational "yellow" journalism, and nationalistic statements from officials such as Assistant Secretary of the Navy Theodore Roosevelt encouraged popular support for direct American military intervention on behalf of Cuban independence. President McKinley, however, proceeded cautiously through 1897.

Britain and Venezuela (1895)

The dispute over the border of Britain's colony of Guiana threatened war with Venezuela, especially after gold was discovered in the area. Although initially at odds with Britain, the United States eventually came to support British claims against Venezuela when Britain agreed to recognize the Monroe Doctrine in Latin America. Britain also sought U.S. cooperation in its dispute with Germany in South Africa. This rivalry would in time lead to the Boer War. The realignment of the United States and Britain would play a significant role during World War I.

The Sino-Japanese War, 1894–1895

Japan's easy victory over China signaled to the United States and other nations trading in Asia that China's weakness might result in its colonization by industrial powers, and the closing of the China market. The U.S. resolved to seek a naval base in the Pacific to protect its interests. The opportunity to annex the Philippines after the war with Spain was in part motivated by the desire to protect America's trade and future potential in Asia. This concern would also lead the U.S. to announce the Open Door policy with China in 1899 and 1900 designed to protect equal opportunity of trade, and China's political independence.

Latin America

When revolutions broke out in 1894 in both Brazil and Nicaragua, the United States supported the existing governments in power to maintain political stability and favorable trade treaties. Secretaries of State Walter Q. Gresham, Richard Olney and John Sherman continued to support James G. Blaine's Pan American policy.

The Pacific

The United States intervened in the Hawaiian revolution (1893) to overthrow the anti-American government of Queen Liliuokalani. President Cleveland rejected American annexation of Hawaii in 1894, but President McKinley agreed to annex it in 1898.

WAR AND THE AMERICANIZATION OF THE WORLD, 1897–1902

In 1900 an Englishman named William T. Stead authored a book entitled *The Americanization of the World* in which he predicted that American productivity and economic strength would propel the United States to the forefront of world leadership in the twentieth century. The Spanish-American War and the events following it indicated that the U.S. would be a force in the global balance of power for years to come. Few, however, would have predicted that as early as 1920 the U.S. would achieve the pinnacle of world power as a result of the debilitating policies pursued by European political leaders during World War I (1914–1919). One question remained: Would the American people be prepared to accept the responsibility of world leadership?

POLITICS OF THE PERIOD, 1897–1902

President McKinley's wartime leadership and tragic assassination closed one door in American history, but opened another door to the leadership of Theodore Roosevelt, the first "progressive" president.

Election of 1900

The unexpected death of Vice President Garrett Hobart led the Republican Party to choose the war hero and reform governor of New York, Theodore Roosevelt, as President William McKinley's vice presidential running mate. Riding the crest of victory against Spain, the G.O.P. platform called for upholding the gold standard for full economic recovery, promoting economic expansion and power in the Caribbean and the Pacific, and building a canal in Central America. The Democrats once again nominated William Jennings Bryan and Adlai Stevenson on a platform condemning imperialism and the gold standard. McKinley easily won reelection by about 1 million votes (7.2 million to 6.3 million), and the Republicans retained control of both houses of Congress.

Other Parties

The fading Populists nominated Wharton Barker (Pennsylvania) and Ignatius Donnelly (Minnesota) on a pro-inflation platform but only received 50,000 votes. The Socialist Democratic Party nominated Eugene V. Debs (Indiana) and Job Harriman (California) on a platform urging the nationalization of major industries. Debs received 94,000 votes. The Prohibition Party nominated John Woolley (Illinois) and Henry Metcalf (Rhode Island) and called for a ban on alcohol production and consumption. They received 209,000 votes.

McKinley Assassination (1901)

While attending the Pan American Exposition in Buffalo, New York, the president was shot on September 6 by Leon Czolgosz, an anarchist sworn to destroy all governments. The president died on September 14 after many officials had said they thought he would recover. Theodore Roosevelt became the nation's twenty-fifth president and—at age 42—its youngest to that time.

THE ECONOMY, 1897–1902

The war with Spain provided the impetus for economic recovery. President Roosevelt promised a "square deal" for all Americans, farmers, workers, consumers and businessmen. Progressive economic reform was geared to the rejuvenation of free enterprise capitalism following the 1893 depression, and the destruction of illegal monopolies. In this way, radicals would be denied an audience for more revolutionary and violent change.

War with Spain (1898)

The financial cost of the war was $250 million. Eastern and Midwestern industrial cities tended to favor war and benefit from it. Northeastern financial centers were more cautious about war until March 1898, and questioned the financial gains of wartime production at the expense of peacetime expansion and product/market development.

Federal Bankruptcy Act (1898)

This act reformed and standardized procedures for bankruptcy, along with the responsibilities of creditors and debtors.

Erdman Act (1898)

This act provided for mediation by the chair of the Interstate Commerce Commission and the commissioner of the Bureau of Labor in unresolved railroad labor controversies.

Currency Act (1900)

The United States standardized the amount of gold in the dollar at 25.8 grains 9/10 fine. A separate gold reserve was set apart from other general funds, and government bonds were sold to maintain the reserve.

Technology

Between 1860 and 1900 railroad trackage grew from 36,800 miles to 193,350 miles. U.S. Steel Corp. was formed in 1901, Standard Oil Company of New Jersey in 1899.

SOCIAL AND CULTURAL DEVELOPMENTS, 1897–1902

Debates about the war and territorial acquisitions, and the state of the economy, tended to dominate thought and literature.

Yellow Journalism

Joseph Pulitzer's *New York World* and William Randolph Hearst's *New York Journal* competed fiercely to increase circulation through exaggeration of Spanish atrocities in Cuba. Such stories whipped up popular resentment of Spain, and helped to create a climate of opinion receptive to war.

DeLôme Letter and Sinking of the *Maine*

On February 9, 1898, the newspapers published a letter written by the Spanish minister in Washington, Depuy de Lôme, personally criticizing President McKinley in insulting terms. On February 15, the Battleship U.S.S. *Maine* was blown up in Havana harbor with a loss of 250 Americans. The popular demand for war with Spain grew significantly even though it was likely that the *Maine* was blown up by accident when spontaneous combustion in a coal bunker caused a powder magazine to explode.

U.S. Military

Facing its first war since the Civil War, the U.S. Army was not prepared for a full-scale effort in 1898. Although 245,000 men served in the war (with over 5,000 deaths), the Army at the outset consisted of only 28,000 troops. The volunteers who signed up in the early stages were surprised to be issued winter uniforms to train in the tropics for war in Cuba. Cans of food stockpiled since the Civil War were reissued. After getting past these early problems, the War Department settled down to a more effective organizational procedure. Sadly, more deaths resulted from disease and food poisoning than from battlefield casualties. The U.S. Navy (26,000 men) was far better prepared for war as a result of past years of modernization.

Territories

After the United States had defeated Spain (see "Foreign Policy"), it was faced with the issue of what to do with such captured territories as the Philippines, Puerto Rico, the Isle of Pines, and Guam. A major public debate ensued with critics of land acquisition forming the Anti-Imperialist League with the support of Mark Twain, William James, William Jennings Bryan, Grover Cleveland, Charles Francis Adams, Carl Schurz, Charles W. Eliot, David Starr Jordan, Andrew Carnegie and Samuel Gompers among others. Supporters of colonialism included Theodore Roosevelt, Mark Hanna, Alfred Thayer Mahan, Henry Cabot Lodge, Albert Beveridge, President McKinley and many others. Ironically, many individuals in both camps favored U.S. economic expansion, but had difficulty with the idea that a democracy would actually accept colonies and overseas armies of occupations.

Literature

Thorstein Veblen's *Theory of the Leisure Class* (1899) attacked the "predatory wealth" and "conspicuous consumption" of the new rich in the gilded age. Veblen added evidence and argument to a critique begun by Jacob Riis in *How the Other Half Lives* (1890), documenting the gnawing poverty, illness, crime and despair of New York's slums. Frank Norris's *McTeague* (1899) chronicled a man's regression to brutish animal behavior in the dog-eat-dog world of unbridled and unregulated capitalist competition. His novel *The Octopus* (1901) condemned monopoly.

FOREIGN POLICY, 1897–1902

The summer war with Spain, and the expansion of American interests in Asia and the Caribbean were dominant factors.

Decision for War (1898)

Loss of markets, threats to Americans in Cuba, and the inability of both Spain and Cuba to resolve the Cuban revolution either by force or diplomacy led to McKinley's request of Congress for a declaration of war. The sinking of the *Maine* in February 1898, and the return of Vermont Senator Redfield Proctor from a fact-finding mission on March 17, 1898, revealed how poor the situation was in Cuba.

McKinley's Ultimatum

On March 27, President McKinley asked Spain to call an armistice, accept American mediation to end the war, and end the use of concentration camps in Cuba. When Spain refused to comply, McKinley requested Congress declare war. On April 21, Congress declared war on Spain with the objective of establishing Cuban independence (Teller Amendment).

Cuba

After the first U.S. forces landed in Cuba on June 22, 1898, the United States proceeded to victories at El Caney and San Juan Hill. By July 17, Admiral Sampson's North Atlantic Squadron destroyed the Spanish fleet, Santiago surrendered, and American troops quickly went on to capture Puerto Rico.

The Philippines

As early as December 1897, Commodore Perry's Asiatic Squadron was alerted to possible war with Spain. On May 1, 1898, the Spanish fleet in the Philippines was destroyed and Manila surrendered on August 13. Spain agreed to a peace conference to be held in Paris in October 1898.

Treaty of Paris

Secretary of State William Day led the American negotiating team, which secured Cuban independence, the ceding of the Philippines, Puerto Rico and Guam to the U.S., and the payment of $20 million to Spain for the Philippines. The treaty was ratified by the Senate February 6, 1900.

Philippines Insurrection

Filipino nationalists under Emilio Aguinaldo rebelled against the United States (February 1899) when they learned the Philippines would not be given independence. The United States used 70,000 men to suppress the revolutionaries by June 1902. A special U.S. commission recommended eventual self-government for the Philippines.

Hawaii and Wake Island

During the war with Spain, the U.S. annexed Hawaii on July 7, 1898. In 1900 the U.S. claimed Wake Island, 2,000 miles west of Hawaii.

China

Fearing the break-up of China into separate spheres of influence, Secretary of State John Hay called for acceptance of the Open Door Notes by all nations trading in the China market to guarantee equal opportunity of trade (1899), and the sovereignty of the Manchu government of China (1900). With Manila as a base of operations, the United States was better able to protect its economic and political concerns in Asia. Such interests included the American China Development Co. (1898), a railway and mining concession in south China, and various oil, timber, and industrial investments in Manchuria.

Boxer Rebellion (1900)

Chinese nationalists ("Boxers") struck at foreign settlements in China, and at the Ch'ing dynasty Manchu government in Beijing for allowing foreign industrial nations such as Britain, Japan, Russia, France, Germany, Italy, Portugal, Belgium, The Netherlands, and the United States large concessions within Chinese borders. An international army helped to put down the rebellion, and aided the Chinese government to remain in power.

Platt Amendment (1901)

Although Cuba was granted its independence, the Platt Amendment provided that Cuba become a virtual protectorate of the United States. Cuba could not 1) make a treaty with a foreign state impairing its independence, or 2) contract an excessive public debt. Cuba was required to 1) allow the U.S. to preserve order on the island, and 2) lease a naval base for 99 years to the U.S. at Guantanamo Bay.

Hay-Pauncefote Treaty (1901)

This treaty between the U.S. and Britain abrogated an earlier agreement (1850, Clayton-Bulwer Treaty) to build jointly an isthmian canal. The United States was free unilaterally to construct, fortify and maintain a canal that would be open to all ships.

Insular Cases (1901–1903)

The Supreme Court decided that constitutional rights did not extend to territorial possessions, thus the Constitution did not follow the flag. Congress had the right to administer each island possession without constitutional restraint. Inhabitants of those possessions did not have the same rights as American citizens.

THEODORE ROOSEVELT AND PROGRESSIVE REFORMS, 1902–1907

As a Republican progressive reformer committed to honest and efficient government designed to serve all social classes in America, Theodore Roosevelt restored the presidency to the high eminence it had held through the Civil War era, and redressed the balance of power with old guard leaders in Congress.

POLITICS OF THE PERIOD, 1902–1907

President Roosevelt did much to create a bipartisan coalition of liberal reformers whose objective was to restrain corporate monopoly and promote economic competition at home and abroad. Roosevelt won the support of enlightened business leaders, the middle class, consumers, and urban and rural workers with his promise of a "square deal" for all.

Roosevelt's Anti-Trust Policy, 1902

The president pledged strict enforcement of the Sherman Anti-Trust Act (1890) to break up illegal monopolies and regulate large corporations for the public good through honest federal government administration.

Progressive Reform in the States

Taking their cue from Washington, many states enacted laws creating honest and efficient political and economic regulatory standards. Political reforms included enacting laws establishing primary elections (Mississippi, Wisconsin), initiative and referendum (South Dakota, Oregon), and the rooting out of political bosses on the state and municipal levels (especially in New York, Ohio, Michigan, and California).

Commission Form of Government, 1903

After a hurricane and tidal wave destroyed much of Galveston, Texas, progressive businessmen and Texas state legislators removed the ineffective and corrupt mayor and city council and established a city government of five elected commissioners who were experts in their fields to rebuild Galveston. Numerous other cities adopted the commission form of government to replace the mayor/council format.

State Leaders

Significant state reformers in the period were Robert LaFollette of Wisconsin, Albert Cummins of Iowa, Charles Evans Hughes of New York, James M. Cox of Ohio, Hiram Johnson of California, William S. Wren of Oregon, Albert Beveridge of Indiana, and Woodrow Wilson of New Jersey.

City Reformers

Urban leaders included John Purroy Mitchell of New York City, Tom L. Johnson and Newton Baker of Cleveland, Hazen Pingree of Detroit, Sam Jones of Toledo, and Joseph Folk of St. Louis.

Election of 1904

Having assured Republican Party leaders that he wished to reform corporate monopolies and railroads, but not interfere with monetary policy or tariffs, Roosevelt was nominated for president along with Charles Fairbanks (Indiana) for vice president. The Democratic Party nominated New York judge Alton B. Parker for president and Henry G. Davis (West Virginia) for vice president on a platform that endorsed Roosevelt's "trust-busting," which called for even greater power for such regulatory agencies as the Interstate Commerce Commission, and accepted the conservative gold standard as the basis for monetary policy. Roosevelt easily defeated Parker by about two million votes, and the Republicans retained control of both houses of Congress.

Hepburn Act, 1906

Membership of the Interstate Commerce Commission was increased from five to seven. The I.C.C. could set its own fair freight rates, had its regulatory power extended over pipelines, bridges, and express companies, and was empowered to require a uniform system of accounting by regulated transportation companies. This act and the Elkins Act (1903—reiterated illegality of railroad rebates) gave teeth to the original interstate Commerce Act of 1887.

Pure Food and Drug Act (1906)

Prohibited the manufacture, sale and transportation of adulterated or fraudulently labeled foods and drugs in accordance with consumer demands to which Theodore Roosevelt was especially sensitive.

Meat Inspection Act (1906)

Provided for federal and sanitary regulations and inspections in meat packing facilities. Wartime scandals in 1898 relating to spoiled canned meats were a powerful force for reform.

Immunity of Witness Act (1906)

Corporate officials could no longer make a plea of immunity to avoid testifying in cases dealing with their corporation's illegal activities.

Conservation Laws

From 1902 to 1908 a series of laws and executive actions were enacted to create federal irrigation projects, national parks and forests, develop water power (Internal Waterways Commission), and establish the National Conservation Commission to oversee the nation's resources.

THE ECONOMY, 1902–1907

Anti-trust policy and government regulation of the economy gave way to a more lenient enforcement of federal laws after the panic of 1907. Recognition of the rights of labor unions was enhanced.

Anti-Trust Policy (1902)

In order to restore free competition, President Roosevelt ordered the Justice Department to prosecute corporations pursuing monopolistic practices. Attorney General P.C. Knox first brought suit against the Northern Securities Company, a railroad holding corporation put together by J. P. Morgan; then he moved against Rockefeller's Standard Oil Company. By the time he left office in 1909, Roosevelt brought indictments against 25 monopolies.

Department of Commerce and Labor (1903)

A new Cabinet position was created to address the concerns of business and labor. Within the department, the Bureau of Corporations was empowered to investigate and report on the illegal activities of corporations.

Coal Strike (1902)

Roosevelt interceded with government mediation to bring about negotiations between the United Mine Workers union and the anthracite mine owners after a bitter strike over wages, safety conditions and union recognition. This was the first time that the government intervened in a labor dispute without automatically siding with management.

Panic of 1907

A brief economic recession and panic occurred in 1907 as a result, in part, of questionable bank speculations, a lack of flexible monetary and credit policies, and a conservative gold standard. This event called attention to the need for banking reform which would lead to the Federal Reserve System in 1913. Although Roosevelt temporarily eased the pressure on anti-trust activity, he made it clear that reform of the economic system to promote free-enterprise capitalism would continue.

St. Louis World's Fair (1904)

The World's Fair of 1904 celebrated the centennial of the Louisiana Purchase, and brought the participation of Asian nations to promote foreign trade.

SOCIAL AND CULTURAL DEVELOPMENTS, 1902–1907

Debate and discussion over the expanding role of the federal government commanded the attention of the nation.

Progressive Reforms

There was not one unified progressive movement, but a series of reform causes designed to address specific social, economic, and political problems. Middle-class men and women were especially active in attempting to correct the excessive powers of giant corporations, and the radical extremes of Marxist revolutionaries and radicals among intellectuals and labor activists. However, mainstream of business and labor leaders were moderate in their desire to preserve economic opportunities and the free enterprise system.

Varieties of Reform

Progressive reform goals included not only honest government, economic regulation, environmental conservation, labor recognition, and new political structures. Reformers also called for gender equality for men and women in the work force (Oregon Ten Hour Law), an end to racial segregation (National Association for the Advancement of Colored People), child labor laws, prison reform, regulation of the stock market, direct election of senators, and a more efficient foreign service among other reform activities.

Muckrakers

Muckrakers (a term coined by Roosevelt) were investigative journalists and authors who were often the publicity agents for reforms. Popular magazines included *McClure's, Collier's, Cosmopolitan*, and *Everybody's*. Famous articles that led to reforms included "The Shame of the Cities" by Lincoln Steffens, "History of Standard Oil Company" by Ida Tarbell, "The Treason of the Senate" by David Phillips, and "Frenzied Finance" by Thomas Lawson.

Literature

Works of literature with a social message included *Following the Color Line* by Ray Stannard Baker, *The Bitter Cry of the Children* by John Spargo, *Poverty* by Robert Hunter, *The Story of Life Insurance* by Burton Hendrick, *The Financier* by Theodore Dreiser, *The Jungle* by Upton Sinclair, *The Boss* by Henry Lewis, *Call of the Wild, The Iron Heel* and *The War of the Classes* by Jack London, *A Certain Rich Man* by William Allen White, and *The Promise of American Life* by Herbert Croly.

Inventions

The Wright brothers made the first piloted flight of a heavier-than-air machine at Kitty Hawk, North Carolina, in 1903. News of their feat traveled slowly and was widely doubted.

FOREIGN RELATIONS, 1902–1907

Theodore Roosevelt's "Big Stick" diplomacy and economic foreign policy were characteristics of the administration.

Panama Canal

Roosevelt used executive power to engineer the separation of Panama from Colombia, and the recognition of Panama as an independent country. The Hay-Bunau-Varilla Treaty of 1903 granted the United States control of the canal zone in Panama for $10 million and an annual fee of $250,000 beginning nine years after ratification of the treaty by both parties. Construction of the canal began in 1904 and was completed in 1914.

Roosevelt Corollary to the Monroe Doctrine

The U.S. reserved the right to intervene in the internal affairs of Latin American nations to keep European powers from using military force to collect debts in the Western Hemisphere. The U.S. eventually intervened in the affairs of Venezuela, Haiti, the Dominican Republic, Nicaragua, and Cuba by 1905 as an international policeman brandishing the "big stick" against Europeans and Latin Americans.

Rio de Janeiro Conference (1906)

Secretary of State Elihu Root attempted to de-emphasize U.S. military and political intervention in order to promote political goodwill, economic development, trade and finances in Latin America. President Roosevelt was actually moving away from "big stick" diplomacy and toward "dollar diplomacy" before he left office. The United States also promoted the Pan American Railway project at this meeting of the International Bureau of American Republics.

China

In pursuit of the Open Door policy of equal opportunity of trade and the guaranteed independence of China, the United States continued to promote its trade interests in Asia. Segregation and restrictions of Chinese immigrants in California and other states led Chinese national leaders to call for a boycott in 1905 of U.S. goods and services in both China and the United States. The boycott ended in 1906 without significant changes in state laws.

Russo-Japanese War (1904–1905)

With American encouragement and financial loans, Japan pursued and won a war against tsarist Russia. Roosevelt negotiated the Treaty of Portsmouth, New Hampshire, which ended the war, and for which the President ironically received the Nobel Peace Prize in 1906. Japan, however, was disappointed at not receiving more territory and financial compensation from Russia and blamed the United States.

Taft-Katsura Memo, 1905

The United States and Japan pledged to maintain the Open Door principles in China. Japan recognized American control over the Philippines and the United States granted a Japanese protectorate over Korea.

Gentleman's Agreement with Japan, 1907

After numerous incidents of racial discrimination against Japanese in California, Japan agreed to restrict the emigration of unskilled Japanese workers to the U.S.

Great White Fleet, 1907

In order to show American strength to Japan and China, Roosevelt sent the great white naval fleet to Asian ports.

Algeciras Conference, 1906

The United States participated in the Algeciras Conference with eight European states to guarantee equal opportunity of trade for Morocco. The independence granted the sultan of Morocco was reminiscent of the Open Door policy initiated by the U.S. with China at the turn of the century. The conference (held at Algeciras, Spain, January 16–April 7, 1906), however, created tension between Germany and France, which would end up at war in the next decade.

The Second Hague Conference, 1907

Forty-six nations, including the United States, met in the Netherlands to discuss disarmament and the creation of an international court of justice. Little was accomplished except for the adoption of a resolution banning the use of military force for the collection of foreign debts.

THE REGULATORY STATE AND THE ORDERED SOCIETY, 1907–1912

The progressive presidencies of Roosevelt, Taft and Wilson brought the concept of big government to fruition. A complex corporate society needed rules and regulations as well as powerful agencies to enforce those measures necessary to maintain and enhance democratic free enterprise competition. The search for political, social and economic standards designed to preserve order in American society while still guaranteeing political, social and economic freedom was a difficult, but primary task. The nation increasingly looked to Washington to protect the less powerful segments of the republic from the special interests that had grown up in the late 19th century. A persistent problem for the federal government was how best to preserve order and standards in a complex technological society while not interfering with the basic liberties Americans came to cherish in the Constitution and throughout their history. The strain of World War I after 1914 would further complicate the problem.

POLITICS OF THE PERIOD, 1907–1912

The continuation of progressive reforms by both Republican and Democratic leaders helped to form a consensus for the establishment of regulatory standards.

Election 1908

Deciding not to run for re-election, Theodore Roosevelt opened the way for William H. Taft (Ohio) and James S. Sherman (New York) to run on a Republican platform calling for a continuation of anti-trust enforcement, environmental conservation, and a lower tariff policy to promote international trade. The Democrats nominated William Jennings Bryan for a third time with John Kern (Indiana) for vice president on an anti-monopoly and low tariff platform. The Socialists once again nominated Eugene V. Debs. Taft easily won by over a million votes, and the Republicans retained control of both houses of Congress. For the first time, the American Federation of Labor entered national politics officially with an endorsement of Bryan. This decision began a long alliance between organized labor and the Democratic Party in the 20th century.

Taft's Objectives

The president had two primary political goals in 1909. One was the continuation of Roosevelt's trust-busting policies, and the other was the reconciliation of the old guard conservatives and young progressive reformers in the Republican Party.

Anti-Trust Policy

In pursuing anti-monopoly law enforcement, Taft chose as his Attorney General George Wickersham, who brought 44 indictments in anti-trust suits.

Political Rift

Taft was less successful in healing the Republican split between conservatives and progressives over such issues as tariff reform, conservation, and the almost dictatorial power held by the reactionary Republican Speaker of the House, Joseph Cannon (Illinois). Taft's inability to bring both wings of the party together led to the hardened division which would bring about a complete Democratic victory in the 1912 elections.

The Anti-Cannon Crusade

In 1910, Republican progressives joined with Democrats to strip Speaker Cannon of his power to appoint the Committee on Rules and serve on it himself.

Critical of Cannon, Taft failed to align himself with the progressives. Democrats gained control of the House in the 1910 elections, and a Republican Democratic coalition ran the Senate.

Ballinger-Pinchot Dispute (1909–1910)

Progressives backed Gifford Pinchot, chief of the U.S. Forest Service, in his charge that the conservative Secretary of the Interior, Richard Ballinger, was giving away the nation's natural resources to private corporate interests. A congressional investigatory committee found that Ballinger had done nothing illegal, but did act in a manner contrary to the government's environmental policies. Taft had supported Ballinger through the controversy, but negative public opinion forced Ballinger to resign in 1911. Taft's political standing with progressive Republicans was hurt going into the election of 1912.

The Sixteenth Amendment

Congress passed in 1909 a graduated income tax amendment to the Constitution which was ratified in 1913.

Mann-Elins Act (1910)

This act extended the regulatory function of the Interstate Commerce Commission over cable and wireless companies, and telephone and telegraph lines; gave the I.C.C. power to begin its own court proceedings and suspend questionable rates; and set up a separate but temporary commerce court to handle rate-dispute cases.

Election of 1912

This election was one of the most dramatic in American history. President Taft's inability to maintain party harmony led Theodore Roosevelt to return to national politics. When denied the Republican nomination, Roosevelt and his supporters formed the Progressive Party (Bull Moose) and nominated Roosevelt for president and Hiram Johnson (California) for vice president on a political platform nicknamed "The New Nationalism." It called for stricter regulation on large corporations, creation of a tariff commission, women's suffrage, minimum wages and benefits, direct election of senators, initiative, referendum and recall, presidential primaries, and prohibition of child labor. Roosevelt also called for a Federal Trade Commission to regulate the broader economy, a stronger executive, and more government planning. Theodore Roosevelt did not see big business as evil, but a permanent development that was necessary in a modern economy.

The Republicans

President Taft and Vice President Sherman retained control of the Republican Party after challenges by Roosevelt and Robert LaFollette, and were nominated on a platform of "Quiet Confidence" calling for a continuation of progressive programs pursued by Taft over the past four years.

The Democrats

After forty-five ballots without a nomination, the Democratic convention finally worked out a compromise whereby William Jennings Bryan gave his support to New Jersey Governor Woodrow Wilson on the forty-sixth ballot. Thomas Marshall (Indiana) was chosen as the vice presidential candidate. Wilson called his campaign the "New Freedom" based on progressive programs similar to those in the Progressive and Republican parties. Wilson, however, did not agree with Roosevelt on the issue of big business, which Wilson saw as morally evil. Therefore, Wilson called for breaking up large corporations rather than just regulating them. He differed from the other two party candidates by favoring independence for the Philippines, and the exemption from prosecution of labor unions under the Sherman Anti-Trust Act. Wilson also supported such measures as lower tariffs, a graduated income tax, banking reform, and direct election of senators. Philosophically, Wilson was skeptical of big business and big government. In some respects, he hoped to return to an earlier and simpler concept of a free enterprise republic. After his selection, however, he would modify his views to conform more with those of Theodore Roosevelt.

Election Results

The Republican split clearly paved the way for Wilson's victory. Wilson received 6.2 million votes, Roosevelt 4.1 million, Taft 3.5 million, and the Socialist Debs 900,000 votes. In the electoral college, Wilson received 435 votes, Roosevelt 88, Taft 8. Although a minority president, Wilson garnered the largest electoral majority in American history to that time. Democrats won control of both houses of Congress.

The Wilson Presidency

The Wilson administration brought together many of the policies and initiatives of the previous Republican administrations, and reform efforts in Congress by both parties. Before the outbreak of World War I in 1914, President Wilson, working with cooperative majorities in both houses of Congress, achieved much of the remaining progressive agenda including lower tariff reform (Underwood-Simmons Act, 1913), the 16th Amendment (graduated income tax, 1913), the 17th Amendment (direct election of senators, 1913), Federal Reserve Banking System (which provided regulation and flexibility to monetary policy, 1913), Federal Trade Commission (to investigate unfair business practices, 1914), and the Clayton Anti-Trust Act (improving the old Sherman Act and protecting labor unions and farm cooperatives from prosecution, 1914).

Other goals such as the protection of children in the work force (Keating-Owen Act, 1916), credit reform for agriculture (Federal Farm Loan Act, 1916), and an independent tariff commission (1916) came later. By the end of Wilson's presidency, the New Freedom and the New Nationalism merged into one government philosophy of regulation, order and standardization in the interest of an increasingly diverse and pluralistic American nation.

THE ECONOMY, 1907–1912

The short-lived panic of 1907 revealed economic weaknesses in U.S. banking and currency policy addressed by Presidents Roosevelt, Taft, and Wilson, and by Congress. Fortunately, the American economy was strengthened just in time to meet the challenges of World War I.

National Monetary Commission, 1908

Chaired by Senator Nelson Aldrich of Rhode Island, the 18-member National Monetary Commission recommended what later became the basis for the Federal Reserve System in 1913 with a secure Treasury reserve and branch banks to add and subtract currency from the monetary supply to accommodate the needs of the economy.

Payne-Aldrich Tariff, 1909

Senate amendments added to the Payne-Aldrich Tariff of 1909 turned the bill, originally intended to lower the tariff, into a protective measure. Progressive reformers felt betrayed by special interests opposed to consumer-price concerns. President Taft made the political mistake of endorsing the tariff.

Postal Savings Banks, 1910

On the recommendation of President Taft, certain U.S. post offices were authorized to receive deposits and pay interest. This was an idea that had been championed early on by the Populist Party.

New Battleship Contract, 1910

The State Department arranged for Bethlehem Steel Corporation to receive a large contract to build battleships for Argentina. This was an example of Taft's "dollar diplomacy" in action.

Anti-Trust Proceedings

Although a friend to the business community, President Taft ordered 90 legal proceedings against monopolies, and 44 anti-trust suits including the one which broke up the American Tobacco Trust (1911). It was also under Taft that the government succeeded with its earlier suit against Standard Oil.

Canadian Reciprocity, 1911

A reciprocal trade agreement between the United States and Canada was repudiated by the Canadian legislature which feared economic and political domination by the United States.

New Cabinet Posts, 1913

The Department of Commerce and Labor was divided into two separate autonomous Cabinet-level positions.

Automobiles

In 1913 Henry Ford introduced the continuous-flow process on the automobile assembly line.

SOCIAL AND CULTURAL DEVELOPMENTS, 1907–1912

Progressive reform and government activism were important themes in American society.

Social Programs

States led the way with programs such as public aid to mothers of dependent children (Illinois, 1911), and the first minimum wage law (Massachusetts, 1912).

Race and Ethnic Attitudes

Despite the creation of the NAACP in 1909, many progressive reformers tended to be Anglo-Saxon elitists critical of the lack of accomplishments of Native American Indians, African-Americans, and Asian, Southern and Eastern European immigrants. In 1905, the African-American intellectual militant W. E. B. DuBois founded the Niagara Movement calling for federal legislation to protect racial equality, and full rights of citizenship.

Radical Labor

Although moderate labor unions as represented by the A.F. of L. functioned within the American system, a radical labor organization called the Industrial

Workers of the World (I.W.W. or Wobblies, 1905–1924) was active in promoting violence and revolution. Led by colorful figures such as Carlo Tresca, Elizabeth Gurley Flynn (the Red Flame), Daniel DeLeon, "Mother" Mary Harris Jones, the maverick priest Father Thomas Hagerty, and "Big Bill" Haywood, among others, the I.W.W. organized effective strikes in the textile industry in 1912, and among a few Western miners groups, but generally had little appeal to the average American worker. After the Red Scare of 1919, the government worked to smash the I.W.W. and deport many of its immigrant leaders and members.

White Slave Trade

In 1910, Congress made interstate prostitution a federal crime with passage of the Mann Act.

Literature

Enthused by the self-confidence exuded by political reformers, writers remained optimistic in their realism, and put their faith in the American people to solve social and economic problems with honest and efficient programs.

Motion Pictures

By 1912 Hollywood had replaced New York and New Jersey as the center for silent film production. There were 13,000 movie houses in the United States and Paramount Pictures had just been formed as a large studio resembling other large corporations. Serials, epic features and Mack Sennett comedies were in production. All of these developments contributed to the "star system" in American film entertainment.

Science

The X-ray tube was developed by William Coolidge in 1913. Robert Goddard patented liquid rocket fuel in 1914. Plastics and synthetic fibers such as rayon were developed in 1909 by Arthur Little and Leo Baekeland, respectively. Adolphus Busch applied the Diesel engine to the submarine in 1912.

FOREIGN RELATIONS, 1907–1912

The expansion of American international interests through Taft's "dollar diplomacy," and world tensions foreshadowing the First World War were dominant themes.

Dollar Diplomacy

President Taft sought to avoid military intervention, especially in Latin America, by replacing "big stick" policies with "dollar diplomacy" in the expectation that American financial investments would encourage economic, social and political stability. This idea proved an illusion as investments never really filtered through all levels of Latin American societies, nor did such investments generate democratic reforms.

Mexican Revolution (1910)

Francisco I. Madero overthrew the dictator Porfirio Diaz (1911) declaring himself a progressive revolutionary akin to reformers in the United States. American and European corporate interests (especially oil and mining) feared national interference with their investments in Mexico. President Taft recognized Madero's government, but stationed 10,000 troops on the Texas border (1912) to protect Americans from the continuing fighting. In 1913 Madero was assassinated by General Victoriano Huerta. Wilson urged Huerta to hold democratic elections and adopt a constitutional government. When Huerta refused his advice, Wilson invaded Mexico with troops at Vera Cruz in 1914. A second U.S. invasion came in northern Mexico in 1916. War between the U.S. and Mexico might have occurred had not World War I intervened.

Latin American Interventions

Although Taft and Secretary of State P. C. Knox created the Latin American Division of the State Department in 1909 to promote better relations, the United States kept a military presence in the Dominican Republic and Haiti, and intervened militarily in Nicaragua (1911) to quiet fears of revolution and help manage foreign financial problems.

Arbitration Treaties

Taking a page from Roosevelt's book, Taft promoted arbitration agreements as an alternative to war in Latin America and in Asia.

Lodge Corollary to the Monroe Doctrine, 1911

When a Japanese syndicate moved to purchase a large tract of land in Mexico's Lower California, Senator Lodge introduced a resolution to block the Japanese investment. The Corollary went further to exclude non-European powers from the Western Hemisphere under the Monroe Doctrine.

Bryan's Arbitration Treaties (1913–1915)

Wilson's Secretary of State, William Jennings Bryan, continued the policies of Roosevelt and Taft to promote arbitration of disputes in Latin America and elsewhere. Bryan negotiated about 30 such treaties.

Root-Takahira Agreement (1908)

This agreement reiterated the status quo in Asia established by the United States and Japan by the Taft-Katsura Memo (1905).

China Consortium (1909)

American bankers and the State Department demanded entry into an international banking association with Britain, France, and Germany to build a railway network (Hukuang) in southern and central China. Wilson withdrew the U.S. from participation in 1913 as the Chinese revolution deteriorated into greater instability.

Manchuria

President Taft and Secretary Knox attempted to force the sale of Japanese and Russian railroad interests in Manchuria to American investment interests. When this diplomacy failed, Knox moved to construct a competing rail system. The Chinese government, however, refused to approve the American plan. Both Japan and Russia grew more suspicious of United States interests in Asia.

Chinese Revolution, 1911

Chinese nationalists overthrew the Manchu Dynasty and the last emperor of China, Henry Pu Yi. Although the military war lord Yuan Shih-Kai seized control, decades of factionalism, revolution, and civil war destabilized China and its market potential for American and other foreign investors.

HISTORICAL TIMELINE

Industrialism, War, and the Progressive Era (1877–1912)

1877	San Francisco anti-chinese riots
1878	Bland-Allison Act
1879	Edison invents the light bulb
1881	President Garfield assassinated Helen Hunt Jackson writes *A Century of Dishonor*
1882	Standard Oil Trust formed Chinese Exclusion Act
1883	Pendleton Civil Service Act
1885	First skyscraper built in Chicago
1886	Haymarket Square bombing in Chicago American Federation of Labor formed
1887	Dawes Act
1889	Jane Addams founds Hull House in Chicago
1890	Sioux massacred at Wounded Knee Sherman Antitrust Act Sherman Silver Purchase Act U.S. Census declares frontier's end Alfred Mahan writes *The Influence of Sea Power upon History*
1891	Populist Party formed
1892	Homestead Steel Strike
1893	Panic of 1893 Great Northern Railroad completed

1894	Pullman strike Coxey's Army
1895	Booker T. Washington's Atlanta Compromise speech
1896	*Plessy v. Ferguson* upholds separate but equal McKinley defeats Bryan for president
1898	U.S.S. *Maine* sinks in Havana Harbor Spanish-American War Dewey captures Philippine Islands Hawaii annexed by U.S.
1899	Aguinaldo leads Filipinos against Americans Treaty of Paris ends Spanish-American War Open Door Policy in China
1900	Boxer Rebellion in China
1901	Theodore Roosevelt becomes president
1902	Platt Amendment President Roosevelt settles coal strike
1903	U.S. recognizes Panama's independence
1904	Northern Securities Trust dissolved Roosevelt Corollary declared
1906	Upton Sinclair writes *The Jungle* Pure Food and Drug Act Hepburn Act passed President Roosevelt wins Nobel Peace Prize
1908	*Muller v. Oregon* limits women's working hours Taft elected president
1909	NAACP formed
1911	Triangle Shirtwaist Fire Mexican Revolution erupts
1912	Roosevelt forms Progressive Party to challenge Taft Wilson elected president

10 WILSON AND WORLD WAR I (1912–1920)

IMPLEMENTING THE NEW FREEDOM: THE EARLY YEARS OF THE WILSON ADMINISTRATION

The New President

Woodrow Wilson was only the second Democrat (Cleveland was the first) elected president since the Civil War. He was born in Virginia in 1856, the son of a Presbyterian minister, and was reared and educated in the South. After earning a doctorate at Johns Hopkins University, he taught history and political science at Princeton, and in 1902 became president of that university. In 1910 he was elected governor of New Jersey as a reform or progressive Democrat.

The Cabinet

The key appointments were William Jennings Bryan as secretary of state and William Gibbs McAdoo as secretary of the treasury.

The Inaugural Address

Wilson called the Congress, now controlled by Democrats, into a special session beginning April 7, 1913, to consider three topics: Reduction of the tariff, reform of the national banking and currency laws, and improvements in the antitrust laws. On April 8 he appeared personally before Congress, the first president since John Adams to do so, to promote his program.

The Underwood-Simmons Tariff Act of 1913

Average rates were reduced to about 29 percent as compared with 37 to 40 percent under the previous Payne-Aldrich Tariff. A graduated income tax was included in the law to compensate for lost tariff revenue. It ranged from a tax of one percent on personal and corporate incomes over $4,000, a figure well above the annual income of the average worker, to seven percent on incomes over $500,000. The 16th Amendment to the Constitution, ratified in February 1913, authorized the income tax.

The Federal Reserve Act of 1913

Following the Panic of 1907, it was generally agreed that there was need for more stability in the banking industry and for a currency supply which would expand and contract to meet business needs.

Three points of view on the subject developed. Most Republicans backed the proposal of a commission headed by Senator Nelson W. Aldrich for a large central bank controlled by private banks. Bryanite Democrats, pointing to the Wall Street influence exposed by the 1913 Pujo Committee investigation of the money trust, wanted a reserve system and currency owned and controlled by the government. Conservative Democrats favored a decentralized system privately owned and controlled but free from Wall Street.

The bill which finally passed in December 1913 was a compromise measure. The law divided the nation into twelve regions with a Federal Reserve bank in each region. Commercial banks in the region owned the Federal Reserve Bank by purchasing stock equal to six percent of their capital and surplus, and elected the directors of the bank. National banks were required to join the system, and state banks were invited to join. The Federal Reserve Banks held the gold reserves of their members. Federal Reserve Banks loaned money to member banks by rediscounting their commercial and agricultural paper; that is, the money was loaned at interest less than the public paid to the member banks, and the notes of indebtedness of businesses and farmers to the member banks were held as collateral. This allowed the Federal Reserve to control interest rates by raising or lowering the discount rate.

The money loaned to the member banks was in the form of a new currency, Federal Reserve Notes, which was backed sixty percent by commercial paper and forty percent by gold. This currency was designed to expand and contract with the volume of business activity and borrowing. Checks on member banks were cleared through the Federal Reserve System.

The Federal Reserve System serviced the financial needs of the federal government. The system was supervised and policy was set by a national Federal Reserve Board composed of the secretary of the Treasury, the comptroller of the currency, and five other members appointed by the president of the United States.

The Clayton Antitrust Act of 1914

This law supplemented and interpreted the Sherman Antitrust Act of 1890. Under its provisions, stock ownership by a corporation in a competing corporation was prohibited. Interlocking directorates of competing corporations were prohibited; that is, the same persons could not manage competing corporations. Price discrimination (charging less in some regions than in others to undercut the competition) and exclusive contracts which reduced competition were prohibited. Officers of corporations could be held personally responsible for violations of antitrust laws. Lastly, labor unions and agricultural organizations were not to be considered "combinations or conspiracies in restraint of trade" as defined by the Sherman Antitrust Act.

The Federal Trade Commission Act of 1914

The law prohibited all unfair trade practices without defining them, and created a commission of Eve members appointed by the president. The commission was empowered to issue cease and desist orders to corporations to stop actions considered to be in restraint of trade, and to bring suit in the courts if the orders were not obeyed. Firms could also contest the orders in court. Under previous antitrust legislation, the government could act against corporations only by bringing suit.

Evaluation

The Underwood-Simmons Tariff, the Federal Reserve Act, and the Clayton Act were clearly in accord with the principles of the New Freedom, but the Federal Trade Commission reflected a move toward the kind of government regulation advocated by Roosevelt in his New Nationalism. Nonetheless, in 1914 and 1915 Wilson continued to oppose federal government action in such matters as loans to farmers, child labor regulation, and woman suffrage.

THE TRIUMPH OF NEW NATIONALISM

Political Background

The Progressive Party dissolved rapidly after the election of 1912. The Republicans made major gains in Congress and in the state governments in the 1914 elections, and their victory in 1916 seemed probable. Early in 1916 Wilson and the Democrats abandoned most of their limited government and states' rights positions in favor of a legislative program of broad economic and social reforms designed to win the support of the former Progressives for the Democratic Party in the election of 1916. The urgency of their concern was increased by the fact that Theodore Roosevelt intended to seek the Republican nomination in 1916.

The Brandeis Appointment

Wilson's first action marking the adoption of the new program was the appointment on January 28, 1916, of Louis D. Brandeis, considered by many to be the principal advocate of social justice in the nation, as an associate justice of the Supreme Court.

The Federal Farm Loan Act of 1916

The law divided the country into twelve regions and established a Federal Land Bank in each region. Funded primarily with federal money, the banks made farm mortgage loans at reasonable interest rates. Wilson had threatened to veto similar legislation in 1914.

The Child Labor Act of 1916

This law, earlier opposed by Wilson, forbade shipment in interstate commerce of products whose production had involved the labor of children under fourteen or sixteen, depending on the products. The legislation was especially significant because it was the first time that Congress regulated labor within a state using the interstate commerce power. The law was declared unconstitutional by the Supreme Court in 1918 on the grounds that it interfered with the powers of the states.

The Adamson Act of 1916

This law mandated an eight-hour day for workers on interstate railroads with time and a half for overtime and a maximum of sixteen hours in a shift. Its passage was a major victory for railroad unions, and averted a railroad strike in September 1916.

The Kerr-McGillicuddy Act of 1916

This law initiated a program of workmen's compensation for federal employees.

THE ELECTION OF 1916

The Democrats

The minority party nationally in terms of voter registration, the Democrats nominated Wilson and adopted his platform calling for continued progressive reforms and neutrality in the European war. "He kept us out of war" became the principal campaign slogan of Democratic politicians.

The Republicans

The convention bypassed Theodore Roosevelt, who had decided not to run as a Progressive and had sought the Republican nomination. On the first ballot it chose Charles Evans Hughes, an associate justice of the Supreme Court and formerly a progressive Republican governor of New York. Hughes, an ineffective campaigner, avoided the neutrality issue because of divisions among the Republicans, and found it difficult to attack the progressive reforms of the Democrats. He emphasized what he considered the inefficiency of the Democrats, and failed to find a popular issue.

The Election

Wilson won the election with 277 electoral votes and 9,129,000 popular votes, almost three million more than he received in 1912. Hughes received 254 electoral votes and 8,538,221 popular votes. The Democrats controlled Congress by a narrow margin. While Wilson's victory seemed close, the fact that he had increased his popular vote by almost fifty percent over four years previous was remarkable. It appears that most of his additional votes came from people who had voted for the Progressive or Socialist tickets in 1912.

SOCIAL ISSUES IN THE FIRST WILSON ADMINISTRATION

Blacks

In 1913 Treasury Secretary William G. McAdoo and Postmaster General Albert S. Burleson segregated workers in some parts of their departments with no objection from Wilson. Many Northern blacks and whites protested, especially black leader W. E. B. DuBois, who had supported Wilson in 1912. William Monroe Trotter, militant editor of the Boston Guardian, led a protest delegation to Washington and clashed verbally with the president. No further segregation in government agencies was initiated, but Wilson had gained a reputation for being inimical to civil rights.

Women

The movement for woman suffrage, led by the National American Woman Suffrage Association, was increasing in momentum at the time Wilson became president, and several states had granted the vote to women. Wilson opposed a federal woman suffrage amendment, maintaining that the franchise should be controlled by the states. Later he changed his view and supported the 19th Amendment.

Immigration

Wilson opposed immigration restrictions which were proposed by labor unions and some reformers. He vetoed a literacy test for immigrants in 1915, but in 1917 Congress overrode a similar veto.

WILSON'S FOREIGN POLICY AND THE ROAD TO WAR

Wilson's Basic Premise: New Freedom Policy

Wilson promised a more moral foreign policy than that of his predecessors, denouncing imperialism and dollar diplomacy, and advocating the advancement of democratic capitalist governments throughout the world.

Conciliation Treaties

Secretary Bryan negotiated treaties with 29 nations under which they agreed to submit disputes to international commissions for conciliation, not arbitration.

They also included provisions for a cooling-off period, usually one year, before the nations would resort to war. While the treaties probably had no practical effect, they illustrated the idealism of the administration.

Dollar Diplomacy

Wilson signaled his repudiation of Taft's dollar diplomacy by withdrawing American involvement from the six-power loan consortium of China.

Japan

In 1913 Wilson failed to prevent passage of a California law prohibiting land ownership by Japanese aliens. The Japanese government and people were furious, and war seemed possible. Relations were smoothed over, but the issue was unresolved. In 1915 American diplomatic pressure made Japan back off from its 21 demands on China, but in 1917 the Lansing-Ishii Agreement was signed wherein Japan recognized the Open Door in China but the United States recognized Japan's special interest in that nation.

The Caribbean

Like his predecessors, Wilson sought to protect the Panama Canal, which opened in 1914, by maintaining stability in the area. He also wanted to encourage diplomacy and economic growth in the underdeveloped nations of the region. In applying his policy, he became as interventionist as Roosevelt and Taft.

In 1912 American marines had landed in Nicaragua to maintain order, and an American financial expert had taken control of the customs. The Wilson administration kept the marines in Nicaragua, and negotiated the Bryan-Chamorro Treaty of 1914 which gave the United States an option to build a canal through the country. In effect, Nicaragua became an American protectorate, although treaty provisions authorizing such action were not ratified by the Senate.

Claiming that political anarchy existed in Haiti, Wilson sent marines in 1915 and imposed a treaty making the country a protectorate, with American control of its finances and constabulary. The marines remained until 1934.

In 1916 Wilson sent marines to the Dominican Republic to stop a civil war, and established a military government under an American naval commander.

Wilson feared in 1915 that Germany might annex Denmark and its Caribbean possession, the Danish West Indies or Virgin Islands. After extended negotiations, the United States purchased the islands from Denmark by treaty on August 4, 1916 for $25 million, and took possession of them on March 31, 1917.

In 1913 Wilson refused to recognize the government of Mexican military dictator Victoriano Huerta, and offered unsuccessfully to mediate between

Huerta and his Constitutionalist opponent, Venustiano Carranza. When the Huerta government arrested several American seamen in Tampico in April 1914, American forces occupied the port of Veracruz, an action condemned by both Mexican political factions. In July 1914 Huerta abdicated his power to Carranza, who was soon opposed by his former general Francisco "Pancho" Villa. Seeking American intervention as a means of undermining Carranza, Villa shot sixteen Americans on a train in northern Mexico in January 1916, and burned the border town of Columbus, New Mexico, in March 1916, killing 19 people. Carranza reluctantly consented to Wilson's request that the United States be allowed to pursue and capture Villa in Mexico, but did not expect the force of about six thousand Army troops under the command of General John J. Pershing which crossed the Rio Grande on March 18. The force advanced over three hundred miles into Mexico, failed to capture Villa, and became, in effect, an army of occupation. The Carranza government demanded an American withdrawal, and several clashes with Mexican troops occurred. War threatened, but in January 1917 Wilson removed the American forces.

Pan American Mediation, 1914

John Barrett, head of the Pan American Union (formerly Blaine's International Bureau of American Republics) called for multilateral mediation to bring about a solution to Mexico's internal problems, and extract the United States from its military presence in Mexico. Although Wilson initially refused, Argentina, Brazil, and Chile did mediate among the Mexican factions and Wilson withdrew American troops. Barrett hoped to replace the unilateral Monroe Doctrine with a multilateral Pan American policy to promote collective responses and mediation to difficult hemispheric problems. Wilson, however, refused to share power with Latin America.

THE ROAD TO WAR IN EUROPE

American Neutrality

When World War I broke out in Europe, Wilson issued a proclamation of American neutrality on August 4, 1914. Despite that action, the United States drifted toward closer ties with the Allies, especially Britain and France. While many Americans were sympathetic to the Central Powers, the majority, including Wilson, hoped for an Allied victory. Although British naval power effectively prevented American trade with the Central Powers and European neutrals, often in violation of international law, the United States limited itself to formal diplomatic protests. The value of American trade with the Central Powers fell from $169 million in 1914 to almost nothing in 1916, but trade with the Allies rose from $825 million to $3.2 billion during the same period. In addition, the British and French had borrowed about $3.25 billion from American sources by 1917. The United States had become a major supplier of Allied munitions, food, and raw materials.

The Submarine Crisis of 1915

The Germans began the use of submarines in 1915, announced a submarine blockade of the Allies on February 4, and began to attack unarmed British passenger ships in the Atlantic. Wilson insisted to the Germans that Americans had a right as neutrals to travel safely on such ships, and that international law required a war ship to arrange for the safe removal of passengers before attacking such a ship. The sinking of the British liner Lusitania off the coast of Ireland on May 7, 1915, with the loss of 1,198 lives, including 128 Americans, brought strong protests from Wilson. Secretary of State Bryan, who believed Americans should stay off belligerent ships, resigned rather than insist on questionable neutral rights, and was replaced by Robert Lansing. Following the sinking of another liner, the Arabic, on August 19, the Germans gave the "Arabic pledge" to stop attacks on unarmed passenger vessels.

The Gore-McLemore Resolution

During the latter part of 1915 the British began to arm their merchant ships. Many Americans thought it in the interest of United States neutrality that Americans not travel on the vessels of belligerents. Early in 1916 the Gore-McLemore Resolution to prohibit American travel on armed ships or on ships carrying munitions was introduced in Congress, but it was defeated in both houses after intensive politicking by Wilson.

The Sussex Pledge

When the unarmed French channel steamer Sussex was torpedoed but not sunk on March 24, 1916, with seven Americans injured, Wilson threatened to sever relations unless Germany ceased all surprise submarine attacks on all shipping, whether belligerent or neutral, armed or unarmed. Germany acceded with the "Sussex pledge" at the beginning of May, but threatened to resume submarine warfare if the British did not stop their violations of international law.

The House-Grey Memorandum

Early in 1915 Wilson sent his friend and adviser, Colonel Edward M. House, on an unsuccessful visit to the capitals of the belligerent nations on both sides to offer American mediation in the war. Late in the year House returned to London to propose that Wilson call a peace conference, and, if Germany refused to attend or was uncooperative at the conference, the United States would probably enter the war on the Allied side. An agreement to that effect, called the House-Grey Memorandum, was signed by the British foreign secretary, Sir Edward Grey, on February 22, 1916.

Preparedness

In November 1915 Wilson proposed a major increase in the Army and the abolition of the National Guard as a preparedness measure. Americans divided on the issue, with organizations like the National Security League proposing stronger military forces, and others like the League to Enforce Peace opposing. After opposition by Southern and Western antipreparedness Democrats, Congress passed a modified National Defense Act in June 1916 which increased the Army from about 90,000 to 220,000, and enlarged the National Guard under federal control. In August over $500 million was appropriated for naval construction. The additional costs were met by increased taxes on the wealthy.

The Election of 1916

Wilson took the leadership on the peace issue, charging that the Republicans were the war party and that the election of Charles Evans Hughes would probably result in war with Germany and Mexico. His position was popular with many Democrats and progressives, and the slogan "He kept us out of war" became the principal theme of Democratic campaign materials, presumably contributing to his election victory.

Wilson's Final Peace Efforts, 1916–1917

On December 12, 1916, the Germans, confident of their strong position, proposed a peace conference, a step which Wilson previously had advocated. When Wilson asked both sides to state their expectations, the British seemed agreeable to reasonable negotiations, but the Germans were evasive and stated that they did not want Wilson at the conference. In an address to Congress on January 22, 1917, Wilson made his last offer to serve as a neutral mediator. He proposed a "peace without victory," based not on a "balance of power" but on a "community of power," alluding to his proposal of May 1916 for an "association of nations."

Unlimited Submarine Warfare

Germany announced on January 31, 1917, that it would sink all ships, belligerent or neutral, without warning in a large war zone off the coasts of the Allied nations in the eastern Atlantic and the Mediterranean. The Germans realized that the United States might declare war, but they believed that, after cutting the flow of supplies to the Allies, they could win the war before the Americans could send any sizable force to Europe. Wilson broke diplomatic relations with Germany on February 3. During February and March several American merchant ships were sunk by submarines.

The Zimmerman Telegram

The British intercepted a secret message from the German foreign secretary, Arthur Zimmerman, to the German minister in Mexico, and turned it over to the United States on February 24, 1917. The Germans proposed that, in the event of a war between the United States and Germany, Mexico attack the United States. After the war, the "lost territories" of Texas, New Mexico, and Arizona would be returned to Mexico. In addition, Japan would be invited to join the alliance against the United States. When the telegram was released to the press on March 1, many Americans became convinced that war with Germany was necessary.

The Declaration of War

Wilson, on March 2, 1917, called Congress to a special session beginning April 2. When Congress convened, he requested a declaration of war against Germany. The declaration was passed by the Senate on April 4 by a vote of 82 to 6, by the House on April 6 by a vote of 373 to 50, and signed by Wilson on April 6.

Wilson's Reasons

Wilson's decision to ask for a declaration of war seems to have been based primarily on four considerations. He believed that the Zimmerman Telegram showed that the Germans were not trustworthy and would eventually go to war against the United States. He also felt that armed neutrality could not adequately protect American shipping. The democratic government established in Russia after the revolution in March 1917 also provided more acceptable as an ally than the Tsarist government. Finally, he was convinced that the United States could hasten the end of the war and insure for itself a major role in designing a lasting peace.

WORLD WAR I: THE MILITARY CAMPAIGN

Raising an Army

Despite the enlistment of many volunteers, it was apparent that a draft would be necessary. The Selective Service Act was passed on May 18, 1917, after bitter opposition in the House led by the speaker, "Champ" Clark. Only a compromise outlawing the sale of liquor in or near military camps secured passage. Originally including all males 21 to 30, the limits were later extended to 17 and 46. The first drawing of 500,000 names was made on July 20, 1917. By the end of the war 24,231,021 men had been registered and 2,810,296 had been inducted. In addition, about two million men and women volunteered.

Women and Minorities in the Military

Some women served as clerks in the Navy or in the Signal Corps of the Army. Originally nurses were part of the Red Cross, but eventually some were taken into the Army. About 400,000 black men were drafted or enlisted, despite the objections of Southern political leaders. They were kept in segregated units, usually with white officers, which were used as labor battalions or for other support activities. Some black units did see combat, and a few blacks became officers, but did not command white troops.

The War at Sea

In 1917 German submarines sank 6.5 million tons of Allied and American shipping, while only 2.7 million tons were built. German hopes for victory were based on the destruction of Allied supply lines. The American Navy furnished destroyers to fight the submarines, and, after overcoming great resistance from the British navy, finally began the use of the convoy system in July 1917. Shipping losses fell from almost 900,000 tons in April 1917 to about 400,000 tons in December 1917, and remained below 200,000 tons per month after April 1918. The American Navy transported over 900,000 American soldiers to France, while British transports carried over 1 million. Only two of the well-guarded troop transports were sunk. The Navy had over 2,000 ships and over half a million men by the end of the war.

The American Expeditionary Force

The soldiers and marines sent to France under the command of Major General John J. Pershing were called the American Expeditionary Force, or the AEF. From a small initial force which arrived in France in June 1917, the AEF increased to over two million by November 1918. Pershing resisted efforts by European commanders to amalgamate the Americans with the French and British armies, insisting that he maintain a separate command. American casualties included 112,432 dead, about half of whom died of disease, and 230,024 wounded.

Major Military Engagements

The American force of about 14,500 which had arrived in France by September 1917 was assigned a quiet section of the line near Verdun. As numbers increased, the American role became more significant. When the Germans mounted a major drive toward Paris in the spring of 1918, the Americans experienced their first important engagements. In June they prevented the Germans from crossing the Marne at Chateau-Thierry, and cleared the area of Belleau Woods. In July, eight American divisions aided French troops in attacking the German line between Reims and Soissons. The American First Army with over half a million men under Pershing's immediate command was assembled in August 1918, and began a major offensive at St. Mihiel on the southern part of the front on September 12. Following the successful operation, Pershing began a drive against the German defenses between Verdun and Sedan, an action called the Meuse-Argonne offensive, and reached Sedan on November 7. During the same period the English in the north and the French along the central front also broke through the German lines. The fighting ended with the armistice on November 11, 1918.

MOBILIZING THE HOME FRONT

Industry

The Council of National Defense, comprised of six cabinet members and a seven-member advisory commission of business and labor leaders, was established in 1916 before American entry into the war to coordinate industrial mobilization, but it had little authority. In July 1917 the council created the War Industries Board to control raw materials, production, prices, and labor relations. The military forces refused to cooperate with the civilian agency in purchasing their supplies, and the domestic war effort seemed on the point of collapse in December 1917 when a Congressional investigation began. In 1918 Wilson took stronger action under his emergency war powers which were reinforced by the Overman Act of May 1918. In March 1918 Wilson appointed Wall Street broker Bernard M. Baruch to head the WIB, assisted by an advisory committee of 100 businessmen. The WIB allocated raw materials, standardized manufactured products, instituted strict production and purchasing controls, and paid high prices to businesses for their products. Even so, American industry was just beginning to produce heavy armaments when the war ended. Most heavy equipment and munitions used by the American troops in France were produced in Britain or France.

Food

The United States had to supply not only its own food needs but those of Britain, France, and some of the other Allies as well. The problem was compounded by bad weather in 1916 and 1917 which had an adverse effect on agriculture. The Lever Act of 1917 gave the president broad control over the production, price, and distribution of food and fuel. Herbert Hoover was appointed by Wilson to head a newly-created Food Administration. Hoover fixed high prices to encourage the production of wheat, pork, and other products, and encouraged the conservation of food through such voluntary programs as "Wheatless Mondays" and "Meatless Tuesdays." Despite the bad harvests in 1916 and 1917, food exports by 1919 were almost triple those of the pre-war years, and real farm income was up almost 30 percent.

Fuel

The Fuel Administration under Harry A. Garfield was established in August 1917. It was concerned primarily with coal production and conservation because coal was the predominant fuel of the time and was in short supply during the severe winter of 1917–1918. "Fuelless Mondays" in nonessential industries to conserve coal and "Gasless Sundays" for automobile owners to save gasoline were instituted. Coal production increased about 35 percent from 1914 to 1918.

Railroads

The American railroad system, which provided most of the inter-city transportation in the country, seemed near collapse in December 1917 because of the wartime demands and heavy snows which slowed service. Wilson created the United States Railroad Administration under William G. McAdoo, the secretary of the Treasury, to take over and operate all the railroads in the nation as one system. The government paid the owners rent for the use of their lines, spent over $500 million on improved tracks and equipment, and achieved its objective of an efficient railroad system.

Maritime Shipping

The United States Shipping Board was authorized by Congress in September 1916, and in April 1917 it created a subsidiary, the Emergency Fleet Corporation, to buy, build, lease, and operate merchant ships for the war effort. Edward N. Hurley became the director in July 1917, and the corporation constructed several large shipyards which were just beginning to produce vessels when the war ended. By seizing German and Dutch ships, and by the purchase and requisition of private vessels, the board had accumulated a large fleet by September 1918.

Labor

To prevent strikes and work stoppages in war industries, the War Labor Board was created in April 1918 under the joint chairmanship of former president William Howard Taft and attorney Frank P. Walsh with members from both industry and labor. In hearing labor disputes the WLB in effect prohibited strikes, but it also encouraged higher wages, the eight-hour day, and unionization. Union membership doubled during the war from about 2.5 million to about 5 million.

War Finance and Taxation

The war is estimated to have cost about $33.5 billion by 1920, excluding such future costs as veterans' benefits and debt service. Of that amount at least

$7 billion was loaned to the Allies, with most of the money actually spent in the United States for supplies. The government raised about $10.5 billion in taxes, and borrowed the remaining $23 billion. Taxes were raised substantially in 1917, and again in 1918. The Revenue Act of 1918, which did not take effect until 1919, imposed a personal income tax of six percent on incomes up to $4,000, and twelve percent on incomes above that amount. In addition, a graduated surtax went to a maximum of 65 percent on large incomes, for a total of 77 percent. Corporations paid an excess profits tax of 65 percent, and excise taxes were levied on luxury items. Much public, peer, and employer pressure was exerted on citizens to buy Liberty Bonds which covered a major part of the borrowing. An inflation of about one hundred percent from 1915 to 1920 contributed substantially to the cost of the war.

The Committee on Public Information

The committee, headed by journalist George Creel, was formed by Wilson in April 1917. Creel established a successful system of voluntary censorship of the press, and organized about 150,000 paid and volunteer writers, lecturers, artists, and other professionals in a propaganda campaign to build support for the American cause as an idealistic crusade, and to portray the Germans as barbaric and beastial Huns. The CPI set up volunteer Liberty Leagues in every community, and urged their members, and citizens at large, to spy on their neighbors, especially those with foreign names, and to report any suspicious words or actions to the Justice Department.

War Hysteria

A number of volunteer organizations sprang up around the country to search for draft dodgers, enforce the sale of bonds, and report any opinion or conversation considered suspicious. Perhaps the largest such organization was the American Protective League with about 250,000 members, which claimed the approval of the Justice Department. Such groups publicly humiliated people accused of not buying war bonds and persecuted, beat, and sometimes killed people of German descent. As a result of the activities of the CPI and the vigilante groups, German language instruction and German music were banned in many areas, German measles became "liberty measles," pretzels were prohibited in some cities, and the like. The anti-German and anti-subversive war hysteria in the United States far exceeded similar public moods in Britain and France during the war.

The Espionage and Sedition Acts

The Espionage Act of 1917 provided for fines and imprisonment for persons who made false statements which aided the enemy, incited rebellion in the military, or obstructed recruitment or the draft. Printed matter advocating treason or insurrection could be excluded from the mails. The Sedition Act of May 1918 forbade any criticism of the government, flag, or uniform, even if there were not detrimental consequences, and expanded the mail exclusion. The laws sounded reasonable, but they were applied in ways which trampled on civil liberties. Eugene V. Debs, the perennial Socialist candidate for president, was given a ten-year prison sentence for a speech at his party's convention in which he was critical of American policy in entering the war and warned of the dangers of militarism. Movie producer Robert Goldstein released the movie *The Spirit of'76* about the Revolutionary War. It naturally showed the British fighting the Americans. Goldstein was fined $10,000 and sentenced to ten years in prison because the film depicted the British, who were now fighting on the same side as the United States, in an unfavorable light. The Espionage Act was upheld by the Supreme Court in the case of *Shenk v. United States* in 1919. The opinion, written by Justice Oliver Wendell Holmes Jr., stated that Congress could limit free speech when the words represented a "clear and present danger," and that, in effect, a person cannot cry "fire" in a crowded theater. The Sedition Act was similarly upheld in *Abrams v. United States* a few months later. Ultimately 2,168 persons were prosecuted under the laws, and 1,055 were convicted, of whom only ten were charged with actual sabotage.

WARTIME SOCIAL TRENDS

Women

With approximately 16 percent of the normal labor force in uniform and demand for goods at a peak, large numbers of women, mostly white, were hired by factories and other enterprises in jobs never before open to them. They were often resented and ridiculed by male workers. When the war ended, almost all returned to traditional "women's jobs" or to homemaking. Returning veterans replaced them in the labor market. Women continued to campaign for woman suffrage. In 1917 six states, including the large and influential states of New York, Ohio, Indiana, and Michigan, gave the vote to women. Wilson changed his position in 1918 to advocate woman suffrage as a war measure. In January 1918 the House of Representatives adopted a suffrage amendment to the constitution which was defeated later in the year by Southern forces in the Senate. The way was paved for the victory of the suffragists after the war.

Racial Minorities

The labor shortage opened industrial jobs to Mexican-Americans and to blacks. W. E. B. DuBois, among the most prominent black leaders of the time, supported the war effort in the hope that a war to make the world safe for democracy would bring a better life for blacks in the United States. About half a million rural Southern blacks migrated to cities, mainly in the North and

Midwest, to obtain employment in war and other industries, especially in steel and meatpacking. Some white Southerners, fearing the loss of labor when cotton prices were high, tried forceably to prevent their departure. Some white Northerners, fearing job competition and encroachment on white neighborhoods, resented their arrival. In 1917 there were race riots in twenty-six cities North and South, with the worst in East St. Louis, Illinois. Despite the opposition and their concentration in entry-level positions, there is evidence that the blacks who migrated generally improved themselves economically.

Prohibition

Proponents of prohibition stressed the need for military personnel to be sober and the need to conserve grain for food, and depicted the hated Germans as disgusting beer drinkers. In December 1917 a constitutional amendment to prohibit the manufacture and sale of alcoholic beverages in the United States was passed by Congress and submitted to the states for ratification. While alcohol consumption was being attacked, cigarette consumption climbed from 26 billion in 1916 to 48 billion in 1918.

PEACEMAKING AND DOMESTIC PROBLEMS, 1918–1920

The Fourteen Points

From the time of the American entry into the war, Wilson had maintained that the war would make the world safe for democracy. He insisted that there should be peace without victory, meaning that the victors would not be vindictive toward the losers, so that a fair and stable international situation in the postwar world would insure lasting peace. In an address to Congress on January 8, 1918, he presented his specific peace plan in the form of the Fourteen Points. The first five points called for open rather than secret peace treaties, freedom of the seas, free trade, arms reduction, and a fair adjustment of colonial claims. The next eight points were concerned with the national aspirations of various European peoples and the adjustment of boundaries, as, for example, in the creation of an independent Poland. The fourteenth point, which he considered the most important and had espoused as early as 1916, called for a "general association of nations" to preserve the peace. The reception of the Fourteen Points was mixed in Europe, as there was a great desire to punish Germany. In the United States, however, many people opposed a peace plan that risked American involvement in another European war.

The Election of 1918

On October 25, 1918, a few days before the congressional elections, Wilson appealed to the voters to elect a Democratic Congress, saying that to do otherwise would be a repudiation of his leadership in European affairs. Republicans, who had loyally supported his war programs, were affronted. The voters, probably influenced more by domestic and local issues than by foreign policy, gave the Republicans a slim margin in both houses in the election. Wilson's statement had undermined his political support at home and his stature in the eyes of world leaders.

The Armistice

The German Chancellor, Prince Max of Baden, on October 3, 1918, asked Wilson to begin peace negotiations based on his concepts of a just peace and the Fourteen Points. Wilson insisted that the Germans must evacuate Belgium and France and form a civilian government. By early November the Allied and American armies were advancing rapidly and Germany was on the verge of collapse. The German Emperor fled to the Netherlands and abdicated. Representatives of the new German republic signed the armistice on November 11, 1918, to be effective at 11:00 a.m. that day, and agreed to withdraw German forces to the Rhine and to surrender military equipment, including 150 submarines.

The Versailles or Paris Peace Conference

Wilson decided that he would lead the American delegation to the peace conference which opened in Paris on January 12, 1919. In doing so he became the first president to leave the country during his term of office. The other members of the delegation were Secretary of State Robert Lansing, General Tasker Bliss, Colonel Edward M. House, and attorney Henry White. Wilson made a serious mistake in not appointing any leading Republicans to the commission and in not consulting the Republican leadership in the Senate about the negotiations. In Paris, Wilson joined Prime Minister David Lloyd George of Great Britain, Premier Georges Clemenceau of France, and Prime Minister Vittorio Orlando of Italy to form the "Big Four" which dominated the conference. In the negotiations, which continued until May 1919, Wilson found it necessary to make many compromises in forging the text of the treaty.

The Soviet Influence

Russia was the only major participant in the war which was not represented at the peace conference. Following the Communist Revolution of 1917, Russia had made a separate peace with Germany in March 1918. Wilson had resisted Allied plans to send major military forces to Russia to oust the Communists and bring Russia back into the war. An American force of about five thousand was sent to Murmansk in the summer of 1918 in association with British and French troops to prevent the Germans from taking military supplies, and was soon active in assisting Russian anti-Bolsheviks. It remained in the area until June 1919. In July 1918 Wilson also sent about ten thousand soldiers to Siberia where they took over the operation of the railroads to assist a Czech army which was escaping from the Germans by crossing Russia. They were also to counterbalance a larger Japanese force in the area, and remained until April 1920. Wilson believed that the spread of communism was the greatest threat to peace and international order. His concern made him reluctant to dispute too much with the other leaders at the Versailles Conference, and more agreeable to compromise, because he believed it imperative that the democracies remain united in the face of the communist threat.

Important Provisions of the Versailles Treaty

In the drafting of the treaty Wilson achieved some of the goals in the Fourteen Points, compromised on others, and failed to secure freedom of the seas, free trade, reduction of armaments, or the return of Russia to the society of free nations. Some major decisions were as follows:

1) The League of Nations was formed, implementing the point which Wilson considered the most important. Article X of the Covenant, or charter, of the League called on all members to protect the "territorial integrity" and "political independence" of all other members.
2) Germany was held responsible for causing the war, and required to agree to pay the Allies for all civilian damage and veterans' costs, which eventually were calculated at $33 billion; the German army and navy were limited to tiny defensive forces; and the west bank of the Rhine was declared a military-free zone forever and occupied by the French for fifteen years. These decisions were clearly contrary to the idea of peace without victory.
3) New nations of Yugoslavia, Austria, Hungary, Czechoslovakia, Poland, Lithuania, Latvia, Estonia, and Finland partially fulfilled the idea of self-determination for all nationalities, but the boundaries drawn at the conference left many people under the control of other nationalities.
4) German colonies were made mandates of the League of Nations, and given in trusteeship to France, Japan, and Britain and its Dominions.

Germany and the Signing of the Treaty

The German delegates were allowed to come to Versailles in May 1919 after the completion of the treaty document. They expected to negotiate on the basis of the draft, but were told to sign it "or else," probably meaning an economic boycott of Germany. They protested, but signed the Versailles Treaty on June 28, 1919.

The Senate and the Treaty

Following a protest by 39 senators in February 1919, Wilson obtained some changes in the League structure to exempt the Monroe Doctrine and domestic matters from League jurisdiction. Then, on July 26, 1919, he presented the treaty with the League within it to the Senate for ratification. Almost all of the 47 Democrats supported Wilson and the treaty, but the 49 Republicans were divided. About a dozen were "irreconcilables" who thought that the United States should not be a member of the League under any circumstances. The remainder included 25 "strong" and 12 "mild" reservationists who would accept the treaty with some changes. The main objection centered on Article X of the League Covenant, where the reservationists wanted it understood that the United States would not go to war to defend a League member without the approval of Congress. The leader of the reservationists was Henry Cabot Lodge of Massachusetts, the chairman of the Foreign Relations Committee. More senators than the two-thirds necessary for ratification favored the treaty either as written or with reservations.

Wilson and the Senate

On September 3, 1919, Wilson set out on a national speaking tour to appeal to the people to support the treaty and the League, and to influence their senators. He collapsed after a speech in Pueblo, Colorado, on September 25, and returned to Washington where he suffered a severe stroke on October 2 which paralyzed his left side. He was seriously ill for several months, and never fully recovered. In a letter to the Senate Democrats on November 18, Wilson urged them to oppose the treaty with the Lodge reservations. In votes the next day, the treaty failed to get a two-thirds majority either with or without the reservations.

The Final Vote

Many people, including British and French leaders, urged Wilson to compromise with Lodge on reservations, including the issue of Article X. Wilson, instead, wrote an open letter to Democrats on January 8, 1920, urging them to make the election of a Democratic president in 1920 a "great and solemn referendum" on the treaty as written. Such partisanship only acerbated the situation. Many historians think that Wilson's ill health impaired his judgment, and that he would have worked out a compromise had he not had the stroke. The Senate took up the treaty again in February 1920, and on March 19 it was again defeated both with and without the reservations. The United States officially ended the war with Germany by a resolution of Congress signed on July 2, 1921, and a separate peace treaty was ratified on July 25. The United States did not join the League.

Consequences of War

The impact of the war was far-reaching in the twentieth century. The United States emerged as the economic and political leader of the world—

even if the American people were not prepared to accept the responsibility. The Russian revolution overthrew the tsar and inaugurated a communist dictatorship. Britain, France, Austria, and Turkey went into various states of decline. Germany was devastated at the Versailles Peace Conference. Revenge and bitterness would contribute to the rise of Adolf Hitler and the Nazi movement. The European industrial nations would never recover from the cost of the war. Lingering economic problems would contribute to the Crash of 1929 and the Great Depression of the 1930s. The seeds of World War II had been planted.

DOMESTIC PROBLEMS AND THE END OF THE WILSON ADMINISTRATION

Demobilization

The AEF was brought home as quickly as possible in early 1919, and members of the armed forces were rapidly discharged. Congress provided for wounded veterans through a system of veteran's hospitals under the Veteran's Bureau, and funded relief, especially food supplies, for war-torn Europe. The wartime agencies for the control of the economy, such as the War Industries Board, were soon disbanded. During 1919 Congress considered various plans to nationalize the railroads or continue their public operation, but then passed the Esch-Cummings or Transportation Act of 1920 which returned them to private ownership and operation. It did extend Interstate Commerce Commission control over their rates and financial affairs, and allowed supervised pooling. The fleet of ships accumulated by the Shipping Board during the war was sold to private owners at attractive prices.

Final Reforms of the Progressive Era

In January 1919 the 18th Amendment to the Constitution prohibiting the manufacture, sale, transportation, or importation of intoxicating liquors was ratified by the states, and it became effective in January 1920. The 19th Amendment providing for woman suffrage, which had been defeated in the Senate in 1918, was approved by Congress in 1919. It was ratified by the states in time for the election of 1920.

The Postwar Economy

Despite fear of unemployment with the return of veterans to the labor force and the end of war purchases, the American economy boomed during 1919 and the first half of 1920. Consumers had money from high wages during the war, and the European demand for American food and manufactured products continued for some months after the war. The demand for goods resulted in a rapid inflation. Prices in 1919 were 77 percent above the prewar level, and in 1920 they were 105 percent above that level.

Strikes

The great increase in prices prompted 2,655 strikes in 1919 involving about four million workers or twenty percent of the labor force. Unions were encouraged by the gains they had made during the war and thought they had the support of public opinion. However, the Communist Revolution in Russia in 1917 soon inspired in many Americans, including government officials, a fear of violence and revolution by workers. While most of the strikes in early 1919 were successful, the tide of opinion gradually shifted against the workers.

Four major strikes received particular attention. In January 1919 all unions in Seattle declared a general strike in support of a strike for higher pay by shipyard workers. The action was widely condemned, the federal government sent marines, and the strike was soon abandoned.

In September 1919 Boston police struck for the right to unionize. Governor Calvin Coolidge called out the National Guard and stated that there was "no right to strike against the public safety by anybody, anywhere, anytime." The police were fired and a new force was recruited.

The American Federation of Labor attempted to organize the steel industry in 1919. When Judge Elbert H. Gary, the head of U.S. Steel, refused to negotiate, the workers struck in September. After much violence and the use of federal and state troops, the strike was broken by January 1920.

The United Mine Workers of America under John L. Lewis struck for shorter hours and higher wages on November 1, 1919. Attorney General A. Mitchell Palmer obtained injunctions and the union called off the strike. An arbitration board later awarded the miners a wage increase.

The Red Scare

Americans feared the spread of the Russian Communist Revolution to the United States, and many interpreted the widespread strikes of 1919 as communist-inspired and the beginning of the revolution. Bombs sent through the mail to prominent government and business leaders in April 1919 seemed to confirm their fears, although the origin of the bombs has never been determined. The membership of the two communist parties founded in the United States in 1919 was less than one hundred thousand, but many Americans were sure that many workers, all foreign-born persons, radicals, and members of the International Workers of the World (also known as "Wobblies"), a radical union in the western states, were communists. The anti-German hysteria of the war years was transformed into the anti-communist and anti-foreign hysteria of 1919 and 1920, and continued in various forms through the twenties.

The Palmer Raids

Attorney General A. Mitchell Palmer was one of the targets of the anonymous bombers in the spring of 1919. He was also an aspirant for the Democratic nomination for president in 1920, and he realized that many Americans saw the threat of a communist revolution as a grave danger. In August 1919 he named J. Edgar Hoover to head a new Intelligence Division in the Justice Department to collect information about radicals. In November 1919 Palmer's agents arrested almost seven hundred persons, mostly anarchists, and deported forty-three of them as undesirable aliens. On January 2, 1920, Justice Department agents, local police, and vigilantes in thirty-three cities arrested about four thousand people accused of being communists. It appears that many people caught in the sweep were neither communists nor aliens. Eventually 556 were shown to be communists and aliens, and were deported. Palmer then announced that huge communist riots were planned for major cities on May Day, May 1, 1920. Police and troops were alerted, but the day passed with no radical activity. Palmer was discredited and the Red Scare subsided.

The Race Riots of 1919

During the war about half a million blacks had migrated from the South to industrial cities, mostly in the North and Midwest, to find employment. After the war, white hostility based on competition for lower-paid jobs and black encroachment into neighborhoods led to race riots in twenty-five cities with hundreds killed or wounded and millions of dollars in property damage. Beginning in Longview, Texas, the riots spread, among other places, to Washington, D.C., and Chicago. The Chicago riot in July was the worst, lasting 13 days and leaving 38 dead, 520 wounded, and 1,000 families homeless. Fear of resuming black veterans in the South lead to an increase of lynchings from 34 in 1917 to 60 in 1918 and 70 in 1919. Some of the victims were veterans still in uniform.

HISTORICAL TIMELINE

Wilson and World War I (1912–1920)

1912	Wilson elected president
1913	Underwood Tariff Federal Reserve Act 16th Amendment (income tax) ratified 17th Amendment (direct senator election) ratified
1914	Clayton Antitrust Act Panama Canal opens World War I begins
1915	Germans sink *Lusitania*
1916	Margaret Sanger organizes New York Birth Control League Gen. Pershing pursues Pancho Villa in Mexico
1917	Germany resumes unrestricted submarine warfare U.S. declares war on Germany War Industries Board established Espionage Act passed Russian Revolution Committee on Public Information established
1918	Wilson proposes Fourteen Points Armistice ends war U.S. troops intervene in Russia
1919	Treaty of Versailles Red Scare and Palmer raids Senate rejects U.S. role in League of Nations 18th Amendment (Prohibition) ratified Over 20 percent of U.S. labor force goes on strike *Schenck v. United States* Race riots and lynchings throughout U.S.
1920	19th Amendment (women's suffrage) ratified

11 THE ROARING TWENTIES AND ECONOMIC COLLAPSE (1920–1929)

THE ELECTION OF 1920

The Political Climate

It seemed to many political observers in 1920 that the Republicans had an excellent chance of victory. The Wilson administration was blamed by many for the wartime civil liberties abuses, the League of Nations controversy, and the strikes and inflation of the postwar period.

The Republican Convention

The principal contenders for the nomination were General Leonard Wood, who had the support of the followers of the deceased Theodore Roosevelt, and Governor Frank O. Lowden of Illinois, the pick of many of the party bosses. When the convention seemed to deadlock, Henry Cabot Lodge, the convention chairman, and several other leaders arranged for the name of Senator Warren G. Harding of Ohio to be introduced as a dark-horse candidate. Harding was nominated on the tenth ballot, and Governor Calvin Coolidge of Massachusetts was chosen as the vice presidential nominee. The platform opposed the League, and promised low taxes, high tariffs, immigration restriction, and aid to farmers.

The Democratic Convention

The front-runners were William Gibbs McAdoo, the secretary of the Treasury and Wilson's son-in-law, and Attorney General A. Mitchell Palmer. Governor James Cox of Ohio was entered as a favorite son. Wilson expected the convention to deadlock, at which point his name would be introduced and he would be nominated for a third term by acclamation. His plan never materialized. McAdoo and Palmer contended for thirty-seven ballots with neither receiving the two-thirds necessary for nomination. Palmer then released his delegates, most of whom turned to Cox. Cox was nominated on the forty-fourth ballot, and Franklin D. Roosevelt, an assistant secretary of the Navy and distant cousin of Theodore, was selected as his running mate. The platform endorsed the League, but left the door open for reservations.

The Campaign

Harding's managers decided that he should speak as little as possible, but he did address visiting delegations from his front porch in Marion, Ohio. It was impossible to tell where he stood on the League issue, but he struck a responsive chord in many people when he urged that the nation should abandon heroics, nostrums, and experiment, and return to what he called normalcy. Cox and Roosevelt travelled extensively, speaking mostly in support of the League. Many found neither presidential candidate impressive.

The Election

Harding received 16,152,200 popular votes, 61 percent of the total, for 404 electoral votes. Cox received 9,147,353 popular votes for 127 electoral votes. Socialist candidate Eugene V. Debs, in federal prison in Atlanta for an Espionage Act conviction, received 919,799 votes. The Democrats carried only states in the Solid South, and even there lost Tennessee. It appears that people voted Republican more as a repudiation of Wilson's domestic policies than as a referendum on the League. Wilson had alienated German-Americans, Irish-Americans, antiwar progressives, civil libertarians, and Midwestern farmers, all groups which had given the Democrats considerable support in 1916.

THE TWENTIES: ECONOMIC ADVANCES AND SOCIAL TENSIONS

The Recession of 1920–1921

The United States experienced a severe recession from mid-1920 until the end of 1921. Europe returned to normal and reduced its purchases in America, and domestic demand for goods not available in wartime was filled. Prices fell, and unemployment exceeded twelve percent in 1921.

Prosperity and Industrial Productivity

Though overall the economy was strong between 1922 and 1929, certain segments of the economy—notably agriculture—did not share in the nation's general prosperity. Improved industrial efficiency, which resulted in lower prices for goods, was primarily responsible. Manufacturing output increased about 65 percent, and productivity, or output per hour of work increased about forty percent. The number of industrial workers actually decreased from 9 million to 8.8 million during the decade. The increased productivity resulted from improved machinery, which in turn came about for several reasons. Industry changed from steam to electric power, allowing the design of more intricate machines which replaced the work of human hands. By 1929, 70 percent of industrial power came from electricity. The moving assembly line, first introduced by Henry Ford in the automobile industry in 1913 and 1914, was widely adopted. Scientific management, exemplified by the time and motion studies pioneered by Frederick W. Taylor before the war, led to more efficient use of workers and lower labor costs. Larger firms began, for the first time, to fund major research and development activities to find new and improved products, reduce production costs, and utilize by-products, and the like.

The Automobile

The principal driving force of the economy of the 1920s was the automobile. There were 8,131,522 motor vehicles registered in the United States in 1920, and 26,704,825 in 1929. Annual output of automobiles reached 3.6 million in 1923, and remained at about that level throughout the decade. By 1925 the price of a Ford Model T had been reduced to $290, less than three months' pay for an average worker. Ford plants produced nine thousand Model Ts per day, and Henry Ford cleared about $25,000 a day throughout the decade. Just as information technology has been credited with enhancing, and even driving, innovation and productivity growth in the economy of early-twenty-first-century America, Henry Ford's use of electric motors to power automobile assembly lines led to the reorganization of a major production process. In turn, automobile manufacturing stimulated supporting industries such as steel, rubber, and glass, as well as gasoline refining and highway construction. It was during the 1920s that the United States became a nation of paved roads. Mileage of paved roads increased from 387,000 miles in 1921, most of which was in urban areas, to 662,000 in 1929. Highway construction costs averaged over one billion dollars a year in the late 1920s, in part due to the Federal Highway Act of 1916 which started the federal highway system and gave matching funds to the states for construction. One estimate stated that the automobile industry directly or indirectly employed 3.7 million people in 1929.

Other Leading Industries

The electrical industry also expanded rapidly during the 1920s. The demand for power for industrial machinery as well as for business and some lighting increased dramatically, and a host of electrical appliances such as stoves, vacuum cleaners, refrigerators, toasters, and radios became available. About two-thirds of American homes had electricity by 1929, leaving only those in rural areas without it. Home and business construction also experienced a boom from 1922 until 1928. Other large industries which grew rapidly were chemicals and printing. The movie industry expanded rapidly, especially after the introduction of sound films, and employed about 325,000 people by 1930. New industries which began in the period were radio and commercial aviation.

Consumer Credit and Advertising

Unlike earlier boom periods which had involved large expenditures for capital investments such as railroads and factories, the prosperity of the 1920s depended heavily on the sale of consumer products. Purchases of "big ticket" items such as automobiles, refrigerators, and furniture were made possible by installment or time payment credit. The idea was not new, but the availability of consumer credit expanded tremendously during the 1920s. Consumer interest and demand was spurred by the great increase in professional advertising using newspapers, magazines, radio, billboards, and other media. By 1929 advertising expenditures reached $3.4 billion, more than was spent on education at all levels.

The Dominance of Big Business

There was a trend toward corporate consolidation during the 1920s. By 1929 the 200 largest corporations held 49 percent of the corporate wealth and received 43 percent of corporate income. The top 5 percent of the corporations in the nation received about 85 percent of the corporate income. Corporate profits and dividends increased about 65 percent during the decade. In most fields an oligopoly of two to four firms dominated, exemplified by the automobile industry, where Ford, General Motors, and Chrysler produced 83 percent of the nation's vehicles in 1929. Firms in many fields formed trade associations which represented their interests to the public and the government, and which claimed to stabilize each industry. Government regulatory agencies such as the Federal Trade Commission and the Interstate Commerce Commission were passive and generally controlled by persons from the business world. The public generally accepted the situation and viewed the businessmen with respect. Illustrating the attitudes of the time, *The Man Nobody Knows*, a book by advertising executive Bruce Barton published in 1925, became a best-seller. It described Jesus as the founder of modern business and his apostles as an exemplary business management team.

Banking and Finance

As with other industries, there was a trend toward consolidation in banking. Bank assets increased about 66 percent from 1919 to 1929. There was a growth in branch banking, and in 1929 the 3.2 percent of the banks with branch operations controlled 46 percent of the banking resources. Because corporations were raising much of their money through the sale of stocks and bonds, the demand for business loans declined. Commercial banks then put more of their funds into real estate loans, loans to brokers against stocks and bonds, and the purchase of stocks and bonds themselves. By doing so they made themselves vulnerable to economic disaster when the depression began in late 1929. Even during the prosperous 1920s, 5,714 banks failed, most of them in rural areas or in Florida. Banks in operation in 1929 numbered 25,568.

Labor

The National Association of Manufacturers and its state affiliates began a drive in 1920 to restore the "open shop," or nonunion, workplace. As an alternative, firms sought to provide job satisfaction so that the workers would not want a union. Company-sponsored pension and insurance plans, stock purchase plans, efforts to ensure worker safety and comfort, social and sporting events, and company magazines were undertaken. Company unions, designed to give workers some voice with management under company control, were organized by 317 firms. The American Federation of Labor and other unions, which had prospered during World War I, found themselves on the defensive. Leaders, especially William Green, president of the American Federation of Labor after 1924, were conservative and nonaggressive. Union membership dropped about twenty percent, from five million to about four million, during the decade. The most violent labor confrontations occurred in the mining and southern textile industries. The United Mine Workers of America, headed by John L. Lewis, was involved in bitter strikes in Pennsylvania, West Virginia, Kentucky, and Illinois, but by 1929 had lost most of its power. The United Textile Workers failed to organize southern textile workers in a campaign from 1927 to 1929, but violent strikes occurred in Tennessee, North Carolina, and Virginia.

The Farm Problem

Farmers did not share in the prosperity of the twenties. Farm prices had been high during World War I because of European demand and government price fixing. By 1920 the European demand had dropped considerably, and farm prices were determined by a free market. Farm income dropped from $10 billion annually in 1919 to about $4 billion in 1921, and then leveled off at about $7 billion a year from 1923 through 1929. During the same period farm expenses rose with the cost of more sophisticated machinery and a greater use of chemical fertilizers.

AMERICAN SOCIETY IN THE 1920s

Population

During the 1920s the population of the U.S. increased by 16.1 percent, from 105,710,620 in 1920 to 122,775,046 in 1930, a slower percentage of growth than in previous decades. The birthrate was also lower than in former times, dropping from 27.7 per 100,000 in 1920 to 21.3 per 100,000 in 1930. About 88 percent of the people were white.

Urbanization

In 1920 for the first time a majority of Americans, 51 percent, lived in an urban place with a population of 2,500 or more. By 1930 the figure had increased to 56 percent. In terms of Standard Metropolitan Areas, which are defined as areas with central cities of at least 50,000 population, 44 percent of the people lived in an SMA in 1920, and 50 percent in 1930. Farm residents dropped from 26 percent of the total population in 1920 to 21 percent in 1930. A new phenomenon of the 1920s was the tremendous growth of suburbs and satellite cities, which grew more rapidly than the central cities. Streetcars, commuter railroads, and automobiles contributed to the process, as well as the easy availability of financing for home construction. The suburbs had once been the domain of the wealthy, but the technology of the twenties opened them to working-class families.

The Standard of Living

Improved technology and urbanization led to a sharp rise in the standard of living. Urban living improved access to electricity, natural gas, telephones, and piped water. Two-thirds of American homes had electricity by 1929. The use of indoor plumbing, hot water, and central heating increased dramatically. Conveniences such as electric stoves, vacuum cleaners, refrigerators, washing machines, toasters, and irons made life less burdensome. Improved machinery produced better-fitting and more comfortable ready-made clothing and shoes. Diet improved as the consumption of fresh vegetables increased 45 percent and canned vegetables 35 percent. Sales of citrus fruit and canned fruit were also up. Correspondingly, per capita consumption of wheat, corn, and potatoes fell. Automobiles, radios, phonographs, and commercial entertainment added to the enjoyment of life. Yet enjoyment of the new standard of living was uneven. The one-third of the households which still did not have electricity in 1929 lacked access to many of the new products. For those who had access, the new standard of living required more money than had been necessary in former times. Despite heavy sales of appliances, by 1929 only 25 percent of American families had vacuum cleaners, and only 20 percent had electric toasters. The real income of workers increased about 11 percent during the decade, but the benefits of prosperity were not spread evenly across the nation. It is estimated that the bottom 93 percent of the population actually saw a 4 percent drop in real disposable per capita income from 1923 to 1929. In 1929 about 12 million families, or 43 percent of the total, had annual incomes under $1,500, which was considered by many to be the poverty line. About 20 million families, or 72 percent, had incomes under $2,500, the family income deemed necessary for a decent standard of living with reasonable comforts.

The Sexual Revolution

Traditional American moral standards regarding premarital sex and marital fidelity were widely questioned for the first time during the 1920s. There was a popular misunderstanding by people who had not read his works that Sigmund Freud had advocated sexual promiscuity. Movies, novels, and magazine stories were more sexually explicit and sensational. The "flaming youth" of the "Jazz

Age" emphasized sexual promiscuity and drinking, as well as new forms of dancing considered erotic by the older generation. The automobile, by giving people mobility and privacy, was generally considered to have contributed to sexual license. Journalists wrote about "flappers," young women who were independent, assertive, and promiscuous. Birth control, though illegal, was promoted by Margaret Sanger and others, and was widely accepted. The sexual revolution occurred mostly among some urban dwellers, middle class people, and students, who were an economically select group at the time. Many continued to adhere to the old ways. Compared with the period from 1960 to the present, it was a relatively conservative time.

Women

Many feminists believed that the passage of the 19th Amendment in 1920 providing women suffrage would solve all problems for women. When it became apparent that women did not vote as a block, political leaders gave little additional attention to the special concerns of women. The sexual revolution brought some emancipation. Women adopted less bulky clothing with short skirts and bare arms and necks. They could smoke and socialize with men in public more freely than before. Birth control was more acceptable. Divorce laws were liberalized in many states at the insistence of women. In 1920 there was one divorce for every 7.5 marriages. By 1929 the ratio was 1 in 6. The number of employed women rose from 8.4 million in 1920 to 10.6 million in 1929, but the total work force increased in about the same proportion. Black and foreign-born women comprised 57 percent of the female work force, and domestic service was the largest job category. Most other women workers were in traditional female occupations such as secretarial and clerical work, retail sales, teaching, and nursing. Rates of pay were below those for men. Most women still pursued the traditional role of housewife and mother, and society accepted that as the norm.

Blacks

The migration of Southern rural blacks to the cities continued, with about 1.5 million moving during the 1920s. By 1930 about 20 percent of blacks lived in the North, with the largest concentrations in New York, Chicago, and Philadelphia. While they were generally better off economically in the cities than they had been as tenant farmers, they tended to hold low-paying jobs and were confined to segregated areas of the cities. The Harlem section of New York City, with a black population of 73,000 in 1920 and 165,000 in 1930, was the largest black urban community, and became the center for black writers, musicians, and intellectuals. Blacks throughout the country developed jazz and blues as music forms which enjoyed widespread popularity. W. E. B. DuBois, the editor of *The Crisis*, continued to call for integration and to attack segregation despite his disappointment with the lack of progress after World War I. The National Association for the Advancement of Colored People was a more conservative but active voice for civil rights, and the National Urban League concentrated on employment and economic advancement. Lynchings continued in the South, and the anti-black activities of the Ku Klux Klan are mentioned under Social Conflicts later in this chapter.

Marcus Garvey and the UNIA

A native of Jamaica, Marcus Garvey founded the Universal Negro Improvement Association there in 1914, and moved to New York in 1916. He advocated black racial pride and separatism rather than integration, and a return of blacks to Africa. Some of his ideas soon alienated the older black organizations. He developed a large following, especially among Southern blacks, but his claim of six million members in 1923 may be inflated. An advocate of black economic self-sufficiency, he urged his followers to buy only from blacks, and founded a chain of businesses, including grocery stores, restaurants, and laundries. In 1921 he proclaimed himself the provisional president of an African empire, and sold stock in the Black Star Steamship Line, which would take migrants to Africa. The line went bankrupt in 1923, Garvey was convicted and imprisoned for mail fraud in the sale of the line's stock, and then deported. His legacy was an emphasis on black pride and self-respect.

Mexicans and Puerto Ricans

Mexicans had long migrated to the southwestern part of the United States as agricultural laborers, but in the 1920s they began to settle in cities such as Los Angeles, San Antonio, and Denver. Like other immigrants, they held low-paying jobs and lived in poor neighborhoods, which they called *barrios*. The 1920s also saw the first large migration of Puerto Ricans to the mainland, mostly to New York City. There they were employed in manufacturing, in service industries such as restaurants, and in domestic work. They lived in barrios in Brooklyn and Manhattan.

Education

Free elementary education was available to most students in 1920, except for many black children. Growth of elementary schools in the 1920s reflected population growth and the addition of kindergartens. High school education became more available, and the number of public secondary schools doubled from 2.2 million in 1920 to 4.4 million in 1930. High school instruction shifted from an emphasis on college preparation to include vocational education, which was funded in part by the Smith-Hughes Act of 1917; this act provided federal funding for agricultural and technical studies, including home economics. There was also a substantial growth in enrollment in higher education from 600,000 in 1920 to 1.1 million in 1930.

Religion

Church and synagogue membership increased more rapidly than the population during the 1920s despite much religious tension and conflict. Most Protestants had been divided North and South since before the Civil War. By the 1920s, there was another major division between the modernists who accommodated their thinking with modern biblical criticism and evolution, and fundamentalists who stressed the literal truth of the Bible and creationism. There was also division on social issues such as support of labor. The only issue which united most Protestants, except Lutherans, was prohibition. The Roman Catholic Church and Jewish congregations were assimilating the large number of immigrants who had arrived prior to 1922. They also found themselves under attack from the Ku Klux Klan and the immigration restrictions.

Popular Culture

The trend whereby entertainment shifted from the home and small social groups to commercial profit-making activities had begun in the late nineteenth century and reached maturity in the 1920s. Spending for entertainment in 1929 was $4.3 billion. The movies attracted the most consumer interest and generated the most money. Movie attendance averaged 40 million a week in 1922 and 90 million a week in 1929. Introduction of sound with *The Jazz Singer* in 1927 generated even more interest. Stars like Douglas Fairbanks, Gloria Swanson, Rudolph Valentino, Clara Bow, and Charlie Chaplin were tremendously popular. Americans spent ten times more on movies than on all sports, the next attraction in popularity. It was called the golden age of major-league baseball, with an attendance increase of over 50 percent during the decade. Millions followed the exploits of George Herman "Babe" Ruth and other stars. Boxing was popular, and made Jack Dempsey and others famous. College football began to attract attention with Knute Rockne coaching at Notre Dame and Harold "Red" Grange playing for the University of Illinois. When Grange signed with the Chicago Bears in 1926, professional football began to grow in popularity. Commercial radio began when station KDKA in Pittsburgh broadcasted the election results in November 1920. By 1929 over 10 million families, over one-third of the total, had radios. National network broadcasting began when the National Broadcasting Company was organized in 1926, followed by the Columbia Broadcasting System in 1927. Radio was free entertainment, paid for by advertising. Despite the many new diversions, Americans continued to read, and millions of popular magazines were sold each week. Popular books of the period included the Tarzan series and Zane Grey's Westerns, as well as literary works, some of which are mentioned under Literary Trends below.

Literary Trends

Many talented writers of the 1920s were disgusted with the hypocrisy and materialism of contemporary American society, and expressed their concern in their works. Often called the "Lost Generation," many of them, such as novelists Ernest Hemingway and F. Scott Fitzgerald and poets Ezra Pound and T.S. Eliot, moved to Europe. Typical authors and works include Hemingway's *The Sun Also Rises* (1926) and *A Farewell to Arms* (1929); Sinclair Lewis's *Babbitt* (1922), *Arrowsmith* (1925), and *Elmer Gantry* (1927); F. Scott Fitzgerald's *The Great Gatsby* (1925) and *Tender Is the Night* (1929); John Dos Passos' *Three Soldiers* (1921); and Thomas Wolfe's *Look Homeward, Angel* (1929). H. L. Mencken, a journalist who began publication of the *American Mercury* magazine in 1922, ceaselessly and vitriolicly attacked the "booboisie," as he called middle-class America, but his literary talent did not match that of the leaders of the period.

SOCIAL CONFLICTS

A Conflict of Values

The rapid technological changes represented by the automobile, the revolution in morals, and the rapid urbanization with many immigrants and blacks inhabiting the growing cities brought a strong reaction from white Protestant Americans of older stock who saw their traditional values gravely threatened. In many ways their concerns continued the emotions of wartime hysteria and the Red Scare. The traditionalists were largely residents of rural areas and small towns, and the clash of farm values with those of an industrial society of urban workers was evident. The conflict is often called a rural-urban conflict, and to a great extent it was, but some think the lines of division were not that neat. The traditionalist backlash against modern urban industrial society expressed itself primarily through intolerance.

The Ku Klux Klan

On Thanksgiving Day in 1915 the Knights of the Ku Klux Klan, modeled on the organization of the same name in the 1860s and 1870s, was founded near Atlanta by William J. Simmons. Its purpose was mainly to intimidate blacks, who were experiencing an apparent rise in status during World War I. The Klan remained small until 1920 when two advertising experts, Edward Y. Clark and Elizabeth Tyler, were hired by the leadership. Clark and Tyler used modern advertising to recruit members, charged a ten dollar initiation fee of which they received \$2.50, and made additional money from the sale of regalia and emblems. By 1923 the Klan had about five million members throughout the nation. The largest concentrations of members were in the South, the Southwest, the Midwest, California, and Oregon. The use of white hoods, masks, and robes, and secret ritual and jargon, seemed to appeal mostly to lower middle class men in towns and small cities. The Klan stood for "100 percent pure Americanism" to preserve "native, white, Protestant supremacy." It opposed blacks and Catholics primarily. In addition, Jews and the foreign-born were often its targets. It also attacked bootleggers, drunkards, gamblers, and adulterers for violating moral standards. The Klan's methods of repression included cross burnings, tar and featherings, kidnappings, lynchings, and burnings. The Klan was not a political party, but it endorsed and opposed candidates, and exerted considerable control over elections and politicians in at least nine states. The Klan began to decline after 1925 when it was hit by scandals, especially the murder conviction of Indiana Grand Dragon David Stephenson. The main reason for its decline was the staunch opposition of courageous editors, politicians, and other public figures who exposed its lawlessness and terrorism in the face of great personal danger of violence. Many historians see the Klan as the American expression of fascism, which was making headway in Italy, Germany, and other European nations during the twenties.

Immigration Restriction

There had been calls for immigration restriction since the late nineteenth century. Labor leaders believed that immigrants depressed wages and impeded unionization. Some progressives believed that they created social problems. In June 1917 Congress, over Wilson's veto, had imposed a literacy test for immigrants and excluded many Asian nationalities. During World War I and the Red Scare, almost all immigrants were considered radicals and communists, and the tradition was quickly picked up by the Klan. With bad economic conditions in postwar Europe, over 1.3 million came to the United States during the three years from 1919 through 1921. As in the period before the war, they were mostly from southern and eastern Europe and mostly Catholics and Jews, the groups most despised by nativist Americans. In 1921 Congress quickly passed the Emergency Quota Act, which limited immigration by nation to three percent of the number of foreign-born persons from that nation in the United States in 1910. In practice, the law admitted about as many as wanted to come from such nations as Britain, Ireland, and Germany, while severely restricting Italians, Greeks, Poles, and eastern European Jews. It became effective in 1922 and reduced the number of immigrants annually to about 40 percent of the 1921 total. Congress then passed the National Origins Act of 1924 which set the quotas at two percent of the number of foreign-born persons of that nationality in the United States in 1890, excluded all Asians, and imposed an annual maximum of 164,000.

Immigration from Western Hemisphere nations, including Canada and Mexico, was not limited. The law further reduced the number of southern and eastern Europeans, and cut the annual immigration to 20 percent of the 1921 figure. In 1927 the annual maximum was reduced to 150,000. The quotas were not fully calculated and implemented until 1929. Objections to the law were not aimed at the idea of restriction, but at the designation of certain nationalities and religious groups as undesirable. The law was resented by such groups as Italian- and Polish-Americans.

Prohibition

The 18th Amendment, which prohibited the manufacture, sale, or transportation of intoxicating liquors, took effect in January 1920. It was implemented by the Volstead Act, signed into law in October 1919, which defined intoxicating beverages as containing one-half of 1 percent alcohol by volume and imposed criminal penalties for violations. Many states had authorized the sale of light beer, believing that it was not covered by the amendment, but Anti-Saloon League lobbyists pushed through the Volstead Act. Many historians believe that prohibition of hard liquor might have been successful if light wine and beer had been allowed. As things turned out, the inexpensive light beverages were less available while expensive illegal hard liquor was readily available. Prohibition was enforceable only if many people in the society accepted and supported it. Enforcement was reasonably effective in some rural Southern and Midwestern states that had been dry before the amendment. In urban areas where both foreign-born and native citizens often believed that their liberty had been infringed upon, neither the public nor their elected officials were interested in enforcement. Speakeasies, supposedly secret bars operated by bootleggers, replaced the saloons. Smuggled liquor flowed across the boundaries and coastlines of the nation, and the manufacture of "bathtub gin" and similar beverages was undertaken by thousands. Organized crime, which previously had been involved mainly with prostitution and gambling, grew tremendously to meet the demand. Al Capone of Chicago was perhaps the most famous of the bootlegging gangsters. The automobile was used both to transport liquor and to take customers to speakeasies. Women, who had not gone to saloons in the pre-prohibition period, frequented speakeasies and began to drink in public. By the mid-1920s, the nation was badly divided on the prohibition issue. Support continued from rural areas and almost all Republican office-holders. The Democrats divided between the urban Northerners who advocated repeal, and rural, especially Southern, Democrats who supported prohibition. Some people who originally favored prohibition changed their views because of the public hypocrisy and criminal activity which it caused.

Creationism and the Scopes Trial

Fundamentalist Protestants, under the leadership of William Jennings Bryan, began a campaign in 1921 to prohibit the teaching of evolution in the schools, and thus protect belief in the literal Biblical account of creation. The idea was especially well-received in the South. In 1925 the Tennessee legislature passed a law that forbade any teacher in the state's schools or colleges to teach evolution. The American Civil Liberties Union found a young high school biology teacher, John Thomas Scopes, who was willing to bring about a test case by breaking the law. Scopes was tried in Dayton, Tennessee, in July 1925. Bryan came to assist the prosecution, and Chicago trial lawyer Clarence Darrow defended Scopes. The trial attracted national attention through newspaper and radio coverage. The judge refused to allow expert testimony, so the trial was a duel of words between Darrow and Bryan. As was expected, Scopes was convicted and fined one hundred dollars. Bryan died of exhaustion a few days after the trial. Both sides claimed a moral victory. The anti-evolution crusaders continued their efforts, and secured enactment of a statute in Mississippi in 1926. They failed after a bitter fight in North Carolina in 1927, and in several other states until Arkansas in 1928 passed an anti-evolution law by use of the initiative.

Sacco and Vanzetti

On April 15, 1920, two unidentified gunmen robbed a shoe factory and killed two men in South Braintree, Massachusetts. Nicola Sacco and Bartolomeo Vanzetti, Italian immigrants and admitted anarchists, were tried for murder. Judge Webster Thayer clearly favored the prosecution, which based its case on the political radicalism of the defendants. After they were convicted and sentenced to death in July 1921, there was much protest in the United States and in Europe that they had not received a fair trial. After six years of delays, they were executed on August 23, 1927. A debate on their innocence and the possible perversion of American justice continued long afterward. The men were ultimately vindicated by Governor Michael Dukakis in 1977.

GOVERNMENT AND POLITICS IN THE 1920s: THE HARDING ADMINISTRATION

Warren G. Harding

Harding was a handsome and amiable man of limited intellectual and organizational abilities. He had spent much of his life as the publisher of a newspaper in the small city of Marion, Ohio. He recognized his limitations, but hoped to be a much-loved president. He showed compassion by pardoning socialist Eugene V. Debs for his conviction under the Espionage Act and inviting him to dinner at the White House. He also persuaded U.S. Steel to give workers the eight-hour day. A convivial man, he liked to drink and play poker with his friends, and kept the White House stocked with bootleg liquor despite prohibition. He was accused of keeping a mistress, Nan Britton. His economic philosophy was conservative.

The Cabinet and Government Appointments

Harding appointed some outstanding persons to his Cabinet, including Secretary of State Charles Evans Hughes, a former Supreme Court justice and presidential candidate; Secretary of the Treasury Andrew Mellon, a Pittsburgh aluminum and banking magnate and reportedly the richest man in America; and Secretary of Commerce Herbert Hoover, a dynamic multimillionaire mine owner who was famous for wartime relief efforts. Less impressive was his appointment of his cronies Albert B. Fall as Secretary of the Interior and Harry M. Daugherty as Attorney General. Other cronies, some dishonest, were appointed to other government posts.

Tax Reduction

Mellon believed in low taxes and government economy to free the rich from "oppressive" taxes and thus encourage investment. The farm bloc of Midwestern Republicans and Southern Democrats in Congress prevented cuts in the higher tax brackets as great as Mellon recommended. The Revenue Acts of 1921 and 1924 cut the maximum tax rates to 50 percent and then to 40 percent. Taxes in lower brackets were also reduced, but inheritance and corporate income taxes were retained. Despite the cuts, Mellon was able to reduce the federal debt by an average of $500 million a year.

The Fordney-McCumber Tariff

Mellon sought substantial increases in the tariffs, but again there was a compromise with the farm bloc. The Fordney-McCumber Tariff of September 1922 imposed high rates on farm products and protected such infant industries as rayon, china, toys, and chemicals. Most other items received moderate protection, and a few items including farm equipment, were duty-free. The president could raise or lower rates to a limit of 50 percent on recommendation of the Tariff Commission. The average rate was about 33 percent, compared with about 26 percent under the previous tariff.

The Budget

As a result of the Budget and Accounting Act of 1921, the federal government had a unified budget for the first time. The law also provided for a director of the budget to assist in its preparation, and a comptroller general to audit government accounts.

The Harding Scandals

Harding apparently was completely honest, but several of his friends whom he appointed to office became involved in major financial scandals. Most of the information about the scandals did not become public knowledge until after Harding's death.

The "Teapot Dome" Scandal began when Secretary of the Interior Albert B. Fall in 1921 secured the transfer of several naval oil reserves to his jurisdiction. In 1922 he secretly leased reserves at Teapot Dome in Wyoming to Harry F. Sinclair of Monmouth Oil and at Elk Hills in California to Edward Doheny of Pan-American Petroleum. A Senate investigation later revealed that Sinclair had given Fall $305,000 in cash and bonds and a herd of cattle, while Doheny had given him a $100,000 unsecured loan. Sinclair and Doheny were acquitted in 1927 of charges of defrauding the government, but in 1929 Fall was convicted, fined, and imprisoned for bribery.

Another scandal involved Charles R. Forbes, appointed by Harding to head the new Veterans' Bureau. He seemed energetic and efficient in operating the new hospitals and services for veterans. It was later estimated that he had stolen or squandered about $250 million in bureau funds.

Scandal also tainted Attorney General Daugherty who, through his intimate friend Jesse Smith, took bribes from bootleggers, income tax evaders, and others in return for protection from prosecution. When the scandal began to come to light, Smith committed suicide in Daugherty's Washington apartment in May 1923. There was also evidence that Daugherty received money for using his influence in returning the American Metal Company, seized by the government during the war, to its German owners.

Harding's Death

Depressed by the first news of the scandals, Harding left in June 1923 for an extended trip that included a tour of Alaska. On his return to California, he died suddenly in San Francisco on August 2, 1923, apparently of a heart attack. Rumors of foul play or suicide persisted for years.

Coolidge Becomes President

Vice President Calvin Coolidge became president to complete Harding's term. As the scandals of the deceased president's administration came to light, Coolidge was able to avoid responsibility for them. He had a reputation for honesty, although he did not remove Daugherty from the Cabinet until March 1924.

THE ELECTION OF 1924

The Republicans

Progressive insurgents failed to capture the convention. Calvin Coolidge was nominated on the first ballot with Charles G. Dawes as his running mate. The platform endorsed business development, low taxes, and rigid economy in government. The party stood on its record of economic growth and prosperity since 1922.

The Democrats

The party had an opportunity to draw farmers and labor into a new progressive coalition. An attractive Democratic candidate would have had a good chance against the bland Coolidge and the Harding scandals. Instead, two wings of the party battled to exhaustion at the convention. The Eastern wing, led by Governor Alfred E. Smith of New York, wanted the platform to favor repeal of prohibition and to condemn the Ku Klux Klan. Southern and Western delegates, led by William G. McAdoo and William Jennings Bryan, narrowly defeated both proposals. Smith and McAdoo contested for 103 ballots with neither receiving the two-thirds necessary for nomination. John W. Davis, a conservative Wall Street lawyer, was finally chosen as a dark horse with Charles W. Bryan, brother of William Jennings, as the vice presidential candidate. The platform favored a lower tariff, but otherwise was similar to the Republican document.

The Progressives

Robert M. LaFollette, after failing in a bid for the Republican nomination, formed a new Progressive Party with support from Midwest farm groups, socialists, and the American Federation of Labor. The platform attacked monopolies and called for the nationalization of railroads, the direct election of the president, and other reforms.

The Campaign

Neither Coolidge nor Davis were active or effective campaigners. Republican publicity concentrated on attacking LaFollette as a communist. LaFollette campaigned vigorously, but he lacked money and was disliked by many for his 1917 opposition to entrance into World War I.

The Election

Coolidge received 15,725,016 votes and 382 electoral votes, more than his two opponents combined. Davis received 8,385,586 votes and 136 electoral votes, while LaFollette had 4,822,856 votes and 13 electoral votes from his home state of Wisconsin.

THE COOLIDGE ADMINISTRATION

Calvin Coolidge

Coolidge was a dour and taciturn man. Born in Vermont, his adult life and political career were spent in Massachusetts. "The business of the United States is business," he proclaimed, and "the man who builds a factory builds a temple." His philosophy of life was stated in the remark that "four-fifths of all our troubles in this world would disappear if only we would sit down and keep still." Liberal political commentator Walter Lippmann wrote that "Mr. Coolidge's genius for inactivity is developed to a very high point." He intentionally provided no presidential leadership.

The McNary-Haugen Bill

In 1921 George Peek and Hugh S. Johnson, farm machinery manufacturers in Illinois, developed a plan to raise prices for basic farm products. The government would buy and resell in the domestic market a commodity such as wheat at the world price plus the tariff. The surplus would be sold abroad at the world price, and the difference made up by an equalization fee on all farmers in proportion to the amount of the commodity they had sold. When farm conditions did not improve, the idea was incorporated in the McNary-Haugen Bill, which passed Congress in 1927 and 1928, but was vetoed both times by Coolidge. The plan was a forerunner of the agricultural programs of the 1930s.

Muscle Shoals

During World War I the government had constructed a dam and two nitrate plants on the Tennessee River at Muscle Shoals, Alabama. In 1925 Senator George W. Norris of Nebraska led the defeat of a plan to lease the property to private business, but his proposal for government operation was vetoed by Coolidge in 1928. The facility was to become the nucleus of the Tennessee Valley Authority in the 1930s.

Veterans' Bonus

Legislation to give veterans of World War I 20-year endowment policies with values based on their length of service was passed over Coolidge's veto in 1924.

The Revenue Act of 1926

Mellon's tax policies were finally implemented by the Revenue Act of 1926, which reduced the basic income tax, cut the surtax to a maximum of 20 percent, abolished the gift tax, and cut the estate tax in half.

THE ELECTION OF 1928

The Republicans

Coolidge did not seek another term, and the convention quickly nominated Herbert Hoover, the secretary of commerce, for president, and Charles Curtis as his running mate. The platform endorsed the policies of the Harding and Coolidge administrations.

The Democrats

Governor Alfred E. Smith of New York, a Catholic and an anti-prohibitionist, controlled most of the non-Southern delegations. Southerners supported his nomination with the understanding that the platform would not advocate repeal of prohibition. Senator Joseph T. Robinson of Arkansas, a Protestant and a prohibitionist, was the vice presidential candidate. The platform differed little from that of the Republicans, except in advocating lower tariffs.

The Campaign

Hoover asserted that Republican policies would end poverty in the country. Smith was also economically conservative, but he attacked prohibition and bigotry. He was met in the South by a massive campaign headed by Bishop James Cannon Jr. of the Methodist Episcopal Church South, attacking him as a Catholic and a wet.

The Election

Hoover received 21,392,190 votes and 444 electoral votes, carrying all of the North except Massachusetts and Rhode Island, and seven states in the Solid South. Smith had 15,016,443 votes for 87 electoral votes in eight states.

FOREIGN POLICY IN THE TWENTIES

The Washington Conference

At the invitation of Secretary of State Charles Evans Hughes, representatives of the United States, Great Britain, France, Japan, Italy, China, the Netherlands, Belgium, and Portugal met in Washington in August 1921 to discuss naval limitations and Asian affairs. Three treaties resulted from the conference.

The Five Power Pact or Treaty, signed in February 1922, committed the United States, Britain, Japan, France, and Italy to end new construction of capital naval vessels, to scrap some ships, and to maintain a ratio of 5:5:3:1.67:1.67 for tonnage of capital or major ships in order of the nations listed. Hughes did not realize that the treaty gave Japan naval supremacy in the Pacific.

The Nine Power Pact or Treaty was signed by all of the participants at the conference. It upheld the Open Door in China by binding the nations to respect the sovereignty, independence, and integrity of China.

The Four Power Pact or Treaty bound the United States, Great Britain, Japan, and France to respect each other's possessions in the Pacific, and to confer in the event of disputes or aggression in the area.

War Debts, Reparations, and International Finance

The United States had lent the Allies about $7 billion during World War I and about $3.25 billion in the postwar period, and insisted on full payment of the debts. Meanwhile, Germany was to pay reparations to the Allies, but by

1923 Germany was bankrupt. The Dawes Plan, proposed by American banker Charles G. Dawes, was accepted in 1924. Under it, American banks made loans of $2.5 billion to Germany by 1930. Germany paid reparations of over $2 billion to the Allies during the same period, and the Allies paid about $2.6 billion to the United States on their war debts. The whole cycle was based on loans from American banks.

The Kellogg-Briand Pact

A group of American citizens campaigned during the 1920s for a treaty which would outlaw war. In 1927 the French foreign minister, Aristide Briand, proposed such a treaty with the United States. Frank B. Kellogg, Coolidge's secretary of state, countered by proposing that other nations be invited to sign. At Paris, in August 1928, almost all major nations signed the treaty, which renounced war as an instrument of national policy. It outlawed only aggression, not self-defense, and had no enforcement provisions.

Latin America

American investment in Latin America almost doubled during the 1920s to $5.4 billion, and relations with most nations in the region improved. Coolidge removed the Marines from Nicaragua in 1925, but a revolution erupted and the Marines were returned. Revolutionary General Augusto Sandino fought against the marines until they were replaced by an American-trained national guard under Anastasio Somoza. The Somoza family ruled Nicaragua until 1979 when they were overthrown by revolutionaries called the Sandinistas.

THE GREAT DEPRESSION: THE CRASH

Hoover Becomes President

Herbert Hoover, an Iowa farm boy and an orphan, graduated from Stanford University with a degree in mining engineering. He became a multimillionaire from mining and other investments around the world. After serving as the director of the Food Administration under Wilson, be became secretary of commerce under Harding and Coolidge. He believed that an associative economic system with voluntary cooperation of business and government would enable the United States to abolish poverty through continued economic growth.

The Stock Market Boom

Stock prices increased throughout the decade. The boom in prices and volume of sales was especially active after 1925, and was intensive during 1928–29. The Dow Jones Industrial Average finished the year 1924 at 120; for the month of September 1929 it was 381; and for the year 1932 it dropped to 41. Stocks were selling for more than 16 times their earnings in 1929, well above the rule of thumb at the time of ten times their earnings.

The Stock Market Crash

Careful investors, realizing that stocks were overpriced, began to sell to take their profits. During October 1929 prices declined as more stock was sold. On "Black Thursday," October 24, 1929, almost 13 million shares were traded, a large number for that time, and prices fell precipitously. Investment banks tried to boost the market by buying, but on October 29, "Black Tuesday," the market fell about 40 points, with 16.5 million shares traded. A long decline followed until early 1933, and with it, depression.

HISTORICAL TIMELINE

The Roaring Twenties and Economic Collapse (1920–1929)

1920	Sacco and Vanzetti arrested Harding elected president First commercial radio broadcast
1921	Washington Naval Conference Emergency Quota Act restricts immigration
1923	Teapot Dome scandal Marcus Garvey claims 6 million followers Ku Klux Klan claims 5 million members
1924	National Origins Act sets 2 percent quotas for immigration
1925	*Scopes* Tennessee evolution trial Model T Ford drops to cost of $290 (three months' wages)
1927	Lindbergh's solo flight across the Atlantic Sacco and Vanzetti executed Babe Ruth hits 60 home runs for the Yankees Al Jolson stars in *The Jazz Singer*, the first talking film
1928	Hoover elected president Fifty-two nations sign Kellogg-Briand Pact renouncing war
1929	Stock Market crashes in October

12 THE GREAT DEPRESSION AND THE NEW DEAL (1929–1941)

REASONS FOR THE DEPRESSION

A stock market crash does not mean that a depression must follow. A similar crash in October 1987, for example, did not lead to depression. In 1929 a complex interaction of many factors caused the decline of the economy.

Many people had bought stock on a margin of ten percent, meaning that they had borrowed ninety percent of the purchase through a broker's loan, and put up the stock as collateral. Broker's loans totaled $8.5 billion in 1929, compared with $3.5 billion in 1926. When the price of a stock fell more than ten percent, the lender sold the stock for whatever it would bring and thus further depressed prices. The forced sales brought great losses to the banks and businesses which had financed the broker's loans, as well as to the investors.

There were already signs of recession before the market crash in 1929. Because the gathering and processing of statistics was not as advanced then as it is now, some factors were not so obvious to people at the time. The farm economy, which involved almost twenty-five percent of the population, had been depressed throughout the decade. Coal, railroads, and New England textiles had not been prosperous. After 1927 new construction declined and auto sales began to sag. Many workers had been laid off before the crash of 1929.

Many scholars believe that there was a problem of underconsumption, meaning that ordinary workers and farmers, after using their consumer credit, did not have enough money to keep buying the products which were being produced. One estimate says that the income of the top one percent of the population increased at least 75 percent during the decade, while that of the bottom 93 percent increased only 6 percent. The process continued after the depression began. After the stock market crash, people were conservative and saved their money, thus reducing the demand for goods. As demand decreased, workers were laid off or had wage reductions, further reducing their purchasing power and bringing another decrease in demand.

With the decline in the economy, Americans had less money for foreign loans and bought fewer imported products. That meant that foreign governments and individuals were not able to pay their debts in the United States. The whole reparations and war debts structure collapsed. American exports dropped, further hurting the domestic economy. The depression eventually spread throughout the world.

Economic Effects of the Depression

During the early months of the depression most people thought it was just an adjustment in the business cycle which would soon be over. Hoover repeatedly assured the public that prosperity was just around the corner. As time went on, the worst depression in American history set in, reaching its bottom point in early 1932. The gross national product fell from $104.6 billion in 1929 to $56.1 billion in 1933. Unemployment reached about 13 million in 1933, or about 25 percent of the labor force excluding farmers. National income dropped 54 percent from $87.8 billion to $40.2 billion. Labor income fell about 41 percent, while farm income dropped 55 percent from $11.9 billion to $5.3 billion. Industrial production dropped about 51 percent. The banking system suffered as 5,761 banks, over 22 percent of the total, failed by the end of 1932.

The Human Dimension of the Depression

As the depression grew worse, more and more people lost their jobs or had their wages reduced. Many were unable to continue credit payments on homes, automobiles, and other possessions, and lost them. Families doubled up in houses and apartments. Both the marriage rate and the birth rate declined as people put off family formation. Hundreds of thousands became homeless and lived in groups of makeshift shacks called Hoovervilles in empty spaces around cities. Others traveled the country by foot and boxcar seeking food and work. State and local government agencies and private charities were overwhelmed in their attempts to care for those in need, although public and private soup kitchens and soup lines were set up throughout the nation. Malnutrition was widespread but few died of starvation, perhaps because malnourished people are susceptible to many fatal diseases.

HOOVER'S DEPRESSION POLICIES

The Agricultural Marketing Act

Passed in June 1929 before the market crash, the Agricultural Marketing Act, proposed by the president, created the Federal Farm Board with a revolving fund of $500 million to lend the agricultural cooperatives to buy commodities such as wheat and cotton, and hold them for higher prices. Until 1931 it did keep agricultural prices above the world level. Then world prices plummeted, the board's funds ran out, and there was no period of higher prices in which the cooperatives could sell their stored commodities.

The Hawley-Smoot Tariff

The Hawley-Smoot Tariff, passed in June 1930, raised duties on both agricultural and manufactured imports. It did nothing of significance to improve the economy, and historians argue over whether or not it contributed to the spread of the international depression.

Voluntarism

Hoover believed that voluntary cooperation would enable the country to weather the depression. He held meetings with business leaders at which he urged them to avoid lay-offs of workers and wage cuts, and he secured no-strike pledges from labor leaders. He urged all citizens to contribute to charities to help alleviate the suffering. While people were generous, private charity could not begin to meet the needs.

Public Works

In 1930 Congress appropriated $750 million for public buildings, river and harbor improvements, and highway construction in an effort to stimulate employment.

The Reconstruction Finance Corporation

Chartered by Congress in 1932, the RFC had an appropriation of $500 million and authority to borrow $1.5 billion for loans to railroads, banks, and other financial institutions. It prevented the failure of basic firms on which many other elements of the economy depended, but was criticized by some as relief for the rich.

The Federal Home Loan Bank Act

The Federal Home Loan Bank Act, passed in July 1932, injected $125 million of capital into newly created home loan banks so that loans could be made to building and loan associations, savings banks, and insurance companies to help them avoid foreclosures on homes.

Relief

Hoover staunchly opposed the use of federal funds for relief for the needy. In July 1932 he vetoed the Garner-Wagner Bill, which would have appropriated funds for relief. He did compromise by approving legislation authorizing the RFC to lend $300 million to the states for relief, and to make loans to states and cities for self-liquidating public works.

The Bonus Army

The Bonus Expeditionary Force, which took its name from the American Expeditionary Force of World War I, was a group of about fourteen thousand unemployed veterans who went to Washington in the summer of 1932 to lobby Congress for immediate payment of the bonus which had been approved in 1926 for payment in 1945. At Hoover's insistence, the Senate did not pass the bonus bill, and about half of the BEF accepted a congressional offer of transportation home. The remaining five or six thousand, many with wives and children, continued to live in shanties along the Anacostia River and to lobby for their cause. After two veterans were killed in a clash with the police, Hoover, calling them insurrectionists and communists, ordered the Army to remove them. On July 28, 1932, General Douglas MacArthur, the Army chief of staff, assisted by Majors Dwight D. Eisenhower and George S. Patton, personally commanded the removal operation. With machine guns, tanks, cavalry, infantry with fixed bayonets, and tear gas, MacArthur drove the veterans from Washington and burned their camp.

The Farm Holiday Association

Centered in Iowa, the Farm Holiday Association, headed by Milo Reno and others, called a farm strike in August 1932. They urged farmers not to take their products to market in an effort to raise farm prices. The picketing of markets led to violence, and the strike collapsed.

THE ELECTION OF 1932

The Republicans

At the Republican convention in Chicago, Hoover was nominated on the first ballot. The platform called for a continuation of his depression policies.

The Democrats

Franklin D. Roosevelt, the popular governor of New York, gained the support of many Southern and Western delegates through the efforts of his managers, Louis Howe and James Farley. When the Democratic convention opened in Chicago, he had a majority of delegates, but not the necessary two-thirds for nomination. House speaker John Nance Garner, a favorite son candidate from Texas, threw support to Roosevelt, who was nominated on the fourth ballot. Garner then became the vice presidential candidate. Roosevelt took the unprecedented step of flying to the convention to accept the nomination in person, declaring that he pledged a "new deal" for the American people. The platform called for the repeal of prohibition, government aid for the unemployed, and a twenty five percent cut in government spending.

The Campaign

Hoover declared that he would lead the nation to prosperity with higher tariffs and the maintenance of the gold standard. He warned that the election of Roosevelt would lead to grass growing in the streets of the cities and towns of America. Roosevelt called for "bold, persistent experimentation," and expressed his concern for the "forgotten man" at the bottom of the economic heap, but he did not give a clear picture of what he intended to do. Roosevelt had a broad smile and amiable disposition which attracted many people, while Hoover was aloof and cold in his personal style.

The Election

Roosevelt received 22,809,638 votes for 57.3 percent of the total, and 472 electoral votes, carrying all but six Northeastern states. Hoover had 15,758,901 votes and 59 electoral votes. Despite the hard times, Norman Thomas, the Socialist candidate, received only 881,951 votes. The Democrats also captured the Senate, and increased their majority in the House.

THE FIRST NEW DEAL

Franklin D. Roosevelt

The heir of a wealthy family and a fifth cousin of Theodore Roosevelt, Franklin was born in 1882 on the family estate at Hyde Park, New York. He graduated from Harvard and the Columbia Law School, married his distant cousin Anna Eleanor Roosevelt in 1905, and practiced law in New York City. He entered state politics, then served as assistant secretary of the Navy under Wilson, and was the Democratic vice-presidential candidate in 1920. In 1921 he suffered an attack of polio which left him paralyzed for several years and on crutches or in a wheelchair for the rest of his life. In 1928 he was elected governor of New York to succeed Al Smith, and was reelected in 1930. As governor, his depression programs for the unemployed, public works, aid to farmers, and conservation attracted national attention.

The Cabinet

Important Cabinet appointments included Senator Cordell Hull of Tennessee as secretary of state; Henry A. Wallace as secretary of agriculture; Harold L. Ickes as secretary of the interior; Frances Perkins, a New York social worker, as secretary of labor and the first woman appointed to a Cabinet post; and James A. Farley, Roosevelt's political manager, as postmaster general.

The Brain Trust

Roosevelt's inner circle of unofficial advisors, first assembled during the campaign, was more influential than the Cabinet. Prominent in it were agricultural economist Rexford G. Tugwell, political scientist Raymond Moley, lawyer Adolph A. Berle Jr., the originators of the McNary-Haugen Bill—Hugh S. Johnson and George Peek—and Roosevelt's personal political advisor, Louis Howe.

The New Deal Program

Roosevelt did not have a developed plan of action when he took office. He intended to experiment and to find that which worked. As a result, many programs overlapped or contradicted others, and were changed or dropped if they did not work.

Repeal of Prohibition

In February 1933, before Roosevelt took office, Congress passed the 21st Amendment to repeal prohibition, and sent it to the states. In March the new Congress legalized light (lower alcohol content) beer. The amendment was ratified by the states and took effect in December 1933.

The Banking Crisis

In February 1933, as the inauguration approached, a severe banking crisis developed. Banks could not collect their loans or meet the demands of their depositors for withdrawals, and runs occurred on many banks. Eventually banks in thirty-eight states were closed by the state governments, and the remainder were open for only limited operations. An additional 5,190 banks failed in 1933, bringing the depression total to 10,951.

The Inaugural Address

By the time Roosevelt was inaugurated on March 4, 1933, the American economic system seemed to be on the verge of collapse. Roosevelt assured the nation that "the only thing we have to fear is fear itself," called for a special session of Congress to convene on March 9, and asked for "broad executive powers to wage war against the emergency." Two days later, he closed all banks, and forbade the export of gold or the redemption of currency in gold.

LEGISLATION OF THE FIRST NEW DEAL

The Hundred Days and the First New Deal

The special session of Congress, from March 9 to June 16, 1933, passed a great body of legislation which has left a lasting mark on the nation, and the period has been referred to ever since as the "Hundred Days." Over the next two years legislation was added, but the basic recovery plan of the Hundred Days remained in operation. Hence, the period from 1933 to 1935 is called the First New Deal. A new wave of programs beginning in 1935 is called the Second New Deal. The distinction was not known at the time, but is a device of historians to differentiate between two stages in Roosevelt's administration.

Economic Legislation of the Hundred Days

The banking crisis was the most immediate problem facing Roosevelt and the Congress. A series of laws were passed to deal with the crisis and to reform the American economic system.

Emergency Banking Relief Act was passed on March 9, the first day of the special session. The law provided additional funds for banks from the RFC and the Federal Reserve, allowed the Treasury to open sound banks after ten days and to merge or liquidate unsound ones, and forbade the hoarding or export of gold. Roosevelt on March 12 assured the public of the soundness of the banks in the first of many "fireside chats," or radio addresses. People believed him and most banks were soon open with more deposits than withdrawals.

The Banking Act of 1933, or the Glass-Steagall Act, established the Federal Deposit Insurance Corporation (FDIC) to insure individual deposits in commercial banks, and separated commercial banking from the more speculative activity of investment banking.

The Truth-in-Securities Act required that full information about stocks and bonds be provided by brokers and others to potential purchasers.

The Home Owners Loan Corporation (HOLC) had authority to borrow money to refinance home mortgages and thus prevent foreclosures. Eventually it lent over $3 billion to over 1 million home owners.

Gold was taken out of circulation following the president's order of March 6, and the nation went off the gold standard. Eventually, on January 31, 1934, the value of the dollar was set at $35 per ounce of gold, 59 percent of its former value. The object of the devaluation was to raise prices and help American exports.

Later Economic Legislation of the First New Deal

The Securities and Exchange Commission was created in 1934 to supervise stock exchanges and to punish fraud in securities trading.

The Federal Housing Administration (FHA) was created by Congress in 1934 to insure long-term, low-interest mortgages for home construction and repair.

Relief and Employment Programs of the Hundred Days

Roosevelt's relief and employment programs were intended to provide temporary relief for people in need, and to be disbanded when the economy improved.

The Federal Emergency Relief Act appropriated $500 million for aid to the poor to be distributed by state and local governments. Half of the funds were to be distributed on a one to three matching basis with the states. It also established the Federal Emergency Relief Administration under Harry Hopkins. Additional appropriations were made many times later.

The Civilian Conservation Corps enrolled 250,000 young men ages 18 to 24 from families on relief to go to camps where they worked on flood control, soil conservation, and forest projects under the direction of the War Department. A small monthly payment was made to the family of each member. By the end of the decade, 2.75 million young men had served in the corps.

The Public Works Administration, under Secretary of the Interior Harold Ickes, had $3.3 billion to distribute to state and local governments for building projects such as schools, highways, and hospitals. The object was to "prime the pump" of the economy by creating construction jobs. Additional money was appropriated later.

Later Relief Efforts

After the Hundred Days, in November 1933, Roosevelt established the Civil Works Administration under Harry Hopkins with $400 million from the Public Works Administration to hire four million unemployed workers. The temporary and makeshift nature of the jobs, such as sweeping streets, brought much criticism, and the experiment was terminated in April 1934.

Agricultural Programs of the Hundred Days

The Agricultural Adjustment Act of 1933 created the Agricultural Adjustment Administration (AAA), which was headed by George Peek. It sought to return farm prices to parity with those of the 1909 to 1914 period. Farmers agreed to reduce production of principal farm commodities and were paid a subsidy in return. The money came from a tax on the processing of the commodities. Farm prices increased, but tenants and sharecroppers were hurt when owners took land out of cultivation. The law was declared unconstitutional in January 1936 on the grounds that the processing tax was not constitutional.

The Federal Farm Loan Act consolidated all farm credit programs into the Farm Credit Administration to make low-interest loans for farm mortgages and other agricultural purposes.

Later Agricultural Programs

The Commodity Credit was established in October 1933 by the AAA to make loans to corn and cotton farmers against their crops so that they could hold them for higher prices.

The Frazier-Lemke Farm Bankruptcy Act of 1934 allowed farmers to defer foreclosure on their land while they obtained new financing, and helped them to recover property already lost through easy financing.

The National Industrial Recovery Act

The National Industrial Recovery Act, passed on June 16, 1933, the last day of the Hundred Days, was viewed as the cornerstone of the recovery program. It sought to stabilize the economy by preventing extreme competition, labor-management conflicts, and over-production. A board composed of industrial and labor leaders in each industry or business drew up a code for that industry which set minimum prices, minimum wages, maximum work hours, production limits, and quotas. The antitrust laws were temporarily suspended. The approach was based on the idea of many economists at the time; because a mature industrial economy produced more goods than could be consumed, it would be necessary to create a relative shortage of goods in order to raise prices and restore prosperity. The idea was proved wrong by the expansion of consumer goods after World War II. Section 7a of the law also provided that workers had the right to join unions and to bargain collectively. The National Recovery Administration (NRA) was created under the leadership of Hugh S. Johnson to enforce the law and generate public enthusiasm for it. In May 1935 the law was declared unconstitutional in the case of *Schechter v. United States*, on the grounds that Congress had delegated legislative authority to the code-makers, and that Schechter, who slaughtered chickens in New York, was not engaged in interstate commerce. It was argued later that the NRA had unintentionally aided big firms to the detriment of smaller ones because the representatives of the larger firms tended to dominate the code-making process. It was generally unsuccessful in stabilizing small businesses such as retail stores, and was on the point of collapse when it was declared unconstitutional.

The Tennessee Valley Authority

Different from the other legislation of the Hundred Days which addressed immediate problems of the depression, the Tennessee Valley Authority, a public corporation under a three-member board, was proposed by Roosevelt as the first major experiment in regional public planning. Starting from the nucleus of the government's Muscle Shoals property on the Tennessee River, the TVA built 20 dams in an area of 40,000 square miles to stop flooding and soil erosion, improve navigation, and generate hydroelectric power. It also manufactured nitrates for fertilizer, conducted demonstration projects for farmers, engaged in reforestation, and attempted to rehabilitate the whole area. It was fought unsuccessfully in the courts by private power companies. Roosevelt believed that it would serve as a yardstick to measure the true cost of providing electric power.

Effects of the First New Deal

The economy improved but remained far from recovered between 1933 and 1935. The gross national product rose from $74.2 billion in 1933 to $91.4 billion in 1935. Manufacturing salaries and wages increased from $6.24 billion in 1933 to over $9.5 billion in 1935, with average weekly earnings going from $16.73 to $20.13. Farm income rose from $1.9 billion in 1933 to $4.6 billion in 1935. The money supply, as currency and demand deposits, grew from $19.2 billion to $25.2 billion. Unemployment dropped from about 25 percent of nonfarm workers in 1933 to about 20.1 percent, or 10.6 million, in 1935. While the figure had improved, it was a long way from the 3.2 percent of pre-depression 1929, and suffering as a result of unemployment was still a major problem.

THE SECOND NEW DEAL: OPPOSITION FROM THE RIGHT AND LEFT

FDR Weathers Criticism

The partial economic recovery brought about by the first New Deal provoked criticism from the right for doing too much, and from the left for doing too little. Conservatives and businessmen criticized the deficit financing, which accounted for about half of the federal budget, federal spending for relief, and government regulation of business. They frequently charged that the New Deal was socialist or communist in form, and some conservative writers labeled the wealthy Roosevelt "a traitor to his class." People on the lower end of the economic scale thought that the New Deal, especially the NRA, was too favorable to big business. Small-business people and union members complained that the NRA codes gave control of industry to the big firms, while farmers complained that the NRA set prices too high. The elderly thought that nothing had been done to help them. Several million people who were or had been tenant farmers or sharecroppers were badly hurt. When the AAA paid farmers to take land out of production, the landowners took the money while the tenants and sharecroppers lost their livelihood. Several opposition organizations and persons were particularly active in opposing Roosevelt's policies.

The American Liberty League was formed in 1934 by conservatives to defend business interests and promote the open shop. While many of its members were Republicans and it was financed primarily by the Du Pont family, it also attracted conservative Democrats like Alfred E. Smith and John W. Davis. It supported conservative congressional candidates of both parties in the election of 1934 with little success.

The Old Age Revolving Pension Plan was advanced by Dr. Francis E. Townsend, a retired California physician. The plan proposed that every retired person over sixty receive a pension of $200 a month, about double the average worker's salary, with the requirement that the money be spent within the month. The plan would be funded by a national gross sales tax. Townsend claimed that it would end the depression by putting money into circulation, but economists thought it fiscally impossible. Some three to five million older Americans joined Townsend Clubs.

The Share Our Wealth Society was founded in 1934 by Senator Huey "The Kingfish" Long of Louisiana. Long was a populist demagogue who was elected governor of Louisiana in 1928, established a practical dictatorship over the state, and moved to the United States Senate in 1930. He supported Roosevelt in 1932, but then broke with him, calling him a tool of Wall Street for not doing more to combat the depression. Long called for the confiscation of all fortunes over five million dollars and a tax of one hundred percent on annual incomes over one million. With the money, the government would provide subsidies so that every family would have a "homestead" of house, car, and furnishings worth at least $5,000, a minimum annual income of $2,000, and free college education for those who wanted it. His slogan was "Every Man a King." Long talked of running for president in 1936, and published a book entitled My First Days in the White House. His society had over five million members when he was assassinated on the steps of the Louisiana Capitol on September 8, 1935. The Reverend Gerald L.K. Smith appointed himself Long's successor as head of the society, but he lacked Long's ability.

The National Union for Social Justice was headed by Father Charles E. Coughlin, a Catholic priest in Royal Oak, Michigan, who had a weekly radio program. Beginning as a religious broadcast in 1926, Coughlin turned to politics and finance, and attracted an audience of millions of many faiths. He supported Roosevelt in 1932, but then turned against him. He advocated an inflationary currency and was anti-Semitic, but beyond that his fascist-like program was not clearly defined.

THE SECOND NEW DEAL BEGINS

Roosevelt's Position

With millions of Democratic voters under the sway of Townsend, Long, and Coughlin, with the destruction of the NRA by the Supreme Court imminent, and with the election of 1936 approaching the next year, Roosevelt began to push through a series of new programs in the spring of 1935. Much of the legislation was passed during the summer of 1935, a period sometimes called the Second Hundred Days.

Legislation and Programs of the Second New Deal

The Works Progress Administration (WPA) was started in May 1935 following the passage of the Emergency Relief Appropriations Act of April 1935. Headed by Harry Hopkins, the WPA employed people from the relief rolls for thirty hours of work a week at pay double the relief payment but less than private employment. There was not enough money to hire all of the unemployed, and the numbers varied from time to time, but an average of 2.1 million people per month were employed. By the end of the program in 1941, 8.5 million people had worked at some time for the WPA at a total cost of $11.4 billion. Most of the projects undertaken were in construction. The WPA built hundreds of thousands of miles of streets and roads, and thousands of schools, hospitals, parks, airports, playgrounds, and other facilities. Hand work was emphasized so that the money would go for pay rather than equipment, provoking much criticism for inefficiency. Unemployed artists painted murals in public buildings; actors, musicians, and dancers performed in poor neighborhoods; and writers compiled guide books and local histories.

The National Youth Administration (NYA) was established as part of the WPA in June 1935 to provide part-time jobs for high school and college students to enable them to stay in school, and to help young adults not in school to find jobs.

The Rural Electrification Administration (REA) was created in May 1935 to provide loans and WPA labor to electric cooperatives to build lines into rural areas not served by private companies.

The Resettlement Administration (RA) was created in the Agriculture Department in May 1935 under Rexford Tugwell. It relocated destitute families from seemingly hopeless situations to new rural homestead communities or to suburban greenbelt towns.

The National Labor Relations or Wagner Act was passed in May 1935 to replace the provisions of Section 7a of the NIRA. It reaffirmed labor's right to unionize, prohibited unfair labor practices, and created the National Labor Relations Board (NLRB) to oversee and insure fairness in labor-management relations.

The landmark Social Security Act was passed in August 1935. It established a retirement plan for persons over age sixty-five funded by a tax on wages paid equally by employee and employer. The first benefits, ranging from $10 to $85 per month, were paid in 1942. Another provision of the act had the effect of forcing the states to initiate unemployment insurance programs. It imposed a payroll tax on employers which went to the state if it had an insurance program, and to the federal government if it did not. The act also provided matching funds to the states for aid to the blind, handicapped, and dependent children, and for public health services. The American Social Security system was limited compared with those of other industrialized nations, and millions of workers were not covered by it. Nonetheless, it marked a major change in American policy.

The Banking Act of 1935 created a strong central Board of Governors of the Federal Reserve System with broad powers over the operations of the regional banks.

The Public Utility Holding Company or Wheeler-Rayburn Act of 1935 empowered the Securities and Exchange Commission to restrict public utility holding companies to one natural region and to eliminate duplicate holding companies. The Federal Power Commission was created to regulate interstate electrical power rates and activities, and the Federal Trade Commission received the same kind of power over the natural gas companies.

The Revenue Act of 1935 increased income taxes on higher incomes, and also inheritance, large gift, and capital gains taxes.

The Motor Carrier Act of 1935 extended the regulatory authority of the Interstate Commerce Commission to cover interstate trucking lines.

THE ELECTION OF 1936

The Democrats

At the convention in Philadelphia in June, Roosevelt and Garner were renominated by acclamation on the first ballot. The convention also ended the requirement for a two-thirds vote for nomination. The platform promised an expanded farm program, labor legislation, more rural electrification and public housing, and enforcement of the antitrust laws. In his acceptance speech Roosevelt declared that "this generation of Americans has a rendezvous with destiny." He further proclaimed that he and the American people were fighting for democracy and capitalism against the "economic royalists," business people he charged with seeking only their own power and wealth, and opposing the New Deal.

The Republicans

Governor Alfred M. Landon of Kansas, a former progressive supporter of Theodore Roosevelt, was nominated on the first ballot at the convention in Cleveland in June. Frank Knox, a Chicago newspaper publisher, was chosen as his running mate. The platform criticized the New Deal for operating under unconstitutional laws, and called for a balanced budget, higher tariffs, and lower corporate taxes. It did not call for the repeal of all New Deal legislation, and promised better and less expensive relief, farm, and labor programs. In effect, Landon and the Republicans were saying that they would do about the same thing, but do it better.

The Union Party

Dr. Francis Townsend, Father Charles Coughlin, and the Reverend Gerald L. K. Smith, Long's successor in the Share Our Wealth Society, organized the Union Party to oppose Roosevelt. The nominee was Congressman William Lemke of North Dakota, an advocate of radical farm legislation but a bland campaigner. Vicious attacks by Smith and Coughlin on Roosevelt brought a backlash against them, and American Catholic leaders denounced Coughlin.

The Election

Roosevelt carried all of the states except Maine and Vermont with 27,757,333 votes, or 60.8 percent of the total, and 523 electoral votes. Landon received 16,684,231 votes and 8 electoral votes. Lemke had 891,858 votes for 1.9 percent of the total. Norman Thomas, the Socialist candidate, received 187,000 votes, only 21 percent of the 881,951 votes he received in 1932.

The New Deal Coalition

Roosevelt had put together a coalition of followers who made the Democratic Party the majority party in the nation for the first time since the Civil War. While retaining the Democratic base in the Solid South and among white ethnics in the big cities, Roosevelt also received strong support from Midwestern farmers. Two groups which made a dramatic shift into the Democratic ranks were union workers and blacks. Unions took an active political role for the first time since 1924, providing both campaign funds and votes. Blacks had traditionally been Republican since emancipation, but by 1936 about three-fourths of the black voters, who lived mainly in the Northern cities, had shifted into the Democratic Party.

THE LAST YEARS OF THE NEW DEAL

Court Packing

Frustrated by a conservative Supreme Court which had overturned much of his New Deal legislation, Roosevelt, after receiving his overwhelming mandate in the election of 1936, decided to curb the power of the court. In doing so, he overestimated his own political power and underestimated the force of tradition. In February 1937 he proposed to Congress the Judicial Reorganization Bill which would allow the president to name a new federal judge for each judge who did not retire by the age of 70 ½. The appointments would be limited to a maximum of fifty, with no more than six added to the Supreme Court. At the time, six justices were over the proposed age limit. Roosevelt cited a slowing of the judicial process due to the infirmity of the incumbents, and the need for a modern outlook. The president was astonished by the wave of opposition from Democrats and Republicans alike, and uncharacteristically refused to compromise. In doing so, he not only lost the bill but he lost control of the Democratic Congress which he had dominated since 1933. Nonetheless, the Court changed its position as Chief Justice Charles Evans Hughes and Justice Owen Roberts began to vote with the more liberal members. The National Labor Relations Act was upheld in March 1937, and the Social Security Act in April. In June a conservative justice retired, and Roosevelt had the opportunity to make an appointment.

The Recession of 1937–1938

Most economic indicators rose sharply between 1935 and 1937. The gross national product had recovered to the 1930 level, and unemployment, if WPA workers were considered employed, had fallen to 9.2 percent. Average yearly earnings of the employed had risen from $1,195 in 1935 to $1,341 in 1937, and average hourly manufacturing earnings from 55 cents to 62 cents. During the same period there were huge federal deficits. In fiscal 1936, for example, there was a deficit of $4.4 billion in a budget of $8.5 billion. Roosevelt decided that the recovery was sufficient to warrant a reduction in relief programs and a move toward a balanced budget. The budget for fiscal 1938, from July 1937 to June 1938, was reduced to $6.8 billion, with the WPA experiencing the largest cut. During the winter of 1937–1938 the economy slipped rapidly and unemployment rose to 12.5 percent. In April 1938 Roosevelt requested and received from Congress an emergency appropriation of about $3 billion for the WPA, as well as increases for public works and other programs. In July 1938 the economy began to recover, and it regained the 1937 levels in 1939.

Legislation of the Late New Deal

With the threat of adverse Supreme Court rulings removed, Roosevelt rounded out his program during the late 1930s.

The Bankhead-Jones Farm Tenancy Act, passed in July 1937, created the Farm Security Administration (FSA) to replace the Resettlement Administration. The FSA continued the homestead projects, and loaned money to farmers to purchase farms, lease land, and buy equipment. It also set up camps for migrant workers and established rural health care programs.

The National Housing, or Wagner-Steagall Act, passed in September 1937, established the United States Housing Authority (USHA) which could borrow money to lend to local agencies for public housing projects. By 1941 it had loaned $750 million for 511 projects.

The Second Agricultural Adjustment Act of February 1938 appropriated funds for soil conservation payments to farmers who would remove land from production. The law also empowered the Agriculture Department to impose market quotas to prevent surpluses in cotton, wheat, corn, tobacco, and rice if two-thirds of the farmers producing that commodity agreed.

The Fair Labor Standards Act, popularly called the minimum wage law, was passed in June 1938. It provided for a minimum wage of 25 cents an hour which would gradually rise to 40 cents, and a gradual reduction to a work week of 40 hours, with time and a half for overtime. Workers in small businesses and in public and nonprofit employment were not covered. The law also prohibited the shipment in interstate commerce of manufactured goods on which children under 16 worked.

SOCIAL DIMENSIONS OF THE NEW DEAL ERA

Blacks and the New Deal

Blacks suffered more than other people from the depression. Unemployment rates were much higher than for the general population, and before 1933 they were often excluded from state and local relief efforts. Blacks did benefit from many New Deal relief programs, but about forty percent of black workers were sharecroppers or tenants who suffered from the provisions of the first Agricultural Adjustment Act. Roosevelt seems to have given little thought to the special problems of black people, and he was afraid to endorse legislation such as an anti-lynching bill for fear of alienating the southern wing of the Democratic party. Eleanor Roosevelt and Harold Ickes strongly supported civil rights, and a "Black Cabinet" of advisors was assembled in the Interior Department. More blacks were appointed to government positions by Roosevelt than ever before, but the number was still small. When government military contracts began to flow in 1941, A. Philip Randolph, the president of the Brotherhood of Sleeping Car Porters, proposed a black march on Washington to demand equal access to defense jobs. To forestall such an action, Roosevelt issued an executive order on June 25, 1941, establishing the Fair Employment Practices Committee to insure consideration for minorities in defense employment.

Native Americans and the New Deal

John Collier, the commissioner of the Bureau of Indian Affairs, persuaded Congress to repeal the Dawes Act of 1887 by passing the Indian Reorganization Act of 1934. The law restored tribal ownership of lands, recognized tribal constitutions and government, and provided loans to tribes for economic development. Collier also secured the creation of the Indian Emergency Conservation Program, a Native American CCC for projects on the reservations. In addition, he helped Native Americans secure entry into the WPA, NYA, and other programs.

Mexican Americans and the New Deal

Mexican Americans benefitted the least from the New Deal, for few programs covered them. Farm owners turned against them as farm workers after they attempted to form a union between 1933 and 1936. By 1940 most had been replaced by whites dispossessed by the depression. Many returned to Mexico, and the Mexican American population dropped almost forty percent from 1930 to 1940.

Women During the New Deal

The burden of the depression fell on women as much or more as it did on men. Wives and mothers found themselves responsible for stretching meager budgets by preparing inexpensive meals, patching old clothing, and the like. "Making do" became a slogan of the period. In addition, more women had to supplement or provide the family income by going to work. In 1930 there were 10.5 million working women comprising 29 percent of the work force. By 1940 the figures had grown to over 13 million and 35 percent. There was much criticism of working women based on the idea that they deprived men of jobs. Male job losses were greatest in heavy industry such as factories and mills, while areas of female employment such as retail sales were not hit as hard. Unemployed men seldom sought jobs in the traditional women's fields.

LABOR UNIONS

Unions During the First New Deal

Labor unions had lost members and influence during the twenties, and slipped further during the economic decline of 1929 to 1933. The National Industrial Recovery Act gave them new hope when Section 7a guaranteed the right to unionize, and during 1933 about 1.5 million new members joined unions. It soon became clear that enforcement of the industrial codes by the NRA was ineffective, and labor leaders began to call it the "National Run Around." As a result in 1934 there were many strikes, sometimes violent, including a general strike in San Francisco involving about 125,000 workers.

Craft Versus Industrial Unions

The passage of the National Labor Relations, or Wagner, Act in 1935 resulted in a massive growth of union membership, but only at the expense of bitter conflict within the labor movement. The American Federation of Labor was made up primarily of craft unions. Some leaders, especially John L. Lewis, the dynamic president of the United Mine Workers, wanted to unionize the mass production industries, such as automobiles and rubber, with industrial unions. In 1934 the AFL convention authorized such unions, but the older unions continued to try to organize workers in those industries by crafts. In November 1935 Lewis and others established the Committee for Industrial Organization to unionize basic industries, presumably within the AFL. President William Green of the AFL ordered the CIO to disband in January 1936. When the rebels refused, they were expelled by the AFL executive council in March 1937. The insurgents then reorganized the CIO as the independent Congress of Industrial Organizations to be composed of industrial unions.

The Growth of the CIO

During its organizational period the CIO sought to initiate several industrial unions, particularly in the steel, auto, rubber, and radio industries. In late 1936 and early 1937 it used a tactic called the sit-down strike, with the strikers occupying the workplace to prevent any production. There were 477 sit-down strikes involving about 400,000 workers. The largest was in the General Motors plant in Flint, Michigan, as the union sought recognition by that firm. In February 1937 General Motors recognized the United Auto Workers as the bargaining agent for its 400,000 workers. When the CIO established its independence in March 1937, it already had 1.8 million members, and it reached a membership of 3.75 million six months later. The AFL had about 3.4 million members at that time. By the end of 1941 the CIO had about 5 million members, the AFL about 4.6 million, and other unions about one million. Union members comprised about 11.5 percent of the work force in 1933, and 28.2 percent in 1941.

CULTURAL TRENDS OF THE 1930s

Literary Developments

The writers and intellectuals who had expressed disdain for the middle class materialism of the 1920s found it even more difficult to deal with the meaning of the crushing poverty in America and the rise of fascism in Europe during the 1930s. Some turned to communism, including the fifty-three writers who signed an open letter endorsing the Communist presidential candidate in 1932. Some turned to proletarian novels, such as Jack Conroy in *The Disinherited* (1933) and Robert Cantwell in *The Land of Plenty* (1934). Ernest Hemingway seemed to have lost his direction in *Winner Take All* (1933) and *The Green Hills of Africa* (1935), but in *To Have and Have Not* (1937), a strike novel, he turned to social realism, and *For Whom the Bell Tolls* (1941) expressed his concern about fascism. Sinclair Lewis also dealt with fascism in *It Can't Happen Here* (1935), but did not show the power of his works of the 1920s. John Dos Passos depicted what he saw as the disintegration of American life from 1900 to 1929 in his trilogy *U.S.A.* (1930–1936). William Faulkner sought values in Southern life in *Light in August* (1932), *Absalom! Absalom!* (1936), and *The Unvanquished* (1938). The endurance of the human spirit and personal survival were depicted in James T. Farrell's trilogy *Studs Lonigan* (1936) about the struggles of lower-middle-class Irish Catholics in Chicago, while Erskine Caldwell's *Tobacco Road* (1932) dealt with impoverished Georgia sharecroppers, and John Steinbeck's *The Grapes of Wrath* (1939) depicted "Okies" migrating from the dust bowl to California in the midst of the depression.

Popular Culture

The depression greatly reduced the amount of money available for recreation and entertainment. There was an increase in games and sports among family groups and friends. The WPA and the CCC constructed thousands of playgrounds, playing fields, picnic areas, and the like for public use. Roosevelt and Harry Hopkins, the director of the WPA, hoped to develop a mass appreciation of culture through the WPA murals in public buildings, with traveling plays, concerts, and exhibits, and with community arts centers. Beyond some revival of handicrafts, it is doubtful that the program had much effect. There were, however, several popular forms of entertainment.

Radio was the favorite form of daily entertainment during the depression because, after the initial cost of the instrument, it was free. There were about forty million radios in the United States by 1938. It provided comedy and mystery shows, music, sports and news. A study at the time indicated that radio tended to make Americans more uniform in their attitudes, taste, speech, and humor.

While radio was the form of entertainment most used, the movies were the most popular. By 1939 about 65 percent of the people went to the movies at least once a week. The movie industry was one of the few which did not suffer financially from the depression. Movies were the great means of escape, providing release from the pressures of the depression by transporting people to a make-believe world of beauty, mystery, or excitement. Spectacular musicals with dozens of dancers and singers, such as *Broadway Melody of 1936*, were popular. The dance team of Fred Astaire and Ginger Rogers thrilled millions in *Flying Down to Rio* and *Shall We Dance?* Shirley Temple charmed the public as their favorite child star. Judy Garland rose to stardom in *The Wizard of Oz*, while animated films like *Snow White* appealed to children of all ages. People enjoyed the triumph of justice and decency in *Mr. Smith Goes to Washington* and *You Can't Take It with You* with Jimmy Stewart. Dozens of light comedies starred such favorites as Cary Grant, Katharine Hepburn, Clark Gable, and Rosalind Russell, while Errol Flynn played in such larger-than-life roles as Robin Hood. A different kind of escape was found in gangster movies with Edward G. Robinson, James Cagney, or George Raft. Near the end of the decade *Gone with the Wind*, released in 1939 starring Clark Gable and Vivien Leigh, became a timeless classic, while *The Grapes of Wrath* in 1940 commented on the depression itself.

The popular music of the decade was swing, and the big bands of Duke Ellington, Benny Goodman, Glenn Miller, Tommy Dorsey, and Harry James vied for public favor. The leading popular singer was Bing Crosby. City African Americans refined the country blues to city blues, and interracial audiences enjoyed both city blues and jazz. African American musicians were increasingly accepted by white audiences.

Comic strips existed before the thirties, but they became a standard newspaper feature as well as a source of comic books during the decade. "Dick Tracy" began his war on crime in 1931, and was assisted by "Superman" after 1938. "Tarzan" began to swing through the cartoon jungles in 1929, and "Buck Rogers" began the exploration of space in 1930.

NEW DEAL DIPLOMACY AND THE ROAD TO WAR

The Good Neighbor Policy

Roosevelt and Secretary of State Cordell Hull continued the policies of their predecessors in endeavoring to improve relations with Latin American nations, and formalized their position by calling it the Good Neighbor Policy.

Nonintervention

At the Montevideo Conference of American Nations in December of 1933 the United States renounced the right of intervention in the internal affairs of Latin American countries. In 1936, in the Buenos Aires Convention, the United States further agreed to submit all American disputes to arbitration. Accordingly, the Marines were removed from Haiti, Nicaragua, and the Dominican Republic by 1934. The Haitian protectorate treaty was allowed to expire in 1936, the right of intervention in Panama was ended by treaty in 1936, and the receivership of the finances of the Dominican Republic ended in 1941.

Cuba

The United States did not intervene in the Cuban revolution in the spring of 1933, but it did back a coup by Fulgencio Batista to overthrow the liberal regime of Ramon Grau San Martin in 1934. Batista was given a favorable sugar import status for Cuba in return for establishing a conservative administration. In May 1934 the United States abrogated its Platt Amendment rights in Cuba except for control of the Guantanamo Naval Base.

Mexico

The Mexican government of Lazaro Cardenas began to expropriate American property, including oil holdings, in 1934. Despite calls for intervention, Roosevelt insisted only on compensation. A joint commission worked out a settlement which was formally concluded on November 19, 1941.

The London Economic Conference

An international conference in London in June 1933 tried to obtain tariff reduction and currency stabilization for the industrialized nations. Roosevelt would not agree to peg the value of the dollar to other currencies because he feared that it might impede his recovery efforts. The conference failed for lack of American cooperation.

Recognition of Russia

The United States had not had diplomatic relations with the Union of Soviet Socialist Republics since it was established after the 1917 revolution. In an effort to open trade with Russia, mutual recognition was negotiated in November 1933. The financial results were disappointing.

Philippine Independence

The Tydings-McDuffie Act of March 1934 forced the Philippines to become independent on July 4, 1946, rather than granting the dominion status which the Filipinos had requested.

The Reciprocal Trade Agreement Act

The Reciprocal Trade Agreement, the idea of Cordell Hull, was passed in June 1934. It allowed the president to negotiate agreements which could vary from the rates of the Hawley-Smoot Tariff up to 50 percent. By 1936 lower rates had been negotiated with 13 nations, and by 1941 almost two-thirds of all American foreign trade was covered by agreements.

UNITED STATES NEUTRALITY LEGISLATION

Isolationism

Belief that the United States should stay out of foreign wars and problems began in the 1920s and grew in the 1930s. It was fed by House and Senate investigations of arms traffic and the munitions industry in 1933 and 1934, especially an examination of profiteering by bankers and munitions makers in drawing the United States into World War I by Senator Gerald Nye of North Dakota. Books of revisionist history which asserted that Germany had not been responsible for World War I and that the United States had been misled were also influential during the 1930s. A Gallup poll in April 1937 showed that almost two-thirds of those responding thought that American entry into World War I had been a mistake. Such feelings were strongest in the Midwest and among Republicans, but were found in all areas and across the political spectrum. Leading isolationists included Congressman Hamilton Fish of New York, Senator William Borah of Idaho, and Senator George Norris of Nebraska, all Republicans. Pacifist movements, such as the Fellowship of Christian Reconciliation, were influential among college and high school students and the clergy.

The Johnson Act of 1934

When European nations stopped payment on World War I debts to the United States, the Johnson Act of 1934 prohibited any nation in default from selling securities to any American citizen or corporation.

The Neutrality Acts of 1935

Isolationist sentiment prompted Senator Key Pittman, a Nevada Democrat, to propose these laws. Roosevelt would have preferred more presidential flexibility, but Congress wanted to avoid flexibility and the mistakes of World War I. The laws provided that, on outbreak of war between foreign nations, all exports of American arms and munitions to them would be embargoed for six months. In addition, American ships were prohibited from carrying arms to any belligerent, and the president was to warn American citizens not to travel on belligerent ships.

The Neutrality Acts of 1936

The Neutrality Acts of 1936 gave the president authority to determine when a state of war existed, and prohibited any loans or credits to belligerents.

The Neutrality Acts of 1937

The Neutrality Acts of 1937 gave the president authority to determine if a civil war was a threat to world peace and covered by the Neutrality Acts, prohibited all arms sales to belligerents, and allowed the cash and carry sale of nonmilitary goods to belligerents.

THREATS TO WORLD ORDER

The Manchurian Crisis

In September 1931 the Japanese army invaded and seized the Chinese province of Manchuria. The action violated the Nine Power Pact and the Kellogg-Briand Pact. When the League of Nations sought consideration of some action against Japan, Hoover refused to consider either economic or military sanctions. The only American action was to refuse recognition of the action or the puppet state of Manchukuo which the Japanese created.

Ethiopia

Following a border skirmish between Italian and Ethiopian troops, the Italian army of Fascist dictator Benito Mussolini invaded Ethiopia from neighboring Italian colonies in October 1935. The League of Nations failed to take effective action, the United States looked on, and Ethiopia fell in May 1936.

Occupation of the Rhineland

In defiance of the Versailles Treaty, Nazi dictator Adolf Hitler sent his German army into the demilitarized Rhineland in March 1936.

The Rome-Berlin Axis

Germany and Italy, under Hitler and Mussolini, formed an alliance called the Rome-Berlin Axis on October 25, 1936.

The Sino-Japanese War

The Japanese launched a full-scale invasion of China in July 1937. When Japanese planes sank the American Gunboat *Panay* and three Standard Oil tankers on the Yangtze River in December 1937, the United States accepted a

Japanese apology and damage payments while the American public called for the withdrawal of all American forces from China.

The "Quarantine the Aggressor" Speech

In a speech in Chicago in October 1937 Roosevelt proposed that the democracies unite to quarantine the aggressor nations. When public opinion did not pick up on the idea, he did not press the issue.

German Expansion

Hitler brought about a union of Germany and Austria in March 1938, took the German-speaking Sudetenland from Czechoslovakia in September 1938, and occupied the rest of Czechoslovakia in March 1939.

The Invasion of Poland and the Beginning of World War II

On August 24, 1939, Germany signed a nonaggression pact with Russia which contained a secret provision to divide Poland between them. German forces then invaded Poland on September 1, 1939. Britain and France declared war on Germany on September 3 because of their treaties with Poland. By the end of September Poland had been dismembered by Germany and Russia, but the war continued in the west along the French-German border.

THE AMERICAN RESPONSE TO THE WAR IN EUROPE

Preparedness

Even before the outbreak of World War II, Roosevelt began a preparedness program to improve American defenses. In May 1938 he requested and received a naval construction appropriation of about one billion dollars. In October, Congress provided an additional $300 million for defense, and in January 1939 a regular defense appropriation of $1.3 billion with an added $525 million for equipment, especially airplanes. Defense spending increased after the outbreak of war. In August 1939 Roosevelt created the War Resources Board to develop a plan for industrial mobilization in the event of war. The next month he established the Office of Emergency Management in the White House to centralize mobilization activities.

The Neutrality Act of 1939

Roosevelt officially proclaimed the neutrality of the United States on September 5, 1939. He then called Congress into special session on September 21 and urged it to allow the cash-and-carry sale of arms. Despite opposition from isolationists, the Democratic Congress, in a vote that followed party lines, passed a new Neutrality Act in November. It allowed the cash-and-carry sale of arms and short-term loans to belligerents, but forbade American ships to trade with belligerents or Americans to travel on belligerent ships. The new law was helpful to the Allies because they controlled the Atlantic.

Changing American Attitudes

Hitler's armies invaded and quickly conquered Denmark and Norway in April 1940. In May, German forces swept through the Netherlands, Belgium, Luxembourg, and France. The British were driven from the continent, and France surrendered on June 22. Almost all Americans recognized Germany as a threat. They divided on whether to aid Britain or to concentrate on the defense of America. The Committee to Defend America by Aiding the Allies was formed in May 1940, and the America First Committee, which opposed involvement, was incorporated in September 1940.

Greenland

In April 1940 Roosevelt declared that Greenland, a possession of conquered Denmark, was covered by the Monroe Doctrine, and he supplied military assistance to set up a coastal patrol there.

Defense Mobilization

In May 1940 Roosevelt appointed a Council of National Defense chaired by William S. Knudson, the president of General Motors, to direct defense production and especially to build fifty thousand planes. The Council was soon awarding defense contracts at the rate of $1.5 billion a month. The Office of Production Management was created to allocate scarce materials, and the Office of Price Administration was established to prevent inflation and protect consumers. In June, Roosevelt made Republicans Henry L. Stimson and Frank Knox secretaries of war and the Navy, respectively, partly as an attempt to secure bipartisan support.

Selective Service

Congress approved the nation's first peacetime draft, the Selective Service and Training Act, in September 1940. Men ages 21 to 35 were registered, and many were called for one year of military training.

Destroyers for Bases

Roosevelt had determined that to aid Britain in every way possible was the best way to avoid war with Germany. He ordered the army and navy to turn over all available weapons and munitions to private dealers for resale to Britain. In September 1940 he signed an agreement to give Britain fifty American destroyers in return for a 99-year lease on air and naval bases in British territories in Newfoundland, Bermuda, and the Caribbean.

THE ELECTION OF 1940

The Republicans

Passing over their isolationist front-runners, Senator Robert A. Taft of Ohio and New York attorney Thomas E. Dewey, the Republicans nominated Wendell L. Willkie of Indiana, a dark horse candidate. Willkie was a liberal Republican who had been a Democrat most of his life, and the head of an electric utility holding company which had fought against the TVA. The platform supported a strong defense program, but severely criticized the New Deal domestic policies.

The Democrats

Roosevelt did not reveal his intentions regarding a third term, but he neither endorsed another candidate nor discouraged his supporters. When the convention came in July, he sent a message to the Democratic National Committee implying that he would accept the nomination for a third time if it were offered. He was then nominated on the first ballot, breaking a tradition which had existed since the time of Washington. Only with difficulty did Roosevelt's managers persuade the delegates to accept his choice of vice president, Secretary of Agriculture Henry A. Wallace, to succeed Garner. The platform endorsed the foreign and domestic policies of the administration.

The Campaign

Willkie's basic agreement with Roosevelt's foreign policy made it difficult for him to campaign. Willkie had a folksy approach which appealed to many voters, but he first attacked Roosevelt for the slowness of the defense program, and then, late in the campaign, called him a warmonger. Roosevelt, who lost the support of many Democrats, including his adviser James Farley, over the third term issue, campaigned very little. When Willkie began to gain on the warmongering issue, Roosevelt declared on October 30 that "your boys are not going to be sent into any foreign wars."

The Election

Roosevelt won by a much narrower margin than in 1936, with 27,243,466 votes, 54.7 percent, and 449 electoral votes. Willkie received 22,304,755 votes and 82 electoral votes. Socialist Norman Thomas had 100,264 votes, and Communist Earl Browder received 48,579.

AMERICAN INVOLVEMENT WITH THE EUROPEAN WAR

The Lend-Lease Act

The British were rapidly exhausting their cash reserves with which to buy American goods. In January 1941 Roosevelt proposed that the United States provide supplies to be paid for in goods and services after the war. The Lend-Lease Act was passed by Congress and signed on March 11, 1941, and the first appropriation of $7 billion was provided. In effect, the law changed the United States from a neutral to a nonbelligerent on the Allied side.

The Patrol of the Western Atlantic

The Germans stepped up their submarine warfare in the Atlantic to prevent the flow of American supplies to Britain. In April 1941 Roosevelt started the American Neutrality Patrol. The American navy would search out but not attack German submarines in the western half of the Atlantic, and warn British vessels of their location.

Greenland

In April 1941, United States forces occupied Greenland and in May the president declared a state of unlimited national emergency.

Occupation of Iceland

American Marines occupied Iceland, a Danish possession, in July 1941 to protect it from seizure by Germany. The American Navy began to convoy American and Icelandic ships between the United States and Iceland.

The Atlantic Charter

On August 9, 1941, Roosevelt and Winston Churchill, the British prime minister, met for the first time on a British battleship off Newfoundland. They issued the Atlantic Charter, which described a postwar world based on self-determination for all nations. It also endorsed the principles of freedom of speech and religion and freedom from want and fear, which Roosevelt had proposed as the Four Freedoms earlier that year.

Aid to Russia

Germany invaded Russia in June 1941, and in November the United States extended lend-lease assistance to the Russians.

The Shoot-on-Sight Order

The American destroyer *Greer* was attacked by a German submarine near Iceland on September 4, 1941. Roosevelt ordered the American military forces to shoot on sight at any German or Italian vessel in the patrol zone. An undeclared naval war had begun. The American destroyer *Kearny* was attacked by a submarine on October 16, and the destroyer *Reuben James* was sunk on October 30, with 115 lives lost. In November, Congress authorized the arming of merchant ships.

THE ROAD TO PEARL HARBOR

A Japanese Empire

Following their invasion of China in 1937, the Japanese began to speak of the Greater East Asia Co-Prosperity Sphere, a Japanese empire of undefined boundaries in east Asia and the western Pacific. Accordingly, they forced out American and other business interests from occupied China, declaring that the Open Door policy had ended. Roosevelt responded by lending money to China and requesting American aircraft manufacturers not to sell to Japan.

The Embargo of 1940

Following the fall of France, a new and more militant Japanese government in July 1940 obtained from the German-controlled Vichy French government the right to build air bases and to station troops in northern French Indochina. The United States, fearing that the step would lead to further expansion, responded in late July by placing an embargo on the export of aviation gasoline, lubricants, and scrap iron and steel to Japan, and by granting an additional loan to China. In December the embargo was extended to include iron ore and pig iron, some chemicals, machine tools, and other products.

The Tripartite Pact

Japan joined with Germany and Italy to form the Rome-Berlin-Tokyo Axis on September 27, 1940, when it signed the Tripartite Pact or Triple Alliance with the other Axis powers.

The Embargo of 1941

In July 1941 Japan extracted a new concession from Vichy France by obtaining military control of southern Indochina. Roosevelt reacted by freezing Japanese funds in the United States, closing the Panama Canal to Japan, activating the Philippine militia, and placing an embargo on the export of oil and other vital products to Japan.

Japanese-American Negotiations

Negotiations to end the impasse between the United States and Japan were conducted in Washington between Secretary Hull and Japanese Ambassador Kichisaburo Nomura. Hull demanded that Japan withdraw from Indochina and China, promise not to attack any other area in the western Pacific, and withdraw from the Tripartite Pact in return for the reopening of American trade. The Japanese offered to withdraw from Indochina when the Chinese war was satisfactorily settled, to promise no further expansion, and to agree to ignore any obligation under the Tripartite Pact to go to war if the United States entered a defensive war with Germany. Hull refused to compromise.

A Summit Conference Proposed

The Japanese proposed in August 1941 that Roosevelt meet personally with the Japanese prime minister, Prince Konoye, in an effort to resolve their differences. Such an action might have strengthened the position of Japanese moderates, but Roosevelt replied in September that he would do so only if Japan agreed to leave China. No meeting was held.

Final Negotiations

In October 1941 a new military cabinet headed by General Hideki Tojo took control of Japan. The Japanese secretly decided to make a final effort to negotiate, and to go to war if no solution was found by November 25. A new round of talks followed in Washington, but neither side would make a substantive change in its position, and on November 26, Hull repeated the American demand that the Japanese remove all their forces from China and Indochina immediately. The Japanese gave final approval on December 1 for an attack on the United States.

Japanese Attack Plans

The Japanese planned a major offensive to take the Dutch East Indies, Malaya, and the Philippines in order to obtain the oil, metals, and other raw materials which they needed. At the same time they would attack Pearl Harbor in Hawaii to destroy the American Pacific fleet to keep it from interfering with their plans.

American Awareness of Japanese Plans

The United States had broken the Japanese diplomatic codes, and knew that trouble was imminent. Between December 1 and December 6, 1941, it became clear to administration leaders that Japanese task forces were being ordered into battle. American commanders in the Pacific were warned of possible aggressive action there, but not forcefully. Apparently most American leaders thought that Japan would attack the Dutch East Indies and Malaya, but would avoid American territory so as not to provoke action by the United States. Some argue that Roosevelt wanted to let the Japanese attack so that the American people would be squarely behind the war.

The Pearl Harbor Attack

At 7:55 a.m. on Sunday December 7, 1941, the first wave of Japanese carrier-based planes attacked the American fleet in Pearl Harbor. A second wave followed at 8:50 a.m. American defensive action was almost nil, but by the second wave a few anti-aircraft batteries were operating and a few Army planes from another base in Hawaii engaged the enemy. The United States suffered the loss of two battleships sunk, six damaged and out of action, three cruisers and three destroyers sunk or damaged, and a number of lesser vessels destroyed or damaged. All of the 150 aircraft at Pearl Harbor were destroyed on the ground. Worst of all, 2,323 American servicemen were killed and about 1,100 wounded. The Japanese lost 29 planes, five midget submarines, and one fleet submarine.

The Declaration of War

On December 8, 1941, Roosevelt told a joint session of Congress that the day before had been a "date that would live in infamy." Congress declared war on Japan with one dissenting vote. On December 11, Germany and Italy declared war on the United States.

HISTORICAL TIMELINE

The Great Depression and the New Deal (1929–1941)

1929	Agricultural Marketing Act attempts to support farm prices
1930	Hawley-Smoot Tariff raises duties on farm products and manufactured goods
1931	Japan invades Manchuria
1932	Reconstruction Finance Corporation attempts to support industry Bonus Expeditionary Force marches on Washington, D.C. Franklin Roosevelt wins presidency
1933	Prohibition repealed Hundred Days of legislation follows FDR's inauguration Banks closed after over 6,000 fail FDIC established by Glass-Steagall Act Agricultural Adjustment Act passed National Industrial Recovery Act passed Tennessee Valley Authority established Civilian Conservation Corps enrolls 250,000 young men Hitler becomes chancellor of Germany
1934	Securities and Exchange Commission established Huey Long begins Share Our Wealth clubs Dr. Francis Townsend promotes Old Age Revolving Pension Plan Nye Committee probes World War I profiteering by American industrialists
1935	*Schecter v. United States* rules NIRA unconstitutional Works Progress Administration established National Labor Relations (Wagner) Act protects workers' rights Social Security Act passed Congress passes first of annual Neutrality Acts

1936	FDR defeats Republican Landon and third-party Union Party for president General Motors sitdown strike Germany occupies the Rhineland Spanish Civil War begins Ethiopia falls to Italy
1937	FDR proposes court-packing plan, which fails Japan invades China U.S. gunship *Panay* sunk by Japanese in Yangtze River
1938	Appeasement at Munich by England's Chamberlain as Germany takes Sudetenland
1939	Czechoslovakia falls to Germany Austria votes to be annexed by Germany Germany invades Poland Neutrality Act allows cash-and-carry for military purchases Germany and Soviet Union sign nonaggression pact
1940	Germany conquers Denmark, Norway, the Netherlands, Belgium, and France Congress approves first peace-time draft U.S. and Great Britain sign destroyers for bases deal America First Committee established, urging U.S. neutrality Italy, Germany, and Japan form the Rome-Berlin-Tokyo Axis FDR wins unprecedented third term for president
1941	Lend-Lease Act allows U.S. to financially assist Allied nations FDR and Churchill sign Atlantic Charter, pledging self-determination for all nations Germany invades Soviet Union Japan attacks Pearl Harbor, Hawaii, on December 7, killing 2,323 U.S. servicemen U.S. declares war on Japan on December 8

13 WORLD WAR II AND THE POSTWAR ERA (1941–1960)

DECLARED WAR BEGINS

Declaration of War

On December 8, Congress declared war on Japan. Three days later the Axis powers, Germany and Italy, declared war on the United States. Great Britain and the United States then established the Combined Chiefs of Staff, headquartered in Washington, to direct Anglo-American military operations.

Declaration of the United Nations

On January 1, 1942, representatives of 26 nations met in Washington, D.C., and signed the Declaration of the United Nations, pledging themselves to the principles of the Atlantic Charter and promising not to make a separate peace with their common enemies.

THE HOME FRONT

War Production Board

The War Production Board was established in 1942 by President Franklin D. Roosevelt for the purpose of regulating the use of raw materials.

Wage and Price Controls

In April 1942 the General Maximum Price Regulation Act froze prices and extended rationing. In April 1943 prices, wages, and salaries were all frozen.

Revenue Act of 1942

The Revenue Act of 1942 extended the income tax to the majority of the population. Payroll deduction for the income tax began in 1944.

Social Changes

Rural areas lost population while coastal areas increased rapidly. Women entered the work force in increasing numbers. Blacks moved from the rural

South to Northern and Western cities with racial tensions often resulting, most notably in the June 1943 racial riot in Detroit.

Smith-Connolly Act

Passed in 1943, the Smith-Connolly Antistrike Act authorized government seizure of a plant or mine idled by a strike if the war effort was impeded. It expired in 1947.

Korematsu v. United States

In 1944 the Supreme Court upheld President Roosevelt's 1942 order that Issei (Japanese Americans who had emigrated from Japan) and Nisei (native-born Japanese Americans) be relocated to concentration camps. The camps were closed in March 1946.

Smith v. Allwright

In 1944 the Supreme Court struck down the Texas primary elections, which were restricted to whites, for violating the 15th Amendment.

Presidential Election of 1944

President Franklin D. Roosevelt, together with new vice-presidential candidate Harry S. Truman of Missouri, defeated his Republican opponent, Governor Thomas Dewey of New York.

Death of Roosevelt

Roosevelt died on April 12, 1945, at Warm Springs, Georgia. Harry S. Truman became president.

THE NORTH AFRICAN AND EUROPEAN THEATRES

Nearly 400 ships were lost in American waters of the Atlantic to German submarines between January and June 1942.

The United States joined in the bombing of the European continent in July 1942. Bombing increased during 1943 and 1944 and lasted to the end of the war.

The Allied army under Dwight D. Eisenhower attacked French North Africa in November, 1942. The French surrendered.

In the Battle of Kassarine Pass, February 1943, North Africa, the Allied army met General Erwin Rommel's Africa Korps. Although the battle is variously interpreted as a standoff or a defeat for the U.S., Rommel's forces were soon trapped by the British moving in from Egypt. In May 1943, Rommel's Africa Korps surrendered.

Allied armies under George S. Patton invaded Sicily from Africa in July 1943 and gained control by mid-August. Moving from Sicily, the Allied armies invaded the Italian mainland in September. Benito Mussolini had already fallen from power and his successor, Marshal Pietro Badoglio surrendered. The Germans, however, put up a stiff resistance with the result that Rome did not fall until June 1944.

In March 1944, the Soviet Union began pushing into Eastern Europe.

On "D-Day," June 6, 1944, Allied armies under Dwight D. Eisenhower, now commander in chief of Supreme Headquarters, Allied Expeditionary Forces, began an invasion of Normandy, France. Allied armies under General Omar Bradley took the transportation hub of St. Lo, France in July.

Allied armies liberated Paris in August. By mid-September they had arrived at the Rhine, on the edge of Germany.

Beginning December 16, 1944, at the Battle of the Bulge, the Germans counter-attacked, driving the Allies back about 50 miles into Belgium. By January the Allies were once more advancing toward Germany.

The Allies crossed the Rhine in March 1945. In the last week of April, Eisenhower's forces met the Soviet army at the Elbe.

On May 7, 1945, Germany surrendered.

THE PACIFIC THEATRE

By the end of December 1941, Guam, Wake Island, the Gilbert Islands, and Hong Kong had fallen to the Japanese. In January 1942, Raboul, New Britain fell, followed in February by Singapore and Java, and in March by Rangoon, Burma.

The U.S. air raids on Tokyo in April 1942 were militarily inconsequential but they raised Allied morale.

U.S. forces surrendered at Corregidor, Philippines, on May 6, 1942.

In the Battle of the Coral Sea, May 7–8, 1942 (northeast of Australia, south of New Guinea and the Solomon Islands), planes from the American carriers *Lexington* and *Yorktown* forced Japanese troop transports to turn back from attacking Port Moresby. The battle stopped the Japanese advance on Australia.

At the Battle of Midway, June 4–7, 1942, American air power destroyed four Japanese carriers and about 300 planes while the U.S. lost the carrier Yorktown and one destroyer. The battle proved to be the turning point in the Pacific.

A series of land, sea, and air battles took place around Guadalcanal in the Solomon Islands from August 1942 to February 1943, stopping the Japanese.

The Allied strategy of island hopping, begun in 1943, sought to neutralize Japanese strongholds with air and sea power and then move on. General Douglas MacArthur commanded the land forces moving from New Guinea toward the Philippines, while Admiral Chester W. Nimitz directed the naval attack on important Japanese islands in the central Pacific.

U.S. forces advanced into the Gilberts (November 1943), the Marshalls (January 1944), and the Marianas (June 1944).

In the Battle of the Philippine Sea, June 19–20, 1944, the Japanese lost three carriers, two submarines, and over 300 planes while the Americans lost 17 planes. After the American capture of the Marianas, General Tojo resigned as premier of Japan.

The Battle of Leyte Gulf, October 25, 1944, involved three major engagements that resulted in Japan's loss of most of its remaining naval power. It also brought the first use of the Japanese kamikaze, or suicide, attacks by Japanese pilots who crashed into American carriers.

Forces under General Douglas MacArthur liberated Manila in March 1945.

Between April and June 1945, in the battle for Okinawa, nearly 50,000 American casualties resulted from the fierce fighting which virtually destroyed Japan's remaining defenses.

THE ATOMIC BOMB

The Manhattan Engineering District was established by the Army engineers in August 1942 for the purpose of developing an atomic bomb. The mission eventually became known as the Manhattan Project. J. Robert Oppenheimer directed the design and construction of a transportable atomic bomb at Los Alamos, New Mexico.

On December 2, 1942, Enrico Fermi and his colleagues at the University of Chicago produced the first atomic chain reaction.

On July 16, 1945, the first atomic bomb was exploded at Alamogordo, New Mexico.

The *Enola Gay* dropped an atomic bomb on Hiroshima, Japan, on August 6, 1945, killing about 78,000 people and injuring 100,000 more. On August 9, a second bomb was dropped on Nagasaki, Japan. Some 40,000 people were killed in the explosion. Thousands more died later from burns, injuries, and radiation exposure.

On August 8, 1945, the Soviet Union entered the war against Japan.

Japan surrendered on August 15, 1945. The formal surrender was signed on September 2.

DIPLOMACY

Casablanca Conference

On January 14–25, 1943, Franklin D. Roosevelt and Winston Churchill, prime minister of Great Britain, declared a policy of unconditional surrender for "all enemies."

Moscow Conference

In October 1943, Secretary of State Cordell Hull obtained Soviet agreement to enter the war against Japan after Germany was defeated and to participate in a world organization after the war was over.

Declaration of Cairo

Issued on December 1, 1943, after Roosevelt met with General Chiang Kai-shek in Cairo from November 22 to 26, the Declaration of Cairo called for Japan's unconditional surrender and stated that all Chinese territories occupied by Japan would be returned to China and that Korea would be free and independent.

Teheran Conference

The first "Big Three" (Roosevelt, Churchill, and Stalin) conference, met at Teheran from November 28 to December 1, 1943. Stalin reaffirmed the Soviet commitment to enter the war against Japan and discussed coordination of the Soviet offensive with the Allied invasion of France.

Yalta Conference

On February 4–11, 1945 the "Big Three" met to discuss post-war Europe. Stalin said that the Soviet Union would enter the Pacific war within three months after Germany surrendered and agreed to the "Declaration of Liberated Europe" which called for free elections. They called for a conference on world organization, to meet in the U.S. beginning on April 25, 1945, and agreed that the Soviets would have three votes in the General Assembly and that the U.S., Great Britain, the Soviet Union, France, and China would be permanent members of the Security Council. Germany was divided into occupation zones, and a coalition government of communists and non-communists was agreed to for Poland. Roosevelt accepted Soviet control of Outer Mongolia, the Kurile Islands, the southern half of Sakhalin Island, Port Arthur (Darien), and participation in the operation of the Manchurian railroads.

Potsdam Conference

From July 17 to August 2, 1945, Truman, Stalin, and Clement Atlee (who during the conference replaced Churchill as prime minister of Great Britain) met at Potsdam. During the conference, Truman ordered the dropping of the atomic bomb on Japan. The conference disagreed on most major issues but did establish a Council of Foreign Ministers to draft peace treaties for the Balkans. Approval was also given to the concept of war-crimes trials and the demilitarization and denazification of Germany.

THE EMERGENCE OF THE COLD WAR AND CONTAINMENT

Failure of U.S.–Soviet Cooperation

By the end of 1945 the Soviet Union controlled most of Eastern Europe, Outer Mongolia, parts of Manchuria, Northern Korea, the Kurile Islands, and Sakhalin Island. In 1946–47 it took over Poland, Hungary, Rumania, and Bulgaria.

Iron Curtain

In a speech in Fulton, Missouri, in 1946, Winston Churchill stated that an Iron Curtain had been spread across Europe separating the democratic from the authoritarian communist states.

Containment

In 1946, career diplomat and Soviet expert George F. Kennan warned that the Soviet Union had no intention of living peacefully with the United States. The next year, in July 1947 he wrote an anonymous article for Foreign Affairs in which he called for a counter-force to Soviet pressures for the purpose of "containing" communism.

Truman Doctrine

In February 1947 Great Britain notified the United States that it could no longer aid the Greek government in its war against communist insurgents. The next month President Harry S. Truman asked Congress for $400 million in military and economic aid for Greece and Turkey. He argued in what became known as the "Truman Doctrine" that the United States must support free peoples who were resisting communist domination.

Marshall Plan

Secretary of State George C. Marshall proposed in June 1947 that the United States provide economic aid to help rebuild Europe. Meeting in July, representatives of the European nations agreed on a recovery program jointly financed by the United States and the European countries. The following March, Congress passed the European Recovery Program, popularly known as the Marshall Plan, providing more than $12 billion in aid.

Czechoslovakia

In February 1948 the Soviets sponsored a coup d'état in Czechoslovakia, thereby extending communism in Europe.

Berlin Crisis

After the United States, France, and Great Britain announced plans to create a West German Republic out of their German zones, the Soviet Union in June 1948 blocked surface access to Berlin. The U.S. then instituted an airlift to transport supplies to the city until the Soviets lifted their blockade in May 1949.

NATO

In April 1949 the North Atlantic Treaty Organization was signed by the United States, Great Britain, France, Italy, Belgium, the Netherlands, Luxembourg, Denmark, Norway, Portugal, Iceland, and Canada. The signatories pledged that an attack against one would be considered an attack against all. Greece and Turkey joined the alliance in 1952 and West Germany in 1954. The Soviets formed the Warsaw Treaty Organization in 1955 to counteract NATO.

Atomic Bomb

The Soviet Union exploded an atomic device in September 1949.

INTERNATIONAL COOPERATION

Bretton Woods, New Hampshire

Representatives from Europe and the U.S. at a conference held July 1–22, 1944, signed agreements for an international bank and a world monetary fund to stabilize international currencies and rebuild the economies of war-torn nations.

Yalta Conference

In February 1945 Roosevelt, Churchill, and Stalin called for a conference on world organization to meet in April 1945 in the United States.

United Nations

From April to June 1945, representatives from 50 countries met in San Francisco to establish the United Nations. The U.N. charter created a General Assembly composed of all member nations which would act as the ultimate policy-making body. A Security Council, made up of 11 members, including the United States, Great Britain, France, the Soviet Union, and China as permanent members and six additional nations elected by the General Assembly for two-year terms, would be responsible for settling disputes among U.N. member nations.

CONTAINMENT IN ASIA

Japan

General Douglas MacArthur headed a four-power Allied Control Council which governed Japan, allowing it to develop economically and politically.

China

Between 1945 and 1948 the United States gave over $2 billion in aid to the Nationalist Chinese under Chiang Kai-shek and sent George C. Marshall to settle the conflict between Chiang's Nationalists and Mao Tse-tung's Communists. In 1949, however, Mao defeated Chiang and forced the Nationalists to flee to Formosa (Taiwan). Mao established the People's Republic of China on the mainland.

Korean War

On June 25, 1950, North Korea invaded South Korea. President Truman committed U.S. forces commanded by General MacArthur but under United Nations auspices. By October, the U.N. (mostly American) had driven north of the 38th parallel which divided North and South Korea. Chinese troops attacked MacArthur's forces on November 26, pushing them south of the 38th parallel, but by spring 1951, the U.N. forces had recovered their offensive. MacArthur called for a naval blockade of China and bombing north of the Yalu River, criticizing the president for fighting a limited war. In April 1951, Truman removed MacArthur from command.

Armistice

Armistice talks began with North Korea in the summer of 1951. In June 1953 an armistice was signed leaving Korea divided along virtually the same boundary that had existed prior to the war.

EISENHOWER-DULLES FOREIGN POLICY

John Foster Dulles

Dwight D. Eisenhower, elected president in 1952, chose John Foster Dulles as secretary of state. Dulles talked of a more aggressive foreign policy, calling for "massive retaliation" and "liberation" rather than containment. He wished to emphasize nuclear deterrents rather than conventional armed forces. Dulles served as secretary of state until ill health forced him to resign in April 1959. Christian A. Herter took his place.

Hydrogen Bomb

The U.S. exploded its first hydrogen bomb in November 1952 while the Soviets followed with theirs in August 1953.

Soviet Change of Power

Josef Stalin died in March 1953. After an internal power struggle that lasted until 1955, Nikita Khrushchev emerged as the Soviet leader. He talked of both "burying" capitalism and "peaceful coexistence."

Asia

In 1954 the French asked the U.S. to commit air forces to rescue French forces at Dien Bien Phu, Vietnam, as they were besieged by the nationalist forces led by Ho Chi Minh, but Eisenhower refused. In May 1954 Dien Bien Phu surrendered.

Geneva Accords

France, Great Britain, the Soviet Union, and China signed the Geneva Accords in July 1954, dividing Vietnam along the 17th parallel. The North would be under Ho Chi Minh and the South under Emperor Bao Dai. Elections were scheduled for 1956 to unify the country, but Ngo Dinh Diem overthrew Bao Dai and prevented the elections from taking place. The United States supplied economic aid to South Vietnam.

Southeast Asia Treaty Organization

Dulles attempted to establish a Southeast Asia Treaty Organization parallel to NATO but was able to obtain only the Philippine Republic, Thailand, and Pakistan as signatories in September 1954.

Quemoy and Matsu

The small islands of Quemoy and Matsu off the coast of China were occupied by the Nationalist Chinese under Chiang Kai-shek but claimed by the People's Republic of China. In 1955, after the mainland Chinese began shelling these islands, Eisenhower obtained authorization from Congress to defend Formosa (Taiwan) and related areas.

Middle East—The Suez Canal Crisis

The United States had agreed to lend money to Egypt, under the leadership of Colonel Gamal Abdul Nasser, to build the Aswan Dam but refused to give arms. Nasser then drifted toward the Soviet Union and in 1956 established diplomatic relations with the People's Republic of China. In July 1956 the U.S. withdrew its loan to Egypt. In response, Nasser nationalized the Suez Canal. France, Great Britain, and Israel then attacked Egypt but Eisenhower demanded that they pull out. On November 6 a cease-fire was announced.

Eisenhower Doctrine

President Eisenhower announced in January 1957 that the U.S. was prepared to use armed force in the Middle East against communist aggression. Under this doctrine, U.S. marines entered Beirut, Lebanon in July 1958 to promote political stability during a change of governments. The Marines left in October.

Summit Conference with the Soviet Union

In July 1955 President Eisenhower met in Geneva with Anthony Eden, prime minister of Great Britain, Edgar Faure, premier of France, and Nikita Khrushchev and Nikolai Bulganin, at the time co-leaders of the Soviet Union. They discussed disarmament and reunification of Germany but made no agreements.

Atomic Weapons Test Suspension

Eisenhower and Khrushchev voluntarily suspended in October 1958 atmospheric tests of atomic weapons.

Soviet-American Visitations

Vice President Richard M. Nixon visited the Soviet Union and Soviet Vice-Premier Anastas I. Mikoyan came to the United States in the summer of 1959. In September Premier Khrushchev toured the United States and agreed to another summit meeting.

U-2 Incident

On May 1, 1960, an American U-2 spy plane was shot down over the Soviet Union and pilot Francis Gary Powers was captured. Eisenhower ultimately took responsibility for the spy plane and Khrushchev angrily called off the Paris summit conference which was to take place in a few days.

Latin America

The U.S. supported the overthrow of President Jacobo Arbenz Guzman of Guatemala in 1954 because he began accepting arms from the Soviet Union.

Vice President Nixon had to call off an eight nation goodwill tour of Latin America after meeting hostile mobs in Venezuela and Peru in 1958.

In January 1959 Fidel Castro overthrew Fulgencio Batista, dictator of Cuba. Castro soon began criticizing the United States and moved closer to the Soviet Union, signing a trade agreement with the Soviets in February 1960. The United States prohibited the importation of Cuban sugar in October 1960 and broke off diplomatic relations in January 1961.

THE POLITICS OF AFFLUENCE: DEMOBILIZATION AND DOMESTIC POLICY

Truman Becomes President

Harry S. Truman, formerly a senator from Missouri and vice president of the United States, became president on April 12, 1945. In September 1945 he proposed a liberal legislative program, including expansion of unemployment insurance, extension of the Employment Service, a higher minimum wage, a permanent Fair Employment Practices Commission, slum clearance, low-rent housing, regional TVA-type programs, and a public works program, but was unable to put it through Congress.

Employment Act of 1946

This act established a three member Council of Economic Advisors to evaluate the economy, advise the president, and set up a Congressional Joint Committee on the Economic Report. The act declared that the government was committed to maintaining maximum employment.

Atomic Energy

Congress created the Atomic Energy Commission in 1946, establishing civilian control over nuclear development and giving the president sole authority over the use of atomic weapons in warfare.

Price Controls

Truman vetoed a weak price control bill passed by Congress, thereby ending the wartime price control program. When prices quickly increased about 6 percent, Congress passed another bill in July 1946. Although Truman signed this bill, he used its powers inconsistently, especially when—bowing to pressure—he ended price controls on beef. In late 1946, he lifted controls on all items except rents, sugar, and rice.

Labor

In early 1946, the United Auto Workers, under Walter Reuther, struck General Motors, and steelworkers, under Philip Murray, struck U.S. Steel, demanding wage increases. Truman suggested an 18 cent-per-hour wage increase and in February allowed U.S. Steel to raise prices to cover the increase. This formula became the basis for settlements in other industries. After John L. Lewis's United Mine Workers struck in April 1946, Truman ordered the government to take over the mines and then accepted the union's demands, which included safety and health and welfare benefits. The president averted a railway strike by seizing the railroads and threatening to draft strikers into the Army.

Demobilization

By 1947 the total armed forces had been cut to 1.5 million. The Army fell to 600,000 from a WWII peak of 8 million. The Serviceman's Readjustment Act (G.I. Bill of Rights) of 1944, provided $13 billion in aid ranging from education to housing.

Taft-Hartley Act

The Republicans, who had gained control of Congress as a result of the 1946 elections, sought to control the power of the unions through the Taft-Hartley Act, passed in 1947. This act made the "closed-shop" illegal; labor unions could no longer force employers to hire only union members although it allowed the "union shop" in which newly hired employees were required to join the union. It established an 80 day cooling-off period for strikers in key industries; ended the practice of employers collecting dues for unions; forbade such actions as secondary boycotts, jurisdictional strikes, featherbedding, and contributing to political campaigns; and required an anti-communist oath of union officials. The act slowed down efforts to unionize the South and by 1954, 15 states had passed "right to work" laws, forbidding the "union shop."

Reorganization of Armed Forces

In 1947 Congress passed the National Security Act creating a National Military Establishment, National Security Council, Joint Chiefs of Staff, and Central Intelligence Agency (CIA). Together these organizations were intended to coordinate the armed forces and intelligence services.

Government Reorganization

Truman in 1947 appointed former President Herbert Hoover to head a Commission on Organization of the Executive Branch. The Commission's 1949 report led to the Organization Act of 1949 which allowed the president to make organizational changes subject to congressional veto.

Civil Rights

In 1946 Truman appointed the President's Committee on Civil Rights, which a year later produced its report *To Secure These Rights*. The report called for the elimination of all aspects of segregation. In 1948 the president banned racial discrimination in federal hiring practices and ordered desegregation of the armed forces.

Presidential Succession

The Presidential Succession Act of 1947 placed the speaker of the House and the president pro tempore of the Senate ahead of the secretary of state and after the vice president in the line of succession. The 22nd Amendment to the Constitution, ratified in 1951, limited the president to two terms.

Election of 1948

Truman was the Democratic nominee but the Democrats were split by the States' Rights Democratic Party (Dixiecrats) which nominated Governor Strom Thurmond of South Carolina and the Progressive Party which nominated former Vice-President Henry Wallace. The Republicans nominated Governor Thomas E. Dewey of New York. After traveling widely and attacking the "do-nothing Congress," Truman won a surprise victory.

THE FAIR DEAL

The Fair Deal Program

Truman sought to enlarge and extend the New Deal. He proposed increasing the minimum wage, extending Social Security to more people, maintaining rent controls, clearing slums and building public housing, and providing more money to TVA, rural electrification, and farm housing. He also introduced bills dealing with civil rights, national health insurance, federal aid to education, and repeal of the Taft-Hartley Act. A coalition of Republicans and Southern Democrats prevented little more than the maintenance of existing programs.

Farm Policy

Because of improvements in agriculture, overproduction continued to be a problem. Secretary of Agriculture Charles F. Brannan proposed a program of continued price supports for storable crops and guaranteed minimum incomes to farmers of perishable crops. It was defeated in Congress and surpluses continued to pile up.

ANTICOMMUNISM

Smith Act

The Smith Act of 1940, which made it illegal to advocate the overthrow of the government by force or to belong to an organization advocating such a position, was used by the Truman administration to jail leaders of the American Communist Party.

Loyalty Review Board

In response to criticism, particularly from the House Committee on Un-American Activities, that his administration was "soft on communism," Truman established this board in 1947 to review government employees.

The Hiss Case

In 1948 Whittaker Chambers, formerly a communist and then an editor of *Time,* charged Alger Hiss, a former State Department official and then president of the Carnegie Endowment for International Peace, with having been a communist who supplied classified American documents to the Soviet Union. In 1950 Hiss was convicted of perjury, the statute of limitations on his alleged spying having run out.

McCarran Internal Security Act

Passed in 1950, this act required communist-front organizations to register with the attorney general and prevented their members from defense work and travel abroad. It was passed over Truman's veto.

Rosenberg Case

In 1950 Julius and Ethel Rosenberg, as well as Harry Gold, were charged with giving atomic secrets to the Soviet Union. The Rosenbergs were convicted and executed in 1953.

Joseph McCarthy

On February 9, 1950, Senator Joseph R. McCarthy of Wisconsin stated that he had a list of known communists who were working in the State Department. He later expanded his attacks to diplomats and scholars and contributed to the electoral defeat of two senators. After making charges against the army, he was censured and discredited by the Senate in 1954 and died in 1957.

EISENHOWER'S DYNAMIC CONSERVATISM

1952 Election

The Republicans nominated Dwight D. Eisenhower, most recently NATO commander, for the presidency and Richard M. Nixon, senator from California, for the vice-presidency. The Democrats nominated Governor Adlai E. Stevenson of Illinois for president. Eisenhower won by a landslide; for the first time since Reconstruction the Republicans won some Southern states.

Conservatism

Eisenhower sought to balance the budget and lower taxes but did not attempt to roll back existing social and economic legislation. Eisenhower first described his policy as "dynamic conservatism" and then as "progressive moderation." The administration abolished the Reconstruction Finance Corporation, ended wage and price controls, and reduced farm price supports. It cut the budget and in 1954 lowered tax rates for corporations and individuals with high incomes; an economic slump, however, made balancing the budget difficult.

Social Legislation

Social Security was extended in 1954 and 1956 to an additional 10 million people, including professionals, domestic and clerical workers, farm workers, and members of the armed services. In 1959 benefits were increased 7 percent. In 1955 the minimum wage was raised from 75 cents to $1.00 an hour.

Public Power

Opposed to the expansion of TVA, the Eisenhower administration supported a plan to have a privately owned power plant (called Dixon-Yates) built to supply electricity to Memphis, Tennessee. After two years of controversy and discovery that the government consultant would financially benefit from Dixon-Yates, the administration turned to a municipally owned power plant. The Idaho Power Company won the right to build three small dams on the Snake River rather than the federal government establishing a single large dam at Hell's Canyon. The Atomic Energy Act of 1954 allowed the construction of private nuclear power plants under Atomic Energy Commission license and oversight.

Farm Policy

The Rural Electrification Administration announced in 1960 that 97 percent of American farms had electricity. In 1954 the government began financing the export of farm surpluses in exchange for foreign currencies and later provided surpluses free to needy nations, including milk to school children and to the poor in exchange for governmentally issued food stamps.

Public Works

In 1954 Eisenhower obtained congressional approval for joint Canadian-U.S. construction of the St. Lawrence Seaway, giving ocean-going vessels access to the Great Lakes. In 1956 Congress authorized construction of the Interstate Highway System, with the federal government covering 90 percent of the cost and the states 10 percent. The program further undermined the American railroad system.

Supreme Court

Eisenhower appointed Earl Warren, formerly governor of California, chief justice of the Supreme Court in 1953. That same year he appointed William J. Brennan associate justice. Although originally perceived as conservatives, both justices used the court as an agency of social and political change.

Election of 1956

The 1956 election once again pitted Eisenhower against Stevenson. The president won easily, carrying all but seven states.

Space and Technology

The launching of the Soviet space satellite Sputnik on October 4, 1957, created fear that America was falling behind technologically. Although the U.S. launched Explorer I on January 31, 1958, the concern continued. In 1958 Congress established the National Aeronautics and Space Administration (NASA) to coordinate research and development and passed the National Defense Education Act to provide grants and loans for education.

Sherman Adams Scandal

In 1958 the White House chief of staff, Sherman Adams, resigned after it was revealed that he had received a fur coat and an oriental rug in return for helping a Boston industrialist deal with the federal bureaucracy. This became known as the Sherman Adams Scandal.

Labor

The Landrum-Griffen Labor-Management Act of 1959 sought to control unfair union practices by establishing rules such as penalties for misuse of funds.

New States

On January 3, 1959, Alaska became the forty-ninth state and on August 21, 1959, Hawaii became the fiftieth.

CIVIL RIGHTS

Initial Eisenhower Actions

Eisenhower completed the formal integration of the armed forces, desegregated public services in Washington, D.C., naval yards, and veteran's hospitals, and appointed a Civil Rights Commission.

Legal Background to *Brown*

In *Ada Lois Sipuel v. Board of Regents* (1948) and *Sweatt v. Painter* (1950) the Supreme Court ruled that African Americans must be allowed to attend integrated law schools in Oklahoma and Texas.

Brown v. Board of Education of Topeka

In *Brown v. Board of Education of Topeka*, a 1954 case, NAACP lawyer Thurgood Marshall challenged the doctrine of "separate but equal" (*Plessy v. Ferguson*, 1896). The Court declared that separate educational facilities were inherently unequal. In 1955 the Court ordered states to integrate "with all deliberate speed."

Southern Reaction

Although at first the South reacted cautiously, by 1955 there were calls for "massive resistance" and White Citizens Councils emerged to spearhead the resistance. State legislatures used a number of tactics to get around Brown. By the end of 1956 desegregation of the schools had advanced very little.

Little Rock

Although he did not personally support the Supreme Court decision, Eisenhower sent 10,000 National Guardsmen and 1,000 paratroopers to Little Rock, Arkansas, to control mobs and enable blacks to enroll at Central High in September 1957. A small force of soldiers was stationed at the school throughout the year.

Emergence of Non-Violence

On December 1, 1955, in Montgomery, Alabama, Rosa Parks, a black woman, refused to give up her seat on a city bus to a white passenger and was arrested. Under the leadership of Martin Luther King Jr., a black pastor, blacks of Montgomery organized a bus boycott that lasted for a year, until in December 1956 the Supreme Court refused to review a lower court ruling that stated that separate but equal was no longer legal.

Civil Rights Acts

Eisenhower proposed the Civil Rights Act of 1957, that established a permanent Civil Rights Commission and a Civil Rights Division of the Justice Department which was empowered to prevent interference with the right to vote. The Civil Rights Act of 1960 gave the federal courts power to register African American voters.

Ending "Massive Resistance"

In 1959 state and federal courts nullified Virginia laws which prevented state funds from going to integrated schools. This proved to be the beginning of the end for "massive resistance."

Sit-Ins

In February 1960 four black students who had been denied service staged a sit-in at a segregated Woolworth lunch counter in Greensboro, North Carolina. This inspired sit-ins elsewhere in the South and led to the formation of the Student Nonviolent Coordinating Committee (SNCC). SNCC's primary aims included the end of segregation in public accommodations and winning voting rights.

THE ELECTION OF 1960

The Nominations

Vice President Richard M. Nixon won the Republican presidential nomination while the Democrats nominated Senator John F. Kennedy for the presidency with Lyndon B. Johnson, majority leader of the Senate, as his running mate.

Catholicism

Kennedy's Catholicism was a major issue until, on September 12, he told a gathering of Protestant ministers that he accepted the separation of church and state and that he would not allow Catholic leaders to tell him how to act as president.

Debates

A series of televised debates between Kennedy and Nixon helped create a positive image for Kennedy and may have been a turning point in the election.

Kennedy's Victory

Kennedy won the election by slightly over 100,000 popular votes and 94 electoral votes, based on majorities in New England, the Middle Atlantic, and the South.

SOCIETY AND CULTURE

Gross National Product

The GNP almost doubled between 1945 and 1960, growing at an annual rate of 3.2 percent from 1950 to 1960. Inflation meanwhile remained under 2 percent annually throughout the 1950s. Defense spending was the most important stimulant, and military-related research helped create or expand the new industries of chemicals, electronics, and aviation. The U.S. had a virtual monopoly over international trade, because of the devastation of the World War. Technological innovations contributed to productivity, which jumped 35 percent between 1945 and 1955. After depression and war, Americans had a great desire to consume. Between 1945 and 1960 the American population grew by nearly 30 percent, which contributed greatly to consumer demand.

Consumption Patterns

Home ownership grew by 50 percent between 1945 and 1960. These new homes required such appliances as refrigerators and washing machines, but the most popular product was television, which increased from 7,000 sets in 1946 to 50 million sets in 1960. *TV Guide* became the fastest-growing magazine and advertising found the TV medium especially powerful. Consumer credit increased 800 percent between 1945 and 1957 while the rate of savings dropped to about 5 percent of income. The number of shopping centers rose from 8 in 1945 to 3,840 in 1960. Teenagers became an increasingly important consumer group, making—among other things—a major industry of rock 'n' roll music, with Elvis Presley as its first star, by the mid-1950s.

DEMOGRAPHIC TRENDS

Population Growth

In the 1950s population grew by over 28 million, 97 percent of which was in urban and suburban areas. The average life expectancy increased from 66 in 1955 to 71 in 1970. Dr. Benjamin Spock's *The Commonsense Book of Baby and Child Care* sold an average of 1 million copies a year between 1946 and 1960.

The Sun Belt

Aided by use of air conditioning, Florida, the Southwest, and California grew rapidly, with California becoming the most populous state by 1963. The Northeast, however, remained the most densely populated area.

Suburbs

The suburbs grew six times faster than the cities in the 1950s. William Levitt pioneered the mass-produced housing development when he built 10,600 houses (Levittown) on Long Island in 1947, a pattern followed widely elsewhere in the country. The Federal Housing Administration helped builders by insuring up to 95 percent of a loan and buyers by insuring their mortgages. Thanks in part to the development of the interstate highway system during the Eisenhower administration, auto production increased from 2 million in 1946 to 8 million in 1955, which further encouraged the development of suburbia. As increasing numbers of African Americans moved into the Northern and Midwestern cities, whites moved to the suburbs, a process dubbed "white flight." About 20 percent of the population moved their residence each year.

Middle Class

The number of American families that were classified as middle class changed from 5.7 million in 1947 to more than 12 million by the early 1960s.

Jobs

The number of farm workers dropped from 9 million to 5.2 million between 1940 and 1960. By 1960 more Americans held white-collar than blue-collar jobs.

CONFORMITY AND SECURITY

Corporate Employment

Employees tended to work for larger organizations. By 1960, 38 percent of the workforce was employed by organizations with over 500 employees. Such environments encouraged the managerial personality and corporate cooperation rather than individualism.

Homogeneity

Observers found the expansion of the middle class an explanation for emphasis on conformity. David Riesman argued in *The Lonely Crowd* (1950) that American were moving from an inner-directed to an outer-directed orientation. William Whyte's *The Organization Man* (1956) saw corporate culture as emphasizing the group rather than the individual. Sloan Wilson's *The Man in the Grey Flannel Suit* (1955) expressed similar concerns in fictional form.

Leisure

The standard work week shrank from six to five days. Television became the dominant cultural medium, with over 530 stations by 1961. Sales of books, especially paperbacks, increased annually.

Women

A cult of feminine domesticity re-emerged after World War II. Marynia Farnham and Ferdinand Lundberg published *Modern Woman: The Lost Sex* in 1947; Farnham suggested that science supported the idea that women could find fulfillment only in domesticity. Countless magazine articles also promoted the notion that a woman's place was in the home.

Religion

From 1940, when less than half the population belonged to a church, membership rose to more than 65 percent by 1960. Catholic Bishop Fulton J. Sheen had a popular weekly television show, "Life Worth Living," while Baptist evangelist Billy Graham held huge crusades. Norman Vincent Peale best represented the tendency of religion to emphasize reassurance with his best-seller *The Power of Positive Thinking* (1952). Critics noted the shallowness of this religion. Will Herberg in *Protestant-Catholic-Jew* (1955) said that popular religiosity lacked conviction and commitment. Reinhold Niebuhr, the leading neo-orthodox theologian, criticized the self-centeredness of popular religion and its failure to recognize the reality of sin.

SEEDS OF REBELLION

Intellectuals

Intellectuals became increasingly critical of American life. John Kenneth Galbraith in *The Affluent Society* (1958) argued that the public sector was underfunded. John Keats's *The Crack in the Picture Window* (1956) criticized the homogeneity of suburban life in the new mass-produced communities. The adequacy of American education was questioned by James B. Conant in *The American High School Today* (1959).

Theatre and Fiction

Arthur Miller's *Death of a Salesman* (1949) explored the theme of the loneliness of the other-directed person. Novels also took up the conflict between the individual and mass society. Notable works included J.D. Salinger's *The Catcher in the Rye* (1951), James Jones's *From Here to Eternity* (1951), Joseph Heller's *Catch-22* (1955), Saul Bellow's *The Adventures of Augie March* (1953), and John Updike's *Rabbit, Run* (1960).

Art

Painter Edward Hopper portrayed isolated, anonymous individuals. Jackson Pollock, Robert Motherwell, Willem de Kooning, Arshile Gorky, and Mark Rothko were among the leaders in abstract expressionism, in which they attempted spontaneous expression of their subjectivity.

The Beats

The Beats were a group of young men alienated by twentieth-century life. Their movement began in Greenwich Village, New York, with the friendship of Allen Ginsburg, Jack Kerouac, William Burroughs, and Neal Cassady. They emphasized alcohol, drugs, sex, jazz, Buddhism, and a restless vagabond life, all of which were vehicles for their subjectivity. Ginsberg's long poem *Howl* (1956) and Kerouac's novel *On the Road* (1957) were among the more important literary works to emerge from the Beat movement.

HISTORICAL TIMELINE

World War II and the Postwar Era (1941–1960)

1941	Axis Powers declare war on the U.S. three days after Pearl Harbor
1942	Japan captures Philippine Islands as Bataan and Corregidor fall War Production Board established U.S. begins interning Japanese-American citizens Germany sinks 400 American ships Battle of Coral Sea Battle of Midway U.S. attacks Vichy forces and Germans in North Africa Manhattan Project begins
1943	Casablanca Conference Americans seize Guadalcanal Island Soviets defeat Germans at Stalingrad Allies invade Italy Teheran Conference
1944	Allies invade France at Normandy (D-Day) June 6 Battle of Leyte Gulf Roosevelt elected president for fourth term Island-hopping campaign retakes Guam Island Battle of the Bulge
1945	Yalta Conference U.S. bombing raids destroy 250,000 buildings in Tokyo 50 nations approve United Nations Charter in San Francisco Conference Hitler commits suicide in Berlin bunker V-E Day Americans recapture the Philippine Islands Potsdam Conference Bomb dropped on Hiroshima Soviets declare war on Japan Bomb dropped on Nagasaki V-J Day
1946	Churchill gives "Iron Curtain" speech George Kennan proposes containment policy
1947	Truman Doctrine aids nations resisting communism Marshall Plan provides economic aid to Europe House Un-American Activities Committee investigates Hollywood Jackie Robinson breaks color line in baseball Taft-Hartley Act slows growth of labor unions

1948	Soviets block access to West Berlin in Berlin Airlift Alger Hiss case begins Truman signs armed forces desegregation order Israel becomes a nation Truman defeats Dewey in presidential election
1949	NATO formed Soviet Union explodes atomic bomb Mao leads communist takeover in China
1950	Korean War begins U.S. troops invade North Korea Chinese troops enter war Rosenberg spy trial begins McCarthy begins anti-communist campaign U.S. begins hydrogen bomb program
1951	Gen. MacArthur relieved of command in Korea Peace negotiations begin in Panmunjon, Korea
1952	U.S. ends Japan occupation Eisenhower elected president
1953	Korean War ends with truce and demilitarized zone Stalin dies
1954	*Brown v. Topeka Board of Education* Army-McCarthy hearings French surrender at Dienbienphu in Vietnam Sen. McCarthy censured by Senate
1955	Martin Luther King Jr. begins Montgomery Bus Boycott
1956	Suez crisis Soviets crush Hungarian revolt
1957	Soviets launch Sputnik Eisenhower Doctrine commits economic aid to Middle East Little Rock school desegregation crisis
1959	Castro takes over in Cuba Soviet Premier Khrushchev visits U.S.

14 THE NEW FRONTIER, VIETNAM, AND SOCIAL UPHEAVAL (1960–1972)

KENNEDY'S "NEW FRONTIER" AND THE LIBERAL REVIVAL

Legislative Failures

Kennedy was unable to get much of his program through Congress because of an alliance of Republicans and southern Democrats. He proposed plans for federal aid to education, urban renewal, medical care for the aged, reductions in personal and corporate income taxes, and the creation of a Department of Urban Affairs. None of these proposals passed.

Kennedy did gain congressional approval for raising the minimum wage from $1.00 to $1.25 an hour and extending it to 3 million more workers.

Housing Act

The 1961 Housing Act provided nearly $5 billion over four years for the preservation of open urban spaces, development of mass transit, and the construction of middle-class housing.

CIVIL RIGHTS

Freedom Riders

In May 1961, blacks and whites, sponsored by the Congress on Racial Equality, boarded buses in Washington, D.C., and traveled across the South to New Orleans to test federal enforcement of regulations prohibiting discrimination. They met violence in Alabama but continued to New Orleans. Others came into the South to test the segregation laws.

Justice Department

The Justice Department, under Attorney General Robert F. Kennedy (1925–1968), the president's brother, began to push for civil rights, including desegregation of interstate transportation in the South, integration of schools, and supervision of elections.

Mississippi

In the fall of 1962, President Kennedy called the Mississippi National Guard to federal duty to enable an African American, James Meredith, to enroll at the University of Mississippi.

March on Washington

Kennedy presented a comprehensive civil rights bill to Congress in 1963. It banned racial discrimination in public accommodations, gave the attorney general power to bring suits on behalf of individuals for school integration, and withheld federal funds from state-administered programs that practiced discrimination. While the bill was held up in Congress, 200,000 people marched on August 28, 1963, in Washington, D.C. During their demonstration, Martin Luther King Jr. gave his seminal "I Have a Dream" speech.

THE COLD WAR CONTINUES

Bay of Pigs

Under Eisenhower, the Central Intelligence Agency had begun training some 2,000 men for an invasion of Cuba to overthrow Fidel Castro, the left-leaning revolutionary who had taken power in 1959. On April 19, 1961, this force invaded at the Bay of Pigs, but was pinned down and forced to surrender. Some 1,200 men were captured.

Berlin Wall

After a confrontation between Kennedy and Khrushchev in Berlin, Kennedy called up reserve and National Guard units and asked for an increase in defense funds. In August 1961, Khrushchev responded by closing the border between East and West Berlin and ordering the erection of the Berlin Wall.

Nuclear Testing

The Soviet Union began the testing of nuclear weapons in September 1961. Kennedy then authorized resumption of underground testing by the United States.

Cuban Missile Crisis

On October 14, 1962, a U-2 reconnaissance plane brought photographic evidence that missile sites were being built in Cuba. Kennedy, on October 22, announced a blockade of Cuba and called on Khrushchev to dismantle the missile bases and remove from Cuba all weapons capable of attacking the United States. Six days later, Khrushchev backed down, withdrew the missiles, and Kennedy lifted the blockade. The United States promised not to invade Cuba, and removed missiles from bases in Turkey, claiming they had planned to do so anyway.

Afterwards, a "hot line" telephone connection was established between the White House and the Kremlin to effect quick communication in threatening situations.

Nuclear Test Ban

In July 1963, a treaty banning the atmospheric testing of nuclear weapons was signed by all the major powers except France and China.

Alliance for Progress

In 1961, Kennedy announced the Alliance for Progress, which would provide $20 million in aid to Latin America.

Peace Corps

The Peace Corps, established in 1961, sent young volunteers to third-world countries to contribute their skills in locally sponsored projects.

JOHNSON AND THE GREAT SOCIETY

Kennedy Assassination

On November 22, 1963, Kennedy was assassinated by Lee Harvey Oswald in Dallas, Texas. Jack Ruby, a nightclub owner, killed Oswald two days later. Conspiracy theories emerged. Chief Justice Earl Warren led an investigation of the murder and concluded that Oswald had acted alone, but questions remain.

Lyndon Johnson

Succeeding Kennedy, Johnson had extensive experience in both the House and Senate, and as a Texan, was the first southerner to serve as president since Woodrow Wilson. He pushed hard for Kennedy's programs, which were languishing in Congress.

A tax cut of more than $10 billion passed Congress in 1964, and an economic boom resulted.

Civil Rights Act

The 1964 Civil Rights Act outlawed racial discrimination by employers and unions, created the Equal Employment Opportunity Commission to enforce the law, and eliminated the remaining restrictions on African-American voting.

Election of 1964

Lyndon Johnson was nominated for president by the Democrats, with Senator Hubert H. Humphrey of Minnesota for vice-president. The Republicans nominated Senator Barry Goldwater, a conservative from Arizona. Johnson won more than 61 percent of the popular vote and could now launch his own "Great Society" program.

Health Care

The Medicare Act of 1965 combined hospital insurance for retired people with a voluntary plan to cover physician's bills. Medicaid provided grants to states to help the poor below retirement age.

Education

In 1965, the Elementary and Secondary Education Act provided $1.5 billion to school districts to improve the education of poor people. Head Start prepared educationally disadvantaged children for elementary school.

Immigration

The Immigration Act of 1965 discontinued the national origin system, basing immigration instead on such things as skills and the need for political asylum.

Cities

The 1965 Housing and Urban Development Act provided 240,000 housing units and $2.9 billion for urban renewal. The Department of Housing and Urban Affairs was established in 1966, and rent supplements for low-income families also became available.

Space

Fulfilling a goal established by Kennedy, Neil Armstrong and Edwin "Buzz" Aldrin became the first humans to walk on the moon, on July 20, 1969.

EMERGENCE OF BLACK POWER

Voting Rights

In 1965, Martin Luther King Jr. announced a voter registration drive. With help from the federal courts, he dramatized his effort by leading a march from Selma to Montgomery, Alabama, between March 21 and 25. The Voting Rights Act of 1965 authorized the attorney general to appoint officials to register voters.

Racial Riots

Seventy percent of African-Americans lived in city ghettos across the country. It did not appear that the tactics used in the South would help them.

Frustration built up. In August 1965, Watts, an area of Los Angeles, erupted in riot. More than 15,000 National Guardsmen were brought in; 34 people were killed, 850 wounded, and 3,100 arrested. Property damage reached nearly $200 million. In 1966, New York and Chicago experienced riots, and the following year there were riots in Newark and Detroit. The Kerner Commission, appointed to investigate the riots, concluded that they were directed at a social system that prevented African Americans from getting good jobs and crowded them into ghettos.

Black Power

Stokely Carmichael, chairman of SNCC, was by 1964 unwilling to work with white civil-rights activists. In 1966, he called for the civil rights movements to be "black-staffed, black-controlled, and black-financed." Later, he moved on to the Black Panthers, self-styled urban revolutionaries based in Oakland, California. Other leaders such as H. Rap Brown also called for Black Power.

King Assassination

On April 4, 1968, Martin Luther King Jr. was assassinated in Memphis. James Earl Ray pleaded guilty and was convicted of the murder. Riots in more than 100 cities followed. Ray died in prison in 1998.

Black Officials

Despite the rising tide of violence, the number of African-Americans achieving elected and appointed office increased. Among the more prominent were Associate Justice of the Supreme Court Thurgood Marshall, Secretary of Housing and Urban Affairs Robert Weaver, and Senator Edward W. Brooke.

ETHNIC ACTIVISM

United Farm Workers

Cesar Chavez founded the United Farm Workers' Organizing Committee to unionize Mexican-American farm laborers. He turned a grape pickers strike in Delano, California, into a national campaign by attacking the structure of the migrant labor system through a boycott of grapes.

Native Americans

The American Indian Movement (AIM) was founded in 1968. At first it staged sit-ins to bring attention to Native American demands. By the early 1970s, it was turning to the courts.

THE NEW LEFT

Demographic Origins

By the mid-1960s, the majority of Americans were under age 30. College enrollments increased fourfold between 1945 and 1970.

Students for a Democratic Society

Students for a Democratic Society was organized by Tom Hayden and Al Haber of the University of Michigan in 1960. Hayden's Port Huron Statement (1962) called for "participatory democracy." SDS drew much of its ideology from the writings of C. Wright Mills, Paul Goodman, and Herbert Marcuse.

Free-Speech Movement

Students at the University of California, Berkeley, staged sit-ins in 1964 to protest the prohibition of political canvassing on campus. Led by Mario Savio, the movement changed from emphasizing student rights to criticizing the bureaucracy of American society. In December, police broke up a sit-in; protests spread to other campuses around the nation.

Vietnam

Student protests began focusing on the Vietnam War. In the spring of 1967, 500,000 gathered in Central Park in New York City to protest the war, many burning their draft cards. SDS became more militant and willing to use violence. It turned to Lenin for its ideology.

1968

More than 200 large campus demonstrations took place in the spring, culminating in the occupation of buildings at Columbia University to protest the university's involvement in military research and its poor relations with minority groups. Police wielding clubs eventually broke up the demonstration. In August, thousands gathered in Chicago to protest the war during the Democratic convention. Although police violence against the demonstrators aroused anger, the antiwar movement began to split between those favoring violence and those opposed to it.

Decline

Beginning in 1968, SDS began breaking up into rival factions. After the more radical factions began using bombs, Tom Hayden left the group. By the early 1970s, the New Left had lost political influence, having abandoned its original commitment to democracy and nonviolence.

THE COUNTERCULTURE

Origins

Like the New Left, the founders of the counterculture were alienated by bureaucracy, materialism, and the Vietnam War, but they turned away from politics in favor of an alternative society. In many respects, they were heirs of the Beats.

Counterculture Expression

Many young people formed communes in such places as San Francisco's Haight-Ashbury district or in rural areas. "Hippies," as they were called, experimented with Eastern religions, drugs, and sex, but most were unable to establish a self-sustaining lifestyle. Leading spokesmen included Timothy Leary, Theodore Roszak, and Charles Reich.

WOMEN'S LIBERATION

Betty Friedan

In *The Feminine Mystique* (1963), Betty Friedan argued that middle-class society stifled women and did not allow them to use their individual talents. She attacked the cult of domesticity.

National Organization for Women

Friedan and other feminists founded the National Organization for Women (NOW) in 1966, calling for equal employment opportunities and equal pay.

Problems

The women's movement was largely limited to the middle class. The Equal Rights Amendment failed to pass. Abortion rights stirred up a counter "right-to-life" movement.

VIETNAM

Background

After the French defeat in 1954, the United States sent military advisors to South Vietnam to aid the government of Ngo Dinh Diem. The pro-Communist Vietcong forces gradually grew in strength, partly because Diem failed to follow through on promised reforms. They received support from North Vietnam, the Soviet Union, and China. The U.S. government supported a successful military coup against Diem in the fall of 1963.

Escalation

In August 1964—after claiming that North Vietnamese gunboats had fired on American destroyers in the Gulf of Tonkin—Lyndon Johnson pushed the Gulf of Tonkin resolution through Congress, authorizing him to use military force in Vietnam. After a February 1965 attack by the Vietcong on Pleiku, Johnson ordered operation "Rolling Thunder," the first sustained bombing of North Vietnam. Johnson then sent combat troops to South Vietnam; under the leadership of General William C. Westmoreland, they conducted search and destroy operations. The number of troops increased to 184,000 in 1965, 385,000 in 1966, 485,000 in 1967, and 538,000 in 1968.

Defense of American Policy

"Hawks" defended the president's policy and, drawing on containment theory, said that the nation had the responsibility to resist aggression. Secretary of State Dean Rusk became a major spokesman for the domino theory, which justified government policy by analogy with England's and France's failure to stop Hitler prior to 1939. If Vietnam should fall, it was said, all Southeast Asia would eventually go. The administration stressed its willingness to negotiate the withdrawal of all "foreign" forces from the war.

Tet Offensive

On January 31, 1968, the first day of the Vietnamese new year (Tet), the Vietcong attacked numerous cities and towns, American bases, and even Saigon. Although they suffered large losses, the Vietcong won a psychological victory, as American opinion began turning against the war.

ELECTION OF 1968

Eugene McCarthy

In November 1967, Senator Eugene McCarthy of Minnesota announced his candidacy for the 1968 Democratic presidential nomination, running on the issue of opposition to the war.

New Hampshire

In February, McCarthy won 42 percent of the Democratic vote in the New Hampshire primary, compared with Johnson's 48 percent. Robert F. Kennedy then announced his candidacy for the Democratic presidential nomination.

Johnson's Withdrawal

Lyndon Johnson withdrew his candidacy on March 31, 1968, and Vice-President Hubert H. Humphrey took his place as a candidate for the Democratic nomination.

Kennedy Assassination

After winning the California primary over McCarthy, Robert Kennedy was assassinated by Sirhan Sirhan, a young Palestinian. This event assured Humphrey's nomination.

The Nominees

The Republicans nominated Richard M. Nixon, who chose Spiro T. Agnew, governor of Maryland, as his running mate in order to appeal to southern voters. Governor George C. Wallace of Alabama ran for the presidency under the banner of the American Independent party, appealing to fears generated by left-wing protestors and big government.

Nixon's Victory

Johnson suspended air attacks on North Vietnam shortly before the election. Nonetheless, Nixon, who emphasized stability and order, defeated Humphrey by a margin of 1 percent. Wallace's 13.5 percent was the best showing by a third-party candidate since 1924.

THE NIXON CONSERVATIVE REACTION

Civil Rights

The Nixon administration sought to block renewal of the Voting Rights Act and delay implementation of court-ordered school desegregation in Mississippi. After the Supreme Court ordered busing of students in 1971 to achieve school desegregation, the administration proposed an antibusing bill, which was blocked in Congress.

Supreme Court

In 1969, Nixon appointed Warren E. Burger, a conservative, as chief justice, but ran into opposition with the nomination of southerners Clement F. Haynesworth, Jr., and G. Harrold Carswell. After these nominations were defeated, he nominated Harry A. Blackmun, who received Senate approval. He later appointed Lewis F. Powell Jr. and William Rehnquist as associate justices. Although more conservative than the Warren court, the Burger court did declare the death penalty, as used at the time, unconstitutional in 1972, and struck down state anti-abortion legislation in 1973.

Revenue Sharing

The heart of Nixon's "New Federalism," passed by Congress in 1972, was a five-year plan to distribute $30 billion of federal revenues to the states.

Congressional Legislation

Congress passed bills giving 18-year-olds the right to vote (1970), increasing Social Security benefits and funding for food stamps (1970), as well as establishing the Occupational Safety and Health Act (1970), the Clean Air Act (1970), laws to control water pollution (1970, 1972), and the Federal Election Campaign Act (1972). None was supported by the Nixon administration.

Economic Problems and Policy

Unemployment climbed to 6 percent in 1970, real gross national product declined in 1970, and in 1971 the United States experienced a trade deficit. Inflation reached 12 percent by 1974. These problems resulted from federal deficits in the 1960s, growing international competition, and rising energy costs.

In 1969, Nixon cut spending and raised taxes. He encouraged the Federal Reserve Board to raise interest rates. The economy worsened. In 1970, Congress gave the president the power to regulate prices and wages. Nixon used this power in August 1971 by declaring a 90-day price and wage freeze and taking the United States off the gold standard. At the end of the 90 days he established mandatory guidelines for wage and price increases. Finally, in 1973, he turned to voluntary wage and price controls, except on health care, food, and construction. When inflation increased rapidly, Nixon cut back on government expenditures, impounding funds already appropriated by Congress.

VIETNAMIZATION

Nixon proposed that all non–South Vietnamese troops be withdrawn in phases, and that an internationally supervised election be held in South Vietnam. The North Vietnamese rejected this plan.

The president then turned to "Vietnamization," the effort to build up South Vietnamese forces while withdrawing American troops. In 1969, Nixon reduced American troop strength by 60,000, but at the same time ordered the bombing of Cambodia, a neutral country, in the interests of flushing out Vietcong.

Protests

Two Moratorium Days in 1969 brought out several hundred thousand protesters, and reports of an American massacre of Vietnamese at My Lai reignited controversy over the nature of the war, but Nixon continued to defend his policy. Troop withdrawals continued, and a lottery system was instituted in 1970 to make the draft more equitable. In 1973, Nixon abolished the draft and established an all-volunteer army.

Cambodia

In April 1970, Nixon announced that Vietnamization was succeeding and that another 150,000 American troops would be out of Vietnam by the end of the year. A few days later, he sent troops into Cambodia to clear out Vietcong sanctuaries and resumed bombing of North Vietnam.

Kent State

Protests against escalation of the war were especially strong on college campuses. During a May 1970 demonstration at Kent State University in Ohio, National Guardsmen opened fire on protestors, killing four students. Soon after, two black students were killed by a Mississippi state policeman at Jackson State University. Several hundred colleges were soon closed down by student strikes, as moderates joined the radicals. Congress repealed the Gulf of Tonkin Resolution.

Pentagon Papers

The publication in 1971 of "the Pentagon Papers," classified Defense Department documents that were leaked to the press, revealed that the government had misled the Congress and the American people about its intentions in Vietnam during the mid-1960s.

End of U.S. Involvement

In the summer of 1972, negotiations between the United States and North Vietnam began in Paris. By October, a draft agreement was developed which included provisions for a cease-fire, the return of American prisoners of war, and the withdrawal of U.S. forces from Vietnam. A few days before the 1972 presidential election, Henry Kissinger, the president's national security advisor, declared that "peace was at hand."

Resumption of Bombing

Nixon resumed bombing of North Vietnam in December 1972, claiming that the North Vietnamese were not bargaining in good faith. In January 1973, the opponents reached a settlement in which the North Vietnamese retained control over large areas of the South and agreed to release American prisoners of war within 60 days. After the prisoners were released, the United States would withdraw its remaining troops. On March 29, 1973, the last American combat troops left South Vietnam. Nearly 60,000 Americans had been killed and 300,000 more wounded; the war's financial cost to the United States was $109 billion.

War Powers Act

Later in 1973, the War Powers Act was passed. It required congressional approval of any commitment of combat troops beyond 90 days.

FOREIGN POLICY

China

With his national security advisor, Henry Kissinger, Nixon took some bold diplomatic initiatives. Kissinger traveled to China and the Soviet Union for secret sessions to plan summit meetings with the Communists. In February 1972, Nixon and Kissinger went to China to meet with Mao Tse-tung and his associates. The United States agreed to support China's admission to the United Nations and to pursue economic and cultural exchanges.

Soviet Union

At a May 1972 meeting with the Soviets, the Strategic Arms Limitation Treaty (SALT) was signed. The signatories agreed to stop making nuclear ballistic missiles and to reduce the number of antiballistic missiles to 200 for each power.

Middle East

Following the Arab-Israeli war of 1973, Arab states staged an oil boycott to push the Western nations into forcing Israel to withdraw from lands controlled since the Six-Day War of 1967. Kissinger, now secretary of state, negotiated the withdrawal of Israel from some of the lands and the Arabs lifted their boycott. The five-member Organization of Petroleum Exporting Countries (OPEC)—composed of Venezuela, Saudi Arabia, Kuwait, Iraq, and Iran—then raised the price of oil from about $3.00 to $11.65 a barrel. U.S. gas prices doubled and inflation shot above 10 percent.

ELECTION OF 1972

George McGovern

The Democrats nominated Senator George McGovern of South Dakota for president and Senator Thomas Eagleton for vice president. After the press revealed that Eagleton had been treated for psychological problems, McGovern eventually forced him off the ticket, replacing him with Sargent Shriver.

George Wallace

George Wallace, a longtime segregationist, ran once again as the American Independent party candidate. While campaigning at a Maryland shopping center on May 15, 1972, he became the victim of an assassination attempt that left him paralyzed below the waist. Arthur Bremer, 21, was sentenced to 63 years for shooting Wallace and three others.

Richard M. Nixon

Richard M. Nixon and Spiro T. Agnew, who had been renominated by the Republicans, won a landslide victory, receiving 521 electoral votes to McGovern's 17.

HISTORICAL TIMELINE

The New Frontier, Vietnam, and Social Upheaval (1960–1972)

1960	Kennedy and Nixon participate in first televised presidential debates Greensboro sit-in protests Kennedy defeats Nixon
1961	Bay of Pigs invasion fails Freedom rides Berlin Wall built Peace Corps established Alliance for Progress established
1962	Cuban Missile Crisis Students for a Democratic Society formed
1963	Rev. King begins Birmingham desegregation efforts University of Alabama admits first black student Civil Rights March on Washington Premier Diem of South Vietnam toppled by U.S.-approved coup President Kennedy assassinated
1964	President Johnson announces war on poverty Freedom summer vote registration campaign in Mississippi Civil Rights Act passed VISTA established Berkeley Free Speech Movement Gulf of Tonkin Resolution passed U.S. begins bombing of North Vietnam Johnson elected president
1965	Medicare funding begins Race riots in Watts Malcolm X assassinated American combat troops sent to Vietnam
1966	National Organization for Women (NOW) formed Stokely Carmichael leads black power movement
1967	Race riots in Detroit and Newark Massive antiwar protest in Washington, D.C. Israel, Arab neighbors fight Six-Day War

1968	Viet Cong launch Tet Offensive Johnson withdraws from presidential race Dr. Martin Luther King Jr. assassinated Robert Kennedy assassinated Protests at Chicago Democratic Convention Nixon elected president
1969	Woodstock festival Apollo 11 crew lands on moon Stonewall Riots launch gay liberation movement
1970	U.S. invades Cambodia Kent State Massacre
1972	Nixon visits People's Republic of China Détente begins with Soviet Union SALT I Treaty signed with Soviet Union

15 WATERGATE, CONSERVATISM'S RISE, AND POST–COLD WAR CHALLENGES (1972–2005)

THE WATERGATE SCANDAL

The Break-In

What became known as the Watergate crisis began during the 1972 presidential campaign. Early on the morning of June 17, James McCord, a security officer for the Committee for the Re-election of the President, and four other men broke into Democratic headquarters at the Watergate apartment complex in Washington, D.C., and were caught while going through files and installing electronic eavesdropping devices. On June 22, Nixon announced that the administration was in no way involved in the burglary attempt.

James McCord

The trial of the burglars began in early 1973, with all but McCord (who was convicted) pleading guilty. Before sentencing, McCord wrote a letter to U.S. District Court Judge John J. Sirica arguing that high Republican officials had known in advance about the burglary and that perjury had been committed at the trial.

Further Revelations

Soon Jeb Stuart Magruder, head of the Nixon re-election committee, and John W. Dean, Nixon's attorney, revealed that they had been involved. Dean testified before a Senate Watergate committee that Nixon had been involved in covering up the incident. Over the next several months, extensive involvement of the White House administration, including payment of "hush" money to the burglars, destruction of FBI records, forgery of documents, and wiretapping, was revealed. Dean was fired and H. R. Haldeman and John Ehrlichman, who headed the White House staff, and Attorney General Richard Kleindienst, resigned. Nixon claimed that he had not personally been involved in the cover-up but refused, on the grounds of executive privilege, to allow investigation of White House documents.

White House Tapes

Under considerable pressure, Nixon agreed to the appointment of a special prosecutor, Archibald Cox of Harvard Law School. When Cox obtained a subpoena for tape recordings of White House conversations (whose existence had been revealed in testimony during the Senate hearings)—and the administration lost an appeal in the appellate court—Nixon ordered Elliot Richardson, the attorney general, to fire Cox. Both Richardson and his subordinate, William Ruckelshaus, resigned, leaving Robert Bork, the solicitor general, to carry out the order. This "Saturday Night Massacre," which took place on October 20, 1973, caused a storm of controversy. The House Judiciary Committee, headed by Peter Rodino of New Jersey, began looking into the possibility of impeachment. Nixon agreed to turn the tapes over to Judge Sirica and named Leon Jaworski as the new special prosecutor. But it soon became known that some of the tapes were missing and that a portion of another had been erased.

The Vice-Presidency

Vice-President Spiro Agnew was accused of income tax fraud and having accepted bribes while a local official in Maryland. He resigned the vice-presidency in October 1973 and was replaced by Congressman Gerald R. Ford of Michigan under provisions of the new 25th Amendment.

Nixon's Taxes

Nixon was accused of paying almost no income taxes between 1969 and 1972, and of using public funds for improvements to his private residences in California and Florida. The IRS reviewed the president's tax return and assessed him nearly $500,000 in back taxes and interest.

Indictments

In March 1974 a grand jury indicted Haldeman, Ehrlichman, former Attorney General John Mitchell, and four other White House aides, and named Nixon as an unindicted coconspirator.

Calls for Resignation

In April, Nixon released edited transcripts of the White House tapes, the contents of which led to further calls for his resignation. Jaworski subpoenaed 64 additional tapes, which Nixon refused to turn over, and the case went to the Supreme Court.

Impeachment Debate

Meanwhile, the House Judiciary Committee televised its debate over impeachment, adopting three articles of impeachment. It charged the president with obstructing justice, misusing presidential power, and failing to obey the committee's subpoenas.

Resignation

Before the House began to debate impeachment, the Supreme Court ordered the president to release the subpoenaed tapes to the special prosecutor. On August 5, Nixon, under pressure from his advisors, made public the tape of June 23, 1972. This tape, recorded less than a week after the break-in, revealed that Nixon had used the CIA to keep the FBI from investigating the case. Nixon announced his resignation on August 8, 1974, to take effect at noon the following day. Gerald Ford then became president.

Legislative Response

Congress responded to the Vietnam War and Watergate by enacting legislation intended to prevent such situations. In 1974 Congress limited the amounts of contributions and expenditures in presidential campaigns. It also strengthened the 1966 Freedom of Information Act by requiring the government to act promptly when asked for information and to prove its case for classification when attempting to withhold information on grounds of national security.

THE FORD PRESIDENCY

Gerald Ford

Gerald Ford was in many respects the opposite of Nixon. Although a partisan Republican, he was well liked and free from any hint of scandal. Ford almost immediately encountered controversy when, in September 1974, he offered to pardon Nixon. Nixon accepted the offer, although he admitted no wrongdoing and had not yet been charged with a crime.

The Economy

Ford also faced major economic problems, which he approached somewhat inconsistently. Saying that inflation was the major problem, he called for voluntary restraints and asked citizens to wear "Whip Inflation Now," or WIN, buttons. The economy went into decline. Ford asked for tax cuts to stimulate business and argued against spending for social programs.

When New York City teetered on the verge of bankruptcy in 1975, Ford at first opposed federal aid but changed his mind when the Senate and House Banking Committees guaranteed the loans.

Vietnam

As North Vietnamese forces pushed back the South Vietnamese, Ford asked Congress to provide more arms for the South. Congress rejected the request, and in April 1975 Saigon fell to the North Vietnamese.

Election of 1976

Ronald Reagan, formerly a movie actor and governor of California, opposed Ford for the Republican nomination, but Ford won by a slim margin. The Democrats nominated James Earl Carter, formerly governor of Georgia, who ran on the basis of his integrity and lack of Washington connections. Carter, with Senator Walter Mondale of Minnesota as his vice-presidential candidate, narrowly defeated Ford.

CARTER'S MODERATE LIBERALISM

Policy Orientation in the Carter Administration

Carter sought to conduct the presidency on democratic and moral principles. The former peanut farmer, however, often misread political sentiment on Capitol Hill: the administration typically proposed complex programs but failed to support them through the legislative process.

The Economy

Carter approached economic problems inconsistently. In 1978, he proposed voluntary wage and price guidelines. Although somewhat successful, the guidelines did not apply to oil, housing, and food. Carter then named Paul A. Volcker as chairman of the Federal Reserve Board. Volcker tightened the money supply in order to reduce inflation, but this action caused interest rates to go even higher. High interest rates depressed sales of automobiles and houses, which in turn increased unemployment. By 1980, unemployment stood at 7.5 percent, interest at 20 percent, and inflation at 12 percent.

Domestic Achievements

Carter offered amnesty to Americans who had fled the draft and gone to other countries during the Vietnam War. He established the Departments of Energy and Education and placed the civil service on a merit basis. He created a "superfund" for cleanup of chemical waste dumps, established controls over strip mining, and protected 100 million acres of Alaskan wilderness from development.

CARTER'S FOREIGN POLICY

Human Rights

Carter sought to base foreign policy on human rights, but was criticized for inconsistency and lack of attention to American interests.

Panama Canal

Carter negotiated a controversial treaty with Panama, affirmed by the Senate in 1978, that provided for the transfer of ownership of the canal to Panama in 1999 and guaranteed its neutrality.

China

Carter ended official recognition of Taiwan and in 1979 recognized the People's Republic of China. Conservatives called the decision a "sell-out."

SALT II

In 1979, Carter signed the Strategic Arms Limitation Treaty II with the Soviet Union. The treaty set a ceiling of 2,250 bombers and missiles for each side, and set limits on warheads and new weapons systems. It never reached the Senate floor.

Camp David Accords

In 1978 Carter negotiated the Camp David Accords between Israel and Egypt. Bringing Anwar Sadat, president of Egypt, and Menachem Begin, prime minister of Israel, to Camp David, Maryland, for two weeks in September 1978, Carter sought to end the state of war that existed between the two countries. Israel promised to return occupied land in the Sinai to Egypt in exchange for Egyptian recognition, a process completed in 1982. An agreement to negotiate the Palestinian refugee problem proved ineffective.

Afghanistan

The policy of detente went into decline. Carter criticized Soviet restrictions on political freedom and reluctance to allow dissidents and Jews to emigrate. In December 1979 the Soviet Union invaded Afghanistan. In response, Carter stopped shipments of grain and technology to the Soviets, withdrew his support for SALT II, and barred Americans from competing in the 1980 Moscow Summer Olympics.

THE IRANIAN CRISIS

The Iranian Revolution

In 1978 a revolution forced the shah of Iran to flee the country, replacing him with a religious leader, Ayatollah Ruhollah Khomeini. Because the United States had supported the shah with arms and money, the revolutionaries were strongly anti-American, calling the United States the "Great Satan."

Hostages

After Carter allowed the exiled shah to come to the United States for medical treatment in October 1979, some 400 Iranians broke into the American embassy in Teheran on November 4, taking the occupants captive. They demanded that the shah be returned to Iran for trial and that his wealth be confiscated and given to Iran. Carter rejected these demands; instead, he froze Iranian assets in the United States and established a trade embargo against Iran. He also appealed to the United Nations and the World Court. The Iranians eventually freed the African-American and women hostages, but kept 52 others.

In April 1980 Carter ordered a marine rescue attempt, but it collapsed after several helicopters broke down and another crashed, killing eight men. Secretary of State Cyrus Vance resigned in protest before the raid began, and Carter was widely criticized for its failure.

THE ELECTION OF 1980

The Democrats

Carter, whose approval rating in public opinion polls had dropped to about 25 percent in 1979, successfully withstood a challenge from Senator Edward M. Kennedy of Massachusetts for the Democratic presidential nomination.

The Republicans

The Republicans nominated Ronald Reagan of California, who had narrowly lost the 1976 nomination and was the leading spokesman for American conservatism. Reagan chose George Bush, a New Englander transplanted to Texas and former CIA director, as his vice-presidential candidate. One of Reagan's opponents, Congressman John Anderson of Illinois, continued his presidential campaign on a third-party ticket.

The Campaign

While Carter defended his record, Reagan heavily favored increased defense spending, but also called for reductions in government spending and taxes. Reagan talked of granting more power to the states. He advocated what were coming to be called traditional values—family, religion, hard work, and patriotism.

Reagan's Victory

Reagan won by a large electoral majority, and the Republicans gained control of the Senate and increased their representation in the House.

American Hostages

After extensive negotiations with Iran, in which Algeria acted as an intermediary, Carter released Iranian assets and the hostages were freed on January 20, 1981—the day of Reagan's inaugural. It had been 444 days since they had been taken captive.

THE REAGAN PRESIDENCY: ATTACKING BIG GOVERNMENT

Tax Policy

An ideological though pragmatic conservative, Ronald Reagan acted quickly and forcefully to change the direction of government policy. He placed priority on cutting taxes. His approach was based on "supply-side" economics, the idea that if government left more money in the hands of the people, they would invest rather than spend the excess on consumer goods. The results would be greater production, more jobs, and greater prosperity, and thus more income for the government despite lower tax rates.

Economic Recovery Tax Act

Reagan asked for a 30 percent tax cut, and despite fears of inflation on the part of Congress, in August 1983 obtained a 25 percent cut, spread over three years. The percentage was the same for everyone; hence high-income people received greater savings than middle- and low-income individuals. To encourage investment, capital gains, gift, and inheritance taxes were reduced and business taxes liberalized. Anyone with earned income was also allowed to invest up to $2,000 a year in an Individual Retirement Account (IRA), deferring all taxes on both the principal and its earnings until retirement.

Government Spending

Congress passed the Budget Reconciliation Act in 1981, cutting $39 billion from domestic programs, including education, food stamps, public housing, and the National Endowments for the Arts and Humanities. While cutting domestic programs, Reagan increased the defense budget by $12 billion.

SDI

Reagan concentrated on obtaining funding for the development of a computer-controlled Strategic Defense Initiative (SDI) system, dubbed by the press "Star Wars" after the movie of that name. SDI would destroy incoming enemy missiles from outer space. Skeptical about its technological feasibility and fearful of enormous costs, Congress balked and scaled back the proposal during Reagan's second term.

Increasing Revenue

Because of rising deficits, Reagan and Congress increased taxes in various ways. The 1982 Tax Equity and Fiscal Responsibility Act reversed some concessions made to business in 1981. Social Security benefits became taxable income in 1983. In 1984, the Deficit Reduction Act increased taxes by another $50 billion. But the deficit continued to increase.

Assassination Attempt

John W. Hinckley shot Reagan in the chest on March 30, 1981. The president was wounded but made a swift recovery. His popularity increased, possibly helping his legislative program.

Antitrust

Reagan ended ongoing antitrust suits against IBM and AT&T, thereby fulfilling his promise to reduce government interference with business.

Women and Minorities

Although Reagan appointed Sandra Day O'Connor to the Supreme Court, his administration gave fewer of its appointments to women and minorities than had the Carter administration. The Reagan administration also opposed "equal pay for equal work" and renewal of the Voting Rights Act of 1965.

Problems with Appointed Officials

A number of Reagan appointees were accused of conflict of interest, including Anne Gorsuch Burford and Rita Lavelle of the Environmental Protection Agency, Edwin Meese, presidential advisor and later attorney general, and Michael Deaver, the deputy chief of staff. Ray Donovan, secretary of labor, was indicted but later acquitted of charges that he had made payoffs to government officials while he was in private business. By the end of Reagan's term, more than 100 of his officials had been accused of questionable activities.

ASSERTING AMERICAN POWER

Soviet Union

Reagan took a hard line against the Soviet Union, calling it an "evil empire." He placed new cruise missiles in Europe, despite considerable opposition from Europeans.

ELECTION OF 1984

The Democrats

Walter Mondale, a former senator from Minnesota and vice president under Carter, won the Democratic nomination over Senator Gary Hart and Jesse Jackson, an African American civil-rights leader. Mondale chose Geraldine Ferraro, a congresswoman from New York, as his running mate. Mondale criticized Reagan for his budget deficits, high unemployment and interest rates, and reduction of spending on social services.

The Reagan Victory

The Republicans renominated Ronald Reagan and George Bush. Reagan drew support from groups such as the Moral Majority, founded by Fundamentalist evangelist Jerry Falwell. (The Fundamentalists had become a major political presence, voicing opposition to abortion, advocating an amendment to allow prayer in public schools, and identifying with the cause of Israel and a strong military defense budget.) Reagan's appeal also derived from an in-your-face anti-Soviet stance and decreased inflation, interest rates, and unemployment during his watch. He defeated Mondale handily, gaining nearly 60 percent of the vote by breaking apart the Democratic coalition of industrial workers, farmers, and the poor that had existed since FDR's time. Yet his coattails proved short: the GOP lost two seats in the Senate and gained little in the House.

SECOND-TERM FOREIGN CONCERNS

Libya

Reagan challenged Muammar al-Qadhafi, the anti-American leader of Libya, by sending Sixth Fleet ships within the Gulf of Sidra, which Qadhafi claimed. When Libyan gunboats challenged the American ships, American planes destroyed the gunboats and bombed installations on the Libyan shoreline. Soon after, a West German night club popular among American servicemen was bombed, killing a soldier and a civilian. Reagan, believing the bombing was ordered directly by Qadhafi, launched an air strike from Great Britain against Libyan bases in April 1986.

Soviet Union

After Mikhail S. Gorbachev became the premier of the Soviet Union in March 1985 and took a more flexible approach toward both domestic and foreign affairs, Reagan softened his anti-Soviet stance. But despite the Soviets' assurances that they would honor the unratified SALT II agreement, Reagan argued that they in fact had not adhered to the pact; as a result, he sought to expand and modernize the American defense system.

Arms Control

Reagan and Gorbachev had difficulty in reaching an agreement on arms limitations at summit talks in 1985 and 1986. Finally, in December 1987, they signed an agreement eliminating medium-range missiles from Europe.

Iran-Contra

Near the end of 1986, a scandal arose involving William Casey, head of the CIA, Lieutenant Colonel Oliver North of the National Security Council, Admiral John Poindexter, national security advisor, and Robert McFarlane, former national security advisor. In 1985 and 1986, they had sold arms to the Iranians in hopes of encouraging them to use their influence in getting American hostages in Lebanon released. The profits from these sales were then diverted to the Nicaraguan *Contras* in an attempt to get around congressional restrictions on funding the *Contras*. The president was forced to appoint a special prosecutor, and Congress held hearings on the affair in May 1987.

Nicaragua

The Reagan administration did not support a peace plan signed by five Central American nations in 1987, but the following year the *Sandinistas* and the *Contras* agreed on a cease-fire.

SECOND-TERM DOMESTIC AFFAIRS

Tax Reform

The Tax Reform Act of 1986 lowered tax rates, changing the highest rate on personal income from 50 percent to 28 percent and on corporate taxes from 46 percent to 34 percent. At the same time, it removed many tax shelters and tax credits. The law did away with the concept of progressive taxati on, the requirement that the percentage of income taxed increased as income increased. Instead, over a two-year period it established two rates, 15 percent on incomes below $17,850 for individuals and $29,750 for families and 28 percent on incomes above these amounts. The tax system would no longer be used as an instrument of social policy.

Economic Patterns

Unemployment declined, reaching 6.6 percent in 1986, while inflation fell as low as 2.2 percent during the first quarter of that year. The stock market was bullish through mid-1987.

Agriculture

With the general slowing of inflation, and the decline of world agricultural prices, many American farmers began to descend into bankruptcy in the mid-1980s, often dragging the rural banks that had made them the loans into bankruptcy as well. Although it lifted the ban on wheat exports to the Soviet Union, the Reagan administration reduced price supports and opposed debt relief passed by Congress.

Deficits

The federal deficit reached $179 billion in 1985. At about the same time, the United States experienced trade deficits of more than $100 billion annually, partly because management and engineering skills had fallen behind Japan and Germany, and partly because the United States provided an open market to foreign businesses. In the mid-1980s, the United States became a debtor nation for the first time since World War I. Consumer debt also rose from $300 billion in 1980 to $500 billion in 1986.

Black Monday

On October 19, 1987, labeled "Black Monday" on Wall Street, the Dow Jones Industrial Average dropped more than 500 points, or over 20 percent. Between August 25 and October 20, the market lost over a trillion dollars in paper value. Fearing a recession, Congress in November 1987 reduced 1988 taxes by $30 billion.

NASA Tragedy

The explosion of the space shuttle *Challenger* soon after liftoff on January 28, 1986, damaged NASA's credibility and reinforced doubts about the complex technology required to implement the Strategic Defense Initiative. All aboard perished, including a New Hampshire teacher who was the first private citizen to go into space.

Supreme Court

Reagan reshaped the Court. In 1986, he replaced Chief Justice Warren C. Burger with Associate Justice William H. Rehnquist, probably the most conservative member of the Court. Although failing in his nomination of Robert Bork for associate justice, Reagan successfully appointed other conservatives to the Court: Sandra Day O'Connor, Antonin Scalia, and Anthony Kennedy.

ELECTION OF 1988

The Candidates

After a sex scandal eliminated Senator Gary Hart from the race for the Democratic presidential nomination, Governor Michael Dukakis of Massachusetts emerged as the victor over his major challenger, Jesse Jackson. He chose Senator Lloyd Bentsen of Texas as his vice-presidential running mate. Vice

President George Bush, after a slow start in the primaries, won the Republican nomination. He chose Senator Dan Quayle of Indiana as his running mate. Bush easily defeated Dukakis, but the Republicans were unable to make any inroads in Congress.

BUSH ABANDONS REAGANOMICS

Budget Deficit

Soon after George H. W. Bush took office as president on January 20, 1989, the budget deficit for 1990 was estimated at $143 billion. With deficit estimates continuing to grow, Bush held a "budget summit" with congressional leaders in May 1990, and his administration continued talks throughout the summer. In September, the administration and Congress agreed to increase taxes on gasoline, tobacco, and alcohol, establish an excise tax on luxury items, and raise Medicare taxes. Cuts were also to be made in Medicare and other domestic programs. The 1991 deficit was now estimated to be over $290 billion. The following month, Congress approved the plan, hoping to cut a cumulative amount of $500 billion from the deficit over the next five years. In a straight party vote—Republicans voting against and Democrats voting in favor— Congress in December gave the power to decide whether new tax and spending proposals violated the deficit-cutting agreement to the Congressional Budget office. This power had been in the hands of the White House Office of Management and Budget.

Savings and Loan Debacle

With the savings and loan industry in financial trouble in February 1989, largely because of bad real-estate loans, Bush proposed to close or sell 350 institutions, to be paid for by the sale of government bonds. In July he signed a bill that created the Resolution Trust Corporation to oversee the closure and merging of savings and loans, and which provided $166 billion over 10 years to cover the bad debts. Estimates of the total cost of the debacle ran to upward of $300 billion.

Scandals in the Financial Markets

Charges of insider trading, stock manipulation, and falsification of records resulted in Drexel Burnham Lambert, a major securities firm, pleading guilty in December 1988 to six violations of federal law. The company filed for bankruptcy and Michael Milken, its "junk bond king" (junk bonds are bonds below an investment grade of BB or Bb, which because of their risk carry a two- to three-point interest advantage) pleaded guilty to conspiracy, among other charges, in 1990. Meanwhile, in July 1989, 46 futures traders at the Chicago Mercantile Exchange were charged with racketeering.

Economic Slowdown

The gross national product slowed from 4.4 percent in 1988 to 2.9 percent in 1989. Unemployment gradually began to increase, reaching 6.8 percent in March 1991, a three-year high. Every sector of the economy except for medical services and all geographical areas experienced the slowdown. The "Big Three" automakers posted record losses and Pan American World Airways and Eastern Airlines entered bankruptcy proceedings. In September 1991, the Federal Reserve lowered the interest rate.

OTHER DOMESTIC ISSUES UNDER BUSH

Exxon Valdez Accident

After the *Exxon Valdez* spilled more than 240,000 barrels of oil into Alaska's Prince William Sound in March 1989, the federal government ordered Exxon Corporation to develop a clean-up plan, which it carried out until the weather prevented it from continuing in September. The *Valdez* captain, Joseph Hazelwood, was found guilty of negligence the following year. Exxon, the state of Alaska, and the U.S. Justice Department reached a settlement in October 1991 requiring Exxon to pay $1.025 billion in fines and restitution through 2001.

Congressional Ethics Violations

After the House Ethics Committee released a report charging that Speaker Jim Wright had violated rules regulating acceptance of gifts and outside income, Wright resigned in May 1989. A short time later, the Democratic whip Tony Coelho resigned because of alleged improper use of campaign funds.

Pollution

The Clean Air Act, passed in October 1990 and updating the 1970 law, mandated that the level of emissions was to be reduced 50 percent by the year 2000. Cleaner gasolines were to be developed, cities were to reduce ozone (an ingredient in photo-chemical smog), and nitrogen oxide emissions were to be cut by one-third.

Civil Rights

The Americans with Disabilities Act, passed in July 1990, barred discrimination against people with physical or mental disabilities. In October 1990, Bush vetoed the Civil Rights Act on the grounds that it established quotas, but a year later he accepted a slightly revised version that, among other things, required that employers in discrimination suits prove that their hiring practices are not discriminatory.

Supreme Court Appointments

Bush continued to reshape the Supreme Court in a conservative direction when, upon the retirement of Justice William J. Brennan, he successfully nominated Judge David Souter of the U.S. Court of Appeals in 1989. Two years later, Bush nominated a conservative African American, Judge Clarence Thomas, also of the U.S. Court of Appeals, upon the retirement of Justice Thurgood Marshall. Thomas's nomination stirred up opposition from the NAACP and other liberal groups, which supported affirmative action and abortion rights. Dramatic charges of sexual harassment against Thomas from Anita Hill, a University of Oklahoma law professor, were revealed only days before the nomination was to go to the Senate. The charges provoked a reopening of Judiciary Committee hearings, which were nationally televised. Nonetheless, Thomas narrowly won confirmation in October 1991.

BUSH'S ACTIVIST FOREIGN POLICY

Panama

Since coming to office, the Bush administration had been concerned with Panamanian dictator Manuel Noriega because he allegedly provided an important link in the drug traffic between South America and the United States. After economic sanctions, diplomatic efforts, and an October 1989 coup failed to oust Noriega, Bush ordered 12,000 troops into Panama on December 20. The Americans installed a new government headed by Guillermo Endara, who had earlier apparently won a presidential election which was then nullified by Noriega. On January 3, 1990, Noriega surrendered to the Americans and was taken to the United States to stand trial on drug-trafficking charges, a trial that began in September 1991. Found guilty in 1992, he was sentenced to 40 years' imprisonment. Twenty-three United States soldiers and three American civilians were killed in the Panamanian operation. The Panamanians lost nearly 300 soldiers and more than 500 civilians.

China

After the death in April 1989 of reformer Hu Yaobang, formerly general secretary and chairman of the Chinese Communist party, students began prodemocracy marches in Beijing. By the middle of May, more than one million people were gathering in Beijing's Tiananmen Square and elsewhere in China, calling for political reform. Martial law was imposed and in early June the army fired on the demonstrators. Estimates of the death toll in the wake of the nationwide crackdown on demonstrators ranged between 500 and 7,000. In July 1989 U.S. National Security Advisor Brent Scowcroft and Deputy Secretary of State Lawrence Eagleburger secretly met with Chinese leaders. When they again met the Chinese in December and revealed their earlier meeting, the Bush administration faced a storm of criticism for its policy of "constructive engagement" from opponents arguing that sanctions were needed. Although establishing sanctions on China in 1991 on high-technology satellite-part exports, Bush continued to support renewal of China's Most Favored Nation trading status.

COLLAPSE OF EAST EUROPEAN COMMUNISM

Bush-Gorbachev Summits

Amid the collapse of communism in Eastern Europe, Bush met with Mikhail Gorbachev in Malta from December 1 through 3, 1989; the two leaders appeared to agree that the Cold War was over. On May 30 and 31, 1990, Bush and Gorbachev met in Washington to discuss the possible reunification of Germany, and signed a trade treaty between the United States and the Soviet Union. The meeting of the two leaders in Helsinki on September 9 addressed strategies for the developing Persian Gulf crisis. At the meeting of the "Group of 7" nations (Canada, France, Germany, Italy, Japan, the United Kingdom, and the United States) in July 1991, Gorbachev requested economic aid from the West. A short time later, on July 30 and 31, Bush met Gorbachev in Moscow, where they signed the Strategic Arms Reduction Treaty (START), which cut United States and Soviet nuclear arsenals by 30 percent, and pushed for Middle Eastern talks.

PERSIAN GULF CRISIS

July 1990: Saddam Hussein of Iraq charged that Kuwait had conspired with the United States to keep oil prices low and began massing troops at the Iraq-Kuwait border.

August 1990: On August 2 Iraq invaded Kuwait, an act that Bush denounced as "naked aggression." One day later, 100,000 Iraqi soldiers were poised south of Kuwait City, near the Saudi Arabian border. The United States quickly banned most trade with Iraq, froze Iraq's and Kuwait's assets in the United States, and sent aircraft carriers to the Persian Gulf. After the U.N. Security Council condemned the invasion, Bush on August 6 ordered the deployment of air, sea, and land forces to Saudi Arabia, dubbing the operation "Desert Shield." At the end of August there were 100,000 American soldiers in Saudi Arabia.

September 1990: Bush encouraged Egypt to support American policy by forgiving Egypt its debt to the United States. He also obtained pledges of financial support from Saudi Arabia, Kuwait, and Japan, among other nations, to help pay for the operation.

October 1990: On October 29 the Security Council warned Hussein that further actions might be taken if he did not withdraw from Kuwait.

November 1990: In November, Bush ordered that U.S. forces be increased to more than 400,000. On November 29 the United Nations set January 15, 1991, as the deadline for Iraqi withdrawal from Kuwait.

January 1991: On January 9 Iraq's foreign minister, Tariq Aziz, rejected a letter written by Bush to Hussein. Three days later, after an extensive debate, Congress authorized the use of force in the gulf. On January 17 an international force that included the U.S., Great Britain, France, Italy, Saudi Arabia, and Kuwait launched an air and missile attack on Iraq and occupied Kuwait. The United States called the effort "Operation Desert Storm." Under the overall command of the army's General H. Norman Schwarzkopf, the military effort emphasized high-technology weapons, including F-15E fighter bombers, F-117A stealth fighters, Tomahawk cruise missiles, and Patriot antimissile missiles. Beginning on January 17, Iraq sent SCUD missiles into Israel in an effort to draw that country into the war and hopefully break up the U.S.-Arabian coalition. On January 22 and 23, Hussein's forces set Kuwaiti oil fields on fire and spilled oil into the gulf.

February 1991: On February 23 the allied ground assault began. Four days later, Bush announced that Kuwait was liberated and ordered offensive operations to cease. The United Nations established the terms for the cease-fire: Iraqi annexation of Kuwait to be rescinded, Iraq to accept liability for damages and return Kuwaiti property, Iraq to end all military actions and identify mines and booby traps, and Iraq to release captives.

April 1991: On April 3 the Security Council approved a resolution to establish a permanent cease-fire; Iraq accepted U.N. terms on April 6. The next day the United States began airlifting food to Kurdish refugees on the Iraq-Turkey border who were fleeing the Kurdish rebellion against Hussein, a rebellion that was seemingly encouraged by Bush, who nonetheless refused to become militarily involved. The United States estimated that 100,000 Iraqis had been killed during the war, while the Americans had lost about 115 lives.

Toward a Middle East Conference

On February 6, 1991, the United States had set out its postwar goals for the Middle East. These included regional arms control and security arrangements, international aid for reconstruction of Iraq and Kuwait, and resolution of the Israeli-Palestinian conflict. Immediately after cessation of the conflict, Secretary of State James Baker toured the Middle East attempting to promote a conference to address the problems of the region. After several more negotiating sessions, Saudi Arabia, Syria, Jordan, and Lebanon had accepted the United States proposal for an Arab-Israeli peace conference by the middle of July; Israel conditionally accepted in early August. Despite continuing conflict with Iraq, including U.N. inspections of its nuclear capabilities, and new

Israeli settlements in disputed territory which kept the conference agreement tenuous, the nations met in Madrid, Spain, at the end of October. Bilateral talks in early November between Israel and the Arabs concentrated on procedural issues.

BREAKUP OF THE SOVIET UNION

Collapse of Soviet Communism and the End of the Cold War

The Soviet Union began to break up in 1990, when Lithuania declared its independence. In the aftermath of an attemped coup by hard-line Communists later that year, other Soviet republics followed suit. For the United States, the collapse of the U.S.S.R. meant that the Cold War, which had begun in 1945, was finally over. The United States was now the world's only superpower. In September 1991 President Bush announced that the U.S. would carry out the unilateral removal and destruction of ground-based tactical nuclear weapons in Europe and Asia, removal of nuclear-armed Tomahawk cruise missiles from surface ships and submarines, immediate destruction of intercontinental ballistic missiles covered by the START treaty, and an end to the 24-hour alert for strategic bombers which the United States had maintained for decades. Gorbachev responded the next month by announcing the immediate deactivation of intercontinental ballistic missiles covered by START, removal of all short-range missiles from Soviet ships, submarines, and aircraft, and destruction of all ground-based tactical nuclear weapons. He also said that the Soviet Union would reduce its forces by 700,000 troops, and he placed all long-range nuclear missiles under a single command.

New foreign policy challenges emerged, however. Yugoslavia broke up into several different nations, and the region was plunged into a brutal war. Conflict threatened other parts of the world as well. The disintegration of the Soviet Union meant more nations had nuclear weapons, as several of the former Soviet republics had access to them.

THE ELECTION OF 1992

William Jefferson Clinton, governor of Arkansas, overcame several rivals and won the Democratic presidential nomination, choosing Senator Al Gore of Tennessee as his candidate for vice-president. Clinton and Reform Party candidate H. Ross Perot, emphasized jobs and the economy, as well as the debt. Bush stressed traditional values and his foreign policy accomplishments. In the general election Clinton won 43 percent of the popular vote and 370 electoral votes, thereby defeating George Bush, who received 38 percent of the vote, and independent candidate Ross Perot, who took 19 percent of the vote but no electoral votes.

THE CLINTON PRESIDENCY

Rocky Start Upon taking office, Clinton created a storm of protest when he proposed lifting the ban on homosexuals in the military. In July 1993 a compromise "Don't ask, don't tell" policy was struck, requiring gays and lesbians to be discreet about their sexual orientation and not to engage in homosexual acts. On the legislative front, Clinton was strongly rebuffed in a first-term attempt, led by the First Lady, to comprehensively reform the nation's healthcare system. In the 1994 mid-term elections, in what Clinton himself considered a repudiation of his administration, the Republicans took both houses of Congress from the Democrats and voted in Newt Gingrich of Georgia as Speaker of the House. Gingrich had helped craft the Republican congressional campaign strategy to dramatically shrink the federal government and give more power to the states.

Clinton, however, was not without his successes, both on the legislative and diplomatic fronts. He signed a bill establishing a five-day waiting period for handgun purchases, and he signed an anti-crime bill emphasizing community policing. He signed the Family and Medical Leave Act, which required large companies to provide up to 12 weeks' unpaid leave to workers for family and medical emergencies. He also championed welfare reform (a central theme of his campaign), but made it clear that the legislation he signed into law in August 1996 radically overhauling FDR's welfare system disturbed him on two counts—its exclusion of legal immigrants from getting most federal benefits and its deep cut in federal outlays for food stamps; Clinton said these flaws could be repaired with further legislation. In foreign affairs, Clinton signed the North American Free Trade Agreement (NAFTA), which, as of January 1994, lifted most trade barriers with Mexico and Canada. Clinton sought to ease tensions between Israelis and Palestinians, and he helped bring together Itzhak Rabin, prime minister of Israel, and Yasir Arafat, chairman of the Palestine Liberation Organization, for a White House summit. Ultimately, the two Middle East leaders signed a 1994 accord establishing Palestinian self-rule in the Gaza Strip and Jericho. In October 1994 Israel and Jordan signed a treaty to begin the process of establishing full diplomatic relations. Rabin was assassinated a year later by a radical, right-wing Israeli. The Clinton administration also played a key role in hammering out a peace agreement in 1995 in war-torn former Yugoslavia—where armed conflict had broken out in 1991 between Serbs, Croats, Bosnian Muslims, and other factions and groups.

Controversy Swirls Around the President The president came to be dogged by a number of controversies, including his and his wife's role in a complex Arkansas real estate deal called Whitewater, the removal of employees from the White House travel office, the suicide of Deputy White House Counsel Vince Foster, and a sexual harassment suit (later settled out of court) brought against the president by Paula Jones, a former Arkansas state employee. Whitewater spawned the Justice Department's appointment of an independent counsel, Robert B. Fiske, to look into it. Fiske's successor, Kenneth W. Starr, would expand the scope of the investigation. (Congress ultimately soured on the independent counsel law—enacted as a kind of coda to Watergate—and allowed it to expire in mid-1999.)

THE ELECTION OF 1996

Clinton recaptured the Democratic nomination without a serious challenge, while longtime GOP Senator Robert Dole of Kansas, the Senate majority leader, had to overcome several opponents but orchestrated a harmonious nominating convention with running mate Jack Kemp, a former New York congressman and Cabinet member during the Bush administration. In November 1996, with most voters citing a healthy economy and the lack of an enticing alternative in Dole or the Reform Party's Perot, Clinton received 49 percent of the vote (47 million popular votes and 379 electoral votes), becoming the first Democrat to be returned to the White House since FDR, in 1936. Dole won 41 percent (39 million popular votes, 159 electoral votes) and Perot polled eight percent of the total (8 million popular votes). The GOP retained control of both houses of Congress.

The Election of 1998 In the congressional elections of 1998, the Democrats gained seats in both the House and the Senate. Seldom does the president's party gain seats in a mid-term election, so it was widely believed that this—in part—might have been backlash to the continued Republican-led prosecution of Clinton for alleged perjury and obstruction of justice.

Domestic Policy Clinton sought a legacy as a preservationist by signing executive orders that set aside vast expanses of public lands, especially in the West.

Foreign Policy During his second term, Clinton faced continued political unrest and civil war in the Balkans. In 1999 the Serbian government attacked ethnic Albanians in Kosovo, a province of Serbia. In response, NATO forces, led by the United States, bombed Serbia. Several weeks of bombing forced Serbian forces to withdraw from Kosovo. Meanwhile, Clinton was instrumental in bringing about a historic peace agreement in Northern Ireland, while the land-for-peace accord he tried to broker between the Palestinians and Israel proved elusive. Clinton also continued to seek a policy of expanding international trade by relaxing or eliminating trade barriers.

Campaign Finance Reform Fails to Pass Though the issue of the influence of money on politics was not new, increasingly high levels of campaign spending and the contributions necessary to make such spending possible began to receive significant attention. Several bills were proposed in Congress, and Clinton pledged to support reform; by the end of his presidency in January 2001, however, no bill had passed.

Historic Economic Boom Falters As of February 1, 2000, the U.S. economy had enjoyed its longest stretch of uninterrupted growth in the nation's history. Much of this growth, which had begun in March 1991, was fueled by a new industry, electronic commerce on the Internet. Stock prices generally rose, but share prices for Internet companies rose especially fast, soaring to extraordinary heights. In 2000, investors came to see e-businesses' and high-tech stock prices as unreasonably high. A number of such stocks tumbled, with some losing as much as 90 percent of their value. Soon many formerly high-flying Internet companies were folding and by the close of 2000 the future of the surviving e-businesses, as well as the economy as whole, was uncertain.

Impeachment and Acquittal In December 1998 Clinton was impeached by the House and in January and February 1999 he was tried and acquitted by the Senate on charges that he had lied about an adulterous affair with a White House intern. The affair had been uncovered by Starr.

THE ELECTION OF 2000

The Democrats nominated Vice-President Al Gore for president and Senator Joseph Lieberman for vice president. The Republican Party nominated Texas Governor George W. Bush (son of President George H. W. Bush). After some conflict, the Reform party nominated Patrick Buchanan. The Green Party ran Ralph Nader. After one of the tightest presidential elections ever, highlighted by a withdrawn initial concession by Gore, a recount in Florida, and several court challenges, Bush was declared the winner.

AMERICAN SOCIETY AT THE DAWN OF THE TWENTY-FIRST CENTURY

Terrorism Hits Home Major symbols of U.S. economic and military might—the World Trade Center in New York and the Pentagon just outside Washington, D.C.—were attacked on September 11, 2001, when hijackers deliberately crashed commercial jetliners into the buildings, toppling the trade center's 110-story twin towers. Thousands died in the worst act of terrorism in American history. The prime suspect, said President Bush, was Saudi exile Osama bin Laden, the alleged mastermind of previous attacks on U.S. interests overseas. Terrorist attacks had continued to be a grim reality overseas through the 1980s and early 1990s, with Americans frequently targeted. Yet such incidents had come to be viewed as something the United States wouldn't have to face on its own soil—until February 26, 1993, when a terrorist bomb ripped through the underground parking garage of the World Trade Center in New York City, killing six people and injuring more than 1,000. Convicted and sentenced to 240 years each were four Islamic militants. On April 19, 1995, the Oklahoma City federal building was bombed, killing 168 people and injuring 500. Timothy James McVeigh, a member of the American militia movement who had expressed hatred toward the U.S. government and was aggrieved over its assault two years earlier on a self-proclaimed prophet's compound in Waco, Texas, was put to death for the crime in May 2001. A second defendant, Terry Nichols, was convicted on federal charges of conspiracy and involuntary manslaughter and sentenced to life in prison.

A Modern Plague Descends on America In 1981 scientists announced the discovery of Acquired Immune Deficiency Syndrome, or AIDS, which was especially prevalent among—but not confined to—homosexual males and intravenous drug users. Widespread fear resulted, with an upsurge in homophobia. The revelation that a Florida dentist, who died in 1990, had transmitted human immunodeficiency virus, or HIV, to six patients led to calls for mandatory testing of healthcare workers. There were calls as well for fast-tracking drug approvals. In 1998 the federal Centers for Disease Control and Prevention estimated that between 400,000 and 650,000 Americans were HIV-positive, meaning that they had the virus that causes AIDS.

Urban America Rebounds America's cities showed renewed promise at the dawn of the new century—though much remained to be done to attack a host of social and economic ills. *The Economist* reported in January 1998 that unemployment in the 50 biggest cities had fallen by a third over the prior four years, to about 6 percent. Rates for serious crime fell to their lowest in a generation. Cities such as New York—which two decades before had nearly gone bankrupt—and Los Angeles, victim of race riots and an earthquake during the early and mid-'90s, were "growing in both population and confidence." There were also comebacks like that of New Brunswick, N.J. Moribund in the 1970s, it forged a public–private partnership that resulted in more than $1 billion in investments over 25 years. In 1999 this city of 42,000 boasted a vibrant downtown (with small-business loans awarded to city-based businesses topping $1.2 million), a jobless rate of 6.6 percent (down from as high as 11.8 percent in 1993), a 34 percent drop in crime since 1991 for which so-called community policing got much of the credit, and the U.S. Department of Education's coveted Blue Ribbon Award for one of its elementary schools.

Writers Explore the Kaleidoscope of U.S. Life The 1980s and 1990s saw the emergence of writers who threw light on various, sometimes hidden facets of national life—from the immigrant experience as told by Amy Tan in *The Joy-Luck Club* (1989) and Oscar Hijuelos in *The Mambo Kings Play Songs of Love* (1990) to Tom Wolfe's satirical take on greed and class and racial tensions in New York City in *The Bonfire of the Vanities* (1987) and, later, his look behind the patina of Deep South gentility in *A Man in Full* (1998). Toni Morrison's *Beloved* (1987) dramatized the African-American slave experience.

The U.S. Counts Its People The 2000 decennial census counted 281,421,906 Americans, a 13.2 percent increase since 1990. The most populous state was California (33,871,648), the least populous, Wyoming (493,782).

HISTORICAL TIMELINE

Watergate, Conservatism's Rise, and Post–Cold War Challenges (1972–2005)

1972	Watergate break-in occurs at Democratic Headquarters Nixon defeats McGovern for presidency Haiphong Harbor in North Vietnam mined by U.S.
1973	U.S., North Vietnam sign Paris Peace Accords *Roe v. Wade* expands abortion rights Yom Kippur War in Israel Vice-President Agnew resigns in disgrace
1974	Impeachment proceedings begin against Pres. Nixon *U.S. v. Richard Nixon* rules that tapes must be turned over Nixon resigns; Vice-President Ford succeeds him Ford pardons Nixon
1975	U.S. abandons South Vietnam as it falls to North Vietnam
1978	*Bakke vs. University of California Regents* affirmative action case Camp David Accords between Israel and Egypt
1979	U.S. and China establish diplomatic relations Iran deposes shah Iran militants capture U.S. embassy and take hostages Soviet Union invades Afghanistan Three-Mile Island nuclear accident Sandinistas overthrow Somoza in Nicaragua
1980	U.S. boycotts Moscow Olympics Reagan elected president
1981	Iran releases hostages Reagan breaks air traffic controller strike Sandra Day O'Connor named first female Supreme Court justice AIDS epidemic reaches U.S.
1982	241 Marines killed in Lebanon U.S. invades Grenada
1985	Gorbachev takes power in Soviet Union
1986	Iran-Contra affair *Challenger* space shuttle explodes after takeoff
1989	*Exxon Valdez* runs aground in Alaska Students begin pro-democracy demonstrations in China Berlin Wall falls

1990	Saddam Hussein of Iraq invades Kuwait
1991	Operation Desert Storm ends Iraq's occupation of Kuwait Soviet Union breaks up as Cold War ends
1992	Los Angeles riots follow Rodney King verdict Clinton elected president
1993	North American Free Trade Agreement approved
1995	U.S., NATO forces enforce peace in Bosnia
1999	Clinton acquitted following House impeachment
2000	George W. Bush defeats Gore in disputed election
2001	Hijackers crash planes into World Trade Center towers and Pentagon U.S. invades Afghanistan to overthrow Taliban government Patriot Act gives U.S. broad powers to investigate terrorism
2004	George W. Bush re-elected president
2006	President Bush urges Congress to reauthorize the USA Patriot Act

THE SAT SUBJECT TEST IN

United States History

PRACTICE TEST 1

This test is also on CD-ROM in our special interactive SAT United States History TEST*ware*®. It is highly recommended that you first take this exam on computer. You will then have the additional study features and benefits of enforced timed conditions and instantaneous, accurate scoring. See page ix for guidance on how to get the most out of our SAT United States History software.

SAT United States History

Practice Test 1

1. (A) (B) (C) (D) (E)
2. (A) (B) (C) (D) (E)
3. (A) (B) (C) (D) (E)
4. (A) (B) (C) (D) (E)
5. (A) (B) (C) (D) (E)
6. (A) (B) (C) (D) (E)
7. (A) (B) (C) (D) (E)
8. (A) (B) (C) (D) (E)
9. (A) (B) (C) (D) (E)
10. (A) (B) (C) (D) (E)
11. (A) (B) (C) (D) (E)
12. (A) (B) (C) (D) (E)
13. (A) (B) (C) (D) (E)
14. (A) (B) (C) (D) (E)
15. (A) (B) (C) (D) (E)
16. (A) (B) (C) (D) (E)
17. (A) (B) (C) (D) (E)
18. (A) (B) (C) (D) (E)
19. (A) (B) (C) (D) (E)
20. (A) (B) (C) (D) (E)
21. (A) (B) (C) (D) (E)
22. (A) (B) (C) (D) (E)
23. (A) (B) (C) (D) (E)
24. (A) (B) (C) (D) (E)
25. (A) (B) (C) (D) (E)
26. (A) (B) (C) (D) (E)
27. (A) (B) (C) (D) (E)
28. (A) (B) (C) (D) (E)
29. (A) (B) (C) (D) (E)
30. (A) (B) (C) (D) (E)
31. (A) (B) (C) (D) (E)
32. (A) (B) (C) (D) (E)
33. (A) (B) (C) (D) (E)
34. (A) (B) (C) (D) (E)
35. (A) (B) (C) (D) (E)
36. (A) (B) (C) (D) (E)
37. (A) (B) (C) (D) (E)
38. (A) (B) (C) (D) (E)
39. (A) (B) (C) (D) (E)
40. (A) (B) (C) (D) (E)
41. (A) (B) (C) (D) (E)
42. (A) (B) (C) (D) (E)
43. (A) (B) (C) (D) (E)
44. (A) (B) (C) (D) (E)
45. (A) (B) (C) (D) (E)
46. (A) (B) (C) (D) (E)
47. (A) (B) (C) (D) (E)
48. (A) (B) (C) (D) (E)
49. (A) (B) (C) (D) (E)
50. (A) (B) (C) (D) (E)
51. (A) (B) (C) (D) (E)
52. (A) (B) (C) (D) (E)
53. (A) (B) (C) (D) (E)
54. (A) (B) (C) (D) (E)
55. (A) (B) (C) (D) (E)
56. (A) (B) (C) (D) (E)
57. (A) (B) (C) (D) (E)
58. (A) (B) (C) (D) (E)
59. (A) (B) (C) (D) (E)
60. (A) (B) (C) (D) (E)
61. (A) (B) (C) (D) (E)
62. (A) (B) (C) (D) (E)
63. (A) (B) (C) (D) (E)
64. (A) (B) (C) (D) (E)
65. (A) (B) (C) (D) (E)
66. (A) (B) (C) (D) (E)
67. (A) (B) (C) (D) (E)
68. (A) (B) (C) (D) (E)
69. (A) (B) (C) (D) (E)
70. (A) (B) (C) (D) (E)
71. (A) (B) (C) (D) (E)
72. (A) (B) (C) (D) (E)
73. (A) (B) (C) (D) (E)
74. (A) (B) (C) (D) (E)
75. (A) (B) (C) (D) (E)
76. (A) (B) (C) (D) (E)
77. (A) (B) (C) (D) (E)
78. (A) (B) (C) (D) (E)
79. (A) (B) (C) (D) (E)
80. (A) (B) (C) (D) (E)
81. (A) (B) (C) (D) (E)
82. (A) (B) (C) (D) (E)
83. (A) (B) (C) (D) (E)
84. (A) (B) (C) (D) (E)
85. (A) (B) (C) (D) (E)
86. (A) (B) (C) (D) (E)
87. (A) (B) (C) (D) (E)
88. (A) (B) (C) (D) (E)
89. (A) (B) (C) (D) (E)
90. (A) (B) (C) (D) (E)
91. (A) (B) (C) (D) (E)
92. (A) (B) (C) (D) (E)
93. (A) (B) (C) (D) (E)
94. (A) (B) (C) (D) (E)
95. (A) (B) (C) (D) (E)

United States History

PRACTICE TEST 1

TIME: 60 Minutes
95 Questions

DIRECTIONS: Each of the questions or incomplete statements below is followed by five suggested answers or completions. Select the one that is best in each case.

1. Which of the following was NOT characteristic of American industry in the post-Civil War period?

   (A) Government successfully broke up large business concentrations.

   (B) The corporation became an increasingly popular form of organization.

   (C) Trusts and holding companies emerged.

   (D) Trade names began appearing for the first time.

   (E) Monopolies were formed both horizontally and vertically.

2. Adoption of the "direct primary" by every state changed which of the following?

   (A) the procedure for choosing a presidential candidate

   (B) the procedure for recalling an elected official

   (C) the procedure for making new laws

   (D) the procedure for selecting candidates for governor and other high state offices

   (E) the procedure for forcing the state legislature to hear a particular bill

3. Which of the following is NOT associated with the atomic bomb?

   (A) Manhattan Project (B) J. Robert Oppenheimer

(C) General Billy Mitchell
(D) Nagasaki and Hiroshima
(E) Los Alamos, New Mexico

4. All of the following were early explorers of North America EXCEPT

(A) Francisco Coronado.
(B) Robert La Salle.
(C) Samuel de Champlain.
(D) Francisco Pizarro.
(E) Jacques Marquette.

5. Which of the following best characterizes Southern society before the Civil War?

(A) Half of the slaveowners owned five or fewer slaves.
(B) Most white families owned slaves.
(C) Most slaveowners owned several hundred slaves.
(D) The percentage of slaveowners was consistent throughout the South.
(E) Most slaveowners lived in urban areas.

6. Which of the following states first gave women the right to vote?

(A) Colorado
(B) Wyoming
(C) New York
(D) Utah
(E) Idaho

7. Between 1806 and 1809 non-importation, non-intercourse, and embargo sought to

(A) bring peace between France and Great Britain.
(B) encourage domestic American manufacturing.
(C) force Great Britain to recognize American rights.
(D) balance Southern and Northern economic power.
(E) help Britain in the Napoleonic wars.

8. Which of the following was the first important means of transportation in the United States after independence?

(A) canals
(B) turnpikes

(C) steamboats

(D) railroads

(E) clipper ships

9. The Missouri Compromise of 1820 did all of the following EXCEPT

(A) bring in Maine as a free state.

(B) bring in Missouri as a slave state.

(C) prohibit slavery north of latitude 36°30′.

(D) maintain the balance of slave and free states.

(E) establish the principle of popular sovereignty south of 36°30′.

10. John Foster Dulles' negotiation of the SEATO and CENTO defense pacts in the 1950s was an example of what policy?

(A) Liberation

(B) Brinkmanship

(C) Massive Retaliation

(D) Containment

(E) Peaceful Coexistence

11. In which of the following crises did the United States side with the Soviet Union?

(A) the shelling of Quemoy and Matsu

(B) the Hungarian Revolution

(C) the Suez crisis

(D) the Korean conflict

(E) the U-2 incident

12. Most modern historians believe that Reconstruction was characterized by

(A) extensive military occupation of the South.

(B) black misrule of the South.

(C) government corruption of the South.

(D) limited military occupation of the South.

(E) Northern takeover of the economy and government of the South.

13. Which of the following territories was won from Mexico in 1848?

(A) Oregon
(B) California
(C) Texas
(D) Florida
(E) Louisiana

14. The Declaration of Independence stated that

(A) men are created unequal.
(B) governments derive their powers from God.
(C) it was not right that a small island should rule a large continent.
(D) people have the right to abolish governments destructive of their rights.
(E) there shall be no taxation without representation.

15. According to the Treaty of Paris of 1783, the boundaries of the United States were

(A) Canada, the Gulf of Mexico, and the Mississippi River.
(B) Canada, Florida, and the Mississippi River.
(C) Canada, Florida, and the Missouri River.
(D) Canada, Florida, and the Appalachian Mountains.
(E) Canada, the Gulf of Mexico, and the Missouri River.

16. In 1858 at Freeport, Illinois, Stephen Douglas argued that

(A) Congress should bar slavery from the territories.
(B) slavery should be abolished in Washington, D.C.
(C) slavery could be kept out of the territories if people in the territories failed to pass laws to protect it.
(D) the slave trade should be declared illegal.
(E) slavery should be allowed in all the territories.

17. The Second Bank of the United States performed all of the following functions EXCEPT

(A) receiving and paying out federal funds.
(B) stabilizing the money supply.

(C) shifting funds from the West and South to the Northeast.

(D) keeping a check on the loans of other banks.

(E) making loans to the federal government.

18. Which of the following was NOT involved in the "triangular trade" of the colonial period?

(A) rum

(B) molasses

(C) cotton

(D) slaves

(E) tobacco

19. Those who supported ratification of the Constitution were called

(A) Federalists.

(B) Democrats.

(C) Whigs.

(D) Antifederalists.

(E) Republicans.

20. The Populists advocated

(A) the ten-hour work day.

(B) an income tax.

(C) private ownership of the railroads.

(D) government financed health care.

(E) deflation.

21. Robert E. Lee surrendered to Ulysses Grant at

(A) Spotsylvania.

(B) Appomattox.

(C) Cold Harbor.

(D) Raleigh.

(E) Richmond.

22. Horace Mann was associated with which of the following reforms?

(A) education

(B) temperance

(C) care of the mentally ill

(D) health

(E) anti-slavery

23. Which of the following is true of women in the Iroquois society?

    (A) The elder women selected the male chief.

    (B) They sometimes became chiefs.

    (C) They were largely responsible for hunting and fishing activities

    (D) The served as the religious priests.

    (E) They controlled all aspects of tribal life.

24. "In all things that are purely social we can be separate as the fingers, yet one as the hand in all things essential to human progress." This statement reflects the philosophy of which of the following?

    (A) A. Philip Randolph
    (B) W.E.B. DuBois
    (C) Booker T. Washington
    (D) Martin Luther King
    (E) Frederick Douglass

25. A government-sponsored healthcare program for people over sixty-five was passed during whose presidential administration?

    (A) Harry S. Truman
    (B) Dwight D. Eisenhower
    (C) John F. Kennedy
    (D) Lyndon B. Johnson
    (E) Richard M. Nixon

26. The Spanish-American War resulted in which of the following?

    (A) a guerrilla war between Americans and Filipinos

    (B) American colonization of Cuba

    (C) Theodore Roosevelt's election as president in 1900

    (D) the decline of the anti-imperialist movement

    (E) independence of Puerto Rico

27. The French and Indian War took place during

    (A) 1740–1748
    (B) 1754–1763
    (C) 1689–1699
    (D) 1702–1713
    (E) 1776–1783

28. The Waltham system

    (A) purified melted iron with oxygen.

    (B) combined spinning and weaving in a single factory.

    (C) introduced the idea of interchangeable parts.

    (D) combined public and private capital in business enterprise.

    (E) established government bounties for the creation of new businesses.

29. Which of the following does NOT describe Franklin D. Roosevelt's New Deal or its consequences?

    (A) New Deal policies were often inconsistent.

    (B) The New Deal created a large federal bureaucracy without central control.

    (C) The New Deal set up public works projects to help the unemployed and provided direct relief to the unemployed.

    (D) The New Deal gave Americans greater economic security than they had known before.

    (E) The New Deal weakened the position of workers in relationship to employers.

30. Colonial law generally defined slaves as chattels. This meant that slaves were considered as

    (A) human beings with limited rights.

    (B) servants who served for a limited period of time.

    (C) slaves who received freedom upon the death of their masters.

    (D) pieces of property with no rights.

    (E) employees who received pay for their work.

31. The United States began mobilizing for war after September 1939 through which of the following?

    (A) the Neutrality Act of 1939

    (B) the Selective Service Acts of 1940 and 1941

    (C) the establishment of Lend-Lease in 1941

    (D) the Declaration of Panama

    (E) the exchange of American destroyers for British naval bases in the Caribbean

32. All of the following contributed to American entrance into World War I EXCEPT

    (A) German submarine warfare.

    (B) cultural and economic ties with Great Britain.

    (C) the Zimmerman telegram.

    (D) the presidential election of 1916.

    (E) the February 1917 revolution in Russia.

33. Which of the following best describes black Americans after 1965?

    (A) They called for an end to legalized segregation.

    (B) They called for voting rights legislation.

    (C) They sought to end discrimination in the North and improve their economic condition.

    (D) They rejected integration in favor of black separatism.

    (E) They rejected non-violence in favor of force.

34. The Kentucky and Virginia Resolutions of 1798 introduced which of the following ideas?

    (A) that Federal laws take precedent over state wishes

    (B) that the years of residence required for naturalization be increased from five to 14

    (C) that it is illegal to make "false, scandalous, malicious" statements against the federal government

    (D) that individual states could nullify or set aside federal laws with which they disagreed

    (E) that a protective tariff was harmful to the economic interests of the South

35. The unbalanced distribution of income that characterized the 1920s led to which of the following consequences?

    (A) inability of people to buy all the consumer goods that were being produced

    (B) a reduction in the percentage of national income going to the wealthiest 5 percent of the population

    (C) a major increase in wages relative to the increase of corporate profits

(D) a decrease in stock purchases "on the margin"

(E) an increase in the building of new houses and sales of automobiles after 1925

36. Prior to declaring war in December 1941, the United States became an unofficial enemy of Germany and Italy through all of the following EXCEPT

(A) American ships convoyed British shipping across the Atlantic.

(B) The U.S. imprisoned German and Italian seamen.

(C) The U.S. froze all axis-held property within its borders.

(D) The U.S. occupied Greenland and Iceland.

(E) American and British merchant and war ships were repaired in American shipyards.

37. The Social Security program of 1935 provided which of the following?

(A) federally administered unemployment insurance

(B) old age pensions paid for by taxes on employers and workers

(C) unemployment insurance administered by the federal government

(D) old age pensions paid for by taxes on employees

(E) federally administered assistance to the blind and disabled

38. The Judiciary Act of 1789 established

(A) a nine-judge Supreme Court.

(B) thirteen circuit courts.

(C) three district courts.

(D) the office of attorney general.

(E) the power of the Supreme Court to review the constitutionality of federal laws.

39. Which of the following characterized the economy of the 1920s?

(A) an emphasis on heavy industry, such as the production of locomotives

(B) an emphasis on cash rather that credit purchases

(C) a drop in the real wages of workers

(D) a shift to the production of consumer goods

(E) increasing wealth for the agricultural sector

40. Alexander Hamilton's legislative program for the new republic included all of the following EXCEPT

(A) the Bank of the United States.

(B) organization of the federal judiciary.

(C) assumption of Confederation and state debts.

(D) promotion of domestic manufacturing.

(E) a system of excise taxes.

41. Which of the following would be INCONSISTENT with the isolationism that generally characterized American foreign policy in the 1920s?

(A) the Washington Armament Conference

(B) the Stimson Non-Recognition Doctrine

(C) American membership in the World Court

(D) the Dawes and Young Commissions

(E) the Fordney-McCumber Tariff

42. Which of the following best characterizes the counterculture of the 1960s?

(A) It rejected use of drugs in favor of natural living.

(B) It sought to break down the communication gap between young people and older Americans.

(C) It supported the American war effort in Vietnam.

(D) It promoted traditional moral and cultural standards.

(E) It emphasized the non-rational over the rational.

43. The 25th Amendment to the Constitution provides for which of the following?

(A) filling the office of vice president between elections

(B) lowering the voting age to 18

(C) equal rights for women

(D) prohibition of the poll tax

(E) limiting presidential terms to two

44. Which of the following was not involved in the anti-communist crusade of the 1940s and 1950s?

    (A) A. Mitchell Palmer

    (B) Richard M. Nixon

    (C) Whittaker Chambers

    (D) Joseph R. McCarthy

    (E) House Un-American Activities Committee

45. According to the following table, by what year did the majority of the American population live in urban areas?

Year	*Urban*	*Rural*
1890	22,106,000	40,841,000
1900	30,160,000	45,835,000
1910	41,999,000	49,973,000
1920	54,158,000	51,552,000
1930	68,955,000	53,821,000

    (A) 1890
    (B) 1900
    (C) 1910
    (D) 1920
    (E) 1930

46. "Reaganomics" was based upon which of the following theories?

    (A) Cutting taxes would stimulate investment which would in turn increase employment and tax revenue.

    (B) Government must "prime" the economic pump by large expenditures in order to produce prosperity.

    (C) The United States was an undertaxed country where taxes must be increased substantially and the money spent on public needs.

    (D) The government must institute wage and price controls in order to control inflation.

    (E) The government must turn to tight controls on the money supply in order to cut inflation.

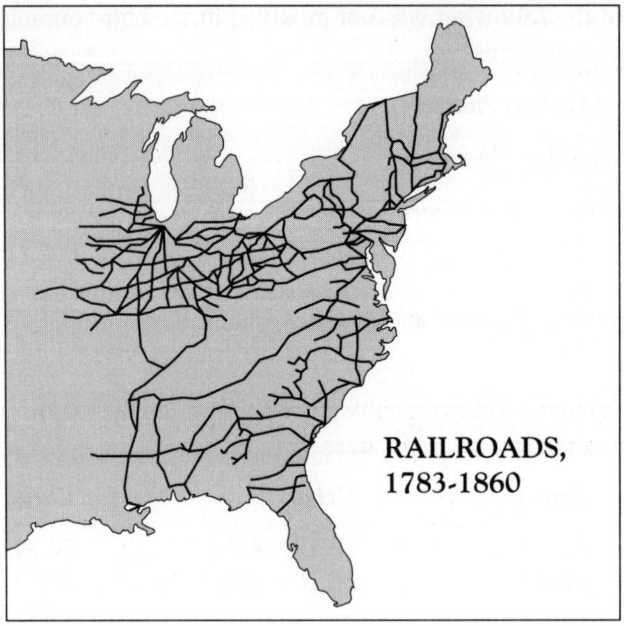

47. According to the map above, which of the following statements is most correct?

    (A) The South had the most extensively developed railroad system.

    (B) The transportation system ran primarily east-west.

    (C) The West had a poorly developed transportation system.

    (D) The South depended upon canals for transportation.

    (E) The United States had developed few railroad lines prior to 1860.

48. The leading scientist in colonial America was

    (A) John Peter Zenger.
    (B) Jonathan Edwards.
    (C) William Byrd.
    (D) Benjamin Franklin.
    (E) George Whitefield.

49. Which of the following correctly describes women's rights in mid-nineteenth-century America?

    (A) A married woman controlled her own property.

    (B) Husbands were forbidden to beat their wives.

    (C) Women could freely enter professions such as medicine and law.

(D) Women could not claim money they had earned.

(E) Women had the right to vote in federal elections.

50. Under Lincoln's plan of Reconstruction, Southern states could resume their part in the Union after

(A) 50 percent of the voters as of 1860 took an oath of allegiance.

(B) 10 percent of the voters as of 1860 took an oath of allegiance.

(C) allowing blacks to vote.

(D) adopting the 13th Amendment, which abolished slavery.

(E) repudiating debts accumulated under the Confederacy.

Source: New York Public Library

RE-CONSTRUCTION,
OR "A WHITE MAN'S GOVERNMENT".

51. Which of the following best expresses the point of view of the above cartoon?

(A) Southern whites and blacks can never be reconciled.

(B) Southern whites would willingly be reconciled with blacks.

(C) Blacks have no interest in reconciliation with Southern whites.

(D) The president must take a forceful role in reconciling Southern whites and blacks.

(E) Reconciliation of Southern whites and blacks is simply a matter of recognizing the new realities.

52. The effect of the neutrality acts of 1935–1937 was to

    (A) halt all trade between the U.S. and belligerent nations.

    (B) encourage aggressor nations because they knew in advance that the U.S. would not become involved.

    (C) prevent United States involvement in European wars.

    (D) encourage trade between the United States and belligerent nations.

    (E) encourage peaceful settlement of problems between potentially belligerent nations.

53. Which of the following was NOT characteristic of pre–Civil War American cities?

    (A) rapidly rising death rates

    (B) increase of crime

    (C) extensive sewer systems

    (D) growth of slums

    (E) increase of population

54. Which of the following gave people jobs building such things as schools, airports, and roads?

    (A) Civilian Conservation Corps

    (B) Civil Works Administration

    (C) Agricultural Adjustment Administration

    (D) National Industrial Recovery Administration

    (E) Tennessee Valley Authority

55. The issue that most influenced voters in choosing Bill Clinton over President Bush in 1992 was

    (A) the aftermath of the Persian Gulf War.

    (B) the condition of the U.S. economy.

    (C) U.N. relief efforts in Somalia.

    (D) reports of ethnic cleansing in the former Yugoslavia.

    (E) the breakup of the Soviet Union.

56. The first armed conflict in 1775 between the Americans and British soldiers took place at

(A) Fort Ticonderoga.
(B) Bunker Hill.
(C) Lexington-Concord.
(D) Boston.
(E) Yorktown.

57. John Hay's "Open Door" policy of 1899 sought which of the following?

(A) American freedom to trade with China
(B) the opening of Japan to Western trade
(C) a sphere of influence for the United States in Asia
(D) an end to the Russian-Japanese War
(E) prevention of Japanese interference in the Philippines

58. By opening territory north of 36°30' to slavery, the Kansas-Nebraska Act repealed the

(A) Dred Scott decision.
(B) Compromise of 1850.
(C) Wilmot Proviso.
(D) Missouri Compromise.
(E) Northwest Ordinance.

59. The last Indian uprising took place in

(A) 1890.
(B) 1876.
(C) 1864.
(D) 1862.
(E) 1871.

60. Political machines in the late nineteenth century performed which of the following functions?

(A) provided honest and efficient government
(B) provided aid to immigrants
(C) promoted reform of city government
(D) promoted reform of the civil service
(E) expanded the power of the federal government

61. By February 1, 1861, what group of states had seceded from the Union?

    (A) Mississippi, Florida, Alabama, Georgia, Louisiana, Texas, South Carolina

    (B) Mississippi, Arkansas, Missouri, Alabama, Georgia, Florida

    (C) Arkansas, Tennessee, North Carolina, Virginia

    (D) Texas, Louisiana, Arkansas, Mississippi, Alabama

    (E) Kentucky, Mississippi, Arkansas, Missouri, Alabama, Georgia

62. In 1819 the United States obtained Florida from

    (A) Great Britain.

    (B) Spain.

    (C) France.

    (D) Mexico.

    (E) Portugal.

63. The Ballenger-Pinchot affair involved which of the following issues?

    (A) reduction of tariff rates

    (B) the Insurgents' move against Speaker of the House Joseph Cannon

    (C) conservation of public lands

    (D) regulation of the railroads

    (E) the importation of farm products from Canada without tariff duties

64. The "Bonus Army" of 1932 called for which of the following?

    (A) a pension for all citizens over 65

    (B) relief money for the unemployed

    (C) the establishment of the Social Security system

    (D) a $1,000 payment for World War I veterans

    (E) the creation of an unemployment insurance system

65. Which of the following does NOT describe the Louisiana Purchase of 1803?

    (A) The United States purchased Louisiana from France for $15 million.

    (B) Jefferson expanded the powers of the presidency.

    (C) French power expanded in the Western Hemisphere.

    (D) The United States doubled in size.

    (E) The treaty of cession left some of the boundaries vague.

66. When no presidential candidate obtains a majority of the electoral vote, who chooses the president?

(A) the Senate

(B) the House of Representatives

(C) the Supreme Court

(D) the Senate and House of Representatives combined

(E) the Electoral College

67. During World War II, which of the following served as an American commander in the Pacific Theater?

(A) George S. Patton, Jr.

(B) Douglas MacArthur

(C) Dwight D. Eisenhower

(D) Omar Bradley

(E) Bernard Montgomery

68. Which Supreme Court chief justice oversaw the development of the Court's power to judge the constitutionality of acts of Congress?

(A) John Marshall

(B) John Jay

(C) Roger Taney

(D) Alexander Hamilton

(E) Oliver Wendell Holmes, Jr.

69. Speaking of the need to expand American power into Central and South America, one nineteenth-century American said, "… can anyone doubt that the result of this competition will be the 'survival of the fittest'?" This statement reflects what philosophy?

(A) social Darwinism

(B) realism

(C) idealism

(D) communism

(E) anarchism

70. What territory gained independence in 1836?

(A) California

(B) Oregon

(C) Texas

(D) Kansas-Nebraska

(E) Missouri

71. After World War II, the United States sought to strengthen Western Europe through all of the following EXCEPT

(A) the establishment of NATO.

(B) Lend-Lease.

(C) the establishment of West Germany.

(D) the Marshall Plan.

(E) the Berlin airlift.

72. The Whiskey Rebellion of 1794 protested

(A) prohibition.

(B) a 25 percent tax on whiskey.

(C) government regulation of whiskey production.

(D) the lifting of import duties on whiskey.

(E) a 30 percent drop in whiskey prices.

73. Antiwar protests became more intense in the early 1970s because

(A) Richard Nixon turned to a policy of Vietnamization.

(B) Congress voted to repeal the Gulf of Tonkin Resolution.

(C) Richard Nixon extended the war into Cambodia.

(D) Attorney General John Mitchell placed FBI and CIA spies within the protest movement.

(E) the United States had rejected holding peace talks with the North Vietnamese.

74. Which of the following critics of the New Deal advocated a "Share-the-Wealth" program?

(A) Huey Long

(B) Frances Townsend

(C) Charles E. Coughlin

(D) William Lemke

(E) Alfred Landon

75. The National Origins Act of 1924

(A) restricted immigrants from Northern and Western Europe.

(B) removed all immigration restrictions.

(C) discriminated against immigrants from Southern and Eastern Europe.

(D) opened up immigration to Orientals.

(E) restricted disproportionately against immigrants from the Eastern Hemisphere.

76. Which of the following best describes the First Bank of the United States?

(A) It was solely a private business enterprise.

(B) It was solely a federal government enterprise.

(C) It was a joint private-public enterprise.

(D) It was a joint state-federal government enterprise.

(E) It was a joint state-private enterprise.

77. Which of the following correctly describes the Puritans?

(A) Their primary goal was to find gold.

(B) They established the Virginia colony.

(C) They established an economy based on tobacco.

(D) They wanted to build a society based upon biblical teachings.

(E) They established religious toleration.

78. Which of the following groups is not matched to its correct geographical region?

(A) Anasazi—American Southwest

(B) Aztecs—Mexico City region

(C) Natchez—California and the Pacific Northwest

(D) Maya—Yucatán peninsula

(E) Mohawk—Eastern Woodland

79. The Federal Constitution

(A) abolished slavery.

(B) did not count slaves for purposes of representation.

(C) counted 3/5 of slaves for purposes of representation.

(D) explicitly legalized slavery.

(E) counted all slaves for purposes of representation.

80. The agreement that lifted most trade barriers between the United States, Canada, and Mexico was

(A) SALT.
(B) START.
(C) SDI.
(D) NAFTA.
(E) the Gulf of Tonkin Resolution.

81. "Underneath the surface … the activity of privilege appears, the privileges of the street railways, the gas, the water, the telephone, and the electric-lighting companies. The connection of these industries with politics explains the power of the boss and the machine." Who would most likely have made this statement?

(A) a Puritan
(B) a Muckraker
(C) a Populist
(D) a Transcendentalist
(E) an Isolationist

82. The Northwest Ordinance of 1787 established what precedent for new territories?

(A) support for public education
(B) equality of new states with old
(C) fair treatment of Indians
(D) prohibition of slavery
(E) popular sovereignty

83. Martin Luther King Jr. emerged as a civil rights leader during which of the following events?

(A) the 1957 desegregation of the Little Rock schools
(B) Greensboro, N.C., sit-ins of 1960

(C) Montgomery Bus Boycott of 1956

(D) 1941 March on Washington

(E) *Brown v. Board of Education of Topeka* 1954

84. In the controversy over the lands belonging by treaty to the "Five Civilized Tribes," the Jackson administration

    (A) destroyed the tribes militarily.

    (B) forced Georgia to restore the lands to the Indians.

    (C) forced the Indians to be removed to the West.

    (D) called upon the Supreme Court to decide the issue.

    (E) divided the lands between Georgia and the Indians.

85. Formation of the Organization of Petroleum Exporting Countries in 1972 contributed to which of the following in the United States?

    (A) less dependence on imported oil

    (B) a rise in oil prices and general inflation

    (C) laws restricting the use of oil

    (D) an improved balance of trade

    (E) a shift to nuclear power

86. Which of the following statements best describes the ethnic makeup of colonial America?

    (A) French Huguenots settled heavily in New England.

    (B) Germans concentrated in Pennsylvania.

    (C) The Scots- (or Scotch-) Irish moved into the southern tidewater area.

    (D) Maryland was largely a Dutch-dominated colony.

    (E) Spanish and Portuguese Jews settled in the Appalachian backcountry.

87. Which of the following correctly describes American railroads in the late nineteenth century?

(A) All shippers received rebates on their freight charges.

(B) Railroads had little influence in Congress.

(C) Railroads received public land.

(D) After 1886 the states had the power to regulate railroads.

(E) Railroads were built only to serve population centers.

88. Based upon the following table, which statement best describes the impact of the Civil War on Southern manufacturing?

	1850	**1860**	**1870**	**1880**
Value of products	*51*	*100*	*128*	*155*

(A) The rate of growth stayed the same after 1860.

(B) The rate of growth increased after 1860.

(C) The rate of growth increased temporarily after 1860 and then slowed to pre-war levels.

(D) The rate of growth decreased after 1860.

(E) The rate of growth decreased temporarily after 1860 and then increased at pre-1860 rates.

89. The American public protested the Jay Treaty of 1794 because

(A) it failed to get British soldiers out of the Northwest posts.

(B) it arranged compensation for slaves freed by the British during the Revolution.

(C) it allowed extensive trade with the West Indies.

(D) it did nothing about British seizure of American vessels in the French West Indies.

(E) it settled Canadian boundary questions.

90. Who served as a Union general?

(A) Joseph Johnston
(B) Thomas Jackson
(C) William T. Sherman
(D) Robert E. Lee
(E) Jeb Stuart

91. The central compromise of the Constitutional Convention involved the issue of

(A) balance of powers within the federal government.
(B) relationship of state and federal powers.
(C) abandonment of the Articles of Confederation.
(D) representation of large and small states.
(E) the powers of the presidency.

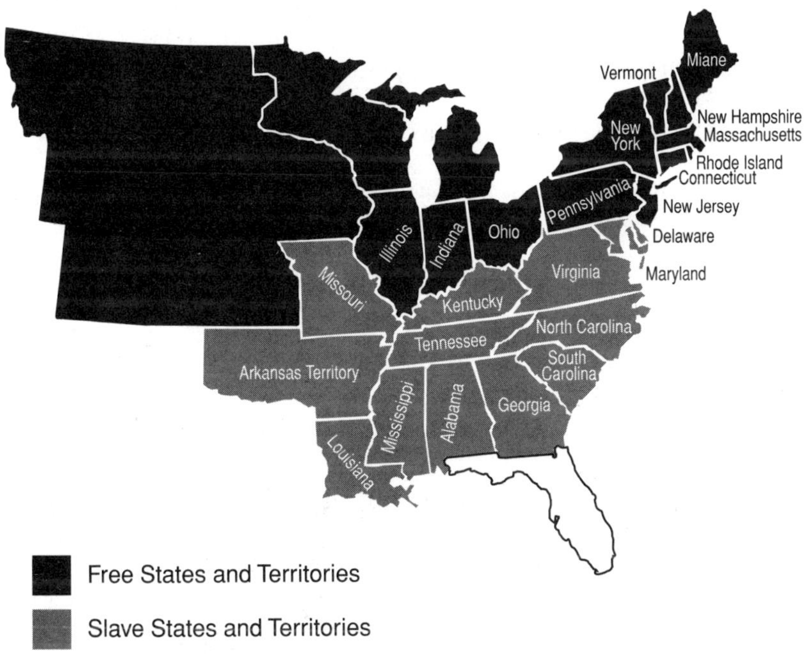

92. This map represents the United States in what year?

(A) 1804 (B) 1821 (C) 1845 (D) 1848 (E) 1853

93. Which of the following was NOT a cause of the Panic of 1837?

(A) the building up of surpluses in the nation's factories

(B) destruction of the Second Bank of the United States

(C) overextension of bank credit

(D) a poor wheat crop

(E) the Specie Circular of 1836

94. This cartoon blames the depression of 1893–1896 on which of the following?

(A) foreign competition with American products

(B) the power of the trusts

(C) the failure to coin silver after 1873

(D) the lack of labor unions

(E) the indebtedness of farmers

95. "There is a twofold liberty, natural (I mean as our nature is now corrupt) and civil or federal. The first is common to man with beasts and other creatures. By this, man, as he stands in relation to man simply, hath liberty to do what he lists; it is a liberty to evil as well as to good.... The other kind of liberty I call civil or federal, it may also be termed moral, in reference to the covenant between God and man, in the moral law, and the politic covenants and constitutions, amongst men themselves. This liberty is the proper end and object of authority, and cannot subsist without it; and it is a liberty to that only which is good, just, and honest." John Winthrop, 1630.

In this passage, liberty is understood

(A) primarily in communal terms.

(B) as the most important value.

(C) as something incompatible with Puritan society.

(D) primarily in individual terms.

(E) as something to be achieved only in the future, not in the present.

SAT United States History

Practice Test 1
ANSWER KEY

1.	(A)	26.	(A)	51.	(E)	76.	(C)
2.	(D)	27.	(B)	52.	(B)	77.	(D)
3.	(C)	28.	(B)	53.	(C)	78.	(C)
4.	(D)	29.	(E)	54.	(B)	79.	(C)
5.	(A)	30.	(D)	55.	(B)	80.	(D)
6.	(B)	31.	(B)	56.	(C)	81.	(B)
7.	(C)	32.	(D)	57.	(A)	82.	(B)
8.	(B)	33.	(C)	58.	(D)	83.	(C)
9.	(E)	34.	(D)	59.	(A)	84.	(C)
10.	(D)	35.	(A)	60.	(B)	85.	(B)
11.	(C)	36.	(A)	61.	(A)	86.	(B)
12.	(D)	37.	(D)	62.	(B)	87.	(C)
13.	(B)	38.	(D)	63.	(C)	88.	(D)
14.	(D)	39.	(D)	64.	(D)	89.	(D)
15.	(B)	40.	(B)	65.	(C)	90.	(C)
16.	(C)	41.	(B)	66.	(B)	91.	(D)
17.	(C)	42.	(E)	67.	(B)	92.	(B)
18.	(C)	43.	(A)	68.	(A)	93.	(A)
19.	(A)	44.	(A)	69.	(A)	94.	(C)
20.	(B)	45.	(D)	70.	(C)	95.	(A)
21.	(B)	46.	(A)	71.	(B)		
22.	(A)	47.	(B)	72.	(B)		
23.	(A)	48.	(D)	73.	(C)		
24.	(C)	49.	(D)	74.	(A)		
25.	(D)	50.	(B)	75.	(C)		

Detailed Explanations of Answers

PRACTICE TEST 1

1. **(A)** Although the Sherman Antitrust Act of 1890 gave the government power to break up large business combinations, the Supreme Court in the *United States v. E.C. Knight Co.* (1895) took away that power.

2. **(D)** The direct primary replaced the party caucus as the procedure for choosing candidates for governor and other high state offices. Adopted by most states during the Progressive period, it was more popular than the initiative (E), referendum (C), and recall (B). Not all states use the primary in choosing presidential candidates.

3. **(C)** General Billy Mitchell was an advocate of air power and preparedness in the 1920s and 1930s. The Manhattan Project was the name for the secret effort to develop the atomic bomb. Oppenheimer was one of the leading scientists to work on the project, which was carried out at Los Alamos, N.M., and Oak Ridge, Tenn. The bombs were dropped on Nagasaki and Hiroshima in August 1945.

4. **(D)** Francisco Pizarro explored Peru while Francisco Coronado travelled through the area of Texas, Oklahoma, and Kansas. Robert La Salle and Jacques Marquette pursued the Mississippi River, and Samuel de Champlain explored the New England coast, Lake Champlain, and the Great Lakes.

5. **(A)** Of the 400,000 slaveholders, about 200,000 owned 5 or fewer slaves. Only about 1 in 4 white Southerners belonged to a slaveholding family, but the percentage varied from region to region. Relatively few slaveholders lived in urban areas.

6. **(B)** The Western states led in giving women the right to vote. Wyoming granted the right in territorial elections in 1869 and continued the right when it became a state in 1890. Colorado (1893), Idaho (1896), and Utah (1896) also established women's right to vote. New York (1917) became the first Eastern state to do so.

7. **(C)** Non-importation (1806), embargo (1807), and nonintercourse (1809) all sought to force the British to recognize American rights on the sea.

8. **(B)** Turnpikes became popular in the 1790s and canals after completion of the Erie Canal in 1825. The steamboat was introduced in 1807 and became particularly popular in the 1830s.

9. **(E)** The Missouri Compromise, engineered by Henry Clay, maintained the balance of slave and free states by bringing in Maine as a free state and Missouri as a slave state. It sought to diffuse slavery as an issue in westward expansion by prohibiting slavery north of latitude 36°30', but it said nothing about popular sovereignty south of that line.

10. **(D)** Despite proclaiming a more aggressive stance toward the communist world through such terminology as "liberation," "brinkmanship," and "massive retaliation," Dulles in many respects carried on the policy of containment. Nikita Khruschev, premier of the Soviet Union, spoke of "peaceful coexistence."

11. **(C)** The United States joined the Soviet Union in 1956 in demanding that Great Britain and France pull out of Egypt. During the Hungarian Revolution of 1956 the U.S. remained silent, but the U-2 incident of 1960 brought tension between the Soviets and the U.S. The Korean conflict (1950-1953) and the shelling of Quemoy and Matsu (1954) both involved tensions with China.

12. **(D)** Modern historians have generally rejected the traditional view that Reconstruction of the South was characterized by black misrule, government corruption, Northern takeover of the Southern government and economy, and extensive military occupation. Only about 20,000 troops were stationed in the South and that number was only for a short time.

13. **(B)** The Oregon boundary was settled with Britain in 1846. Louisiana was purchased from France in 1803 and Florida from Spain in 1819. Texas had won its independence from Mexico in 1836 and was annexed by the United States in 1845.

14. **(D)** The Declaration argued that all men are created equal and are endowed with rights, that government is instituted for the purpose of preserving these rights and gains its powers from the governed, and that people have the right of revolution when government becomes despotism. It was Thomas Paine's *Common Sense* that argued that a small island should not rule a large continent. No taxation without representation was a popular phrase of Americans after the Stamp Act of 1765.

15. **(B)** The Treaty recognized Canada, Florida, and the Mississippi River as the boundaries of the United States. Florida went to Spain. The Missouri River lies west of the Mississippi while the Appalachians lay within the United States of 1783.

16. **(C)** In response to Lincoln's question of how he could support both popular sovereignty and the Dred Scott decision, Stephen Douglas said that slavery could not be kept out of the territories if people there failed to pass laws to protect it. This became known as the Freeport Doctrine and lost Douglas support in the South.

17. **(C)** The Second Bank of the United States shifted funds from the wealthy East for investment in the underdeveloped West and South.

18. **(C)** Cotton did not become a major product until the invention of the cotton gin in the 1790s. Sugar or molasses was purchased in the West Indies and taken to New England where it was manufactured into rum. The rum was then traded in Africa for slaves. In other forms of the triangular trade, tobacco was a major product.

19. **(A)** Those who supported the Constitution were called Federalists while the Antifederalists opposed it. The Whigs, Republicans, and Democrats were political parties that emerged later in the country's history.

20. **(B)** The Populist Party, which emerged in the late 1880s and early 1890s, called for the eight-hour day, an income tax, and government ownership of the railroads as well as restrictions on immigration, the secret ballot, popular election of senators, and freeing the money supply from the price of gold.

21. **(B)** Lee surrendered to Grant at Appomattox Courthouse on April 9, 1865. Spotsylvania and Cold Harbor were battles between Lee and Grant that preceded the surrender. Joseph E. Johnston surrendered to William T. Sherman at Raleigh on April 17, 1865. Richmond was the capital of the Confederacy.

22. **(A)** Horace Mann served as secretary of the Massachusetts State Board of Education. Lyman Beecher advocated temperance reforms. Dorothea Dix promoted better care of the mentally ill. And Sylvester Graham pushed health reform.

23. **(A)** In the matrilineal system of Iroquois government, women played an important role in the political and social life of the tribe. Clan mothers selected the representatives to speak at tribal meetings. Property passed from mother to daughter, and women had the responsibility of nominating the male chiefs and also removing them if duties were not correctly performed. Women participated in tribal discussions and were consulted in all matters of importance to the community and the Iroquois Confederacy.

24. **(C)** Booker T. Washington made this statement in his "Atlanta Compromise" speech of 1895. His contemporary, W.E.B. DuBois, strongly opposed Washington's compromise approach in favor of strong advocacy of civil rights. Frederick Douglass was active in the pre-Civil War anti-slavery movement while Martin Luther King was a civil rights leader of the 1950s and 1960s.

25. **(D)** Medicare and Medicaid were passed in 1965 during Johnson's presidency. Harry Truman had first proposed a national health insurance program in the 1940s but was unable to gain congressional approval.

26. **(A)** When the U.S. refused to grant independence to the Philippines, Filipino rebels mounted guerrilla warfare against the Americans until defeated in 1902. Cuba became an American protectorate rather than a colony while Puerto Rico became an unincorporated U.S. territory. Anti-imperialism grew as a result of the war and its aftermath. Roosevelt was elected vice president in 1900.

27. **(B)** The French and Indian War was the culmination of a series of wars between France and England: King William's War (1689–1697), Queen Anne's War (1700–1713), King George's War (1740–1748), and the French and Indian War (1754–1763). The American Revolution took place between 1776 and 1783.

28. **(B)** In 1814 Francis Cabot Lowell built the first integrated textile factory at Waltham, Massachusetts. In 1851 William Kelly developed a method for purifying iron with oxygen. Eli Whitney and Simeon North were associated with interchangeable parts in the early nineteenth century. Many nineteenth century businesses used both private and public capital. Alexander Hamilton had proposed government bounties for the establishment of new manufacturing businesses.

29. **(E)** The New Deal years strengthened the position of the worker through such legislation as the Wagner Act (1936), which gave unions a strong legal basis, and the Fair Labor Standards Act (1938), which established a minimum wage.

30. **(D)** "Chattel" was the legal term for a piece of property. Black slaves were not considered human beings and therefore had no rights, nor were they employees. Servants who served for a limited period of time were called indentured servants. Individual masters might grant slaves freedom in their wills, but this happened infrequently.

31. **(B)** The Selective Service Act was the only action specifically for the purpose of building up American forces. "Cash and Carry," exchanges of destroyers for naval bases, and Lend-Lease attempted to strengthen Great Britain. The Declaration of Panama declared a war-free zone in the Atlantic around the American continents south of Canada.

32. **(D)** The presidential election of 1916 indicated the country's desire for peace. Ties with Great Britain led to sympathy with that country from the beginning of the war. The German submarine warfare and, to a lesser extent, the Zimmerman Telegram, were major elements in Wilson's decision to go to war. The revolution in Russia eased his doubts about joining the Allied cause.

33. **(C)** After passage of the Civil Rights Act of 1964 and the Voting Rights Act of 1965, blacks turned their attention to ending discrimination in the North and improving their economic situation. Although some advocated separatism and use of force, most blacks rejected these approaches.

34. **(D)** The Kentucky and Virginia Resolutions (1798) introduced the idea of nullification in response to the Alien and Sedition Acts (1798), which changed the years of residence necessary for naturalization and placed sharp limits on freedom of speech.

35. **(A)** The unbalanced distribution of income in the 1920s meant that an increasing percentage of the national income went to the wealthiest 5 percent of the population. This resulted in an inability to purchase all the consumer products being produced, including a flattening of automobile and new home sales after 1925.

36. **(A)** American ships convoyed British shipping across the western third of the Atlantic. The British picked up the convoy in the eastern third.

37. **(D)** The Social Security Act of 1936 set up an old age pension fund paid for by taxes on both employers and employees. It also set up state administered unemployment insurance and assistance to the blind and disabled.

38. **(D)** The Judiciary Act of 1789 provided for a six-justice Supreme Court, 13 district courts, three circuit courts, and the office of attorney general. It gave the Supreme Court the power to review state laws that conflicted with federal statutes.

39. **(D)** In the 1920s consumer goods such as cars and radios became the dominant elements in the economy. Installment purchasing became popular. Real wages increased, but farming did not participate in the prosperity.

40. **(B)** As secretary of the treasury, Hamilton was concerned with economic issues, thus he promoted the Bank of the United States, assumption of Confederation and state debts, excise taxes, and manufacturing, though the latter was unsuccessful in Congress. Congress passed the Judiciary Act in 1789, but it was not Hamilton's proposal.

41. **(B)** The Washington Armament Conference (or Naval Conference) of 1921–22 was a major effort at international cooperation. On the other hand, the U.S. did not become a member of the World Court, raised tariffs, and through the Dawes and Young commissions insisted that the European war debts be paid. The Stimson Doctrine was issued in 1931 in response to the Japanese invasion of Manchuria.

42. **(E)** The counterculture emphasized the non-rational over the rational. This was one of the reasons it was attracted to drug use. It also opposed the Vietnam War, undermined traditional morals and values, and was suspicious of older (over 30, it was said) Americans.

43. **(A)** The 25th Amendment provided for filling the office of vice president between elections. The 26th Amendment lowered the voting age to 18, the 24th Amendment prohibited the poll tax, and the 22nd Amendment limited presidential terms to two for any one individual. The Equal Rights Amendment was not ratified.

44. **(A)** A. Mitchell Palmer was a leader in the Red Scare following World War I. The HUAC carried out widespread investigations of communist influence and one of its members, Richard Nixon, with information from Whittaker Chambers, pursued Alger Hiss, formerly a member of the State Department. Joseph R. McCarthy became one of the most notorious of the anti-communists.

45. **(D)** 1920 was the first year that the census reported more people living in urban areas than living in rural areas.

46. **(A)** "Reaganomics," often called "supply-side" economics, was based on the idea that a tax cut would stimulate investment, which in turn would increase both employment and tax revenues. Although the Federal Reserve during the early Reagan years tightened interest rates, it was largely independent of Reagan's economic policy.

47. **(B)** There were few roads or railroad lines connecting the North and South in 1860. Most transportation routes in both the North and South ran east-west.

48. **(D)** Benjamin Franklin made important discoveries regarding electricity. John Peter Zenger was a newspaper editor involved in a 1735 libel case. Jonathan Edwards was the New England preacher who probably started the Great Awakening. William Byrd was one of the leading Virginia planters of the early 18th century. George Whitefield was a British itinerant evangelist who preached throughout the American colonies during the Great Awakening.

49. **(D)** In most states women had no claim to money they earned; it was controlled by their husbands, as was their own property. Husbands could legally beat their wives "with a reasonable instrument." And the professions were largely closed to women. Women did not have the right to vote in federal elections until the passage of the 19th Amendment in 1920.

50. **(B)** According to Lincoln's plan, the former Confederate states could resume their part in the Union after 10% of the voters as of 1860 took an oath of allegiance to the United States Constitution. The Wade-Davis Bill, which Lincoln killed by a pocket veto, required 50% of the voters as of 1860 to take an oath of allegiance. The 13th Amendment was not adopted until after Lincoln's death, although Lincoln did require states to abolish slavery. Neither black voting rights nor Confederate debts were part of Lincoln's plan.

51. **(E)** This cartoon portrays a rather passive role for President Grant, suggesting that Southerners need only heed his advice to accept the new social realities and all will be well. There is no hint that the federal government might need to bring its weight to bear upon the situation.

52. **(B)** The neutrality acts encouraged such aggressor nations as Italy and Germany because they knew in advance that the U.S. would not help the other side.

53. **(C)** The population growth of pre-Civil War cities generally outdistanced the sewer systems. This contributed to the increasing death rate, especially in the growing slums. With the growth of slums came an increase in crime.

54. **(B)** The Civil Works Administration, established in 1933, hired people to work on various government construction projects. The Civilian Conservation Corps hired young men to work in conservation and related projects. The AAA and NIRA attempted to address structural problems in agriculture and industry. The TVA administered the building and operation of dams in the Tennessee Valley.

55. **(B)** Opinion polls showed that the election's outcome came down overwhelmingly to the widespread perception that the economy had sagged on President Bush's watch. The unemployment rate had climbed to 7.8 percent, an eight-year high, and GNP growth was averaging an anemic 0.5 percent. Combine those factors with the Clinton campaign's relentless pounding of economic themes and you have a strategy and set of circumstances that put Clinton in the White House.

56. **(C)** The conflict at Lexington-Concord occurred April 19, 1775. Fort Ticonderoga was captured by the Americans on May 10, 1775, and the Battle of Bunker Hill took place on June 17. The British were forced to leave Boston in March 1776 and surrendered to Washington at Yorktown in 1781.

57. **(A)** The "Open Door" policy sought to establish American freedom of trade with China, where European powers had established "spheres of influence." Japan had been "opened" in 1854. The Treaty of Portsmouth (1905) ended the Russo-Japanese War while the Japanese in 1905 agreed not to interfere in the Philippines.

58. **(D)** By organizing Kansas-Nebraska on the basis of popular sovereignty, the Kansas-Nebraska Act repealed the Missouri Compromise of 1820 which had barred slavery north of 36°30´. The Wilmot Proviso was not passed by Congress. The Compromise of 1850 had nothing directly to do with slavery north of 36°30´. Dred Scott would not be decided until 1857. The Northwest Ordinance of 1787 had outlawed slavery in the western lands given up by the original 13 states.

59. **(A)** The last Indian uprising took place in 1890, ending at Wounded Knee, South Dakota. In 1862 the Sioux went on the warpath in the northern Great Plains. In 1864 militia attacked Cheyenne and Arapaho at Sand Creek, Colorado. Custer's "Last Stand" occurred in 1876, and the Arapaho-Apache War took place in 1871.

60. **(B)** The political machines served as a crude welfare system for the immigrant population, although they were corrupt and expensive. Reformers sought to wrest control away from the machines.

61. **(A)** The first group of states to secede were Mississippi, Florida, Alabama, Georgia, Louisiana, Texas, and South Carolina. After Lincoln called up troops in April, 1861 Arkansas, Tennessee, North Carolina, and Virginia seceded. Missouri, Kentucky, Maryland, and Delaware were slave states that never seceded.

62. **(B)** England had returned Florida to Spain in 1783. In 1819 through the Adams-Onis Treaty, Spain ceded Florida to the United States in return for an American promise to pay $5 million to American citizens for claims against Mexico.

63. **(C)** Of the various controversies that took place during the Taft presidency (1909–1913), the Ballenger-Pinchot affair dealt with conservation. Taft supported the regulation of railroads (Mann-Elkins Act, 1910) but compromised on the Payne-Aldrich Tariff. He sided with Cannon in a losing battle with the "insurgents" in Congress, and his proposal for tariff-free Canadian farm products stirred up even more controversy.

64. **(D)** The "Bonus Army" marched on Washington to demand early payment of a promised $1,000 bonus for WW I veterans. Social Security and unemployment insurance did not become national issues until the Franklin D. Roosevelt administration.

65. **(C)** The Louisiana Purchase effectively ended Napoleon's dream of power in the Western Hemisphere. He sold the territories, which he had purchased from Spain, because of difficulties in Haiti and need of money.

66. **(B)** According to the 12th Amendment to the Constitution, the House of Representatives shall choose the president from the two or three candidates with the highest electoral votes.

67. **(B)** Douglas MacArthur served in the Pacific theater. Patton, Bradley, and Eisenhower served in the European theater. Montgomery was a British commander in the European theater.

68. **(A)** John Marshall served as chief justice from 1801 to 1835, during which the Court successfully claimed the power to determine the constitutionality of acts of Congress. John Jay served as chief justice from 1789 to 1794 and Roger B. Taney served from 1836 to 1864. Alexander Hamilton never served on the Supreme Court.

69. **(A)** Social Darwinism, which traces its origins to Herbert Spencer rather than Charles Darwin, advocated survival of the fittest. Realism and idealism were philosophical and artistic theories, while communism and anarchism sought to move beyond the "survival of the fittest" in the social and economic realms.

70. **(C)** Texas won independence from Mexico in 1836 through rebellion. California briefly became independent in 1846. The other territories never became independent.

71. **(B)** Lend-Lease was begun in 1941 to help in the fight against Germany. The Marshall Plan was created in 1947. West Germany was created in 1948 and was followed shortly by the Berlin Airlift. NATO was established in 1949.

72. **(B)** The 1794 Whiskey Rebellion opposed a 25 percent tax on whiskey proposed by Hamilton and passed by Congress; Government regulation of whiskey production, import duties, and prohibition did not emerge as issues until much later.

73. **(C)** In 1969 Nixon extended the Vietnam War into Cambodia. "Vietnamization" and repeal of the Tonkin resolution in 1970 had little effect on the protest movement. Although Mitchell proposed placing spies within the protest movement, it was never done. Peace talks with the North Vietnamese began in 1968.

74. **(A)** Huey Long, senator from Louisiana, advocated income redistribution under the phrase "Share-the-Wealth." Frances Townsend advocated a government

pension for everyone over 65. Charles Coughlin, the radio priest, William Lemke of the Union Party, and Alfred Landon, Republican nominee in 1936, promoted various other ideas.

75. **(C)** The National Origins Act limited immigration to 2 percent of the foreign-born residing in the United States in 1890. This effectively discriminated against Southern and Eastern Europeans and Orientals.

76. **(C)** The First Bank of the United States was a joint private-public enterprise, with stock owned by both the federal government and private individuals and representatives of the government and private sector serving as directors.

77. **(D)** The Puritans, who established the Massachusetts Bay Colony, sought to build a society based upon the will of God as revealed in the Bible according to their understanding. Rather than establishing religious toleration, they allowed only their Congregational Church free exercise of religion. It was the founders of the Virginia colony who sought gold and later established tobacco as the basis of their economy.

78. **(C)** The Natchez Indians were part of the Mississippi Valley culture and were not located along the Pacific Ocean. All of the other groups are correctly matched with their regions. The Natchez Indians were among the latest Indian groups to reside in what is now the state of Mississippi. The Natchez Indian culture began around 700 C.E. and lasted until the 1730s, when the tribe was dispersed in a war with the French. Their language is related to the Muskogean language family. Natchez Indian society was organized in chiefdoms with two major ranks (nobles and commoners), with membership determined by matrilineal descent. The Natchez chief was called Great Sun and inherited his position of leadership from his mother's family. The Natchez were farmers of squash, beans, and corn and also hunted and fished.

79. **(C)** The Constitution in Article 1, Section 2 counted 3/5 of "other persons" than free persons for the purposes of representation. It otherwise ignored the issue of slavery, except for providing for the return of runaway slaves in Article 1, Section 9.

80. **(D)** From the protests of organized labor and presidential candidates Pat Buchanan and Ross Perot to the ringing endorsement of most Republicans and large business interests, NAFTA, the North American Free Trade Agreement was widely debated in the months leading up to Congress's passage in November 1993. NAFTA, which is to be phased in over 15 years, went into effect in January 1994, one year into Clinton's first term.

81. **(B)** In the 1890s and early twentieth century, muckraking journalists uncovered the corruption lying underneath the surface of American politics and business. The Populists had been primarily concerned with the problems of the farmers.

82. **(B)** While the Northwest Ordinance provided support for public education, prohibited slavery, and sought fair treatment of Indians, the only precedent it established was a procedure for a territory to become a state equal with all existing states. Popular sovereignty emerged later as a policy to allow states to decide for themselves whether to be slave or free.

83. **(C)** Martin Luther King organized the Montgomery Bus Boycott of 1956. The 1941 March on Washington was organized by A. Philip Randolph, but never took place. King participated in the 1963 March on Washington. He was not directly connected with *Brown v. Topeka Board of Education,* desegregation of the public schools in Little Rock, or the sit-ins in Greensboro, North Carolina.

84. **(C)** The Jackson administration forced the tribes to be removed to the West. The Seminoles of Florida, however, resisted for several years. The Supreme Court had decided the issue in the Indians' favor but Jackson ignored the decision.

85. **(B)** OPEC quadrupled the price of oil within five years which contributed to general inflation. Growing dependence on imported oil resulted in a worsening balance of trade for the United States. Although efforts were made to emphasize nuclear energy, environmental concerns and cost-overruns prevented its extensive development.

86. **(B)** The Germans, known as the Pennsylvania Dutch, settled heavily in Pennsylvania. The French Huguenots could be found in New York and South Carolina. The Scots-Irish settled the frontier areas of the Middle and Southern colonies. The Dutch were concentrated in New York, although the English were the dominant ethnic group even in that colony. Spanish and Portuguese Jews could be found in the urban areas of New York, Rhode Island, and South Carolina.

87. **(C)** The railroads received large land grants from the federal government. They paid rebates only to their large customers and had considerable influence in Congress. In 1886 the Supreme Court decided that only the federal government had the right to regulate the railroads. Railroads were often built to encourage growth of new cities rather than serve existing ones.

88. **(D)** The rate of growth for the two decades 1860 to 1880 was only slightly more than the single decade before the Civil War.

89. **(D)** The Jay Treaty of 1794 said nothing about British seizure of American vessels in the French West Indies, a major problem for Americans. Although the Treaty arranged to get British soldiers out of the Northwest posts, it obtained only limited trading rights with the West Indies and did nothing about compensation for slaves.

90. **(C)** William T. Sherman directed the "march to the sea" of 1864, capturing Savannah and splitting the Confederacy. Joseph Johnston served the Confederacy at the Battle of Seven Pines (1862) and Vicksburg (1862–1863). Thomas "Stonewall"

Jackson played important roles for the Confederacy at the Second Battle of Bull Run (1862) and Chancellorsville (1863). Robert E. Lee commanded the Army of Virginia at such battles as Antietam (1862) and Gettysburg (1863). J.E.B. Stuart fought for the Confederacy at the Second Battle of Bull Run (1862), Chancellorsville (1863), and Gettysburg (1863).

91. **(D)** The central compromise was the agreement that all states would be represented equally in the Senate and by population in the House. There was general agreement that the Articles must be abandoned, that the federal government must be more powerful than the states, and that the legislative and executive powers must be balanced.

92. **(B)** The Missouri Compromise of 1820 brought Missouri into the Union as a slave state in 1821 and Maine as a free state in 1820.

93. **(A)** The United States still had a basically agricultural economy, hence factories had only a marginal effect on the total economy. The destruction of the Bank of the United States took away the major control over the state chartered banks and many of them became overextended. Many banks failed after the 1836 Specie Circular. A poor wheat crop also forced the U.S. to use gold and silver to purchase grain from other countries.

94. **(C)** Although there were many elements that contributed to the depression which began in 1873, this cartoon from W.H. Harvey's *Coin's Financial School* clearly blames the situation on the "Crime of '73," the decision by the U.S. Treasury to stop purchasing silver for the money supply.

95. **(A)** In this statement liberty is understood in terms of the group rather than the individual. Rather than being the primary value, liberty is subordinate to the good. In this sense, liberty is compatible with Puritan society and achievable in the present, although these ideas do not appear directly in the passage quoted.

THE SAT SUBJECT TEST IN

United States History

PRACTICE TEST 2

This test is also on CD-ROM in our special interactive SAT United States History TEST*ware*®. It is highly recommended that you first take this exam on computer. You will then have the additional study features and benefits of enforced timed conditions and instantaneous, accurate scoring. See page ix for guidance on how to get the most out of our SAT United States History software.

SAT United States History

Practice Test 2

1. Ⓐ Ⓑ Ⓒ Ⓓ Ⓔ
2. Ⓐ Ⓑ Ⓒ Ⓓ Ⓔ
3. Ⓐ Ⓑ Ⓒ Ⓓ Ⓔ
4. Ⓐ Ⓑ Ⓒ Ⓓ Ⓔ
5. Ⓐ Ⓑ Ⓒ Ⓓ Ⓔ
6. Ⓐ Ⓑ Ⓒ Ⓓ Ⓔ
7. Ⓐ Ⓑ Ⓒ Ⓓ Ⓔ
8. Ⓐ Ⓑ Ⓒ Ⓓ Ⓔ
9. Ⓐ Ⓑ Ⓒ Ⓓ Ⓔ
10. Ⓐ Ⓑ Ⓒ Ⓓ Ⓔ
11. Ⓐ Ⓑ Ⓒ Ⓓ Ⓔ
12. Ⓐ Ⓑ Ⓒ Ⓓ Ⓔ
13. Ⓐ Ⓑ Ⓒ Ⓓ Ⓔ
14. Ⓐ Ⓑ Ⓒ Ⓓ Ⓔ
15. Ⓐ Ⓑ Ⓒ Ⓓ Ⓔ
16. Ⓐ Ⓑ Ⓒ Ⓓ Ⓔ
17. Ⓐ Ⓑ Ⓒ Ⓓ Ⓔ
18. Ⓐ Ⓑ Ⓒ Ⓓ Ⓔ
19. Ⓐ Ⓑ Ⓒ Ⓓ Ⓔ
20. Ⓐ Ⓑ Ⓒ Ⓓ Ⓔ
21. Ⓐ Ⓑ Ⓒ Ⓓ Ⓔ
22. Ⓐ Ⓑ Ⓒ Ⓓ Ⓔ
23. Ⓐ Ⓑ Ⓒ Ⓓ Ⓔ
24. Ⓐ Ⓑ Ⓒ Ⓓ Ⓔ
25. Ⓐ Ⓑ Ⓒ Ⓓ Ⓔ
26. Ⓐ Ⓑ Ⓒ Ⓓ Ⓔ
27. Ⓐ Ⓑ Ⓒ Ⓓ Ⓔ
28. Ⓐ Ⓑ Ⓒ Ⓓ Ⓔ
29. Ⓐ Ⓑ Ⓒ Ⓓ Ⓔ
30. Ⓐ Ⓑ Ⓒ Ⓓ Ⓔ
31. Ⓐ Ⓑ Ⓒ Ⓓ Ⓔ
32. Ⓐ Ⓑ Ⓒ Ⓓ Ⓔ
33. Ⓐ Ⓑ Ⓒ Ⓓ Ⓔ
34. Ⓐ Ⓑ Ⓒ Ⓓ Ⓔ
35. Ⓐ Ⓑ Ⓒ Ⓓ Ⓔ
36. Ⓐ Ⓑ Ⓒ Ⓓ Ⓔ
37. Ⓐ Ⓑ Ⓒ Ⓓ Ⓔ
38. Ⓐ Ⓑ Ⓒ Ⓓ Ⓔ
39. Ⓐ Ⓑ Ⓒ Ⓓ Ⓔ
40. Ⓐ Ⓑ Ⓒ Ⓓ Ⓔ
41. Ⓐ Ⓑ Ⓒ Ⓓ Ⓔ
42. Ⓐ Ⓑ Ⓒ Ⓓ Ⓔ
43. Ⓐ Ⓑ Ⓒ Ⓓ Ⓔ
44. Ⓐ Ⓑ Ⓒ Ⓓ Ⓔ
45. Ⓐ Ⓑ Ⓒ Ⓓ Ⓔ
46. Ⓐ Ⓑ Ⓒ Ⓓ Ⓔ
47. Ⓐ Ⓑ Ⓒ Ⓓ Ⓔ
48. Ⓐ Ⓑ Ⓒ Ⓓ Ⓔ
49. Ⓐ Ⓑ Ⓒ Ⓓ Ⓔ
50. Ⓐ Ⓑ Ⓒ Ⓓ Ⓔ
51. Ⓐ Ⓑ Ⓒ Ⓓ Ⓔ
52. Ⓐ Ⓑ Ⓒ Ⓓ Ⓔ
53. Ⓐ Ⓑ Ⓒ Ⓓ Ⓔ
54. Ⓐ Ⓑ Ⓒ Ⓓ Ⓔ
55. Ⓐ Ⓑ Ⓒ Ⓓ Ⓔ
56. Ⓐ Ⓑ Ⓒ Ⓓ Ⓔ
57. Ⓐ Ⓑ Ⓒ Ⓓ Ⓔ
58. Ⓐ Ⓑ Ⓒ Ⓓ Ⓔ
59. Ⓐ Ⓑ Ⓒ Ⓓ Ⓔ
60. Ⓐ Ⓑ Ⓒ Ⓓ Ⓔ
61. Ⓐ Ⓑ Ⓒ Ⓓ Ⓔ
62. Ⓐ Ⓑ Ⓒ Ⓓ Ⓔ
63. Ⓐ Ⓑ Ⓒ Ⓓ Ⓔ
64. Ⓐ Ⓑ Ⓒ Ⓓ Ⓔ
65. Ⓐ Ⓑ Ⓒ Ⓓ Ⓔ
66. Ⓐ Ⓑ Ⓒ Ⓓ Ⓔ
67. Ⓐ Ⓑ Ⓒ Ⓓ Ⓔ
68. Ⓐ Ⓑ Ⓒ Ⓓ Ⓔ
69. Ⓐ Ⓑ Ⓒ Ⓓ Ⓔ
70. Ⓐ Ⓑ Ⓒ Ⓓ Ⓔ
71. Ⓐ Ⓑ Ⓒ Ⓓ Ⓔ
72. Ⓐ Ⓑ Ⓒ Ⓓ Ⓔ
73. Ⓐ Ⓑ Ⓒ Ⓓ Ⓔ
74. Ⓐ Ⓑ Ⓒ Ⓓ Ⓔ
75. Ⓐ Ⓑ Ⓒ Ⓓ Ⓔ
76. Ⓐ Ⓑ Ⓒ Ⓓ Ⓔ
77. Ⓐ Ⓑ Ⓒ Ⓓ Ⓔ
78. Ⓐ Ⓑ Ⓒ Ⓓ Ⓔ
79. Ⓐ Ⓑ Ⓒ Ⓓ Ⓔ
80. Ⓐ Ⓑ Ⓒ Ⓓ Ⓔ
81. Ⓐ Ⓑ Ⓒ Ⓓ Ⓔ
82. Ⓐ Ⓑ Ⓒ Ⓓ Ⓔ
83. Ⓐ Ⓑ Ⓒ Ⓓ Ⓔ
84. Ⓐ Ⓑ Ⓒ Ⓓ Ⓔ
85. Ⓐ Ⓑ Ⓒ Ⓓ Ⓔ
86. Ⓐ Ⓑ Ⓒ Ⓓ Ⓔ
87. Ⓐ Ⓑ Ⓒ Ⓓ Ⓔ
88. Ⓐ Ⓑ Ⓒ Ⓓ Ⓔ
89. Ⓐ Ⓑ Ⓒ Ⓓ Ⓔ
90. Ⓐ Ⓑ Ⓒ Ⓓ Ⓔ
91. Ⓐ Ⓑ Ⓒ Ⓓ Ⓔ
92. Ⓐ Ⓑ Ⓒ Ⓓ Ⓔ
93. Ⓐ Ⓑ Ⓒ Ⓓ Ⓔ
94. Ⓐ Ⓑ Ⓒ Ⓓ Ⓔ
95. Ⓐ Ⓑ Ⓒ Ⓓ Ⓔ

United States History

PRACTICE TEST 2

TIME: 60 Minutes
95 Questions

DIRECTIONS: Each of the questions or incomplete statements below is followed by five suggested answers or completions. Select the one that is best in each case.

1. All of the following literary works dealt with the effects of the depression in the 1930s EXCEPT

   (A) *The Sun Also Rises.*
   (B) *The Grapes of Wrath.*
   (C) *Studs Lonigan Trilogy.*
   (D) *USA Trilogy.*
   (E) *Tobacco Road.*

2. Which of the following opposed rechartering the Second Bank of the United States?

   (A) Nicholas Biddle
   (B) Henry Clay
   (C) Daniel Webster
   (D) Andrew Jackson
   (E) John Marshall

3. Under the Articles of Confederation, the Congress lacked the power to

   (A) control foreign affairs.
   (B) coin money.
   (C) settle disputes among the states.
   (D) tax.
   (E) borrow money.

4. Writers such as F. Scott Fitzgerald, Ernest Hemingway, and H. L. Mencken
   (A) viewed American entrance into World War I resulting from bankers' and munitions makers' desire for wartime profits.
   (B) argued for the continuing relevance of traditional values.
   (C) attempted to revive the progressive movement in the 1920s.
   (D) warned that the prosperity of the 1920s would be undermined by overproduction.
   (E) questioned the basic assumptions of middle class society.

5. The essential element of the policy of containment was
   (A) a commitment to rolling back communism.
   (B) a commitment to working with the Soviet Union.
   (C) a rejection of involvement in affairs outside the Western Hemisphere.
   (D) a commitment to fight a defensive war against the Japanese while taking the offensive against Germany.
   (E) a commitment to holding communism within the Soviet Union and Eastern Europe.

6. The Stimson Doctrine of 1931 was directed against
   (A) the Italian invasion of Ethiopia.
   (B) the German reoccupation of the Rhineland.
   (C) the Japanese invasion of Manchuria.
   (D) the Mexican nationalization of all foreign-owned holdings within its territory.
   (E) the German annexation of Austria.

7. In the election of 1860, Abraham Lincoln won
   (A) a majority of the popular vote.
   (B) the electoral votes of Kentucky and Maryland.
   (C) less than half of the electoral vote.
   (D) the Northern and Midwestern states.
   (E) the electoral votes of Virginia and Tennessee.

8. Which of the following groups tended to support the Federalists?

(A) small farmers

(B) small businessmen

(C) wealthy merchants

(D) Baptist and Methodist ministers

(E) skilled craftsmen

9. Henry Kissinger was involved in all of the following EXCEPT

(A) detente with the Soviet Union.

(B) the peace treaty between Egypt and Israel.

(C) shuttle diplomacy in the Middle East.

(D) Richard Nixon's visit to China.

(E) peace talks with the North Vietnamese.

10. The Wagner Act of 1935 helped which of the following groups?

(A) labor

(B) businesspeople

(C) farmers

(D) veterans

(E) homeowners

11. According to the following table, by what year did the major source of immigration to the United States shift from Northern and Western Europe to Southern and Eastern Europe?

Year	*North & West Eur.*	*South & East Eur.*
1870	318,792	5,409
1880	658,904	21,211
1890	459,246	103,357
1900	103,719	206,134
1910	202,198	465,366

(A) 1870

(B) 1880

(C) 1890

(D) 1900

(E) 1910

12. Prior to 1763 the British policy of "salutary neglect"

    (A) did not enforce the Navigation Acts.

    (B) allowed royal colonies to elect their own governors.

    (C) took the Royal Navy off the high seas.

    (D) encouraged colonists to establish their own parliament.

    (E) withdrew British soldiers from North America.

13. What do Gabriel Prosser, Denmark Vesey, and Nat Turner have in common?

    (A) They were active in the Second Great Awakening.

    (B) They were early railroad tycoons.

    (C) They organized slave rebellions.

    (D) They helped form the Whig party.

    (E) They were leading New England abolitionists.

14. Woodrow Wilson failed to obtain ratification of the Versailles treaty because

    (A) a majority of the senators opposed the treaty and the League of Nations under any circumstances.

    (B) he was unwilling to publicly campaign for the treaty.

    (C) he was unwilling to make any compromises with Henry Cabot Lodge.

    (D) the Republican senators wanted a stronger League of Nations.

    (E) he made too many compromises with the Republican opposition.

15. Who was President Clinton's second secretary of state?

    (A) Sandra Day O'Connor

    (B) Ann Richards

    (C) James Baker

    (D) Jeane Kirkpatrick

    (E) Madeleine Albright

16. The *Marbury v. Madison* decision of 1803 established the principle that

    (A) the federal government had the power to regulate commerce.

    (B) the Supreme Court had the power to declare acts of Congress unconstitutional.

(C) the federal government had the power under the contract clause to protect property rights.

(D) a state lacked the power to block the operation of a federal agency.

(E) that states had the power to determine whether acts of Congress applied within their borders.

17. The 22nd Amendment to the Constitution did which of the following?

(A) established prohibition

(B) repealed prohibition

(C) gave women the right to vote

(D) limited the president to two terms

(E) gave Congress the power to enact an income tax

18. The Pinckney Treaty with Spain in 1795 gave Americans the "right of deposit" at New Orleans. This meant that

(A) Americans could land goods at New Orleans and ship them out again without paying taxes.

(B) America had full trading rights with the Spanish.

(C) Americans could ship their goods in Spanish vessels.

(D) New Orleans became an American possession.

(E) American banks could be established in New Orleans.

19. Which of the following contributed to Harry Truman's victory in the presidential election of 1948?

(A) emergence of the "Dixiecrat" Party

(B) Democratic Party opposition to civil rights legislation

(C) labor union support for Truman

(D) the candidacy of Henry Wallace

(E) the "solid South"

POPULATION 1860

■ - Population density 45+ per square mile

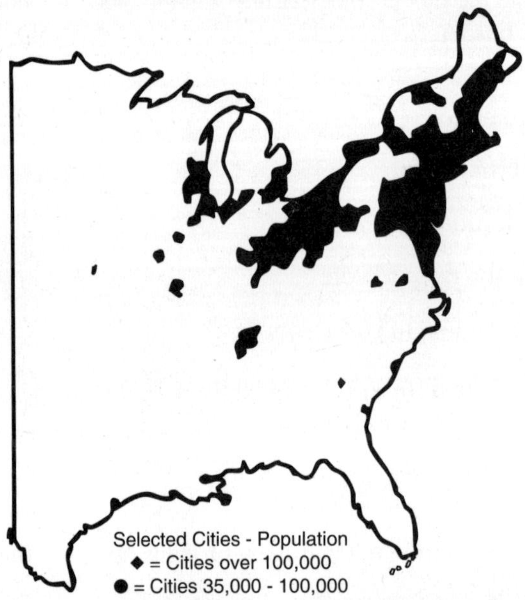

● Albany, NY	◆ Chicago, IL	● Montgomery, AL	● Pittsburgh, PA
◆ Baltimore, MD	◆ Cincinnati, OH	● New Haven, CT	● Providence, RI
◆ Boston, MA	● Cleveland, OH	◆ New Orleans, LA	● Richmond, VA
◆ Brooklyn, NY	● Detroit, MI	◆ New York, NY	◆ St. Louis, MO
● Buffalo, NY	● Lowell, MA	● Newark, NJ	● Troy, NY
● Charleston, SC	● Louisville, KY	◆ Philadelphia, PA	● Washington, D.C.

20. According to this map and table, which state had the greatest degree of urbanization in 1860?

    (A) New York
    (B) Pennsylvania
    (C) Illinois
    (D) Massachusetts
    (E) Virginia

21. The 1896 decision of *Plessy v. Ferguson*

    (A) overturned the Civil Rights Act of 1875.
    (B) said the 14th Amendment applied only to state actions.
    (C) established the doctrine of "separate but equal."
    (D) gave blacks the right to vote.
    (E) ended the segregation of the public schools.

"The Upright Bench" Source: U.S. Library of Congress

22. This 1871 cartoon by Thomas Nast suggests that

(A) justice prevails in New York.

(B) political influence is sold for cash.

(C) the wealthy control New York politics.

(D) New York government is inefficient.

(E) the people are being well-served by New York government.

23. Herbert Hoover's Reconstruction Finance Corporation of 1932 did which of the following?

    (A) gave direct federal relief to the unemployed

    (B) financed major public-works programs such as Boulder Dam

    (C) loaned money to banks which in turn would loan it to businesses

    (D) hired unemployed men to perform unskilled labor for the government

    (E) reorganized the banking system and established deposit requirements

24. American factory workers of the pre-Civil War period

    (A) formed powerful unions.

    (B) worked long hours.

    (C) had excellent working conditions.

    (D) included few children.

    (E) were attracted to socialism.

25. What single event was most important in signalling renewed strength in the American labor movement?

    (A) the air traffic controllers' strike

    (B) the Teamsters Union strike against UPS

    (C) the Teamsters Union strike against Federated Department Stores

    (D) President Clinton's September 1997 address before a major union group

    (E) the election of Ron Carey to head the Teamsters Union

26. The Emancipation Proclamation of 1863

    (A) freed all slaves.

    (B) freed slaves in the "border states."

    (C) freed slaves in areas controlled by the Union army.

    (D) freed slaves in areas still in rebellion.

    (E) freed slaves in Washington, D.C.

27. Which of the following was NOT a new religious group that emerged in America during the nineteenth century?

(A) Latter-Day Saints
(B) Adventists
(C) Methodists
(D) Spiritualists
(E) Christian Scientists

28. The Neutrality Act of 1939 enabled the United States to

(A) sell military and non-military goods on credit to belligerent nations and transport them on American ships.

(B) sell military and non-military goods for cash to belligerent nations and transport them on American ships.

(C) sell military and non-military goods on credit to belligerent nations if transported on another nation's ships.

(D) sell only non-military goods for cash to belligerent nations if transported on another nation's ships.

(E) sell non-military and military goods for cash to belligerent nations if transported on another nation's ships.

29. Theodore Roosevelt contributed to the Progressive movement in all of the following EXCEPT

(A) he strengthened the presidency.

(B) he opposed trusts and other big business combinations.

(C) he advertised progressive ideas.

(D) he promoted conservation.

(E) he expanded the power of the ICC.

30. The Proclamation of 1763

(A) ordered that settlement be stopped west of the peaks of the Appalachians.

(B) stated that those who broke the trade laws were to be tried in the admiralty courts.

(C) ended the French and Indian War.

(D) forbade trade with the French, Dutch, and Spanish West Indies.

(E) established new taxes on trade.

31. The Nullification Controversy of 1828 to 1833 arose in response to congressional support for

    (A) restrictions on slavery.

    (B) protective tariffs.

    (C) internal improvements.

    (D) the Second Bank of the United States.

    (E) popular sovereignty.

32. In 1913 Woodrow Wilson withheld recognition of the Huerta government of Mexico for which of the following reasons?

    (A) Huerta did not really control the country.

    (B) Huerta was unwilling to carry out his country's obligations to other countries.

    (C) Wilson disapproved of Huerta's actions.

    (D) Pancho Villa had raided Columbus, New Mexico.

    (E) American sailors had been arrested at Tampico.

33. Debate over ratification of the Constitution in New York resulted in the publication of

    (A) *The American Commonwealth.*

    (B) *The Federalist Papers.*

    (C) *Common Sense.*

    (D) *The Age of Reason.*

    (E) *Defense of the Constitutions of Government of the United States of America.*

34. Who helped guide the Lewis and Clark expedition and aided in dealing with Indians?

    (A) Sacajawea

    (B) Zebulon Pike

    (C) Sitting Bull

    (D) James Wilkinson

    (E) Tecumseh

35. The Knights of Labor
    (A) excluded women and blacks.
    (B) organized workers by craft.
    (C) were concerned only with wages, hours, and working conditions.
    (D) admitted both skilled and unskilled workers into membership.
    (E) advocated destruction of the federal government.

36. Which of the following was part of the Compromise of 1850?
    (A) abolition of the slave trade
    (B) a new fugitive slave law
    (C) California's entry into the Union on the basis of popular sovereignty
    (D) Utah and New Mexico territories to be free
    (E) a new eastern border for Texas

37. All of the following led to the Spanish-American War of 1898 EXCEPT
    (A) the deLome letter.
    (B) yellow journalism.
    (C) explosion of the *Maine*.
    (D) the push to annex Hawaii.
    (E) influence of Cuban exiles.

38. *Common Sense* was written by
    (A) Thomas Paine.
    (B) Patrick Henry.
    (C) John Locke.
    (D) Thomas Jefferson.
    (E) John Adams.

39. As president, Dwight D. Eisenhower gave the LEAST support to which of the following?
    (A) St. Lawrence Seaway
    (B) Civil rights for blacks
    (C) extension of Social Security
    (D) creation of the Interstate Highway System
    (E) reduction of military expenditures

40. An indentured servant differed from a slave in that he or she

(A) received wages for their work.

(B) worked for a limited period of time, usually seven years, to repay their passage to America.

(C) was used only for agricultural work.

(D) was held in servitude for life.

(E) was ineligible for the 50 acres of land given under Virginia's headright system.

41. Television played an important role in the 1950s in all of the following EXCEPT

(A) encouraging women to pursue careers outside the home.

(B) shaping consumer buying habits.

(C) creating political images.

(D) offering mass entertainment.

(E) reducing the popularity of "going to the movies."

42. Which of the following does NOT correctly describe the Progressives?

(A) They favored government regulation of business on behalf of the public interest.

(B) They were concerned with the social and economic conditions of the city.

(C) They represented farmers and the working class.

(D) They advocated a more orderly and efficient society.

(E) They called for a stronger state and federal government.

43. Who supported the free coinage of silver in the 1890s?

(A) large corporations

(B) bankers

(C) Populists

(D) Republicans

(E) international traders

44. Alexander Hamilton believed that the United States should

(A) repudiate the debts of the Confederation but assume those of the states.

(B) assume the debts of the Confederation but not those of the states.

(C) assume the debts of both the Confederation and the states.

(D) repudiate the debts of both the Confederation and the states.

(E) assume the debts of the Confederation, the states, and local governments.

45. The Vietnam War ultimately had its roots in which of the following?

(A) French colonialism

(B) the Japanese invasion of Southeast Asia

(C) the Korean War

(D) the Geneva Accords

(E) the Gulf of Tonkin Resolution

46. The Bill of Rights guarantees all of the following EXCEPT

(A) the freedom of religion.

(B) the right to a fair trial.

(C) powers not delegated to the federal government by the constitution are reserved to the states.

(D) the right to bear arms.

(E) the right of women to vote.

47. Which of the following tribes was the ancestor of the Pueblo Indians?

(A) Oneida

(B) Creek

(C) Choctaw

(D) Anasazi

(E) Aztecs

48. The followers of Andrew Jackson established what political party?

(A) Whig

(B) Republican

(C) Democratic

(D) Federalist

(E) Populist

49. Beginning in the 1830s, William Lloyd Garrison called for

 (A) colonization of slaves.
 (B) immediate emancipation of the slaves.
 (C) free soil.
 (D) step-by-step emancipation of the slaves.
 (E) popular sovereignty.

50. The growth of suburbs during the 1950s resulted in which of the following?

 (A) loss of white population in the central cities
 (B) a growing dependence on public transportation
 (C) a reduction in the migration of blacks to the cities
 (D) a decline in automobile sales
 (E) a rejection of mass-produced housing

51. The Great Awakening of the 1740s resulted in

 (A) the establishment of the Church of England.
 (B) a split between religious traditionalists and religious radicals.
 (C) an outbreak of witch hunting, resulting in the Salem witchcraft trials.
 (D) the hanging of Quakers in Boston.
 (E) a revival of denominationalism.

52. George Washington's army faced which of the following problems during the American Revolution?

 (A) The British public unanimously supported the policy of its government.
 (B) Two-thirds of the colonists opposed the war.
 (C) The army was dependent on poorly trained militia.
 (D) The army used conventional military tactics.
 (E) The British government was able to give its full attention to the war.

53. After 1890 most immigrants to America came from

(A) Northern and Western Europe.
(B) Southern and Eastern Europe.
(C) Great Britain and Ireland.
(D) Asia.
(E) Mexico.

54. Regarding interpretation of the Constitution, Alexander Hamilton wrote:

"It leaves, therefore, a criterion of what is constitutional, and of what is not so. This criterion is the *end*, to which the measure relates as a *means*. If the *end* be clearly comprehended within any of the specified powers, and if the measure have an obvious relation to that *end*, and is not forbidden by any particular provision of the Constitution, it may safely be deemed to come within the compass of the national authority."

In this passage Hamilton is arguing that

(A) the Constitution delegates implied powers to the federal government.
(B) the Constitution must specifically state that the federal government has the power to take a particular action.
(C) constitutional questions are to be settled by the Supreme Court.
(D) all implied powers are reserved to the states.
(E) the Constitution states both the ends and means of government action.

55. The Roosevelt corollary to the Monroe Doctrine established which of the following?

(A) The right of European nations to forcefully collect debts in the Western Hemisphere
(B) The right of the United States to build and fortify an Atlantic-Pacific canal
(C) The independence of Panama from Columbia
(D) The right of the U.S. to act as a police power in the Western Hemisphere nations
(E) The right of the United States to act as an arbitrator in European conflicts with Western Hemisphere nations.

56. Which of the following was NOT a major writer of the pre-Civil War period?

(A) Ralph Waldo Emerson
(B) William Dean Howells
(C) Nathaniel Hawthorne
(D) Herman Melville
(E) Washington Irving

57. The Red Scare of 1919 was influenced by all of the following EXCEPT

(A) the October Russian Revolution.
(B) labor strikes in several areas of the U.S.
(C) terrorist bombings.
(D) the continuation of World War I.
(E) formation of the American Communist Party.

58. According to the Dred Scott decision,

(A) only people living within a territory could forbid slavery there.
(B) slaves were citizens of the United States.
(C) Congress had no power over slavery in the territories.
(D) the Missouri Compromise was constitutional.
(E) slaves taken temporarily into a free state were free.

59. Great Britain sought to control colonial trade because

(A) it did not want competition with its own manufacturers.
(B) colonial products were inferior to British products.
(C) colonial products were too expensive.
(D) the colonies were seeking political independence.
(E) the colonies were unable to establish trade with Spain and France.

60. Each of the following expanded the right to vote in some way EXCEPT

(A) the 23rd Amendment to the Constitution.
(B) the 24th Amendment to the Constitution.
(C) *Gideon v. Wainright* (1963).

(D) *Wesberry v. Sanders* (1964).

(E) Voting Rights Act (1964).

61. In what election did blacks begin to overwhelmingly support the Democratic party?

(A) 1928 (B) 1932 (C) 1936 (D) 1948 (E) 1960

62. The Owens-Glass Federal Reserve Act of 1913 provided for which of the following?

(A) a commission to oversee big business

(B) an enlarged list of illegal business activities

(C) a graduated tax on income

(D) the popular election of U.S. senators

(E) a central banking system for the United States

63. Which of the following was NOT a Northern advantage in the Civil War?

(A) It was fighting a defensive war.

(B) It had greater manufacturing capacity.

(C) It owned greater railroad trackage.

(D) It had a larger population.

(E) The mountain chains ran north and south.

64. The Axis alliance of World War II included which of the following?

(A) Soviet Union, Germany, Italy

(B) Soviet Union, Germany, Japan

(C) France, Germany, Italy

(D) Germany, Italy, Japan

(E) France, Germany, Japan

65. Which of the following does NOT apply to the Monroe Doctrine?

(A) It forbade Spain from attempting to restore control over its former colonies in the Western Hemisphere.

(B) It was based upon the assumption that the British navy would defend the principles of the Doctrine.

(C) It allowed the United States to take action in European affairs.

(D) It blocked a possible move by Russia to possess the Pacific Coast.

(E) It allowed European nations to use force of arms in order to collect debts from Latin American nations.

66. Which of the following was NOT a women's rights reformer?

(A) Phoebe Palmer
(B) Lucretia Mott
(C) Elizabeth Cady Stanton
(D) Susan B. Anthony
(E) Margaret Fuller

67. A revolution in what country made American neutrality an issue in the 1790s?

(A) Great Britain
(B) Spain
(C) Netherlands
(D) France
(E) Germany

68. The Confederacy raised money for their war effort by all of the following means EXCEPT

(A) borrowing money from abroad.

(B) raising taxes.

(C) printing money.

(D) establishing an income tax.

(E) borrowing money from its citizens.

69. The Constitutional Convention took place in

(A) 1776. (B) 1789. (C) 1787. (D) 1781. (E) 1800.

70. The colonial South was divided into all of the following EXCEPT

(A) the Piedmont.
(B) the Great Plains.
(C) the Backcountry.
(D) the Tidewater.
(E) the Fall Line.

71. Which of the following appealed to black pride and urged separation of the races?

(A) Paul Robeson
(B) A. Philip Randolph
(C) Marcus Garvey
(D) Claude McKay
(E) Langston Hughes

72. What became the South's major cash crop for sale in the international market in the nineteenth century?

(A) tobacco
(B) cotton
(C) corn
(D) rice
(E) indigo

73. All of the following correctly describe Gerald Ford as president EXCEPT

(A) he pardoned Richard Nixon.
(B) he was the first president not elected to a national office.
(C) he gave federal help when New York City faced bankruptcy.
(D) he aided South Vietnam militarily when it was about to collapse.
(E) he cut inflation from 12 percent to 6 percent.

74. Andrew Jackson's Specie Circular sought to

(A) pay off the government debts.
(B) slow down speculation in public land.
(C) replace the Bank of the United States with an independent treasury.
(D) end the financial panic of 1837.
(E) establish the free coinage of silver.

75. American involvement in World War I brought about which of the following social and economic changes in the United States?

(A) extensive black migration to the North
(B) decline of trade unions
(C) a loosening of controls on freedom of speech
(D) reduction of the number of women in the workplace
(E) a strengthening of anti-trust laws

76. The "spoils system" refers to

(A) the practice of supporting government projects for one's own congressional district.

(B) the practice of appointing relatives to political office.

(C) the practice of giving government jobs to one's political supporters.

(D) the practice of turning to unofficial advisors for council regarding official actions.

(E) the practice of turning to political action committees for campaign funds.

77. The "Intolerable Acts" of 1774 included all of the following EXCEPT

(A) the closing of Boston harbor.

(B) new taxes on glass, tea, lead, and paper.

(C) making the Massachusetts council and judiciary appointive.

(D) allowing trials of accused colonial officials to be moved to England.

(E) authorizing the governor to limit town meetings to as few as one a year.

78. Who was the first woman to serve as a cabinet member?

(A) Jane Addams

(B) Lillian Wald

(C) Sandra Day O'Connor

(D) Betty Friedan

(E) Frances Perkins

79. According to the Constitution, the president is chosen by

(A) the House of Representatives.

(B) popular vote of the people.

(C) the electoral college.

(D) the Senate.

(E) both Houses of Congress.

80. The "Wisconsin Idea" of Robert LaFollette included which of the following?

(A) close cooperation with the University of Wisconsin in the writing of legislation

(B) strong support of labor unions

(C) reduction of business and income taxes

(D) subsidies to agriculture

(E) establishment of Social Security

81. All of the following events took place during the Kennedy administration EXCEPT

(A) the Bay of Pigs invasion.

(B) the building of the Berlin Wall.

(C) a limited test ban treaty signed by the United States, the Soviet Union, and Great Britain.

(D) the Cuban missile crisis.

(E) the U-2 incident.

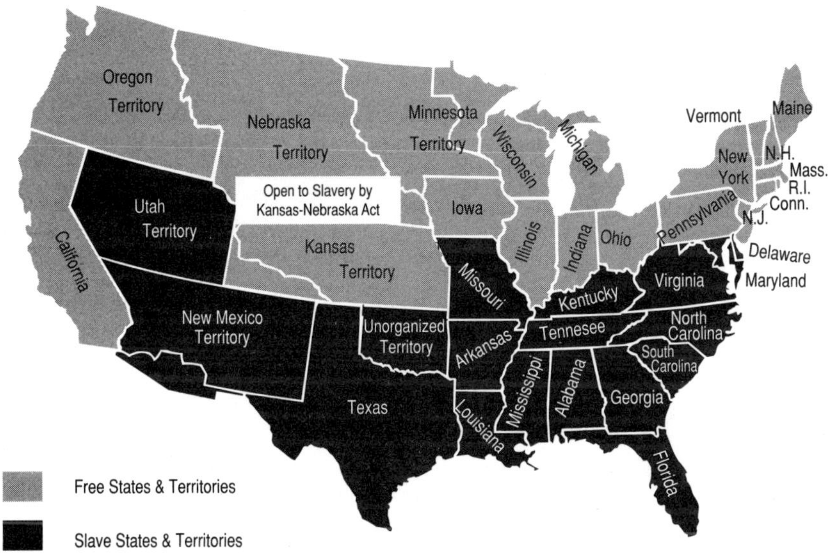

82. This map represents the United States in what year?

(A) 1804 (B) 1821 (C) 1845 (D) 1848 (E) 1853

83. Which of the following did NOT take place during the Grant presidency?

(A) John Wesley Powell's exploration of the Grand Canyon

(B) Last federal troops removed from the South

(C) Settlement of the Alabama claims

(D) Completion of the first transcontinental railroad

(E) Credit Mobilier scandal

84. According to the U.S. State Department, China fell to communism in 1947 because of which of the following?

    (A) Inadequate American aid to Chiang Kai-Shek

    (B) Ccommunist influence within the U.S. government

    (C) Soviet development of the atomic bomb

    (D) The incompetence and corruption of Chiang Kai-Shek's government

    (E) The poor advice of General Joseph Stillwell, U.S. commander in China during World War II.

85. The following table represents the amount of continental currency required to buy $1.00 in specie. In what year did the currency's value decline by the largest percentage?

1777	*January*	1.25	*October*	3.00
1778	*January*	4.00	*October*	5.00
1779	*January*	8.00	*October*	30.00
1780	*January*	42.50	*October*	77.50
1781	*January*	100.00	*April*	167.50

    (A) 1777

    (B) 1778

    (C) 1779

    (D) 1780

    (E) 1781

86. The Tennessee Valley Authority did all of the following EXCEPT

    (A) provide flood control.

    (B) provide low-cost electric power.

    (C) discourage private industry from moving into the valley.

(D) manufacture fertilizer.

(E) raise the average income of those living in the area.

87. The term "Middle Colonies" refers to which of the following groupings?

(A) New York, Pennsylvania, New Jersey, Delaware

(B) Georgia, South Carolina, Virginia, Maryland

(C) New Hampshire, New York, Virginia

(D) Massachusetts, New Hampshire, Connecticut, Rhode Island

(E) North Carolina, Virginia, Maryland, Delaware

88. In 1968 who challenged President Lyndon Johnson in the New Hampshire primary, ultimately forcing him to withdraw from the presidential race?

(A) Hubert H. Humphrey

(B) Robert Kennedy

(C) Edmund Muskie

(D) Eugene McCarthy

(E) George C. Wallace

89. Frederick Jackson Turner's "Frontier Thesis" included all of the following EXCEPT

(A) American democracy developed out of the frontier experience.

(B) The frontier acted as a safety-valve for social ferment.

(C) The frontier moved throughout American history.

(D) The frontier had disappeared by 1890.

(E) The frontier contributed to higher levels of civilization.

90. The 14th Amendment to the Constitution provided for which of the following?

(A) gave blacks federal and state citizenship

(B) disallowed any former Confederate officeholder from becoming a U.S. Senator under any circumstances

(C) repudiated federal war debts

(D) allowed a state to limit the voting of blacks

(E) required the former Confederate states to pay off their debts incurred during the Civil War

91. Which of the following does NOT describe colonial government in America?

(A) During the 1700s the assemblies became more powerful.

(B) In royal colonies the governor could summon or dismiss the assembly.

(C) Compared with England, the right to vote was limited to a few individuals.

(D) The assemblies controlled the raising and spending of tax money.

(E) In proprietary colonies the proprietor appointed the governor.

92. Which of the following worked for women's suffrage in the latter part of the 19th century?

(A) Abigail Adams

(B) Margaret Fuller

(C) Dorothea Dix

(D) Lucy Stone

(E) Germaine Greer

93. Northerners were interested in the Oregon Territory for all of the following reasons EXCEPT

(A) it would maintain the balance of slave and free territory.

(B) it had a large amount of rich farmland.

(C) it offered excellent harbors.

(D) the Russians were expressing interest in the area.

(E) missionary reports described the territory in glowing terms.

94. The War of 1812 resulted in which of the following?

(A) new territory for the United States

(B) resumption of the status quo prior to the war

(C) defeat of the United States

(D) the strengthening of the Federalist party

(E) loss of United States territory

95. The point of view expressed in this cartoon would have pleased

(A) Daniel Webster.

(B) Henry Clay.

(C) William Lloyd Garrison.

(D) John C. Calhoun.

(E) George Fitzhugh.

SAT United States History

Practice Test 2 ANSWER KEY

1.	(A)	26.	(D)	51.	(B)	76.	(C)
2.	(D)	27.	(C)	52.	(C)	77.	(B)
3.	(D)	28.	(E)	53.	(B)	78.	(E)
4.	(E)	29.	(B)	54.	(A)	79.	(C)
5.	(E)	30.	(A)	55.	(D)	80.	(A)
6.	(C)	31.	(B)	56.	(B)	81.	(E)
7.	(D)	32.	(C)	57.	(D)	82.	(D)
8.	(C)	33.	(B)	58.	(C)	83.	(B)
9.	(B)	34.	(A)	59.	(A)	84.	(D)
10.	(A)	35.	(D)	60.	(C)	85.	(C)
11.	(D)	36.	(B)	61.	(C)	86.	(C)
12.	(A)	37.	(D)	62.	(E)	87.	(A)
13.	(C)	38.	(A)	63.	(A)	88.	(D)
14.	(C)	39.	(B)	64.	(D)	89.	(E)
15.	(E)	40.	(B)	65.	(C)	90.	(D)
16.	(B)	41.	(A)	66.	(A)	91.	(C)
17.	(D)	42.	(C)	67.	(D)	92.	(D)
18.	(A)	43.	(C)	68.	(D)	93.	(D)
19.	(C)	44.	(C)	69.	(C)	94.	(B)
20.	(A)	45.	(A)	70.	(B)	95.	(C)
21.	(C)	46.	(E)	71.	(C)		
22.	(B)	47.	(D)	72.	(B)		
23.	(C)	48.	(C)	73.	(D)		
24.	(B)	49.	(B)	74.	(B)		
25.	(B)	50.	(A)	75.	(A)		

Detailed Explanations of Answers

PRACTICE TEST 2

1. **(A)** Ernest Hemingway's *The Sun Also Rises* was published in 1926. John Steinbeck's *The Grapes of Wrath* appeared in 1939; James T. Farrell published the *Studs Lonigan Triology* between 1932 and 1935; John Dos Passos's *USA* appeared between 1930 and 1935; and Erskine Caldwell's *Tobacco Road* appeared in 1932.

2. **(D)** Andrew Jackson vetoed in 1832 the rechartering of the Second Bank of the United States. Nicholas Biddle served as president of the Second Bank of the United States and Henry Clay and Daniel Webster supported its rechartering in Congress. John Marshall served as chief justice of the Supreme Court.

3. **(D)** Under the Articles of Confederation, Congress had the power to control foreign affairs, make war, settle disputes between the states, and coin or borrow money, but it did not have the power to tax.

4. **(E)** Fitzgerald, Hemingway, and Mencken, in various ways, reflected the disillusionment with traditional values that appeared in the wake of World War I. They had little interest in political and economic problems.

5. **(E)** Containment, generally attributed to George F. Kennan, was the policy of holding communism within the Soviet Union and Eastern Europe. John Foster Dulles sought a more aggressive policy of "rolling back" communism while Richard Nixon sought to work with the Soviet Union through "detente." Isolationism sought to avoid involvement in affairs outside the Western Hemisphere.

6. **(C)** Henry L. Stimson stated in 1931 that the U.S. would not recognize any territorial acquisition brought about by force. This was in response to the Japanese invasion of Manchuria. Italy invaded Ethiopia in 1935. Germany reoccupied the Rhineland in 1936 and annexed Austria in 1938. Mexico nationalized its oil fields in 1938.

7. **(D)** Although Lincoln won only 40 percent of the popular vote and none of the Southern or border states, he won the electoral votes of the Northern and Midwestern states as well as California and Oregon. He would have won even if all the votes against him had gone to a single candidate.

8. **(C)** Wealthy merchants, holders of government bonds, owners of large plantations, former officers of the Continental Army, Episcopal and Congregational

ministers, important lawyers, and those involved in export and shipping tended to support the Federalists.

9. **(B)** Egypt and Israel signed a peace treaty in 1979 through the influence of President Jimmy Carter.

10. **(A)** The Wagner Act or National Labor Relations Act of 1936 gave workers the right to form unions and established the National Labor Relations Board to oversee the establishment of unions and hear complaints of unfair labor practices.

11. **(D)** In 1900 there were nearly twice as many immigrants from Southern and Eastern Europe as there were from Northern and Western Europe. This shift is called the "new immigration."

12. **(A)** The policy of "salutary neglect," described by Prime Minister Robert Walpole in the 1720s, made little attempt to enforce the Navigation Acts, passed in the 1660s to control colonial trade. The royal navy remained on the high seas and royal governors continued to be appointed by the king. Britain never encouraged the American colonies to establish their own parliament.

13. **(C)** Gabriel Prosser plotted a rebellion in Virginia in 1800 but was betrayed. Denmark Vesey similarly organized an uprising in South Carolina in 1822 but was discovered. Nat Turner led a rebellion in Virginia in 1831 that resulted in over 60 deaths.

14. **(C)** Wilson refused to make any compromises, and instructed his followers to vote against the treaty with Lodge's amendment. Wilson became ill while publicly campaigning for the treaty and soon suffered a debilitating stroke. Although most senators wanted some changes in the treaty, few opposed it under any circumstances.

15. **(E)** Madeleine Albright became the nation's first woman secretary of state upon the retirement of Warren Christopher, who had served through Clinton's first term.

16. **(B)** In *Marbury v. Madison* the Supreme Court claimed the power to determine the constitutionality of acts of Congress. In *Gibbons v. Ogden* (1824) it gave the federal government the power to regulate commerce. *Dartmouth College v. Woodward* (1819) extended federal protection to property rights under the contract clause, and *McCulloch v. Maryland* (1819) declared that a state could not block a federal agency. Nullification was the doctrine that a state could declare a federal law inoperative within its borders, a position advocated by South Carolina in the 1830s.

17. **(D)** In response to Franklin Roosevelt's four terms as president, the 22nd Amendment, passed in 1951, limited the president to two terms.

18. **(A)** The "right of deposit" meant that Americans could land their goods at New Orleans and ship them out again without paying taxes. The treaty also opened the Mississippi to American shipping for three years and settled the boundary with Florida.

19. **(C)** Labor contributed significantly to Truman's victory. Democratic support for civil rights legislation led to a splitting off of the "Dixiecrats," who took four Southern states, thereby breaking up the "solid South." The candidacy of Henry Wallace, on the other hand, took the most liberal voters out of the Democratic Party.

20. **(A)** New York had two cities over 100,000 in population and three with between 35,000 and 100,000.

21. **(C)** *Plessy v. Ferguson* (1896) established the doctrine of separate but equal. In 1883 the Court disallowed the Civil Rights Act of 1875, saying that the 14th Amendment applied to state governments, not individuals.

22. **(B)** Boss Tweed's moneybag and the dollar and cent signs indicate that political influence was up for sale. The cartoon does not say who was buying influence nor does it bring up the issue of efficiency.

23. **(C)** The RFC loaned money to banks which in turn loaned it to businesses. Although the Hoover administration sponsored some public works projects, it was unwilling to give aid directly to the unemployed or hire the unemployed for unskilled jobs.

24. **(B)** During the first half of the nineteenth century, American factory workers labored from 60 to 72 hours a week. Although some attempted to form unions, none were long-lasting. Working conditions allowed little concern for health and safety. Children made up a significant proportion of the work force. Socialism was not yet an important movement in the United States.

25. **(B)** The Teamsters' strike against UPS, the nation's largest parcel shipper, showed the union getting key concessions from management, mainly regarding the employment of part-time workers and the use of the union's pension fund.

26. **(D)** The Emancipation Proclamation of January 1, 1863 freed slaves in areas still in rebellion. The 13th Amendment (1865) abolished slavery entirely.

27. **(C)** The Methodists came to America during the late colonial period. Latter-Day Saints or Mormons began about 1830 under the leadership of Joseph Smith. Adventists grouped around William Miller's prediction that Christ would return in 1844. Modern Spiritualism began with the "rappings" experienced by the Fox sisters in 1848. Christian Science was founded in 1866 by Mary Baker Eddy.

28. **(E)** According to the Neutrality Act of 1939, the U.S. could sell both military and non-military goods on a "cash-and-carry" basis to belligerent nations.

29. **(B)** Roosevelt distinguished between "good" and "bad" trusts, unlike many other progressives. Although popularly known as the "trust-buster," he initiated only 25 cases against trusts in contrast to Taft, regarded as a conservative, who pursued more than 50 such cases.

30. **(A)** The Proclamation of 1763 ordered the ending of settlement west of the peaks of the Appalachians because of increasing problems with the Indians. The Peace of Paris (1763) ended the French and Indian War while the Sugar Act (1764) forbade trade with the non-English West Indies and required trials for those breaking the law to be held in Admiralty Courts, which had no juries. Numerous new taxes were placed on trade beginning in 1765.

31. **(B)** The Nullification Controversy arose in response to the Tariff of 1828 (Tariff of Abominations) and the Tariff of 1832. South Carolina declared the tariffs "null, void, and no law" in their state after February 1, 1833. A compromise tariff in 1833 diffused the situation. Popular sovereignty refers to the policy of having a state decide whether it would be slave or free.

32. **(C)** Wilson introduced a policy of non-recognition because of disapproval of a government. Before Wilson's action, recognition had depended only on whether a government controlled a country and was willing to carry out its obligations. The Tampico incident took place in 1914 and Villa raided New Mexico in 1916.

33. **(B)** *The Federalist Papers* were written by John Jay, Alexander Hamilton, and James Madison to support ratification of the Constitution in New York state. Thomas Paine wrote *Common Sense* during the conflict with Great Britain and *The Age of Reason* to support rational religion. James Bryce, an Englishman, wrote *The American Commonwealth* in the late nineteenth century. John Adams's *Defense of the Constitutions of Government of United States of America* was a history of republican government.

34. **(A)** Sacajawea was an Indian guide and interpreter for Lewis and Clark. Sitting Bull was a Sioux chief of the late nineteenth century. Zebulon Pike was an army officer who explored the West while James Wilkinson served as governor of the Louisiana Territory and may have been involved in a plan to establish part of the region as a separate nation. Tecumseh led an Indian confederacy in revolt against the United States just prior to the War of 1812.

35. **(D)** The Knights of Labor was a general labor union that organized workers without regard to occupation or industry, in contrast to the AFL which organized only skilled workers by craft. The Knights also admitted women and blacks. The anarchists advocated the destruction of all government.

36. **(B)** A new fugitive slave law was adopted but the slave trade was abolished only in Washington, D.C. California was to enter the union as a free state while Utah and Mexico were left undetermined in regard to slavery. The western border of Texas was also settled.

37. **(D)** Although the Hawaiian Islands were annexed during the Spanish-American War, they had nothing directly to do with that conflict.

38. **(A)** Thomas Paine published *Common Sense* in 1776. Thomas Jefferson drafted the "Declaration of Independence" that same year. Patrick Henry became famous for his "Give me liberty or give me death" speech in Virginia in 1775. All three men were indebted to the natural rights philosophy of the British writer John Locke. John Adams wrote *Defense of the Governments of the United States of America* in the mid-1780s.

39. **(B)** Eisenhower privately opposed the 1954 *Brown v. Board of Education of Topeka* decision and only reluctantly supported the 1957 and 1960 Civil Rights Acts.

40. **(B)** Indentured servants sold their services for a limited period of time to repay their passage to America. In contrast, slaves were held in servitude for life. Both slaves and indentured servants were used for all types of manual labor but neither received wages for their work, except in special circumstances. At the end of their indenture, servants usually received 50 acres of land.

41. **(A)** Television in both its programming and commercials portrayed women primarily as homemakers.

42. **(C)** In contrast to the Populists, who represented farmers and to a lesser extent the working class, the Progressives came primarily from the middle class.

43. **(C)** The Populists supported the coinage of silver because it would bring about inflation which would help farmers in paying off their debts. Representatives of the large corporations and banks supported the gold standard and were influential in the Republican party. Those involved in international trade opposed attempts at inflation.

44. **(C)** Alexander Hamilton believed that the United States should assume the debts of both the Confederation and the states in order to draw people's loyalty from the states to the federal government, as explained in his *Report on Public Credit* (1790).

45. **(A)** Independence movements against France had emerged in the 1920s. The WW II invasion of the Japanese temporarily forced the French to withdraw. During the Korean War the U.S. gave aid to the French in Vietnam. The Geneva Accords of 1954 divided the two Vietnams. The Gulf of Tonkin Resolution of 1964 gave the

president the power to take military action in Vietnam. Although all of these options relate to the Vietnam War, the key word in the question is "ultimately."

46. **(E)** The Bill of Rights, or first 10 amendments to the Constitution, placed limits on the power of the federal government, including freedom of religion, speech, press, and assembly, right to keep and bear arms, limits on the quartering of troops, limits on the right of government to search, various rights for accused persons, and nonenumerated rights and powers reserved by the states and people.

47. **(D)** The Pueblo tribes, which currently reside in the American Southwest, are descendants of the Anasazi people. Beginning in about 1050, the Anasazi began building large apartment-like dwellings under the overhangs of cliffs. These cliff dwellings, located where the current states of Utah, Colorado, Arizona, and New Mexico intersect, were as much as five stories high. Within 300 years the dwellings were abandoned. A severe drought and internal fighting may have caused the culture's decline. The term *anasazi* is the Navajo word for "ancient enemies," causing some modern-day descendents to consider it a derogatory name. These modern tribes, which include the Pueblo and the Hopi, use the name Hisatsinom, which in Hopi means "ancient people."

48. **(C)** The followers of Andrew Jackson established the Democratic Party, whose roots could be loosely traced back to the Democratic-Republican (or Republican) Party of Thomas Jefferson. The Federalists had died out since 1814 and the Whigs arose in the 1830s in opposition to Jackson and the Democrats. The Populists emerged in the 1880s.

49. **(B)** In 1831 William Lloyd Garrison called for immediate emancipation. He rejected colonization, free soil, and any other step-by-step emancipation as insufficient.

50. **(A)** The growth of suburbs resulted in a loss of the white population in the central cities, as people moved from one to the other. Suburbanites depended on cars rather than public transportation and purchased great amounts of mass-produced housing, e.g., Levittown. Blacks continued to migrate from the South to the central cities.

51. **(B)** The Great Awakening, which took place primarily in New England, split both the Congregational and Presbyterian churches between those who emphasized spiritual enthusiasm and those who preferred a more staid, rational approach. The Awakening was interdenominational in character, particularly through the evangelism of George Whitefield. The hanging of Quakers and the witchcraft trials both took place in the seventeenth century. The Church of England was not an established, or state supported, church in New England, where Congregationalism was established.

52. **(C)** Washington was dependent upon poorly trained militia to man his army. The British public was divided in its support of Britain's policy while about one

third of the American colonists opposed the war. Washington did not depend on conventional military tactics and began fighting in ways new to the English. The attention of the British government was also diverted by continuing conflict with France.

53. **(B)** By the 1890s most immigrants came from Southern and Eastern Europe (Italy, Austria-Hungary, Russia, and the Balkans) rather than Northern and Western Europe (Great Britain, Ireland, Scandinavia, and Germany) which had dominated earlier immigration. Mexico at this time provided few immigrants.

54. **(A)** Alexander Hamilton was arguing for "broad construction" of the Constitution, asserting that as long as the Constitution did not prohibit an action it was allowable when it carried out an end or goal of the Constitution. Thomas Jefferson argued for "strict construction," saying that the Constitution must specifically give the federal government a power in order for that power to be constitutional. Hamilton was saying nothing about the Supreme Court and rejected the idea that implied powers were reserved to the states.

55. **(D)** In response to European efforts to collect debts from Western Hemisphere nations by force, Theodore Roosevelt in 1904 claimed the right of the U.S. to act as an international police power in the area. The U.S. had acted as an arbitrator earlier that year in a dispute between Germany and Great Britain with Venezuela.

56. **(B)** William Dean Howells emerged as a major writer after the Civil War. Irving, Emerson. Hawthorne, and Melville all wrote their major works before the Civil War although Emerson and Melville lived beyond the war itself.

57. **(D)** World War I had ended in 1918, but the social and economic dislocation resulting from its end contributed to the anxiety that produced the Red Scare.

58. **(C)** In the 1857 Dred Scott decision, the Supreme Court decided that neither Congress nor the people living in a territory could bar slavery from that territory; therefore the Missouri Compromise was unconstitutional. It also decided that slaves were not citizens, thus Scott had no right to bring his case to the Court.

59. **(A)** Great Britain sought to discourage products that would compete with those of its own manufacturers. Most colonial products were raw materials and therefore equality was not a major problem. Although British prices were low, the government was interested in preventing sale of colonial goods to other countries, rather than directly controlling prices.

60. **(C)** *Gideon v. Wainright* guaranteed the right of a lawyer to persons charged with a serious crime. The 23rd Amendment gave voting rights in presidential elections to the District of Columbia. The 24th Amendment prohibited the poll tax. *Wesberry v. Sanders* established the principle of one person one vote. The Voting Rights Act prohibited the use of literacy tests in voting.

61. **(C)** In 1936, 75 percent of the black vote went to Franklin Roosevelt, in contrast to 21 percent in 1932.

62. **(E)** The Federal Reserve Act set up the Federal Reserve System of 12 district banks under the supervision of a Federal Reserve Board. The Underwood Tariff of 1913 lowered tariffs by 10 percent. The Federal Trade Commission Act of 1914 established a commission for overseeing big business. The Clayton Antitrust Act expanded the list of illegal business activities, and the 17th Amendment provided for the popular election of U.S. senators.

63. **(A)** The North was fighting an offensive war, for it had to invade the South in order to win.

64. **(D)** Germany, Italy, and Japan constituted the Axis alliance, formed in 1940. After being overrun by Germany, France became a collaborationist power. The Soviet Union signed a non-aggression pact with Germany in 1939.

65. **(C)** The Monroe Doctrine of 1823 pledged that the U.S. would not intervene in European affairs. Because of previous discussions with the British, Monroe knew that the British navy would support the U.S. in opposing Russian or Spanish expansion in the Western Hemisphere.

66. **(A)** Phoebe Palmer was a Methodist layworker who pioneered social welfare projects in New York. Lucretia Mott, Elizabeth Cady Stanton, and Susan B. Anthony were all active in the women's rights movement, which held its first convention at Seneca Falls, New York in 1848. Margaret Fuller was a transcendentalist who wrote *Woman in the Nineteenth Century* (1845).

67. **(D)** The French Revolution, beginning in 1789, made the maintenance of neutrality difficult for the United States for the next two decades.

68. **(D)** The Confederacy borrowed about $15 million from abroad and $100 million from its citizens, raised over $100 million through taxation, and printed over $1 billion in paper money. No income tax was established.

69. **(C)** The Constitutional Convention took place in 1787. The Declaration of Independence was signed in 1776, the Articles of Confederation ratified in 1781, and George Washington became president in 1789. Thomas Jefferson was elected to the presidency in 1800.

70. **(B)** The Great Plains refers to the trans-Mississippi West. The Tidewater refers to the area near the sea, the Piedmont includes the foothills on the eastern side of the Appalachians, while the backcountry lay in the Appalachians themselves and westward. The Fall Line is the dividing point between the Tidewater and the Piedmont where the water falls rapidly to the lower land.

71. **(C)** Although Robeson (singer), Randolph (union leader), McKay (writer), and Hughes (writer), all appealed to black pride, only Marcus Garvey explicitly argued for separation of the races. His Universal Negro Improvement Association served as a vehicle for his ideas.

72. **(B)** Although more corn was grown than cotton, it was the latter that was the South's major cash crop for the international market. Tobacco, rice, and indigo were grown only in a few areas.

73. **(D)** Although Ford wanted to aid South Vietnam in 1975, he was unable to gain congressional support to do so.

74. **(B)** The Specie Circular of 1836 sought to slow down speculation in public land by requiring payment in gold and silver rather than bank notes. Sales of public lands were helping pay off the public debt. The Independent Treasury was not established until the 1840s.

75. **(A)** Between 1916 and 1919 about 500,000 blacks moved to the North, most looking for work in the factories. Women also worked in the factories. Trade unions gained more power and antitrust laws were weakened. Greater controls were placed over freedom of speech.

76. **(C)** The "spoils system" or "patronage," largely introduced by Andrew Jackson at the federal level, was the practice of giving government jobs to one's political supporters. "Pork barreling" refers to promoting government projects for one's own political district. "Nepotism" is the practice of appointing relatives to political office. And "Kitchen Cabinet" was the phrase used during Jackson's presidency to describe his unofficial advisors.

77. **(B)** The Townshend Duties of 1767 placed new duties on glass, tea, lead, and paper. The "Intolerable" or "Coercive Acts" were passed in response to the Boston Tea Party and closed Boston Harbor until the tea was paid for, gave the governor greater powers, made the colony's council appointive rather than elective, and provided that colonial officials accused of capital crimes could have their trials moved to England.

78. **(E)** Frances Perkins served as Franklin D. Roosevelt's Secretary of Labor beginning in 1933. Jane Addams and Lillian Wald were early leaders — as was Frances Perkins — in what became known as social work. Sandra Day O'Connor was the first woman member of the Supreme Court. And Betty Friedan was a women's rights leader of the 1960s and 1970s.

79. **(C)** The electoral college is made up of electors, chosen by the people, and equal in number to the total number of representatives and senators from each state. These electors choose the president.

80. **(A)** During the first quarter of the twentieth century Robert M. LaFollette, as governor and then senator from Wisconsin, promoted close cooperation with University of Wisconsin professors in the writing of legislation. He also established higher taxes on business and introduced the income tax. Support for labor unions and subsidies for agriculture did not really begin until the New Deal of the 1930s.

81. **(E)** The U-2 incident took place in 1960 during the Eisenhower administration. The Bay of Pigs invasion and the building of the Berlin Wall occurred in 1961. The Cuban Missile Crisis happened in 1961 and the Test Ban Treaty was signed in 1963.

82. **(D)** The Treaty of Guadalupe Hidalgo (1848) which ended the Mexican War, gave the United States New Mexico and Upper California and established the Rio Grande as the southern border of Texas.

83. **(B)** Grant served as president from 1869 to 1877. Powell explored the Grand Canyon in 1869, the same year the transcontinental railroad was completed. The Alabama claims were settled in 1872. The Credit Mobilier scandal broke open in 1972. Federal troops were removed from the South in 1877, after Hayes became president.

84. **(D)** A State Department "White Paper" of 1949 blamed the loss of China on the incompetence and corruption of Chiang Kai-Shek's government and military, something Stillwell had pointed out years earlier. Anti-communists such as McCarthy blamed the situation on lack of American aid and communist influence on the State Department. The Soviets did not develop the atomic bomb until 1949.

85. **(C)** Although the largest dollar amount that the currency declined was $67.50 between January and April, 1781, the largest percentage was in 1779 when it declined 375 percent.

86. **(C)** The TVA, by providing low electrical rates, encouraged private industry to move into the valley. It also provided flood control and manufactured fertilizers. Its overall effect was to raise the average income in the area.

87. **(A)** The "Middle Colonies" include New York, Pennsylvania, New Jersey, and Delaware. "New England" refers to Massachusetts, New Hampshire, Connecticut, and Rhode Island. The "Southern Colonies" were Georgia, South Carolina, Virginia, and Maryland.

88. **(D)** Eugene McCarthy challenged Johnson as an anti-war candidate. Kennedy came into the race after McCarthy's near-victory in New Hampshire. Humphrey, Johnson's vice president, became the Democratic nominee with Muskie as his running mate. Wallace was the candidate of the American Independent Party.

89. **(E)** Turner argued in 1893 that the frontier, as it moved westward, continually broke down the established civilization that was taken to it, forcing people to rebuild their culture from the ground up.

90. **(D)** The 14th Amendment promised that federal war debts would be paid but forbade the payment of Confederate war debts by the United States or any states. It allowed limitations on black voting but provided for a reduction in representation in such cases. It gave blacks federal and state citizenship.

91. **(C)** The right to vote was more widespread in the American colonies than in England because ownership of land was more open. The assemblies gained in power throughout the 1700s because they controlled the "purse strings." Royal governors had the power to summon or dismiss these assemblies, but the assemblies controlled the payment of the governor's salary.

92. **(D)** Lucy Stone was a leader in the women's suffrage movement from the 1840s until her death in 1893. Abigail Adams was the wife of John Adams, and Margaret Fuller was active in the Transcendentalist movement of the 1830s and 1840s, while Dorothea Dix campaigned about the same time for better treatment of the mentally ill. Germaine Greer was active in the women's movement of the 1960s and 1970s.

93. **(D)** Oregon would balance the slave state of Texas. The Willamette Valley offered fertile farmland while Puget Sound contained excellent harbors. The territory also held excellent potential for fur trapping. All of these things were reported by the missionaries such as Marcus Whitman who went to Oregon.

94. **(B)** The Treaty of Ghent (1814) restored the ante-bellum status quo. Although the United States had attempted to take Canada, it had failed. Despite defeats in many battles and the burning of Washington, D.C., the U.S. was not defeated in the war. The Federalists, who opposed the war and were moving toward supporting secession of the Northeast, were seriously weakened when the war ended.

95. **(C)** William Lloyd Garrison was a leading abolitionist who would have approved of this cartoon condemning the Fugitive Slave Law of 1850. Daniel Webster (portrayed in the cartoon) and Henry Clay both played roles in bringing about the Compromise of 1850, of which the law was a part. John C. Calhoun and George Fitzhugh were staunch defenders of slavery.

THE SAT SUBJECT TEST IN

United States History

PRACTICE TEST 3

SAT United States History

Practice Test 3

1. (A) (B) (C) (D) (E)
2. (A) (B) (C) (D) (E)
3. (A) (B) (C) (D) (E)
4. (A) (B) (C) (D) (E)
5. (A) (B) (C) (D) (E)
6. (A) (B) (C) (D) (E)
7. (A) (B) (C) (D) (E)
8. (A) (B) (C) (D) (E)
9. (A) (B) (C) (D) (E)
10. (A) (B) (C) (D) (E)
11. (A) (B) (C) (D) (E)
12. (A) (B) (C) (D) (E)
13. (A) (B) (C) (D) (E)
14. (A) (B) (C) (D) (E)
15. (A) (B) (C) (D) (E)
16. (A) (B) (C) (D) (E)
17. (A) (B) (C) (D) (E)
18. (A) (B) (C) (D) (E)
19. (A) (B) (C) (D) (E)
20. (A) (B) (C) (D) (E)
21. (A) (B) (C) (D) (E)
22. (A) (B) (C) (D) (E)
23. (A) (B) (C) (D) (E)
24. (A) (B) (C) (D) (E)
25. (A) (B) (C) (D) (E)
26. (A) (B) (C) (D) (E)
27. (A) (B) (C) (D) (E)
28. (A) (B) (C) (D) (E)
29. (A) (B) (C) (D) (E)
30. (A) (B) (C) (D) (E)
31. (A) (B) (C) (D) (E)
32. (A) (B) (C) (D) (E)
33. (A) (B) (C) (D) (E)
34. (A) (B) (C) (D) (E)
35. (A) (B) (C) (D) (E)
36. (A) (B) (C) (D) (E)
37. (A) (B) (C) (D) (E)
38. (A) (B) (C) (D) (E)
39. (A) (B) (C) (D) (E)
40. (A) (B) (C) (D) (E)
41. (A) (B) (C) (D) (E)
42. (A) (B) (C) (D) (E)
43. (A) (B) (C) (D) (E)
44. (A) (B) (C) (D) (E)
45. (A) (B) (C) (D) (E)
46. (A) (B) (C) (D) (E)
47. (A) (B) (C) (D) (E)
48. (A) (B) (C) (D) (E)
49. (A) (B) (C) (D) (E)
50. (A) (B) (C) (D) (E)
51. (A) (B) (C) (D) (E)
52. (A) (B) (C) (D) (E)
53. (A) (B) (C) (D) (E)
54. (A) (B) (C) (D) (E)
55. (A) (B) (C) (D) (E)
56. (A) (B) (C) (D) (E)
57. (A) (B) (C) (D) (E)
58. (A) (B) (C) (D) (E)
59. (A) (B) (C) (D) (E)
60. (A) (B) (C) (D) (E)
61. (A) (B) (C) (D) (E)
62. (A) (B) (C) (D) (E)
63. (A) (B) (C) (D) (E)
64. (A) (B) (C) (D) (E)
65. (A) (B) (C) (D) (E)
66. (A) (B) (C) (D) (E)
67. (A) (B) (C) (D) (E)
68. (A) (B) (C) (D) (E)
69. (A) (B) (C) (D) (E)
70. (A) (B) (C) (D) (E)
71. (A) (B) (C) (D) (E)
72. (A) (B) (C) (D) (E)
73. (A) (B) (C) (D) (E)
74. (A) (B) (C) (D) (E)
75. (A) (B) (C) (D) (E)
76. (A) (B) (C) (D) (E)
77. (A) (B) (C) (D) (E)
78. (A) (B) (C) (D) (E)
79. (A) (B) (C) (D) (E)
80. (A) (B) (C) (D) (E)
81. (A) (B) (C) (D) (E)
82. (A) (B) (C) (D) (E)
83. (A) (B) (C) (D) (E)
84. (A) (B) (C) (D) (E)
85. (A) (B) (C) (D) (E)
86. (A) (B) (C) (D) (E)
87. (A) (B) (C) (D) (E)
88. (A) (B) (C) (D) (E)
89. (A) (B) (C) (D) (E)
90. (A) (B) (C) (D) (E)
91. (A) (B) (C) (D) (E)
92. (A) (B) (C) (D) (E)
93. (A) (B) (C) (D) (E)
94. (A) (B) (C) (D) (E)
95. (A) (B) (C) (D) (E)

United States History

PRACTICE TEST 3

TIME: 60 Minutes
95 Questions

DIRECTIONS: Each of the questions or incomplete statements below is followed by five suggested answers or completions. Select the one that is best in each case.

1. The key difference between the functions of a grand jury and a petit jury in the American legal system is

   (A) the grand jury is larger in size.

   (B) only the petit jury determines innocence or guilt.

   (C) there is no presiding judge at a grand jury.

   (D) a grand jury does not examine evidence.

   (E) the petit jury does not hear criminal cases.

2. Cloture is a parliamentary device designed by the _____ to stop _____.

   (A) president … a veto override

   (B) Senate … filibustering

   (C) House of Representatives … filibustering

   (D) Senate … impoundment

   (E) president … inflation

3. In the nineteenth century, American farmers supported an economic policy of inflation because inflation generally favors

   (A) debtor groups.

   (B) creditor groups.

   (C) high food costs.

   (D) a dynamic monetary system.

   (E) a barter system.

4. At the time President George H. W. Bush spoke of building "a new world order," the most significant concern confronting his administration was

(A) the outbreak of civil war throughout the Balkans and the Caucasus.

(B) the threat of massive destruction from nuclear war.

(C) the rapid democratization of the former Soviet bloc.

(D) Henry Kissinger's shuttle diplomacy in the Middle East.

(E) global concern regarding Acquired Immune Deficiency Syndrome.

5. A "closed shop" requires workers to

(A) receive national security clearance.

(B) promise not to join a union.

(C) join a union to secure a job.

(D) receive their pay in cash.

(E) apply for unemployment benefits.

6. Article I of the U.S. Constitution establishes

(A) freedom of speech.

(B) the powers of the presidency.

(C) freedom of assembly.

(D) the powers of Congress.

(E) the powers of the Supreme Court.

7. In order for a treaty to become law, the _____ must ratify the treaty after it has been negotiated by the _____ .

(A) House of Representatives ... Senate

(B) Congress ... president

(C) Supreme Court ... Senate

(D) Senate ... president

(E) president ... Senate

8. The first presidential election that relied upon the popular vote to select the Electoral College was held in

   (A) 1789.
   (B) 1800.
   (C) 1824.
   (D) 1916.
   (E) 1928.

9. The American commitment to the "unalienable rights" of "life, liberty, and the pursuit of happiness" is most clearly expressed in

   (A) the U.S. Constitution.
   (B) the Declaration of Independence.
   (C) the Bill of Rights.
   (D) the 25th Amendment.
   (E) *Plessy v. Ferguson.*

10. The only president to be elected to more than two terms in office was

   (A) John Adams.
   (B) George Washington.
   (C) Woodrow Wilson.
   (D) Andrew Jackson.
   (E) Franklin D. Roosevelt.

COTTON PRODUCTION AND SLAVE POPULATION, 1790-1860

Year	*Cotton Bales Produced*	*Number of Slaves*
1790	4,000	697,897
1820	73,222	1,538,098
1840	1,347,640	2,487,213
1860	3,841,416	3,957,760

11. The table above shows which of the following for the period 1790 to 1860?

   (A) Cotton was the largest crop in the South.
   (B) Slaves were efficient workers.
   (C) Slavery was profitable.
   (D) Cotton production was a primary cause for the growth of slavery.
   (E) Northern textile mills required more Southern cotton.

12. The Mayflower Compact of 1620 established
    (A) a land of religious freedom.
    (B) the colony of Massachusetts.
    (C) a royal colony.
    (D) Plymouth colony.
    (E) the colony of Rhode Island.

13. On the eve of Columbus' first arrival in 1492, the native Indian population of the Western Hemisphere is estimated to have been at
    (A) 1–5 million.
    (B) 10–20 million.
    (C) 25–40 million.
    (D) 50–60 million.
    (E) 80–100 million.

14. Columbus undertook his 1492 voyage to the Americas to
    (A) Christianize the Indian population.
    (B) prove that the Earth was round.
    (C) discover new worlds.
    (D) test the geographic theories of Ptolemy.
    (E) secure wealth and power for himself and the Spanish throne.

15. Jamestown survived as the first permanent English settlement in America because
    (A) the settlers followed the example of Roanoke.
    (B) of the emergence of tobacco as a cash crop.
    (C) of the religious convictions of its first settlers.
    (D) of the mild climate of Virginia.
    (E) of its use of Indian slaves as a labor force.

16. Roger Williams is best known in American history as
    (A) advocating the uniting of church and state into a theocracy.
    (B) an early champion of religious freedom.
    (C) the chief justice at the Salem witch trials.

(D) the founder of New Hampshire.

(E) the first royal governor of Massachusetts.

17. Indentured servants in colonial America experienced

(A) great upward economic mobility.

(B) political power.

(C) racial harmony with black slaves.

(D) a high standard of living.

(E) low social status.

18. During the seventeenth century, black slaves in the Southern colonies

(A) came directly from East Africa.

(B) grew slowly as a labor force.

(C) were treated the same as slaves in the British West Indies.

(D) were allowed to set their children free.

(E) lived mostly in urban areas.

19. The Dominion of New England was

(A) the title of the first book published in America.

(B) the name given to Massachusetts by John Winthrop.

(C) an attempt to reorganize the British Empire by James II.

(D) the first American public school.

(E) the official name of the Puritan religion.

20. William Penn's plans for a Quaker colony in Pennsylvania included all of the following EXCEPT

(A) establishing peaceful relations with the Indians.

(B) allowing for religious freedom.

(C) establishing a democracy.

(D) the making of an economic profit.

(E) establishing a colony loyal to Great Britain.

21. At the close of the Seven Years' War in 1763, France ceded to Great Britain

(A) the French West Indies.
(B) Florida.
(C) Canada.
(D) the African slave trade.
(E) the Louisiana Territory.

22. England passed the Stamp Act in 1765 to

(A) punish Americans for protests to the Sugar Act.
(B) control the American press.
(C) raise money to reduce England's national debt.
(D) allow for illegal search-and-seizure of smugglers.
(E) allow Americans to settle the Ohio River Valley.

23. The eighteenth century population in British North America

(A) nearly doubled every 25 years.
(B) became increasingly more homogeneous.
(C) had a life expectancy of 45 years for males.
(D) was clustered inside the new cities of the colonies.
(E) was composed of less than 2 percent African-Americans.

24. All of the following were major figures in the Enlightenment EXCEPT

(A) Benjamin Franklin.
(B) William Bradford.
(C) John Locke.
(D) Sir Isaac Newton.
(E) Thomas Jefferson.

25. After the American Revolution, the Loyalists did NOT

(A) return to Great Britain.
(B) emigrate to Canada.
(C) sue America for property loss.
(D) settle in the West Indies.
(E) create their own American colony in Ohio.

26. The Articles of Confederation created for the 13 states

(A) a strong national government.

(B) a sound national economy.

(C) a league of friendship among 13 independent countries.

(D) the Bill of Rights.

(E) interstate trade agreements.

27. During the winter of 1786, Shays' Rebellion indicated to most Americans

(A) the political dangers of the post-war recession.

(B) the weaknesses of state government.

(C) the need to reform the Articles of Confederation.

(D) the desperation of the yeoman farmer in America.

(E) All of the above.

28. In seventeenth century New England, married women were denied the right to

(A) vote for elected officials.

(B) divorce their husbands.

(C) arrange marriages for their children.

(D) own property.

(E) All of the above.

29. The passage of the Declaratory Act in 1766 by Parliament was greeted in America by

(A) the creation of the Continental Congress.

(B) mob violence against British merchants.

(C) refusal to pay these new taxes.

(D) little attention to its statement of parliamentary sovereignty.

(E) Tories fleeing to Canada.

30. During the Washington administration, the secretary of the Treasury, Alexander Hamilton, proposed an economic program which included all of the following EXCEPT

(A) establishing close ties between the national government and American business.

(B) establishing a national bank.

(C) having the states pay off the total war debt.

(D) imposing new taxes through customs duties and excise taxes.

(E) retiring the full national debt and deficit government spending.

31. During the 1790s, Federalists and Republicans openly disagreed over

(A) the extent of popular control of government.

(B) foreign policy toward England and France.

(C) the activities of Citizen Genet.

(D) the fiscal policies of the national government.

(E) All of the above.

32. The Alien and Sedition Acts included all of the following EXCEPT

(A) increasing the residency requirements for U.S. citizenship.

(B) extended presidential powers to remove foreign residents of the United States.

(C) a threat to the jury system.

(D) restriction of an opposition press.

(E) the curtailment of free speech in America.

33. At the close of the American Revolution, a group of American writers and artists sought to establish a distinctly American national culture. Which of the following artists do not belong to this movement?

(A) Noah Webster

(B) Philip Freneau

(C) Hector St. Jean Crèvecoeur

(D) Cotton Mather

(E) Joel Barlow

34. President John Adams' "Midnight Appointments" were the primary issue in the Supreme Court's ruling in

(A) *Marbury v. Madison.*
(B) *Gibbons v. Ogden.*
(C) *Martin v. Hunter's Lessee.*
(D) *Dartmouth v. Woodward.*
(E) *Fletcher v. Peck.*

35. Chief Justice John Marshall established the power of judicial review for the Supreme Court in 1803. This doctrine grants

(A) the Court the power of original jurisdiction.
(B) the power of strict constructionism.
(C) the power of the government to regulate big business.
(D) the power of the Court to determine what the laws of America are.
(E) the power of the Court to select its own members.

36. "We prefer war to the putrescent pool of ignominious peace." This quote best represents the attitudes of which individual and/or group during the War of 1812?

(A) Oliver Ellsworth and New England merchants
(B) Henry Clay and Westerners
(C) the British nobility
(D) James Madison and the Republicans
(E) Harrison Gay Otis and the Federalists

37. The primary goal of the Hartford Convention was

(A) to have New England secede from the United States.
(B) to assert a doctrine of states' rights.
(C) to establish a public school system in the nation.
(D) to establish direct trade with Japan.
(E) to plan the invasion of Cuba.

38. The fragility of the Era of Good Feelings was shattered by the

(A) War of 1812.
(B) Chesapeake Affair.
(C) Missouri Compromise.
(D) Non-Intercourse Act.
(E) Jay Treaty.

39. The American population grew from _____ million in 1820 to _____ million in 1850.

(A) 1 … 6

(B) 20 … 40

(C) 9 … 23

(D) 62 … 88

(E) 40 … 44

40. During the 1820s, the ideal American family was portrayed as a family in which

(A) the home served as a refuge from a hostile world.

(B) the children were the center.

(C) there existed separate spheres for men and women.

(D) the mother primarily was responsible for raising the children.

(E) All of the above.

41. The popular theology of Charles Finney during the Second Great Awakening stressed

(A) human perfectibility.

(B) an Old Testament God.

(C) original sin.

(D) rational Christianity.

(E) None of the above.

42. Which of the following American authors sought to recreate the everyday experiences of ordinary Americans in his writings?

(A) Edgar Allan Poe

(B) Nathaniel Hawthorne

(C) Herman Melville

(D) Walt Whitman

(E) Frances Trollope

43. The Tariff Act of 1832 resulted in

(A) near war between the United States and South Carolina.

(B) a rift between President Jackson and Vice President Calhoun.

(C) the revival of a states' rights doctrine.

(D) a compromise solution proposed by Henry Clay.

(E) All of the above.

44. The American Colonization Society was an anti-slavery organization that

(A) advocated racial equality.

(B) sought full political rights for blacks.

(C) favored immediate emancipation.

(D) advocated the forced shipment of freed slaves to Africa.

(E) relied upon governmental action to end slavery.

45. The vast majority of Southern slaves lived on plantations holding

(A) less than 20 slaves.

(B) 50–100 slaves.

(C) 200–500 slaves.

(D) 500–1,000 slaves.

(E) more than 1,000 slaves.

46. Gabriel Prosser, Denmark Vesey, and Nat Turner were

(A) the secret French agents X,Y & Z.

(B) leaders of slave rebellions.

(C) members of the Hudson River School.

(D) famous African-American poets.

(E) the founders of the Abolitionists.

47. Nativism was a movement seeking to

(A) use emotionalism in painting.

(B) keep the United States out of World War II.

(C) protect the American environment.

(D) restrict America to a land of white Anglo-Saxons only.

(E) gain full citizenship for the Amerindian.

48. The doctrine of Manifest Destiny argued for all of the following EXCEPT

(A) It was America's natural right to occupy all lands to the Pacific coast.

(B) The American economy needed new lands for new markets.

(C) America should remain first and foremost a nation of farmers.

(D) The nation needed new lands to safeguard democracy.

(E) U.S. annexation of Great Britain.

49. Which of the following events occurred first?

    (A) the Kansas-Nebraska Act

    (B) the Nat Turner Rebellion

    (C) the Seneca Falls Convention

    (D) the Lincoln-Douglas debates

    (E) the Homestead Act

50. "I wish to speak today, not as a Massachusetts man, nor as a Northern man, but as an American for the preservation of the Union." Daniel Webster delivered this speech in defense of

    (A) Dartmouth College.

    (B) the Charles River Bridge.

    (C) Abraham Lincoln.

    (D) the Compromise of 1850.

    (E) the Second Bank of the United States.

51. Stephen Douglas' advocacy of popular sovereignty in the Kansas-Nebraska Act ignited rather than dispelled the flames of sectionalism. Popular sovereignty sought to

    (A) allow blacks to vote in the Kansas-Nebraska territories.

    (B) let the residents of Kansas-Nebraska areas determine their own laws on slavery through elections.

    (C) force the Supreme Court to rule on slavery's constitutionality.

    (D) remove the slavery issue from politics.

    (E) None of the above.

52. The "Secret Six" were the financial supporters of

    (A) the attack on Fort Sumter.

    (B) John Brown's raid on Harper's Ferry.

    (C) Lincoln's presidential candidacy.

    (D) Southern secession.

    (E) King Cotton Diplomacy.

53. The final four states to secede from the United States after the firing on Fort Sumter were

    (A) Alabama, Georgia, South Carolina, and North Carolina.

    (B) Virginia, Arkansas, Tennessee, and North Carolina.

    (C) Georgia, Mississippi, South Carolina, and Texas.

    (D) South Carolina, Kentucky, Maryland, and Delaware.

    (E) Florida, Georgia, Maryland, and South Carolina.

54. During the Civil War, the Copperheads were

    (A) anti-Lincoln Republicans.

    (B) Northern pro-war Democrats.

    (C) pro-Union Southerners.

    (D) Northern anti-war Democrats, or Peace Democrats.

    (E) part of the Union League.

55. The Southern strategy of gaining a European ally against the North was attempted through a policy referred to as

    (A) the Stars and Bars.

    (B) the war of attrition.

    (C) King Cotton Diplomacy.

    (D) nullification

    (E) mercantilism.

56. The Great Plains Indian culture in the 1840s can best be described as all of the following EXCEPT

    (A) nomadic.

    (B) centered around the buffalo.

    (C) at its zenith.

    (D) animistic in its reverence for the spiritual power of nature.

    (E) forging close ties with whites.

57. Lincoln's Reconstruction plan for the defeated Southern states included all of the following EXCEPT

    (A) abolition of slavery.

    (B) free education for the ex-slaves.

    (C) republican state governments.

    (D) a required 10 percent of all voters in a state to take a loyalty oath to the United States.

    (E) citizenship for the ex-slaves.

58. The Wade-Davis Bill best represents the views of

    (A) President Andrew Johnson.

    (B) the Radical Republicans.

    (C) the carpetbaggers.

    (D) the scalawags.

    (E) the Democratic Party.

59. The 13th Amendment established

    (A) the legal end of slavery in America.

    (B) the two-term presidency.

    (C) the right to vote for the ex-slaves.

    (D) the income tax.

    (E) woman suffrage.

60. In trying to impeach President Andrew Johnson, Congress used the

    (A) the Morrill Act.

    (B) the Tenure of Office Act.

    (C) the Civil Rights Act.

    (D) *Ex Parte* Milligan.

    (E) the Bill of Rights.

61. The corporate merger was first used successfully by J. Pierpont Morgan with

    (A) the Bank of the United States.

    (B) Sinclair Oil Company.

    (C) Standard Oil Corporation.

(D) United States Steel Corporation.

(E) American Telephone & Telegraph.

62. The late nineteenth century labor union most identified with the motto "pure and simple unionism" was

(A) the Knights of Labor.

(B) the American Federation of Labor.

(C) the National Labor Union.

(D) the IWW.

(E) the Molly Maguires.

63. In 1890, Jacob Riis vividly portrayed life in an American urban slum in his work

(A) *Ragged Dick.*

(B) *The Jungle.*

(C) *Maggie, Girl of the Streets.*

(D) *How the Other Half Lives.*

(E) *The Octopus.*

64. The doctrine of "separate but equal" was established in

(A) *Munn v. Illinois.*

(B) *Plessy v. Ferguson.*

(C) *Scopes v. Tennessee.*

(D) *Brown v. Board of Education of Topeka.*

(E) *Schecter v. The United States.*

65. Booker T. Washington's Atlanta Compromise included all of the following positions EXCEPT

(A) black economic self-improvement.

(B) vocational training for blacks.

(C) black acceptance of segregation.

(D) black accommodation to racism.

(E) black political power.

66. The Pendleton Act of 1883 sought to reform

(A) the illegal corporate trust.
(B) Amerindian reservations.
(C) the Grange.
(D) the civil service.
(E) trade unions.

67. All the following Populist platform issues were later accepted by Americans EXCEPT

(A) the graduated income tax.
(B) direct election of United States senators.
(C) the use of the Australian ballot.
(D) the eight-hour day for labor.
(E) government ownership of telegraph and telephone industries.

68. The only American president to be awarded a Nobel Peace Prize was

(A) Woodrow Wilson.
(B) Herbert Hoover.
(C) Theodore Roosevelt.
(D) Jimmy Carter.
(E) John F. Kennedy.

QUESTIONS 69-70: Each of these questions requires you to identify the correct person/persons associated with the following quotations.

69. "Look away from first things…and look towards last things."

(A) Ralph Waldo Emerson
(B) William James
(C) Frank Lloyd Wright
(D) B. F. Skinner
(E) Jane Addams

70. "I saw the best minds of my generation destroyed by madness, starving hysterical naked."

(A) Herman Melville
(B) Allen Ginsberg
(C) Gerald Ford
(D) Walt Whitman
(E) Dwight Eisenhower

71. The Platt Amendment to the Cuban Constitution of 1900 restricted Cuban independence by allowing the United States to do all of the following EXCEPT

(A) establish an American naval base in Cuba.

(B) control the Cuban monetary system.

(C) compel Cuba to use American shipping for all its trade.

(D) directly intervene in Cuban affairs.

(E) approve all treaties between Cuba and another country.

72. The phrase "yellow journalism" is associated with _____ during (the) _____.

(A) Bernard Baruch … World War I

(B) William Randolph Hearst … Spanish-American War

(C) Daniel Ellsberg … Vietnam War

(D) Ernie Pyle … World War II

(E) Earl Warren … World War II

73. All of the following were members of the Progressive movement EXCEPT

(A) Theodore Roosevelt.

(B) Woodrow Wilson.

(C) Robert LaFollette.

(D) William H. Taft.

(E) William McKinley.

74. The 18th Amendment to the United States Constitution

(A) prohibits the sale of alcoholic beverages.

(B) recognizes women's right to vote.

(C) limits the president to two terms.

(D) establishes the direct election of United States senators.

(E) establishes the federal income tax.

75. The Chicago School of Architecture's motto "form follows function" was expressed by Frank Lloyd Wright's

(A) geodesic domes.

(B) pseudo-Gothic structures.

(C) neo-classical buildings.

(D) prairie house designs.

(E) English Classicism.

76. The achievements of Woodrow Wilson's "New Freedom" program included all of the following EXCEPT

(A) creation of the Federal Reserve Board.

(B) creation of the Federal Trade Commission.

(C) the first federal income tax.

(D) the Clayton Antitrust Act.

(E) a laissez-faire attitude on monopolies.

77. The following were all measures of the first New Deal EXCEPT

(A) the Tennessee Valley Authority.

(B) the bank holiday.

(C) Securities and Exchange Commission.

(D) Social Security.

(E) the Civilian Conservation Corps.

78. In 1924, Congress wrote into law the National Origins Act, which

(A) established the federal census every ten years.

(B) established immigration quotas that restricted immigration from Southern and Eastern Europe.

(C) required all public officeholders to be native-born citizens.

(D) created an open border policy between Canada and the United States.

(E) required all Americans traveling abroad to acquire a passport.

79. Place the following four events in the proper order in which they occurred.

I. the rise of the flapper

II. the creation of the National Organization for Women

III. *Roe v. Wade*

IV. the creation of "Rosie the Riveter"

(A) IV–II–III–I
(B) I–IV–II–III
(C) I–IV–III–II
(D) II–I–IV–III
(E) I–II–III–IV

80. The Civil Rights Act of 1964 accomplished all of the following EXCEPT

(A) barring racial discrimination in public hotels.

(B) authorizing the attorney general to bring suit to desegregate the public schools.

(C) outlawing discriminatory employment practices.

(D) barring racial discrimination in restaurants.

(E) outlawing literacy tests used to prevent citizens from voting.

81. The Bonus Army was

(A) the nickname given to black army volunteers during the Civil War.

(B) Japanese-American victims of relocation camps in World War II.

(C) a 1932 protest group against Herbert Hoover's economic policies.

(D) an American volunteer cavalry unit during the Spanish-American War.

(E) Vietnam War veterans.

82. The diplomatic strategy behind the Lend-Lease program was

(A) to continue American neutrality at all costs during World War II.

(B) to support non-Communist nations at the close of World War II.

(C) to support England's war efforts against Germany without the United States entering World War II.

(D) to stimulate the growth of Third World nations' economies.

(E) to aid American business interests in Latin America.

83. Place the following events of World War II in the correct order in which they occurred.

I. the attack on Pearl Harbor

II. the German invasion of the Soviet Union

III. the D-Day Invasion

IV. the dropping of the atomic bomb on Hiroshima

(A) I–III–II–IV
(B) II–III–I–IV
(C) II–I–IV–III
(D) II–I–III–IV
(E) III–II–I–IV

84. The Soviet Union's launching of Sputnik in 1957 immediately led to
   (A) an easing of U.S.-USSR tensions.
   (B) massive federal aid to American higher education.
   (C) the Suez Crisis.
   (D) the Geneva Summit's endorsement of Open Skies.
   (E) the U-2 incident.

85. During the Vietnam War, the Tet Offensive immediately led to
   (A) the invasion of Cambodia by the United States.
   (B) the Gulf of Tonkin Resolution.
   (C) the Hanoi Peace Talks.
   (D) President Johnson's decision not to seek a second term in office.
   (E) the creation of the Viet Cong.

86. Clarence Earl Gideon earned fame in 1963 by
   (A) being the first American to orbit Earth.
   (B) establishing the accused's right to legal counsel in all criminal cases.
   (C) being impeached from the Supreme Court.
   (D) authoring *Catch 22*.
   (E) breaking Babe Ruth's home run record.

87. McCarthyism refers to
   (A) the illegal practice of redistricting to favor the political party in power.
   (B) the hysterical search for Communists and their sympathizers in American government.
   (C) the post-World War II economic recovery programs for Western Europe.
   (D) corrupt urban politicians.
   (E) the United States policy toward Latin America in the 1950s.

88. The term "detente" refers to

(A) easing of tensions between the United States and the Soviet Union.

(B) the Russian term for "Cold War."

(C) United States relations with Latin America in the 1960s.

(D) Nixon's invasion of Cambodia.

(E) Kennedy's strategy during the Berlin Airlift.

89. The event considered the deadliest act of domestic terrorism in U.S. history is the

(A) Japanese attack on Pearl Harbor.

(B) mail bombings perpetrated by the so-called Unabomber.

(C) World Trade Center car bombing.

(D) crash of TWA Flight 800.

(E) bombing of the Alfred P. Murrah Federal Building in Oklahoma City, Oklahoma.

90. During the 1980s, neo-conservatives advocated all of the following positions EXCEPT

(A) limited government.

(B) traditional religious values.

(C) reinvigorated patriotism.

(D) decreased military spending.

(E) restoration of the nuclear family.

91. A 1982 crisis over the War Power Resolution Act between Congress and President Reagan was narrowly averted when the president withdrew American ground forces from

(A) Iran.

(B) Grenada.

(C) Lebanon.

(D) Israel.

(E) Libya.

92. The first humans to inhabit North America came

(A) by migrating from Asia across the Bering Strait.

(B) on rafts from Polynesia.

(C) in giant canoes from Africa.

(D) in sailing vessels from Scandinavia.

(E) with advanced Iron Age skills and written languages.

93. This cartoon of 1978 depicts the Supreme Court's decision in *Bakke v. the Regents of the University of California* as

(A) ending affirmative action programs based on race.

(B) ending debate on issues of reverse discrimination.

(C) ambiguous on the issue of affirmative action programs and the issue of reverse discrimination.

(D) a clear statement on race relations.

(E) a racist backlash against minority quota systems

94. President Jimmy Carter achieved major success in dealing with

(A) inflation.

(B) the Iranian hostage crisis.

(C) the energy crisis.

(D) Middle East peace.

(E) unemployment.

95. The "Reagan Revolution" was launched through the budget of 1981 which

(A) reduced government spending across all areas equally.

(B) reduced government spending primarily in the domestic area.

(C) reduced government spending primarily in the military arena.

(D) increased personal income taxes.

(E) increased corporate taxes.

SAT United States History

Practice Test 3 ANSWER KEY

1.	**(B)**	26.	**(C)**	51.	**(B)**	76.	**(E)**
2.	**(B)**	27.	**(E)**	52.	**(B)**	77.	**(D)**
3.	**(A)**	28.	**(A)**	53.	**(B)**	78.	**(B)**
4.	**(C)**	29.	**(D)**	54.	**(D)**	79.	**(B)**
5.	**(C)**	30.	**(E)**	55.	**(C)**	80.	**(E)**
6.	**(D)**	31.	**(E)**	56.	**(E)**	81.	**(C)**
7.	**(D)**	32.	**(C)**	57.	**(E)**	82.	**(C)**
8.	**(C)**	33.	**(D)**	58.	**(B)**	83.	**(D)**
9.	**(B)**	34.	**(A)**	59.	**(A)**	84.	**(B)**
10.	**(E)**	35.	**(D)**	60.	**(B)**	85.	**(D)**
11.	**(D)**	36.	**(B)**	61.	**(D)**	86.	**(B)**
12.	**(D)**	37.	**(B)**	62.	**(B)**	87.	**(B)**
13.	**(E)**	38.	**(C)**	63.	**(D)**	88.	**(A)**
14.	**(E)**	39.	**(C)**	64.	**(B)**	89.	**(E)**
15.	**(B)**	40.	**(E)**	65.	**(E)**	90.	**(D)**
16.	**(B)**	41.	**(A)**	66.	**(D)**	91.	**(C)**
17.	**(E)**	42.	**(D)**	67.	**(E)**	92.	**(A)**
18.	**(B)**	43.	**(E)**	68.	**(C)**	93.	**(C)**
19.	**(C)**	44.	**(D)**	69.	**(B)**	94.	**(D)**
20.	**(C)**	45.	**(A)**	70.	**(B)**	95.	**(B)**
21.	**(C)**	46.	**(B)**	71.	**(C)**		
22.	**(C)**	47.	**(D)**	72.	**(B)**		
23.	**(A)**	48.	**(E)**	73.	**(E)**		
24.	**(B)**	49.	**(B)**	74.	**(A)**		
25.	**(E)**	50.	**(D)**	75.	**(D)**		

Detailed Explanations of Answers

PRACTICE TEST 3

1. **(B)** The main function of the petit jury is to determine innocence or guilt; the main function of the grand jury is to examine evidence and inform the prosecution if the evidence is strong enough to warrant the accused's indictment to stand trial. Most petit juries consist of 12 members, while grand juries are generally much larger. Thus, although Answer (A) is correct by itself, it does not answer questions regarding the functions of juries, only about their size. A judge is always present at grand jury proceedings and petit juries are empowered to hear criminal cases. It should be noted that grand juries are most generally used by the federal courts, while the state courts bypass the grand jury system by allowing prosecutors to file a bill of information to the court during pre-trial hearings to establish bail.

2. **(B)** Cloture is a device available only to the Senate according to the Senate's rules. Unlike the larger House of Representatives, the Senate allows unlimited debate on all bills. Because of its fear that a small minority of Senators may wish to thwart the will of the majority through a filibuster (a tactic whereby a senatorial minority block a bill from coming to a vote by talking on the floor endlessly), three-fifths of the Senate may invoke cloture and limit debate to one hundred hours on a bill. This procedure of cloture was designed to allow the principle of majority rule to reign in the Senate. Only the Senate is in need of cloture to ensure democratic majoritarianism and thus all other national branches of government would not use it.

3. **(A)** In the American economic system, a person who holds a fixed rate loan is aided by inflation. Inflation, as a condition where too many dollars are chasing too few goods, actually reduces the real purchasing power of the dollar over time. Therefore, a person who is indebted over 20 years would be paying the same dollar amount per year from year one to year 20. Yet, the value of year 20 dollars would be worth much less than year one dollars because of inflation. Because nineteenth century American farmers always borrowed money on the promise of a future harvest, they were traditionally a debtor group. Because all loans of the nineteenth century were at fixed interest rates, farmers supported inflationary policies to better their financial condition. Although food costs do rise under inflation, there is no guarantee that the producer of the food (the farmer) would receive more profit in a commercial agricultural system. Also, the farmer would suffer higher costs under inflation as do all consumers. A dynamic monetary system and a barter system by themselves do nothing to better the farmer economically. In short, inflation assisted the debtor and not the creditor in the nineteenth century.

4. **(C)** The rapid democratization of the Soviet bloc would cause an avalanche of change. The Union of Soviet Socialist Republics would break up into separate nations and a Russia pressured by threats of further disintegration. Later, (A) the rise of nationalism in areas of repression would cause the outbreak of civil wars and independent attitudes. The communist party in many countries would be repudiated. Although (B) there was concern about nuclear weapons, it was not as great as concern during the cold war. Henry Kissinger (D) worked during the Nixon administration. President Bush made no concerted effort to combat AIDS (E).

5. **(C)** The closed shop was one where a worker was required to join a union as a condition of receiving a job. This practice started in the late nineteenth century and continued until 1947 when the Taft-Hartley Act declared the closed shop illegal. This Act was passed by a Congress dominated by the Republican Party over President Truman's veto. The Act was designed by the Republicans to weaken the power of labor unions.

6. **(D)** Article I of the Constitution deals exclusively with Congress, the legislative branch of government. In this section of the Constitution, the powers and duties of Congress are carefully enumerated in detailed fashion. The most famous section of this article is Article I, Section 8, the "necessary and proper clause," which allows for a broad expanse of Congress' powers to make law. The powers of the presidency are covered in Article II, while those of the Supreme Court in Article III. Guarantees of freedom of speech and assembly are to be found in the first 10 amendments to the Constitution, the Bill of Rights.

7. **(D)** According to Article II, Section 2 (II,2) of the United States Constitution, the Senate is granted the sole authority to ratify a treaty while the president, or any delegated representative he appoints, alone can negotiate treaties with a foreign nation. This division of power is part of the elaborate checks and balances established in our Constitution by the founding fathers in 1788. This principle is one of the key characteristics of a republican form of government. The system was utilized to prevent one branch of government from becoming too powerful and dictatorial. Neither the Supreme Court nor the House of Representatives was included in this process. In recent years, American presidents have utilized increasingly the device of "executive agreements" with foreign nations to bypass the requirement of Senate approval of treaties. In 1937, the Supreme Court ruled in *United States v. Belmont* that although executive agreements are approved only by the president, they enjoy the same legal status as treaties.

8. **(C)** In the election of 1824, the members of the Electoral College were selected by popular vote for the first time. Despite the public's misconceptions, the American president is selected by the Electoral College and not the popular vote. Prior to 1824 members of the Electoral College were selected by some agency of state government and as a result, the American electorate had little direct say in presidential elections. Today, a candidate requires 270 out of 535 electoral votes to become president. Members of the Electoral College are chosen on a state-by-state basis according to party affiliation with the candidate. Each state is granted the same

number of electors as its membership in Congress. In a winner-take-all format, a vote for a presidential candidate really is a vote for his party's state candidates to the Electoral College and an indication to the electors from your state as to your candidate of choice. The November presidential election really is an election of the Electoral College, which meets in December to select the president.

9. **(B)** It is in the Declaration of Independence that Thomas Jefferson expressed the American devotion to these rights. The rights are considered "unalienable" in that they are afforded every human by birth and can be neither given away nor taken away. Jefferson adapted these three rights of life, liberty, and the pursuit of happiness from the seventeenth century English philosopher John Locke, who listed the rights as life, liberty, and prosperity. Jefferson prudently left the task of applying the specific meaning of these rights for every future generation of Americans to determine for themselves. The U.S. Constitution adds to these rights in its first ten amendments, known as the Bill of Rights. The 25th Amendment deals only with the disability of a president, while the Supreme Court decision of 1896 in *Plessy v. Ferguson* established a doctrine of "separate but equal" and sanctioned *de jure* racial segregation.

10. **(E)** Franklin Roosevelt was the only president to serve more than two terms in office. Roosevelt was elected to four terms from 1932–1945 and died in office during his fourth term. The two-term standard had been established by George Washington and was only a tradition until Roosevelt broke from it owing to the crises of the Depression and World War II. The two-term rule became law in 1951 with the ratification of the 22nd Amendment. Washington, Jackson, and Wilson all were two-term presidents, while Adams served only one term and was defeated in his re-election efforts by Thomas Jefferson in 1800.

11. **(D)** The only relationship established by the table is between cotton production and slave laborers. As a result, we do not know from the table if the South produced more wheat than cotton. Nor do we know if slavery was profitable, as we do not see statistics on the cost of slaves and profits from the sale of cotton over time. We do not know from the table how many slaves were actually used to grow cotton and thus cannot judge labor efficiency. Finally, we do not know from the table where the cotton was exported. The only correlation that is revealed is that increases in cotton production always were accompanied by increases in the number of slaves, thus directing one toward the conclusion that slavery grew along with the demand for increased cotton production.

12. **(D)** The original settlers of the Plymouth colony actually had purchased a tract of land in Northern Virginia from the Virginia Company. They lost their course in crossing the Atlantic and upon arriving at Cape Cod decided to stay. The settlers feared that, because they were occupying land not legally granted to them, they would be forced to return to England. As a result, they drew up a contract among all the settlers called the Mayflower Compact to legally establish their existence. The Pilgrim settlers in Plymouth did not establish religious freedom as they only desired freedom for their religion and came to America to erect a religious utopia.

In addition, Plymouth did not become part of Massachusetts until 1692 and indeed Puritans and Pilgrims had much dislike for each other and lived as separate, often hostile, colonies until 1692. Rhode Island was founded in 1644 by Roger Williams.

13. **(E)** In recent years, students of population analysis, demographers, have greatly revised the long accepted population estimates of James Mooney in 1925 for the Amerindian in pre-Columbian times. Mooney has estimated that fewer than 25 million Indians resided in the Americas around the year 1500. The main problem with Mooney's figures is that they were based primarily upon white European eyewitness accounts of the sixteenth and seventeenth centuries. Today archaeological findings and sophisticated demographic computer analysis have established the Indian population of the Western Hemisphere at nearly 100 million prior to Columbus' arrival. It should be noted that the Indian population stood at its lowest ebb in America in 1886 when there were less than 250,000 Amerindians. In the 1980 census, the Amerindian population had grown to 1.2 million.

14. **(E)** In his contract with the Spanish monarchy, Columbus established that he and his heirs would receive 40 percent of all wealth taken from the lands to which he was about to sail; he would receive the title, Admiral of the Ocean Seas; and he would be named governor of any unchartered areas he came into contact with. Columbus' motives are clear from this contract as power, glory, and wealth. Few educated people in Europe believed that the Earth was flat and Columbus had no desire to serve as a missionary for Christianity. Columbus did not come to America as an explorer; he came as a colonizer, seeking wealth and power. Once he landed in the Americas in 1492, he had proven Ptolemy wrong—a fact seldom mentioned by Columbus during the remainder of his life.

15. **(B)** The establishment of Jamestown in 1607 as the first permanent English settlement in North America came dangerously close to failure. England had already failed in its initial venture in the 1580s at Roanoke, Virginia. Upon the first arrival of the Jamestown settlers, they indicated they had learned little from Roanoke and repeated the myopic quest for gold and silver rather than plant and secure a food supply. As with Roanoke, during the first harsh winter more than half the settlers perished. Hostile Indians did not bode well for the colony either. It was the combination of the efforts of John Smith and the discovery of tobacco as a cash crop for export to Europe that made the colony able to be economically profitable. According to most historians, the Anglican faith played a minimal role in Virginia throughout the seventeenth century.

16. **(B)** Roger Williams was forced to flee Massachusetts because of his unorthodox religious beliefs. Although a Puritan minister, Williams warned the ministry in Massachusetts that they exerted too much political power and were being corrupted by their theocracy. He was to be put on trial for heresy when he fled to Rhode Island, not New Hampshire. Williams allowed complete religious toleration to all settlers. He died well before the Salem witch trials of 1692–1694. He never served as governor of Massachusetts.

17. **(E)** Recent historical research has indicated that indentured servants, popular myths to the contrary, remained for the most part in the lower sections of colonial society throughout their lives. The low social status was especially true in the Southern colonies throughout the colonial period. Indentured servants generally signed a contract with their masters, trading their labor for room and board, and the learning of a skilled craft for a set number of years (usually seven years). The servants were in many cases treated harshly by their masters and emerged from their servitude impoverished with few skills mastered. Although servants supported Bacon in his rebellion in Virginia, they never gained political power throughout the colonial period. Most servants were very hostile toward black slaves in the South and showed little sympathy for the slave's loss of legal status as a human, a condition never applied to the indentured servant. In sum, the indentured generally arrived in America on the edge of poverty and remained there for the bulk of their lives.

18. **(B)** Slavery as an institution grew very slowly in America, unlike in the British West Indies. Although the first American slaves arrived in 1619 in Jamestown, it was not until the 1790s that slavery as an institution grew substantially. Throughout the 1600s, most Southerners had yet to determine if they would seek their labor pool through white servants or black slaves. The incident of Bacon's Rebellion convinced many Southern planters that slaves ultimately were easier to control. Few Americans imported their slaves directly from East Africa, preferring their slaves from this region to have been seasoned a few years in the British West Indies. Unlike North American slavery, the slave system in the West Indies was exceptionally brutal, often working slaves to death within seven years of purchase. The children of slaves were always born slaves in the American slave system.

19. **(C)** Upon taking the crown of England in 1686, James II sent Edmund Andros to Boston with a master plan to unite Massachusetts, New Hampshire, New York, New Jersey, and Connecticut into a single colony with Andros as its governor. James was seeking to administer the colonies more closely and hoped to unify the growing empire under this system of consolidation. Andros ruled in such a tyrannical fashion in Massachusetts that he caused an uprising known as the Glorious Revolution where he was imprisoned. A similar uprising took place a year later in 1690 and is known as Leisler's revolt. During this period, James was removed from the throne by Parliament in a separate affair also called the Glorious Revolution. In England, growing fears of James' Catholic leanings led the Protestant Parliament to granting the throne to William and Mary of the Netherlands. All other answers to this question simply are not relevant.

20. **(C)** William Penn established a frame of government that granted the bulk of power to the Penn family and their advisors. Only reluctantly, and after much difficulty with the settlers, did Penn allow them a small voice in government in the colony. Indeed, the term "democracy" was used as a pejorative term throughout the colonial and Revolutionary periods. For the most part, democracy was a nineteenth and twentieth century political development in America. Few colonials believed the people capable of self-rule without some elite guidance and most used the term synonymously with "mobocracy." Penn did establish religious toleration under

Quaker control in Pennsylvania and during his lifetime the colony enjoyed peaceful relations with the Indians. Penn always envisioned the colony as part of the British Empire and was adamant about making the colony a financial success, which was achieved.

21. **(C)** In 1763, William Pitt had led England to a great victory over France. As he entered the peace talks, Pitt was debating the French offer of all of Canada *or* the West Indies sugar islands of Martinique and Guadaloupe as his fruits of victory. Although Pitt knew England was on the verge of bankruptcy and needed the revenue of the islands, he opted for Canada. This combination of a removed French menace from the North and a growing concern over the British national debt would ultimately prove two long-term causes of the American Revolution. France controlled neither Florida, Louisiana, nor the slave trade at the time of the peace.

22. **(C)** The primary purpose behind all of England's measures to raise a tax in America after 1763 was to reduce England's national debt. During the Seven Years' War with France, England was put on the verge of bankruptcy and could not tax its own subjects any higher. As a result, England turned to its colonies to raise the sorely needed revenue. The colonies had enjoyed the fruits of the empire and a policy of salutary neglect where they evaded taxes openly. The Stamp Act required all legal and published documents to bear a stamp issued from England with a small fee attached. Unlike the mild and sporadic protests against the Sugar Act earlier, Americans responded to the new tax with determined and forceful protests, led by merchants, lawyers, and printers. England had already angered the colonists by refusing their settlement west of Pennsylvania in the Ohio Territory by the Proclamation Line Act of 1763 and allowed illegal searches through the Writs of Assistance in 1760. The Stamp Act was not designed to control the American press.

23. **(A)** The health of the American colonies in the eighteenth century was proven to most Americans by their explosive growth in population—doubling every generation. In the eighteenth century, a rapidly growing population was considered the ultimate sign of a healthy nation. Along with its rapid growth, the colonies were growing more diverse as a people. New arrivals to America from areas other than England (Germans, Scotch-Irish, and Africans) made the middle and Southern colonies more pluralistic. The African-American population now composed about 20 percent of the total population, indicating the South's increased reliance upon slaves as a labor source. The five American cities in the eighteenth century held less than 10 percent of the total population but enjoyed a major role in colonial affairs. Life expectancy for men still remained at or about 70 years of age throughout the colonies.

24. **(B)** William Bradford was one of the earliest settlers in Plymouth colony and was a major political force among the Pilgrims into the 1620s. He earned great fame in America for his history of the Pilgrims, *Of Plimouth Plantation*. The Enlightenment as a movement had its genesis in 1686 with the publication of Sir Isaac Newton's *Principia*. Both Franklin and Jefferson were considered the leading American figures of the Enlightenment, as was John Locke in England. The

Enlightenment placed great faith in a rational universe and natural laws. Its followers believed that through the use of human reason man could discover the laws of nature and achieve perfection through a rational ordering of life. The Enlightenment placed great faith in human progress and believed that a science of human affairs was possible.

25. **(E)** The Loyalists for the most part emigrated out of America. Many returned to England during the war rather than suffer political and economic persecution by the colonials. Some Loyalists founded new settlements during the Revolution and its aftermath in Canada and the West Indies. It is estimated that Loyalists composed about 20 percent of the American population during the Revolution. For those who fled the country, England offered modest pensions. These pensions could not replace the loss of their confiscated property by the patriots, an issue of longstanding difference between England and America after the Revolutionary War. There was no Loyalist settlement in the Ohio Territory.

26. **(C)** The Articles of Confederation existed as the government of the United States from 1781 through 1788 when it was replaced by the United States Constitution. The Articles existed as a unicameral legislature in which each state had one vote. It was granted no coercive powers over the states and cannot be considered a national government, as it could not act directly on citizens. Because it could not raise taxes directly, but could only request moneys from the states, the Articles had little control over the states' finances. It paid for the war through an inflationary currency that at times was nearly worthless. After the war, the Articles proved unable to control interstate trade conflicts that led indirectly to the writing of the Constitution. The Bill of Rights was not ratified until 1791, two years after the Articles had expired. At best, it kept the 13 states from dividing through the use of a common enemy, England, during the War.

27. **(E)** In the immediate aftermath of the Revolutionary War in 1783, the British sought to do economically what they had been unsuccessful at militarily. British merchants indebted Americans heavily by extending credit and then in 1785 demanding full payment in gold. American merchants demanded full payment from yeoman farmers and would not accept barter payment as tender. The result was that by 1786, 35 percent of American farmers were in danger of losing their farms through mortgages. The farmers of western Massachusetts requested aid from the state government and, when none came, took matters into their own hands. The angry farmers closed down the courts to stop foreclosure proceedings against farmers. Massachusetts requested aid from the Articles but the central government was unable to assist Massachusetts. Massachusetts eventually put down the rebellion with a show of force and the rebels scattered. Shays' Rebellion shocked most conservatives in America into recognizing that the Articles were sorely in need of reform. A convention was called for the summer of 1787 to meet in Philadelphia. The 55 delegates to that convention produced the Constitution of the United States.

28. **(A)** Seventeenth century married and single women were denied the right to vote in colonial elections. According to seventeenth century law, married women

(*feme coverts*) did retain the authority to divorce their husbands by proving just cause (i.e., extreme physical cruelty, abandonment, impious behavior). Also, mothers were considered equal partners with fathers in following the New England practice of parental arrangements of marriage for their children as a means of socio-economic mobility. Finally, women were allowed to own personal property while married, and in many cases land and businesses as well. The denial of political rights to women in colonial America was based on the belief that women were unable to know public affairs as they were restricted in their affairs to the private domain of the household.

29. **(D)** The Declaratory Act was largely ignored by Americans because of their rejoicing over the repeal of the hated Stamp Act of 1765. As its title indicates, the Declaratory Act simply stated that although the notorious Stamp Act had been repealed, Parliament still retained its sovereignty over the American colonies. As a result, the Declaratory Act did not add new taxes, resulted in the temporary "end" of American protests, and actually strengthened the position of the Tories who were loyal to British authority in America. The creation of America's first Continental Congress, as the creation of an extralegal form of government was an extremely radical act and did not occur until 1774.

30. **(E)** Although Hamilton publicly advocated retirement of the bulk of America's wartime debt to restore faith, he desired to retain a portion of the debt to cement creditors closer to the national government out of their self-interest. As a result, Hamilton supported the notion of deficit spending as a means of attracting creditors to the national government. It was imperative to Hamilton that business interests be attracted to the national government and not state governments. As a result, Hamilton demanded that the new national government assume the war debt of each individual state. In order to pay this sum, he proposed the raising of revenue through customs duties and excise taxes. To conclude his plan, Hamilton sought to create a national bank with business leaders and government officials in the controlling interest. By these means, Hamilton sought to achieve his goal of uniting business leaders to the new national government during the 1790s. His program was directly opposed by Jefferson and Madison.

31. **(E)** Political parties burst across the nation's political horizon in the 1790s. The existence of political parties had been denounced by the Revolutionary War generation as evil and opposed to the common good of the republic. As a result, political parties virtually were non-existent prior to 1790. However, with the emergence of the Hamiltonian economic program and the start of war between England and France, two viewpoints of the "common good" of America emerged: the Federalists who supported Hamilton, favored England over France, and desired a government dominated by an elite group of politicians; the Democratic-Republicans who supported a nation of small farmers rather than business class, supported Revolutionary France over England, and expressed deep faith in democracy. The two parties openly split over the arrival of the new French minister to the United States in 1793, Edmund "Citizen" Genet. Genet sought to use American public opinion to swing support to France rather than maintain the course of neutrality under Washington.

32. **(C)** The Alien and Sedition Acts of 1797–1798 were a direct and bold attempt by President Adams to crush the opposition party of Madison-Jefferson, the Democratic-Republicans. Adams feared that Jefferson's party was bent on establishing a French-styled class revolution in America. To ensure that his party, the Federalists, remained in power, Adams pushed through the Federalist Congress a series of laws known as the Alien and Sedition Acts. These Acts increased the residency requirement for citizenship from five to 14 years. (Thus, new immigrants to America who tended to support Jefferson would be disenfranchised for 14 years.) In addition, the president was granted broad powers to remove "undesirable" aliens, thus putting a political muzzle on aliens. In addition, the laws established large monetary fines and sentences to prison for anyone who attacked the American government (the Adams administration) in print or speech. The laws never included an attack on the jury system and indeed relied upon juries to determine guilt or innocence in all seditious libel cases.

33. **(D)** Cotton Mather was a leading Puritan minister and intellectual who died a half-century prior to the American Revolution. Mather was a leading figure in the Salem witch trials of 1692–1694 and earned great fame for the publication of his book, *Magnalia Christi Americana*, which was a homage to great Puritan Americans, in 1704. Noah Webster was one of the greatest champions of an American culture in late eighteenth century America and designed his dictionary to create a national language. Freneau, Crèvecoeur, and Barlow all sought to exalt a new American culture at the close of the Revolution. Through their essays, poems, and plays, each supported the view of a special historical mission for America and its people for the cause of freedom and liberty in world history.

34. **(A)** After losing the election of 1800 to Thomas Jefferson and the Democratic-Republicans, President John Adams sought to use the national courts to block Jefferson from radical programs over the next four years. On the night before Jefferson's inaugural, Adams appointed several new federal judges from the Federalist Party. Upon learning of this later, Jefferson sought to remove the midnight appointments through a test case of one appointment, William Marbury. In 1803, Marbury sued Secretary of State James Madison for his judgeship and petitioned the Supreme Court. In *Marbury v. Madison*, Chief Justice John Marshall correctly ruled that the issue was not a matter for the Supreme Court but Congress. In so doing, however, Marshall declared the Judiciary Act of 1789 unconstitutional and granted the Supreme Court the power of judicial review. (This power allows the Court to be the final arbiter on the constitutionality of all laws enacted by Congress.) In *Fletcher* (1810), Marshall extended the Court's power of judicial review over state governments; in *Gibbons* (1824), Marshall extended governmental power over commerce; in *Martin* (1816), Marshall extended judicial review to the state courts; in *Dartmouth* (1819), Marshall offered views of contracts and corporations that would greatly influence the economy throughout the nineteenth century.

35. **(D)** See answer to Question 34. The power of judicial review allows the Supreme Court as the last voice on the constitutionality of law in America. Only the U.S. Constitution grants the Court the power of original jurisdiction in Article

III. "Strict constructionism" is a judicial viewpoint of recent years that argues one cannot liberally interpret pre-existing laws to decide a case. As a result, it is a theory and not a power. The Court does not select its own members; Article III provides that presidents nominate justices upon the advice and consent of the U.S. Senate's approval of a nominee. Finally, the Court's ability to regulate big business was never granted; the regulation of big business comes under the domain of congressional and Executive Department regulatory agencies (Federal Trade Commission, Environmental Protection Agency; Federal Communications Commission, etc.).

36. **(B)** The speech cited was delivered by Henry Clay to his Western supporters in Congress in 1811. Clay and his group, nicknamed the "war hawks," supported American war with Great Britain to advance the westward push of the country to enhance their land speculations in this region and end the "Indian menace." The Federalists and New England merchants were both vehemently opposed to the War of 1812, while President Madison sought to negotiate a peaceful settlement with England and reluctantly went to war in 1812. The British nobility generally were opposed to the war as well.

37. **(B)** New England dissatisfaction with the War of 1812 was evident from the start. Because of the trade embargoes of Jefferson and Madison, the New England merchant community was suffering from a depression that affected the entire region economically. New Englanders called for a meeting in Hartford, Connecticut, in 1814 to discuss the region's options. Few delegates supported a movement to secede from the nation. Instead, the delegates, under the leadership of the Federalist Party, advanced a view of states' rights identical to the position of the South during the Civil War. Tired of being treated as a neglected minority in the nation under Republican presidents, the New England delegates accomplished little at the Convention. The news of the Treaty and the Battle of New Orleans doomed the Convention and the Federalists in the eyes of most Americans as unpatriotic. Neither Japanese trade nor a Cuban invasion were ever discussed at the Convention.

38. **(C)** In 1819, the cooperative nationalism that America had enjoyed since the end of the War of 1812 was ended when the issue of slavery and the statehood of Missouri came before Congress. From 1815 through 1819, the nation had focused on programs of public improvements and advanced views of a monolithic patriotism. When Missouri applied for statehood in 1819, however, the Northern states feared the growing power of the South and the institution of slavery. As debates heated and sectionalism dominated nationalism in the Congress, Henry Clay of Kentucky formed a compromise that allowed the sectional balance of slave and free states to continue. Clay allowed Missouri to enter as a slave state with Maine arriving as a free state; thus, there were 12 slave and 12 free states. Secondly, the Compromise divided the issue of slavery along the 36°30' line: all territories north of the line would be free while areas south could enter as slave areas. The War of 1812 occurred prior to the Era of Good Feelings; the Chesapeake affair took place in 1807 and involved the British navy's impressment of American sailors; the Non-Intercourse Act occurred in 1807 and was Jefferson's feeble effort to avoid war with England. The Jay Treaty occurred in 1794 prior to the Era of Good Feelings.

39. **(C)** The period from 1820 through 1850 marked one of tremendous population growth for the United States. As the figures indicate, the nation's population more than doubled during this single generation from both new waves of immigration and natural increases.

40. **(E)** During the 1820s, the image of the American family underwent a major transformation from that of a work force based on discipline to an agency that was child centered and based upon love. Historians have labeled this process of change the domestification of the family. In the seventeenth and eighteenth centuries, the family was a reflection of society at large and seen primarily as a working unit on the farm. Strict discipline and adult domination were its mainstays. However, in the 1820s, Americans now viewed the home as a refuge from the outside world where one could escape from societal demands. In addition, love replaced discipline as the bonds of the family, with children now occupying center stage in familial matters. Finally, women were seen as operating in separate spheres from their husbands: the woman raised the children and ran the home; the males made money in the outside world. What emerged was a kind of separate but equal doctrine for female-male roles.

41. **(A)** The tremendous religious revival that swept through America during the 1830s was largely the result of the new theology offered by Charles Finney. Finney touched off this Second Great Awakening in western New York state where he offered a view of human perfectibility that rejected the older Calvinistic theology. Finney exhorted his audiences to achieve perfection through God's love and to overcome original sin in their lives. Finney's God was a New Testament God of love, rather than the vengeful Old Testament God depicted in the First Great Awakening in the 1730s. Finney stressed each person's emotional bonds to God and downplayed approaching religion through dry abstract reasoning. As a result, many of his revivals became scenes of emotional outpourings. His appeal to a "self-made" Christian obviously struck a cord with a society advocating the self-made man.

42. **(D)** In his essay, "The American Scholar," Ralph Waldo Emerson implored American writers to cast their works in the everyday lives of ordinary Americans. The only American writer of the group listed who followed that charge proved to be Walt Whitman whose poems were odes to the average American. Whitman depicted the typical American as a noble individual who lived a great morality play in his or her everyday workings. Hawthorne, Poe, and Melville all used either exotic settings (the distant past and ocean voyages) or focused on unusual characters (Captain Ahab and Hester Prynne) to portray the human weaknesses of pride, guilt, and revenge. Poe especially focused on the theme of decline and regression rather than progress, exemplified by his *The Fall of the House of Usher* (1839). Hawthorne's *House of the Seven Gables* (1850) and *The Scarlet Letter* (1851) both re-examined the Puritan past as one complete with misgivings and doom. In Melville's *Moby Dick* (1851), pessimism about the human character prevails and results in tragedy.

43. **(E)** The Tariff Act of 1832 led directly to the Nullification Crisis between South Carolina and the United States. The Tariff Act established high import fees for all European manufactured goods in an effort to protect Northern industries.

South Carolina balked at the policy which offered no protection for Southern farmers and forced them to pay higher prices as consumers. Under the leadership of Vice President John C. Calhoun, South Carolina re-established the states' rights view (the doctrine argues the states and not the national government are sovereign and therefore each state can decide which national laws to obey) and refused to pay the tariff by nullifying it. President Jackson threatened to force South Carolina to obey by armed invasion and South Carolina threatened to secede from the nation. Speaker of the House of Representatives, Henry Clay, intervened in the matter averting war with a compromise solution that effectively allowed South Carolina to avoid paying the tariff duties without advancing states' rights doctrines.

44. **(D)** In 1817, Benjamin Lundy formed the American Colonization Society as the first anti-slavery organization in America. The group advocated gradual emancipation of slaves on an individual basis and refused to see abolition of slavery as a political affair. Comprised mostly of ministers, the Society sought to appeal to the Christian conscience of each slave owner to emancipate their slaves. Once freed, the ex-slaves would then be shipped back immediately to Africa as the Society was extremely racist in its views of the inherent inferiority of blacks to whites. The Society believed there was no place for African-Americans in the nation and sought to remove all blacks from American soil rather than promote racial equality and full political rights for blacks.

45. **(A)** Despite the images of large plantations in novels and movies, the vast majority of slaves in the nineteenth century lived on farms that held less than 20 slaves. In 1860, 80 percent of all Southern slaves lived on such farms. The notion of a large plantation relying on the labor of hundreds and even thousands of slaves is not supported by historical fact.

46. **(B)** Prosser, Vesey, and Turner have all earned fame in American history as leaders of slave uprisings. Both the Prosser planned uprising in Virginia in 1800 and the Vessey plot in 1822 in South Carolina were betrayed by other slaves and thwarted before they could materialize. However, in Hampton County, Virginia in 1831, Nat Turner led the bloodiest slave rebellion in American history. In that year, Turner, an itinerant black preacher, gathered about 15 slaves and went on a two-day rampage killing 55 whites. Turner was captured and executed but not before the publication of his *Confessions of Nat Turner* displayed to Southerners the deep hatred of their slaves toward the peculiar institution.

47. **(D)** The forces of Nativism have been unleashed during both the 1830s and the 1920s. On both occasions, the white Anglo-Saxon Protestant (WASP) responded to new waves of immigrants from non-English and non-Protestant regions with protest and violence. The voiced fears of the WASP was that the new immigrants would "water down" the superior genetic stock of the WASP and bring about the decline of America. The WASP was convinced that the new immigrants from Germany, Ireland, Italy, Russia, and Asia were inferior by birth to the American WASP. As a result, riots, persecutions, and anti-immigrant legislation all sought to reduce the new immigrants to second class citizenship during both the 1830s and the 1920s.

Nativism was not expressed in painting, nor were nativists concerned with the natural environment. Nativists never supported citizenship for the Amerindian.

48. **(E)** The rise of the doctrine of Manifest Destiny in the 1820s and 1830s championed the viewpoint that it was America's natural God-given destiny to create a mighty nation stretching from the Atlantic to the Pacific shores. The advocates of this view contended that the health of the American economy demanded new markets from this push westward and that an expanding frontier guaranteed that the nation would remain a democracy of small, independent yeoman farmers. This belief remained powerful in the country throughout the nineteenth century.

49. **(B)** The Nat Turner Rebellion occurred in 1831 as the bloodiest slave uprising in American history when 55 whites were killed by about 15 slaves in Virginia. The Kansas-Nebraska Act was passed in 1854 and sought to establish the principle of popular sovereignty in the two territories on the issue of slavery to promote the presidential ambitions of Senator Stephen Douglas of Illinois. The Seneca Falls Convention convened in 1848 as a militant expression of women's rights led by Lucretia Mott and Elizabeth Cady Stanton. The Lincoln-Douglas debates took place in 1858 as both candidates vied for the Senate seat in Illinois. The Homestead Act was passed by Congress in 1862 and granted a free 160-acre farm in the Far West (Great Plains region) to any American citizen 21 years of age or older who would work the land for five years.

50. **(D)** This speech by Daniel Webster delivered in defense of the Compromise of 1850 on the floor of the House of Representatives is considered one of the most famous speeches in American history. As Webster was closing out his illustrious political career, he ushered forth all his political and rhetorical skills to combat the growing spirit of sectionalism that was threatening his beloved America. Webster used all his power to gain passage of the act and completed his efforts with this brilliant appeal to patriotic nationalism. His defense of Dartmouth College before the Supreme Court gave rise to a rhetorical flourish of "only a small college, but there are, sirs, those who love it." Webster never delivered major addresses on Lincoln, the Bank, or the Bridge case.

51. **(B)** In 1854, Stephen Douglas harbored ambitions for the presidency in 1856. In order to attract the Southern votes required for his victory, Douglas proposed an Act to amend the Missouri Compromise line of 36°30' in the case of the Kansas-Nebraska territories. Although both areas were north of the line, Douglas argued the settlers of the regions should decide for themselves on slavery. The result was civil war in the two regions as pro-Southern settlers openly battled with anti-slavery forces over the next two years. Douglas never was a champion of the black vote and believed Congress, not the Supreme Court, could solve the slave crisis.

52. **(B)** The Secret Six were a group of New York millionaires who provided the financial backing for John Brown's raid on Harper's Ferry, Virginia in 1859. Brown, a militant abolitionist, sought to seize a federal arsenal in the South and distribute weapons to slaves to lead a massive slave uprising. When information about Brown's

ties to the Secret Six surfaced during his trial, the South began to seriously consider secession as its only course of action against the abolitionists. The Secret Six felt Lincoln much too soft on slavery in 1860 to offer him support. In fact, their support of Brown's raid displays their view that violence and not politics would end slavery in America.

53. **(B)** On April 12, 1861, the Confederate forces began their bombardment on Fort Sumter. With the Fort's surrender and Lincoln's proclamation that an insurrection existed, the states of the Upper South (Virginia, Arkansas, Tennessee, and North Carolina) joined the Lower South (South Carolina, Alabama, Mississippi, Florida, Georgia, Louisiana, and Texas) who had seceded in February, 1861, to form the Confederate States of America.

54. **(D)** The American Civil War was an unpopular war in the North. Lincoln constantly was troubled by draft riots and the threats of Northern anti-war Democrats, called the Copperheads. Anti-Lincoln Republicans adopted the name Radical Republicans and pro-Union Southerners were labeled scalawags after the war. Lincoln masterfully was able to maintain control over his Party during the war and was narrowly re-elected in 1864, owing in large part to some eleventh-hour Northern military victories. At the close of the War, the Copperheads were treated with severe hatred in the North, especially after Lincoln's assassination.

55. **(C)** King Cotton Diplomacy was the sole foreign policy strategy of the Confederacy. The South refused to export cotton to Europe in the hopes that this embargo would lead to a depression in the European textile industry and force Western Europe to ally with the South because of their dependance upon cotton. This strategy failed because Europeans had been stockpiling American cotton since 1855 in anticipation of the Civil War and found a new source of cotton in Egypt. The Stars and Bars was the nickname for the Confederate flag, while a war of attrition was General Grant's military strategy for ending the Civil War. Mercantilism was Great Britain's economic policy toward its American colonies in the seventeenth and eighteenth centuries, while nullification was the attempt by South Carolina not to pay new tariff rates in 1831.

56. **(E)** In the 1840s, the Indians of the Great Plains were at their height as a civilization. Not yet in close contact with whites, the Plains Indians lived a nomadic existence hunting the plentiful buffalo who provided the Indians with food, clothing, and shelter. The Plains tribes were noted for their deep reverence of the forces of nature and believed all natural elements held a soul and were to be treated with respect.

57. **(E)** In 1864, Lincoln announced his plan to allow the South to re-enter the Union. The plan, known as his Reconstruction Plan, was extremely lenient to the defeated South. Lincoln proposed the South re-enter on a state by state basis after having agreed to abolish slavery, educate the ex-slaves, establish republican state governments, and have 10 percent of Southern citizens take an oath of loyalty to the Union. The Radical Republicans in Congress opposed Lincoln's plan as too lenient

and criticized the plan for not allowing for the citizenship of the ex-slaves which the Radicals established under the 14th Amendment in 1867.

58. **(B)** In 1864, the Radical Republicans openly broke from President Lincoln's Reconstruction plans with the passage of the Wade-Davis Act. This Act presented the Radicals' Reconstruction plans and sought to treat the South as a conquered territory under military rule. Rather than the quick readmission of Southern states that Lincoln envisioned, the Act demanded readmission only after 50 percent of the voters of each state could prove their loyalty to the Union during the Civil War. Lincoln vetoed the Act. President Johnson did not support Wade-Davis, nor did the Democratic Party. Both the scalawags and carpetbaggers had little association with the measure as Southerners who cooperated during Reconstruction with the North and carpetbaggers who went down South to work on rebuilding the devastated South after the War.

59. **(A)** Slavery was ended by Congress' ratification of the 13th Amendment to the U.S. Constitution in 1865. The Radical Republicans were in control of Congress and passed the amendment in the aftermath of Lincoln's assassination by John Wilkes Booth. The 15th Amendment (1867) extended the vote to ex-slaves; who were granted citizenship under the 14th Amendment in 1867. The 19th Amendment (1920) extended the vote to women, while the 16th Amendment (1913) established the federal income tax. The 22nd Amendment, passed in 1951, established the two-term limit on the presidency.

60. **(B)** In the impeachment proceedings against President Johnson, Congress cited his violation of the Tenure of Office Act in removing Secretary of War Stanton without Senate approval. Of the 11 charges of impeachment brought by the House against Johnson, nine were based on the Tenure of Office Act. The Morrill Act was passed in 1862 to establish publicly financed land grant colleges in the states. The Civil Rights Act was passed in 1866 and directed against the black codes in Southern governments, not Johnson. In *Ex Parte* Milligan (1866), the U.S. Supreme Court ruled that civilian courts should have been allowed to function during the Civil War rather than the military tribunals Lincoln established.

61. **(D)** Morgan achieved his greatest use of the corporate merger when he purchased the United States Steel Corporation from Andrew Carnegie in 1901, along with Carnegie's eight largest competitors in the steel industry. Thus, Morgan had used the merger to engineer a virtual monopoly of the steel industry in America. Morgan paid the then unheard of price of $400 million for Carnegie's U.S. Steel. The Bank of the United States was never involved in merger acquisitions. The Sinclair and Standard Oil companies used the Teapot Dome scandal and the trust to effectively gain their industrial status as corporate giants. The activities of AT&T regarding mergers were undertaken long after Morgan paved the way with the U.S. Steel deal.

62. **(B)** Of all labor unions in the late nineteenth century, only Samuel Gompers' skilled craftsman union, the American Federation of Labor, claimed a partnership

in capitalism with management and saw itself as "pure and simple unionism" in its quest for higher wages and other bread and butter issues. The Industrial Workers of the World preached one great union for all workers and worker ownership of the means of production as did the Knights of Labor. The National Labor Union held onto an idealistic vision of the American craftsman as the rugged individual entrepreneur that was an anachronism in the late nineteenth century. The Molly Maguires were a group of unionists active in the coal industry who preached the violent overthrow of the managerial class to gain worker benefits.

63. **(D)** Jacob Riis's most famous work, *How the Other Half Lives*, was a collection of essays and photographs documenting the living conditions of urban slum dwellers in 1890. The author of *Ragged Dick*, Horatio Alger, used his novels to promote rugged individual enterprise and self-help for the urban poor. In Upton Sinclair's *The Jungle*, the horrors of the meat industry without federal inspection were graphically illustrated. Stephen Crane's *Maggie* details the life of a young woman who runs away from her family—and the slums of New York—with a man who later abandons her to a life of prostitution and living on the street. Frank Norris's *The Octopus* was a searing indictment of the railroads and their monopolistic abuses.

64. **(B)** In 1896, the Supreme Court sanctioned *de jure* (sanctioned by law) segregation in the United States in the case of *Plessy v. Ferguson*. In this case of separate compartments on a New Orleans trolley, the Court ruled segregation laws were legal as long as the facilities provided to blacks and whites were "equal" in quality. Thus, the Court sanctioned existing Jim Crow laws under the separate but equal doctrine. The Court left it up to state agencies to determine if facilities were indeed equal, a situation that resulted in substandard facilities for blacks throughout the South, until 1954 when *Brown v. Board of Education of Topeka* ruled segregation unconstitutional. The *Munn* case (1877) and the *Schecter* case (1935) both deal with the right of government to regulate private industry. *Scopes* is the 1925 Tennessee case involving a high school teacher using a Darwinian textbook in violation of existing state statutes.

65. **(E)** Booker T. Washington never advocated the quest for black political power. Instead, Washington believed that economic progress would provide the key to black advancement in America. Washington encouraged blacks to accept whatever menial job was offered and accept the social aspects of racism and segregation from whites. Washington preached black patience in a steady climb up the economic ladder to put an end to racism over many generations. Washington founded his famous Tuskegee Institute to train blacks in agriculture and janitorial work as the path to eventual economic equality.

66. **(D)** In 1883, the Pendleton Act was passed by Congress to reform the spoils system of the civil service. The assassination of President James Garfield in 1881 was the driving force to end full-scale patronage in the federal bureaucracy. Despite its intentions of establishing a bipartisan commission to provide jobs to the best qualified candidates rather than personal patronage, the Pendleton Act only covered about 10 percent of the jobs in the federal bureaucracy. By the close of the

century, however, 50 percent of all bureaucrats had received their positions through a competitive examination. The Act had nothing to do with corporate trusts, reservations, trade unions, or the Grange. Instead, the Act was strictly designed to reform the rapidly growing federal bureaucracy and curtail the corruptive practices of the spoils system through patronage.

67. **(E)** Despite their failure as a third political party, the Populists saw nearly all of their platform issues accepted into American life except the government's ownership of the telegraph and telephone industries. The graduated income tax was established in 1913 as the 16th Amendment and direct election of Senators was law under the 17th Amendment in the same year. The eight-hour work day became the norm in America during World War I and the use of the secret ballot was accepted early in the twentieth century. The closest the U.S. government ever came to operating the telegraph and telephone industries was under the War Industries Board during World War I. This action was only seen as a temporary wartime measure and ended in 1919.

68. **(C)** Theodore Roosevelt proved the only president to win a Nobel Prize for Peace in 1904 with his negotiation of the treaty to end the Russo-Japanese War in Portsmouth, New Hampshire. Roosevelt was able to get Japan to agree to a treaty only by offering to end discrimination on the West Coast toward Japanese-Americans, a promise he did little to keep. Neither Wilson, Hoover, Carter, nor Kennedy received a nomination and award while president.

69. **(B)** These words appeared in William James' 1907 book, *Pragmatism*. James was the founder of this distinctly American philosophy which advocated a practical approach to all issues in life. The prime questions were on results rather than means; truth became a function of it if it produced the proper results.

70. **(B)** This a line from Allen Ginsberg's 1955 poem "Howl." In his early writings, Ginsberg, along with other writers such as Jack Kerouac, gave rise to the cultural movement of the 1950s known as "the Beat Generation." The focus of their writings was on the alienated youth of an America of materialistic middle- class comforts.

71. **(C)** Under the restrictions listed under the Platt Amendment, Cuban independence was curtailed by the United States. Because of our major role in securing Cuban independence from Spain during the Spanish-American War, the United States received from Cuba the right to establish a naval base for the U.S. Navy in Cuba, the right to have American bankers control the Cuban economy, the right to intervene directly in Cuban affairs, and the right of approval before all treaties between Cuba and other nations were law. In essence, the Platt Amendment reduced Cuba to a protectorate of the United States. We did not demand Cuba rely exclusively upon American trading vessels.

72. **(B)** The expression "yellow journalism" refers to the practice of sensationalism in news reporting first associated with William Randolph Hearst and the Spanish-American War. Hearst was able to increase circulation of his New York *Journal* dramatically by publishing emotional accounts of Spanish atrocities in

Cuba without the benefit of facts to support his claims. Hearst and other editors like Joseph Pulitzer used this tactic to arouse the American people for war against Spain in 1898. Bernard Baruch was the head of the War Industries Board in World War I. Daniel Ellsberg was the Pentagon official who leaked the "Pentagon Papers" to the press thus detailing the Pentagon's "secret" history of Vietnam. Earl Warren was governor of California in World War II. Ernie Pyle was a roving reporter covering World War II in Europe.

73. **(E)** William McKinley was the Republican president from 1896 until his assassination in 1901. As president, McKinley was a strong proponent of big business interests and opposed to government interference in the economy. Theodore Roosevelt, who succeeded McKinley in office in 1901, became a national symbol for Progressivism with his assault on the Northern Securities Railroad Company in the Pacific Northwest, as well as his conservation measures and faith in government regulatory agencies over big business. President Taft followed in Roosevelt's steps as president and in fact had a stronger record as a "trustbuster" of big business than did Roosevelt. Wilson's New Freedom platform in 1912 was a purely progressive ideology, a policy he followed as president until U.S. entry into World War I in 1917. As governor of Wisconsin, Robert LaFollette was considered the leading statewide Progressive politician in America.

74. **(A)** The Volstead Act of 1918 established the 18th Amendment to the Constitution which prohibited the sale, manufacture, and transportation of alcoholic beverages in America. This Act touched off the prohibition movement that sought to end American consumption of alcohol. Much support for the measure was gained by believing this act would "clean-up" the new immigrants by ending their alcohol consumption. The Act was poorly enforced and only succeeded in granting organized crime in America a rich source for revenue. The 18th Amendment was repealed in 1933 by the 21st Amendment.

75. **(D)** Frank Lloyd Wright is most famous for his prairie house designs that sought to mold design totally to function. His work was in direct contrast to the ornate neo-classical and pseudo-Gothic structures of the early twentieth century. Wright later extended his views to urban planning where he championed the concept of suburbia in *Broadacres*. Geodesic domes are associated with the plans of R. Buckminster Fuller in the 1960s in America and English Classicism drew from Palladio.

76. **(E)** On the contrary, Wilson strengthened the Sherman Antitrust Act with the Clayton Antitrust Act of 1914 to combat price discrimination and holding companies. Under his 1912 New Freedom Program, he was able to create the Federal Reserve Board to place control of currency in the hands of the government rather than private banks. He established the first federal income tax to force the managerial class to carry their burden of the tax load, rather than rely solely upon property taxes that worked unfairly against the farmers. Finally, he established the Federal Trade Commission in 1914 to restore competition through a government regulatory agency to police "unfair trade practices."

77. **(D)** A cornerstone measure of Roosevelt's second New Deal Program was the Social Security Act of 1935. Here Roosevelt clearly abandoned his earlier concept of voluntary government partnership with business under the first New Deal for liberal reform of the economic system by using government to directly aid the dispossessed and downtrodden in society. The Tennessee Valley Authority, the bank holiday, the Securities and Exchange Commission, and the Civilian Conservation Corps were all measures of FDR's first New Deal, a hodgepodge of action seeking to satisfy as many groups as possible. Very often, Roosevelt's New Deal Programs from 1932–1935 are labeled "alphabet soup."

78. **(B)** The National Origins Act of 1924 was passed through Congress by a wave of anti-immigrant fervor sweeping the country in the 1920s. The act restricted total immigration to under 200,000 per year, with the groups arriving to be based on a quota system determined from the 1890 American census of ethnic groups. This measure was directed against immigrants from Southern and Eastern Europe, as well as Asia, and in support of immigrants from the British Isles. The federal census is established by the Constitution of 1788 and there is no law banning naturalized citizens from holding public office, save for the presidency. Canadian-American relations were not part of this act, nor were passport requirements.

79. **(B)** The "flapper" was the new liberated American woman of the 1920s who drew attention because of her clothing styles and public behavior such as smoking in public. "Rosie the Riveter" was the symbol of American women who entered the field of manual labor during World War II to support the war effort. The creation of NOW took place in 1966, while the Supreme Court's decision on abortion in *Roe v. Wade* was handed down in 1973.

80. **(E)** The ending of literacy tests to discourage minority groups from voting was brought about by the Voting Rights Act of 1965 and not the Civil Rights Act of 1964. The main focus of the Civil Rights Act was to bar racial discrimination in public areas and in the hiring systems of companies and to hasten the desegregation of public schools. The Act was a hallmark of President Johnson's Great Society of the 1960s. Both Acts were renewed by President Reagan in 1989.

81. **(C)** The Bonus Army was a group of World War I veterans who marched on Washington, D.C., to demand immediate payment of their promised wartime bonus fees. President Hoover acted with undue force and crushed the protestors with U.S. calvary units under Douglas MacArthur. Vietnam War veterans were labeled "winter soldiers" because of their unpopularity in America during the 1960s and 1970s. The Spanish-American War unit under Theodore Roosevelt was called the "Rough Riders."

82. **(C)** President Roosevelt unveiled the Lend-Lease Program as England's efforts in 1939 against Germany began to falter. England was on the verge of bankruptcy and possible military defeat. As a result, Roosevelt allowed the British to purchase American munitions on credit or a lend/lease program. At the same time,

Roosevelt was trying to goad the Germans into attacking American merchant marine convoys in the North Atlantic. It would take the Japanese attack on Pearl Harbor on December 7, 1941, to force the United States into World War II. During the 1930s, Roosevelt slowly brought along American public opinion to support our entry into World War II.

83. **(D)** The German invasion of the Soviet Union occurred on June 22, 1941. The attack on Pearl Harbor by the Japanese occurred on December 7, 1941; the D-Day Invasion of the Allies against Germany occurred in 1944; and the American bombing of Hiroshima took place in 1945.

84. **(B)** American reaction to the launching of the Soviet satellite Sputnik was immediate. Fearing that the United States had fallen behind the Soviets in scientific and mathematical research, there was pushed through Congress a massive aid act to increase federal aid to higher education. The Geneva Summit took place in 1955 prior to the launching of Sputnik in 1957. The Suez Crisis occurred in 1956, while the U-2 incident, involving the Soviet capture of an American spy plane, occurred in 1960. Sputnik's launching led to heightened tensions globally for the US and USSR.

85. **(D)** In January 1968, the combined forces of the Viet Cong and NVRN troops launched a major offensive against US military bases in Vietnam. Although the attack was repelled by the Americans, the American public was shocked by this show of strength and began to step up its criticism of Johnson's handling of the war. Two months later, President Johnson announced that he would not seek re-election. The invasion of Cambodia was undertaken in 1970 under President Nixon. The Gulf of Tonkin incident occurred in 1964 and granted Johnson an open hand by Congress to run the Vietnam War. The Hanoi Peace talks were initiated in 1972 and the Viet Cong were formed early in the 1950s.

86. **(B)** Clarence Earl Gideon earned fame in American civil liberties by being the defendant in the case that led to the Supreme Court's ruling in 1963 that the accused has a right to legal counsel in all criminal cases. Prior to this ruling, free legal counsel was supplied to the accused usually only in cases that involved capital offenses.

87. **(B)** McCarthyism was the name attached to the domestic political situation in the early 1950s which involved the American search for Communists and their sympathizers in government offices. Named after Senator Joseph McCarthy of Wisconsin, the movement relied upon the Cold War fears of Americans and never resulted in the discovery of large numbers of Communists. The movement was brought to a close through the televised Army-McCarthy hearings in 1954 when Senator McCarthy repeatedly badgered witnesses in trying to uncover nonexistent Communists in military command. The illegal practice of redistricting is referred to as gerrymandering. The post-World War II economic recovery programs for Western Europe were part of the Marshall Plan. A corrupt urban politician generally is called a "boss," and Eisenhower sought to re-establish Roosevelt's 1930s Good Neighbor policy toward Latin America.

88. **(A)** Detente was the foreign policy of the Nixon administration toward the Soviet Union in the early 1970s. Through the efforts of Henry Kissinger, secretary of state, detente sought to ease tensions with the Soviet Union through a series of arrangements based upon "realpolitik." Although relations did improve under this strategy, the Cold War clash between the world's superpowers continued throughout the decade. Detente did, however, move American foreign policy away from a reliance on force in dealing with the Soviet Union and toward recognition of China in 1971. The Strategic Arms Limitation Treaty, which reduced nuclear weapons between the United States and the Soviet Union, was signed in 1972.

89. **(E)** The bombing of the Oklahoma City, Oklahoma, federal building has the grim distinction of being the deadliest act of domestic terrorism: 168 people were killed and 500 injured.

90. **(D)** The rise of the neo-conservative movement in the 1980s as a challenge to the liberal welfare state model strongly endorsed reducing the role of government in American society and thus sought to reverse a trend that had been continuous since the New Deal. The neo-conservatives also supported a return to traditional religious values and social mores, including the restoration of the nuclear family. As part of their faith in American patriotism, the neo-conservatives supported increased military spending in an effort to re-establish American hegemony in global affairs.

91. **(C)** The War Powers Resolution Act (also referred to as the Cooper-Church Amendment) was passed by Congress in 1974. The act stipulates that a president can use American ground forces in a foreign land without Congressional authorization for up to 60 days. At the close of 60 days, Congress then has the authority to either call for the return of the troops or continue the action. The act was passed to prevent another Vietnam conflict from occurring without the authorization of Congress. No American president has recognized the constitutionality of this act and the closest it has come to being used was in 1982 when President Reagan dispatched American ground forces to keep the peace in war-torn Lebanon. As he approached the 60-day deadline, President Reagan was convinced to withdraw the forces by his military advisors and thus narrowly avoided a showdown with Congress.

92. **(A)** Historians and archaeologists believe that the first humans came to North America in several waves over a land bridge between Siberia and Alaska in what is now the Bering Strait. This is one of the world's oldest known migrations. These Indian ancestors then spread out over what are now North and South America over a period of thousands of years. It is believed that the first wave of migrants were hunters of big game, such as bison and mammoths, and were the ancestors of the Indians of South America and most North American Indians. The second wave may have occurred at the same time along the southernmost coast of the Bering land mass and were the ancestors of Eskimos and Aleuts. The third group of migrants probably came several thousand years later than the first two and were nomadic hunter-gatherers.

93. **(C)** By declaring both parties the winner in the Bakke case, the Supreme Court left the American public confused on the issues of reverse discrimination and affirmative action programs. The cartoonist captures this sentiment well with this image of a boxing match ending not in a draw, but double winners.

94. **(D)** During his presidency, Jimmy Carter (1977–1981) was beset by a seemingly endless series of crises. His policies to combat inflation proved ineffective and ultimately led to the election of the Republican Party's Ronald Reagan. In addition, Carter was unable to effectively combat soaring rates of unemployment (giving rise to the phenomenon called "stagflation," high unemployment and rapid inflation) or the continuing energy crisis. His gravest crisis came when, in 1979, Iranians took 53 Americans hostage. They were not released until right after Reagan's inauguration in 1980. The one shining triumph for President Carter occurred in 1978, when he negotiated a peace accord between Egypt (Anwar Sadat) and Israel (Menachem Begin) known as the Camp David Accords. Both Begin and Sadat won the Nobel Prize for Peace for their efforts.

95. **(B)** In his budget of 1981, President Reagan presented the fiscal details of his "Reagan Revolution." The budget reflected severe reductions in government spending primarily in domestic programs of Lyndon Johnson's Great Society Program of 1964–1965. Reagan at the same time increased military spending, and promised in 1982 to sponsor a reduction in personal and corporate taxes. Reagan claimed this 1981 budget was designed specifically to curb inflation by reducing our national debt by reducing deficit spending. The result was a drop in the inflation rate and in unemployment; at the same time, a mounting federal deficit added to the national debt.

THE SAT SUBJECT TEST IN

United States History

PRACTICE TEST 4

SAT United States History

Practice Test 4

1. Ⓐ Ⓑ Ⓒ Ⓓ Ⓔ
2. Ⓐ Ⓑ Ⓒ Ⓓ Ⓔ
3. Ⓐ Ⓑ Ⓒ Ⓓ Ⓔ
4. Ⓐ Ⓑ Ⓒ Ⓓ Ⓔ
5. Ⓐ Ⓑ Ⓒ Ⓓ Ⓔ
6. Ⓐ Ⓑ Ⓒ Ⓓ Ⓔ
7. Ⓐ Ⓑ Ⓒ Ⓓ Ⓔ
8. Ⓐ Ⓑ Ⓒ Ⓓ Ⓔ
9. Ⓐ Ⓑ Ⓒ Ⓓ Ⓔ
10. Ⓐ Ⓑ Ⓒ Ⓓ Ⓔ
11. Ⓐ Ⓑ Ⓒ Ⓓ Ⓔ
12. Ⓐ Ⓑ Ⓒ Ⓓ Ⓔ
13. Ⓐ Ⓑ Ⓒ Ⓓ Ⓔ
14. Ⓐ Ⓑ Ⓒ Ⓓ Ⓔ
15. Ⓐ Ⓑ Ⓒ Ⓓ Ⓔ
16. Ⓐ Ⓑ Ⓒ Ⓓ Ⓔ
17. Ⓐ Ⓑ Ⓒ Ⓓ Ⓔ
18. Ⓐ Ⓑ Ⓒ Ⓓ Ⓔ
19. Ⓐ Ⓑ Ⓒ Ⓓ Ⓔ
20. Ⓐ Ⓑ Ⓒ Ⓓ Ⓔ
21. Ⓐ Ⓑ Ⓒ Ⓓ Ⓔ
22. Ⓐ Ⓑ Ⓒ Ⓓ Ⓔ
23. Ⓐ Ⓑ Ⓒ Ⓓ Ⓔ
24. Ⓐ Ⓑ Ⓒ Ⓓ Ⓔ
25. Ⓐ Ⓑ Ⓒ Ⓓ Ⓔ
26. Ⓐ Ⓑ Ⓒ Ⓓ Ⓔ
27. Ⓐ Ⓑ Ⓒ Ⓓ Ⓔ
28. Ⓐ Ⓑ Ⓒ Ⓓ Ⓔ
29. Ⓐ Ⓑ Ⓒ Ⓓ Ⓔ
30. Ⓐ Ⓑ Ⓒ Ⓓ Ⓔ
31. Ⓐ Ⓑ Ⓒ Ⓓ Ⓔ
32. Ⓐ Ⓑ Ⓒ Ⓓ Ⓔ
33. Ⓐ Ⓑ Ⓒ Ⓓ Ⓔ
34. Ⓐ Ⓑ Ⓒ Ⓓ Ⓔ
35. Ⓐ Ⓑ Ⓒ Ⓓ Ⓔ
36. Ⓐ Ⓑ Ⓒ Ⓓ Ⓔ
37. Ⓐ Ⓑ Ⓒ Ⓓ Ⓔ
38. Ⓐ Ⓑ Ⓒ Ⓓ Ⓔ
39. Ⓐ Ⓑ Ⓒ Ⓓ Ⓔ
40. Ⓐ Ⓑ Ⓒ Ⓓ Ⓔ
41. Ⓐ Ⓑ Ⓒ Ⓓ Ⓔ
42. Ⓐ Ⓑ Ⓒ Ⓓ Ⓔ
43. Ⓐ Ⓑ Ⓒ Ⓓ Ⓔ
44. Ⓐ Ⓑ Ⓒ Ⓓ Ⓔ
45. Ⓐ Ⓑ Ⓒ Ⓓ Ⓔ
46. Ⓐ Ⓑ Ⓒ Ⓓ Ⓔ
47. Ⓐ Ⓑ Ⓒ Ⓓ Ⓔ
48. Ⓐ Ⓑ Ⓒ Ⓓ Ⓔ
49. Ⓐ Ⓑ Ⓒ Ⓓ Ⓔ
50. Ⓐ Ⓑ Ⓒ Ⓓ Ⓔ
51. Ⓐ Ⓑ Ⓒ Ⓓ Ⓔ
52. Ⓐ Ⓑ Ⓒ Ⓓ Ⓔ
53. Ⓐ Ⓑ Ⓒ Ⓓ Ⓔ
54. Ⓐ Ⓑ Ⓒ Ⓓ Ⓔ
55. Ⓐ Ⓑ Ⓒ Ⓓ Ⓔ
56. Ⓐ Ⓑ Ⓒ Ⓓ Ⓔ
57. Ⓐ Ⓑ Ⓒ Ⓓ Ⓔ
58. Ⓐ Ⓑ Ⓒ Ⓓ Ⓔ
59. Ⓐ Ⓑ Ⓒ Ⓓ Ⓔ
60. Ⓐ Ⓑ Ⓒ Ⓓ Ⓔ
61. Ⓐ Ⓑ Ⓒ Ⓓ Ⓔ
62. Ⓐ Ⓑ Ⓒ Ⓓ Ⓔ
63. Ⓐ Ⓑ Ⓒ Ⓓ Ⓔ
64. Ⓐ Ⓑ Ⓒ Ⓓ Ⓔ
65. Ⓐ Ⓑ Ⓒ Ⓓ Ⓔ
66. Ⓐ Ⓑ Ⓒ Ⓓ Ⓔ
67. Ⓐ Ⓑ Ⓒ Ⓓ Ⓔ
68. Ⓐ Ⓑ Ⓒ Ⓓ Ⓔ
69. Ⓐ Ⓑ Ⓒ Ⓓ Ⓔ
70. Ⓐ Ⓑ Ⓒ Ⓓ Ⓔ
71. Ⓐ Ⓑ Ⓒ Ⓓ Ⓔ
72. Ⓐ Ⓑ Ⓒ Ⓓ Ⓔ
73. Ⓐ Ⓑ Ⓒ Ⓓ Ⓔ
74. Ⓐ Ⓑ Ⓒ Ⓓ Ⓔ
75. Ⓐ Ⓑ Ⓒ Ⓓ Ⓔ
76. Ⓐ Ⓑ Ⓒ Ⓓ Ⓔ
77. Ⓐ Ⓑ Ⓒ Ⓓ Ⓔ
78. Ⓐ Ⓑ Ⓒ Ⓓ Ⓔ
79. Ⓐ Ⓑ Ⓒ Ⓓ Ⓔ
80. Ⓐ Ⓑ Ⓒ Ⓓ Ⓔ
81. Ⓐ Ⓑ Ⓒ Ⓓ Ⓔ
82. Ⓐ Ⓑ Ⓒ Ⓓ Ⓔ
83. Ⓐ Ⓑ Ⓒ Ⓓ Ⓔ
84. Ⓐ Ⓑ Ⓒ Ⓓ Ⓔ
85. Ⓐ Ⓑ Ⓒ Ⓓ Ⓔ
86. Ⓐ Ⓑ Ⓒ Ⓓ Ⓔ
87. Ⓐ Ⓑ Ⓒ Ⓓ Ⓔ
88. Ⓐ Ⓑ Ⓒ Ⓓ Ⓔ
89. Ⓐ Ⓑ Ⓒ Ⓓ Ⓔ
90. Ⓐ Ⓑ Ⓒ Ⓓ Ⓔ
91. Ⓐ Ⓑ Ⓒ Ⓓ Ⓔ
92. Ⓐ Ⓑ Ⓒ Ⓓ Ⓔ
93. Ⓐ Ⓑ Ⓒ Ⓓ Ⓔ
94. Ⓐ Ⓑ Ⓒ Ⓓ Ⓔ
95. Ⓐ Ⓑ Ⓒ Ⓓ Ⓔ

United States History

PRACTICE TEST 4

TIME: 60 Minutes
95 Questions

DIRECTIONS: Each of the questions or incomplete statements below is followed by five suggested answers or completions. Select the one that is best in each case.

1. The economic theory that relies upon large scale government intervention in the economy to stimulate investment and consumption is known as

(A) monetarist.
(B) Keynesian economics.
(C) supply-side economics.
(D) classical economics.
(E) laissez-faire.

2. Which of the following statements characterizes the requirements to serve as a justice on the U.S. Supreme Court?

(A) Must be at least 35 years old.
(B) Must be a member of the bar.
(C) Must have already served as a Federal Judge.
(D) Must have a law degree.
(E) There are no specific qualifications.

3. In 1958, the number of _____ workers outnumbered the _____ workers for the first time in American history.

(A) factory .. farm
(B) factory .. white collar
(C) white collar .. blue collar
(D) blue collar .. factory
(E) unemployed .. employed

4. Which of the following is true of the Mayas?

   (A) They created a writing system that used both syllables and written characters.

   (B) Their city-states remained at peace throughout their history.

   (C) They had no known religion.

   (D) They had no knowledge of astronomy.

   (E) Their cultures survived and even thrived after Spanish contact.

5. A policy of *caveat emptor* offers the consumer

   (A) legal redress for the purchase of unsatisfactory products.

   (B) no legal redress for the purchase of unsatisfactory products.

   (C) only union produced products.

   (D) only imported products.

   (E) an exemption from a state sales tax.

6. In the impeachment process against the president, which of the following determines guilt or innocence?

   (A) House of Representatives

   (B) Senate

   (C) Supreme Court

   (D) Cabinet

   (E) American people

7. The right to a speedy trial is guaranteed Americans by

   (A) the Declaration of Independence.

   (B) the First Amendment.

   (C) the Third Amendment.

   (D) the Sixth Amendment.

   (E) Article II of the Constitution.

8. The U.S. House of Representatives has how many members?

   (A) 100

   (B) 435

   (C) 535

   (D) 120

   (E) 648

9. According to Article II of the U.S. Constitution, the sole authority to suspend the writ of *habeas corpus* resides in

(A) the Supreme Court.
(B) the president.
(C) the attorney general.
(D) the Congress.
(E) the state governors.

10. In James Madison's "Federalist Paper Number Ten," the most dangerous threat to the U.S. Constitution was presented by

(A) the president's war powers.
(B) factions.
(C) the Supreme Court.
(D) a standing army.
(E) freedom of speech.

FEDERAL SPENDING & FEDERAL DEFICIT, 1890-1940

(in billions)

Year	***Federal Budget***	***Federal Surplus/Deficit***
1890	$ 0.318	+ 0.09
1900	0.521	+ 0.05
1910	0.694	– 0.02
1920	6.357	+ 0.30
1930	3.320	+ 0.70
1940	9.600	– 2.70

11. The table above shows which of the following in regard to the relationship of spending by the national government to our federal deficit from 1890 to 1940.

(A) Increases in federal spending cause increases in national debt.
(B) The rate of federal spending can be used to predict national debt.
(C) The size of the federal budget by itself has little correlation to the federal deficit.
(D) Federal surpluses always result from reductions in federal spending.
(E) Federal surpluses always result from increases in revenue.

12. The Dutch colony at New Netherland was categorized by all of the following EXCEPT

    (A) its great reliance upon the fur trade.

    (B) friendly relations with neighboring Amerindians.

    (C) relatively small population.

    (D) ethnic diversity of settlers.

    (E) a desire for its own wealth.

13. North American Indian cultures were characterized by all of the following EXCEPT

    (A) a diversified economy of hunting, fishing, and farming.

    (B) a division of labor by gender.

    (C) a reliance on oral culture.

    (D) an animistic religion that worshipped the spiritual elements of nature.

    (E) the lack of the presence of warfare.

14. Spanish colonization of the New World was characterized by all of the following EXCEPT

    (A) ruthless exploitation of the Indians.

    (B) establishing African slavery in the Americas.

    (C) reliance upon large families as settlers.

    (D) introduction of the horse to America.

    (E) the creation of large agricultural plantations.

15. The Puritans left England to settle in America in order to

    (A) establish religious freedom for all Christians.

    (B) emulate the Spanish conquistadors.

    (C) create a perfect religious utopia.

    (D) avoid serving in the English army.

    (E) protest the persecution of the Pilgrims.

16. Seventeenth-century English settlers of New England differed from those in Virginia by

    (A) living shorter lives because of the harsh climate.

    (B) importing large numbers of slaves.

    (C) settling on isolated farms.

    (D) living in tightly clustered communities.

    (E) having large families.

17. King Philip's War of 1675–1676 was fought to

    (A) remove Spanish Catholics from Florida.

    (B) end Spanish control over the African slave trade.

    (C) establish New England trade with the West Indies.

    (D) stop the French from settling the Ohio River Valley.

    (E) establish English control over the Indians in New England.

18. The only eighteenth-century North American British colony with a black population majority was

    (A) North Carolina.

    (B) Virginia.

    (C) Maryland.

    (D) South Carolina.

    (E) Georgia.

19. From 1689 until 1763, England fought a series of wars with France for control of North America. Which of the following wars was not part of this series?

    (A) King William's War

    (B) Queen Anne's War

    (C) The Seven Years' War

    (D) King George's War

    (E) King Philip's War

20. Colonial government in British North America did NOT allow

    (A) universal manhood suffrage.

    (B) bicameral legislatures.

    (C) annual elections.

    (D) for a republican form of government.

    (E) local units of government to exist.

21. James Otis earned fame for his defense of American political freedom in
    (A) his book *Common Sense*.
    (B) the Writs of Assistance Case.
    (C) the Virginia House of Burgesses.
    (D) the Second Continental Congress.
    (E) the Boston Tea Party.

22. The Boston Massacre occurred after which of the following events?
    (A) the Intolerable Acts
    (B) the Townshend Duties
    (C) the First Continental Congress
    (D) the Battle of Lexington and Concord
    (E) the Boston Tea Party

23. The most significant political development in British North America from 1700 to 1763 was
    (A) the use of the secret ballot.
    (B) the rise of the assembly as the major force in colonial government.
    (C) the rise of the Constitutional Convention.
    (D) the creation of political parties.
    (E) the extension of the vote to the poor.

24. The Great Awakening was
    (A) the name given to the colonization of Georgia in 1732.
    (B) a major religious revival in the colonies.
    (C) the pseudonym of Thomas Paine.
    (D) a scientific society established by Benjamin Franklin.
    (E) the name of the first American newspaper.

25. The Battle of Saratoga in October 1777 was best known for
    (A) near total defeat of Washington by Howe.
    (B) securing America an alliance with France.

(C) the first signs of Benedict Arnold's treason.

(D) being the first battle in the South.

(E) the splitting of the American states in half by the Howe brothers.

26. In 1632, England allowed its first proprietary colony as a refuge for Catholics in

(A) Connecticut.

(B) Maryland.

(C) New York.

(D) New Hampshire.

(E) Delaware.

27. Prior to 1763, the British policy of mercantilism encouraged the American colonies to

(A) develop native American manufactures.

(B) trade with the French West Indies.

(C) cease importing African slaves.

(D) supply England with raw materials.

(E) All of the above.

28. At the Philadelphia Convention of 1788, the author of the Great Compromise to the U.S. Constitution was

(A) Patrick Henry.

(B) John Adams.

(C) Thomas Jefferson.

(D) Roger Sherman.

(E) James Madison.

29. During the ratification contest, the Antifederalist critique of the proposed U.S. Constitution contained all of the following arguments EXCEPT

(A) a lack of a written Bill of Rights.

(B) the lack of a popular vote for the presidency.

(C) the location of the new government in Washington, D.C.

(D) the powers of the Supreme Court.

(E) the large territory of the United States.

30. Opposition to the Jay Treaty in the U.S. Senate centered around

    (A) the opening of American trade with the West Indies.

    (B) the British refusal to withdraw troops from American soil.

    (C) the settlement of American debts to British merchants.

    (D) its inability to stop the practice of British impressment.

    (E) None of the above.

31. "Millions for defense, not one cent for tribute" became the nation's rallying cry during

    (A) the Whiskey Rebellion.

    (B) the Jay Treaty.

    (C) Hamilton's fiscal policies.

    (D) the XYZ Affair.

    (E) the Fries Rebellion.

32. In the election of 1800, the House of Representatives selected the president because of the deadlocked election between

    (A) John Adams and Thomas Jefferson.

    (B) Thomas Jefferson and Aaron Burr.

    (C) Thomas Jefferson and Charles Pickney.

    (D) James Madison and John Adams.

    (E) George Washington and John Adams.

33. Women emerged from the American Revolution with the prescribed new responsibility of

    (A) enjoying the vote.

    (B) serving in local political office.

    (C) becoming public school teachers.

    (D) raising sons and daughters as good republican citizens.

    (E) paying income taxes.

34. The Lewis and Clark expedition occurred AFTER which event?

    (A) the War of 1812

    (B) the Louisiana Purchase

    (C) the Embargo of 1807

(D) the Nullification Controversy

(E) the Missouri Compromise

35. The Burr Conspiracy refers to

(A) Aaron Burr's attempt to steal the presidency from Thomas Jefferson in 1800.

(B) Burr's scheme to create a new nation from the Southern territory of the United States.

(C) Burr's attempt to assassinate President James Madison.

(D) Burr's attempt to defraud the Bank of the United States of $20 million.

(E) loot the U.S. Treasury.

36. During the War of 1812, the battle waged AFTER the signing of the peace at Ghent was the

(A) Invasion of Canada.

(B) Battle of Lake Erie.

(C) Burning of Washington, D.C.

(D) Battle of New Orleans.

(E) Battle of Bull Run.

37. The principle that "American continents [were not]...subjects for future colonizations by any European power" is expressed directly in

(A) George Washington's farewell address.

(B) the Monroe Doctrine.

(C) the Truman Doctrine.

(D) *McCulloch v. Maryland.*

(E) the Bill of Rights.

38. "John Marshall has made his decision; now let him enforce it," refers to which Supreme Court decision scorned by President Andrew Jackson?

(A) *Gibbons v. Ogden*

(B) *McCulloch v. Maryland*

(C) Dred Scott case

(D) *Cherokee Nation v. Georgia*

(E) *Marbury v. Madison*

39. The rise of the "market economy" in the 1820s refers to

    (A) the rise of the New England textile industry.
    (B) the rise of commercial agriculture.
    (C) the rise of subsistence agriculture.
    (D) the rise of American factories.
    (E) the rise of the Second Bank of the United States.

40. All of the following were New World crops that enhanced European diets EXCEPT

    (A) tomatoes.
    (B) potatoes.
    (C) coffee.
    (D) maize (corn).
    (E) chocolate.

41. Andrew Jackson referred to the Election of 1824 as "the corrupt bargain" because of

    (A) the Whig election smear campaign against him.
    (B) widescale fraud in the popular vote.
    (C) the selection of Henry Clay as President John Quincy Adams' secretary of state.
    (D) the Senate's choice of John Quincy Adams as president.
    (E) the lack of a popular vote for the Electoral College.

42. Which of the following statements is INCORRECT about Andrew Jackson's impact on the office of the presidency?

    (A) He used the veto as a political weapon.
    (B) He relied on the so-called Kitchen Cabinet.
    (C) He relied on the spoils system.
    (D) He lent a keen ear to public opinion.
    (E) He weakened the power of the presidency.

43. Jackson's reasons for his veto of the Second Bank of the United States included all of the following EXCEPT

    (A) The Bank of the United States was a monopoly.

(B) Jackson feared foreign control of the United States through the bank.

(C) Jackson opposed the Bank's political uses of its funds.

(D) The Bank was unconstitutional.

(E) Large blocks of voters favored the bank.

44. The historian most associated with the view of slavery as crushing African-Americans into a "Sambo personality" is

(A) Herbert Aptheker.
(B) George Fitzhugh.
(C) Harriet Beecher Stowe.
(D) Eugene Genovese.
(E) Stanley Elkins.

45. The slavery as a "positive good" argument was presented by

(A) Benjamin Lundy.
(B) Henry Clay.
(C) George Fitzhugh.
(D) Stephen Douglas.
(E) William Lloyd Garrison.

46. Although Texas claimed its independence from Mexico in 1837, it was not admitted as an American state until 1845 because

(A) of prolonged treaty negotiations with Mexico.

(B) of the doctrine of Manifest Destiny.

(C) of Sam Houston's hatred of President Martin Van Buren.

(D) of the North's fear of a growing slave power in the United States.

(E) of strong anti-American sentiment among Texas settlers.

47. Select the statement which BEST represents Abraham Lincoln's public position on slavery in the Election of 1860.

(A) "We must purge this land by blood."

(B) "We consider the slaveholder a relentless tyrant."

(C) "On the issue of slavery I will not retreat a single inch."

(D) "If I can maintain the Union with slavery I shall; if I can maintain the Union without slavery I shall."

(E) "Slavery is the most dreaded disease known to civilized mankind."

48. The Mexican-American War resulted in Mexico ceding all of the following territories to the United States EXCEPT

(A) Texas.
(B) New Mexico.
(C) California.
(D) Nevada.
(E) Washington.

49. Which of the following events occurred last?

(A) the Kansas-Nebraska Act
(B) the Nat Turner Rebellion
(C) the Seneca Falls Convention
(D) the Lincoln-Douglas debates
(E) the Homestead Act

50. Northern denunciation of the Compromise of 1850 was directed primarily toward

(A) the Fugitive Slave Law.
(B) statehood for California.
(C) the acquisition of New Mexico and Utah as slave territories.
(D) the gag rule in the House of Representatives.
(E) continuation of the African slave trade.

51. The Dred Scott decision in 1857 by Chief Justice Roger Taney declared

(A) African-Americans were citizens.
(B) slaves legally could sue in federal courts.
(C) slaves were not property.
(D) the Missouri Compromise was unconstitutional.
(E) that the Bank of the United States be ended.

52. In the election of 1860, Abraham Lincoln's total of the popular vote was

(A) 80 percent.
(B) 70 percent.
(C) 60 percent.
(D) 50 percent.
(E) 40 percent.

53. The Emancipation Proclamation freed the slaves

    (A) throughout the United States.

    (B) only in the border states.

    (C) throughout the South only.

    (D) in Maryland and Tennessee.

    (E) in areas then in rebellion against the U.S. government.

54. Because of its acceptance of the states' rights doctrine, the Confederacy most closely resembled

    (A) the British constitution.

    (B) the Articles of Confederation.

    (C) Napoleonic France.

    (D) the United States Constitution.

    (E) the Magna Carta.

55. During the Civil War, President Lincoln gave evidence of his democratic beliefs by sponsoring

    (A) the Homestead Act.

    (B) the recruitment of black soldiers into the Northern Army.

    (C) the Emancipation Proclamation.

    (D) the 14th Amendment.

    (E) his actions during his first four months in office.

56. The vast majority of settlers who traveled to the Far West because of the Homestead Act's grant of a free 160-acre farm

    (A) proposed and established democracy in the region.

    (B) were supporters of the Democratic Party.

    (C) returned East after failing as farmers.

    (D) were ex-slaves.

    (E) were recent immigrants from Eastern Europe.

57. According to most historians, the major failure of Northern Reconstruction was its inability to

(A) educate the ex-slaves.

(B) provide the vote to ex-slaves.

(C) provide economic independence to ex-slaves.

(D) control the Northern desire to punish the South.

(E) establish civil rights for the ex-slaves.

58. The president associated with the Sellout of 1876 was

(A) U.S. Grant.

(B) Ben Tilden.

(C) Andrew Johnson.

(D) Rutherford B. Hayes.

(E) William Howard Taft.

59. The Dawes Severalty Act of 1887 attempted to do all of the following EXCEPT

(A) end the practice of reservations for the Amerindian.

(B) establish the Amerindian family rather than the tribe as the center of Amerindian society.

(C) transform the Great Plains Indians from nomads to farmers.

(D) offer a final plan for the "Indian problem."

(E) relocate Native Americans to Canada.

60. The "robber barons" included all of the following EXCEPT

(A) John D. Rockefeller.

(B) Andrew Carnegie.

(C) Henry Clay Frick.

(D) J. Pierpont Morgan.

(E) Edward Bellamy.

61. Between 1870 and 1914, approximately _____ million new immigrants arrived in America from Eastern and Southern Europe.

(A) 2

(B) 8

(C) 10

(D) 22

(E) 75

62. The incident that transformed Eugene Debs into the foremost socialist leader in America was

(A) the Haymarket Square Massacre.
(B) the Pullman Railroad Strike.
(C) World War I.
(D) the Great Depression.
(E) the Spanish-American War.

63. The Settlement House Movement sought to do all of the following EXCEPT

(A) improve working conditions for women.
(B) outlaw child labor.
(C) strip the "new immigrants" of their native cultures.
(D) seize political power from the urban boss.
(E) restrict immigration.

64. "You shall not crucify mankind on a cross of gold" was what candidate's rallying cry in the election of 1896?

(A) William McKinley
(B) Eugene Debs
(C) William Jennings Bryan
(D) William Howard Taft
(E) Theodore Roosevelt

65. The Populist Party failed as a third party movement because of all of the following EXCEPT

(A) the Democratic Party stole its platform.
(B) of the discovery of gold in Alaska.
(C) of the expansion of farm exports to European markets.
(D) of the inability to unite farmers with urban workers.
(E) the party's refusal to expand beyond agrarian interests.

66. The campaign slogan, "Ma! Ma! Where's my Pa? / Gone to the White House. Ha! Ha! Ha!" was directed against Grover Cleveland by

(A) the Democratic Party.
(B) the Republican Party.
(C) the Populists.
(D) the Temperance League.
(E) the Suffragettes.

QUESTIONS 67–71: Each of these questions requires you to identify the correct American author with his/her work.

(A) Sinclair Lewis
(B) John Dos Passos
(C) Charlotte Perkins Gilman
(D) F. Scott Fitzgerald
(E) T.S. Eliot

67. *The Waste Land*

68. *Main Street*

69. *The Big Money*

70. *The Yellow Wallpaper*

71. *The Great Gatsby*

72. The number of incarcerated Americans in 1997 was

(A) 50,000
(B) 300,000
(C) 10 million
(D) 1.6 million
(E) 500,000

QUESTIONS 73–75: Each of these questions requires you to identify the correct person/persons associated with the following quotations.

73. "There is nothing to fear but fear itself."

(A) Harry Truman
(B) Calvin Coolidge
(C) Franklin Roosevelt
(D) John F. Kennedy
(E) Lyndon Johnson

74. "There is no right to strike against the public safety by anyone, anywhere, anytime."

(A) Thomas Jefferson
(B) Samuel Gompers
(C) Calvin Coolidge
(D) Caesar Chavez
(E) Woodrow Wilson

75. "I took the isthmus."

(A) General William Westmoreland

(B) Theodore Roosevelt

(C) General Douglas MacArthur

(D) Lewis and Clark

(E) General William Sherman

76. Under the Treaty of Paris ending the Spanish-American War, Spain ceded to the United States

(A) Hawaii.

(B) Puerto Rico and Guam.

(C) the Philippines and the Virgin Islands.

(D) New Mexico.

(E) Florida.

77. During the Progressive Era, the state referred to as "the laboratory of democracy" was

(A) Wisconsin.

(B) Massachusetts.

(C) Connecticut.

(D) Florida.

(E) New York.

78. In the case of the Northern Securities Company, President Theodore Roosevelt contended the company was in violation of the Sherman Antitrust Act because

(A) the Northern Securities Company had consolidated to a degree in restraint of free trade.

(B) it had acted against "due process."

(C) it had violated Roosevelt's embargo of Germany.

(D) it had violated the 14th Amendment.

(E) All of the above.

79. The muckrakers as reformers of social, political, and economic corruption used the _____ as their primary weapon.

(A) radio
(B) Congress
(C) presidency
(D) print media
(E) state legislatures

80. John Dewey's theories on "progressive education" advocated all of the following EXCEPT

(A) rote memorization was an ineffective way of learning.
(B) school's developing a student's social outlook.
(C) children best learn by doing.
(D) knowledge of the facts was the purpose of education.
(E) students should be encouraged to work on group projects.

81. As part of the American mobilization during World War I, all of the following agencies were created except the

(A) War Industries Board.
(B) Office of Food Administration.
(C) Council of National Defense.
(D) McCarran Internal Security Act.
(E) Committee on Public Information.

82. Teapot Dome refers to

(A) the code name for the atomic bomb during World War II .
(B) a school of artistic realism that flourished in the 1920s.
(C) a political scandal during the Harding administration.
(D) the sale of stocks on margin in 1929.
(E) the migrant farm community in John Steinbeck's *Grapes of Wrath.*

83. The liberal views of the Earl Warren Court are displayed in all of the following Supreme Court decisions EXCEPT

(A) *Baker v. Carr.*
(B) *Roe v. Wade.*

(C) *Brown v. Board of Education of Topeka.*

(D) *Miranda v. Arizona.*

(E) *Engel v. Vitale.*

84. A major cause of the Great Depression was

(A) the stock market crash.

(B) reliance upon a single metallic base for currency.

(C) the inability of wages to keep pace with production increases.

(D) the inability of production to keep pace with wage increases.

(E) federal budget increases during the New Deal.

85. All of the following were outspoken critics of the New Deal EXCEPT

(A) Francis Townsend.

(B) Huey Long.

(C) Father Charles Coughlin.

(D) Frances Perkins.

(E) Upton Sinclair.

86. The formation of the North Atlantic Treaty Organization (NATO) in 1949 is an example of the policy known as

(A) appeasement.

(B) brinkmanship.

(C) containment.

(D) imperialism.

(E) détente.

87. President Eisenhower's domestic strategy of "modern Republicanism" advocated

(A) acceptance of existing New Deal programs.

(B) increasing military spending.

(C) continuation of McCarthyism.

(D) large deficit spending to finance socialized medicine.

(E) support of civil rights activism.

88. The first black appointed to the United States Supreme Court was

(A) Warren Burger.
(B) Earl Warren.
(C) William Rehnquist.
(D) Thurgood Marshall.
(E) Sandra Day O'Connor.

89. Modeled after the New Deal, Lyndon Johnson's Great Society Program included all of the following EXCEPT

(A) Medicare.
(B) the Fair Housing Act.
(C) the Voting Rights Act.
(D) Project Headstart.
(E) the Department of Energy.

90. The Cuban Missile Crisis of 1962 resulted in

(A) Soviet deployment of offensive nuclear missiles in Cuba.
(B) the closing of the American naval base in Cuba.
(C) Fidel Castro coming to power.
(D) an American pledge not to invade Cuba.
(E) increased American reliance on the policy of brinkmanship.

91. In 1973, the OPEC oil boycott sought to

(A) drive President Nixon from office.
(B) bankrupt American oil companies.
(C) restrict United States support of Israel during the Yom Kippur War.
(D) make Americans more environmentally responsible.
(E) reduce Americans' oil consumption.

92. The longest war in American history was

(A) the War of 1812.
(B) World War I.
(C) the Vietnam War.
(D) the Korean War.
(E) World War II.

93. During his second term, President Reagan faced his gravest foreign policy challenge from Congress over his support for

(A) the Sandinistas.
(B) the Contras.
(C) the MX missile system.
(D) Iraq.
(E) Margaret Thatcher.

Source: New York Public Library

94. This famous cartoon of 1754 by Benjamin Franklin offered a warning to the 13 colonies if they

(A) refused to enter the Seven Years' War.
(B) continued to follow the British policy of mercantilism.
(C) did not protest the Stamp Act.
(D) continued trading with French Canada.
(E) rejected the Albany Plan.

95. In 1991, Americans celebrated the bicentennial of

(A) World War II.
(B) the United States Constitution.
(C) the Declaration of Independence.
(D) the Bill of Rights.
(E) the Supreme Court.

SAT United States History

Practice Test 4 ANSWER KEY

1.	(B)	26.	(B)	51.	(D)	76.	(B)
2.	(E)	27.	(D)	52.	(E)	77.	(A)
3.	(C)	28.	(D)	53.	(E)	78.	(A)
4.	(A)	29.	(C)	54.	(B)	79.	(D)
5.	(B)	30.	(D)	55.	(A)	80.	(D)
6.	(B)	31.	(D)	56.	(C)	81.	(D)
7.	(D)	32.	(B)	57.	(C)	82.	(C)
8.	(B)	33.	(D)	58.	(D)	83.	(B)
9.	(D)	34.	(B)	59.	(E)	84.	(C)
10.	(B)	35.	(B)	60.	(E)	85.	(D)
11.	(C)	36.	(D)	61.	(D)	86.	(C)
12.	(B)	37.	(B)	62.	(B)	87.	(A)
13.	(E)	38.	(D)	63.	(E)	88.	(D)
14.	(C)	39.	(B)	64.	(C)	89.	(E)
15.	(C)	40.	(C)	65.	(E)	90.	(D)
16.	(D)	41.	(C)	66.	(B)	91.	(C)
17.	(E)	42.	(E)	67.	(E)	92.	(C)
18.	(D)	43.	(E)	68.	(A)	93.	(B)
19.	(E)	44.	(E)	69.	(B)	94.	(E)
20.	(A)	45.	(C)	70.	(C)	95.	(D)
21.	(B)	46.	(D)	71.	(D)		
22.	(B)	47.	(D)	72.	(D)		
23.	(B)	48.	(E)	73.	(C)		
24.	(B)	49.	(E)	74.	(C)		
25.	(B)	50.	(A)	75.	(B)		

Detailed Explanations of Answers

PRACTICE TEST 4

1. **(B)** It is Keynesian economics that recognizes the government as one of three major forces acting upon an economy. (The other two forces are investment and consumption.) Keynesian economics was adopted by President Franklin Roosevelt in modest forms during the 1930s in an effort to stimulate the stagnated American economy. To one degree or another, American presidents followed Keynesian policies continuously until 1981, when President Reagan abandoned Keynesian policies for an economic policy labeled supply-side or monetarist. By focusing on inflation, supply-siders advocate limited government involvement in the economy with regard to the money supply. Both classical economics and laissez-faire doctrines establish minimal governmental economic activity. Thus, among the theories listed, it was only the policies of the British economist John Maynard Keynes who, in 1929, advanced the view of large-scale government deficit spending to artificially prime an economy.

2. **(E)** The Constitution is silent on qualifications to hold office as a justice of the Supreme Court, as specified in Article III of the Constitution, beyond the "good behavior" clause. Thus, justices need not hold a law degree (40 percent of the justices have had no law degree) or serve as a judge on the lower courts. As many historians have pointed out, the founding fathers were extremely vague in drawing up the Supreme Court in the United States Constitution in 1788.

3. **(C)** The rise of the managerial class, or white collar worker, began in the late nineteenth century and finally surpassed both farm laborers and factory workers (blue collar workers) in 1958. In and of itself, this fact holds little importance. Nonetheless, economists have pointed out that such a development signaled the arrival of a tremendous economic revolution in America; the transition of the American economy from its industrial phase to its post-modern phase. Often referred to as the information economy, this transition is seen by economists as important as the rise of commercial farming in the 1830s and the rapid industrialization of America in the 1880s and 1890s. No longer is the health of the American economy determined by our production of food and industrial products alone. Since 1958, factors of technological improvement (such as the computer and telecommunication satellite) must be considered to accurately assess the state of the American economy.

4. **(A)** The Mayas had a sophisticated writing system; it utilized glyphs, which are symbols composed of both syllables and written characters. More than 800 individual glyphs were used and were paired in columns, which were read together from left to right and from top to bottom. These glyphs could then be combined to form any word or idea, including the names of gods, buildings, numbers, dynastic events, places, and food. Glyphic inscriptions were carved in wood or stone on Maya monuments and architecture or sometimes painted on paper and pottery. The Maya writing system unit is the glyphic cartouche, which is equivalent to the words and sentences of a modern language. Maya cartouches could contain as few as 3 or as many as 50 glyphs. A large number of Maya glyphs have multiple meanings, and many concepts can be written in more than one way. Numbers are represented with numerical symbols or with a picture of a god, or a combination of two symbols. Some glyphs signify more than one sound while also representing an idea. This means that a single concept can be presented in glyphs in a variety of ways. There is no Maya alphabet.

5. **(B)** A policy of *caveat emptor* offers no redress for consumers. The Latin phrase means "let the buyer beware" and allows manufacturers full freedom in the production and marketing of their products. This was the accepted practice in the early phases of industrialization in America and was challenged by the Progressive movement which demanded truth in advertising and federal governmental regulatory agencies to protect the consumer from fraudulent claims and poor merchandise. Under the presidency of Theodore Roosevelt, the Progressive demands made their way into federal law and gave rise to a multitude of consumer protection agencies in our government.

6. **(B)** The impeachment process in American government is actually a two- part process. In Article I, Section 2 (I, 2), the House of Representatives holds the sole right to initiate impeachment against a president. The House acts as a grand jury in this phase and its impeachment of a president only amounts to an announcement to the Senate that the second phase of the process must begin. According to I,3, the Senate, with the chief justice of the Supreme Court presiding, begins a trial on the guilt or innocence of a president regarding the bill of impeachment. If found guilty, the president is removed from office. Thus, the Senate acts as a petit jury and determines innocence and guilt. Only Andrew Johnson, the 17th president, and William Clinton, the 42nd president, have been impeached by the House of Representatives. Johnson escaped removal from office by the Senate by a single vote. President Richard Nixon, who resigned the presidency was neither impeached nor removed from office by this process.

7. **(D)** It is in the Sixth Amendment that Americans are guaranteed the right to a "speedy trial." The entire amendment deals specifically with the rights of the accused in a criminal procedure. The amendment reflects the fears of the Antifederalists that "justice delayed was justice denied" and that the key to the survival of the Constitution, as with all republics, lay foremost in its capacity to administer justice to its citizens. Although the Declaration of Independence advances principles on the fundamental rights of all people, these rights are stated generally and lack the specific language of the Sixth Amendment. The First Amendment focuses on free

speech, assembly, religion, and the right to petition, while the Third Amendment deals with the illegal quartering of soldiers in private homes. Article II focuses on the Congress of the United States and not individual rights.

8. **(B)** The House of Representatives is permanently frozen at 435 members. Originally, the number of members of the House was to be set at one representative per every 25,000 inhabitants. But as the American population grew, so did the House. Out of fear that the House would grow too unwieldy because of too many representatives, the House established a practice of one representative for every 500,000 inhabitants as a minimum guideline with membership not to exceed 435 members. It is the House's policy to adjust representative districts and members every ten years upon the completion of the federal census. It is important to recall that the House's formula for membership was part of the Great Compromise authored by Roger Sherman of Connecticut at the Philadelphia Convention in 1788. There Sherman settled the differences between large and small states by making the legislative branch bicameral: the Senate would be based on equal representation regardless of a state's population, while the House would base its membership on a state's population and thus favor the large states. Today, there are 100 members of the U.S. Senate (two per state) and 435 members of the House of Representatives, who vary by the size of their state's population.

9. **(D)** Only Congress has the authorization to suspend the writ of *habeas corpus*. The writ is one of our judicial system's basic protections for citizens from arbitrary arrest. The writ demands that arresting officers must present their evidence before a court official within 48 hours after the arrest of a suspect. Thus, the accused is presented with charges and evidence quickly to preserve the principle of innocent until proven guilty. The only American president to suspend the writ without Congressional authorization was Abraham Lincoln, who during the Civil War suspended it in Maryland and Tennessee. This action was later approved by Congress as an emergency wartime action. The attorney general was granted similar emergency powers regarding the writ by Congress in the McCarran Internal Security Act of 1950. This power ceased to function in 1970. Neither the Supreme Court nor the state governors have ever been granted this power temporarily by Congress.

10. **(B)** According to most political scientists, James Madison's *Tenth Federalist* ranks behind only the Declaration of Independence and the U.S. Constitution as a document fundamental to American government. During the ratification contest over the Constitution in New York, Madison, along with Alexander Hamilton and John Jay, authored a series of letters in defense of the Constitution that were signed under the pseudonym "Publius." It was Madison's *Tenth* letter that showed how the Constitution differed from all previous political systems in that it allowed for expansive freedom for its citizens, yet still provided an energetic government. According to Madison, however, the only serious threat to the Constitution would arise from a single interest group, or faction, becoming dominant in our government. Madison believed a large territory and diverse population would prevent that from ever occurring. Madison supported a strong president and Supreme Court, and authored the Bill of Rights in 1790–1791.

11. **(C)** The table does not establish a direct correlation between the size of the federal budget and a deficit. A deficit is determined by the relationship between federal spending and tax revenues collected. Thus, an increase in federal spending may result in a surplus if tax revenues are increased as in 1900. A surplus is not always the result of a reduction in federal spending. As the figures for 1930 reveal, growth in federal spending by itself cannot reveal a rate of change in the size of the deficit. In order to achieve the other relationships desired by all answers other than (C), additional materials and statistics are required.

12. **(B)** The Dutch had extremely hostile relations with neighboring Amerindians because of the Dutch exploitation of the fur trade. Indeed, one of the bloodiest European-Indian wars occurred in 1643 between the Dutch and the Algonquian Indians which nearly annihilated the tribe. The Dutch came to America to exploit its land and peoples as did the Spanish. They sought wealth primarily through the lucrative fur trade. Because of their small native population, the Dutch were forced to attract settlers from all over Europe to populate their colony. As a result, New Netherland was ethnically diverse and this often led to internal struggling among the diverse colonists. Because of the harsh economic conditions established by the Dutch patroon system of farming, few European settlers were attracted to New Netherland.

13. **(E)** Prior to the arrival of Columbus, North American Indians had a record of warfare no better nor worse than their European counterparts. The primary cause of intra-tribal warfare was the violation by one tribe of another tribe's territories. The Indians did have a diversified economy with the notable exception of the Great Plains Indians who were nomadic hunters only. Generally, Indian males hunted and fished while women practiced communal farming methods. Because of the large number of language groups in North America, Indian culture remained oral and relied upon face to face communication. Indian religions stressed that all life was sacred and that all of nature contained a spiritual element. As a result, Indian deities tended to be associated with the forces of nature and nature was seen as animistic.

14. **(C)** The ideal colonial for Spain was an unmarried young male bent on achieving sudden fame and wealth through military exploitation of the Indians. During the sixteenth century about 1500 conquistadors arrived per year seeking only to gain a rapid fortune and return to Spain. To achieve this end, the conquistadors conquered the Indians through military force and exploited their labor as slaves on large plantations called adelantados. Only after the Indian population succumbed did the Spanish introduce African slavery to the Americas through the efforts of Charles V and Las Casas. Prior to Columbus' arrival, there were no horses known to the Western Hemisphere.

15. **(C)** As with the Pilgrims, the Puritans sought to create a perfect religious utopia in America. The Puritans believed they were the last hope to establish true Christianity in the world and fled the persecutions of James and Laud to create isolated communities of devoted Puritans. As a result, they feared all outsiders to their ways and punished the practitioners of any other religions in their midst. The

Puritans extended their fear of other religious groups to include the Pilgrims and were especially hateful of the Spanish who were much too worldly and Catholic for the Puritans. The Puritans were not pacifists and proved this during the English Civil War, 1641–1660 and the Pequot War in 1675–1676 in New England.

16. **(D)** Contrary to popular views, New Englanders enjoyed a life expectancy of close to 70 years for men and 62 years for women in the seventeenth century. Earlier estimates of life expectancy too often factored a high infant mortality rate into the equation to conclude with an inaccurate assessment of life expectancies in the forties for both men and women. Both Virginians and New Englanders had average family sizes of between six and eight throughout the seventeenth century. Slavery never grew beyond small portions in New England because of the lack of large plantations in the region. Instead, Puritans tended to reside in highly isolated villages or towns. Here each Puritan community huddled together and worked closely to establish their separate religious utopias. The harsh New England climate, rocky soil, and thick forests all worked to support the Puritan pattern of settlement by townships.

17. **(E)** The Puritan Wars of 1675–1676 with the Wampanoag Indians and other New England tribes was a direct result of white settlement encroaching on traditional Indian lands. After the hanging of three Indians in 1675, Metacomet, or King Philip, organized the Wampanoags into a unified force to drive the English from New England. Despite being outnumbered, the Indians destroyed many New England settlements and drove back the Puritans repeatedly. During the winter of 1675–1676, the Puritans counterattacked and defeated the Wampanoags and Philip. Indian losses were close to 40 percent of their population in New England. The war effectively ended Indian resistance to white settlement in New England.

18. **(D)** South Carolina earned its distinct population ratios with a black:white ratio of 20:1. In large part, this was owing to the harsh work in the colony's rice fields, which were little better than marshes and swamps. Because of the fear of diseases such as malaria and the demanding nature of the work on a rice plantation, South Carolina farmers were unable to attract white indentured servants and were compelled to rely on black slaves almost exclusively as a labor force. All the remaining Southern colonies held a black:white ratio where slaves comprised about 12–15 percent of the total population throughout the colonial period.

19. **(E)** King Philip's War in Massachusetts was not part of the four great imperial wars between England and France for control of North America. (See Question 17 on King Philip's War.) Each of the other wars were fought for control of North America. Of the four wars, only the Seven Years' War (1756–1763) began in America and spread to Europe. In this final war, England and France fought for control of the Ohio Territory. The French were finally defeated and ceded all of Canada to England at the peace treaty. Thus, in 1763, England was the master of the entirety of North America for the first time. The other wars for the most part ended without conclusive victors: King William's War (1690-1697); Queen Anne's War (1702–1713); King George's War (1744–1748).

20. **(A)** Colonial Americans believed that the vote belonged only to those members of society who had a large stake in society's well being. As a result, they allowed only white adult males with sufficient property and, in many cases, the correct religion to vote. In order to vote in most colonies, one had to be white, male, 21 years or older, a property owner, and a Protestant. These electoral qualifications disenfranchised all blacks, women, non-Protestants, and poor from being politically active through the vote. Annual elections were the rule for the lower legislative houses; local government and county government were very active throughout the colonial period; bicameral legislatures were the norm for the colonies; all 13 colonies claimed to have created a republican form of government to replicate that of England's.

21. **(B)** In 1761, the young Massachusetts lawyer, James Otis, burst across the political horizon with his assault on the general search warrants issued to British customs officials in the Writs of Assistance case. Since 1760, England had sought a method to curb colonial smuggling and New England trade with France during the Seven Years' War. The issuance of the writs allowed officials to ransack private homes searching for evidence. In arguing against the writs, Otis advanced the view that an act of Parliament was subject to review by the higher law of the English Constitution. Otis lost the case, but advanced a view of higher law and constitutions that most Americans came to accept. Thomas Paine was the author of *Common Sense*. Otis never spoke in Virginia and during the 1770s was to play a minimal political role because of diminishing psychological faculties.

22. **(B)** Taking place in March 1770, the Boston Massacre occurred AFTER the Townshend Duties of 1767. All other events took place after 1770: Boston Tea Party (1773); First Continental Congress (1774); Intolerable Acts (1774); Lexington and Concord (1775). The massacre itself was a relatively small, local incident involving Boston dock workers and British soldiers that resulted in seven Bostonians being shot. However, the radicals used the incident to their advantage and propagandized the event into a major blow against American freedom.

23. **(B)** The growing power of the assembly at the expense of the governor and the Governor's Council proved the most dramatic political development in America prior to 1763. As the only elected office in colony-wide government (the other two branches were appointed positions), the assembly was depicted as the democratic branch of government. Although comprised of upper-middle and upper class men for the most part, the assembly used this identification with the people in their quest for power. By and large, the assembly used its control over taxes and government spending as its vehicle to increased power. By 1763, the assembly had became nearly equal to the governor in most of the colonies. The use of the secret ballot did not occur until the twentieth century in America (eighteenth century ballots were openly labeled by candidates). The rise of the constitutional convention and political parties did not occur until the 1780s and 1790s respectively. The one man, one vote rule was not accepted in America until the twentieth century.

24. **(B)** The Great Awakening was a major religious revival that burst across the colonies during the 1730s and 1740s. The decline of religion as a major force

in American lives was evident from the exceedingly low numbers of colonists with affiliated church memberships. Indeed, it is believed in New England alone church membership had dropped to about 15 percent of the adults. In addition, the Enlightenment belief in a rational universe governed by a distant and mechanical deistic God had challenged religious faith for many. Amidst all this, a number of young colonial ministers began to preach a message of an angry and vengeful God whose love alone could save one from eternal agony. By emphasizing love and other emotions over reason, by relying on new preaching styles of an highly emotional nature, and by calling for renewed emotional commitment to God, these "New Light" ministers touched off a colony-wide religious revival. Many flocked back to the churches of their fathers, while the Baptists, Methodists, and Presbyterians gained in converts. Opponents of the Awakening were labeled "Old Lights" and stressed a rational Christianity. The rift between the two groups continued down through the American Revolution.

25. **(B)** The major victory of the Americans at Saratoga did much to convince the French to join in an alliance with the Americans against England. According to our French ambassador, Benjamin Franklin, the French were hesitant to assist the Americans because they saw little hope for an American military victory over England. However, General Gates' victory over General Burgoyne gave the Americans new hope and the desperately needed French alliance and loan. Now England faced a war on two fronts. Saratoga was the turning point in the military phase of the American Revolution. Neither Washington nor Howe participated at the Battle of Saratoga which took place in New York.

26. **(B)** In 1632, the English Catholic, Lord Baltimore, purchased the colony of Maryland as a refuge and haven for persecuted English Catholics. As a proprietary colony, Maryland never attracted many Catholics and the settlers constantly were contesting with the Baltimore family for power. New York, New Hampshire, and Delaware were royal colonies directly under the control of the British monarch. Connecticut was a compact/contract colony that remained largely independent of British rule up to the American Revolution.

27. **(D)** The British policy of mercantilism encouraged the American colonists to serve as a source of raw materials (i.e., fish, fur, lumber, food, etc.) for the mother country. The policy of mercantilism was an economic policy for the British Empire in North America. It was first proposed in the 1590s by Richard Hakluyt and guided the British Parliament throughout the seventeenth and eighteenth centuries. Under mercantilism, the American colonies were to engage in exclusive trade with England and not any other foreign powers, including the French West Indies. Mercantilism promoted a system of economic specialization between England and America, whereby the colonies would serve as the suppliers of raw materials and the consumers of British manufactured goods (i.e., hats, paints, carriages, clothing). Thus, the policy of mercantilism discouraged the development of American manufacturing as it would prove an unwanted competitor to British industry. The British Parliament never discouraged Americans from the importation of black slave labor.

28. **(D)** Roger Sherman was the author of the Great Compromise at the Philadelphia Convention. The issue at hand was the proposed Virginia Plan versus the New Jersey Plan at the Convention. The delegates were equally divided between support of the Virginia Plan (a legislature based on population and favoring the large/populous states) and the New Jersey Plan (a legislature granting each state an equal vote and favoring the small states). This division resulted in a deadlock and threatened the ability to produce a new government for the nation. The deadlock was broken when Sherman proposed the creation of a two house (bicameral) legislature/congress, with the Senate based on the New Jersey Plan (two senators per state) and the House of Representatives based on the Virginia Plan (1 representative per 25,000 inhabitants). With the approval of the compromise, the 55 delegates were able to produce the U.S. Constitution. Patrick Henry, as an Antifederalist, never attended the Convention. Adams and Jefferson also were not in attendance as they were serving overseas as America's ambassadors to England and France, respectively. James Madison, as one of the authors of the Virginia Plan, did not author the Compromise.

29. **(C)** The Antifederalists never voiced concern in 1788–1789 over the location of the government in Washington, D.C., because Washington was not proposed as the new seat of government until 1790 with the accepted Constitution already in operation. During the newspaper debates over the Constitution, the Antifederalists expressly and vehemently denounced the powers of the Supreme Court as too broad and that the national court would overshadow the state courts under the Constitution. These opponents of the Constitution also feared the indirect election of the president through the Electoral College system as one that would encourage plots and conspiracies. Finally, the two gravest defects of the Constitution in the eyes of the Antifederalists were that it did not guarantee the rights of its citizens in writing (ultimately, this complaint would lead to the Bill of Rights as the first 10 amendments to the Constitution) and that no single republican form of government could effectively rule over such a large territory as the original American states.

30. **(D)** In 1794, George Washington appointed John Jay as special ambassador to negotiate a treaty with Great Britain. Because of his lack of diplomatic leverage, Jay secured a treaty in which England agreed only to the removal of British troops from American soil. England refused to allow the Americans open trade with the West Indies and refused to stop the impressment of American sailors (a practice whereby Americans virtually were kidnapped into serving 10-20 two-year terms in the British navy). Revolutionary War debts remained open to negotiation by the two parties. Although the Treaty passed the Senate by a single vote, opposition from the Republican Party was most intense over the issue of impressment.

31. **(D)** During his first year as president, John Adams faced a crisis with France that threatened the honor and sovereignty of America. In 1796, the French navy began seizing American ships on the Atlantic and confiscating their cargo. Adams was informed by three French agents, X, Y, & Z were their code names, that French minister Talleyrand would accept a bribe of $250,000 and an interest free loan of

$12 million, to negotiate this issue. Adams prudently leaked this demand to the American press who rallied the nation around the slogan listed in Question 31. Adams was able to avoid war with France, but did not offer the tribute demanded and saved the honor of the new nation. This was the one event in which Adams took greatest pride for the remainder of his life.

32. **(B)** According to the Constitution, the House of Representatives was empowered to select the president from the two top vote getters if no candidate received over 50 percent of the electoral vote. In the election of 1800, John Adams and Charles Pickney were the Federalist Party candidates for president and vice president, while Jefferson and Aaron Burr were the nominees of the Democratic-Republican Party. However, the ballots cast by the Electoral College never indicated who was president and who was vice president. Thus, Jefferson and Burr were tied. Burr sought to steal the presidency from Jefferson and the House cast 37 separate votes before deciding on Jefferson upon the advice of Alexander Hamilton. This election led to the ratification of the 12th Amendment to the Constitution in 1804 which ordered all future ballots to designate a candidate's office.

33. **(D)** After the American Revolution, American women were advised by authors and ministers that they could best serve the nation by becoming "republican mothers." This concept encouraged women to retain their domain in the household and seek to enter the public world vicariously through their sons. Mothers were advised to teach their sons the republican virtues of truth, frugality, sense of public service, honor, and wisdom. Women were not granted the right to vote, hold any public office, or teach in public schools. Instead, they were advised to keep the home as their domain and only take a half-step toward public life.

34. **(B)** In 1803, Thomas Jefferson sought to purchase American trade rights to use the Mississippi from France. Because of Napoleon's need for capital to finance his European wars, he offered to sell Jefferson all of the Louisiana Territory instead. After the purchase of this seemingly tractless wilderness, Jefferson witnessed the Lewis and Clark expedition to explore the region embark in 1804. Lewis and Clark crossed the continental United States and reached the Pacific coast in 1806. The Louisiana Purchase was approved by the Senate in 1803. The Nullification Controversy with South Carolina occurred in 1831–1832 and the Missouri Compromise was in 1819–1820.

35. **(B)** In 1805, Aaron Burr entered into one of the boldest schemes in American history. Because he was removed from the vice-presidency in 1804 and defeated for governor of New York, Burr desperately planned a plot with Spain to kidnap President Jefferson and accept for ransom a large territory in the southwestern United States as a new independent country under his control. Burr was arrested at the 11th hour of the conspiracy and placed on trial for treason. Chief Justice John Marshall used the case to embarrass Jefferson in 1807 and actually acquitted Burr of the treason charges on a very liberal reading of the treason law requiring two eyewitnesses to the same overt act. Burr attempted neither to assassinate Madison nor defraud the Bank of the United States.

36. **(D)** The Treaty of Ghent ending the War of 1812 was signed on December 24, 1815. Two weeks later, because news of the treaty had yet to arrive in America, the Battle of New Orleans was fought on January 8, 1815. The Americans under the leadership of Andrew Jackson earned a major victory, killing over 2,000 British soldiers while suffering only 13 casualties. The invasion of Canada, which ended in American defeat, was in 1812. The Battle of Lake Erie took place in 1813 and proved a major American naval victory. The burning of Washington, D.C., by the British took place in 1814.

37. **(B)** In 1823, President James Monroe announced to Congress his three principles for foreign policy that later were labeled the Monroe Doctrine. In addition to pledging that Americans would remain free of European wars and threatening American war for any future European colonization of the Western Hemisphere, Monroe uttered the words quoted in Question 37. This doctrine established the areas of North and South America as an American sphere of influence. England supported the doctrine primarily to prevent a major European war over the crumbling Spanish empire. The issue of American continents and European colonization was not the focus of any of the other answers. Washington's farewell address of 1796 only warned Americans to avoid future European wars; the Truman Doctrine of 1947 was Truman's outline for combatting worldwide Communism; *McCulloch v. Maryland* involved the rights of the national government over the states in 1819. The Bill of Rights does not deal with foreign policy matters directly.

38. **(D)** In 1832, Jackson is said to have uttered these words in reaction to Chief Justice Marshall's decision in the case of the *Cherokee Nation v. Georgia*. Although Marshall rejected the Cherokee nation's argument that they existed as a "nation within a nation," he nonetheless ruled that the Cherokees could not be legally moved from their lands as the state of Georgia desired. The Cherokees were finally removed in 1837–1838 along the Trail of Tears. In this case, Jackson reminded the Court that its power was totally dependent upon the Executive branch's willingness to enforce the law. In *Gibbons* (1824), the Court ruled on commerce; in *McCulloch* (1819), the court ruled on the superior power of the national government over the states; *Dred Scott* (1857) was a decision by Roger Taney on slavery; on *Marbury* (1803), see question 67.

39. **(B)** During the 1820s, American farmers moved away from subsistence farming (growing food for one's own consumption only) to commercial market farming (growing a single cash crop for export). After the War of 1812, high crop prices enticed most American farmers to venture cash crop production. For many of these farmers, commercial affairs and market demands proved far more complex than they had expected. The result of this venture was short term indebtedness for most farmers and becoming dependent pawns in a trans-Atlantic commercial economy. The symbol of the small, independent yeoman farmer no longer fit the reality of the American economy. The rise of textile industry and factories is generally described under the heading of American industrialization and not the market economy. The Second Bank of the United States under the directorship of Nicholas Biddle earned fame through its struggles with President Andrew Jackson and not as an innovative economic force in the 1820s.

40. **(C)** Tomatoes, potatoes, maize (corn), and chocolate were all New World crops. Coffee was first cultivated in Africa. The Incas in 700 C.E. cultivated tomatoes, which grow wild in the Andes Mountains. The Incas also first grew potatoes as an agricultural crop, with archaeological evidence suggesting its cultivation as early as 200 B.C.E. Maize first appeared in southern Mexico as early as 5000 B.C.E. Chocolate was first consumed by the Aztecs and the Mayas. By 1000 C.E., cocoa beans were used as currency.

41. **(C)** In 1824, no candidate received a clear majority in the Electoral College. Although Jackson had outpolled his nearest rival in the popular vote, 43 percent to 30 percent, the House of Representatives still selected the second candidate, John Quincy Adams, over Jackson. Jackson became outraged when he discovered that Henry Clay, a presidential candidate, swung his support to Adams and was named secretary of state by Adams. Jackson was convinced that a deal had been struck and the popular vote denied. Jackson never discussed fraudulent voting practices and the Whig Party was not identified with campaign smears during this election.

42. **(E)** Andrew Jackson had the single greatest impact on the office of the presidency of any president other than Washington during the nineteenth century. Jackson completely transformed the office from a pawn of political parties to a strong and independent force in American government and politics. He established his power through the use of the veto (i.e., the Maysville Veto, the veto of the Second Bank of the United States, etc.) as an offensive rather than defensive political weapon. In addition, he was able to bypass both congressional and party control of his Cabinet by appointing an unofficial inner circle of top advisors called "the kitchen cabinet." Jackson also used his power to appoint civil servants for the federal government with a vengeance and replaced earlier office holders with officials who were personally loyal to him, creating the "spoils system." Finally, Jackson skillfully used public opinion to back his policies whenever he felt it was required, as in his struggles with Nicholas Biddle over the Second Bank of the United States.

43. **(E)** President Jackson began leading an assault on the Second Bank, which under the directorship of Nicholas Biddle, in 1832. Known as Jackson's Bank War, the president was outraged by the Bank's pro-Eastern and pro-business policies under Biddle. In 1832, Jackson refused to recharter the Bank on the grounds that the Bank was an illegal monopoly and had no constitutional authority to exist. In addition, Jackson publicly rallied the American people around his crusade by stating fears that the Bank's foreign creditors could use the Bank to control American foreign policy and that the Bank catered to the needs and interests of a wealthy elite at the cost of high taxes and no benefits to the American farmer and workingman.

44. **(E)** In 1961, Stanley Elkins published his controversial work, *Slavery*. In this study, Elkins likened the conditions of blacks under slavery to Jewish inmates of Nazi concentration camps during World War II. (It should be remembered that it is a matter of historical record that the Nazis systematically murdered six million Jews.) According to Elkins, the American system of slavery relied upon physical and psychological torture of African-Americans to such a degree that it crushed them

psychologically and produced the "Sambo personality"; infantile-like adults who lacked strong self-esteem and initiative and who often adopted the views of white racism as their own internal values of self-hate. Herbert Aptheker was a Marxist scholar who advanced the view of slaves as heroic rebels. George Fitzhugh was the Southern champion of slavery as a positive good in the 1850s and viewed all black people as innately inferior to whites and as a result they advanced under slavery. Stowe's depiction of slaves in *Uncle Tom's Cabin* displayed blacks as human beings with a full range of virtues and courage. Eugene Genovese is a contemporary historian whose classic *Roll Jordan Roll* examines African-American slave culture and depicts a strong culture grounded by strong and stable people and not "Sambo" personalities.

45. **(C)** In the 1850s, the most ardent defender of Southern slavery was George Fitzhugh. In works such as *Cannibals All*, Fitzhugh pointed out that all great empires and civilizations of the past had relied upon slavery and that slave owners actually were civilizing "savage" Africans as much as could be expected under slavery. Fitzhugh also pointed out that unlike the treatment of "wage slaves" up north (factory workers), slaves were cared for while aged and infirm by the slave owner. It was Fitzhugh's view that because of the community of interest under slavery, slavery actually proved more humane toward its workers (slaves) than Northern capitalism did toward its workers. Benjamin Lundy sought to end slavery through the American Colonization Society, as did William Lloyd Garrison through the Abolitionists or American Anti-Slavery Society. Both Henry Clay and Stephen Douglas sought compromise solutions to the political crisis of slavery that adopted a strong stance on neither side of the slavery issue.

46. **(D)** The delay in admitting Texas to the Union was largely owing to Northern fears that the great size of the Texas territory would produce at least 10 new slave states and thus shift the balance of power established under the Missouri Compromise of 1819 to the slave states. Texas settlers since gaining their independence from Mexico in 1837 had been clamoring for entry into the United States and appealed to the American belief that it was the nation's destiny to reach the Pacific under Manifest Destiny doctrines. Treaty negotiations with Mexico over the extent of Texas' border did not take place until 1845–1846 and led directly to the Mexican-American War. Sam Houston's views toward Van Buren had little impact on the Texas as a state issue.

47. **(D)** During the election of 1860, Lincoln sought to reduce the issue of slavery to a secondary status before the primary concern of keeping the nation united. As a result, Lincoln varied widely in his public views on slavery, but never wavered from his belief that the primary issue in the election was keeping the union together. John Brown in 1859 uttered the words of needing to purge America by blood of the sin of slavery. The quotes from (B), (C), and (E) were all representative of the extreme abolitionist position adopted by William Lloyd Garrison and his followers who desired to end slavery immediately even at the cost of losing the South to secession. Lincoln never advocated the Abolitionist position.

48. **(E)** At the close of the Mexican-American War in 1847, Mexico ceded to the United States portions of present-day Texas, Nevada, New Mexico, California, Utah, Arizona, and Wyoming for $15 million. The state of Washington was part of the Louisiana Purchase of 1803.

49. **(E)** The Nat Turner Rebellion occurred in 1831 as the bloodiest slave uprising in American history when 55 whites were killed by about 15 slaves in Virginia. The Kansas-Nebraska Act was passed in 1854 and sought to establish the principle of popular sovereignty in the two territories on the issue of slavery to promote the presidential ambitions of Senator Stephen Douglas of Illinois. The Seneca Falls Convention convened in 1848 as a militant expression of women's rights led by Lucretia Mott and Elizabeth Cady Stanton. The Lincoln-Douglas debates took place in 1858 as both candidates vied for the Senate seat in Illinois. The Homestead Act was passed by Congress in 1862 and granted a free 160 acre farm in the Far West (Great Plains region) to any American citizen 21 years of age or older who would work the land for five years.

50. **(A)** Northerners were outraged by the measure of the Compromise of 1850 known as the Fugitive Slave Law. Although the North had gained victories in the Compromise in California's admission as a free state and the end of slave auctions in Washington, D.C., they felt the price of victory was too high with the Fugitive Slave Law. Under this law, all Americans legally were required to assist in the return of all runaway or "fugitive" slaves to their masters. Abolitionists like Garrison denounced the act as an attempt to force every Northerner to become part of the dreaded slave system. The importation of African slaves legally had ended in 1808 and the Gag Rule on tabling abolition petitions in Congress without discussion was enacted in 1837. Northern concern over Utah and New Mexico had been voiced during debates over the Wilmot Proviso at the end of the Mexican-American War.

51. **(D)** In 1857, the Supreme Court under Roger Taney sought to offer a final solution to the crisis over slavery in the Dred Scott Case. Here a black slave sued for his freedom on the grounds he was in Northern territory which had outlawed slavery. Taney ruled that Scott could not sue in the Court because blacks were not and could never become citizens of the United States. In addition, Taney ruled the Missouri Compromise of 1819 and all other laws prohibiting slavery unconstitutional as violations of the "due process clause" of the Fifth Amendment regarding property.

52. **(E)** In the election of 1860, the strength of sectionalism in the country was apparent with the nomination of four sectional candidates for president. As the Republican Party's candidate, Lincoln mustered only 40 percent of the popular vote but carried a majority of Electoral College votes to win the election. John Breckinridge for the Southern Democrats earned 18 percent of the popular vote, while Stephen Douglas and the Northern Democrats earned 30 percent. John Bell of the Constitutional Union Party was able to gather only 13 percent of the vote. Thus, Lincoln was seen as a minority president lacking a national mandate and representing only the interests of the North.

53. **(E)** Lincoln's issuance of the Emancipation Proclamation in January 1863 was greeted with joyous celebration in the North. However, a strict legal reading of the document indicates that it effectively did not free a slave. Lincoln's proclamation freed only those slaves in territories in rebellion against the United States, an area in which—by definition—Lincoln had no authority. The proclamation was silent on the issue of those slaves who were held in Maryland and Tennessee, two areas under Lincoln's control. Slavery finally was ended by an act of Congress in 1865 through the 13th Amendment to the Constitution.

54. **(B)** The Confederate government's adoption of a states' rights system of government most closely represents the Articles of Confederation from 1784–1788. Both systems of government rely on the friendly cooperation of its member states, have no coercive power over the states, and cannot act directly on its citizens but must go through the states. The British Constitution, U.S. Constitution, and Napoleonic France all established strong central/national governments with local government units that are subordinate to the national government. Another term for the Confederacy and the Articles used by political scientists is state-centered federalism.

55. **(A)** Lincoln's faith in democracy is best reflected in his sponsorship of the Homestead Act which granted a free 160-acre farm in the Great Plains to any American citizen willing to work the land for five years. This Act gave rise to the great westward migration of up to four million Americans from 1865 to 1900. Lincoln was extremely reluctant to enlist black volunteers during the Civil War and was forced to this action only in 1863 with the creation of the 54th Massachusetts regiment. Black troops, about 185,000, were kept in segregated units under white officers. Lincoln's passage of the Emancipation Proclamation was more an act of political subterfuge than an effort in democracy as the Proclamation never really freed a slave. The 14th Amendment was ratified in 1867, after Lincoln's death. During his first four months in office, Lincoln ran the Civil War as a virtual dictator, usurping Congressional powers of raising and supporting an army while Congress was on leave.

56. **(C)** Despite their great exodus westward under the Homestead Act, the vast majority of the five million homesteaders from 1865 to 1900 failed. The main problems they faced were that a 160-acre farm was too small to support profitable agriculture in this region because of water shortages and soil conditions. The Great Plains required large farming methods that were beyond the means of most homesteaders. Most ex-slaves remained in the South as sharecroppers after the War, although a sizeable minority did serve as cowboys on the Santa Fe cattle drives. Most recent immigrants from Eastern Europe at this time congregated in America's Northern and Eastern cities as factory workers. The homesteaders retained their allegiance to the Republican Party for it had sponsored the Act.

57. **(C)** At the close of the Civil War, the Radical Republicans pledged to the ex-slaves that they would establish the freed blacks' economic independence in the South. The Radicals planned to do this by confiscating all Southern plantations of

more than 200 acres and subdividing these farms into 40 acre farms to be given to the ex-slaves along with a free mule. This "40 acres and a mule" program was never established and most ex-slaves were forced to work for their former masters under sharecropping, a system of exploitation that reduced most Southern blacks to abject poverty. The Radicals did establish the Freedman's Bureau which established free public schools in the South for ex-slaves, provided the vote to the ex-slaves, and protected the black voter before the attacks of white terrorist groups such as the Ku Klux Klan and the White Camelia, and satisfied most Northerners that the South was paying for secession and Civil War.

58. **(D)** The Republican President Hayes is the author of the Sellout of 1876. In the election of 1876, the Republican Hayes and Democrat Tilden ended in an electoral tie for the presidency. Amidst claims of fraudulent election returns, Hayes met with Southern members of the House of Representatives in New Orleans. In return for their votes, Hayes promised to withdraw Union soldiers from the South and end Reconstruction, effectively granting the white South a free hand in dealing with blacks. Hayes won the election in the South and made good on his bargain. Neither Taft, Johnson, nor Grant were involved in the election of 1876.

59. **(E)** The Dawes Severalty Act was the American Congress' final plan to deal with the Amerindian population. Indians were no longer perceived as threats to the United States in 1887 as their population had shrunk to under 300,000. The Dawes-Severalty Act effectively made the conditions of the Homestead Act of 1862 applicable to the Indian, save that a free 160 acre farm was available after 20 years of farming and not the five for whites. This act effectively sought to destroy the Plains culture of the Indians by forcing them to be sedentary farmers rather than nomadic hunters and place the Indian family rather than the tribe as the center of Indian culture. With this act for small farms, the government no longer established designated lands for Indian tribes called reservations.

60. **(E)** Edward Bellamy was an utopian novelist who described a utopian socialist community in Boston in his novel *Looking Backwards* (1887). Rockefeller, Carnegie, Frick, and Morgan were all labeled "robber barons" for their aggressive and oftentimes unscrupulous actions as self-made millionaires and giant industrialists in the late nineteenth century. The term *robber baron* was one of derision seeking to cast blame for the poor working conditions and low wages of manual workers.

61. **(D)** American immigration from 1870 to the outbreak of World War I in 1914 grew at a tremendous pace. Most of these new immigrants arrived from Southern and Eastern Europe, as well as Russia, in record numbers seeking religious and political freedom that America offered. They were welcomed into the country as the manual labor required for America's new factories and industrialization but were greeted with low wages, discrimination, poor working conditions, and slum living conditions in urban areas. Only World War I stopped this immigration and after the war, Congress reduced the number of immigrants allowed into America drastically through such laws as the National Origins Act of 1924 which established immigration quotas for ethnic groupings.

62. **(B)** Eugene Debs was the leader of the American Railway Union when the Pullman Railroad Strike of 1894 started. George Pullman had drastically cut his workers' wages and refused to lower rents or food costs in his company town. When Debs joined the strike with a sympathy strike of the ARU, Pullman convinced President Cleveland to crush the peaceful strikers with federal troops because of their refusal to move the U.S. mail. When the ARU and Debs were sued successfully in the Supreme Court in 1895 for damages, Debs turned toward socialism as he realized the Supreme Court had effectively ruled striking unions illegal. Debs already was a socialist by World War I and the Great Depression of the 1930s, as well as the Spanish-American War of 1898. Although Debs sympathized with striking workers during the Haymarket Square Massacre of 1886, he still at that time advocated unionism rather than socialism.

63. **(E)** The Settlement House Movement of Jane Addams and other middle class social workers sought to improve the living and working conditions of America's new immigrants in urban slum areas. Addams and her workers sought the end to child labor, improved working conditions for women, the end of urban bossism, and education for the new immigrant. The price extracted from the immigrant was to be completely "Americanized" and lose much of their native culture. Addams and her workers moved into slum areas and lived among the people they served.

64. **(C)** William J. Bryan's famous "cross of gold" speech was the rallying cry for farmers throughout the country in the election of 1896. Bryan crisscrossed the country delivering his populist message as the Democratic Party candidate. His opponent, William McKinley, sided clearly with big business interests and was opposed to Bryan's platform of a bimetalic currency (silver and gold standards). McKinley easily won the election. Neither Debs, Taft, nor Roosevelt were presidential candidates in 1896.

65. **(E)** In 1894, the Populist Party appeared ready to became the most powerful third-party movement in American history. Because of the severe economic recession of 1893, the Populist platform of an expanded currency backed by silver and gold was attracting a large following. In the election of 1896, however, the Democratic Party and William Jennings Bryan stole the Populist Party platform, yet lost the election to McKinley and the pro-business Republicans. After the election, the discovery of gold in Alaska expanded the currency, farmer prosperity briefly returned with expanded European markets, and urban workers never identified with the Populists. The result was that the Party collapsed by 1902.

66. **(B)** The election of 1884 was one of the most vicious campaigns in American history. The Republicans sought to smear the candidate of the Democratic Party, Grover Cleveland, with charges of private immorality for having fathered an illegitimate child. Personal attacks on James Blaine, the Republican candidate, abounded as well. Indeed, it is difficult to isolate any issues put forward among these negative campaign tactics of mudslinging by both parties. The Republican strategy backfired and Cleveland won the election. The Populist Party had not come into existence in

1884, while the Temperance League was a group of the 1830s and the Suffragettes would not appear until the early 1900s.

67. **(E)** T.S. Eliot authored the epic poem *The Waste Land* in 1922 on the vacuum of modern life in America.

68. **(A)** Sinclair Lewis authored the classic novel, *Main Street*, in 1920 on the materialism invading small town America.

69. **(B)** John Dos Passos completed his famous USA trilogy with the publication of *The Big Money* in 1931. Dos Passos focused on the increased class, ethnic, and racial biases in America.

70. **(C)** Charlotte Perkins Gilman was a late-nineteenth-century feminist author who compared the life of a mental patient with the confinement of a housewife in *The Yellow Wallpaper* in 1885.

71. **(D)** F. Scott Fitzgerald published *The Great Gatsby* in 1925 as a statement of the loss of direction for America's post-World War I society.

72. **(D)** Between 1987 and 1997, the number of incarcerated Americans doubled, rising from 800,000 to 1.6 million.

73. **(C)** These words were spoken by President Franklin D. Roosevelt as part of his "Fireside Chat" radio broadcasts to the American nation during the 1930s. Roosevelt was seeking to ease American fears about the Great Depression and restore faith and confidence in the government's ability to solve the Depression.

74. **(C)** These words were spoken by Massachusetts Governor Calvin Coolidge in response to the Boston Police Strike of 1919. In calling the national guard to end the strike, Coolidge forwarded the words as a telegram to Samuel Gompers and became an overnight American hero and Republican vice-presidential candidate in 1920 on the Harding ticket.

75. **(B)** These were the words used by President Theodore Roosevelt to justify his backing of the Panamanian revolution against Colombia in 1903. This allowed the United States to gain access to an area to build the Panama Canal, establishing easy water access to both the Atlantic and Pacific coasts.

76. **(B)** The Treaty ceded only Puerto Rico and Guam; Spain sold the Philippines to the United States for $20 million. New Mexico had been purchased after the Mexican-American War of 1848; Hawaii was annexed after the abortive Queen Lil uprisings in 1893 and formally approved for annexation in 1898.

77. **(A)** Wisconsin earned the title, "laboratory of democracy," during the Progressive era because of the reforming actions of its governor, Robert LaFollette.

Wisconsin was the first state to establish governmental regulatory agencies and proved a major testing grounds for legislation that the Progressives would establish on a national scale regarding conservation, consumer protections, and improved working conditions.

78. **(A)** In the Northern Securities Company case, Theodore Roosevelt ordered the Justice Department to seek criminal action on the violation of the Sherman Antitrust Act. Roosevelt contended that this Pacific Northwest railroad conglomerate had monopolized the region in restraint of free trade and was charging exorbitant freight rates to farmers of the region. The Supreme Court upheld Roosevelt's actions and total shock spread through the country as one of the largest American corporations was forced to divest. The company never violated due process and actually sought protection from Roosevelt's actions under the 14th amendment. Roosevelt never established an embargo against Germany.

79. **(D)** The muckrakers were a group of reformers who sought to arouse the American middle class to action against political corruption and economic reform through the exposé in novels, magazines, and reports. They provided momentum for the Progressive movement by their constant attacks upon injustices from big business and the conditions of the working classes in America. The muckrakers left it up to the middle class to mount the political drives to correct the abuses of the American political and economic systems of the times. At the time of their writing, the radio had not yet emerged as a powerful medium in American society.

80. **(D)** John Dewey sought to transform American education's emphasis on the rote memorization of facts. Contending that social knowledge and behavior were vital in a democracy, Dewey charged teachers with becoming more student centered in their teaching methods and encouraged group projects for students to develop their skills at social learning. Dewey's theories were never put in practice in American schools due to many misperceptions about his theories. For Dewey, the classroom environment rather than intelligence of a student was the key to public education.

81. **(D)** The McCarran Internal Security Act was passed in 1950 as part of the Communist scare in America at the close of World War II. The act sought to garner Communist party members to register with the Justice Department and granted the Attorney General sweeping authority in cases of national emergency. The War Industries Board, Office of Food Administration, Council of National Defense, and Committee on Public Information were all agencies created by President Wilson to accelerate the American mobilization efforts for World War I in 1917. These agencies greatly expanded government control over the lives of Americans in order to win the war effort.

82. **(C)** Next to the Watergate scandal, the Teapot Dome scandal of the Harding administration is the biggest political scandal in American history. Under the Harding presidency, the secretary of the treasury, Herbert Falls, secretly leased oil reserves to Harry Sinclair of the Sinclair Oil Company, who refined the petroleum for his company. Secretary Fall pleaded guilty to corruption charges and the lands

were returned to the United States government. The code name for the atomic bomb project in World War II was the Manhattan Project. The Ashcan School is the school of artistic realism that flourished in the 1920s.

83. **(B)** The *Roe v. Wade* decision on abortion was handled by the Burger Court and not the Warren Court. Chief Justice Earl Warren stepped down from the Supreme Court in 1969 (Warren Court, 1954–1969) after rendering his decisions on protecting the rights of the accused in *Miranda* (1966); prohibiting state sponsored school prayer in *Engel* (1962); declaring segregation illegal in public schools in *Brown*, (1954); the one person, one vote principle in state apportionment of legislative districts in *Baker* (1966). Warren Burger was named chief justice of the Court by President Nixon in 1969 and resigned in 1986; President Ronald Reagan replaced him with William Rehnquist.

84. **(C)** The problems that caused the Great Depression were structural in nature and stemmed primarily from the fact that wage increases simply did not keep pace with industrial output in the 1920s. As a result, consumption declined and businesses began to build up inventories. The result was increased layoffs of workers and further declines in consumer spending. Finally, the stock market crash of 1929 pointed to the house of cards that was the American economy. The stock market crash was a symptom and not a cause of the Great Depression. The New Deal was put in place to battle the Depression and the issuance of more money in the economy would only have helped if the inflated currency had found its way to the American consumer.

85. **(D)** Frances Perkins was Roosevelt's longtime secretary of labor and supporter of the New Deal programs. Francis Townsend attacked Roosevelt's First New Deal in 1935 for not being radical enough of a change and not helping the destitute and downtrodden. Huey Long and Upton Sinclair both attacked Roosevelt from the left for ignoring the American farmer and worker under the New Deal. Father Coughlin attacked Roosevelt from both the left and the right on his popular radio shows until Coughlin's severe anti-Semitism forced him from the air waves.

86. **(C)** NATO was formed in 1949 as part of President Truman's strategy of containment against Communism in the Cold War. The policy actually was the brainchild of George Kennan in an effort to slow down the spread of Communism. NATO was designed to unite Western Europe as a strong defensive measure to keep Communism from extending beyond Germany. Appeasement is the policy associated with the British prime minister, Neville Chamberlain, who gave in to Hitler's expansionistic drives in the 1930s. Brinkmanship was the foreign policy strategy under the Eisenhower and Kennedy years that sought to frighten the USSR from aggressive behavior with the threat of nuclear war. Detente was the foreign policy objectives of the Nixon administration to ease US-USSR tensions in the 1970s.

87. **(A)** During his 1952 campaign for the presidency, Eisenhower announced his strategy to modernize the Republican Party to make it more attractive to the Ameri-

can public. Eisenhower declared that he accepted Roosevelt's New Deal programs but refused to advance beyond them in the domestic arena. As a result, he rejected plans for socialized medicine and notions of increased deficit spending. Eisenhower never supported the policies or tactics of Joseph McCarthy's red baiting politics, nor did he approve of increased military spending or civil rights activism.

88. **(D)** Thurgood Marshall was the first and only black appointed to the US Supreme Court in 1967 by President Johnson. Sandra Day O'Connor was the first woman appointed in 1981 by President Reagan. Burger was the chief justice appointed by Nixon in 1969 and Warren was appointed chief justice by Eisenhower in 1954. Rehnquist was first appointed to the Court in 1971 by President Nixon and named chief justice by Reagan in 1986.

89. **(E)** The Cabinet post of secretary of energy was created in 1977 by President Carter; James Schlesinger was named to fill the post. The department was created by Carter in response to the mounting energy crisis in America. President Johnson's Great Society Program included Medicare for the sick and disabled; a Fair Housing Act to end residential segregation; a Voting Rights Act to end the use of the literacy test against blacks who were seeking to vote in the South; Project Headstart for nursery age children of low income families. All these programs were created in 1964–1965 by President Johnson as part of his war on racism and poverty.

90. **(D)** In 1962, the United States and the Soviet Union nearly engaged in nuclear war over the Soviet placement of offensive nuclear weapons in Cuba. The Soviets began placing the missiles in 1962 in reaction to the United States supported abortive invasion of Cuba in 1961 at the Bay of Pigs. With the discovery of the missiles, the United States established a naval blockade of Cuba and narrowly averted a nuclear war when President Kennedy agreed to a pact with Khruschev: the Soviets would remove the missiles if the United States pledged never to support an invasion of Cuba. Fidel Castro has been Cuba's leader since 1957 when his communist guerrilla forces overthrew Batista. The U.S. continued to operate its naval base in Cuba through the 1980s. Finally, President Kennedy was less enamored with the policy of brinkmanship after the missile crisis.

91. **(C)** In 1973, Syria and Egypt launched an attack on Israel. To convince the United States to remain neutral during the conflict, OPEC (Organization of Petroleum Exporting Countries) established an oil boycott to the United States and its allies. This attempt to utilize American imports of Arab oil supplies as a lever for political blackmail did not reach its desired results, but it did touch off an energy crisis that reached severe proportions in 1973–1974 in America. President Nixon responded to the challenge with Project Independence, an attempt to get the American public to conserve fuel and thus reduce our nation's dependency upon foreign oil supplies. The desired end of the boycott by OPEC was to alter American foreign policy in the Middle East, and not drive Nixon from office, make Americans conserve more fuel through conservation awareness, or bankrupt U.S. oil companies as the latter's profits continued to mount throughout the oil crisis.

92. **(C)** The longest war in terms of U.S. involvement was the Vietnam War (1954–1974), which lasted 20 years. The War of 1812 lasted three years (1812–1815); World War I, two years (1917–1919); Korean War, three years (1950–1953); World War II, four years, (1941–1945).

93. **(B)** Throughout his second term in office, President Reagan faced repeated challenges from Congress regarding his support of the Nicaraguan rebels, called the Contras. Reagan continued to support the Contras against the Communist regime of the Sandinistas under the leadership of Daniel Ortega. Congressional restrictions on Contra aid led some members of the Reagan administration to devise the scheme of "arms for hostages" deals to indirectly provide Contra military aid from the sale of weapons to Iran. Former President Reagan was never directly linked to the Iran-Contra affair, while junior members of the National Security Agency, such as Oliver North and John Poindexter, were indicted as co-conspirators for breaking the applicable Congressional statutes. Iran-Contra proved to be President Reagan's worst foreign policy crisis by far.

94. **(E)** Franklin's famous engraving was intended to muster support for his plan for colonial unity known as the Albany Plan. The other delegates to the 1754 Congress rejected Franklin's plan. The 13 colonies would not be united under a single plan of government until the American Revolution through the Continental Congress and later the Articles of Confederation. The Seven Years' War did not begin until 1756, while the Stamp Act was in 1765. The colonies never sought to break from the system of mercantilism and traded with Canada even during the Seven Years' War.

95. **(D)** In 1991, the Bill of Rights was 200 years old. The United States entered World War II in 1941; the Declaration of Independence was written in 1776; the Constitution was ratified in 1789; the Supreme Court began in 1789.

THE SAT SUBJECT TEST IN

United States History

PRACTICE TEST 5

SAT United States History

Practice Test 5

1. Ⓐ Ⓑ Ⓒ Ⓓ Ⓔ
2. Ⓐ Ⓑ Ⓒ Ⓓ Ⓔ
3. Ⓐ Ⓑ Ⓒ Ⓓ Ⓔ
4. Ⓐ Ⓑ Ⓒ Ⓓ Ⓔ
5. Ⓐ Ⓑ Ⓒ Ⓓ Ⓔ
6. Ⓐ Ⓑ Ⓒ Ⓓ Ⓔ
7. Ⓐ Ⓑ Ⓒ Ⓓ Ⓔ
8. Ⓐ Ⓑ Ⓒ Ⓓ Ⓔ
9. Ⓐ Ⓑ Ⓒ Ⓓ Ⓔ
10. Ⓐ Ⓑ Ⓒ Ⓓ Ⓔ
11. Ⓐ Ⓑ Ⓒ Ⓓ Ⓔ
12. Ⓐ Ⓑ Ⓒ Ⓓ Ⓔ
13. Ⓐ Ⓑ Ⓒ Ⓓ Ⓔ
14. Ⓐ Ⓑ Ⓒ Ⓓ Ⓔ
15. Ⓐ Ⓑ Ⓒ Ⓓ Ⓔ
16. Ⓐ Ⓑ Ⓒ Ⓓ Ⓔ
17. Ⓐ Ⓑ Ⓒ Ⓓ Ⓔ
18. Ⓐ Ⓑ Ⓒ Ⓓ Ⓔ
19. Ⓐ Ⓑ Ⓒ Ⓓ Ⓔ
20. Ⓐ Ⓑ Ⓒ Ⓓ Ⓔ
21. Ⓐ Ⓑ Ⓒ Ⓓ Ⓔ
22. Ⓐ Ⓑ Ⓒ Ⓓ Ⓔ
23. Ⓐ Ⓑ Ⓒ Ⓓ Ⓔ
24. Ⓐ Ⓑ Ⓒ Ⓓ Ⓔ
25. Ⓐ Ⓑ Ⓒ Ⓓ Ⓔ
26. Ⓐ Ⓑ Ⓒ Ⓓ Ⓔ
27. Ⓐ Ⓑ Ⓒ Ⓓ Ⓔ
28. Ⓐ Ⓑ Ⓒ Ⓓ Ⓔ
29. Ⓐ Ⓑ Ⓒ Ⓓ Ⓔ
30. Ⓐ Ⓑ Ⓒ Ⓓ Ⓔ
31. Ⓐ Ⓑ Ⓒ Ⓓ Ⓔ
32. Ⓐ Ⓑ Ⓒ Ⓓ Ⓔ
33. Ⓐ Ⓑ Ⓒ Ⓓ Ⓔ
34. Ⓐ Ⓑ Ⓒ Ⓓ Ⓔ
35. Ⓐ Ⓑ Ⓒ Ⓓ Ⓔ
36. Ⓐ Ⓑ Ⓒ Ⓓ Ⓔ
37. Ⓐ Ⓑ Ⓒ Ⓓ Ⓔ
38. Ⓐ Ⓑ Ⓒ Ⓓ Ⓔ
39. Ⓐ Ⓑ Ⓒ Ⓓ Ⓔ
40. Ⓐ Ⓑ Ⓒ Ⓓ Ⓔ
41. Ⓐ Ⓑ Ⓒ Ⓓ Ⓔ
42. Ⓐ Ⓑ Ⓒ Ⓓ Ⓔ
43. Ⓐ Ⓑ Ⓒ Ⓓ Ⓔ
44. Ⓐ Ⓑ Ⓒ Ⓓ Ⓔ
45. Ⓐ Ⓑ Ⓒ Ⓓ Ⓔ
46. Ⓐ Ⓑ Ⓒ Ⓓ Ⓔ
47. Ⓐ Ⓑ Ⓒ Ⓓ Ⓔ
48. Ⓐ Ⓑ Ⓒ Ⓓ Ⓔ
49. Ⓐ Ⓑ Ⓒ Ⓓ Ⓔ
50. Ⓐ Ⓑ Ⓒ Ⓓ Ⓔ
51. Ⓐ Ⓑ Ⓒ Ⓓ Ⓔ
52. Ⓐ Ⓑ Ⓒ Ⓓ Ⓔ
53. Ⓐ Ⓑ Ⓒ Ⓓ Ⓔ
54. Ⓐ Ⓑ Ⓒ Ⓓ Ⓔ
55. Ⓐ Ⓑ Ⓒ Ⓓ Ⓔ
56. Ⓐ Ⓑ Ⓒ Ⓓ Ⓔ
57. Ⓐ Ⓑ Ⓒ Ⓓ Ⓔ
58. Ⓐ Ⓑ Ⓒ Ⓓ Ⓔ
59. Ⓐ Ⓑ Ⓒ Ⓓ Ⓔ
60. Ⓐ Ⓑ Ⓒ Ⓓ Ⓔ
61. Ⓐ Ⓑ Ⓒ Ⓓ Ⓔ
62. Ⓐ Ⓑ Ⓒ Ⓓ Ⓔ
63. Ⓐ Ⓑ Ⓒ Ⓓ Ⓔ
64. Ⓐ Ⓑ Ⓒ Ⓓ Ⓔ
65. Ⓐ Ⓑ Ⓒ Ⓓ Ⓔ
66. Ⓐ Ⓑ Ⓒ Ⓓ Ⓔ
67. Ⓐ Ⓑ Ⓒ Ⓓ Ⓔ
68. Ⓐ Ⓑ Ⓒ Ⓓ Ⓔ
69. Ⓐ Ⓑ Ⓒ Ⓓ Ⓔ
70. Ⓐ Ⓑ Ⓒ Ⓓ Ⓔ
71. Ⓐ Ⓑ Ⓒ Ⓓ Ⓔ
72. Ⓐ Ⓑ Ⓒ Ⓓ Ⓔ
73. Ⓐ Ⓑ Ⓒ Ⓓ Ⓔ
74. Ⓐ Ⓑ Ⓒ Ⓓ Ⓔ
75. Ⓐ Ⓑ Ⓒ Ⓓ Ⓔ
76. Ⓐ Ⓑ Ⓒ Ⓓ Ⓔ
77. Ⓐ Ⓑ Ⓒ Ⓓ Ⓔ
78. Ⓐ Ⓑ Ⓒ Ⓓ Ⓔ
79. Ⓐ Ⓑ Ⓒ Ⓓ Ⓔ
80. Ⓐ Ⓑ Ⓒ Ⓓ Ⓔ
81. Ⓐ Ⓑ Ⓒ Ⓓ Ⓔ
82. Ⓐ Ⓑ Ⓒ Ⓓ Ⓔ
83. Ⓐ Ⓑ Ⓒ Ⓓ Ⓔ
84. Ⓐ Ⓑ Ⓒ Ⓓ Ⓔ
85. Ⓐ Ⓑ Ⓒ Ⓓ Ⓔ
86. Ⓐ Ⓑ Ⓒ Ⓓ Ⓔ
87. Ⓐ Ⓑ Ⓒ Ⓓ Ⓔ
88. Ⓐ Ⓑ Ⓒ Ⓓ Ⓔ
89. Ⓐ Ⓑ Ⓒ Ⓓ Ⓔ
90. Ⓐ Ⓑ Ⓒ Ⓓ Ⓔ
91. Ⓐ Ⓑ Ⓒ Ⓓ Ⓔ
92. Ⓐ Ⓑ Ⓒ Ⓓ Ⓔ
93. Ⓐ Ⓑ Ⓒ Ⓓ Ⓔ
94. Ⓐ Ⓑ Ⓒ Ⓓ Ⓔ
95. Ⓐ Ⓑ Ⓒ Ⓓ Ⓔ

United States History

PRACTICE TEST 5

TIME: 60 Minutes
95 Questions

DIRECTIONS: Each of the questions or incomplete statements below is followed by five suggested answers or completions. Select the one that is best in each case.

1. In 1867, Secretary of State William Seward purchased what area of land?

   (A) Hawaii
   (B) Puerto Rico
   (C) Guam
   (D) Virgin Islands
   (E) Alaska

2. Which of the following was NOT associated with the independence of Panama and the building of the Panama Canal?

   (A) Colombia
   (B) Costa Rica
   (C) Walter Reed
   (D) Theodore Roosevelt
   (E) Great Britain

3. President Woodrow Wilson sent troops into Mexico because

   (A) Mexico would not pay its debts to the United States.
   (B) Mexico nationalized the oil industry.
   (C) Victoriano Huerta assassinated President Francisco Madera and seized power.
   (D) Pancho Villa raided Columbus, New Mexico, killing 17 Americans.
   (E) A Mexican official arrested American sailors near Tampico, Mexico.

4. According to many historians, the first people to arrive in North America came from

(A) Africa.
(B) Asia.
(C) Europe.
(D) the South Pacific.
(E) South America.

5. Which of the following statements best describes American attitudes toward World War I prior to 1917?

(A) American sympathies were divided but they supported the president's policy of neutrality.
(B) Americans generally opposed neutrality and wanted to enter the war on the side of the English.
(C) Americans believed that the war had nothing to do with the United States.
(D) Americans generally opposed neutrality and wanted to enter the war on the side of the Germans.
(E) Americans believed that Congress should forbid Americans from travelling on British and French ships and from selling war materials to nations at war.

6. Which of the following led to European discovery and exploration of the Americas?

(A) the discovery of new land routes to Asia
(B) the breakdown of the Genoese and Venetian monopoly over Mediterranean-European trade
(C) the decline of commercial banking
(D) the development of new navigational instruments
(E) the success of the Crusades in bringing Christian control of the Middle East

7. What World War I battle, in which the Americans were involved, turned the tide against Germany?

(A) Belleau Wood
(B) Somme Offensive
(C) Second Battle of the Marne
(D) Saint Mihiel Salient
(E) Meuse-Argonne Offensive

8. Roger Williams came into conflict with the Puritan authorities for advocating

   (A) that the land belonged by right to the English.

   (B) that government rested upon the consent of the governed.

   (C) that political leaders could have no authority over religious matters.

   (D) that religion should be based on direct intuition of God and his love.

   (E) that no one had the right to worship according to their individual conscience.

9. In what decade did Congress first require that an annual budget be developed?

   (A) 1920s
   (B) 1890s
   (C) 1950s
   (D) 1830s
   (E) 1860s

10. Which of the following was NOT one of the Middle Colonies?

   (A) New Jersey
   (B) Connecticut
   (C) New York
   (D) Delaware
   (E) Pennsylvania

11. The National Labor Relations Act (1935) aided the labor movement by

   (A) legalizing labor organizations.

   (B) establishing government mediation in labor disputes.

   (C) outlawing establishment of company unions.

   (D) creating the National Labor Relations Board.

   (E) guaranteeing the right of collective bargaining.

12. Which of the following does NOT characterize French settlement in the New World?

   (A) The French controlled access to the Mississippi River and the St. Lawrence River.

   (B) The French established trade in furs.

   (C) The French developed widespread settlement in the interior of the continent.

   (D) The French established a single government for all of New France.

   (E) The French generally established good relations with the Indians.

13. A people who dominated a large kingdom in the Andes Mountains of Peru when the first Europeans arrived were the

(A) Incas.
(B) Mayas.
(C) Aztecs.
(D) Mohicans.
(E) Pueblos.

14. Which of the following ethnic groups won the right to U.S. citizenship in 1924?

(A) Blacks
(B) Mexican Americans
(C) Indians
(D) Japanese
(E) Chinese

15. The key British victory in the French and Indian War was at

(A) Louisburg.
(B) Fort Frontenac.
(C) Fort Duquesne.
(D) Crown Point.
(E) Ticonderoga.

16. In the 1920s women were affected by all of the following EXCEPT

(A) the Equal Rights Amendment.
(B) the right to vote in national elections.
(C) increasing opportunities for employment.
(D) labor-saving devices for the home.
(E) a new freedom in social roles.

17. In 1972 Richard Nixon dramatically visited what country?

(A) the Soviet Union
(B) China
(C) Cambodia
(D) South Vietnam
(E) Egypt

18. Which of the following prevented the entrance of Texas into the Union after it gained independence in 1836?

(A) Texas wanted to permit slavery
(B) opposition to Mexicans residing within American territory

(C) inability to control Indian tribes in the area

(D) the influence of Catholicism on Texas

(E) disagreement over the southern boundary of Texas

19. The "Middle Passage" refers to

(A) the route travelled by Louis and Clark through the Rocky Mountains.

(B) the route to the Orient sought by Henry Hudson.

(C) the road established between Cumberland, Maryland and Vandalia, Illinois.

(D) the route across Panama for those heading to the California gold fields.

(E) the voyage between Africa and the Americas taken by the slave traders.

20. The Johnson Act of 1924 favored immigrants from

(A) Asia.

(B) Latin America.

(C) Eastern Europe.

(D) Southern Europe.

(E) Northern Europe.

21. All of the following were advocates of religious toleration EXCEPT

(A) William Penn.

(B) John Winthrop.

(C) Roger Williams.

(D) Lord Baltimore.

(E) Thomas Jefferson.

22. In 1937 the United States joined Great Britain and France by not intervening in a civil war in what European country?

(A) Czechoslovakia

(B) Poland

(C) Greece

(D) Spain

(E) Hungary

23. According to British mercantilist policy, the colonies would perform all of the following functions EXCEPT

(A) provide markets for British goods.

(B) produce manufactured goods.

(C) provide raw materials for British manufacturing.

(D) encourage the growth of a strong merchant fleet.

(E) provide bases for the Royal Navy.

24. Which of the following did NOT contribute to the achieving of Allied initiative in both the Pacific and Europe in 1942?

    (A) surrender of Corregidor

    (B) Battle of the Coral Sea

    (C) invasion of the Solomons

    (D) Battle of El Alamein

    (E) invasion of North Africa

25. The Intolerable Acts of 1774 were passed in response to

    (A) the Boston Tea Party.

    (B) the Boston Massacre.

    (C) formation of the Continental Congress.

    (D) the *Gaspee* affair.

    (E) creation of the Committee of Correspondence.

26. Who was the Supreme Commander of the Allied troops that invaded Western Europe in June, 1944?

    (A) Omar Bradley

    (B) Bernard Montgomery

    (C) Dwight D. Eisenhower

    (D) George S. Patton

    (E) George C. Marshall

27. Which of the following served as an American commander during the American Revolution?

    (A) William Howe

    (B) John Burgoyne

    (C) Nathaniel Greene

    (D) Barry St. Leger

    (E) Henry Clinton

28. As established in 1945, the Security Council of the United Nations was to

    (A) make recommendations for the peaceful settlement of disputes.

    (B) decide legal questions referred to it by disputing nations.

(C) look after the welfare of people in colonial areas.

(D) make recommendations regarding world economic, social, cultural, and health problems.

(E) was to be the police authority, responsible for preventing war.

29. The Constitutional Convention took place in 1787 in what city?

(A) New York

(B) Philadelphia

(C) Washington, D.C.

(D) Baltimore

(E) Boston

30. Right-to-work laws stipulate that

(A) workers must join a union within a specified time after they are hired.

(B) unions are illegal.

(C) workers must join a union before they are hired.

(D) workers cannot be required to join a union.

(E) there must be an 80-day cooling-off period before a strike can go into effect.

31. Alexander Hamilton's "Report on Public Credit" proposed which of the following?

(A) to repudiate the Confederate debts

(B) to establish a protective tariff

(C) to offer bonuses to encourage manufacturing

(D) to assume the state debts

(E) to establish a national bank

32. The U.N. coalition's main objective in Operation Desert Storm, as expressed by President Bush, was to

(A) establish democracy.

(B) expel Iraq from Kuwait.

(C) take over the Iraqi oil supply.

(D) establish an area for new Muslim settlements.

(E) punish Saddam Hussein.

33. Under Thomas Jefferson, the Republicans

(A) reversed Federalist measures for funding the national debt.

(B) renewed the charter of the Bank of the United States.

(C) reduced the federal budget.

(D) enlarged the United States Army.

(E) increased the national debt.

34. Which of the following books argued that Americans were neglecting the public sector in their pursuit of personal wealth?

(A) *Invisible Man*

(B) *The Organization Man*

(C) *The Affluent Society*

(D) *The Man in the Gray Flannel Suit*

(E) *The Lonely Crowd*

35.

Wisconsin Republicans 1897–1903
Percentage Distribution by Occupation

	Farmers	*Merchants*	*Professionals*	*Manufacturers*	*Financiers*	*Workers*
Progressives	20	27	26	13	9	5
Moderates	22	24	29	6	13	6
Conservatives	12	27	32	16	10	3

Based on the above chart, the balance of which of the following groups leaned toward the moderate-progressive wing of the Republican party?

(A) farmers

(B) merchants

(C) professionals

(D) manufacturers

(E) financiers

36. Which of the following does NOT describe farming in the early twentieth century?

(A) Growth of urban populations resulted in a growing demand for farm products.

(B) Farmers increasingly turned to commercial agriculture, concentrating on only a few products.

(C) The federal government gave no aid to agriculture except through the tariff system.

(D) After the turn of the century, farming became increasingly mechanized.

(E) Scientific knowledge began to revolutionize agriculture.

37. Which of the following was NOT a significant factor in the presidential campaign of 1968?

(A) George C. Wallace

(B) Barry Goldwater

(C) Richard M. Nixon

(D) Hubert Humphrey

(E) Eugene McCarthy

38. The income tax was successfully included as a part of what piece of Wilsonian legislation?

(A) Underwood Tariff Act

(B) Federal Reserve Act

(C) Clayton Antitrust Act

(D) Federal Trade Commission Act

(E) Smith-Lever Act

39. Who is the only president to have served by appointment rather than election?

(A) Andrew Johnson

(B) Chester A. Arthur

(C) John Tyler

(D) Gerald Ford

(E) Lyndon Johnson

40. Which of the following has NOT been identified as a cause of the Great Depression of the 1930s?

(A) the high tariffs of the United States

(B) uneven distribution of income

(C) the increasing strength of organized labor

(D) excessive borrowing of money

(E) worldwide dislocation of trade during and after World War I

41. The Adams-Onis Treaty (1819) gave the United States
    (A) Louisiana.
    (B) Oregon.
    (C) Texas.
    (D) California.
    (E) Florida.

42. Which of the following did NOT follow the Montivideo Pact (1933) in which the United States agreed not to interfere in the internal or external affairs of its neighbors?
    (A) cancellation of the Platt Amendment
    (B) withdrawal of American troops from Nicaragua
    (C) removal of American troops from Haiti
    (D) ending of control over customs houses of the Dominican Republic
    (E) giving up of the American right to intervene in the affairs of Panama

43. President Lyndon Johnson sent American troops into what Caribbean nation?
    (A) Haiti
    (B) Cuba
    (C) Grenada
    (D) Jamaica
    (E) Dominican Republic

44. Which of the following is NOT associated with the "American System"?
    (A) a protective tariff to stimulate new industries
    (B) Henry Clay
    (C) the Second Bank of the United States
    (D) federally funded internal improvements
    (E) bonuses to new industries

45. The Kerner Commission (1967–68) investigated what national problem?
    (A) protests against the Vietnam War
    (B) inflation
    (C) energy
    (D) education
    (E) racial violence

46. In her diary, Mary Boykin Chesnut wrote the following:

"God forgive us, but ours is a monstrous system, a wrong and an iniquity! Like the patriarchs of old, our men live all in one house with their wives and their concubines; and the mulattoes one sees in every family partly resemble the white children...."

".... On one side Mrs. Stowe, Greeley, Thoreau, Emerson, Sumner. They live in nice New England homes, clean, sweet-smelling, shut up in libraries, writing books which ease their hearts of their bitterness against us.... Now consider what I have seen of my mother's life, my grandmother's, my mother-in-law's. These people were educated at Northern schools, they read the same books as their Northern contemporaries, the same daily papers, the same Bible. They have the same ideas of right and wrong, are highbred, lovely, good, pious, doing their duty as they conceive it. They live in Negro villages. They do not preach and teach hate as the gospel, and the sacred duty of murder and insurrection; but they strive to ameliorate the condition of these Africans in every particular. They set them the example of a perfect life, a life of utter self-abnegation. Think of these holy New Englanders forced to have a Negro village walk through their houses whenever they see fit, dirty, slatternly, idle, ill-smelling by nature. These women I love ... have a swarm of blacks about them like children under their care, not as Mrs. Stowe's fancy painted them, and they hate slavery worse than Mrs. Stowe does."

Which of the following best characterizes this diary entry by Mary Boykin Chesnut?

(A) Northerners understand slavery better than Southerners.

(B) Southern women who have to live with slavery are more antislavery than Northerners.

(C) Blacks are equal to whites.

(D) Northern writers present an accurate picture of slavery.

(E) The Southern social structure presents a superior moral order to that of the North.

47. The most important difference between the South and other sections of the United States prior to 1860 was which of the following?

(A) slavery

(B) economic diversification

(C) rural patterns of living

(D) development of transportation systems

(E) population growth

48. The 26th Amendment to the Constitution provided for

(A) presidential succession.

(B) the right to vote for 18-year-olds.

(C) limiting the president to two terms.

(D) equal rights for women.

(E) the right of residents of the District of Columbia to participate in national elections.

49. Which of the following does NOT correctly describe the Korean War?

(A) Chinese troops entered the war in December 1950.

(B) The United States bombed China.

(C) United States forces fought as part of the United Nations command.

(D) Douglas MacArthur and President Harry S. Truman disagreed over the blockading of China.

(E) The war resulted in recognition of the division of Korea into two countries.

50. The Jacksonian era was notable for its

(A) decrease in the number of active voters.

(B) destruction of the spoils system.

(C) opposition to party nominating conventions.

(D) support of Indian rights.

(E) rhetorical egalitarianism.

51. What writer probably did more than any other single person in bringing the United States to environmental awareness?

(A) John Kenneth Galbraith

(B) George Gilder

(C) Michael Harrington

(D) Rachel Carson

(E) Betty Friedan

52. Which of the following presidents was most concerned with conservation?

(A) William McKinley

(B) Woodrow Wilson

(C) Grover Cleveland

(D) Theodore Roosevelt

(E) Benjamin Harrison

53. Which of the following statements correctly describes farming on the Great Plains?

(A) Farmers on the Great Plains successfully used the same agricultural techniques they had used in the East.

(B) Farmers on the Great Plains found the 160 acres given by the Homestead Act adequate for their needs.

(C) Farmers on the Great Plains had to turn to new technologies such as barbed wire and windmills in order to succeed.

(D) Farmers and cattle ranchers experienced few conflicts.

(E) Farmers on the Great Plains found abundant wood for buildings and fences.

54. Helen Hunt Jackson's *A Century of Dishonor* (1881) dealt with which of the following?

(A) relations with the Indians

(B) political corruption

(C) treatment of blacks

(D) temperance

(E) industrial monopolies

55. Which of the following statements correctly describes the building of the Western railroads?

(A) The Western railroads were built without government aid.

(B) The Western railroads were built to connect existing cities.

(C) The Western railroads were adequately financed.

(D) The Western railroads were carefully planned to avoid direct competition.

(E) The Western railroads became involved in major political and financial scandals.

56. Which of the following Black leaders was involved in the efforts that led to the establishment of the NAACP?

(A) W.E.B. DuBois

(B) Frederick Douglass

(C) Martin Luther King

(D) Booker T. Washington

(E) A. Philip Randolph

57. The Interstate Commerce Act (1887) provided for which of the following?

(A) allowed railroads to make pooling arrangements

(B) forbade railroads from charging more for a short haul than a long haul over the same line

(C) allowed railroads to give rebates

(D) nationalized the railroads

(E) gave the Interstate Commerce Commission authority to fix rates and enforce its decisions

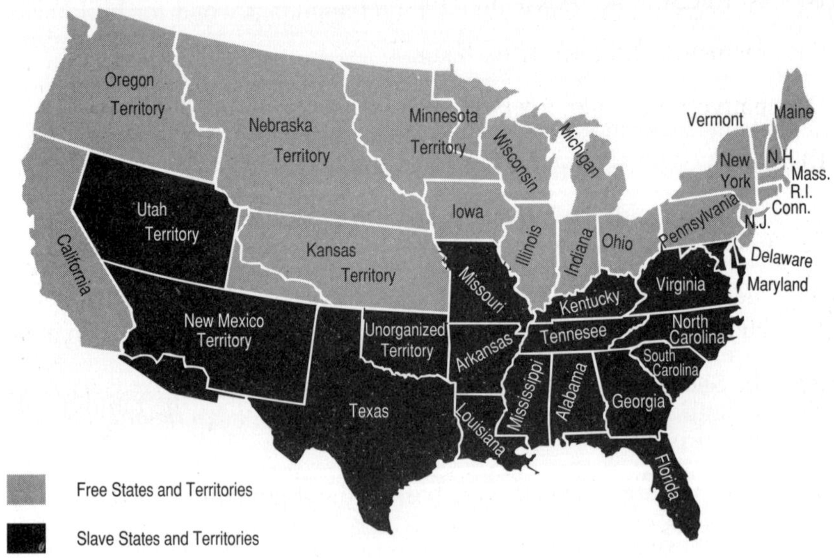

58. This map represents slave and free areas of the United States as of

(A) 1821.
(B) 1850.
(C) 1854.
(D) 1861.
(E) 1865.

59. What group of immigrants prior to the Civil War helped stimulate formation of the American or "Know-Nothing" party?

(A) Italians
(B) Russian Jews
(C) Slavs
(D) Irish
(E) Chinese

60. The immigration of what ethnic group led to tensions on the West Coast in the late nineteenth century?

    (A) Italians
    (B) Blacks
    (C) Jews
    (D) Chinese
    (E) Irish

61. The term "scalawag" was used during Reconstruction to describe

    (A) the freed slaves.
    (B) Northerners who came into the South.
    (C) members of the Ku Klux Klan.
    (D) native-born Southerners who cooperated with the Northerners.
    (E) blacks who served in the Southern state legislatures.

62. The "Crime of '73" refers to

    (A) the Bland-Allison bill which required the Treasury Department to purchase between $2 million and $4 million worth of silver each month.
    (B) the Sherman Silver Purchase Act which required the Treasury Department to purchase 4.5 million ounces of silver each month.
    (C) the removal of silver coins from the list of standard coins.
    (D) the decision to purchase silver at the ratio of 16 to 1 in relation to gold.
    (E) the refusal to coin silver purchased by the Treasury Department.

63. Which of the following events did NOT take place during the Civil War (1861–1865)?

    (A) Morrill Tariff Act
    (B) National Banking Act
    (C) Homestead Act
    (D) Conscription Act
    (E) Tenure of Office Act

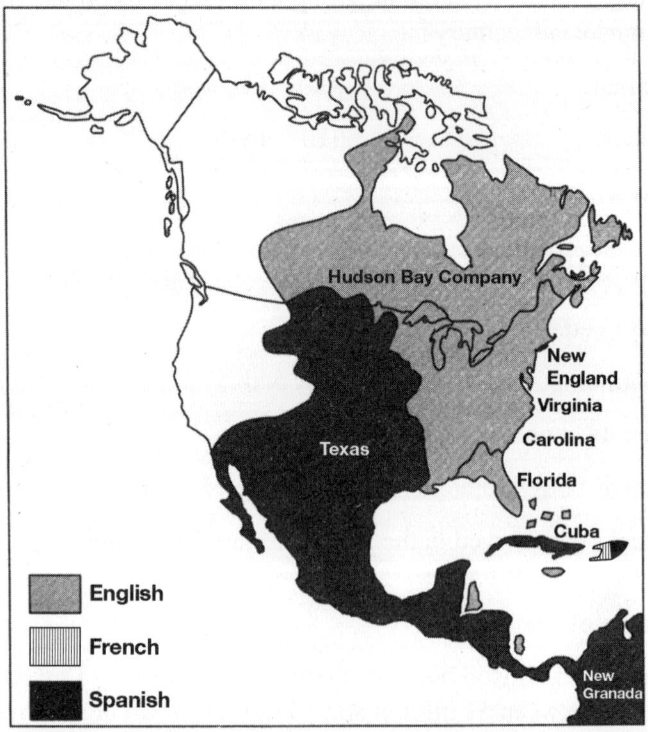

64. This map represents European powers in North America as of

(A) 1600.
(B) 1682.
(C) 1713.
(D) 1763.
(E) 1783.

65. By 1860 approximately how many slaves lived in the South?

(A) 2 million
(B) 3 million
(C) 4 million
(D) 5 million
(E) 6 million

66. Jane Addams is most closely associated with which of the following?

(A) temperance reform
(B) women's suffrage
(C) higher education for women
(D) Protestant missions
(E) the settlement house movement

67. Andrew Jackson contributed to the depression of 1837 by doing which of the following?

    (A) placing federal funds in the Bank of the United States

    (B) issuing the Specie Circular

    (C) establishing the Independent Treasury

    (D) opposing the Ordinance of Nullification

    (E) vetoing the renewal of the charter of the Bank of the United States

68. The 12th Amendment (1804) to the Constitution

    (A) required the Electoral College to vote separately for president and vice president.

    (B) provided for freedom of religion.

    (C) limited the president to two terms.

    (D) prohibited the manufacture and sale of alcoholic beverages.

    (E) gave the right to bear arms.

69. In a 1750 sermon, Jonathan Mayhew stated:

    "... If the end of all civil government be the good of society; if this be the thing that is aimed at in constituting civil rulers; and if the motive and argument for submission to government, be taken from the apparent usefulness of civil authority, it follows, that when no such good end can be answered by submission, there remains no argument or motive to enforce it; if, instead of this good end's being brought about by submission, a *contrary end* is brought about, and the ruin and misery of society effected by it, here is a plain and positive reason against submission in all such cases, should they ever happen.

    And therefore, in such cases, a regard to the public welfare ought to make us withhold from our rulers, that obedience and submission which it would otherwise be our duty to render to them.... Not to discontinue our allegiance, in this case, would be to join with the sovereign in promoting slavery and misery of that society, the welfare of which we ourselves, as well as our sovereign, are indispensably obliged to secure and promote as far as in us lies."

    In this sermon, Mayhew is arguing that

    (A) slavery is a moral evil.

    (B) submission to civil rulers must depend on their contribution to the public good.

    (C) the civil rulers define what is good for the public welfare.

(D) government is founded on the natural rights of the citizens.

(E) Scripture teaches submission to governmental authorities.

70. The Ostend Manifesto of 1854 concerned which of the following?

(A) Hawaii
(B) Alaska
(C) Puerto Rico
(D) Cuba
(E) Guam

71. The Declaratory Act of 1766

(A) required the colonists to provide barracks and supplies for British troops.

(B) forbade the American colonists to issue paper money.

(C) established a new duty on molasses.

(D) stated that Parliament had the power to make laws binding on the colonies.

(E) established a tax on licenses, legal documents, and newspapers.

72. The Chautauqua movement was

(A) a political movement advocating better wages and hours for workers.

(B) an artistic movement which emphasized abstract forms.

(C) a religious movement promoting Protestant missions.

(D) an educational movement utilizing lectures and sermons.

(E) a philosophical movement that defined truth in terms of results.

73. Which of the following writers was NOT a part of the "American Renaissance" of the mid-nineteenth century?

(A) Henry James
(B) Nathaniel Hawthorne
(C) Walt Whitman
(D) Henry David Thoreau
(E) Herman Melville

Source: From the collection of Macculloch Hall Historical Museum, Morristown, NJ

74. In this cartoon Thomas Nast presents Boss Tweed as

    (A) a politician ruled by greed.

    (B) a benefactor of the public.

    (C) a political reformer.

    (D) a politician corruptly influenced by business.

    (E) a politician who rejected business influence.

75. Secessionist feeling during the War of 1812 was strong in

    (A) New England and the West.

    (B) New England.

    (C) the South.

(D) the South and West.

(E) the West.

76. The first nationally important writer from west of the Mississippi was

(A) William Dean Howells.
(B) Samuel L. Clemens.
(C) Edith Wharton.
(D) Edward Eggleston.
(E) Joel Chandler Harris.

77. Which of the following is associated with early English settlement in the New World?

(A) joint-stock companies
(B) encomienda
(C) Prince Henry the Navigator
(D) George III
(E) republicanism

78. As president, John F. Kennedy successfully put through Congress all of the following EXCEPT the

(A) Manpower Development and Training Act.
(B) Trade Expansion Act.
(C) Area Redevelopment Act.
(D) Housing Act.
(E) Civil Rights Act.

79. Who was the first Democratic president to be re-elected since Franklin Delano Roosevelt's election to a second term in 1936?

(A) Harry Truman
(B) Bill Clinton
(C) Lyndon Johnson
(D) Jimmy Carter
(E) Hubert Humphrey

80. By what decade did all of the Southern states segregate Blacks in schools, streetcars, and railroad stations?

(A) 1860s
(B) 1870s
(C) 1880s
(D) 1890s
(E) 1900s

81. By the middle 1760s the most influential citizens in the New England towns were the

(A) ministers.
(B) artisans.
(C) merchants.
(D) farmers.
(E) laborers.

82. Where did the United States Army fight against native revolutionaries in the early twentieth century?

(A) Philippines
(B) Hawaii
(C) Cuba
(D) Samoa
(E) Puerto Rico

83. Which of the following was NOT a Union strategy in the Civil War?

(A) to fight a defensive war
(B) to blockade the Confederate coastline
(C) to seize control of the Mississippi River
(D) to seize Richmond, Virginia
(E) to control the interior railroad lines of the South

84. Which of the following became president upon the assassination of Abraham Lincoln?

(A) Ulysses S. Grant
(B) Andrew Johnson
(C) Rutherford B. Hayes
(D) James A. Garfield
(E) Chester A. Arthur

85. The Pendleton Act (1883) attempted to establish

(A) equal treatment for blacks and whites.

(B) efficient city government.

(C) civil service reform.

(D) limits on business monopolies.

(E) prohibition of alcoholic beverages.

86. Which of the following groups opposed Franklin D. Roosevelt and his New Deal?

(A) blacks

(B) small businessmen

(C) labor

(D) farmers

(E) progressive Republicans

87. Which of the following was NOT a Progressive reform?

(A) direct election of the president

(B) Australian ballot

(C) initiative

(D) referendum

(E) direct election of senators

88. Which of the following worked to improve conditions for prisoners and the mentally ill?

(A) Louisa May Alcott

(B) Margaret Fuller

(C) Lucretia Mott

(D) Dorothea Dix

(E) Sarah Josepha Hale

89. Which of the following became a major exponent of the architectural principle "form follows function"?

(A) Thomas Eakins

(B) August Saint-Gaudens

(C) Frank Lloyd Wright

(D) Winslow Homer

(E) Mary Cassatt

90. The ordinances of 1785 and 1787 established all of the following EXCEPT

(A) division of the Northwestern lands into townships.

(B) reservation of one section in each township for support of public schools.

(C) establishment of territorial government.

(D) protection of slavery.

(E) a procedure for achieving statehood.

91. Which of the following was NOT a significant means of business consolidation in the late nineteenth century?

(A) corporation pools

(B) multinational corporation

(C) trust

(D) holding company

(E) interlocking directorate

92. Henry Ford contributed to the advance of American industry by developing

(A) efficiency engineering.

(B) the moving assembly line.

(C) use of electrical power in industry.

(D) collective bargaining.

(E) interchangeable parts.

93. Which of the following contributed significantly to the growth of anti-slavery sentiment in the 1850s?

(A) the establishment of the American Anti-Slavery Society

(B) publication of *Uncle Tom's Cabin*

(C) William Lloyd Garrison's founding of *The Liberator*

(D) passage of the "Gag" rule by the House of Representatives

(E) creation of the Liberty Party

94. The panic of 1857 fundamentally resulted from

(A) the violence in Kansas.

(B) the economic impact of gold from California.

(C) the Dred Scott decision.

(D) excessive investments in railroads.

(E) the secessionist movement in the South.

95. In the following cartoon Ulysses Grant is presented as

(A) adequately prepared for a third term.

(B) honest and competent.

(C) caught up in several types of corruption.

(D) weeding out corruption.

(E) a powerful president.

Source: U.S. Library of Congress

SAT United States History

Practice Test 5
ANSWER KEY

1.	**(E)**	26.	**(C)**	51.	**(D)**	76.	**(B)**
2.	**(B)**	27.	**(C)**	52.	**(D)**	77.	**(A)**
3.	**(D)**	28.	**(E)**	53.	**(C)**	78.	**(E)**
4.	**(B)**	29.	**(B)**	54.	**(A)**	79.	**(B)**
5.	**(A)**	30.	**(D)**	55.	**(E)**	80.	**(D)**
6.	**(D)**	31.	**(D)**	56.	**(A)**	81.	**(C)**
7.	**(C)**	32.	**(B)**	57.	**(B)**	82.	**(A)**
8.	**(C)**	33.	**(C)**	58.	**(D)**	83.	**(A)**
9.	**(A)**	34.	**(C)**	59.	**(D)**	84.	**(B)**
10.	**(B)**	35.	**(A)**	60.	**(D)**	85.	**(C)**
11.	**(E)**	36.	**(C)**	61.	**(D)**	86.	**(B)**
12.	**(C)**	37.	**(B)**	62.	**(C)**	87.	**(A)**
13.	**(A)**	38.	**(A)**	63.	**(E)**	88.	**(D)**
14.	**(C)**	39.	**(D)**	64.	**(D)**	89.	**(C)**
15.	**(A)**	40.	**(C)**	65.	**(C)**	90.	**(D)**
16.	**(A)**	41.	**(E)**	66.	**(E)**	91.	**(B)**
17.	**(B)**	42.	**(B)**	67.	**(B)**	92.	**(B)**
18.	**(A)**	43.	**(E)**	68.	**(A)**	93.	**(B)**
19.	**(E)**	44.	**(E)**	69.	**(B)**	94.	**(D)**
20.	**(E)**	45.	**(E)**	70.	**(D)**	95.	**(C)**
21.	**(B)**	46.	**(B)**	71.	**(D)**		
22.	**(D)**	47.	**(A)**	72.	**(D)**		
23.	**(B)**	48.	**(B)**	73.	**(A)**		
24.	**(A)**	49.	**(B)**	74.	**(A)**		
25.	**(A)**	50.	**(E)**	75.	**(B)**		

Detailed Explanations of Answers

PRACTICE TEST 5

1. **(E)** Seward purchased Alaska from Russia in 1867 for $7 million, thereby raising a storm of controversy.

2. **(B)** Panama gained its independence, probably with Theodore Roosevelt's help, from Colombia in 1903. Earlier, in 1901, Great Britain had agreed to give up its rights in the building and control of the canal. Walter Reed led the team that conquered yellow fever and made the building of the canal possible.

3. **(D)** In 1916 President Wilson sent American troops under General John J. Pershing into Mexico after Pancho Villa had raided New Mexico. This took place after several years of revolutionary turmoil in Mexico, including the assassination of Madera in 1913 and the arrest of the American sailors in 1914.

4. **(B)** Most historians believe that the first people to come to the Americas travelled from Siberia across what is now the Bering Strait to Alaska and then Southward. These events are dated between 10,000 and 25,000 years ago.

5. **(A)** Because of their ethnic loyalties, American sympathies were divided, but they generally supported the president's policy of neutrality. William Jennings Bryan resigned as secretary of state in 1915 because he believed that the U.S. should forbid Americans from traveling on British and French ships. He also wanted Congress to forbid Americans from selling war materials to nations at war. After the sinking of the *Lusitania*, most Americans realized that the war affected American interests.

6. **(D)** Under Prince Henry of Portugal new navigational instruments, such as the compass and astrolabe, were developed which, along with improvements in sailing ships, made long-distance ocean voyages possible. The Crusades, although not bringing Christian control to the Middle East, helped stimulate the Renaissance, which in turn developed interest in the larger world. The Genoese and Venetian monopoly created interest in finding new routes to the east while the development of banking put together capital for financing the search for new trade routes.

7. **(C)** The Second Battle of the Marne (July 18–August 6, 1918) is generally regarded as the turning point of the war. The other battles took place as follows: Belleau Wood (June 6–July 1, 1918), Somme Offensive (August 8, 1918), Saint Mihiel Salient (Sept. 12–16, 1918), and the Meuse-Argonne Offensive (Sept. 26–Nov. 11, 1918).

8. **(C)** Roger Williams came into conflict with the Puritan authorities because he argued that political leaders could have no authority over religious matters, that the English settlers must buy the land from the Indians, and that individuals had the right to worship according to their individual conscience. After establishing the colony of Rhode Island, Williams included the principle that government rested upon the consent of the governed in the 1644 charter. Anne Hutchinson was exiled from Massachusetts Bay Colony for advocating that religion should be based on direct intuition of God and his love rather than religious authorities.

9. **(A)** With the passage of the Budget and Accounting Act of 1921, Congress required for the first time that an annual budget be prepared. Prior to this time, Congress had made appropriations on a piecemeal basis.

10. **(B)** Connecticut was part of New England. Pennsylvania, Delaware, New Jersey, and New York constituted the Middle Colonies.

11. **(E)** The National Labor Relations Act, or Wagner Act, of 1935 reaffirmed the right of collective bargaining which had first appeared in Section 7a of the National Industrial Recovery Act of 1933. Franklin Roosevelt had created the National Labor Relations Board in 1934; the National Labor Relations Act made this Board a permanent body.

12. **(C)** French settlement was largely confined to the area north of Montreal to the mouth of the St. Lawrence River. In addition to controlling the St. Lawrence River, the French also controlled access to the Mississippi at New Orleans. Unlike the thirteen British Colonies, New France had one central government. And also unlike the British, the French, who emphasized the fur trade, tended not to establish permanent settlements in the interior and therefore did not threaten the forests and game necessary to Indian life. The Six Nations, however, never allied with the French.

13. **(A)** The Incas built the most advanced culture in South America in the Andes Mountains region of Peru. At their height, in the sixteenth century, they may have controlled a population of about 12 million people. Inca society was strictly stratified, and the emperor ruled with the assistance of an aristocratic bureaucracy. The Incas developed an elaborate irrigation system to support their agricultural economy; they grew maize, potatoes, squash, tomatoes, cassava, and cotton. They built an extensive network of roads, one of which was about 2,250 miles long. They also constructed suspension bridges made of vines and dug rock tunnels through the mountains. A message system based on relay runners was able to deliver news as fast as 150 miles a day. The other tribes did not live in South America.

14. **(C)** The entire American Indian population received American citizenship in 1924. Blacks had become citizens in 1868. Mexican-Americans began receiving citizenship in 1848. The Chinese Exclusion Act of 1882 denied American citizenship to Chinese born in China and remained in effect until World War II. The immigration act of 1924 effectively closed the door to both Japanese and Chinese immigration.

15. **(A)** The fall of Louisburg in 1758 gave the British a base from which they could cut off French reinforcements and supplies to America. The British conquered Fort Frontenac and Fort Duquesne in 1758 and Crown Point and Fort Ticonderoga in 1759.

16. **(A)** Although the Woman's Party advocated the Equal Rights Amendment it did not attain passage. The 19th Amendment gave women the right to vote in national elections for the first time in 1920. An increasing number of jobs were available for women in both industries and offices. Devices such as washing machines and vacuum cleaners made housework easier. And women such as the "flappers" rejected older social conventions in favor of such things as lipstick and bobbed hair.

17. **(B)** Richard Nixon visited China in 1972, after 23 years of American non-recognition of the communist regime. This visit paved the way for formal recognition by Jimmy Carter.

18. **(A)** The principal reason for opposition to Texas' entrance into the Union was that it wanted to permit slavery. There was also concern over possible war with Mexico, because it did not recognize Texan independence. Texas entered the Union in 1845.

19. **(E)** The "Middle Passage" refers to the slave traders' route between Africa and the Americas during which thirteen to thirty-three percent of the slaves died. Lewis and Clark crossed the Rocky Mountains at the Bozeman Pass on their 1804–06 expedition. Henry Hudson sought the Northwest Passage in 1609. The National Road was built between 1806 and 1852, connecting Maryland and Illinois. Gold seekers crossed the Isthmus of Panama in 1849.

20. **(E)** By establishing quotas based on a percentage of a national group living in the United States in 1890, the Johnson Act effectively favored Northern Europeans and discriminated against the "New Immigration."

21. **(B)** John Winthrop, Governor of Massachusetts Bay Colony, opposed religious toleration, supporting the banishment of Roger Williams and Anne Hutchinson. William Penn established toleration in Pennsylvania, Roger Williams in Rhode Island, and Lord Baltimore in Maryland. Later Thomas Jefferson wrote the Virginia Statute for Religious Freedom (1786).

22. **(D)** Congress in 1937 banned all shipments of war materials to either side in the Spanish Civil War.

23. **(B)** Through laws such as the Wool Act (1699) colonial manufacturing was severely restricted.

24. **(A)** The Americans and Filipinos surrendered at Corregidor in May 1942. The British-American force defeated the Japanese in the Battle of the Coral Sea in May 1942. The U.S. invaded the Solomons in August of the same year and repelled

a Japanese attempt to retake the islands in November. British General Bernard L. Montgomery forced the German army back at El Alamein and Dwight D. Eisenhower landed with a British, American, and Canadian force in North Africa in November 1942.

25. **(A)** The Intolerable Acts, which included the closing of the Port of Boston, were passed in response to the Boston Tea Party of 1773. The Boston Massacre (1770), Continental Congress (1774), *Gaspee* affair (1772), and the Committee of Correspondence (1772) were other elements in the growing tension between Great Britain and its American colonies.

26. **(C)** Dwight D. Eisenhower was the Supreme Commander of the Allied troops that invaded the Normandy beaches on June 6, 1944. Omar Bradley, Bernard Montgomery, and George S. Patton served under Eisenhower. George C. Marshall served as the chief of staff of the United States Army during World War II.

27. **(C)** Nathaniel Greene served as commander of the American troops in the South. The other individuals were all British commanders during the American Revolution.

28. **(E)** The Security Council was to be the police authority of the world, responsible for preventing war. The General Assembly was to make recommendations for the peaceful settlement of disputes. The International Court of Justice was to decide legal questions referred to it by disputing nations. The Trusteeship Council was to look after colonial areas. The Economic and Social Council was to make recommendations regarding world economic, social, cultural, and health problems.

29. **(B)** The Constitutional Convention met in Philadelphia from May 14 to September 17, 1787. Washington, D.C., did not yet exist.

30. **(D)** Under the Taft-Hartley Act (1947) states were allowed to pass "right-to-work" laws which banned union-shop agreements which required workers to join a union within a specified time after they were hired. The Act also banned closed-shop agreements which required workers to belong to a union before they were hired and gave the president power to require an 80-day cooling off period before a strike went into effect.

31. **(D)** Hamilton's "Report on Public Credit" (1790) proposed to assume both the state debts and the debts of the Confederation. In other proposals he sought the establishment of a national bank, a protective tariff, and bounties to encourage manufacturing.

32. **(B)** After forcing Iraq out of Kuwait and seeing the multinational force advance into Iraq itself, all within a mere four days into the ground war, George Bush ordered the end of offensive actions in the Gulf, stating that liberating Kuwait was the single objective of the United Nations resolution. Some criticized Bush for this, noting that he could have continued into Baghdad and removed Hussein from power.

33. **(C)** Largely by reducing the size of the army and navy, Jefferson was able to reduce the federal budget. Although he opposed the Bank of the United States and assumption of state debts, he did not change Federalist policies. Secretary of the Treasury Albert Gallatin tried to pay off the national debt as rapidly as possible.

34. **(C)** John Kenneth Galbraith's *The Affluent Society* was one of the important books of the 1950s, arguing that America was neglecting the public sector in favor of the private. David Riesman's *The Lonely Crowd*, W.H. Whyte Jr.'s *The Organization Man*, and Sloan Wilson's *The Man in the Gray Flannel Suit* examined in various ways the issue of conformity in American life. Ralph Ellison's novel, *Invisible Man*, dealt with racial problems.

35. **(A)** While farmers made up 20 percent of the Progressives and 22 percent of the Moderates, they made up only 12 percent of the Conservatives. Merchants and professionals were more evenly matched across the political spectrum while financiers were balanced toward the Moderate-Conservative end.

36. **(C)** The federal government aided agriculture in a number of ways. The land-grant colleges created by the Morrill Act of 1862 provided much of the research behind scientific agriculture. The Hatch Act of 1887 had created agricultural experiment stations in each state. The Smith-Lever Act of 1914 established "county extension agents." The Smith-Hughes Act of 1917 provided money for vocational education, including agriculture, in the public schools.

37. **(B)** Barry Goldwater had been the Republican nominee in 1964 but did not play a significant role in the 1968 campaign. George C. Wallace ran as a third party candidate, emphasizing the theme of law and order. Richard M. Nixon and Hubert Humphrey were the Republican and Democratic nominees, respectively. Eugene McCarthy challenged President Lyndon Johnson in the primaries, primarily on the issue of the Vietnam War and forced him out of the campaign after winning more than 40 percent of the vote in New Hampshire.

38. **(A)** The income tax was included in a section of the Underwood Tariff Act (1913), which significantly lowered tariffs. The Federal Reserve Act (1913) set up the Federal Reserve System to establish some control over the nation's banking system. The Clayton Antitrust Act of 1914 gave the government greater regulatory powers than had the Sherman Antitrust Act. The Federal Trade Commission Act (1914) established a commission to oversee interstate and international commerce. The Smith-Lever Act (1914) provided funds for rural education.

39. **(D)** Under the provisions of the 25th Amendment, Gerald Ford was appointed vice president by Richard Nixon upon the resignation of Spiro Agnew from the vice presidency in 1973. Ford became president when Nixon resigned the presidency in 1974. Ford in turn appointed Nelson Rockefeller as vice president.

40. **(C)** During the 1920s, organized labor lost strength after 1920, which contributed to the uneven distribution of income. The Fordney-McCumber Tariff of 1922 once

again introduced high tariffs, which contributed to the inability of world-wide trade to get back on track. Both consumer products and stock were widely purchased on credit. Farmers, among other groups, never participated in the prosperity of the 1920s.

41. **(E)** The Adams-Onis Treaty (1819) with Spain gave the United States both East and West Florida in return for U.S. payment of up to $5 million in claims by American citizens against the Spanish. Louisiana was purchased in 1803 from France. Texas obtained its independence from Mexico in 1836 and entered the Union in 1845. The 49th parallel was accepted as the border between Canada and Oregon by the U.S. and Great Britain in 1846. And California became an American possession through the Treaty of Guadalupe Hidalgo in 1848.

42. **(B)** The U.S. withdrew its troops from Nicaragua, sent there for a second time in 1926, in 1933. The U.S. cancelled the Platt Amendment and removed its troops from Haiti in 1934, gradually ended its control over Dominican Republic customs houses in the mid-1930s, and in 1936 gave up its right to intervene in Panama.

43. **(E)** In 1965 Johnson sent American troops into the Dominican Republic after a revolution there threatened chaos and, according to the president, presented a possible communist takeover. He withdrew the troops when the Organization of American States agreed to maintain order and oversee free elections.

44. **(E)** Bonuses to new industries were part of Alexander Hamilton's "Report on Manufactures" (1791). Henry Clay's American System included the protective tariff, the Second Bank of the United States, and federally funded internal improvement.

45. **(E)** After riots in Detroit, Los Angeles, and elsewhere, Lyndon Johnson appointed a National Advisory Commission on Civil Disorders in 1967. Chaired by Governor Otto Kerner of Illinois, the Committee argued that the nation was moving toward separate and unequal societies, black and white.

46. **(B)** Mary Chesnut argues that Southern women who have to put up with the moral temptations that slavery presents to their husbands and the dirt and filth of the blacks are more anti-slavery than Northerners.

47. **(A)** Although there may be some disagreement among historians, most see slavery as the key element underlying other differences such as the lack of industrialization, rural patterns of living, and slow development of a transportation system, particularly railroads. The existence of slavery also made the South less attractive to immigrants.

48. **(B)** The 26th Amendment (1971) gave 18 year olds the right to vote. The 25th Amendment (1967) provided for a revised line of presidential succession. The 22nd Amendment (1951) limited the president to two terms. The 23rd Amendment gave residents of the District of Columbia the right to participate in national elections. The Equal Rights Amendment failed to be ratified.

49. **(B)** The bombing, in addition to the blockading, of China were issues in the disagreement between President Harry S. Truman and General Douglas MacArthur. When MacArthur appealed to Congress, Truman dismissed him from command, replacing him with General Matthew Ridgeway.

50. **(E)** The Jacksonian era was notable for its rhetorical egalitarianism, hence the term "Jacksonian democracy," but recent research indicates that the period did not experience any significant increase in social mobility. The Jacksonian Democrats supported the spoils system and opposed Indian rights. Both the Democrats and the Whigs used the nominating convention. And the number of active voters increased in response to the new campaign tactics.

51. **(D)** Rachel Carson published *Silent Spring* in 1962, warning that a central problem of the age was contamination of the environment. John Kenneth Galbraith was a prominent liberal economist who, among other things, wrote *The Affluent Society*. George Gilder was a conservative advocate of supply-side economics, as explained in his book *Poverty and Progress*. Michael Harrington was a socialist who brought poverty to national attention in *The Other America*. Betty Friedan was a feminist whose book *The Feminine Mystique* helped launch the feminist movement of the 1970s.

52. **(D)** Although Harrison, Cleveland, and McKinley all set aside national forest reserves, Theodore Roosevelt became the most closely associated with conservation. He supported the Newlands Reclamation Act (1902) and sponsored the White House Conservation Conference of 1908.

53. **(C)** In order to succeed on the arid Great Plains, farmers had to turn to new technologies, including windmills, barbed wire, and new plows as well as new methods such as "dry farming."

54. **(A)** Helen Hunt Jackson's *A Century of Dishonor* (1881) examined the history of the U.S. government's relations with the Indians, emphasizing the broken treaties. It played an important role in the effort to reform government policy.

55. **(E)** The railroads were involved in scandals such as Credit Mobilier, which included several members of Congress, and in the Southwest ruinous rate wars. The government aided the railroads with land grants and government loans. The railroads were often built, particularly in the Northwest, as colonizing enterprises — building ahead of settlement. They often were inadequately financed and, as in the case of Jay Gould in the Southwest, often were severely competitive.

56. **(A)** W.E.B. DuBois criticized Booker T. Washington's emphasis upon manual training and called for greater activism to demand civil rights. This eventually led to the establishment of the NAACP in 1910. Frederick Douglass, a Black leader of the mid-nineteenth century, died in 1895 while King and Randolph were mid-twentieth century black leaders.

57. **(B)** The Interstate Commerce Act forbade railroads from charging more for a short haul than a long haul over the same line, from making pooling arrangements, and from giving rebates. It did not give the ICC authority to fix rates and enforce its decisions. The courts had the final authority.

58. **(D)** This map represents the United States after territories were opened to slavery by the Dred Scott decision of 1857.

59. **(D)** Beginning in the 1830s, the Irish came to America in large numbers, stirring up resentment because of their Catholicism, clannishness, dress, and accents. The other groups all came to America in significant numbers after the Civil War.

60. **(D)** The entrance of nearly 75,000 Chinese by the 1870s led to racial tensions, especially after the depression of 1873. Italians and Jews concentrated largely on the East Coast, while blacks remained mostly in the South. The Irish immigrated to America primarily before the Civil War.

61. **(D)** "Scalawag" referred to native-born Southerners who cooperated, for whatever reasons, with the Northern authorities during Reconstruction.

62. **(C)** In 1873 Congress passed a law taking silver coins off the list of standard coins. The Bland-Allison Act was passed in 1878 and the Sherman Silver Purchase Act in 1890. In 1834 the government had offered to buy silver at a ratio of 16 to 1 in relation to gold. Despite the Sherman Silver Purchase Act, the Treasury Department refused to coin the silver that it purchased.

63. **(E)** The Tenure of Office Act was passed in 1867 in order to reduce the power of President Andrew Johnson. Congress passed the Morrill Tariff Act in 1861, the Conscription Act in 1863, the Homestead Act in 1862, and the National Banking Act in 1863.

64. **(D)** This map represents European powers in North America after the French and Indian War (or Seven Years' War), 1756–63, transferred Canada from France to great Britain.

65. **(C)** By 1860 the South had nearly four million slaves.

66. **(E)** Jane Addams in 1889 opened Hull House in Chicago to provide social services to the poor working class. Inspired by her example, other "settlement houses" were opened in the slum areas of other major cities.

67. **(B)** The issuing of the Specie Circular of 1836, which required that only gold or silver or bank notes backed by gold and silver could be used to pay for public land, helped spark the panic of 1837. Jackson's withdrawal of federal funds from the Bank of the United States after his 1832 veto of the renewal of the charter also contributed to the expansion in the circulation of bank notes which led to his Specie Circular.

68. **(A)** Because of the tie between Jefferson and Burr in the Electoral College vote of 1800, the 12th Amendment required that the College vote separately for president and vice president. The First Amendment provided for freedom of religion; the 22nd Amendment limited the president to two terms; the 18th Amendment prohibited the manufacture and sale of alcoholic beverages; and the Second Amendment gave the right to bear arms.

69. **(B)** Mayhew uses essentially a pragmatic argument, measuring the performance of civil rulers against the good of society. This argument is compatible with natural rights theory but does not necessarily require such theory. Although Mayhew speaks of slavery, it is clear that he is not thinking of the "peculiar institution" but rather the relationship of white citizens to their government.

70. **(D)** In 1854 the American ministers to Great Britain, France, and Spain met in Ostend, Belgium and issued a statement that became known as the Ostend Manifesto. It said that if Spain would not sell Cuba to the United States, the U.S. had the right to seize the island by force.

71. **(D)** The Declaratory Act of 1766, passed after Parliament rescinded the Stamp Act (1765), asserted that Parliament had the power to make laws that were binding on the American colonists. The other acts referred to are (A) the Quartering Act (1765), (B) the Currency Act (1764), (C) The Sugar Act (1764), and (E) the Stamp Act (1765).

72. **(D)** The Chautauqua movement began in 1874 at Chautauqua Lake in upstate New York, providing lectures and sermons to the thousands of Americans who came for a summer vacation. Traveling Chautauquas emerged around 1900.

73. **(A)** Henry James wrote his major novels in the nineteenth and early twentieth centuries. Nathaniel Hawthorne published *The Scarlet Letter* in 1850 and *The House of the Seven Gables* in 1851. Walt Whitman published *Leaves of Grass* in 1855. Henry David Thoreau wrote *Walden* in 1854, and Herman Melville produced *Moby Dick* in 1851.

74. **(A)** This cartoon presents Tweed as ruled by greed. The source of his money is not indicated.

75. **(B)** Secessionist feeling was strongest among the New England Federalists who spoke up strongly for separation from the United States at the Hartford Convention of 1814–15. The Convention, however, only recommended constitutional amendments to weaken Southern power and the Democratic party.

76. **(B)** Samuel L. Clemens (Mark Twain) was from Missouri and won national acclaim for such books as *Roughing It* (1872) and *The Adventures of Tom Sawyer* (1876). William Dean Howells and Edith Wharton were Eastern novelists, while Edward Eggleston was a Midwesterner and Joel Chandler Harris a Southerner.

77. **(A)** The joint-stock company was the form of business organization that established Jamestown and Massachusetts, among others. The encomienda was a grant to Indians who lived on a specific piece of land in the Spanish colonies. Prince Henry financed the development of new navigation techniques in the fifteenth century. George III was king of England during the American Revolution, 1776-1783, a period during which republicanism became the dominant political ideology.

78. **(E)** Kennedy was unable to pass the civil rights bill that he sent to Congress in June 1963. The Manpower Development and Training Act (1962) provided a three-year worker retraining program. The Trade Expansion Act (1962) gave the president considerable powers over the tariff. The Area Redevelopment Act (1961) sought to help depressed areas. The Housing Act (1961) provided loans to stimulate construction of moderate-income housing.

79. **(B)** The correct response is (B), Bill Clinton. All the other choices are Democrats, and all except Hubert Humphrey served as president, but none was re-elected.

80. **(D)** Tennessee passed the first "Jim Crow" law in 1881, requiring blacks to ride in separate railway cars. By the 1890s all of the Southern states had passed such laws for schools, streetcars, and railroad stations. In time segregation would extend to other facilities as well.

81. **(C)** The merchants, together with lawyers and members of the families of the royal governors, were the most influential citizens in the New England towns. Ministers no longer carried the influence they once had.

82. **(A)** The United States gained control of the Philippines as a result of the Spanish-American War. The Filipino leader, Emilio Aguinaldo, fought against American rule. Some 70,000 American troops served in the Philippines until they were victorious in 1902. The United States acquired Hawaii in 1898, several years after Americans had gained control of the island. The U.S. had essentially a protectorate over Cuba after the Spanish-American War and obtained Puerto Rico as a result of the same conflict. In 1899 the Samoan Islands were divided between the U.S. and Germany.

83. **(A)** In contrast to the Confederacy, the North was not fighting a defensive war. Rather, it sought to strangle the Confederacy with a blockade; split the Confederacy by controlling the Mississippi and interior railroad lines; and seize Richmond, Virginia, the Confederacy's capital.

84. **(B)** Andrew Johnson became president upon Lincoln's death, serving until 1869. Grant was president between 1869 and 1877, Hayes from 1877 to 1881, Garfield in 1881, and Arthur from 1881 to 1885.

85. **(C)** The Pendleton Act established a commission to give competitive examinations for federal job-seekers. It also prohibited political parties from asking for campaign contributions from federal jobholders.

86. **(B)** Small businessmen tended to oppose the New Deal because they felt that they had suffered under NRA.

87. **(A)** The Progressives did not promote direct election of the president. The Australian ballot instituted secret rather than open voting. The initiative provided a means for citizens to place a proposal before the voters while the referendum provided a means for placing an action of the state legislature before the voters. In 1913, the 17th Amendment provided for the direct election of senators, replacing the previous procedure of having the state legislatures choose the senators.

88. **(D)** Dorothea Lynde Dix worked first in Massachusetts and then elsewhere to improve conditions for prisoners and the mentally ill. Louisa May Alcott wrote novels, among them *Little Women;* Margaret Fuller wrote *Woman in the Nineteenth Century*; Lucretia Mott was a women's rights activist; Sarah Josepha Hale was editor of *Godey's Lady's Book.*

89. **(C)** Chicago architect Frank Lloyd Wright, following the lead of Louis Sullivan, argued that a well-designed building has a style and uses materials expressive of the purpose of the structure. Eakins, Homer, and Cassatt were late-nineteenth century painters while Saint-Gaudens was a sculptor of the same time period.

90. **(D)** The Northwest Ordinance of 1787 barred slavery from the territories.

91. **(B)** The multinational corporation had not yet emerged as a significant form of business organization. Corporation pools involved several corporations deciding to divide all business opportunities among themselves. In the trust a group called "trustees" gained the control of the stock in several corporations, thereby being able to run them as a single enterprise. A holding company was formed by establishing a company for the sole purpose of buying a controlling share of the stock in two or more companies that produced goods or services. In an interlocking directorate the directors of one company would serve as directors of other companies.

92. **(B)** Henry Ford introduced the moving assembly line in the early twentieth century. Because of its efficiency he was able in 1914 to pay workers $5.00 for an eight-hour day. Frederick W. Taylor was a pioneer in efficiency engineering in the early twentieth century while Eli Whitney had developed interchangeable parts in the early nineteenth century. Collective bargaining would not become established until the 1930s. The use of electrical power began appearing in American industry toward the end of the nineteenth century.

93. **(B)** Harriet Beecher Stowe's *Uncle Tom's Cabin* was published in 1851–52. The American Anti-Slavery society was established in 1833. Garrison founded *The Liberator* in 1831. The "Gag" rule was passed in 1836, and the Liberty Party first appeared in 1840.

94. **(D)** The panic of 1857 resulted primarily from over-speculation in railroad stocks. Many banks failed across the nation, although the North suffered the most

and the South the least. By 1858 the economy began picking up, bolstered by European demand for foodstuffs and cotton.

95. **(C)** This cartoon shows Ulysses Grant caught within several strands of corruption, including the Whiskey Ring and corruption in the Navy Department.

THE SAT SUBJECT TEST IN

United States History

PRACTICE TEST 6

SAT United States History

Practice Test 6

1. (A) (B) (C) (D) (E)
2. (A) (B) (C) (D) (E)
3. (A) (B) (C) (D) (E)
4. (A) (B) (C) (D) (E)
5. (A) (B) (C) (D) (E)
6. (A) (B) (C) (D) (E)
7. (A) (B) (C) (D) (E)
8. (A) (B) (C) (D) (E)
9. (A) (B) (C) (D) (E)
10. (A) (B) (C) (D) (E)
11. (A) (B) (C) (D) (E)
12. (A) (B) (C) (D) (E)
13. (A) (B) (C) (D) (E)
14. (A) (B) (C) (D) (E)
15. (A) (B) (C) (D) (E)
16. (A) (B) (C) (D) (E)
17. (A) (B) (C) (D) (E)
18. (A) (B) (C) (D) (E)
19. (A) (B) (C) (D) (E)
20. (A) (B) (C) (D) (E)
21. (A) (B) (C) (D) (E)
22. (A) (B) (C) (D) (E)
23. (A) (B) (C) (D) (E)
24. (A) (B) (C) (D) (E)
25. (A) (B) (C) (D) (E)
26. (A) (B) (C) (D) (E)
27. (A) (B) (C) (D) (E)
28. (A) (B) (C) (D) (E)
29. (A) (B) (C) (D) (E)
30. (A) (B) (C) (D) (E)
31. (A) (B) (C) (D) (E)
32. (A) (B) (C) (D) (E)
33. (A) (B) (C) (D) (E)
34. (A) (B) (C) (D) (E)
35. (A) (B) (C) (D) (E)
36. (A) (B) (C) (D) (E)
37. (A) (B) (C) (D) (E)
38. (A) (B) (C) (D) (E)
39. (A) (B) (C) (D) (E)
40. (A) (B) (C) (D) (E)
41. (A) (B) (C) (D) (E)
42. (A) (B) (C) (D) (E)
43. (A) (B) (C) (D) (E)
44. (A) (B) (C) (D) (E)
45. (A) (B) (C) (D) (E)
46. (A) (B) (C) (D) (E)
47. (A) (B) (C) (D) (E)
48. (A) (B) (C) (D) (E)
49. (A) (B) (C) (D) (E)
50. (A) (B) (C) (D) (E)
51. (A) (B) (C) (D) (E)
52. (A) (B) (C) (D) (E)
53. (A) (B) (C) (D) (E)
54. (A) (B) (C) (D) (E)
55. (A) (B) (C) (D) (E)
56. (A) (B) (C) (D) (E)
57. (A) (B) (C) (D) (E)
58. (A) (B) (C) (D) (E)
59. (A) (B) (C) (D) (E)
60. (A) (B) (C) (D) (E)
61. (A) (B) (C) (D) (E)
62. (A) (B) (C) (D) (E)
63. (A) (B) (C) (D) (E)
64. (A) (B) (C) (D) (E)
65. (A) (B) (C) (D) (E)
66. (A) (B) (C) (D) (E)
67. (A) (B) (C) (D) (E)
68. (A) (B) (C) (D) (E)
69. (A) (B) (C) (D) (E)
70. (A) (B) (C) (D) (E)
71. (A) (B) (C) (D) (E)
72. (A) (B) (C) (D) (E)
73. (A) (B) (C) (D) (E)
74. (A) (B) (C) (D) (E)
75. (A) (B) (C) (D) (E)
76. (A) (B) (C) (D) (E)
77. (A) (B) (C) (D) (E)
78. (A) (B) (C) (D) (E)
79. (A) (B) (C) (D) (E)
80. (A) (B) (C) (D) (E)
81. (A) (B) (C) (D) (E)
82. (A) (B) (C) (D) (E)
83. (A) (B) (C) (D) (E)
84. (A) (B) (C) (D) (E)
85. (A) (B) (C) (D) (E)
86. (A) (B) (C) (D) (E)
87. (A) (B) (C) (D) (E)
88. (A) (B) (C) (D) (E)
89. (A) (B) (C) (D) (E)
90. (A) (B) (C) (D) (E)
91. (A) (B) (C) (D) (E)
92. (A) (B) (C) (D) (E)
93. (A) (B) (C) (D) (E)
94. (A) (B) (C) (D) (E)
95. (A) (B) (C) (D) (E)

United States History

PRACTICE TEST 6

TIME: 60 Minutes
95 Questions

DIRECTIONS: Each of the questions or incomplete statements below is followed by five suggested answers or completions. Select the one that is best in each case.

1. Americans became interested in the revolution in Cuba in the 1890s for all of the following reasons EXCEPT

   (A) the United States wanted Cuba as a colony.

   (B) José Marti aroused sympathy for Cuba through his magazine articles.

   (C) the Cuban revolutionaries purchased large amounts of arms and ammunition from the United States.

   (D) Americans had large investments in Cuba.

   (E) important American newspapers supported the revolution.

2. Which of the following correctly describes the Open Door Policy of Secretary of State John Hay?

   (A) John Hay announced that American businesses could compete on an equal basis with other nations in China.

   (B) The Treaty of Portsmouth (1905) ended the Open Door Policy.

   (C) Great Britain and France signed an agreement that American businesses could compete on an equal basis with other nations in China.

   (D) The Boxer Rebellion allowed European nations to seize Chinese land and effectively ended the Open Door Policy.

   (E) China and the U.S. signed an agreement that American businesses could compete on an equal basis with other nations in China.

3. The Roosevelt Corollary to the Monroe Doctrine stated that

(A) European powers were not to attempt any further colonization of the Americas.

(B) European powers were not to interfere with independent nations in the Western Hemisphere.

(C) if it was necessary for any European nation to interfere with any independent nation in the Western Hemisphere, the United States would act in its place.

(D) when individuals or nations loaned money to a nation in the Western Hemisphere they did so at their own risk and had no right to use force to collect their debts.

(E) European nations or individuals were not to loan money to any independent nation in the Western Hemisphere.

4. What position did Republican challenger Bob Dole resign from so he could devote all his time to campaigning against President Clinton in 1996?

(A) President of the World Bank

(B) Speaker of the House

(C) Senate majority leader

(D) U.S. ambassador to the United Nations

(E) Kansas state senator

5. Which of the following did NOT contribute to the outbreak of World War I?

(A) nationalism

(B) imperialism

(C) international rivalries

(D) alliance systems

(E) communism

6. Which of the following was NOT characteristic of Spanish civilization in the New World?

(A) the mission system

(B) slavery

(C) the viceroy

(D) the search for gold and silver

(E) republican government

7. Which of the following agencies was NOT established by the federal government to mobilize industry and labor during World War I?

   (A) Fuel Administration

   (B) Agricultural Adjustment Administration

   (C) War Industries Board

   (D) War Finance Corporation

   (E) Railroad Administration

8. All of the following are associated with the Pilgrims EXCEPT

   (A) Separatism.

   (B) Massachusetts Bay Colony.

   (C) Mayflower Compact.

   (D) Squanto.

   (E) Plymouth.

9. Which of the following events brought Calvin Coolidge to national prominence?

   (A) the coal strike of 1919

   (B) the "Red scare" of 1919–1920

   (C) the steel strike of 1919

   (D) the depression of 1919

   (E) the Boston police strike of 1919

10. Which of the following colonies was established so that debtors freed from English prisons could start a new life?

   (A) Georgia

   (B) Maryland

   (C) North Carolina

   (D) New Jersey

   (E) Delaware

11. Which of the following was NOT an object of the Tennessee Valley Authority?

   (A) to establish homestead communities on good land for sharecroppers and tenant farmers

   (B) to prevent soil erosion

(C) to provide inexpensive electricity

(D) to control floods

(E) to restore soil fertility

12. The French and Indian War, or Seven Years' War, resulted in which of the following after the signing of the Treaty of Paris in 1763?

(A) Spain gained control of Florida.

(B) The British occupied Cuba and the Philippines.

(C) The British gained control of Guadeloupe and Martinique.

(D) The Spanish obtained New Orleans and Louisiana.

(E) The French retained Quebec.

13. By the end of the 1920s, what had become the nation's largest industry?

(A) steel

(B) railroads

(C) oil

(D) chemicals

(E) automobiles

14. Which of the following novels described an Oklahoma family forced to move to California by the depression?

(A) *An American Tragedy*

(B) *This Side of Paradise*

(C) *Elmer Gantry*

(D) *The Grapes of Wrath*

(E) *For Whom the Bell Tolls*

15. Which of the following does NOT correctly describe the Southern colonies?

(A) They were the most English of the colonies.

(B) They were largely urban.

(C) The plantations were on the coastal plains.

(D) Tobacco and rice were the chief cash crops.

(E) Most Southerners lived on small farms.

16. Which of the following statements does NOT describe American society in the 1930s?

(A) Radio was the most influential form of entertainment.

(B) Immigration to the United States continued to increase.

(C) More than a million men travelled throughout the United States looking for work.

(D) Some farmers formed roadblocks and stopped trucks, forcing them to dump their milk.

(E) A "Bonus Army" marched on Washington, D.C., in 1932.

17. Which of the following did NOT participate in the transportation boom of the post-World War II period?

(A) commercial aviation

(B) railroads

(C) trucking

(D) automobiles

(E) busing

18. The Treaty of Ghent which ended the War of 1812, included which of the following?

(A) settlement of Canadian border problems

(B) recognition of American neutral rights

(C) restoration of territory taken during the war

(D) cessation of the impressment of American seamen

(E) transfer of Canadian land to the United States

19. The Iroquois Confederation included all of the following Indian tribes EXCEPT

(A) Sioux.

(B) Mohawk.

(C) Seneca.

(D) Oneida.

(E) Cayuga.

20. Which of the following outlawed war as an "instrument of foreign policy"?

(A) Kellogg-Briand Pact

(B) Washington Naval Conference

(C) Stimson Doctrine

(D) Good Neighbor Policy

(E) Neutrality Act of 1935

21. What was the first college to be established in colonial America?

(A) King's College (Columbia)

(B) College of William and Mary

(C) Harvard College

(D) Queen's College (Rutgers)

(E) College of New Jersey (Princeton)

22. Franklin Roosevelt challenged isolationism with which of the following?

(A) Johnson Debt Default Act

(B) the Neutrality Acts

(C) the Quarantine Speech

(D) the *Panay* incident

(E) Trade Agreements Act

23. The British government faced all of the following problems in 1763 EXCEPT

(A) war debts.

(B) defense costs.

(C) independence movements in Colonial America.

(D) government of Florida and Canada.

(E) ownership of the western lands of Colonial America.

24. Which of the following gave material aid to the Allied powers in World War II?

(A) the Declaration of Panama

(B) the Atlantic Charter

(C) the Act of Havana

(D) the Burke-Wadsworth Act

(E) the Lend-Lease Act

25. Which of the following was feared as a mob leader by British colonial authorities?

    (A) Thomas Jefferson
    (B) Patrick Henry
    (C) John Adams
    (D) James Otis
    (E) Samuel Adams

26. Which of the following was agreed to at the Yalta Conference (1945)?

    (A) the invasion of Sicily
    (B) the establishment of a Council of Foreign Ministers to draft peace treaties
    (C) a commitment to open a second front in France
    (D) an agreement to divide Germany into four military zones
    (E) the Soviet Union agreed to enter the war against Japan once Germany was defeated

27. Which of the following does NOT appear in the Declaration of Independence?

    (A) a portrayal of the king as an evil ruler
    (B) an argument for religious toleration
    (C) a statement of the basic principles of democracy
    (D) an announcement that a state of war existed with Great Britain
    (E) an argument for the right of Americans to revolt

28. The Truman Doctrine (1947) proposed to give aid to what countries in order to combat the spread of communism?

    (A) Turkey and Greece
    (B) Czechoslovakia and Poland
    (C) North Korea and the Philippines
    (D) Egypt and Saudi Arabia
    (E) Hungary and Romania

29. The government under the Articles of Confederation had all of the following powers EXCEPT

    (A) regulation of weights and measures.

    (B) establishment of a post office.

    (C) creation of a navy.

    (D) coinage of money.

    (E) taxation.

30. The terms "brinksmanship" and "massive retaliation" are associated with what secretary of state?

    (A) George C. Marshall

    (B) Cordell Hull

    (C) John Foster Dulles

    (D) Christian Herter

    (E) Elihu Root

31. The Jay Treaty (1794) provided for

    (A) the acceptance of American trade with the French West Indies.

    (B) free navigation of the Mississippi.

    (C) an ending of impressment of American seamen.

    (D) the settlement of the Canadian boundary.

    (E) evacuation of English troops from their posts along the Great Lakes.

32. Which of the following statements best characterizes the Eisenhower administration?

    (A) The Eisenhower administration vigorously extended the social and economic legislation of the New Deal-Fair Deal era.

    (B) The Eisenhower administration vigorously repealed the social and economic legislation of the New Deal-Fair Deal era.

    (C) The Eisenhower administration slowly repealed the social and economic legislation of the New Deal-Fair Deal era.

    (D) The Eisenhower administration neither expanded nor repealed the social and economic legislation of the New Deal-Fair Deal era.

    (E) The Eisenhower administration cautiously expanded the social and economic legislation of the New Deal-Fair Deal era.

33. The XYZ affair of 1797–98 resulted in

(A) a new treaty with France.

(B) a quasi-war with France.

(C) an American loan to France.

(D) a declaration of war on France.

(E) an apology to France for remarks that President Adams made to Congress.

34. The *bracero* program

(A) helped Puerto Ricans find jobs in the United States.

(B) enabled Mexican immigrants to become American citizens.

(C) provided financial and social support for refugees from Cuba.

(D) brought contract Mexican farm workers to the United States.

(E) provided English language training for Spanish-speaking immigrants.

Growth of White Population, Massachusetts Bay, 1700-1740

Year	*Total Population*
1700	55,941
1710	62,390
1720	91,008
1730	114,116
1740	151,613

35. Based on the above chart, in what year did the population of Massachusetts Bay grow by the largest percentage?

(A) 1700

(B) 1710

(C) 1720

(D) 1730

(E) 1740

36. Until the 1930s, the Supreme Court objected to social legislation passed by the states to protect workers on the basis that

(A) such laws made American business less competitive.

(B) such laws interfered with the natural order.

(C) such laws were reserved to the federal government.

(D) such laws interfered with the workers' right of contract.

(E) such laws did not contribute to the health and well-being of the citizens.

37. The first federal legislation to provide health insurance for the elderly was passed during the administration of which president?

(A) Lyndon B. Johnson
(B) Harry S. Truman
(C) John F. Kennedy
(D) Franklin D. Roosevelt
(E) Dwight D. Eisenhower

38. Progressives revolted against Speaker of the House Joseph Cannon in 1910 for all of the following reasons EXCEPT

(A) he could determine who spoke during floor debates.

(B) he appointed all House committees.

(C) he appointed himself head of the Rules Committee.

(D) he selected the chairmen of all House committees.

(E) he determined which bills went to House committees.

39. Which of the following statements does NOT correctly describe the Latter-Day Saints?

(A) The Latter-Day Saints were a religious group founded by Joseph Smith.

(B) The Latter-Day Saints successively settled in Ohio, Missouri, Illinois, and Utah.

(C) Joseph Smith led the Latter-Day Saints to Utah.

(D) The Latter-Day Saints practiced polygamy.

(E) The Latter-Day Saints based their faith on *The Book of Mormon.*

40. Which of the following statements correctly describes the presidency of Richard Nixon?

(A) Richard Nixon reduced the powers of the presidency while president.

(B) Richard Nixon expanded the role of the federal government in social issues.

(C) Richard Nixon turned much of the authority of cabinet officers over to his White House staff.

(D) Richard Nixon was impeached by the House of Representatives.

(E) Richard Nixon relied upon a Republican majority in Congress.

41. Who was the top vote-getter in the 1992 and 1996 presidential elections after the two major-party candidates?

(A) Dick Lamb

(B) Michael Dukakis

(C) H. Ross Perot

(D) Patrick Buchanan

(E) Jack Kemp

42. Which of the following was resolved by negotiation soon after the Treaty of Ghent (1814)?

(A) disarmament of the Great Lakes

(B) impressment of American seamen

(C) neutral rights

(D) boundary of the Oregon territory

(E) elimination of land fortification, armaments, and troops along the Canadian border

43. President Lyndon Johnson based his authority to conduct the war in Vietnam on

(A) the Gulf of Tonkin Resolution.

(B) his constitutional powers as commander in chief.

(C) a congressional declaration of war on Vietnam.

(D) the requirements of the Southeast Asia Treaty Organization, of which the U.S. was a member.

(E) the requirements of the Security Council of the United Nations, of which the U.S. was a member.

44. After 1815, the Southern economy was increasingly tied to what crop?

(A) wheat

(B) tobacco

(C) corn

(D) rice

(E) cotton

45. Between 1940 and 1979 from what areas did the largest percentage of immigrants to the United States come?

(A) Asia
(B) Canada
(C) Great Britain
(D) Latin America
(E) Germany

46. In a speech to the Senate in 1900, Albert J. Beveridge stated in regard to the annexation of the Philippines:

"Mr. President, this question is deeper than any question of party politics; deeper than any question of the isolated policy of our country even; deeper even than any question of constitutional power. It is elemental. It is racial. God has not been preparing the English-speaking and Teutonic peoples for a thousand years for nothing but vain and idle self-contemplation and self-admiration. No! He has made us the master organizers of the world to establish system where chaos reigns. He has given us the spirit of progress to overwhelm the forces of reaction throughout the earth. He has made us adept in government that we may administer government among savage and senile peoples. Were it not for such a force as this the world would relapse into barbarism and night. And of all our race He has marked the American people as His chosen nation to finally lead in the regeneration of the world."

What basic assumption did Senator Beveridge make in this speech?

(A) that all peoples are imbued with natural rights
(B) that to be strong, nations must acquire colonies
(C) that the white race is superior to all other peoples and is destined by God to rule them
(D) that evolutionary processes have brought the white race to the forefront of civilization
(E) that the present struggle is one of political principles

47. The Tallmadge Amendment (1819) proposed to

(A) lower the protective tariff.
(B) prohibit the introduction of more slaves into Missouri.
(C) give the states more money for internal improvements.
(D) organize the Western territories to aid in the building of the transcontinental railroad.
(E) allow Maine to enter the Union as a free state.

48. What World War II federal government agency was responsible for setting up a rationing system?

(A) National War Labor Board

(B) Office of Price Administration

(C) War Manpower Commission

(D) War Production Board

(E) Office of War Mobilization

49. From Nixon to Reagan, American presidents used all of the following policies to combat inflation EXCEPT

(A) mandatory wage and price controls.

(B) voluntary wage and price controls.

(C) cuts in federal spending.

(D) tax increases.

(E) tightening of credit.

50. Which of the following states provoked the nullification crisis?

(A) South Carolina

(B) Georgia

(C) Virginia

(D) North Carolina

(E) Alabama

51. The 1979 accident at the Three Mile Island power plant involved what energy source?

(A) coal

(B) hydroelectricity

(C) natural gas

(D) geothermal

(E) nuclear

52. During his presidency, Theodore Roosevelt was associated with all of the following EXCEPT the

(A) Elkins Act

(B) Hepburn Act

(C) Federal Reserve Act

(D) Meat Inspection Act

(E) Pure Food and Drug Act

53. Which of the following did NOT contribute to the end of the open-range cattle industry?

(A) droughts
(B) railroads
(C) sheep herding
(D) farming
(E) barbed wire

54. Which of the following was NOT involved in the Indian-White conflicts on the Great Plains after the Civil War?

(A) Geronimo
(B) Sitting Bull
(C) Chief Joseph
(D) Tecumseh
(E) Crazy Horse

55. Which of the following became less important in the late 1800s?

(A) small general stores
(B) specialty stores
(C) department stores
(D) chain stores
(E) mail order businesses

56. William Marcy Tweed became the political boss of what city in the 1860s and 1870s?

(A) Boston
(B) New York
(C) Philadelphia
(D) Chicago
(E) Washington, D.C.

57. Which of the following was not involved in American exploration of the West?

(A) Meriwether Lewis
(B) Zebulon Pike
(C) John Charles Frémont
(D) Aaron Burr
(E) William Clark

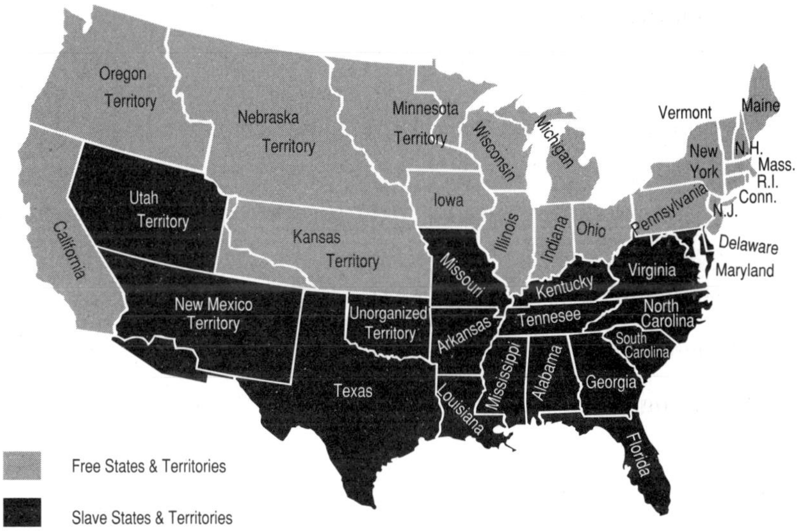

58. The map above represents slave and free areas of the United States as of

(A) 1821. (B) 1850. (C) 1854. (D) 1861. (E) 1865.

59. Who served as president of the Second Bank of the United States?

(A) Roger B. Taney
(B) William Morgan
(C) Nicholas Biddle
(D) Daniel Webster
(E) Robert Y. Hayne

60. Which of the following was organized as a craft union?

(A) National Labor Union
(B) Congress of Industrial Organizations
(C) Knights of Labor
(D) Industrial Workers of the World
(E) American Federation of Labor

61. Which of the following was NOT part of the Radical Republican program for Reconstruction?

(A) division of the South into military districts
(B) the 14th Amendment

(C) enlargement of the powers of the Freedmen's Bureau

(D) division of the plantations and distribution of the land to the freed slaves

(E) guarantees that the freed slaves could vote and hold office

62. One mound-building culture, Cahokia, supported perhaps 40,000 people near what modern-day city?

(A) New York City (D) Seattle

(B) Mexico City (E) Miami

(C) St. Louis

63. During the Civil War, the term "Copperhead" referred to

(A) Northerners who opposed the Civil War.

(B) Northerners who called for the abolition of slavery.

(C) Southerners who opposed the Confederacy.

(D) Southerners who called for the abolition of slavery.

(E) Northerners who supported slavery.

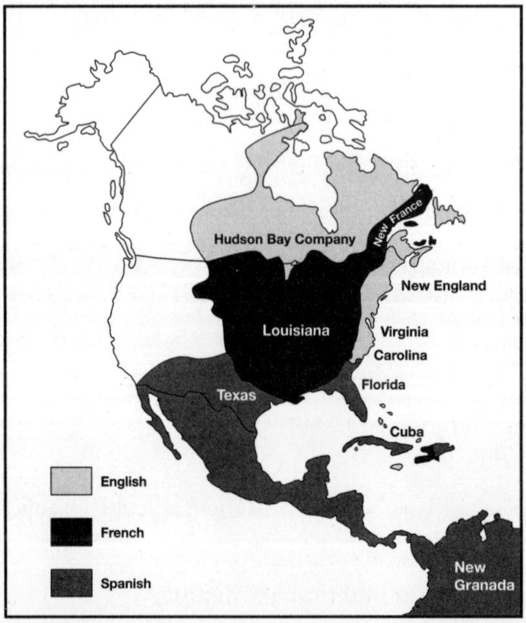

64. The above map represents European powers in North America as of

(A) 1600. (B) 1682. (C) 1713. (D) 1763. (E) 1783.

65. All of the following were associated with the Rocky Mountain Fur Trade EXCEPT

(A) Jim Bridger.

(B) Jedediah Smith.

(C) Jim Beckwourth.

(D) Tom Fitzpatrick.

(E) Marcus Whitman.

66. Which of the following was a major American philosopher and educational theorist?

(A) John Dewey

(B) Josiah Royce

(C) William James

(D) Charles W. Eliot

(E) Andrew D. White

67. The Treaty of Guadalupe Hidalgo (1848) included all of the following EXCEPT

(A) the United States paid Mexico $15 million.

(B) land south of the Gila river.

(C) the United States took over $3 million in debts owed by the Mexican government to Americans.

(D) the United States gained Texas, New Mexico, and Upper California.

(E) the United States promised to respect the religious preferences and civil and property rights of Mexicans in the newly acquired territory.

68. Which of the following was NOT concerned with either slavery or blacks?

(A) Emancipation Proclamation

(B) 13th Amendment

(C) 16th Amendment

(D) Freedmen's Bureau

(E) 14th Amendment

69. In 1786, Thomas Jefferson wrote the following:

"Our present federal limits are not too large for good government, nor will the increase of votes in Congress produce any ill effect. On the contrary it will drown the little divisions at present existing there. Our confederacy must be viewed as the nest from which all America, North and South, is to be peopled.

We should take care too not to think it for the interest of that great continent to press too soon on the Spaniards. Those countries cannot be in better hands. My fear is that they are too feeble to hold them till our population can be sufficiently advanced to gain it from them piece by piece. The navigation of the Mississippi we must have. This is all we are as yet ready to receive."

In this private letter Jefferson is saying all of the following EXCEPT

(A) the American political structure could survive in a larger territory.

(B) the United States is not yet ready to take territory away from the Spanish.

(C) a large territory will enable the political structure to overcome its divisions.

(D) it is possible that the United States might advance too quickly into Spanish territory.

(E) Spain provides good government for its territories.

70. Those who opposed ratification of the Constitution were called

(A) Democrats.

(B) Whigs.

(C) Antifederalists.

(D) Federalists.

(E) Republicans.

71. Which of the following events is placed in an INCORRECT year?

(A) 1854 — Kansas Nebraska Act

(B) 1857 — Dred Scott Decision

(C) 1858 — Lincoln-Douglas debates

(D) 1859 — John Brown's raid on Harper's Ferry

(E) 1861 — South Carolina secedes from the Union

72. Which of the following correctly describes the Progressives?

(A) They were primarily based in rural locations.

(B) They largely represented the working class.

(C) They came to political leadership during a period of depression.

(D) They were concerned with the rights of blacks.

(E) They emphasized such issues as efficiency and morality in government.

73. Horace Mann was involved in which of the following reforms?

(A) peace

(B) health

(C) women's rights

(D) temperance

(E) education

74. What view of the relationship of Congress and business is Thomas Nast presenting in this cartoon?

Source: From the collection of Macculloch Hall Historical Museum, Morristown, NJ

Pan-Ic in Session.
Death to us (the people) and fun for them ("Statesmen").

(A) Congress has established too much regulatory power over business.

(B) Business is the benefactor of the American people.

(C) Congress is the upholder of the national interest.

(D) Congress is subject to the corrupt influence of business.

(E) Business has little influence in national affairs.

75. Which of the following was NOT a major business or financial leader in the late nineteenth century?

(A) Cornelius Vanderbilt
(B) Andrew Carnegie
(C) Horatio Alger
(D) John D. Rockefeller
(E) J. P. Morgan

76. Energy became a major political issue during what decade?

(A) 1940s
(B) 1950s
(C) 1960s
(D) 1970s
(E) 1980s

77. Patroons were which of the following?

(A) a religious group that settled in the Carolinas
(B) an Indian tribe involved in the Pequot War
(C) the founders of Pennsylvania
(D) a colonial farm implement
(E) owners of large tracts of land in New Netherlands

78. The first woman to serve as a member of the Supreme Court was

(A) Sandra Day O'Connor.
(B) Nancy Kassebaum.
(C) Barbara Jordan.
(D) Ella Grasso.
(E) Jane Byrne.

79. Which of the following does NOT apply to the corporation form of business organization?

(A) It gradually replaced individual proprietorship and partnerships as the dominant form of business organization.
(B) It received its charter from the state.
(C) It gave stockholders limited liability.
(D) It was the predominant form of business organization in the 1830s.
(E) It raised capital through the sale of stock.

80. This engraving of the Nat Turner revolt takes what point of view?

HORRID MASSACRE IN VIRGINIA.

The Scenes which the above plate is designed to represent are—Fig 1. a Mother intreating for the lives of her children.—2. Mr. Travis, cruelly murdered by his own slaves.—3. Mr. Barrow, who bravely defended himself until his wife escaped.—4. A comp. of mounted Dragoons in pursuit of the Blacks.

Source: U.S. Library of Congress

(A) The revolt of the slaves was justified.

(B) Northern abolitionists were responsible for the revolt.

(C) The revolt was an attack upon innocent victims.

(D) The slaves were ineffective revolutionaries.

(E) The slave revolt was successful.

81. The largest city in the Southern colonies was

(A) Williamsburg.

(B) Baltimore.

(C) Savannah.

(D) Wilmington.

(E) Charleston.

82. According to Woodrow Wilson, what was the key element of the Treaty of Versailles?

    (A) the Mandate system for Germany's former colonies

    (B) German agreement to pay reparations

    (C) the creation of new independent states

    (D) the League of Nations

    (E) the return of Alsace-Lorraine to France

83. The American colonists were able to control the power of the Royal governors through what means?

    (A) The assemblies controlled all grants of money to be spent by the colonial governments.

    (B) The assemblies appointed the governor.

    (C) The assemblies could dismiss the governor.

    (D) The assemblies established the constitutions that defined the governor's powers.

    (E) The assemblies could pass laws over the governor's veto.

84. "Popular Sovereignty" meant that

    (A) slavery would not be allowed north of 36°30′.

    (B) all territories would be permanently open to slavery.

    (C) the states would decide themselves whether to be slave or free.

    (D) no territories from the Mexican Cession would be open to slavery.

    (E) slavery would be banned in the Southern states.

85. Which of the following served as president of the Confederate States of America?

    (A) Robert E. Lee

    (B) John C. Calhoun

    (C) Robert Y. Hayne

    (D) Jefferson Davis

    (E) Alexander H. Stephens

86. A minimum wage scale and a maximum workweek was established nationally by the

    (A) National Labor Relations Act.

    (B) Fair Employment Practices Committee.

(C) Fair Labor Standards Act.

(D) National Industrial Recovery Administration.

(E) American Federation of Labor.

87. Which of the following did NOT experience a Gold Rush after 1859?

(A) Nevada

(B) Alaska

(C) South Dakota

(D) California

(E) Colorado

88. Which of the following Southern cities became an iron and steel center after the Civil War?

(A) Atlanta

(B) Montgomery

(C) Richmond

(D) Nashville

(E) Birmingham

89. In his book *Progress and Poverty* (1879), Henry George argued that

(A) monopolies were running the industrial economy for their own profit.

(B) silver must be monetized in order to help debtors.

(C) the railroads must be nationalized.

(D) a few people had a monopoly over the best land sites which pushed up rents, thereby raising prices and lowering wages.

(E) with the emergence of the human mind, the evolutionary process could now be controlled, making social engineering possible.

90. Which tribe was a member of the Five Nations of Iroquois?

(A) Aztecs

(B) Mohawks

(C) Anasazi

(D) Incas

(E) Mayas

91. Which of the following correctly describes the attitude of Lincoln and Johnson toward Reconstruction?

(A) They regarded the South as conquered provinces.

(B) They regarded the South as unorganized territory.

(C) They saw the Civil War as a rebellion of individuals.

(D) They supported the establishment of Black Codes.

(E) They believed that Congress had the responsibility for reconstruction.

92. What Union general emerged to prominence in the Western theater of the Civil War?

(A) George B. McClellan
(B) Ulysses S. Grant
(C) Irving McDowell
(D) John Pope
(E) George G. Meade

93. Which of the following best characterizes the cities as they developed in the United States after 1870?

(A) The races were legally separated.

(B) The various ethnic groups and economic classes lived in different neighborhoods.

(C) There was no differentiation between residential, industrial, and commercial areas.

(D) The residences and working places of the various economic classes and ethnic groups were jumbled together throughout the city.

(E) The suburbs became less important toward the end of the nineteenth century.

94. The late-nineteenth-century "managerial revolution" refers to which of the following?

(A) separation of management from ownership

(B) the growing importance of business schools

(C) combination of management and ownership

(D) government regulation of business

(E) the move from regional to national businesses

95. Jimmy Carter's major foreign policy accomplishment was

(A) the release of hostages by Iran.

(B) the Panama Canal treaties.

(C) a peace treaty between Egypt and Israel.

(D) withdrawal of Soviet troops from Afghanistan.

(E) reduction of Soviet influence in Africa.

SAT United States History

Practice Test 6 ANSWER KEY

1.	**(A)**	26.	**(D)**	51.	**(E)**	76.	**(D)**
2.	**(A)**	27.	**(B)**	52.	**(C)**	77.	**(E)**
3.	**(C)**	28.	**(A)**	53.	**(B)**	78.	**(A)**
4.	**(C)**	29.	**(E)**	54.	**(E)**	79.	**(D)**
5.	**(E)**	30.	**(C)**	55.	**(A)**	80.	**(C)**
6.	**(E)**	31.	**(E)**	56.	**(B)**	81.	**(E)**
7.	**(B)**	32.	**(E)**	57.	**(D)**	82.	**(D)**
8.	**(B)**	33.	**(B)**	58.	**(C)**	83.	**(A)**
9.	**(E)**	34.	**(D)**	59.	**(C)**	84.	**(C)**
10.	**(A)**	35.	**(C)**	60.	**(E)**	85.	**(D)**
11.	**(A)**	36.	**(D)**	61.	**(C)**	86.	**(C)**
12.	**(D)**	37.	**(A)**	62.	**(C)**	87.	**(D)**
13.	**(E)**	38.	**(E)**	63.	**(A)**	88.	**(E)**
14.	**(D)**	39.	**(C)**	64.	**(C)**	89.	**(C)**
15.	**(B)**	40.	**(C)**	65.	**(E)**	90.	**(B)**
16.	**(B)**	41.	**(C)**	66.	**(A)**	91.	**(C)**
17.	**(B)**	42.	**(A)**	67.	**(B)**	92.	**(B)**
18.	**(C)**	43.	**(A)**	68.	**(C)**	93.	**(B)**
19.	**(A)**	44.	**(E)**	69.	**(E)**	94.	**(A)**
20.	**(A)**	45.	**(D)**	70.	**(C)**	95.	**(C)**
21.	**(C)**	46.	**(C)**	71.	**(E)**		
22.	**(C)**	47.	**(B)**	72.	**(E)**		
23.	**(C)**	48.	**(B)**	73.	**(E)**		
24.	**(E)**	49.	**(D)**	74.	**(D)**		
25.	**(E)**	50.	**(A)**	75.	**(C)**		

Detailed Explanations of Answers

PRACTICE TEST 6

1. **(A)** The United States had no official interest in Cuba as a colony. The government at first adopted an official policy of neutrality toward the revolution. After the war, the Platt Amendment (1901) declared that no foreign power could take control of the island, although it did contain provisions that essentially established an American protectorate of Cuba.

2. **(A)** In 1899–1900 Secretary of State John Hay sent notes to the great powers demanding that American businesses be allowed to compete on an equal basis with other nations in China. Although most of the responses were noncommittal, in early 1900 Hay announced that the principle of equality was accepted. During the Boxer rebellion of 1900, Hay successfully opposed European acquisition of Chinese territory. The Treaty of Portsmouth (1905), which ended the Russo-Japanese War, maintained the Open Door Policy.

3. **(C)** In 1904, responding to a threat by European nations to use force to collect debts from the Dominican Republic, President Theodore Roosevelt announced that the United States would act in the place of any nation needing to interfere in the Western Hemisphere. The Monroe Doctrine (1823) stipulated that European nations were not to attempt any further colonization of the Americas and were not to interfere with any independent nation in the Western Hemisphere. In 1902 the Argentine Minister of Foreign Affairs argued that when individuals or nations loaned money to a nation in the Western Hemisphere they did so at their own risk and had no right to use force to collect their debts. This became known as the Drago Doctrine.

4. **(C)** Bob Dole was majority leader of the U.S. Senate before deciding to devote all his time to a run for the presidency.

5. **(E)** Communism was not yet a major contributor to international tensions. Nationalism among minority groups created problems in almost every European nation. The struggle for colonies divided European nations into "haves" and "have nots." International rivalries pitted nations against one another as they sought additional territory, and the alliance systems resulted in a chain of military actions once the Archduke of Austria-Hungary was assassinated at Sarajevo, Serbia.

6. **(E)** All authority was centered on the Spanish king, who was represented in the New World by two viceroys, who ruled in his name. The Indians were enslaved

until the 1540s and after that were placed under the *repartimiento*, another system of forced labor. The mission system evangelized the Indians for the Roman Catholic Church. Until the gold and silver ran out, the Spanish used its American colonies to a large extent as a source of these precious metals.

7. **(B)** The Agricultural Adjustment Administration was created in 1933. The other organizations were all created to mobilize various aspects of the economy for the war effort in 1917–18.

8. **(B)** The Massachusetts Bay Colony was founded in 1630 by the Puritans, who wanted to purify rather than separate from the Anglican Church. The Pilgrims were Separatists who established Plymouth in 1620. The Mayflower Compact was an agreement, signed before landing at Plymouth, to obey all the laws that the group adopted. Squanto was an Indian who helped the Pilgrims survive during their first year by teaching them how to use the plants and other natural resources of the new land.

9. **(E)** The Boston police strike of 1919 brought Calvin Coolidge, then governor of Massachusetts, to national prominence. He stated, "There is no right to strike against the public safety by anybody, anywhere, any time." All of the strikes of 1919 were related to the depression of that year.

10. **(A)** James Oglethorpe founded Georgia in 1732 for the purpose of aiding debtors released from British prisons. Sir George Calvert established Maryland in 1632 as a haven for Catholics. North Carolina, then combined with South Carolina, was created in 1663 and unsuccessfully sought to establish a government based on a plan by John Locke. New Jersey was originally part of New Netherlands but after the English takeover was ceded to Lord John Berkeley and Sir George Carteret in 1664. Delaware was founded by Swedes but taken over by the British in 1664 and given to William Penn in 1682, after which it was part of Pennsylvania.

11. **(A)** The Resettlement Administration (1935) had the responsibility to establish homestead communities. The TVA was begun in 1933 as a result of the efforts of Senator George W. Norris.

12. **(D)** In the Treaty of Paris of 1763 France gave up its claims in America except for four islands, including Guadeloupe and Martinique. The Spanish gave up Florida to Great Britain but obtained New Orleans and Louisiana from the French. Although the British occupied Cuba and the Philippines during the war, they returned them to Spain.

13. **(E)** By 1929 the automobile industry had become the nation's largest business. Possibly one of every nine American workers was employed in the automobile industry or an associated business.

14. **(D)** John Steinbeck's *The Grapes of Wrath* (1939) addressed the impact of the depression on an Oklahoma farm family. Theodore Dreiser's *An American*

Tragedy (1925) dealt with a murder case. *Elmer Gantry* (1927) by Sinclair Lewis described a hypocritical evangelist. Ernest Hemingway's *For Whom the Bell Tolls* (1939) described the experience of the Spanish Civil War.

15. **(B)** The Southern colonies were largely rural with only two relatively large cities, Charleston and Baltimore. They were closely tied with England. Tobacco was the main cash crop in Maryland, Virginia, and North Carolina while rice was grown in Georgia and the Carolinas. The population lived largely on the coastal plains (or tidewater area) where plantations dominated the economy but most of the population lived on small farms.

16. **(B)** During the 1930s more people left the United States than entered it and the number of marriages and births slowed.

17. **(B)** The railroads lost nearly half of their freight hauling to the trucking industry and most of their passengers to automobiles, buses, and airplanes.

18. **(C)** The Treaty of Ghent (1814) included only the cessation of hostilities and restoration of territory taken during the War of 1812.

19. **(A)** The Iroquois Confederation, a confederation of Iroquois groups during the seventeenth and eighteenth centuries, included the Seneca, Cayuga, Onondaga, Oneida, and Mohawk tribes, all of which were Eastern woodland groups. In the 1700s the Tuscaroras joined the Confederation. The Sioux lived on the Great Plains.

20. **(A)** The Kellogg-Briand Pact (1928) outlawed war as an instrument of foreign policy; it was signed by 62 nations. The Washington Naval Conference took place in 1921–22 and resulted in agreements to reduce the size of the navies of the U.S., Great Britain, Japan, France, and Italy. The Stimson Doctrine (1932) refused to recognize the Japanese acquisition of Manchuria. The Good Neighbor Policy was the name Franklin D. Roosevelt gave his Latin American policy. The Neutrality Act of 1935 forbade the sale of arms to belligerent nations.

21. **(C)** Harvard was founded in 1636. The colonial colleges included the College of New Jersey (Princeton) (1746), Rhode Island College (Brown) (1764), Queen's College (Rutgers) (1766), King's College (Columbia) (1754), College and Academy of Philadelphia (Pennsylvania) (1755), Dartmouth (1761), College of William and Mary (1693), and Yale College (1716).

22. **(C)** In the "Quarantine Speech" (1937), Roosevelt called for action to prevent the spread of aggression, but the message fell on deaf ears. The Johnson Debt Default Act (1934) forbade the lending of money to any country that had not paid its WW I debts. The Neutrality Acts of 1935–37 in various ways sought to prevent American involvement in a European war. The *Panay* incident occurred when Japanese airplanes bombed some American ships in the Yangtze River in China in 1937. The Trade Agreements Act of 1934 allowed the president to raise or lower the tariff up to 50 percent without Senate approval.

23. **(C)** The independence movement did not begin until after the British began passing new taxes and duties beginning in 1765. In 1763 the British government had a huge debt resulting from the French and Indian War, the need to defend the new territory, and the need to establish British governments for Canada and Florida. It also had to deal with the conflicting claims to land west of the Appalachians by the American colonies.

24. **(E)** The Lend-Lease Act of 1941 appropriated $7 billion for war material for the Allies. The Declaration of Panama (1939) declared a "safety zone" around the Americas. The Atlantic Charter (1941) between Winston Churchill and Franklin D. Roosevelt listed common principles for building a peaceful world. The Act of Havana (1940) provided for mutual defense of the Americas. The Burke-Wads-worth Act (1940) established the first peacetime draft in American history.

25. **(E)** Samuel Adams was active in both the Massachusetts Legislature and on the streets of Boston in arousing opposition to British policies. Patrick Henry and Thomas Jefferson were leaders in the Virginia legislature while John Adams served in the Continental Congress. James Otis wrote a number of pamphlets defending American rights.

26. **(D)** At the Yalta Conference in February 1945, Roosevelt, Stalin, and Churchill agreed to divide Germany into four military zones. The Casablanca Conference of 1943 decided on the invasion of Sicily. The Potsdam Conference of 1945 created the Council of Foreign Ministers to draft peace treaties, and the Teheran Conference of 1943 agreed on the second front in France and the Soviet Union's entrance into the war against Japan.

27. **(B)** There is nothing about religious toleration in the Declaration. The first portion of the Declaration presented the reasons for separation, the second portion outlined a theory of government, and the third section — the final paragraph — announced the existence of a state of war with Great Britain.

28. **(A)** In an early example of the policy of "containment," President Harry S. Truman in 1947 proposed to aid Greece and Turkey. Greek communists were attempting to seize control of the Greek government and the Soviet Union was pressuring Turkey to give up control of the Dardanelles.

29. **(E)** Under the Articles of Confederation the government could only ask the states for money; it could not directly tax the people. Consequently, the government was crippled even in carrying out the powers assigned to it.

30. **(C)** John Foster Dulles used the terms "brinksmanship" and "massive retaliation" to describe the stronger stance against communism that he was leading the Eisenhower administration to take. Christian Herter served as secretary of state under Eisenhower after Dulles's resignation and death in 1959. Marshall served as secretary of state under Truman from 1947 to 1949. Cordell Hull held the same

position under Franklin D. Roosevelt from 1933 to 1944. Elihu Root was secretary of state from 1905 to 1909 under Theodore Roosevelt.

31. **(E)** The Jay Treaty settled the long-standing problem of British troops in American territory but it did not address adequately such maritime issues as impressment of American sailors by the British and trade in the British West Indies. It did move toward settlement of Canadian boundary problems by establishing a commission to study the matter. Navigation of the Mississippi was settled by the Pinckney Treaty (1795) with Spain.

32. **(E)** The Eisenhower administration cautiously expanded the social and economic legislation of the New Deal-Fair Deal era. Examples of these actions were expansion of Social Security and federal aid for housing. In place of fixed price supports for agricultural products, Eisenhower adopted flexible price supports and a "soil bank" program which paid farmers to withdraw land from commercial cultivation.

33. **(B)** Although war was not formally declared, the demand for a bribe before treaty negotiations could begin led to a quasi-war with France in 1797–1798. In addition to the bribe, France had demanded an American loan and an apology for President Adams's remarks regarding France made to the American Congress.

34. **(D)** Under a treaty between the United States and Mexico, Mexicans could enter the U.S. on a temporary basis as farm workers. This program lasted from 1942 to 1962, bringing about 4.5 million Mexican workers into the United States.

35. **(C)** Between 1710 and 1720 the population of Massachusetts Bay grew by 4.6 percent; between 1700 and 1710 it grew 1.2 percent; between 1720 and 1730 it grew 2.6 percent; and between 1730 and 1740 it grew 3.3 percent.

36. **(D)** In turning down laws establishing minimum wages and limits on hours, the Supreme Court argued that they interfered with the workers' right of contract. The Court also used the 5th and 14th Amendments in declaring that such laws deprived owners of their property without "due process of law."

37. **(A)** Medicare was passed in 1965 during the Lyndon Johnson administration. Harry S. Truman and John F. Kennedy had unsuccessfully proposed government medical insurance programs.

38. **(E)** As chairman of the Rules Committee, Cannon determined which bills went to the House floor. He had no power over which bills went to House committees.

39. **(C)** Brigham Young led the Latter-Day Saints or Mormons to Utah after Joseph Smith was killed in Illinois in 1844.

40. **(C)** Richard Nixon turned much of the authority of cabinet officers, who were approved by the Senate, over to his White House staff who were his personal

appointments. He sought to reduce the role of the federal government in social issues and at the same time expanded the powers of the presidency. Although the House Judiciary Committee recommended impeachment, Nixon resigned before the House could take action. Faced with a Democratic majority in Congress, Nixon relied on a coalition of Republicans and conservative — mainly Southern — Democrats.

41. **(C)** H. Ross Perot was the top independent vote-getter in the 1992 and 1996 presidential races. He was viewed as helping to nudge Bill Clinton into office in 1992 by bleeding away support for the incumbent, George Bush.

42 **(A)** In the Rush-Bagot Treaty (1818), Great Britain and the United States agreed to take military ships from the Great Lakes. The other issues either simply faded away or were settled much later.

43. **(A)** The Gulf of Tonkin Resolution, passed in 1964, authorized the president "to take all necessary measures to repel any armed attack against the forces of the United States and to prevent further aggression." The basis of Johnson's authority to conduct the war was unclear, as discovered by the Senate Foreign Relations Committee in a televised hearing in 1968. In 1973 Congress passed the War Powers Act, which said that no president could send troops into combat for more than 60 days without congressional approval.

44. **(E)** With the invention of the cotton gin in 1793 and expansion into the Deep South after 1815, cotton became the dominant cash crop of the Southern economy.

45. **(D)** Latin America, together with the West Indies, provided nearly 34 percent of the immigrants to the United States. Eighteen percent of the immigrants came from Asia, 10 percent from Canada, 6 percent from Great Britain, and 9 percent from Germany.

46. **(C)** Representing the popular Anglo-Saxonism of the day, Beveridge sees the white race as superior in all respects to other peoples and destined by God to rule them.

47. **(B)** James Tallmadge's amendment proposed to outlaw the further introduction of slaves into Missouri. Although not passed, it introduced the problem of the expansion of slavery that led to Henry Clay's "Missouri Compromise" of 1820.

48. **(B)** The Office of Price Administration (1942) established price ceilings and set up a rationing system. The National War Labor Board oversaw wages and salaries. The War Manpower Commission directed workers into the war production effort. The War Production Board allocated raw materials to industrial plants. The Office of War Mobilization was the top policy-making board, unifying the other war agencies.

49. **(D)** Lyndon Johnson put in a tax increase that took effect about the time that Richard Nixon took office. Nixon cut federal spending and encouraged the Federal Reserve to follow a "tight money" policy. He also used both mandatory and voluntary wage and price controls. Gerald Ford cut government spending. Carter increased government spending and cut taxes and called for voluntary wage and price controls. Reagan reduced government spending and instituted a tax cut. The Federal Reserve at the same time followed a tight money policy. The tax cuts of Ford, Carter, and Reagan were attempts to get out of "stagflation," a combination of a stagnant economy and inflation.

50. **(A)** South Carolina provoked the crisis in 1832 by voting to nullify, or not allowing to go into effect within its borders, the tariffs of 1828 and 1832. The crisis was ended by the 1833 compromise tariff, although Andrew Jackson obtained the power to enforce the revenue laws militarily.

51. **(E)** The Three Mile Island nuclear reactor in Pennsylvania experienced a damaged reactor core. Technicians were able to bring the reactor under control before a meltdown occurred.

52. **(C)** The Federal Reserve Act was passed in 1913, during the presidency of Woodrow Wilson. The Elkins Act (1903) and the Hepburn Act (1906) regulated the railroads. The Meat Inspection Act (1906) and the Pure Food and Drug Act (1906) were early ventures into the protection of the public welfare. Roosevelt served as president from 1901–1909.

53. **(B)** Railroads, by providing transportation to markets, encouraged the development of the open range cattle industry. Droughts in the middle 1880s, together with increasing sheep herding and farming, helped bring an end to the open range industry. By the 1890s ranchers as well as farmers were using barbed wire.

54. **(E)** Tecumseh, along with his brother The Prophet, formed a defensive confederation of Eastern Indians in the early 1800s. He was killed in 1813. Sitting Bull and Crazy Horse were Sioux. Chief Joseph was a Nez Percé and Geronimo was an Apache.

55. **(A)** Small general stores became less important. Specialty stores, such as hardware or clothing, were increasingly popular. Wanamaker's, one of the first department stores, opened in Philadelphia in 1876. A&P pioneered the chain store, opening in 1859. And Montgomery Ward's started in the mail order business in 1872.

56. **(B)** William Marcy "Boss" Tweed controlled the Democratic political organization, or "machine," in the 1860s and 1870s, costing the city around $100 million in graft.

57. **(D)** Aaron Burr served as vice president of the United States between 1801 and 1804. He later was involved in an apparent conspiracy to separate the Western

states from the Union. Meriwether Lewis and William Clark led an expedition to the West in 1804–06. Zebulon Pike led a military expedition to Colorado in 1806. John Charles Frémont was involved in several Western expeditions in the 1830s and 1840s.

58. **(C)** This map represents slave and free areas of the United States after passage of the Kansas-Nebraska Act of 1854.

59. **(C)** Nicholas Biddle served as president of the Second Bank of the United States. William Morgan was a former Mason who vanished about 1826 just before he was to publish an exposé about the secret organization. Roger B. Taney served as chief justice of the Supreme Court between 1836 and 1864. Daniel Webster was a leader in the Senate, representing Massachusetts from 1827 to 1850. Robert Y. Hayne represented South Carolina in the Senate between 1822 and 1832, during which he engaged Webster in a famous debate over states' rights.

60. **(E)** The American Federation of Labor organized skilled workers according to their craft in contrast to other unions that organized by industry or as "one big union."

61. **(C)** The Radical Republicans did not favor the distribution of plantation land to the freed slaves. The Reconstruction Act of 1867 temporarily divided the South into military districts and guaranteed that freed slaves could vote and hold office. The Radicals also enlarged the powers of the Freedmen's Bureau over the veto of Andrew Johnson and supported the 14th Amendment, which gave the freed slaves certain civil rights.

62. **(C)** The largest of the mound-building centers, Cahokia, was located near the present-day city of St. Louis. This Mississippi Valley culture built massive earthen mounds of varying size and function. The Cahokia inhabitants erected flat-top mounds for buildings, and other types of mound structures for cemeteries. The largest Cahokia mound, Monks Mount, featured a massive base that measured more than 700,000 square feet, with two terraces, and that was 25 percent larger than the Great Pyramid of Giza. Cahokia's population was greater than any European city of its day, and the first European-American city that matched it in population was eighteenth-century Philadelphia. Other Indian groups settled the other four cities—New York City, Mexico City, Seattle, and Miami.

63. **(A)** Northerners who opposed the Union's war effort were called "Copperheads," after the poisonous snake common in the South. Clement L. Vallandigham, a congressman from Ohio, was the most prominent "Copperhead."

64. **(C)** This map represents European powers in North America in 1713 after the Treaty of Utrecht transferred Acadia and a portion of Newfoundland from France to Great Britain.

65. **(E)** Marcus Whitman was a missionary-physician who with his wife, Narcissa, went to the Oregon Territory in 1836. Whitman was killed by the Indians in 1847. Bridger, Smith, Beckwourth, and Fitzpatrick were all "mountain men."

66. **(A)** John Dewey of the University of Chicago argued for "learning by doing." Josiah Royce and William James were also turn-of-the-century American philosophers, but were not particularly concerned with education. Charles W. Eliot was the president of Harvard University and Andrew D. White the president of Cornell; both were leaders in the modification of the higher education curriculum.

67. **(B)** Through the Gadsden Purchase in 1853 the land south of the Gila River was purchased from Mexico for a possible transcontinental railroad route. Although Texas had entered the Union in 1845, the Treaty of Guadalupe Hidalgo established Mexican recognition of the acquisition and the southern boundary at the Rio Grande River.

68. **(C)** The 16th Amendment, passed in 1913, provided for a national income tax. The Emancipation Proclamation (1862) freed slaves in Confederate territory. The Freedmen's Bureau (1865) was created to help the freed blacks. The 13th Amendment (1865) abolished slavery, while the 14th Amendment made the freed slaves citizens of the United States.

69. **(E)** Jefferson is fearful that the Spanish government is too weak to hold on to its territories long enough for orderly expansion of the United States.

70. **(C)** Those who opposed the Constitution became known as Antifederalists because supporters of the Constitution had adopted the name Federalists. Democrats, Whigs, and Republicans were names of political parties to emerge later in American history.

71. **(E)** South Carolina seceded from the Union in December 1860, prior to Lincoln's inauguration as president.

72. **(E)** The Progressives emphasized such issues as efficiency and morality in government. They were largely urban-based and represented the middle class. They came to leadership during the first decade of the century, a period of prosperity. They generally ignored the rights of blacks.

73. **(E)** Horace Mann worked to establish public education in Massachusetts, becoming its first Secretary of the State Board of Education in 1837.

74. **(D)** In this cartoon Thomas Nast presents a Congress that is ready and willing to be bought.

75. **(C)** Horatio Alger was a popular late nineteenth century novelist who wrote stories based on the themes of self-help and — even more so — luck as the means to financial success.

76. **(D)** Beginning in 1973 when the Organization of Petroleum Exporting Countries increased the price of oil, energy became a major political issue of the 1970s. Under President Jimmy Carter, Congress created the Department of Energy in 1977 and passed a watered-down version of his energy bill.

77. **(E)** Patroon was the term for the owners of large tracts of land in the Dutch colony of New Netherlands, which was taken over by the English in 1664. The Pequot War took place in 1635–67 between the Puritans and the Pequots. The French Huguenots settled in the Carolinas in the seventeenth century, while William Penn founded Pennsylvania in 1681 as a haven for Quakers. Colonial farm implements included such items as the mould board plow, hoe, rake, and grain cradle.

78. **(A)** Sandra Day O'Connor was appointed to the Supreme Court by Ronald Reagan in 1981. Nancy Kassebaum and Barbara Jordan served in Congress, Ella Grasso was governor of Connecticut, and Jane Byrne mayor of Chicago.

79. **(D)** The corporation did not become the predominant form of business organization until the late nineteenth century. Individual proprietorships and partnerships were the prevalent forms until that time.

80. **(C)** This engraving emphasizes the innocence and helplessness of the victims.

81. **(E)** The Southern colonies were largely rural in character. Charleston, South Carolina was the largest city with a population of about 10,000 in the 1750s. Baltimore, the second largest, had a population of 5,000 at this time.

82. **(D)** Woodrow Wilson believed that the League of Nations was the key to maintaining peace. His unwillingness to compromise with Henry Cabot Lodge, however, led to the defeat of the Treaty in the U.S. Senate and fatally weakened the League.

83. **(A)** The colonial assemblies controlled the purse strings of colonial government, including the governor's salary, and therefore were in a strong bargaining position vis-à-vis the Royal governor.

84. **(C)** "Popular Sovereignty," as put forward by Stephen A. Douglas and embodied in the Compromise of 1850 and the Kansas-Nebraska Act of 1854, gave to the states themselves the power to decide whether they were to be slave or free.

85. **(D)** Jefferson Davis served as president of the Confederacy, while Alexander H. Stephens served as vice president. Robert E. Lee was commander of the Confederate forces. Robert Y. Hayne and John C. Calhoun were outspoken supporters of Southern interest while representing South Carolina in the U.S. Senate prior to the Civil War.

86. **(C)** The Fair Labor Standards Act (1938) established a minimum wage of .25 per hour, to be increased to .45 by 1945, and a maximum workweek of 44 hours, to be decreased to 40 hours by 1940. It affected only workers employed in interstate industries. The Fair Employment Practices Committee (1941) was established by Roosevelt to combat racial discrimination in industries that had contracts with the federal government. The National Labor Relations Act (1945) guaranteed the right of labor to organize. The National Industrial Recovery Administration enabled businesses to cooperate in setting production quotas and prices. The American Federation of Labor established wages and hours through each of its contracts.

87. **(D)** California experienced its Gold Rush in 1849. In 1859 both Colorado and Nevada had Gold Rushes, followed by South Dakota in 1874, and Alaska in 1880 and 1896.

88. **(E)** Birmingham was founded in 1871 and soon became known as "the Pittsburgh of the South" because of its iron and steel production.

89. **(C)** George argued that control of land was ultimately responsible for poverty and therefore proposed a single tax to retrieve rising land values for social purposes. The Populists argued for the monetization of silver and nationalization of the railroads. Henry Demarest Lloyd examined business monopolies in *Wealth Against Commonwealth* (1894). Lester Frank Ward examined the social implications of evolution in *Dynamic Sociology* (1883).

90. **(B)** The Mohawks, along with the Cayuga, Oneida, Onondaga, and Seneca, were members of the Five Nations of the Iroquois, a confederation of tribes in the eastern woodland section of what is now the United States. These tribes characterized themselves as the "people of the longhouse." The confederation was probably formed between 1570 and 1600 and is often credited to Dekanawidah, a Huron who persuaded Hiawatha, and Onondaga, to abandon warlike practices and cannibalism. The tribes united in a shared council formed of clan chiefs, with each tribe holding one vote. The Five Nations (later six, when the Tuscarora joined, in 1722) used elaborate ceremonies and rituals in the choice of leaders and other important decisions. The nations did not always act in unison, but they did stay united in their opposition to the French and in the eighteenth century became dependent on the British for goods. All of the other choices lived far from the Iroquois; the Aztecs lived in central Mexico, the Anasazi in the American Southwest, the Incas in South America, and the Mayas in the Yucatán and in Central America.

91. **(C)** Lincoln and Johnson saw the Civil War as a rebellion of individuals. Therefore they emphasized use of the presidential pardon. The Radical Republicans saw the South as either conquered provinces or unorganized territory and believed that Congress had power over Reconstruction. The Southern states passed Black Codes in the aftermath of the War.

92. **(B)** General Ulysses S. Grant emerged to prominence in battles along the Mississippi, including Fort Donelson and Vicksburg. In 1864, Grant became the supreme commander of all the Union armies.

93. **(B)** Increasingly, the nineteenth-century city became a "segregated city" in the sense that the various ethnic groups and economic classes lived in different neighborhoods, in contrast to the antebellum city. Also, residential, industrial, and commercial areas became increasingly differentiated.

94. **(A)** In the late nineteenth century the people who ran the day-to-day affairs of business were increasingly different from those who owned the businesses. This was especially true as the stock market grew in importance.

95. **(C)** Although Carter was successful in obtaining congressional passage of the Panama Canal Treaty in 1978, his major triumph was the treaty between Egypt and Israel in 1979. Carter was unable to obtain release of hostages from Iran—they were freed just a few minutes after he left office—withdrawal of Soviet troops from Afghanistan, or a reduction of Soviet influence in Africa.

INDEX

Index

A

B

E

F

G

I

J

K

M

O

P

Q

R

T

U

V

W

X

Y

Z

INSTALLING REA's TEST*ware*®

SYSTEM REQUIREMENTS

Pentium 75 MHz (300 MHz recommended), or a higher or compatible processor; Microsoft Windows, 98, NT 4 (SP6), ME, 2000, or XP; 64 MB Available RAM; Internet Explorer 5.5 or higher (Internet Explorer 5.5 is included on the CD); minimum 60 MB available hard-disk space; VGA or higher-resolution monitor, 800x600 resolution setting; Microsoft Mouse, Microsoft Intellimouse, or compatible pointing device.

INSTALLATION

1. Insert the SAT United States History TEST*ware*® CD-ROM into the CD-ROM drive.
2. If the installation doesn't begin automatically, from the Start Menu, choose the RUN command. When the RUN dialog box appears, type d:\setup (where *d* is the letter of your CD-ROM drive) at the prompt and click OK.
3. The installation process will begin. A dialog box proposing the directory "Program Files\REA\SAT_US_History" will appear. If the name and location are suitable, click OK. If you wish to specify a different name or location, type it in and click OK.
4. Start the SAT United States History TEST*ware*® application by double-clicking on the icon.

REA's SAT United States History TEST*ware*® is **EASY** to **LEARN AND USE**. To achieve maximum benefits, we recommend that you take a few minutes to go through the on-screen tutorial on your computer.

SSD ACCOMMODATIONS FOR STUDENTS WITH DISABILITIES

Many students qualify for extra time to take the SAT Subject Tests, and our TEST*ware*® can be adapted to accommodate your time extension. This allows you to practice under the same extended-time accommodations that you will receive on the actual test day. To customize your TEST*ware*® to suit the most common extensions, visit our website at *www.rea.com/ssd.*

TECHNICAL SUPPORT

REA's TEST*ware*® is backed by customer and technical support. For questions about **installation or operation of your software**, contact us at:

Research & Education Association
Phone: (732) 819-8880 (9 a.m. to 5 p.m. ET, Monday–Friday)
Fax: (732) 819-8808
Website: www.rea.com
E-mail: info@rea.com

Note to Windows XP Users: In order for the TEST*ware*® to function properly, please install and run the application under the same computer-administrator level user account. Installing the TEST*ware*® as one user and running it as another could cause file access path conflicts.

Research & Education Association
REA
The Best Test Preparation for the
AP*
U.S. & Comparative Government & Politics
8th Edition
Study Smarter & Master the AP!
5 Full-Length Practice Exams
Plus ... Expanded review, glossaries and full index
* AP is a registered trademark of the College Entrance Examination Board, which does not endorse this book.

Research & Education Association
REA
The Best Test Preparation for the
AP*
AP United States History
New! 7th Edition
Timed Practice Exams with Instant Scoring
REA's Software for AP United States History
Expanded! U.S. History Review
Updated! 6 Full-Length Practice Exams with detailed explanations
The AP book more teachers recommend!
* AP is a registered trademark of the College Entrance Examination Board, which does not endorse this book.